BUSINESS CYCLES
AND FORECASTING

BUSINESS CYCLES
and FORECASTING

BY

ELMER CLARK BRATT

Professor and Head
Department of Economics
Lehigh University

FIFTH EDITION

1961

RICHARD D. IRWIN, INC.
HOMEWOOD, ILLINOIS

FIFTH EDITION

First Printing, April, 1961
Second Printing, March, 1962

Library of Congress Catalogue Card No. 61-10590

PRINTED IN THE UNITED STATES OF AMERICA

From BERTHA MARGARET'S HUSBAND

PREFACE

The purpose of this book is to face the issues which are generally recognized as critical in understanding economic conditions. Emphasis is placed on the analysis of *current* conditions. Explanation of the present rests importantly on the perspective of the past. The past provides the building blocks for setting up theories to explain the processes of economic change. Although current conditions grow out of the past, they become meaningful only when seen in relation to the future. Therefore, in addition to dependence on history and theory, this study does not ignore the consequential influence of anticipatory factors. Forecasting methodology is an integral part of our analysis.

As in previous editions, I try to explain economic behavior before grappling with the problems of stabilization. In looking at current conditions, explanatory behavior and anticipatory factors should be recognized before remedial prescriptions are offered. I fully appreciate the importance of examining arguments concerning improvement in the performance of the economy, but I think such arguments should be seen in perspective. First, it is essential to understand how decision makers act in different economic situations and how the outlook may be visualized from the view of current conditions. Rationalization of how to make improvements should follow, rather than precede, efforts to explain the actual situation. After perspective is gained with respect to economic performance, I come to grips with judgments on stabilizing policy in the final chapters of the book. There, policy making in both the domestic and the international spheres is examined.

The application of analysis of current business conditions is by no means limited to control measures. Without question, a better understanding of the way the economy operates will permit more intelligent action by all decision makers in the economy. I place major emphasis on potential improvement, possible as a result of better understanding. For that reason, the principal part of the book relates to characteristic behavior, to explanation of that behavior by considering both expository theories and historical developments, and to background for developing an anticipatory outlook. Discussions on these topics do lead up to the analysis of control policy, but they are at least equally important in their own right.

For the analysis of current economic conditions all types of economic change are relevant. In addition to experiencing cyclical movements, the economy in the past has undergone depressions so deep that their characteristics have differed uniquely from the typical business cycle. Economic growth is increasingly noted as a critical type of economic change. And recently, relatively flat prosperous periods have come to be described as times of "rolling readjustment." The book is written throughout with all of these types of change in mind. For some problems, in which it is unnecessary to differentiate between them, I have tried to cast the analysis in general terms. At least as frequently a preponderant type of change is critical, a reality all analysts now recognize.

In this connection a defense of the title of the book is in order. While the business-cycle type of change is less inclusive than the coverage on economic change in this book, it is a key fluctuation as witnessed by the repeated occurrence of recession in the postwar period. Furthermore, salient interrelations are nearly always found with other types of economic change. In a sense "business cycles" identifies the kind of problems we face as well as any other convenient title would. For instance, while "economic change" more clearly gives recognition to the inclusive nature of the problems, it fails to indicate the area covered as clearly as our title if attention is given to the delicate gradations of meaning business cycles and economic change have assumed among modern analysts. Uncertainty shapes business-cycle variation, and the chief conundrum in economic change is uncertainty.

In advanced editions of a book it is customary to point out changes from earlier editions. In all four revisions, this book has been completely rewritten, and none more thoroughly than the present one. A glance at the Table of Contents will reveal to the reader familiar with earlier editions some of the outstanding changes. New developments in the theory, indicator, and forecasting chapters are clearly apparent. The new part on international repercussions which appears at the end of the book is obviously called for in view of the increasing emphasis on foreign conditions. If the reader scans the pages he will see many new developments, such as an introductory overview, theory based on business inventories, meaning and forecasting of average prices, chapters applying dynamic economics to the problems of individuals and of businesses, and a separate discussion on stabilization goals. With still more attention it will be seen that chapters with approximately unchanged titles show significant reworking.

Illustrations are the new emphasis on cumulation and culmination in explaining the business cycle, the contrast of output with capacity in the growth chapter, a tracing of chronological development in economic theory which finally brought economists to devote serious efforts to an explanation of the business cycle, a historical analysis of the common forces precedent to and arising in the deepest depressions, the concept of a "turning point" model in forecasting, historical testing of fiscal and monetary policy, the position of the Council of Economic Advisers in the coordination of stabilization policy, and the effects on international trade policy of the end of the dollar shortage. Although these points appear most noteworthy to me, others too numerous to mention also absorbed my attention as the book developed.

I feel that I have a far tighter organization than in any of the preceding editions. The six parts into which the book is now divided cover significant divisions of study, and the chapters in each part were designed to flow from one to another. Although the ideas in each part cannot be separated completely from the rest of the book because of the common interrelations which must be recognized, I believe the framework is helpful in an expository way. For instance, ideas on the business cycle (as well as on other types of economic change) are developed from three points of view in Parts One, Two, and Three and references are made back to these parts when pertinent problems arise later in the book.

In the several years in which the writing of this edition has been under way, I have received a wide range of assistance. My first and greatest debt is to other scholars from whom I have drawn more than I am able to recognize in any explicit fashion. I have taken advantage of many new ideas and many new presentations which have appeared in print in recent years. Drafts of the chapters were distributed in preliminary form. Several of these have been used by four successive groups at Lehigh University, including about 400 students. I am indebted to many of these students for useful suggestions. Professor John W. Kendrick of George Washington University provided invaluable assistance in reading the entire manuscript with great care and in furnishing innumerable comments, the influence of which is of major consequence in every chapter. Dr. Harlow D. Osborne of the Office of Business Economics in the Department of Commerce made useful comments on a draft of Chapter 15. Others who made important suggestions on distributed drafts include Dean Carl H. Madden, Professors Nicholas W. Balabkins,

Frederick A. Bradford, Finn B. Jensen, Donald G. Tailby, Eli Schwartz, and Mr. Thomas J. Orsagh of Lehigh University; Professor Dudley W. Johnson of the University of Washington; Mr. Henry Petri of Corning Glass; and my assistant in the course here at Lehigh, Mr. Robert J. Corkhill. My wife, as in earlier editions, picked up where the rest of us stopped. I, myself, happily assume complete responsibility.

ELMER CLARK BRATT

BETHLEHEM, PENNSYLVANIA

March, 1961

TABLE OF CONTENTS

PART ONE: ECONOMIC FLUCTUATION

PART FIVE: PROBLEM OF MAINTAINING REASONABLE STABILITY

PART SIX: INTERNATIONAL REPERCUSSIONS

INDEX

LIST OF CHARTS

LIST OF TABLES

PART ONE

Economic Fluctuation

Chapter	DYNAMIC BEHAVIOR IN
1	THE AMERICAN ECONOMY

The purpose of this chapter is to provide a general impression on the problems of economic change, much as an aerial photograph traces an overview. In the rest of the book, we look at the problems more analytically with a view to the pointing-up of issues and to the provision of conclusions available from the present state of our knowledge. The goal is to attain insight on current economic conditions and to establish the basis for forecasting.

The general movement of activity is traced by industrial production,[1] as pictured in chart 1-1. Although industrial production covers only a third of total output, it represents the variable part. While we must not disregard the importance of the rest of production, if we can explain the changes visible in Chart 1-1, we shall have given consideration to a most important segment of the variability and growth occurring in our economy.

Growth is indicated by the fact that industrial production rose 300 per cent in the forty years shown in the chart. Variability is indicated by the irregularity of the advance. The line almost continuously presents a jagged appearance even though it was adjusted for typical seasonal variation. Nevertheless, we can readily pick out expansions and recessions by the general rises and general falls of the line. Furthermore, unusual rises and falls are clearly seen.

The rapid rise from 1940 to 1943 is due to the expansion of demand arising from World War II. The peak then reached was not reattained until the Korean War in 1952. The violent decline occurring in 1945 was deceptive. It did not represent a significant

---

[1]The industrial production measure covers manufacturing, mineral fuels, and utilities (electric and gas) production. It represents a weighed index of physical output measures. See Board of Governors of the Federal Reserve System, *Industrial Production: 1959 Revision* (Washington, D.C., July, 1960).

CHART 1-1

Change in Industrial Production in the United States
Based on Physical Volume, Adjusted for Seasonal Variation
1957 = 100

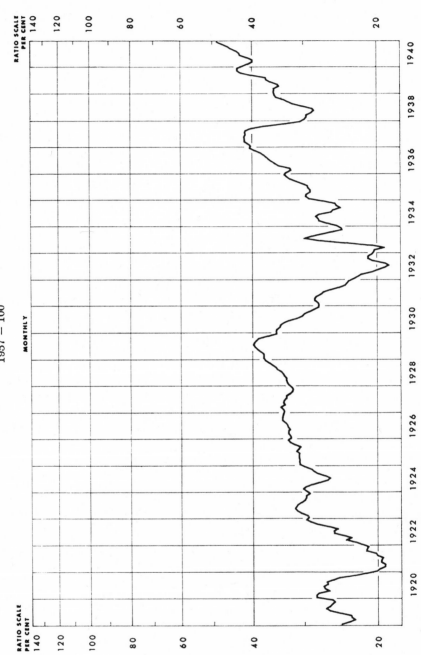

Source: Board of Governors of the Federal Reserve System, *Historical Supplement to Federal Reserve Chart Book on Financial and Business Statistics* (Washington, D.C., September, 1960).

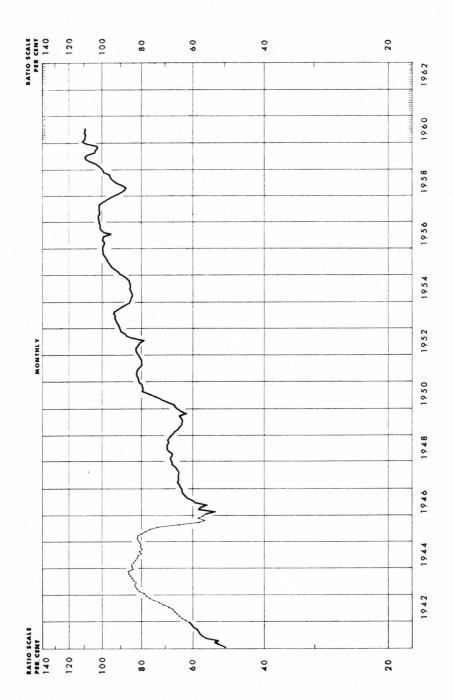

recession in the total economy. This is because some resources were taken out of use as production at a war-draft rate no longer was necessary and because reduced government controls permitted shift to nonindustrial production until more normal proportions were achieved. The decline beginning in 1929 was another matter. It carried all other output down with it. By 1939, industrial production had not advanced significantly above the 1929 level. Special conditions like those in World War II were not involved, and slackness pervaded the economy. In the war and in the postwar era, earlier growth trends reappeared.

Although our growth in industrial production in the forty-year period is a very satisfactory achievement, especially in the postwar, it has been outdistanced by many countries of Asia and Europe. Important differences with European countries are shown in Chart 1–2. The relative rapidity of advance in industrial production in

CHART 1–2

RECENT ADVANCES IN INDUSTRIAL PRODUCTION IN THE UNITED STATES
AND IN EUROPEAN COUNTRIES

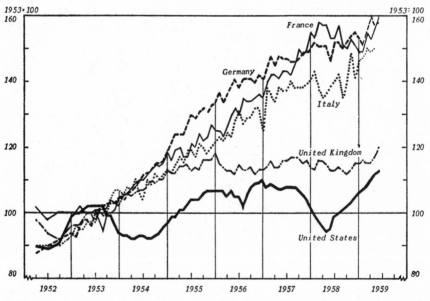

Source: American Bankers Association, *European Trends in Western Europe and the United States* (pamphlet), New York, 1960.

Russia, China, and Japan is even more notable. The most striking reason for the differences is the greater increase in employment in manufacturing in foreign countries, as indicated by Chart 1–3. In

CHART 1-3

RECENT ADVANCES IN MANUFACTURING EMPLOYMENT IN THE UNITED STATES
AND IN EUROPEAN COUNTRIES

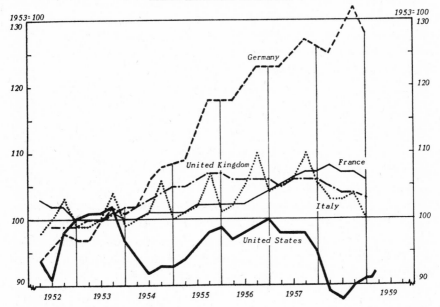

Source: American Bankers Association, *European Trends in Western Europe and the United States* (pamphlet), New York, 1960.

other words, with the greater achievement we have already attained in industrial production, our demands along this line are less pressing than in foreign countries. Therefore, relatively, our efforts have gone more to the making of nonindustrial product (including services). We develop no forecasts of the future differences in growth of industrial production in different countries, but point to the fact that simple trend projections are likely to be unreliable. Too much depends on the growth which has already been attained.

Each age brings its problems. As this is written, a most important one is the higher rate of advance in industrial production in foreign countries. The importance of that problem relates to the "cold war" into which the country has drifted: Our problem of defense will be accentuated if the rest of the world grows faster than we grow. More fundamentally, we can expect a more stable world if development of various countries of the world comes to be more equal. Although it may not add to our insight or perspective, our judgments will mature by realizing that the problems of the past have faded with time. Look to the New Era of the twenties, the secular stagnation of the thirties, the urgency of deferred demand following World

War II, and the fear of secular inflation in the fifties. These ideas do not merely represent fads. They characterize serious problems existing at the time. It is more correct to say we have stumbled through these problems than that we have solved them by design. The current international problem is analyzed in Part Six.

THE INFLATION PROBLEM

The movement of industrial production, pictured in Chart 1–1, provides no clue to the price disturbance which has accompanied activity changes. Prices have been far from stable over the last 150 years, as shown in Chart 1–4. The most notable fact is the high, temporary peak prices which have been achieved after major wars.

A peak was reached after World War II; but so far, there is little indication that it is temporary. On this basis, and founded on plausible reasoning, prices are now commonly expected to experience a slight secular advance over the next decade. Two major arguments adduced are the great increases in demand to be expected with the large growth potential we face and cost-push forces inherent in our institutional setup (notably, it is often held that the effect of wage increases granted to powerful labor unions is to push up prices).

Observe that the onset of a major decline in prices following the rapid upsweep after major wars did not await a major depression in the past. A violent decline of more than a third occurred in prices as the Civil War ended, and the price drop accompanying the following major depression of 1873–79 was somewhat less than a third. Declines following World War I conform to a similar pattern. A 40 per cent drop occurred before the onset of the Great Depression, and the decline during the Great Depression was about a third.

Other interesting price changes may be read from the chart. Note the short, violent rise in prices in the 1830's preceding the onset of a major depression. Note also the general decline in prices in the last quarter of the nineteenth century and the substantial rise which occurred before World War I. Note that interruptions in the rise in prices have occurred since World War II, beginning with the 1949 recession.

The story of the part played by prices in generating economic change carries into nearly every chapter of this book, and one chapter is devoted entirely to a study of the meaning and forecasting of average prices.

CHART 1-4

Change in Wholesale Prices Since 1800
Bureau of Labor Statistics Index, 1947–49 = 100

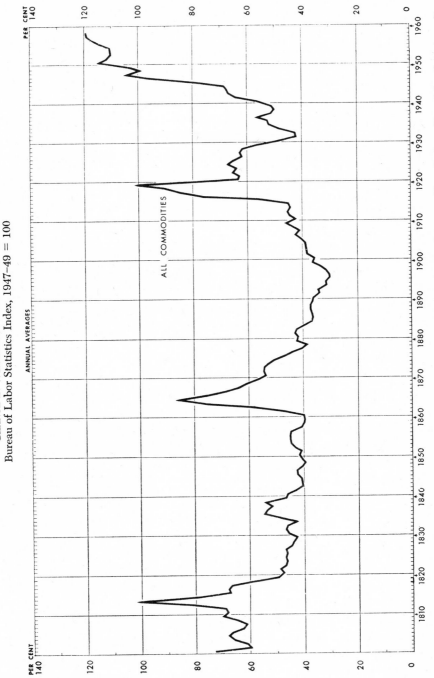

ANNUAL AVERAGES

ALL COMMODITIES

PER CENT

Source: Board of Governors of the Federal Reserve System, *Historical Supplement to Federal Reserve Chart Book on Financial and Business Statistics* (Washington, D.C., September, 1960).

INCREASING IMPORTANCE OF CONSUMER EXPENDITURE

Traditionally, investment expenditure has been assigned critical importance in generating business fluctuation. That investment is predominant in this respect remains unquestioned, but consumer expenditures have become increasingly significant. In every one of the fifteen postwar years the annual dollar total of consumer expenditures has increased, recession or no recession. This, indeed, is a remarkable fact when we recognize that consumer expenditures come to two thirds of total final expenditures in the economy.

The postwar stability of consumer expenditure is notable, but it is not a marked break with past history. It is the very fact that investment has been the unstable factor that has led to the critical position it is given as a generator of instability. Special factors have played an important part in the recent stability of consumer expenditures. One of these is shifting institutional influences, such as rising importance of unemployment benefits, which have added stability to consumer take-home pay. Another, less permanent, factor has been the high level of deferred demand in much of the postwar period. Also, liquid asset holdings have been relatively high in relation to current dollar income.

There are good reasons for believing that unstable factors in consumer expenditures may influence the total more in the future. Chart 1–5 indicates that the stability of consumer expenditures has turned on the rising importance of nondurable goods and of services. A dramatic factor in the rise in expenditure for nondurable goods has been the food component. Its rapid and consistent rise has been related to new food developments and to improved packaging. Although we expect these developments to continue for some time, we doubt that they will continue indefinitely. If food expenditures level off, the relatively unstable clothing component would bring greater instability in the nondurable goods division.

The smooth rise in services is due to a shift to greater demand for services at high standards of living, and to continued lagged advance in the price of services following the large postwar increase in commodity prices. Some of the services now demanded, such as for travel, may be found increasingly discretionary in the future, and it is possible that even the total of service expenditures may come to level off in some future recession.

Consumer expenditures for durable goods are notably unstable, and their variations may increasingly show up in total consumer

CHART 1-5

PERSONAL CONSUMPTION EXPENDITURES

Department of Commerce Estimates; Quarterly Figures Adjusted for Seasonal Variation Annually, 1929-38; Quarterly, 1939

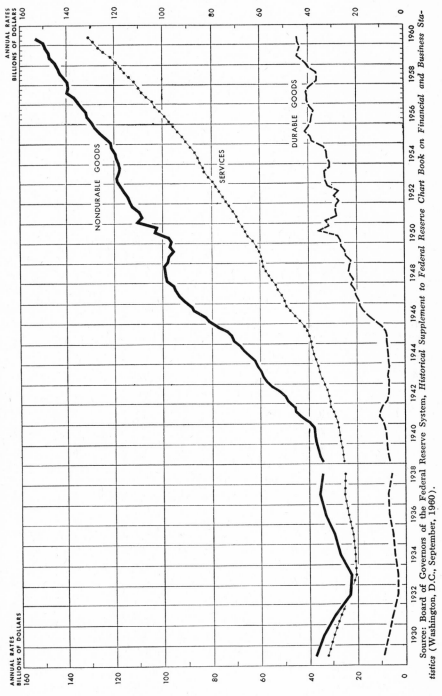

Source: Board of Governors of the Federal Reserve System, Historical Supplement to Federal Reserve Chart Book on Financial and Business Statistics (Washington, D.C., September, 1960).

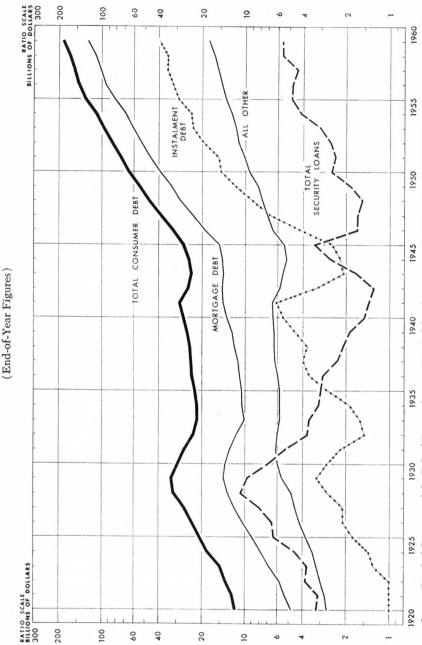

CHART 1-6

CONSUMER DEBT OUTSTANDING

Federal Reserve Estimates

(End-of-Year Figures)

Source: Board of Governors of the Federal Reserve System, *Historical Supplement to Federal Reserve Chart Book on Financial and Business Statistics* (Washington, D.C., September, 1960).

expenditures. This is because they are founded to an important extent on financing by instalment credit. Instalment debt rises in expansions and levels off or falls in recessions, a shown in Chart 1-6. In other words, consumers add to their purchases of durable goods in expansion by borrowing, and reduce such purchases in recession by paying off past debts. A major factor in the argument that investment expenditures create instability in our economy has been the part played by credit in those expenditures. But credit has come to play a major part in financing consumer, as well as business, expenditures.

The stability of consumer expenditures and the instability of investment expenditures are central in the explanations of the business cycle summarized in Part Two on the theory of business fluctuation. The fact that consumer expenditures can be expected to move with increasing independence accounts for some of the uniqueness of current business cycles, as explained in Part Two. Many illustrations of the strategic influence of consumer expenditures at various times in the past are traced in Part Three.

GOVERNMENT EXPENDITURES

Government expenditures for goods and services today are about 20 per cent of total final expenditures, compared with less than half of that before the Great Depression, as shown by Chart 1-7. In addition, transfer expenditures, such as for unemployment benefits, are relatively much more important than they used to be. The high level of government expenditures is often noted as a support which can be counted on to keep total expenditures high.

One weakness of that argument relates to the defense foundation of present government expenditures. If defense expenditures are subtracted, we find that the remaining government expenditures for goods and services amount to only 10 per cent of final expenditures, not materially greater than in 1929. Defense expenditures can be highly unstable, as the postwar period has shown. The "cold war" does not hold a steady temperature. When defense expenditures advance rapidly, activity is increased. But when they are cut back, a recessionary influence is introduced. It is true that transfer expenditures have added a more combative antirecessionary influence, but the increased level of government expenditures should not be looked on as wholly stabilizing.

We find that regard must be given to government expenditures in the discussion of factors responsible for the business cycle in

CHART 1-7

PERCENTAGE OF FINAL EXPENDITURES MADE BY THE GOVERNMENT°

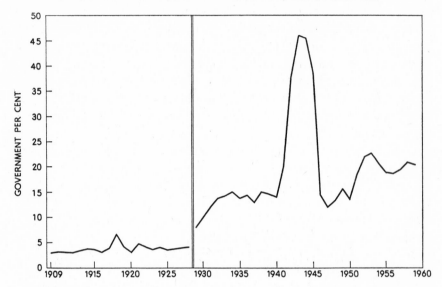

°From 1929, government expenditures for goods and services as a percentage of gross national product. From 1909 to 1923, "general government" expenditures as a percentage of gross national product. The general government expenditures are less inclusive and thus fluctuate at a lower level.

Source: *U.S. Income and Output: A Supplement to the Survey of Current Business* (Washington, D.C.: U.S. Government Printing Office, 1959), and more recent revisions reported in the *Survey of Current Business.*

later chapters in Part One. Furthermore, government expenditures have often been considered a keystone in building reasonable stability, as explained in Part Five.

IS ALL FLUCTUATION BAD AND ALL STABILITY GOOD?

When someone says that if we would pay the price required, we could avoid fluctuation, he is speaking the truth. If there were no psychological revolt, a tradition-bound economy could prevent fluctuation. In the Middle Ages, customs and traditions were so strong that free market fluctuations were largely avoided. Nonetheless, the world of that time was greatly upset by catastrophes. However, we have learned much since then. With the advance in medical science, perhaps no epidemic will again sweep the world as the Black Death did in Europe in the middle of the fourteenth century. With improved agriculture, famines are unlikely.

Great arguments rage on what the restraining influences which would have to be introduced to avoid fluctuations would do to our lives, to our standards of living, and to our progress. Possibly, activity would be stabilized at low levels of activity. Perhaps advancement would be reduced or eliminated. The experience of the Middle Ages tends to confirm such conclusions. The probable loss in flexibility of the economy, tested by the arguments of economists on the operating effectiveness of the market system, leads to the conclusion of stultification. On the other hand, the rapid advance in industrial production in totalitarian countries (notably Russia) is often cited as evidence that progress and stability are available under other systems. The answer we give to these contentions is that a forced advance in industrial production is especially attainable in nonindustrial countries, and that rapid advance after the development approaches the highest productivity achieved in the world will become increasingly difficult. Solutions to these questions are involved and complex, however, and offhand generalizations do not provide satisfactory answers. The problems are more carefully considered in Parts Five and Six.

THE KEY INFLUENCE OF ANTICIPATIONS

For the purposes of facing economic change, the present is a point poised between the relatively well-known past and the anticipated future. Anticipations are formulated by all decision makers. In the case of government, they play a most important part when major changes are made in military expenditures. Those anticipations tend to precede the actual outlays so much that other groups in the economy may show a first reaction, as illustrated by the early days of the Korean War. Consumers were stimulated to increase their expenditures, and it took months to add significantly to military outlays, so that the percentage of government expenditures in 1950 shown on Chart 1–7 is below that of 1949.

Consumers are affected by anticipations in various ways—because of expected future needs, because of expected changes in income, because of expected future prices, because of expected availability of goods, and because of expected holdings of liquid assets. We know these anticipations do play a part; but it is vague because to some degree, consumers buy on impulse rather than according to plan. Furthermore, plans develop in a social milieu, so that the individual frequently does not know what his plans are until he has conferred with others.

Anticipations are most important in the case of business expenditures. The rate at which businessmen purchase or operate their plants depends on anticipated sales. When they are wrong, inventory changes tend to be distressing and may lead to violently higher or lower rates of operation, and thus induce swift changes in the level of business activity.

Another important way in which business anticipations induce changes in the level of business activity is through decisions of businessmen to build plant and equipment. To an increasing extent, durable investment expenditures are founded on careful studies of long-term future needs, but the predominant influence remains current market conditions. Even when long-term plans are made, no businessman can remain blind to current business conditions. While investment remains high and is rising, it induces advances in other types of expenditures and thus encourages businessmen to add further to their investments. Finally, investment activity levels off; and if capacity has been unduly extended, that fact becomes apparent. A high level of capital stock discourages further investment in most lines of business. This induces a decline in other types of expenditures (for instance, workers who are disemployed spend less), and business anticipations are further reduced.

Increased care in formulating business anticipations now in process should improve the stability of business activity. This applies both to inventories and to plant and equipment. If inventory levels come to be judged less by transient demand of the moment and more by requirements over a longer period, the vacillation of inventory investment might be substantially reduced. The use of electronic calculators whereby the businessman obtains a prompter report on his inventory position may help to keep inventories from getting far away from desirable levels. A firmer understanding of the probable levels of future demand will give the businessman more confidence on the use which can be made of the level of investment stock attained. The problem centers on forecasting, which is analyzed in Part Four.

THE FOCUS OF EXPENDITURE

Since market demand is the chief source of orders on the productive resources in our economy, expenditures control business fluctuations. The greater the demand, the higher the level of activity; and also, the greater is the tendency for prices to rise. The sum of various expenditures determines the amount of total activity, and thus the aggregate employment and unemployment rates. Expenditure is also a very important determinant of average prices. These points are so simple that if we are familiar with the way our economy operates, it is difficult to see how different conclusions could be reached. Nineteenth-century economists, however, were so engrossed in the theories of automatic market adjustment and so lacking in facts on the operation of the economy that they failed to see these points clearly, as we explain in Chapter 7.

Actually, there are times when demand does not determine the physical level of activity. When resources are fully or almost fully used, added expenditures raise prices instead of raising the level of activity. Likewise, in all-out war, government demand is so great that resources are insufficient to satisfy all civilian demands. The general rule is that with any unused capacity, added expenditures will increase the level of activity and increase the amount of employment.

The key importance of expenditure in explaining business fluctuation is recognized throughout this book. By contrast, we find in the chapter on growth that long-term development is principally explained by resource availability. In short, demand usually controls fluctuations, and supply usually explains growth.

Chapter 2 | TYPES OF ECONOMIC FLUCTUATION

Total economic change is so complicated that effective generalization requires some breakdown. Everyone recognizes the need to adjust for seasonal variation if changes within the year are to be studied. This is because, over a period of a few months, seasonal changes may be opposite to other fluctuations, and may complicate the interpretation in almost all cases because of the great difference in the causal influence. These points on seasonal variations are developed in the following chapter, and no further consideration will be given to them here.

In like manner, we shall defer the analysis of other variations which occur over a short period until the end of Chapter 4. We shall not dismiss those variations, for they represent more than random or erratic influences; but the fact is that, like seasonal variation, other short-period fluctuations can be considered a disturbance which must be by-passed to get at the more critical types of economic change.

We have left a fluctuation usually known as the business cycle and a representation of development known as growth. The analysis and forecasting of these types of change are the chief functions of this book. The need to consider them separately rests on the fact that business cycle fluctuations are caused by transient changes in demand while growth rests principally on changes in supply conditions.

The way transient changes in demand lead to recurrent expansions and contractions, which are the principal characteristic of the business cycle, is the story told in Chapters 4 and 5. The foundation for the analysis presented there is the historical record, the quintessence of theoretical inquiries on economic change over the last hundred years (which are reviewed in Chapters 7-11), and known institutional behavior patterns in our capitalistic economy.

As we shall see, the observed regularity of the business cycle is impressive, but so also is the uniqueness of each separate business cycle. As a result, the generalizations cannot be summarized in a mathematical function. In the analysis we present, we are therefore closer to traditional economic theory than to mathematical generalization.

Satisfactory growth in our economy, by contrast, reflects effective use of our expanding ability to produce. The movements in the business cycle are by their very nature short-lived, in that they whip up and culminate like a terrestrial storm. The business cycle phases pass and leave a path which, when averaged over time, reflects our growing capacity to produce as long as the market system is effective ultimately in balancing demand and supply. We consider the facility to provide such a balance, if due allowance is made for the derangements arising from the business cycle, a major bulwark of capitalism. Increased activity arising in conformance with advancing ability to produce is called secular growth.

In most of our history, economic development was proceeding satisfactorily enough to be considered secular growth. There were times, however, typified by the 1930's decade, in which growth was completely unsatisfactory. The period is appropriately characterized as the "Great Depression," but as such we are not describing a business cycle movement. For both business cycle expansion and business cycle contraction occurred in the thirties. Our knowledge of the reasons for unsatisfactory growth in the Great Depression is summarized in Chapter 13. The fact is that for over a decade, little or no advance took place in the level of business activity, although our productive capacity had risen substantially. For reasons developed in Chapter 6, the targets visualized by businessmen fell far short of the growing productive capacity of the economy. We designate such growth as secondary to distinguish it from the secular, during which production, on the average over a period of time, achieves an advance in productive activity commensurate with advancing productive ability.

There were, perhaps, limited periods of secondary growth in the nineteenth century, as well as during the Great Depression. Clearly, we cannot guarantee that economic development always will average out to a secular growth level. The output which would have occurred with secular growth, in contrast with the low secondary growth which materialized, obviously was lost forever. Later levels of activity, nevertheless, do not appear to have suffered substantially from the interruption of advance during the period of secondary growth. (Note, for instance, that recent activity could be looked on as a reasonable extension of growth prior to the Great Depression, as indicated by Chart 1-1 on page 4 and by Chart 6-1 on page 104.)

The appearance of periods of secondary growth in the past signifies that they will occur in the future only if we can expect return of the conditions which produced them. As indicated in Chapters 6 and 24, there is some doubt that those conditions will again prevail. If they do not, the critical types of economic change can be limited to business cycles and secular growth. If this pleasant development materializes, the problem of economic change will be much simplified. For secondary growth is poorly understood and much less readily planned than secular growth or even than the business cycle.

Reasonable assurance that secondary trends will not occur fosters the planning of industrial expansion on the basis of secular growth measurements. Developments in the fifties confirm this point. Belief is spreading that the recurrence of a period of secondary growth is becoming increasingly unlikely, and the use of growth forecasting in business has increased at a rapidly expanding rate.

Thus, growth measurements at the present time are used principally to study growth itself. This contrasts with the popularity of growth measurements preceding the Great Depression, when they were more frequently used to study the business cycle. Widespread measurements were made of business cycle changes with the growth measurement divided out. With the advent of secondary growth in the Great Depression, this obviously became an unrewarding exercise, for inadequacy of secular growth measurements made business cycle departures from it wholly unsatisfactory.

We now typically believe that elimination of the growth element is generally unnecessary in a study of business cycle changes. The slow change in growth, relative to business cycle fluctuation, usually means that growth is of second-order importance in the analysis of cyclical swings. The study of growth for its own sake is a different matter.

Thus, the motivation for segregating types of economic change has shifted as time has gone on. The relatively weak basis for measuring growth and eliminating it from economic data to derive a business cycle measurement in the twenties generated considerable dissatisfaction with conventional decomposition procedures. For instance, frequent reference was made to the fact that growth cannot be independent of the expansion which occurs in the business cycle, and doubt was therefore thrown on the growth-eliminated business cycle measurement. No similar argument appears equally valid against the independent study of growth. Planning on the basis of growth necessitates segregation from the business cycle.

The recent motivation for the separation of growth from business cycles does not satisfy one telling argument which has been leveled against this classification for thirty years. That relates to the fact that business cycles, each identified by an expansion followed by a contraction, cover fluctuations of greatly differing intensity and with a few cycles much longer than others. Compare, for example, the 1924–27 cycle with the 1927–33 one. The second is twice as long and far more intense. This is not the place to argue whether or not these cycles have any major features in common, but we believe that they do on the basis of criteria set up in Chapters 4 and 5. On the other hand, differences are fundamental and important. Taking the position that each of these fluctuations represents a business cycle, we hold that the great variation indicated deviates from a common type—the business cycle—although we could wish for some method of analysis involving less variation.

Recognizing the difficulties we have briefly summarized, it is only natural that many efforts should have been made with a view to providing a better method of classifying economic change. We make no effort to catalogue all of these efforts, for most of them have no recognized importance at the present time. In the two following sections, we review methods which are now generally recognized as worthy of consideration.

SCHUMPETER'S CLASSIFICATION OF FLUCTUATIONS

Joseph A. Schumpeter developed an analytical model involving a multiplicity of cycles of different durations occurring simultaneously.[1] If, in reality, many cycles are occurring at the same time, the gross measurement we get in terms of the business cycle when broken down into many cycles occurring at the same time might develop more manageable unit cycles. The cycles of each length might be more nearly alike than business cycles are.

Schumpeter's theory of decomposition as related to his model

---

[1] See his *Business Cycles* (New York: McGraw-Hill Book Co., Inc., 1939). Schumpeter's theories are further discussed in Chapter 7. See pp. 148–49.

has become classic, and it may well be employed as a groundwork for our discussion. Although our interest in this chapter is entirely in decomposition, Schumpeter's position represents a philosophy of technological change, and his contentions on types of change cannot be recognized without some consideration of that philosophy. We shall cover his philosophy rather lightly at this point, for it is too early in our study to probe deeply into theoretical considerations.

Schumpeter's idea of a cycle centers around innovation. He starts with equilibrium in the classical economic sense, except that some unemployment is recognized because of the imperfections of competition. Innovating activity, representing not only reaction to technological change but also reaction to other opportunities such as extended geographical frontiers, arises in capitalism and drives the economy away from equilibrium into a prosperity phase. Prices rise, and capital is expanded on borrowed money. Inevitably, this condition comes to an end, and a period of recession sets in. Schumpeter's "recession" in that sense differs from the type described in this book. His recession comes when the fruits of innovation are reaped; and, at least at first, it involves a *rise* in the output of finished goods, with increased competition and declining prices. Economic conditions are then driven back to the equilibrium level.

As recession proceeds, abnormal liquidation is likely to occur; many firms are then unable to survive under the new equilibrium. Hence, depression may ensue, when adjustments exceed those required by the new equilibrium. It is thought that the depression phase sometimes may not occur and that, even if it does, activity will return to equilibrium levels after some temporary panic. A new cycle begins when advantage is taken of new innovations; and again, activity is driven away from equilibrium into a prosperty phase.

Not just one, but a multiplicity of cycles of different durations are thought to be occurring simultaneously for three reasons:

1. The length of time needed to complete investment projects varies, so that the length of time investment promotes prosperity differs, depending on the kind of investment which is predominant.
2. Major innovations, like the railroads, involve a repeated series of developments, so that the total prosperity effect may be long extended.
3. Many side developments may occur, such as population shifts, the establishment of new cities, and derived economic opportunities, as represented by Western American farms when railroads were extended in the area.

CHART 2-1

COMBINATION OF LONG, INTERMEDIATE, AND SHORT CYCLES

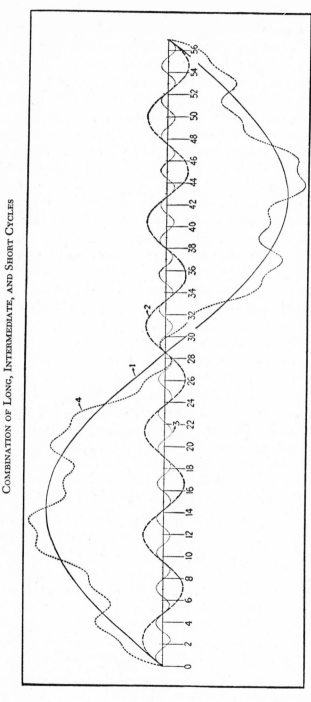

NOTE: Curve 1, long cycle; curve 2, intermediate cycle; curve 3, short cycle; curve 4, sum of 1–3.
Source: Taken with permission from Joseph A. Schumpeter, *Business Cycles, Vol. I* (New York: McGraw-Hill Book Co., Inc., 1939), p. 213.

As a compromise in favor of simplification, Schumpeter chose to analyze a "three-cycle schema," although he felt that five cycles perhaps would be better. He concluded, after some experimentation, that the improvement in the picture of reality would not warrant the increase in cumbersomeness involved in five cycles.

Therefore, we are not justified in criticizing his model wholly on the assumption that *three* simultaneous cycles are involved. The three-cycle model, however, is the one he developed; therefore, it is the one we must face. It is pictured in Chart 2-1. The long, intermediate, and short cycles are spoken of in the literature by the names Schumpeter gave them in recognition of economists who studied cycles of these lengths: the long or 50-year cycle was called a "Kondratieff" after the Russian analyst N. D. Kondratieff; the intermediate or 10-year cycle, a "Juglar" after the French analyst C. Juglar; and the 40-month cycle, a "Kitchin" after the English analyst J. Kitchin. The fact is that, except for the 40-month cycle, which more or less corresponds with the business cycle as we describe it today, these cycles were not satisfactorily identified with historical economic variables.

Although Schumpeter did not think of Kondratieff cycles as the same as "epochs," he associated them with successive industrial revolutions. Measuring from equilibrium point to equilibrium point, the first long wave was said to reflect the Industrial Revolution from about 1790 to 1850; railroad and steel from 1850 to 1900; and automobiles, electric power, and chemistry after 1900. We can accept the position that some such influences as Schumpeter notes were important in first expanding and then decelerating advance in the periods noted, but we need not commit ourselves to the position that recurring cycles of this sort are implied for the future.

It was thought that equilibrium points preceding prosperity were reached in the Juglar cycle in 1843, 1851, 1860, 1869, 1879, 1888, and 1897. These years do identify the beginning of periods of innovation (although there are also other dates which identify such beginnings). But the picture is far less clear in the twentieth century, and questions may be raised as to whether a pattern is indicated which can be expected to prevail in the future.

Schumpeter had some doubts about the part played by innovation in the forty-month cycle. He frequently spoke of this as an "adaptive" fluctuation. As shown later in this book, inventory investment plays an important part in the business cycle, which averages about the length of the Kitchin cycle, and change in inventory investment represents a current adaptation of production schedules to sales. Nevertheless, some innovations, notably in equipment which can be produced fairly quickly, "mature" in a relatively short time. Innovational influences are important in the business cycle, but Schumpeter's major innovations and side developments may be more important over a longer period.

While many innovations mature over a longer period, it is hard to identify them with a ten-year Juglar. In fact, a clearer case can be made for a twenty-year building cycle. Even this is rather vague, partly because of the unsatisfactory nature of the data on which it is based. Also, none of the theoretical analyses which have been made on the forces responsible for a building cycle provide any clear indication that the length of the cycle should be approximately constant or that its average should approach any particular length. As construction in the modern world covers additional facets—a speeding-up in the rate of home depreciation, rapid increases in nonfamily households, expansion of public building, a greater tendency for businessmen to make long-range plans for establishing construction expenditures, and others—some doubt is thrown on the future importance of a building or construction cycle.

Possibly, the ten-year cycle which Schumpeter and other analysts have discovered means little more in the United States than that all recessions or prosperities are not of the same amplitude. If one out of three or four recessions is substantially more severe than the others, the data would appear to indicate a major swing in the order of ten years.

Innovational forces do not satisfactorily explain a cycle of fifty years in length. Some innovational forces do take a long time to work themselves out, but this does not mean that any particular-length cycle—or for that matter, any cycle—will necessarily result. The three Kondratieff cycles Schumpeter thought he identified may or may not be clearly verified by improved production data for the periods covered. Even if they are, they may represent a passing phase of development. In the future, growth may come to be less concentrated on a few kinds of industry. As one type of long-term innovation matures, other types may come along to take its place.

LONG SWINGS IN ECONOMIC GROWTH

A common interpretation of the Kondratieff cycle deviates from that shown in Chart 2-1. Instead of passing through equilibrium, the cycle begins and ends at equilibrium points. It is noted above that the cycle concept as employed by Schumpeter does not necessarily imply a depression phase. If the Kondratieff cycle actually begins and ends along a rising equilibrium line, one interpretation is that the expanding phase shows a period of rapid growth and that the contraction phase shows a period of slower and slower growth, but that growth continues nevertheless as long as activity does not fall below the equilibrium level.

If we maintain that there is to be great uncertainty about the length and nature of long waves in the future, the focus of the analysis is changed materially. The movement may be interpreted as secondary or intermediate growth which sporadically may deviate from the secular growth of which the economy is capable. The past does not necessarily indicate what the future faltering in growth may be. Thus, the Kondratieff movement looks like a kind of unsatisfactory growth (possibly too great to be sustained as the pictured Kondratieff cycle rises rapidly, but too slow to make effective use of our resources as it is pictured to swing downward). That corresponds with the position we explain in Chapter 6.

Norman J. Silberling was the first to state this kind of analysis effectively. The data he developed to illustrate the position over a long period of American history are pictured in Chart 2-2. It will be noted that his intermediate trend corresponds to some extent with the timing Schumpeter found for the Kondratieff cycle, but

CHART 2-2

AMERICAN BUSINESS TRENDS AND CYCLICAL MOVEMENTS, 1700–1940

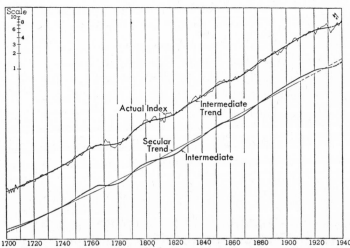

Source: Reproduced by permission from Norman J. Silberling, *The Dynamics of Business* (New York: McGraw-Hill Book Co., Inc., 1943).

Silberling's intermediate trend line has some additional ups and downs. This fact indicates that the most effective way of taking into consideration all of the fluctuations longer than the business cycle may be to incorporate them in a secondary or intermediate growth line.

Moses Abramovitz is conducting a continuing study of long swings in United States economic growth.[2] Chart 2–3, taken from his work, shows some of the basic variations in growth which have occurred. His conclusion is that "growth has taken place in a series

CHART 2–3

VARIATION IN SOME GROWTH FACTORS

(Residential Construction and Capital Expenditures by Railroads and Public Utilities at 1929 prices and Additions to Population, Average Reference Cycle Standings, 1871–1955)

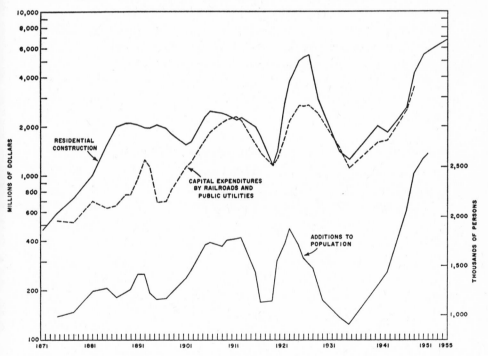

Source: Joint Economic Committee, *Employment, Growth, and Price Levels,* Part 2: *Historical and Comparative Rates of Production, Productivity, and Prices,* Hearings, April 7–10, 1959, 86th Cong., 1st sess. (Washington, D.C.: U.S. Government Printing Office, 1959), p. 452.

[2]See National Bureau of Economic Research, Inc., *Thirty-Ninth Annual Report* (New York, 1959), pp. 23–27; *Fortieth Annual Report* (New York, 1960), pp. 19–21; Joint Economic Committee, *Employment, Growth, and Price Levels,* Part 2: *Historical and Comparative Rates of Production, Productivity, and Prices,* Hearings, April 7–10, 1959, 86th Cong., 1st sess. (Washington, D.C.: U.S. Government Printing Office, 1959), pp. 411–66.

of surges during which growth was especially rapid followed by relapses when growth proceeded much more slowly." And: "The retardation phase of each long swing in output growth has culminated in a depression of unusual severity or in a succession of depressions of lesser severity interrupted by only short-lived or disappointing recoveries." These conclusions appear to conform with our interpretation of Schumpeter's long waves (Kondratieff cycles) plus intermediate movements (Juglar cycles) as a representation of secondary growth.

Visualization of economic change in the *past* as described by a multiplicity of cycles of different duration has proved itself because it has frequently been the most useful classificatory scheme in studying recorded history.[3] To study the current economic situation, to which the present book relates, multiple cycles are of little or no help. Separate cyclical movements cannot be distinguished at an up-dated point of time. Enough difficulty is experienced in breaking the total change down into several cyclical parts in closed periods of history. Furthermore, some doubt, as inferred in the above paragraphs, may be expressed as to whether simultaneous cyclical movements employed to describe the past will be likely to persist in the future.

INDEPENDENT CYCLES IN INDIVIDUAL INDUSTRIES

Thus far, we have assumed that cyclical movements are centered in aggregate activity. If it could be shown that cycles are initiated in individual industries and that the fluctuation in aggregate industry is merely the accidental combination of many independent industry cycles, a different approach would be required.

We may consider two of the best known individual-industry cycles. The cycle in construction, especially in residential building, is noted above. The major explanation of that cycle is successively short supply and excess demand, followed by excess supply and fading demand. This relates to inducements which influence speculative building. Expanded building is induced by rising housing prices available to builders when households turn to new buildings because of unfavorably high rents on old houses. Speculative builders tend to continue to build even after demand for new houses fades; thus, overbuilding develops before building begins

---

[3]Rendigs Fels's use of the Schumpeter type of classification in *American Business Cycles, 1865–1897* (Chapel Hill: University of North Carolina Press, 1959), is an illustration of constructive use along that line.

to decline. By that time, rental rates are declining relative to monthly mortgage payments required at the existing prices for new houses, and housing activity falls for some time. When housing becomes short again, rental rates rise to an unfavorable level relative to housing prices, and the expansion phase of a new cycle starts once more.

Past statistical data are poor enough that, although it is obvious that a variation has occurred in construction, the degree to which cyclical regularity has occurred is questionable. And new factors in building make the future occurrence of construction cycles even more questionable. Such factors as increased demand for second homes in seasonal locations, increases in home ownership, and the flow of contracting to larger and better-informed firms throw doubt on the future cyclical tendency of speculative building. Furthermore, better analysis of past data, poor as it is, brings into question the thesis that housing depressions arose in the past independently of the movement of general business activity.[4]

A two-year textile cycle is recognizable, up in the odd years and down in the even. The best explanation appears to be recurrent flights of pessimism and optimism, founded on cumulative changes occurring in orders and inventories, with the accompanying inducement of price changes. In other words, there is a tendency at the beginning of odd years for unfilled orders to expand, with prices rising and inventories of manufacturers falling. When manufacturers finally get their inventories up to the desired level, they find their unfilled orders shrinking, with prices falling and inventories uncomfortably high. As they later manage to get their inventories down to desired levels, the demand situation again looks favorable, and the cycle is repeated. One factor is an apparent opposition much of the time in the movement of inventories at retail levels, first giving the manufacturer an exaggerated idea of the rise in final sales and later an exaggerated idea of the fall in final sales. Probably, also, the short life of most clothing, together with frequent changes in fashions, induces a two-year wave in final buying.

In addition to the two-year cycle tendency, textile activity always follows the business cycle, especially business cycle recessions. There is little evidence of a pronounced effect on the aggregate economy arising from the textile industry, but there is clear evidence that business cycle recessions influence the textile industry.

---

[4]James S. Duesenberry, *Business Cycles and Economic Growth* (New York: McGraw-Hill Book Co., Inc., 1958), p. 163.

Unquestionably, other illustrations of individual-industry cycles could be supplied. We do not know of any, however, which are better established or more convincing. No effort is made, therefore, to illustrate cycles in other particular industries.

Evidence drawn from the National Bureau of Economic Research is presented in Chapter 4 to show that the cyclical movement in individual industries generally follows that in the aggregate business cycle (with allowance made for some differences in timing [see Chart 4-2 on page 53]). In fact, that evidence is so conclusive and drawn from such a wide group of data that there is no need to pursue the subject further at this point.

SUMMARY

The most effective way of classifying economic change for the purpose of analyzing current economic conditions involves restricting ourselves to one cyclical component, which we shall call the business cycle. The other components are growth elements. These are of two types: (1) what we call secular growth, or a long-term advance, which fairly depicts a reasonable use of potential resources in view of the technological, social, and cultural development existing at the time; and (2) what we call a secondary growth, which involves a long swing in the rate of advance away from secular growth. This may, at times, constitute slower growth than warranted by change in our resource ability. It may represent the appearance of abnormally rapid growth, as might arise, for instance, if investment expenditure came to be extremely high.

Such a situation is represented by Schumpeter's conception of the prosperity phase of a Kondratieff cycle. A very high rate of investment activity usually cannot be sustained indefinitely and thus ultimately leads to a slowing down in the advance. Variation in growth may occur for other reasons, however. Secondary growth may come to fall below secular growth at times and not exceed it at other times. Or possibly, such a deviation may disappear almost entirely. Deviation like that shown in Chart 2–2 may continue in the future, but we cannot be sure. The forces which have created it are not necessarily wholly similar to those which we visualize in the future. The problem of growth is discussed in further detail in Chapter 6.

The study of growth is important for its own sake, because it provides a guide in long-term planning. In a capitalistic society like ours, with continual questions arising as to the desirability of investing in long-lived installations and in prospecting for raw material supplies, a rational basis for estimating the average level of demand in the distant future is indispensable. Growth measurements provide a bench mark for this purpose.

In the study of fluctuations the business cycle is a useful concept. Theoretical formulations show why it reflects transient demand. Looked at in this way, fluctuation is not readily broken down into more than one cycle occurring at the same time (except additionally for the separately generated seasonal variation). The very nature of demand inducement, which lies at the core of business cycle explanations, is that it is all of one piece. All of it reflects anticipation of an uncertain future, and it is not possible effectively to segregate waves of demand founded on the generation of different types of investment, at least not in so far as the present outlook of the United States is concerned.

The resultant business cycle is different from a segregated cycle like Schumpeter's Kitchin. With presumed long-wave motions set apart, less fluctuation has to be explained in the Kitchin cycle. Hence, its average length came out to be somewhat shorter in Schumpeter's computations than the business cycle averages according to the measurements of the National Bureau of Economic Research. We are entitled to look enviously at a mathematically developed measurement which shows less variability than the business cycle; but as long as we explain the fluctuation by induced demand, as we do in later chapters, we find the concept of concomitant cycles of different lengths too cumbersome to employ in explaining current economic change.

FOR REFLECTION AND ANALYSIS

1. Contrast the utility of the concept of a multiplicity of cycles occurring simultaneously with secondary growth as a device in visualizing current economic change.
2. Do cycles occur independently in individual industries? What is their relation to the business cycle?
3. Outline the possibilities one might consider in decomposing time series, and point out why some are more practical than others.

SEASONAL VARIATIONS

In the study of economic change as developed in this book, a knowledge of seasonal variation is needed primarily for the purpose of deriving measurements of economic fluctuations uncomplicated by seasonal variations. Seasonal variations represent economic change just as surely as other variations classified in the preceding chapter, but their explanation differs significantly from that of other types. The major point is that they depend on custom and weather conditions characteristic of particular industries rather than on total demand or total supply, which provides the major basis for other fluctuations and growth.

Seasonal variations must be explained by the conditions in individual industries, not by macroeconomic conditions. No one would look to over-all total industry or to general industry aggregates to find the explanation of seasonal variation in any company or industry. But this is exactly what must be done in the study of growth or of the business cycle. Since this book relates particularly to macroeconomic conditions, interest in seasonal variations is principally subsidiary.

Nevertheless, the simple and special character of seasonal variations in individual industries provides a useful contrast in the study of other types of economic change. Typical seasonal variations are known in advance. This is because their basic cause is ingrained custom or cosmic weather conditions. Planning for seasonal change would be relatively uncomplicated if it were not for other fluctuations with which it sometimes becomes confused.

SEPARATION OF SEASONAL FROM OTHER FLUCTUATIONS

A major difficulty arises from the fact that the seasonal variation which we measure covers only a part of total seasonal fluctuation.

The measured part is the typical seasonal movement, in the sense that it is established by recurrent yearly alternation. This is called typical seasonal variation, in that it characterizes the pattern which can be expected to occur. It is reasonably characteristic of custom-based seasonals—seasonal changes at Christmas and Easter, for instance, do not tend to vary greatly from one year to another. Effectiveness of the typical measurement is more limited in describing weather-based seasonals, for the seasonal variation of weather is more dependent on the particular conditions of a given year. The specific variation of the seasonal, as contrasted with the typical, is unmeasurable and represents an erratic element in business cycle estimates. Since other erratic changes occur, we cannot attribute all such vacillation to seasonal factors. For instance, the sale of air conditioners may rise abnormally because of a hot and humid summer; but other factors, such as shifts in vacation schedules or change in the pattern of ownership of new homes, may also influence the sale of air conditioners.

After making due allowance for the confusion produced by erratic weather influences, adjustment for typical seasonal variation is of major importance in most activity series. Except for relatively few series, no person can be expected to keep in mind all seasonal factors, for these vary greatly between different kinds of activity. The adjustment, which usually amounts to dividing out the typical seasonal variation, puts series on a basis to give a good idea of the movement of nonseasonal fluctuation.[1]

Perhaps the worst confusion which occurs in examination of economic fluctuations is that between typical seasonal and other fluctuations. To evaluate economic conditions, note must be taken of nonseasonal rises and declines. In periods of rapid seasonal expansion, a series may be rising rapidly and yet fall short of seasonal expectations. Instead of presenting an optimistic picture, as might be indicated by a superficial reading, the indication would be pessimistic.

---

[1]Most texts on business statistics provide a satisfactory statement on the measurement of seasonal variation and adjustment to eliminate its influence. See, for instance, Frederick E. Croxton and Dudley J. Cowden, *Practical Business Statistics* (3d ed.; Englewood Cliffs, N.J.: Prentice-Hall, Inc., 1960), pp. 447–71. Particular attention may be called to Julius Shiskin, *Electronic Computers and Business Indicators,* Occasional Paper 57 (New York: National Bureau of Economic Research, Inc., 1957), where the use of electronic calculators in the computation of and adjustment for seasonal variations is discussed.

AMERICAN SEASONAL VARIATIONS

Retail trade experiences a relatively large seasonal variation. This represents the combined effect of customary buying seasons and weather-induced changes in consumer demand. The seasonal variation in total retail trade for the years 1957, 1958, and 1959 is shown in Chart 3-1. (The difference in fluctuation between these

CHART 3-1

SEASONAL VARIATION IN TOTAL RETAIL TRADE IN THE UNITED STATES
1957, 1958, and 1959

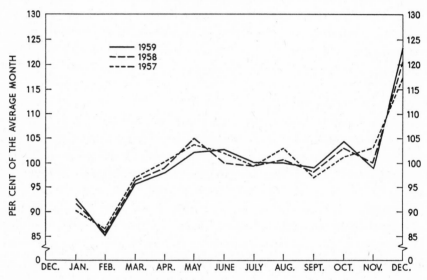

years is largely accounted for by shifting proportions of different types of retail trade; the problem involved is discussed below in connection with seasonal variation in industrial production.) Note the characteristic seasonal high in December and the seasonal low early in the year. This reflects the importance of Christmas sales and the trade relapse in midwinter, partly based on completion of purchases related to winter weather. The Christmas peak is much more pronounced if seasonal-type sales are considered separately. For instance, seasonal sales of department stores in December are 80 per cent above the yearly average and in January are 25 per cent below average.

Seasonal variation in industrial production is less. In 1959 a seasonal low was reached at nearly 6 per cent below average in July, and a seasonal high 3 per cent above average in October. The indicated seasonal stability in total industrial production is somewhat deceptive, however. Seasonal variations differ so much between industries that a considerable offset occurs. As shown in Chart 3–2, for instance, beverage production moves almost oppositely to fuel and lighting. When the weighted figures are added together, a good part of the variation disappears. Furthermore, seasonal variation in total industrial production shifts from year to year because of the change in proportions of total output in different industries. If the relative importance of beverage production should increase, the May seasonal index for total industrial production would be higher. (May is the peak in the beverage seasonal, as shown in Chart 3–2). If the production of equipment should rise faster than the production of consumer goods, seasonal variation in total industrial production would be reduced, as indicated by the first panel of Chart 3–3, which shows that seasonal variation in equipment production is slight.

Seasonal variation in the production of consumer goods differs substantially from that in retail trade. Chart 3–1 shows that retail trade has the wider fluctuation. The variation in retail trade at the end and at the beginning of the year is far greater than that in production. This is accounted for by a policy of inventory building followed by many manufacturing companies in slack seasons when the characteristic of the product warrants it, and the permitting of inventories to run off somewhat at seasons of peak demand. Retail trade, on the other hand, does not fall off as much as production in midsummer when vacation periods tend to be bunched.

Chart 3–4, showing the changing seasonal variation in automobile production, reveals an interesting feature of several postwar seasonals in production. Because of urgency of demand in the early postwar, activity was kept at peak levels throughout the year. After most of the backlog of deferred demand was made up, characteristic seasonal variations reappeared. It should be noted that urgent demand was less influential in retail trade. Although automobiles were purchased any time of the year the consumer could obtain them in the early postwar period, Christmas buying was about as pronounced as ever.

The first panel of Chart 3–5 compares actual with seasonally adjusted civilian employment. The difference between the two lines represents seasonal variation. Employment falls to a seasonal low early in the year and rises to a seasonal high at midyear. Except for the seasonal low in industrial production in July, seasonal varia-

CHART 3-2

SEASONAL PATTERNS IN CONSUMER
GOODS OUTPUT, 1959

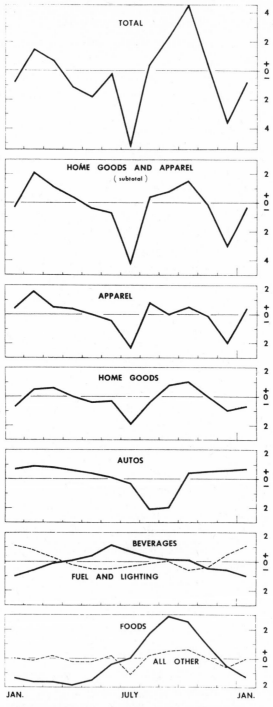

NOTE: Seasonal factors for total shown as points above or below 100. Points for components add to points for total consumer goods.

Source: Board of Governors of the Federal Reserve System, *Industrial Production: 1959 Revision* (Washington, D.C., July, 1960).

CHART 3-3

Seasonal Factors in Industrial Production, 1959

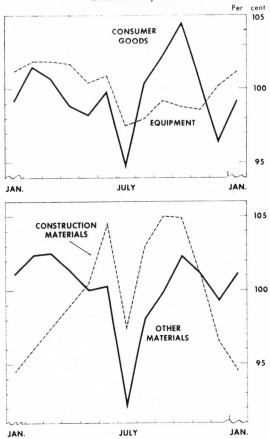

Source: Board of Governors of the Federal Reserve System, *Industrial Production: 1959 Revision* (Washington, D.C., July, 1960).

CHART 3-4

Automobiles—Seasonal Factors

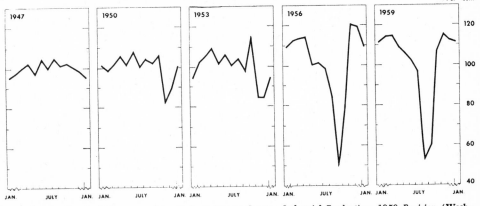

Source: Board of Governors of the Federal Reserve System, *Industrial Production: 1959 Revision* (Washington, D.C., July, 1960).

CHART 3-5

TRENDS IN EMPLOYMENT AND UNEMPLOYMENT

Actual and Seasonally Adjusted
January, 1949, to Date

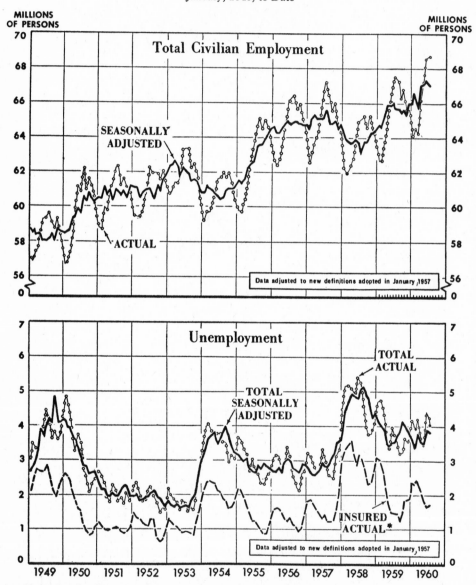

*Insured under following programs: State unemployment insurance, unemployment compensation for federal employees, veterans, ex-servicemen, railroad workers (RRB), and temporary programs (through June, 1959).

Source: United States Department of Labor, Bureau of Labor Statistics, *Monthly Report on the Labor Force* (Washington, D.C.: July, 1960). Beginning in January, 1960, data include Alaska and Hawaii.

tion in civilian employment is greater than that in industrial production. Employees do not move readily to find seasonal employment, but the production index averages seasonally low industries with seasonally high ones when both come at the same time of year.

A comparison of the civilian employment panel with the unemployment panel of Chart 3–5 shows that unemployment does not fall with the rise in civilian employment at midyear. This is because the labor force increases substantially at that time, due to the movement of students into the labor force. Thus, the peak increase in labor demand in early summer, accounted for largely by increased construction and agricultural activity, is accommodated by an increase in the labor force.

Chart 3–6 compares the seasonal variation in total manufacturing inventories with that in total retail trade. While the total stock of manufacturing inventories shows only a small seasonal fluctuation, the seasonal effect is fairly pronounced on inventory investment, which represents changes in inventory stock. Manufacturing inventories are built up from October to December, and then slowly reduced until September. Of course, this does not conform with the practices of many companies in individual industries whose sales patterns deviate from the general average. It does indicate that inventories tend to be reduced to a low point in conformance with a rise in sales to a seasonal peak in the fall. The effect is to curb the variation in production schedules, as noted later in the chapter.

CHART 3–6
SEASONAL VARIATION IN INVENTORIES: MANUFACTURING AND RETAIL TRADE

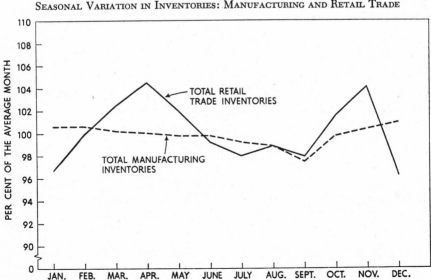

The seasonal variation in retail inventories is somewhat different. Retailers begin to build up inventories in February in anticipation of spring demand. As that demand fades, inventories taper off in the summer, only to be expanded again beginning in September in anticipation of heavy fall demand. Peak inventories are reached in November and allowed to run down with the heavy Christmas trade in December. After a further slight decline in January, the seasonal cycle repeats itself.

Frequent generalizations have implied that the business cycle is related to seasonal variation; but ordinarily, these generalizations have seemed far-fetched. The most likely connection, if any, is with the seasonal variation in inventory accumulation because of the key influence inventories play in the business cycle (see particularly Chapter 11). For instance, it is noted that recessions often become most evident in September. Manufacturers may become alarmed if slow sales result in rising inventories, inasmuch as a seasonal decline in inventories is to be anticipated.

Generally speaking, prices do not show significant seasonal variation. Theoretically, at least, they should not if they do not reflect such an influence as storage costs to carry over seasonal outputs. For instance, a high seasonal demand for construction materials is met by advanced inventorying rather than by increased prices. We note below, however, the possibility of price variation as a method of reducing the variation of seasonal outputs.

SEASONAL FORCES FACED BY THE INDIVIDUAL DECISION MAKER

The basic influences of weather variation and seasonal buying founded on customary holiday periods, such as Christmas, are so ingrained in our way of life that businessmen adapt to them rather than considering the situation which would exist without such seasonal forces. Most businessmen face seasonal variation in supply of raw materials or other purchases as well as in demand for their goods. Weather is the most frequent cause of seasonal variation in supply. The output of many raw materials is dependent on weather and customary buying seasons. Final consumers buy different clothing for winter than for summer and concentrate much of their gift buying at Christmas time. It is easily seen that some businessmen face a complicated set of seasonal patterns.

A company's sales may be considerably more stable than the various seasonal variations would appear to indicate because the company may emphasize different products with alternating seasonal peaks throughout the year. An old familiar illustration is the coal and ice company in small towns at the turn of the century. By the twenties the diversification became much more sophisticated, as in the rubber companies of Ohio. Seasonal shifts in production were made between rubber footwear largely for winter use and rubber tires largely for summer use. As a result, employment by individual companies became more stable than the sale of individual products.

A similar influence grew up with the development of national markets—diversification of regional demands became concentrated with individual companies. Restricted markets had often accentuated seasonal variation. Local demands are founded on a given climate and on the needs of particular industries. The tin-container industry of fifty years ago illustrates this situation. The production of tin containers was localized, so that plants supplied the demands of companies in a very limited territory. Some plants produced containers in fruit and vegetable canning centers and operated at a very low rate except at the season when fruits and vegetables were harvested. Others, which operated in localities specializing in the preparation of fish for market, produced little except when containers were needed for this limited purpose. The growth of large corporations which sell their products throughout the country has reduced the seasonal variation created by local markets.

PLANNING FOR SEASONAL CHANGES

A businessman faces three important types of seasonal planning: with respect to shifts in seasonal requirements for labor, for inventory, and for cash. In most companies, seasonality of sales is great enough that some layoffs of employees are unavoidable. If the seasonal variations occurring in sales are clearly understood, the layoff of employees can be reduced to a minimum. One way is to postpone maintenance and repair work to periods of seasonally low sales. Another is to develop some scheme of seasonal stabilization, such as by diversification among products which experience more or less opposite seasonal variations, or by other methods noted below. Limitation of seasonal layoffs is dramatized by "annual wage" plans, which guarantee an established proportion of workers attached to the company a minimum number of weeks of work each year.

Inventory plans are established to take care of peak seasonal needs, as represented by buildup of inventories in retail stores before the Christmas rush or by the tapering-off of inventories before low seasonal sales. More aggressively, variation in inventory stock may be employed as a method of stabilizing production schedules even though productive capacity might be adequate to provide product for any seasonal expansion in sales. In that scheme, inventories are accumulated in seasonally low periods to keep the labor force employed and to maintain higher efficiency in the use of capacity. Later, at the seasonal peaks, some of the sales are filled out of inventory.

In highly seasonal industries the needs for cash vary greatly. If the pattern of seasonal sales is clearly traced, and if other seasonal plans—such as the postponement of maintenance work to seasonally low periods and the accumulation of inventories in those periods—are clearly recognized, anticipated cash needs can be projected. This will help the company to economize on cash requirements and help to avoid insolvency growing out of temporary cash requirements. Forecasts of sales fluctuations arising from business cycle and other changes are necessary to cover all cash needs; but often, the seasonal variation is the most important one, especially in cyclically stable industries. Most companies find it very worth while to avoid undue increases in cash balances at the end of seasonal expansion in sales and to avoid undue limitation of cash when a seasonal expansion of sales is in the offing.

STABILIZATION OF SEASONAL VARIATIONS

Reference has been made to product diversification and to accommodating inventory changes as methods of dampening seasonal fluctuations in a company's total sales or production schedules. These measures have had important stabilizing effects. Matching products with opposite seasonal movements helps a company to keep regular employment throughout the year and helps to keep capital more effectively employed. When products are storable at reasonable warehouse cost, when physical deterioration can be kept within reasonable limits, and when demand changes are not unpredictable because of such influences as style, the building-up of inventories in off-seasonal periods fills in the seasonal valleys, and using up the inventories at seasonal peaks levels out the seasonal hills.

Another type of diversification frequently advocated is the shifting of employees at different times in the year from seasonal-peak industries to seasonal-trough industries. Although often tried, the method has had little success because of the expense of adding temporary employees, the problem of adapting workers' skills to new types of operation, various institutional factors such as unemployment insurance benefits which reduce the worker's incentive to shift, and the great distance from home of much of the seasonal work which might be available. Forty years ago, when the wheat-harvesting process required a relatively large temporary increase in labor, wages for temporary labor two or three times the regular rate had to be paid.

A possibility that has often appeared attractive represents some kind of manipulation to effect a redistribution of annual sales to provide less variation in the rate of purchase. Three principal approaches may be noted: (1) increased sales activity in off-seasonal periods; (2) offering a price inducement in seasonally slack periods; and (3) encouraging more regular use of the product. As to the first, businessmen find that sales pressure works most effectively in accentuating demand increases rather than in changing the direction of changes in demand. As to the second, there are some illustrations of reducing seasonal variation in sales by offering lower prices in off-seasonal periods, such as so-called "white goods" sales of department stores in February or August, or improved trade-in terms for old-model automobiles as the new models are announced. According to the best evidence, these methods have had only a limited influence.[2] As to the third approach, there is little evidence that buyers, whether final or intermediate, will significantly change their rate of use of a product as a result of a propaganda campaign. When the seasonal variation in sales is effectively shifted, it is most likely that the rate of use will remain largely unchanged, while the buyers will increase their inventory holdings in the seasonally low periods when purchases are increased. A classic illustration is the long-established practice of the Dennison Manufacturing Company in promoting the sale of Christmas cards throughout the year by offering a preseason price advantage. Thus, changes in the seasonal rate of sales turn largely on offering a price advantage which compensates for inventory holding by the buyer.

---

[2]See Oswald W. Knauth, former director of the R. H. Macy Company, "Some Reflections on Retail Prices," *Economic Essays in Honor of Wesley Clair Mitchell* (New York: Columbia University Press, 1935), p. 207. Knauth footnotes the exceptions with the statement: "The August Furniture Sale, August Fur Sale, and January White Sale have become so well established as to create a new seasonal cycle." He also calls attention to the following experience: "In one instance an offering of white curtains at a low price in the middle of February brought a demand for only 600 pairs; in the middle of March, the same curtains at the same price brought a demand for 11,000 pairs."

One type of influence on the seasonal variation of sales the producers can introduce is illustrated by the control of model changes by automobile manufacturers. Chart 3-4 on page 37 principally represents the seasonal variation induced by changing models late in the summer. Probably, the seasonal variation otherwise would represent a higher spring rise and seasonal lows in the late fall and early winter. The separate importance of model changes in the automobile seasonal is recognized to be so important by the Federal Reserve that allowance for the timing and duration of model change-over periods is estimated separately from other seasonal influences.[3] The introduction of model changes appears to have only limited possibilities as an influence on the seasonal variation of sales in other consumer durable products, and practically none in nondurable products.[4]

FORECASTING SEASONAL VARIATION

The problem of forecasting typical seasonal variation is usually very simple because changes seldom occur rapidly. With only limited knowledge of industry and company practices the forecaster can judge whether significant changes in seasonal demand or in stabilizing measures will occur in the near future. If no significant changes are expected, the recent seasonal variation can be confidently projected into the near future.[5] Such procedures are sound for only a few years into the future because practically all seasonals change slowly even though industry practices may remain relatively stable.

At the present time, there is an exciting possibility that we may soon be able to make reasonably effective specific, as contrasted with typical, weather forecasts. This arises from imaginative study of weather changes, but more importantly from a break-through in our knowledge of the universe provided by weather-describing

---

[3] See Board of Governors of the Federal Reserve System, *Industrial Production: 1959 Revision* (Washington, D.C., July, 1960), p. 50.

[4] We may footnote the interesting case of the Federal Reserve preventing a seasonal rise in interest rates in the autumn, when credit demands increase, by providing temporary credit ease. This is a good illustration of seasonal stabilization of interest rates, but the method cannot be applied by businessmen to smooth out activity fluctuation.

[5] The fact that different "product mixes" will occur in totals means that the seasonal component of the total will change even though the basic seasonal patterns of the different products remain the same. See the difference in the plotted lines in Chart 3-1. The new seasonal index for the total can be projected, however, if the new weights can be judged and are applied to the seasonals established for the separate products in the past.

satellites and other new space information. Although it is too early to reduce the new information to quantitative methodology, reasonable promise exists that this may be possible within another decade.[6] If this new achievement materializes, most specific seasonal changes may be effectively forecast, inasmuch as such variation is caused by weather rather than by custom. A new instrument would be available to aid in forecasting consumer demand, for we know that an important factor responsible for seasonal changes in consumer demand is represented by vagaries of the weather. (The importance of summer weather changes is particularly apparent in sales of air conditioners.)

Returning to the question of forecasting the typical seasonal variation for individual products or for the sales of particular companies, the marked contrast with forecasts of other fluctuations should be noted. The typical seasonal movement is expected and clearly understood. As we shall see, that situation is far different from other business fluctuations. The difference is related to the fact that seasonal fluctuations in an individual product or industry are generally unrelated to those of other products or industries, while nonseasonal business fluctuations are induced by combined effects in the total economy. This is the theme with which we started this chapter, and the macroeconomic character of nonseasonal fluctuations is a theme which carries through the rest of the book.

FOR REFLECTION AND ANALYSIS

1. How do seasonally adjusted data lead to better interpretation of current business changes?
2. What tends to happen to unemployment when the greatest seasonal increase in the labor force occurs?
3. Compare seasonal variation in retail trade with that in manufacturing production.
4. Compare seasonal variation in retail trade with seasonal variation in inventories held by retailers.
5. Compare seasonal variation in total employment with that in total production.
6. How would you decide whether planning for seasonal sales in any particular company is most important with respect to requirements for labor, inventory, or cash?

---

[6]Long-range weather forecasting has made considerable progress. This is illustrated by Sverre Petterssen, *Weather Analysis and Forecasting* (2d ed.; New York: McGraw-Hill Book Co., Inc., 1956); and C. G. Abbot, *A Long-Range Forecast of United States Precipitation* (Washington, D.C.: Smithsonian Institution, 1960).

7. Rank methods of seasonal stabilization according to effectiveness. What qualifications would you make about your ranking?

8. What advantages would be achieved with short-term specific weather forecasts? Canvass a few of your friends to see what they think the possibilities are of making specific weather forecasts.

9. Compare the problem of forecasting seasonal variations with that of forecasting business cycle fluctuations.

Chapter 4

FACTORS RESPONSIBLE FOR THE BUSINESS CYCLE

In slightly over a hundred years, there have been 25 business cycles in the United States. We can count 25 business cycle peaks beginning with June, 1857, and ending with July, 1957, as shown in Table 4-1. A simple tabulation of the information in Table 4-1 reveals that 14 of the 25 cycles were three to four years in length, four were shorter (minimum 27 months), and seven were longer (maximum 99 months). Two of the shorter cycles were only marginally less than three to four years, and one of the longer ones only marginally more, so that we can say that two thirds of our business cycles have lasted a modal length of three to four years. Furthermore, all of the longer cycles have been connected either with wars or with deep depressions, and the two cycles significantly shorter than 3 years occurred at the beginning of the Civil War and at the end of World War I. Since 1900 the only cycles significantly longer than four years occurred in World War II, the Korean War, and the Great Depression.

The troughs and peaks show clearly in past history, as indicated, for instance, by the National Bureau of Economic Research method of measurement described below. The period from trough to peak is called expansion, and from peak to trough is called contraction. Except during war periods, expansions have generally ranged from 20 to 30 months in length.[1] The variation in contractions has been much greater, depending on whether or not a serious depression developed. Without serious depression, contractions have been short, usually lasting a little less or a little more than a year.

Frequently, efforts have been made to squeeze from this information more detail in order to provide a fuller description of the

---

[1]Note the exception in the 1930's. This is discussed in Chapter 13.

TABLE 4–1

UNITED STATES BUSINESS CYCLE PEAKS AND TROUGHS*

| TROUGH | PEAK | TROUGH | DURATION IN MONTHS OF: | |
			Expansion	Contraction
Dec., 1854	June, 1857	Dec., 1858	30	18
Dec., 1858	Oct., 1860	June, 1861	22	8
June, 1861	Apr., 1865	Dec., 1867	46	32
Dec., 1867	June, 1869	Dec., 1870	18	18
Dec., 1870	Oct., 1873	Mar., 1879	34	65
Mar., 1879	Mar., 1882	May, 1885	36	38
May, 1885	Mar., 1887	Apr., 1888	22	13
Apr., 1888	July, 1890	May, 1891	27	10
May, 1891	Jan., 1893	June, 1894	20	17
June, 1894	Dec., 1895	June, 1897	18	18
June, 1897	June, 1899	Dec., 1900	24	18
Dec., 1900	Sept., 1902	Aug., 1904	21	23
Aug., 1904	May, 1907	June, 1908	33	13
June, 1908	Jan., 1910	Jan., 1912	19	24
Jan., 1912	Jan., 1913	Dec., 1914	12	23
Dec., 1914	Aug., 1918	Mar., 1919	44	7
Mar., 1919	Jan., 1920	July, 1921	10	18
July, 1921	May, 1923	July, 1924	22	14
July, 1924	Oct., 1926	Nov., 1927	27	13
Nov., 1927	Aug., 1929	Mar., 1933	21	43
Mar., 1933	May, 1937	June, 1938	50	13
June, 1938	Feb., 1945	Oct., 1945	80	8
Oct., 1945	Nov., 1948	Oct., 1949	37	11
Oct., 1949	July, 1953	Aug., 1954	45	13
Aug., 1954	July, 1957	Apr., 1958	35	9
Average, 25 cycles, 1854–1958......................			30.1	19.5

*Reference dates as estimated by the National Bureau of Economic Research.

business cycle. Particularly, recovery has been distinguished from prosperity in expansion and recession from depression in contraction. The difficulty is that no acceptable objective measurement is available to divide the movement into more detailed phases. A likely candidate for making the division is a "normal" or "equilibrium" level, but agreement is lacking on the location of such levels. Even what should constitute the dividing lines is not entirely clear. How low should unemployment reach before we say recovery has shifted to prosperity? It has become the practice in some quarters to describe short contractions as mere recessions, with the implication that depression did not develop. But the idea has not been reduced to a measureable basis.

The substantial cluster of the business cycle at the three- to four-year modal length has presented another irresistible tendency to generalize. It is tempting to look for a mathematical law which will develop a mechanical timing sequence, and considerable effort has gone into such an enterprise. We cannot prove that no such mechanical law exists, but we can show that the evidence is insufficient for accepting it. If there were such a law, extra long cycles should be followed by extra short ones and vice versa, but no such tendency exists. It is possible, of course, that extra long and extra short cycles can be explained by special circumstances, as indicated in the first paragraph of this chapter. But no mathematical law has been devised which excludes these circumstances, and to do so would require great ingenuity. Furthermore, we cannot be sure of the limits of the special circumstances which might occur.

The word "cycle" is appropriately employed in a mathematically imprecise way.[2] To speak mathematically, the term "rhythm" should be used, which implies regular recurrence.

Since the business cycle evidently is not satisfactorily described by a simple rhythm, a tempting generalization is that it is described by a more complicated one. A series of periods of different lengths might be revolving simultaneously. We have seen in Chapter 2 that such ideas have some plausibility, but they are too vague to be helpful in a leading analysis.

Belief that the business cycle is a false summarization of separate and unequal cycles in different industries follows the same general vein. That there are distinctive cyclical movements in some industries appears to have been demonstrated, as summarized in Chapter 2. The idea that nothing more exists than separate industry cycles must, however, be rejected. It fails to explain the pervasiveness and generality of the business cycle, as shown, for instance, by the National Bureau evidence summarized below. It is inconsistent with the logical evidence on interrelated effects among different parts of the economy which is carefully developed in this book.

The timing of peaks and troughs certainly is not all that is factually established about the business cycle, but other information is more complicated and generally less clear. Over the hundred-year period, it is not possible to establish effectively what the amplitude of movement has been, although difference in variation

---

[2]See Wesley C. Mitchell, *Business Cycles: The Problem and Its Setting* (New York: National Bureau of Economic Research, Inc., 1927), pp. 377–78, where Mitchell reports a "conference on cycles" to this effect.

can be shown more clearly in recent cycles. Even now, it is difficult or impossible to state a universally acceptable measure of the degree of variation because of incompleteness of our most satisfactory aggregate measurements. The measurements do indicate a significant difference in variation in different parts of the expansion and contraction, and these differences are summarized in the following chapter.

Finally, we should state more positively what a business cycle is. The definition is a generalization from experience and, as indicated by the above discussion, does not identify a mechanical model. To this date the definition stated by Mitchell in 1927 remains standard:

Business cycles are a type of fluctuation found in the aggregate economic activity of nations that organize their work mainly in business enterprises: a cycle consists of expansions occurring at about the same time in many economic activities, followed by similarly general recessions, contractions, and revivals which merge into the expansion phase of the next cycle; this sequence of changes is recurrent but not periodic; in duration business cycles vary from more than one year to ten to twelve years; they are not divisible into shorter cycles of similar character with amplitudes approximating their own.[3]

As Fabricant stated in 1959: "The heart of the problem of business cycles, Mitchell felt, lay in the question, 'how an economic system of interrelated parts develops internal stresses during expansions, stresses which bring on recessions, and how the uneven contractions of its varied parts pave the way for revivals.'" The burden of this chapter and the following one is to explain that process.

THE NATIONAL BUREAU MEASUREMENT OF BUSINESS CYCLES

The dating of cyclical peaks and troughs, as shown in Table 4–1, is the work of the National Bureau of Economic Research. In its study of the business cycle, these trough and peak months are called reference dates because they are used to compare with the cyclical peaks and troughs found in individual-industry series. The reference dates are timed from a study of more than a thousand individual-industry peaks and troughs. They approximate the modal points shown in groupings of the individual series, although some series are properly considered more important than others in deciding on the particular month which best indicates the peak or trough for total industry.

---

[3]*Ibid.*, p. 468.

The important point for our purposes is to show how closely the reference dates and peaks and troughs of individual-industry cycles correspond. First, we should consider the simple process by which the peaks and troughs of the individual-industry cycles are located. As an initial step, each series is seasonally adjusted, i.e., the typical seasonal variation is divided out. Peaks and troughs of the adjusted series are located by inspection.

For each individual-industry series, an average of the cyclical movement is developed to compare with the showing of the reference dates, as depicted in Chart 4–1. An orderly process is essential in developing this picture. The various cycles occurring over time in most industries are at different absolute levels because of growth or possibly decadence occurring in the industry. The first step, therefore, is to put each cycle, measured from trough to trough, on a comparable basis. The method of doing this involves comparing the months of each cycle with the average level of the cycle. The simple process used involves dividing the figure for each month of each cycle by the average of all months in that cycle. Another way of saying this is that the average month in each cycle is taken to represent 100 per cent.

The standing for the initial trough of the average cycle in any industry is obtained by averaging the percentage standings shown for all of the initial troughs in all of the specific cycle measurements of this series. As shown in Chart 4–1, this average came out to slightly over 70 for coke production. The standings for the peak and terminal trough for the average cycle are obtained in a similar way.

The placing of the peak and terminal trough in Chart 4–1 artificially takes all of the expansions in coke production as of the same length, and likewise for the contractions. This fiction makes it possible to spot average standings at other points in the cycle than at the initial trough, peak, and terminal trough. Each expansion is divided into three parts of equal length. A similar procedure is followed for the contractions. The average standing is found for each of these parts, and then the average is found for each part for all of the expansions and for all of the contractions. Thus, the open-dot points in the expansion and in the contraction are located on Chart 4–1. All told, nine standings result. The initial trough is called Stage I; the peak, Stage V; and the terminal trough, Stage IX. The average standings at the mid-points of the three parts of expansion are called Stages II, III, and IV; and the contraction Stages VI, VII, and VIII are similarly developed. From these meas-

CHART 4-1

SAMPLE CHART OF CYCLICAL PATTERNS
(As Developed by the National Bureau of Economic Research)

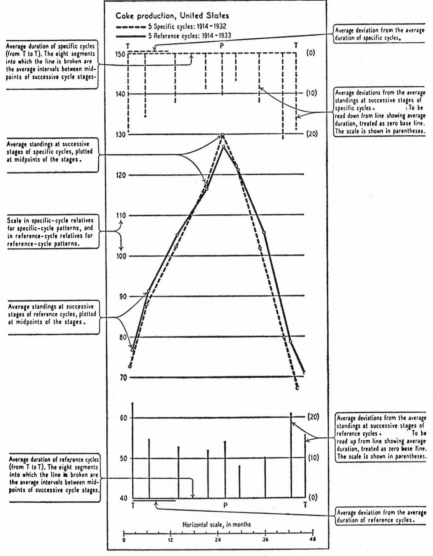

T represents the trough stage (I or IX), P the peak stage (V).

Source: Reproduced with permission from A. F. Burns and W. C. Mitchell, *Measuring Business Cycles* (New York: National Bureau of Economic Research, Inc., 1946), p. 35.

urements, summarizations on the differential rates of change in different parts of the expansion and contraction are inferred, and provide the basis for generalizations in this respect summarized in the following chapter.

The measurements so far obtained represent the specific cycle of the individual industry and are identified by the dash line in Chart 4-1. In order to demonstrate how universally the business cycle of aggregate industry permeates each individual industry, a second set of measurements is developed, using reference dates of aggregate industry for the initial trough, the peak, and the terminal trough instead of the peak and trough dates actually occurring in

CHART 4-2

PERCENTAGE DISTRIBUTION OF 794 SERIES ACCORDING TO THEIR CHARACTERISTIC CYCLICAL TIMING

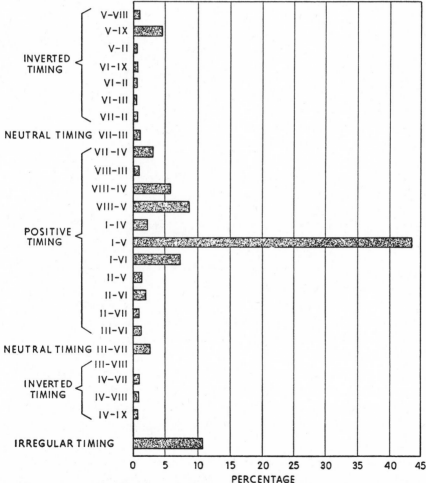

STAGES COVERED
BY EXPANSION

Source: Reproduced with permission from W. C. Mitchell, *What Happens during Business Cycles: A Progress Report* (New York: National Bureau of Economic Research, Inc., 1951), p. 54.

the individual industry. The measurements developed are shown by the solid line in Chart 4-1, and it will be seen that the trough reference dates lag slightly after the coke production troughs, while the peak reference date is timed with that of coke production. Standings between reference dates are similarly shown for coke production by the solid line. These differ slightly from the contrasting standings in the specific cycle.

The striking fact demonstrated by Chart 4-1 is the close similarity between the specific and reference cycle. This result is typical of about 90 per cent of the individual series studied by the National Bureau. It is the simplest and most effective demonstration of how universally the business cycle permeates our economy. The correspondence for a sample of 794 individual-industry series as summarized by the National Bureau is pictured in Chart 4-2.

The 10 per cent which reveal "irregular timing," i.e., show no clear conformity to the business cycle, obviously are unrelated to business cycle conditions. About half of these reflect the movement of farm products or foods, which are more affected by weather conditions than by business cycle variations. About a tenth reflect public works, which proceed independently of the current profit outlook. About 15 per cent represent sticky prices; illustrations are streetcar fares and railway rates. Another 15 per cent represent raw material inventories, such as cattle-hide leather, which are not readily adjusted to business cycle changes.

CUMULATION AND CULMINATION IN THE BUSINESS CYCLE

The key factor in the business cycle is cumulative change arising within the markets of the economy. Various economic factors begin to increase, and expansion occurs. Once the rise attains momentum, it is hard to stop until contractionary forces set up by the expansion itself become powerful. Although the momentum generated in contraction generally is greater than in expansion, a similar broad description applies.

Rising economic factors which will generate cumulation are income and complementary economic factors such as production and employment, also increasing expenditure rates such as in inventory investment or retail trade, as well as prices and wage or profit rates. When a change has occurred in one of these factors, conditions can never again be the same in our interrelated economy. If, for instance, income is increased, at least some proportion of the increase will be spent in the time period; and if the income which was already being received continues to be spent at the same rate, increase in expenditure of the new income will add to total income in the next time period.

The process was reduced to a mechanical principle called the *multiplier* in Keynesian economics. We need not get into the technicalities of this principle now, but we should point out that the simplification achieved depends to a considerable extent on the assumption that multiplication arises from income paid out in limited areas of the economy. Emphasis was placed particularly on income generated by government or private investment expenditure. While these areas have been notably important in generating change in the past, the limitation has been discredited by the increasing importance of changes in consumer expenditure. As usually stated, therefore, the multiplier principle is not sufficiently general to identify the cumulative process.

As limited to income and expenditure, we must recognize that any increase which occurs will tend to maintain higher levels. In this, we assume that the rate at which consumer income is spent remains relatively constant. Under these conditions, increases in expenditure generated by additional income will produce for a limited time a higher income and expenditure level than existed before the increase occurred.

Since all of the increase in income probably will not be spent, however, the new level of income and expenditure, looked at in this limited way, might be expected slowly to decline toward the initial level in existence before the income increase occurred. The reason why that does not happen in business cycle expansions is that the process of cumulative change is broader than can be encompassed in a mechanical statement of income and expenditure relationships. One small increase in income may generate no more side effects than can be recognized in a mechanical statement such as the multiplier, but in business cycle movements the influence is much broader. No one has successfully incorporated the side effects in a broad mechanical principle, but the major types of side effects can be readily recognized.

Increased level of expenditure frequently adds to the desired level of inventory investment, and this adds further to the income level. The higher income level generates further increases in expenditure. Decision makers may come to count on a continuance of the higher level of expenditures and be induced to add further to durable investment expenditures. The higher levels of demand will strengthen prices; and to avoid having to pay still higher prices, businessmen may add further to inventory investment. Higher expenditure levels will induce higher profit rates, if for no other reason than that increased use of already existing plant and equipment will reduce per unit costs. Wage rates will tend to be increased more readily in the optimistic atmosphere, and this may add to the confidence of consumers and induce them to spend more freely. The side effects described here do not necessarily imply major psychological repercussions; but these repercussions frequently become an integral part of the process, and changes may be colored by hysteria and speculation.

The side effects in contraction can be similarly described, the difference, of course, being that side effects of decreases are inducing further decreases. Actually, the side effects of declining income and expenditure have tended to be more powerful than those of increasing income, since hysteria and speculation are more quickly generated under pessimistic conditions. Inventory runoff in early contraction tends to be more drastic than added purchases for inventory early in expansion. Security prices tend to be run down more rapidly than they are run up. New institutional changes, illustrated in the rest of this paragraph, however, are now modifying the extent to which early contraction tends to proceed at a rapid pace. Automatic stabilizers, represented by such factors as unemployment compensation and reduced average rate of income tax on lower income, have played an important part in limiting early declines in disposable income and perhaps have lent consumers some encouragement in maintaining their expenditure rates out of disposable income received. Wage rates are more stable in recession under modern institutional developments, and this tends to have a similar effect. Commodity prices tend to decline less than formerly, and this allays the tendency to cut inventories.

Even so, the tendency is for cumulative change to be more powerful in contraction than in expansion. With the knowledge that declines are likely to continue in economic factors at least for a limited time, the conservative policy is curtailment unless immediate demand is obvious and pressing. Declining income and expenditure are readily reinforced by side effects. Decisions to cut back in contraction are generally made more promptly than decisions to buy in expansion.

As expansion or contraction proceeds, the cumulative forces on which the movement depends begin to weaken, and ultimately they are dissipated. In expansion the rise in economic activity pushes on available capacity, creating shortages. This has three effects. To the extent that resources are not available and adequate substitutes cannot be found, some curtailment occurs. The shortages drive up prices, reducing the profitability of industries buying the resources. Shortages generate demand for additional capacity, the satisfaction of which frequently requires use of short resources, adding further to shortages. As the new capacity is completed, however, the situation is sharply reversed. New supply becomes available, and demand for resources to make new capacity is partially withdrawn. This is one of the major factors which leads to the culmination of expansion.

The movement of inventory investment is another major factor. Generally, the demand for inventory is determined by the level and change in level of sales. Early in expansion, cumulative processes drive up some demand faster than expected so that actual inventory purchase falls behind. Businesses begin to struggle to get inventory to the desired levels. As demand levels off, the battle is won, but reduced inventory demand results. This provides a powerful culminating effect. Expenditures are cut to the extent that less inventory is demanded. The key influence in this factor is the leveling of demand, which is only partially explained in the preceding paragraph. The problem is analyzed in detail in the following chapter.

Apparent overabundance of inventory is closely related to the cumulative processes of decline in contraction. Just as inventory accumulation falls behind in early expansion, inventory runoff falls behind in early contraction. At first, most businessmen find the rate of decline in sales surprising. Production schedules are cut belatedly before the existence of a contraction phase is fully recognized. By that time, they are unhappy about the high level of inventories in relation to current sales. Production schedules are then cut drastically, and better adjustment is achieved. Some relaxation is permitted in production scheduling, and resulting reduction in inventory runoff is a stabilizing effect. Thus, inventory change is important in the culmination of contractions.

Generally, the rate of investment in durable capital (plant and equipment) slows down in recession. An effect opposite to that of change in capacity in expansion is created. Capacity completion slows down some months after the contraction has been under way, since the rate of starting projects declined as contraction started. With a decline in new capacity becoming available, demand comes to be less weakened by the expansion of potential sources of supply.

Psychological factors lead to culmination in both expansion and contraction. Speculation builds up to a climax. Overdevelopment in industries which appeared unusually favorable early in expansion finally comes to be recognized. If consumers have engaged in splurges of demand in some particular areas, such as automobiles or housing, the supply situation ultimately forces unfavorable prices. The general movement of commodity prices which edged upward as shortages appeared tends to level off as the peak is reached.

The purpose of this section is to provide an early preview of the fundamental nature of expansions and contractions. The process is more fully described in the following chapter. In the remainder of the present chapter, we discuss briefly the maintenance of momentum in the business cycle, exogenous forces which influence the business cycle movement, why the business cycle represents disequilibrium conditions, and why short-period variation arises in expansion and contraction

MAINTENANCE OF MOMENTUM

The reader may have heard at one time or another the comment that, instead of there being a business cycle, the level of business conditions represents a purely random situation; i.e., how good business conditions are to be next month is completely independent of how good they are this month. The preceding section shows how untrue such a statement is; cumulative factors create a momentum in our type of capitalistic economy. This fact has long been recognized by students of economic time series. The successive values of time series are related to each other rather than representing independent items; in technical language, they are serially correlated.

The momentum attained by economic activity at any given level is primarily dependent upon the conservatism of consumer expenditure. Consumers spend over 90 per cent of their disposable income except in highly abnormal times, such as in World War II. The percentage tends to rise somewhat in contraction. Since consumer expenditures represent about 65 per cent of total expenditures in all sectors of the economy, it will be seen that a sizable proportion of all income received is spent. Income received is determined by the level of activity in the preceding period.

In prosperity, consumers tend to save more than in contraction, but this is a period when business expenditure is on the rise. In prosperity, then, consumers divert income to financing business expenditure on capital and thus do not contribute to erratic fluctuations by their actions in increasing savings.

Business expenditure is much more variable than that of consumers. It depends more on anticipations than on actual income received; and, as indicated by surges of activity in capital expenditure, anticipations vary much more than actual receipt of income. Business expenditures on capital are powerful influences in moving activity up in expansion and down in contraction; but because of their relatively small proportions, they change the level of activity significantly only over a period of several months.

Government expenditure tends to be a moderating influence under modern conditions. There is a tendency to increase government expenditures in prosperity which probably is still irresistible. Needs for government services appear to increase when demands for output in the private economy increase. But under the modern philosophy of fiscal policy, government expenditures are well maintained in contraction. Government expenditures thus contribute to maintenance of the level achieved.

EXOGENOUS FORCES

The forces we have been describing arise from within the business system, i.e., the effects of the business system itself create them. Business cycle changes are also induced by outside forces. These are forces exogenous to the domestic business system, but nonetheless affect it when they occur. There is no completely satisfactory classification of exogenous forces, which will become clear as we discuss the following types:

1. Cosmic forces
2. Accidents—e.g., fire
3. War and threat of war
4. Other government influences
5. Business cycle conditions in foreign countries
6. Labor disturbances
7. New industries and inventions

The first two of these forces are clearly exogenous, while all of the others may to a greater or less extent be influenced by internal factors.

Unexpected cosmic changes may exert a significant influence. For instance, irregular weather variations clearly influence prices. The price of heating oil is driven up in an extra cold winter. An unusually small or large harvest of some agricultural crop will affect its price. Floods, earthquakes, and windstorms create damage which must usually be replaced, thus leading to increased sales and firmer prices. An illustration is the "big wind," resulting from a hurricane in the fall of 1949, which did a great deal of damage along the East Coast. Important as any such incident is to the persons directly involved, the effect on the course of the business cycle has invariably been minor.

Expected cosmic changes are of no importance in this respect because their influence is discounted ahead of time. Typical seasonal variation represents the principal type. Business action would be taken if such variation failed to occur, rather than the reverse.

Accidents produce effects very similar to unexpected cosmic changes. Fire is the major type of accident influencing over-all economic change, and it sometimes results from storms. However caused, the resulting destruction of property tends to increase sales and to strengthen prices. Actually, in a country as large as ours the over-all influence of fire tends to average out and to remain fairly constant for the economy as a whole.

The most important outside force arises from political decisions, and chief among these is war or threat of war. War is unlikely to be traced directly to changes occurring in the business system. The causes of World War II may be rooted in the Great Depression, but this is different from the tracing of cumulative changes from current movements of business factors. Other government influences are coming more and more to be traceable to changes in the business system, as noted below.

War is the only exogenous factor which clearly has distorted the the business cycle to a major extent. The length and shape of business movements during and following both World War I and World War II certainly greatly differ from what would have happened without war. The Great Depression was rooted to an undetermined degree in the forces produced by World War I. In some quarters the high level of demand in the fifties is traced to World War II. Certainly, the war was a major factor in the high level of demand in the late forties.

A careful analysis of the way wars change the course of business cycles is beyond the scope of this book. The general character of the influence, however, is simple. First, "war prosperity" is created by abnormal increase in extra-economic demand. The financing of war demand is disturbing to a major degree, depending on the extent of the war effort and on the length of the war. Consumer expenditures cannot be permitted to rise commensurately with disposable income. The result is a high, but distorted, postwar demand. This is because of partial deficit financing during the war. More specific influences are traced in Chapter 13, in connection with the description of the influence of World War II.

Other government controls are much less exogenous because, in the modern world, governments have been forced to take economic conditions into consideration in making decisions. In theory, government policy is supposed to offset undesirable business changes, but this is not the invariable result even if planned that way. Public works planned in contraction may, for instance, exert their major expenditure effect at the peak of the following prosperity because of the inevitable lag in getting projects into full operation. And to a major extent, government decisions, especially in state and local governments, are unrelated to the current business situation. Roads and schools have to be built and are geared principally to an estimate of their need rather than to expected effect on total business activity. Taxes are planned to finance activities and depend more on the exigencies of financial solvency and political pressures than on the need for compensatory measures. Even in the federal government, short-run expenditure plans do not always point to a stabilizing effect. For instance, in the summer of 1957, a stretch-out in contracting for defense expenditures was a factor in the downturn which occurred. Nonwar political decisions are somewhat related to current business developments.

The business cycle in other countries is not always in phase with ours. Even though in phase, disturbances may arise in other countries which influence activity in our country. If foreign conditions are better than ours, foreign countries buy more from us, thus adding to sales and strengthening prices; if foreign conditions are worse than ours, they curtail purchases from us, reducing our sales and weakening prices. The inventory situation in foreign countries in recession may be depressive even though cyclical conditions are about in phase. Thus, in the spring of 1958, heavy European inventories of steel and coal added to an unusual extent to the competition in these industries in the United States at the time. Through international trade, relative differences in level of economic conditions tend to be equalized. The smaller and less diversified the country, the more important the foreign influence.

Strikes are definitely influenced by economic decisions, but their timing is dependent principally on the termination of contracts and on other factors independent of current economic changes; they therefore have the principal characteristics of outside forces. It is true, of course, that the nature of settlement will depend importantly on general economic conditions at the time. A more favorable settlement ordinarily will occur in expansion. The settlement is likely to be expansionary in the downswing as well as in the upswing, however. But each settlement must be studied in the light of prevailing opinions and attitudes, and broad generalizations may not be too helpful.

During a strike, both supply and demand are reduced. Frequently, the reduction in supply is a critical one. For instance, the long steel strike in June and July of 1952 eliminated relatively large steel inventories of some rolled products. It then became possible to pay higher wages and to charge higher prices. These added to income receipts in the industry.

New industries and inventions may exert initial effects on the business system comparable to those of an accident. The new industry or invention does not grow out of the gyrations of prices and production which carry cumulative forces along in the business system. Investment required to capitalize on the new industry or invention results from the businessman's decision, but the new technical development on which it is based does not grow out of cumulative business cycle expansions and contractions. Organized research in large corporations has much to do with technical developments, but there is no reason to believe that the fruition of such research will be timed with price and production changes. An interesting illustration is the introduction of a raw material plastic called "Delrin" by du Pont in the summer of 1959 after years of research and after the completion of a plant to produce it.

Good markets may foster scientific development because they lead to greater expenditures on research, but no one expects so many dollars spent on scientific research to produce scientific development in a constant ratio. As we shall see later, profitable experience arising from the application of scientific developments leads to a kind of contagious expansion (called "innovation"), but the original scientific development appears to be largely independent of current business changes. Innovation surges arise only after the scientific development has proved itself in the market.

We have considered in this section the origin of business cycle disturbance in the sense of new influences added to the changes taking place within the business system. Most obviously, new influences originate from outside forces. In a sense, they may also originate from the culmination of forces within the business system. The latter classification has meaning because over-all activity, which traces business cycle changes, represents the sum of activity in many industries and reflects intricate economic processes, none of which moves in exact unison with the rest. When any part of the over-all total falls out of step, its action on other parts of the economy is much like that of an outside force.

Influences spread in the same way that they do when an outside force introduces a sudden change at some point. For instance, decline in replacement demand for some consumer good from three million units one year to two million the next may be contrasted with the market influence of a decline in domestic oil prices caused by an exceptionally warm winter. The recognition of exogenous forces is helpful, but the lines of distinction should not be drawn too fine.

BUSINESS CYCLES REPRESENT DISEQUILIBRIUM CONDITIONS

Cumulative change is indicative of lack of equilibrium. In the static case, forces quickly draw markets back into adjustment. If a drift continues up or down, there must be some explanation for the failure of equilibrating forces to take effect.

A major type of evidence is the positive correlation between prices and output. As activity rises, prices rise. This is, of course, contrary to the movement along a static demand curve. What is happening is that demand is rising. The situation is pictured in Chart 4-3. Moving to the higher demand curve, both higher output and higher prices are indicated. The opposite occurs with a downward shift in demand. In recent contractions, total demand has declined only slightly; and general prices have declined little, because upward readjustments continue to occur in sticky price areas. In highly competitive raw material areas, however, prices have continued to decline significantly with falling demand.

There are two reasons why total demand rises and falls with the business cycle: (1) The business cycle movement is characterized by a rise and fall in total income and in total expenditure. A rise and fall in total expenditure produces a rise and fall in total demand. The shifting demand curves in Chart 4-3 reflect changes in total demand. (2) A business cycle expansion or contraction produces a psychological influence on spending. In expansion, rising prices may come to be anticipated, which will speed up spending, increase total demand, and make prices rise more. In contraction, falling prices may come to be anticipated, which will slow down spending and decrease total demand, thus extending the fall in prices.

As is frequently noted in the following pages, the change in prices becomes an important factor over the business cycle. Price rises tend to induce inventory accumulation. They also lead to an optimistic appraisal of potential markets and thus induce durable capital investment. Price declines tend to induce inventory depletion and lead to a pessimistic appraisal of potential markets, restraining enterprisers in adding to durable capital.

CHART 4–3

SHIFT IN THE DEMAND CURVE

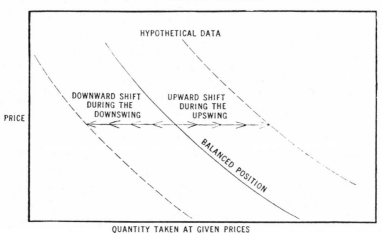

increase total demand, and make prices rise more. In contraction,

Nevertheless, the correlated movement of prices is more indicative of disequilibrating forces arising elsewhere than reflective of the direct influence of changing prices. The shifting demand curve can be principally explained by the influence of investment.

The Acceleration Principle. Investment expenditure represents payment for increasing the stock of capital as well as for replacing the stock which has worn out. To keep the illustration simple, let us ignore changes produced by the replacement of capital until the problem is considered more carefully in Chapter 10. The acceleration principle assumes that capital stock is increased to make possible larger sales. The idea is illustrated in Table 4–2. On the assumption that a dollar of capital is required for every dollar of sales made, it is easy to see how investment made to increase the stock of capital will vary markedly to accommodate slight variations in sales. This is indicated by column 3 in the table, which is equal to the amount of change occurring in column 2. Slight relative changes in sales bring major relative changes in net investment. The increase in column 3 from year 4 to year 6 is 500 per cent, while the assumption is that it is generated by an accompanying increase in sales of less than 10 per cent (from 107 to 116). The main idea of the acceleration principle is that net investment is induced by a change in sales. A change in final demand results in an accelerated demand for capital. While such a principle falls short of describing the complex of investment incentives, it contains enough truth to indicate an important reason why investment requirements rise dramatically in expansion and fall even more dramatically in recession.

TABLE 4–2

CAPITAL IN USE AND ADDED CAPITAL
(Hypothetical Illustration)

Year	(1) Sales	(2) Capital in Use	(3) Added Capital or Net Investment
1	100	100	
2	102	102	2
3	106	106	4
4	107	107	1
5	110	110	3
6	116	116	6
7	116	116	0
8	121	121	5
9	124	124	3
10	123	123	−1

The Multiplier Principle. Any dollar advance in total expenditure is partially kept in the expenditure stream for a considerable time because of the tendency of consumers to spend a large proportion of income received. Consumers ordinarily spend over 90 per cent of their available income, and a large proportion of current income flows to them. As a result, the rise during expansion in the business cycle tends to be well maintained. The term "multiplier," as explained in Chapters 9 and 10, derives from the fact that the amount added by the rounds of consumer expenditure over many time periods will total to a multiple of an initial injection of nonconsumer expenditure. That is not the point, however, that we want to illustrate here. Rather, we wish to recognize that immediately following time periods will involve a higher level of expenditure because of the initial injection. Momentum tends to be maintained at various points in the business cycle, and the multiplier shows the basic reason why that is true.

Doubly Reinforcing Nature of Investment. Since investment does not proceed at a constant rate, it creates a disproportionate effect on demand and supply. This can be most simply illustrated in the case of inventories. While inventories are increasing, they add to income in the process of production, but do not similarly add to the supply of goods put up for sale. The increased income relative to supply put up for sale produces an inflationary situation. Oppositely, inventory runoff increases supply relative to income receipts and produces a deflationary situation.

A similar effect is produced in durable investment. Capacity to make goods is increased only when capital is completed. On the average, this requires several months. As the rate of capital investment increases, income paid out rises disproportionately to the rate at which capacity is completed. As the rate of capital investment slows down, completions hold at a high rate because they are dependent on the rate at which projects were started several months earlier, but the present slower rate of starts reduces the income paid out.

Investment and Credit Expansion. As investment rises to higher and higher levels in expansion, an increasing amount of credit is required for financing. This adds to the income stream, raising demand levels, and therefore is expansionary. Especially is this true since much of the added output is in investment goods which are not a part of the total supply available for consumer purchase.

An opposite situation arises in contraction. As investment drops, especially inventory investment, debt is paid off. This reduces the income stream, cutting down on demand levels, and therefore is contractionary. To the extent that it applies to inventories of consumer goods, the supply for consumer purchase is added to without adding to income payments currently made.

Although credit for financing adds to demand, this principle is not parallel to that stating the doubly reinforcing nature of investment. The latter states that supply and demand distortions are created by investment, especially if started at an irregular rate over time. That is true regardless of whether or not credit is employed in financing. When credit is employed, the effect is more inflationary or more deflationary. But if the credit funds are used in financing consumer purchases, they do not create important distortions between income paid out and the supply of goods made available for sale.

The importance of the effects produced currently, whether in the investment process or in credit extension, depends on the change taking place in the pressures applied. For instance, credit may be extended; but if it is less than in the recent past, the general effect may be contractionary. Likewise, capital completions may not be commensurate with investment expenditures currently being made; but if they are more nearly commensurate than in the recent past, the effect also could be contractionary. The *changes* produced are of major importance in the study of economic change.

Administered Price Effect. Administered (set by the seller) prices are less than warranted by demand conditions in expansion. Thus, demand cumulates more than a more perfect market would permit, and expansionary forces are increased.

Conversely, administered prices are cut little, if any, in contraction, and demand tends to suffer. If prices were immediately cut to the extent warranted by current demand, the contractionary force theoretically would be less. But declining prices would set up contractionary side effects.

Timing of Selling Pressure. Businessmen have learned that selling pressure provides the best return when it is added in a rising market. Therefore, by their efforts, they add more to expansionary markets than they prevent contractionary markets.

Backlogs. Some deferred demand is built up in contraction. The resulting backlog demand adds to the following expansion.

Speculative Gains and Losses. Speculative gains usually predominate in expansion, and they add to total market demand. Speculative losses predominate in contraction, and they reduce total market demand.

Initiating Changes. Some persons assume that cumulative changes are initiated by exogenous forces. In the above paragraphs, we have assumed initiating changes without inquiring into the forces causing them. While exogenous forces frequently do provide enough disturbance that cumulative change is sparked from them, forces within the business system also lead to disproportionate changes significant enough to initiate disturbing influences. This is largely because of the uncertainty businessmen face. Their forecasting is imperfect, and they are sure to conclude that the investment market is much better at one time than at another. The result is a speeding-up and slowing-down of investment expenditure, which accounts for a large part of the initiating changes assumed.

SHORT-PERIOD VARIATION

Expansions and contractions do not represent either straight lines or simple curves. Upward or downward momentum merely sets the general direction of movement. Even the belief that a steady movement is going to occur probably would defeat it. Enterprising individuals probably would anticipate further increases and drive activity up rapidly for a time, only to induce a reaction from such excessively rapid improvement. Overreaching would upset the steady rate. Actually, however, most decision makers do not anticipate a steady rate.

Anticipations do account for a significant part of short-period variation. Exogenous forces also play a part in producing this variation. Finally, short period variation may be related to shifts in demand in a highly prosperous period.

Business anticipations usually run for a period substantially shorter than the total expansion or contraction period, and are quickly revised to adapt to a shifting outlook as new facts appear. The situation is most simply related to inventory policy. If inventories are accumulated for products which sell in a highly competitive market, purchases are likely to be related to the movement of fluctuating prices. Purchases will be made fairly steadily while prices rise; but when they seem to be leveling off, there will be a tendency to delay. When it is believed the bottom has been reached, buying will be speeded up again. The resulting variation in investment expenditure tends to superimpose a saw-tooth fluctuation on total sales.

The idea that decisions slow down or speed up action founded on the current outlook has some application in inventory building or reduction even in products sold in administered-price markets and in other areas, such as regarding the rate at which new employees are added. Ruth Mack has made a thorough study of this problem, and we may quote a conclusion she has reached:

Finally, a type of reciprocating mechanism is implicit in the more or less well-defined time periods to which the long-short market range or the period of option apply in each sort of business. The short end of the range is defined by physical problems of delivery and processing; the long end by seasonal patterns of selling and of suppliers' production, or by the perishability of products with respect to style or physical attributes. Especially for businesses for which seasonal patterns are strong, the long end of the range is well defined. The period of option, also broadly specified, encourages explicit selection of the best time to buy within this period. As the limits to these periods are approached, the risk of further buying tends to increase at a greatly accelerated pace. This is a fact to which the particular buying firm, his supplier, and his banker are all likely to react in a parallel way.[4]

Decisions may be speeded up or slowed down within practicable limits, and some vacillation in economic change is thereby produced. When buying is for the shortest option period, activity is slowed down; and as buying shifts to the longer option period, activity is speeded up.

Nonrecurrent seasonal factors, such as an extra cold or extra warm winter, produce a slight speeding-up or slowing-down in business activity. This kind of seasonal change will not be eliminated from seasonally adjusted data because only the typical seasonal change can be divided out.

Other minor exogenous forces tend to create an undulating appearance in business fluctuations. A law may be passed which produces a short period of uncertainty; but after the initial disturbance, the momentum of business cycle expansion may greatly outweigh its influence. The threat of war may upset markets, but the effect may be slight after the first shock has spent itself. If the relative importance of such an outside force is not great enough to reverse the general cyclical movement, it will at least tend to introduce a slight variation. The variation will be in particular evidence if the outside force acts oppositely to the general direction of movement.

Finally, it is possible that some variation will occur in a highly prosperous period under conditions of "rolling readjustment," without reactions being great enough to produce a general contraction for many months. As the rate of automobile production declined in 1956, for instance, the purchase of consumer nondurable goods expanded, and expenditures for business equipment rose, but the timing of the "rolling" of purchases to new lines was not precisely dovetailed. A similar comment can be made with regard to the

---

[4]Ruth Mack, "Business Expectations and the Buying of Materials," *Expectations, Uncertainty, and Business Behavior* (edited by Mary Jean Bowman; New York: Social Science Research Council, 1958), p. 118. Dr. Mack speaks of short-period variations as "subcycles." Her studies have dealt principally with shoes, leather, and hides. However, considerable work has been done to show short cycles in other industries.

decline of residential construction and rise of nonresidential construction in the same year.

FOR REFLECTION AND ANALYSIS

1. Explain what the idea of the business cycle means to you.
2. What is the difference between the specific and the reference cycle in Chart 4–1?
3. What do stages and standings mean in the National Bureau method?
4. How do the reference dates in Table 4–1 add to our understanding of economic change?
5. Explain side effects, as the term is used in this chapter.
6. Why is the level of business activity during any month partly determined by the level in the preceding month?
7. Explain how most exogenous forces are not wholly independent of internal factors.
8. Why does cumulative change drive business conditions away from equilibrium for a considerable time?
9. Why does investment expenditure vary relatively more than capital stock, as illustrated in Table 4–2?
10. Explain the doubly reinforcing nature of investment.
11. What difference in inflationary effect is produced by credit extended for investment purchases compared to credit extended for financing sales of consumer goods?
12. Explain the determining factors of the short end and the long end of the period of option which influences short-period variation.

Chapter 5   EXPANSION, DOWNTURN, CONTRACTION, AND UPTURN

The purpose of this chapter is to explain how cyclical forces create an expansion, lead to a reversal, produce a contraction, and bring an upturn into expansion again. The description provided is only partially reportorial, for the explanation needed involves an analysis of underlying forces. The differences between cycles are great enough that summary statistical information reveals less about the underlying forces than we would wish. Partly, this is because changing institutional conditions have modified the movement of various processes over the business cycle. Furthermore, the particular demand conditions differ, so that the thread of variation may be through some expenditures in one cycle and through others in another.

Actually, the general direction of movement is not in doubt in expansions or contractions. This is clearly indicated in total industrial production. It is illustrated for total industrial production in four expansions in Chart 5-1. Declines in contractions are dramatic enough that generality and persistence of decline also are not in doubt.

DIFFUSION INDEXES

The tyro has great difficulty in visualizing the forces which turn expansion and contraction around. No effective measurements were available until recently to illustrate this process. The National Bureau of Economic Research has developed a set of measurements which shows that in almost any process the proportion of rising components reaches a peak long before the cyclical downturn and reaches a low long before the cyclical upturn. Thus, the spread of contractionary forces begins well before the general business-cycle

CHART 5–1

INDUSTRIAL PRODUCTION IN FOUR POSTWAR EXPANSIONS
(Seasonally Corrected, in Percentage of 1957 Average)

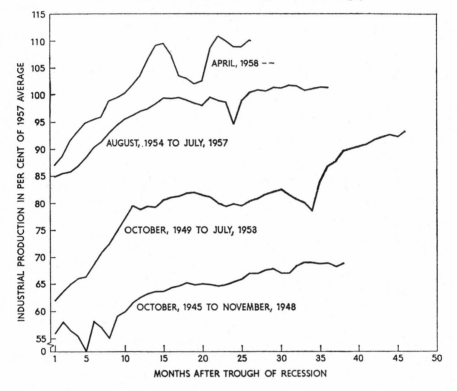

downturn, and the spread of expansionary forces begins well before the general business cycle upturn.

These measurements are called *diffusion indexes*. Such an index is shown in Chart 5–2. The chart discloses that, from 1885 to 1939, somewhere in the order of three fourths of the economc indicators rose to a peak in mid-expansion and dropped to about one fourth in mid-contraction. At the downturn and upturn, in the order of 50 per cent of the series were expanding. This makes sense since the number of series rising and falling might about balance when the aggregate reaches a high or when the aggregate reaches a low.

The diffusion index shows whether the scope of expansion has broadened or narrowed. That the narrowing begins well before the reference peak and the broadening starts again well before the reference trough clearly indicates that forces within the expansion turn the movement downward and that forces within the contraction turn the movement upward. Many measurements of the diffusion index have been developed for the postwar period. These lead to the same general conclusions as the prewar measurements. They are reviewed further in Chapter 17, where we consider the use of diffusion indexes in forecasting.

CHART 5–2

A Diffusion Index for 1885 to 1939

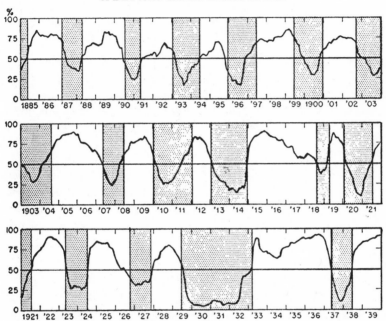

NOTE: Only series which conform well with business cycle movement are included; they number over 300 from 1920 to 1940. Shaded areas represent contractions.

Source: Reproduced with permission from Arthur F. Burns, *New Facts on Business Cycles* (New York: National Bureau of Economic Research, Inc., 1950), p. 12.

Whether or not diffusion indexes have any predictive value, which is beside the point for our present purpose, they should help us understand the spread of expansionary and later contractionary forces within business cycle expansion and the spread of contractionary followed by expansionary forces within the business cycle contraction. Such a description applies to changes within output, employment, prices, or profit. With respect to profits, Arthur Burns rationalizes this process as follows:

In the early stages of an expansion unit costs often decline as industrial facilities are improved or utilized more fully. But as prosperity cumulates, unit costs tend to mount for business firms generally; and since in many instances selling prices cannot be raised, profit margins here and there will narrow, thus offsetting the influence or profits of an increase in sales or reinforcing the effects of an occasional reduction in sales. The "squeeze" on profits becomes more widespread the longer the business expansion continues. In the first place, all firms do not have the same power to advance prices; some are prevented or limited by custom, trade marks, or governmental regulation. Secondly, errors pile up as mounting optimism warps the judgment of an increasing number of businessmen concerning the sales that can be made at profitable prices. Thus, after a business expansion has run for some time, the proportion of firms experiencing rising profits begins to shrink, although the profits of business in the aggregate continue to climb. Such a development spreads doubt or financial pressure to firms whose profits are still rising, and in time moderates their investments in sympathy with that of the growing number of firms whose business fortune is waning. Of course, a check to investment from this source strengthens an emerging tendency to postpone investment projects until a time when, it is felt, construction costs and financing charges will be reduced from the abnormal level to which they have been pushed by prosperity.[1]

EXPANSION

The point in the oscillation at which we begin makes little difference as long as the explanation is carried to the recurrence of that point. Recurrence of the movement and the way it generates itself are the characteristics to be explained. We may conveniently begin at the point where an upturn occurs. Explanation of the upturn may best be deferred.

As shown by the National Bureau measurements, described in Chapter 4, the early stages of expansion are usually rapid. This is shown most clearly in Chart 5-3, which depicts the rapid rate of increase from Stage I to Stage II in several indexes of business activity. An examination of the Industrial Production Index in the postwar reveals a similarly rapid increase in the early part of the expansion phase.

In explaining the early rapid rise in expansion, we must remember that expansion, although not universal, is already under way in particular parts of the economy before the upturn appears for the total economy. In fact, some slight rise in the total economy was achieved in many business cycle instances, although not sustained, before the upturn occurred. In other words, strength and weakness may be about in balance for as long as three or four months before the upturn.

Early rapidity of rise after the upturn is related to resource favorability and the sharpness of culmination at the trough. Capital ca-

---

[1]Arthur F. Burns, *New Facts on Business Cycles* (New York: National Bureau of Economic Research, Inc., 1950), pp. 24–25.

CHART 5-3

REFERENCE CYCLE PATTERNS OF COMPREHENSIVE SERIES

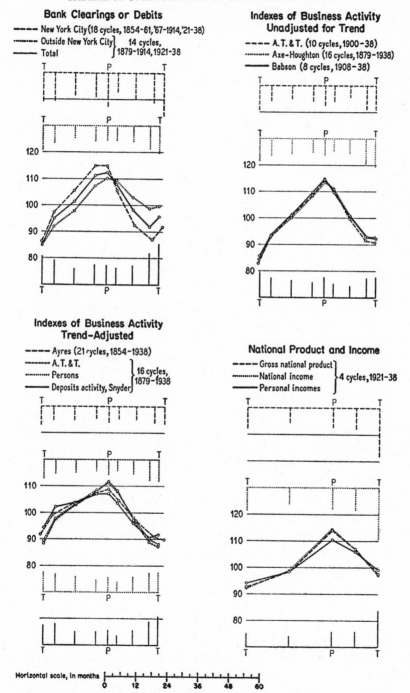

Bank Clearings or Debits
- - - - New York City (18 cycles, 1854-61,'67-1914,'21-38)
- - - - - Outside New York City } 14 cycles,
———— Total } 1879-1914, 1921-38

Indexes of Business Activity Unadjusted for Trend
- - - - A. T. & T. (10 cycles, 1900-38)
- - - - - Axe-Houghton (16 cycles, 1879-1938)
———— Babson (8 cycles, 1908-38)

Indexes of Business Activity Trend-Adjusted
- - - - Ayres (21 cycles, 1854-1938)
- - - - - A.T.&T.
- - - - - Persons } 16 cycles,
———— Deposits activity, Snyder } 1879-1938

National Product and Income
- - - - Gross national product }
- - - - - National income } 4 cycles, 1921-38
———— Personal incomes }

Horizontal scale, in months

Source: Taken from Wesley C. Mitchell, *What Happens during Business Cycles: A Progress Report* (New York: National Bureau of Economic Research, Inc., 1951), p. 267. Reproduced with permission.

pacity is operating under slack conditions, the unemployed are looking for jobs, enterprisers are waiting for favorable opportunities to start new companies, and investment to bring in newer technologies has been held up awaiting the appearance of favorable markets. For instance, business incorporations, which were in the order of ten thousand a month at the trough in early 1958, rose to over fifteen thousand by the year end. Low interest rates are indicative of the slack in use of resources. Early in the upturn at mid-1958, short-term interest rates were near 1 per cent, compared with over 3 per cent a year later.

Sharp culmination in inventory investment is even more important in most business cycles because it represents a direct change in demand conditions. Late in the contraction, businessmen are frantically cutting inventories trying to keep up with the decline in sales. Since this action is in response to unplanned inventory increase early in the recession, it is ruthlessly pursued until adjustment with sales is in sight. A jolting effect is produced on the call for production as inventory runoff is sharply curtailed. An inventory runoff at the annual rate of $5 billion at the trough in the final quarter of 1949 shifted to an inventory accumulation of $3 billion in the first quarter of 1950. No net change occurred in total final sales made in the economy, but production increased by $8 billion to make up for the change in inventory investment.

The early rapid rise stimulates durable investment because the rising market points to many industries where modernization and added capacity will be essential. Substantial increases in plant and equipment expenditures typically follow after the first early fillip in expansion. For a year after an upturn in mid-1954, for instance, rather modest increases occurred in durable investment, while consumer expenditures rose dramatically and inventory investment had risen from the typical runoff, characteristic of the trough, to the prosperity peak level. In the following year—mid-1955 to mid-1956—the rise in consumer expenditure was more modest, but the rise in plant and equipment expenditure was speeding up. Plant and equipment expenditure at the middle part of expansion is the most important influence clinching cumulative rise. A chain reaction is created. The expansion in inventory investment and consumer markets which induced durable investment is further stimulated by the income durable investment provides. Durable investment clearly exhibits its doubly reinforcing characteristic in this part of the expansion because the completion of capacity is lagging far behind the rate at which capital investment is being built. Finally, the stimulated increase in expenditure by consumers and for inventory further induces durable investment.

The expenditure pattern varies somewhat from one cycle to another, but exceptions to the above pattern are due to the movement of expenditures which conform less completely or are accounted for by special circumstances. Residential construction may add substantially to expenditures, as in the 1958 expansion, or fail to do so, as in the 1955–57 expansion. An exogenous factor may intervene, as illustrated by the Korean War starting in 1950. Exceptionally large consumer expenditures were stimulated then. Reacting from so high a rate of accumulation, virtually no further increase occurred in the following year. Because of restrictions, the major stimulation in the latter part of the expansion in 1952–53 came from war and defense expenditure rather than from private investment.

The rounding-off of expansion arises from five sets of influence. (1) By far the most important is an approach to capacity operation. Many different reactions are set up by this influence, as outlined in the immediately following paragraphs. (2) A similar influence is the approach to capacity in limited areas even though operation falls far below aggregate available capacity. (3) Some fading of demand is inevitable as backlogs are filled. (4) Evidence exists that there is at least some tendency for productive efficiency to fall in the prosperous atmosphere. (5) Innovative potentialities become less plentiful.

Approach to Capacity Operation. Expansions, starting at levels of operation which leave some effective capacity unused, rise at a rate too rapid to be sustainable. This means that, because of capacity limitations, the expansion must level off in a limited time. Supply bottlenecks develop in some industries where the rate of expansion rapidly reaches capacity limits. This appears particularly in raw materials used in durable capital expansion. If the necessary raw materials, such as steel, are unavailable, investment will be held up and the rate of expansion thus limited. Some protection from this difficulty is now developing from the use of substitute materials. Other metals and plastics are protecting manufacturers from the shortage of steel. Prestressed concrete is a parallel protection. Similarly, future copper shortages may be less acute because of new substitutions. It is doubtful that substitution will completely eliminate the development of bottlenecks, although it may moderate them.

The bottleneck shortage is accentuated by inducements to add to capacity in raw materials industries. For instance, the building of steel plants requires a substantial quantity of steel and adds to the shortage of steel. The difficulty is now partially alleviated by planning on the basis of growth forecasts, so that less dependence is placed on temporary surges of demand in planning capital expansion. Belief that growth forecasting will entirely displace surges in capital expansion in prosperity in the near future is overoptimistic, however.

The alleviation of capital shortage causes more difficulty than it solves. As capital projects come to be completed at an expanded rate, new sources of supply add to competition, and demand is more readily satisfied. But this means that the strength of the market is reduced, and businessmen are less impelled to start additional investment projects. Slackened advance in durable investment expenditure, coming at the same time as major increases in capacity are becoming available, signifies that income payments in support of demand are slackening as capacity supply is rising. The situation grows out of the phenomenon of double reinforcement in investment, as we have dubbed it.

Similarly, a catching-up occurs in inventory requirements. In many cases the desired inventory accumulation lags in early expansion. As sales level off, however, attempts to bring inventories into adjustment with the higher levels of sales are more readily achieved. The satisfaction produces a lower rate of inventory investment.

Carefully examined, we find that the critical change usually is slackening of investment expansion. As we have said, shortages partly account for this. Another factor, possibly of even greater importance, is that capacity comes to be completed at a more rapid rate than final demand is advancing. The rate of capital completions expands, and inventory stock comes to be considered adequate in relation to sales, as noted in the above paragraphs. Another reason for the slackening of investment expansion; emphasized in earlier business cycle theory,[2] is the increasing cost of borrowing funds.

The demand for investment funds rises so fast in mid-expansion that the required funds are obtained only by paying higher and higher interest rates. Theoretically, this should be a powerful depressive factor, for higher interest rates add proportionately to the cost of the funds borrowed. Over an extended period the power of

---

[2]Notably in the Austrian investment theory. See Chapter 8.

the contractionary influence must become clear. Many investment projects which had a good chance of paying out at lower interest rates will provide inadequate promise at the higher rates. There are many reasons, however, for believing that, in the immediately prospective future of expansion preceding the downturn, the influence of interest rates is readily overestimated. Businessmen have widely testified that the level of the interest rate plays a minor part in their decisions to make investments. One reason for this is the positive correlation between interest rates and optimism. When interest rates are low at depressed aggregate spending levels, businessmen are reluctant to make investments; while when they are high at prosperous aggregate spending levels, investments look promising. Another way of expressing the same thing is to say that demand curves for investment shift to the right in prosperity.[3]

A sharp rise in the current profit rate partially explains the rightward shift in the business demand curve for investment. Although, logically considered, current higher profits may have little to do with the promise of new investment during the future life of its use, it is hard to believe that a change in current profits lacks influence in our uncertain world.

The rising profit rate makes possible accumulation of undistributed profits to be used for investment purposes. Also, financing from outside sources frequently can be done on the standard of the profit rate by flotation of equity issues; one method is the issue of rights. Stock prices may rise even more rapidly than profits because of optimistic anticipations, so that the funds obtained actually are at a lower cost than if financed through debt issues at the current interest rate. This is seen, for instance, in the rapid rise of stock prices in 1959 when the rate of return on common stocks as generally computed fell below the interest rate return on high-grade bonds.

The financial markets must, however, ultimately adjust to recognize the actual promise of investment issues. If the investment demand curve has been driven to the right to an unrealistic extent, ultimately it must shift back, and high interest rates will earmark the investment projects at the lower end of the curve as unprofitable. The exact timing of the contractionary effect of high interest rates is not readily rationalized. Possibly, it does not become of critical importance until investment demand curves generally shift leftward. This would mean that high interest rates are more impor-

---

[3]That demand curve is frequently called the "marginal efficiency of capital" in modern literature. See discussion in Chapter 9.

tant at the downturn, after contractionary forces have already mounted, than in the expansion phase.

In many raw materials, such as copper and lead, less efficient resources have to be tapped as industrial demand mounts. The market is highly competitive in many of these materials, and their prices rise. Costs are increased for a great many manufacturing companies. Also, capacity completions advance rapidly and the prices obtainable for manufactured products tend to be depressed. Prospective profit margins are narrowed. This may be further accentuated by stepped-up increases in wage rates in the prosperity market.

The margin is also pinched by a rise in per unit overhead costs. Early in expansion, with unused capacity and depreciation charged on a stright-line basis (equal yearly charges regardless of the production rate), overhead costs add substantially to unit costs of production as capacity levels of operation are approached. A virtually constant total of overhead costs is no longer divided among an increasing number of units of product produced. Furthermore, full-capacity operation tends to be less efficient than operation at slightly lower levels.

Marginal companies which got started in the more favorable market of earlier expansion, as well as companies which have failed to adjust to changing times, find the going rough as profit margins are squeezed. The failure rate increases. Even the companies in these groups which survive find it desirable to curtail investment expenditures.

New companies are started less readily. Declining profit prospects tend to be discouraging. What may be even more important, the price elasticity of demand declines. Consumers have more satisfactory incomes than ever before. They become less and less inclined to hunt for bargains. They patronize established dealers. Custom and long standing become the major considerations in placing patronage. New firms find the acquisition of a following more and more difficult. A slowing-down in the formation of new companies is more contractionary than an equal reduction in sales of established companies would be because the new company must provide in current investment expenditure for the total capital stock to be employed in producing goods.

Partial Approach to Capacity Operation. The effects described in the preceding section are not wholly limited to times when there is a general approach to capacity conditions. In 1937, for instance, operation in most industries was substantially short of capacity, but approach to capacity in limited areas of the economy had a contractionary effect. Although unemployment was in the order of eight million, some types of skilled labor were acutely short. For instance, because training and apprenticeship programs had been discontinued, there were too few skilled workers to man the rubber plants in Ohio. In some particular industries in which plant and equipment investment had been especially restricted and demand had risen rapidly, operation was at full capacity. The price of many raw materials had risen far above the low levels prevailing at the depth of the depression. Wage rates were rising rapidly because of the new power vested in labor organizations. Partly because of the rise which had taken place in prices and of the higher levels of operation, administrative decisions to stop government stock-piling (Britain) and to eliminate moral support for higher prices (our federal government) tended to stop the rise in wholesale prices. The tendency was to squeeze profit margins.

Elimination of Backlogs. When income is flattened or reduced in contraction, purchases, especially of durable goods, fall below the level required indefinitely to maintain current standards of living. Thus, a backlog of demand is built up. When income rises in expansion, the deficiency is made up in those areas; for instance, the stock of consumer durables is brought up to what consumers consider a more satisfactory condition.

When the stock of durable goods reaches a more satisfactory condition, further purchases may actually decline, as in the case of automobiles in 1956. Some spread is probable to other types of goods and services consumers were formerly unable to afford. The income used for this purpose, however, is more "discretionary."

For a time, there may be a surge to a higher living standard. Most individuals are likely to increase their levels of spending more by jumps than at a regular rate. The purchase of a new home with related accessories may be involved. After so large an outlay, further increase in purchases may be restricted for a time. Since all consumers are affected by prevailing optimism, and since individual spending patterns tend to follow group behavior, the timing of broad advances and approximate plateaus of spending tend toward similarity among individuals.

When deferred demand is made up and/or consumer expenditures level off as a reaction to a preceding broad advance, a contractionary influence is produced. A larger proportion of disposable income is diverted to saving. This tends to depress the consumer market, but there is no tendency for investment activity to take up the slack, for investment activity tends to be geared to current market demand.

Reduction in Effort Expended. Possibly because needs become less pressing, some individuals reduce the effort expended on economic activity. Some relaxation of effort may also be induced by the higher proportion of income taken in taxes.

Perhaps of more importance is a shift in prevailing attitudes. With jobs assured, some psychological letdown may occur among individuals whose work drive was limited in any case. Under thriving economic conditions, managers press less hard for efficient operation. At least, in the 1957–58 contraction, many businessmen cited the achievement of improved efficiencies and heightened work performance of employees. (The opposite testimony is less likely to be available in prosperity.)

Reserve of Innovative Potentialities. Investment requirements in prosperity feed partly on the implementation of new technology. Advantage is taken not only of *current* advances in scientific knowledge but also of similar advances in the preceding contraction or of others passed over for various reasons in the past. At the advanced rate of investment in prosperity, available investment projects to take advantage of new technology are likely to become reduced. Thus, investment expansion tends to slacken because of a fading in profitable projects.

DOWNTURN

The above discussion should make clear the vulnerability of activity levels attained in late expansion. Strategic factors rest on current total market demand. But current market demand is, to a critical extent, transitory in nature, as indicated by (1) the extent to which durable investment depends on overoptimism, (2) the extent to which inventory investment depends on efforts to make up for past inadequacy in the level of inventory stock, and (3) the degree to which consumer demand is dependent upon deferred requirements built up in the preceding contraction.

Many expansions have occurred with flat tops running for many months, during which expansionary and contractionary forces remain in approximate balance. This marks a kind of "rolling readjustment." Shipments come to be made out of unfilled orders which have been long deferred. This may happen even though current orders are slackening off. A cushion of deferred demand protects the present level of activity. To the extent that the unfilled orders are firm, the completion of capacity may actually raise the level of activity. With added capacity, a higher production rate becomes possible. New demands, not covered by unfilled orders, may also arise to employ resources released by areas where demand has slackened. But the indefinite perpetuation of demand rolling into new areas is highly unlikely because of vulnerability reached by the general levels of activity.

As described by Nicholas Kaldor, prosperity is like a difficult steeplechase where a horse has to overcome a series of hurdles and is almost certain to fall at one of the obstacles. Activity might be tripped up by an exogenous factor as it moves along a flat top. Very possibly, the downturn may frequently have been diverted by a month or two on many occasions because of the accidental occurrence of an exogenous factor. But the inherent vulnerability of the general level of activity at such a time makes it clear that forces within the business system will bring a culmination to the prosperity sooner or later.

The inherent instability of prosperity attained is effectively pointed up by the increasing cost of investment funds. The rising cost, as shown by advancing interest rates, is currently offset by a rightward shift of the investment demand curve. The assumption that investment potentialities increase in every expansion as indicated by that curve and contrariwise decline in every contraction is preposterous. Therefore, surely a leftward shift will occur in the curve and the scheduled high interest rates will then be pitched against a much smaller investment potential.

The consumer could play a key role in the timing of the downturn because his proportionate expenditure out of disposable income might shift slightly downward at a critical time. This might occur because of the exhaustion of deferred demand, without new goods appearing attractive enough to the consumer to provoke him to transfer his expenditure to them. Or the general improvement of living standards might reach a plateau, with spending leveling off. These situations could develop as durable investment projects matured, so that capacity would keep rising rapidly, or as inventory stocks increased enough to be considered satisfactory in relation to sales.

The change in inventory levels is most influential. As soon as it is felt that the current level of inventory stocks is entirely satisfactory for the current level of sales and that sales are most likely to taper off in the future, a dramatic change occurs in inventory investment. A rapid shift from sizable inventory accumulation to substantial inventory runoff may happen in a few months, accounting for perhaps a 2 per cent decline in total sales. In dollars, the movement in inventory investment might be from +$5 billion to −$5 billion, stated at annual rates.

The importance of change in inventory investment is not to be denied. But this change does not occur in isolation. It is founded on the extent to which satisfactory inventory stock levels have been achieved and upon the prospect for little further increase in sales. That prospect turns on what has been happening in consumer expenditures and in total investment, upon changes in government expenditures, and as well upon indications of the strength of demand as shown by prices. In other words, weakness in demand brings businessmen to order a dramatic reduction in inventory investment. That change is an almost inevitable accompaniment of the downturn.

CONTRACTION

Rapid shrinkage in investment expenditures for inventory and new equipment sparks the cumulative decline in contraction. Reduced expenditures stemming from these sectors cut off income payments. The lowered income payments, in turn, reduce expenditures of the recipients, although, as noted below, automatic stabilizers and other factors provide considerable support for consumer expenditures. The fact that sales are declining at all is sufficient impetus to drive businessmen to further reductions in investment expenditure in view of the darkened outlook. Aside from changes in final expenditures, businessmen find themselves caught in a web of inventory curtailment proceeding through purchases at successive stages of distribution. Retailers reduce their orders from wholesalers, and wholesalers drastically cut their orders from manufacturers. Manufacturers find their sales shrinking much faster than actual consumption of their products and frequently are unable to get their own inventories into line as rapidly as they would wish. The situation may appear so threatening that production schedules may be cut to a point that just permits meeting current shipments out of available inventories plus current production. In most companies a drastic reduction in current rates of activity results.

Corporate undistributed profits will certainly shrink as profits drop rapidly. Their shrinkage significantly adds to the cautious attitude businessmen are tending to assume. In cases where the rule is to finance out of earnings, many new investment projects may be cut off.

Government receipts automatically decline as the contraction gets under way because tax graduation cuts the rate on receding personal incomes, and the falling-away of corporate profits slices deeply into government revenue. Theoretically, government expenditures should not be cut at such a time, but a cut may be made before the advent of contraction is recognized. Note the stretch-out of the defense program to fight inflation in mid-1957. At first, government finances may be contractionary; but they are, of course, certain to shift later on.

The rate of personal savings has been built up to a relatively high level in prosperity; the reasons are outlined above. The funds made available are readily absorbed in prosperity investment. But the decline in investment often is great enough that all of the funds provided are no longer needed. The normal use of these funds is in financing business investment. When business investment is not great enough to use all of the funds flowing from personal savings, the funds go to liquidate credit somewhere in the economy.

The shrinkage of credit tends to set up a chain reaction. When credit must be paid off, the liquidation of assets is forced. At first, this may cover principally inventories businessmen want to reduce anyway. But once started, credit contraction may lead to apprehension if overextension appears to have occurred in particular areas or if markets show substantial weakness. The two factors are somewhat similar. Overextension of credit in given areas will weaken markets because of forced sales. Markets may be weakened, however, for various reasons other than overextension, such as unsatisfactory financing or inefficient management. Once business failures take hold in an area, even soundly managed companies may find themselves in difficult straits because of widespread liquidation. Capital losses are certain to be an accompaniment of credit shrinkage. Capital losses have had a dramatic effect in the stock market. They set up waves of liquidation; and although they do not immediately change current income levels, they increase caution and spread pessimistic attitudes.

Declining prices are usually contractionary. In addition to the direct losses they may represent in liquidation, for instance, they may generate anticipations that prices will go still lower, especially among business purchasers. The delay induced in purchases may itself lead to still lower prices.

From early in the contraction, consumer expenditures tend to counteract the decline. The wages and salaries of many persons are reduced, and of the disemployed are eliminated entirely. But there are important countering factors. Corporations which find less need for undistributed profits to finance investment projects tend to maintain or even increase dividend payments, although their profits may have fallen substantially. Among persons with reduced income, there is a tendency to maintain living standards at the expense of saving; and among the disemployed, negative saving becomes necessary. As a result, consumers in the aggregate increase their spending relative to disposable income and reduce their saving.

The extent to which this occurs depends on the degree of saturation in consumer durable goods industries. Durable goods already owned may be so satisfactory that purchases are certain to be curtailed with the prevailing pessimistic attitudes. Living standards may be maintained by use of already owned goods. Under other circumstances, new durable products may appear attractive enough that those persons whose income has suffered little may support a high level of durable goods activity. Some variation may therefore occur, but the general tendency will be for consumer expenditure to rise relative to disposable income.

Although fiscal policy measures are not to be expected immediately, they are likely to appear before the contraction has gone very far. Either through increased expenditures or through reduced taxes, the government will become a counteracting influence as the contraction proceeds.

As the contraction wears on, the reduced rate of starting durable capital projects begins to take effect. Completions level off and decline. The rate of adding to capacity is reduced, and the supply situation comes to be less out of balance with demand.

Costs decline. Competitive raw materials come to be produced principally in the more efficient installations, and the reduced output is available at drastically lower prices. Overhead costs level off. As operating rates drop rapidly, per unit overhead costs rise substantially because the same total depreciation cost is distributed over a shrinking number of units. As the operating rate levels out, the per unit overhead cost stabilizes and becomes less disturbing.

Efficiency of individual workers and of management rises. There is increasing evidence that many workers who have poor motivation in prosperity try harder in depression. This was the testimony of many companies in 1957–58. Managements strive to cut unnecessary costs and to introduce efficiencies to meet a difficult competitive situation. Stimulus for doing this is less under prosperous conditions.

If consumer durables and other postponable products slump, a demand backlog is built up. As soon as the income situation becomes more favorable, demand will rise for these products.

With depressed conditions, investment projects are delayed. Research goes forward, and the introduction of new technological methods awaits favorable markets. The growth which has occurred in population in the contraction also is indicative of demand potential which will become effective as soon as incomes begin to rise.

Interest rates are driven down in contraction because the supply of investment funds comes to exceed the demand for them. This is timed with a general reduction in investment demand, so that the low interest rates do not induce additional investment for the time being. But the low cost of funds assures that, when markets become more favorable, investment expenditure will rise.

The most important culminating force in contractions proceeding along lines described above is the reversal of inventory requirements. In most companies, earlier in contraction the inventory situation comes to cause so much apprehension, as noted above, that drastic measures are taken. Inventory runoff is pushed to a rapid rate until inventory stock is at a bare minimum or until an increase in demand arising from other factors makes it obvious that the inventory stock is too low. The very act of reducing inventory runoff is an expansionary factor. If the amount of runoff is cut from $5 billion to $1 billion, productive activity will have to rise $4 billion to support the equivalent demand. This, simply, is because taking less out of inventory forces resort to greater production to maintain the same volume of sales. The record shows that a situation of this kind is typical at the upturn.

Before turning to an analysis of the upturn, attention should be given to the possibility that instead of upturn occurring in accordance with the schedule outlined, deep depression may set in. Culmination does not readily develop when the principal demand disturbance is in durable goods. If a very considerable overcapacity has been achieved, and if the consumer durable goods in use plus secondhand goods awaiting sale appear to provide practically all of consumer requirements, reattainment of a satisfactory demand situation becomes difficult. A culmination is not quickly attained, as contrasted with the situation which develops in the case of rapid inventory runoff.

Reducing the rate of producing durable goods does not lead to a quick reaction. For one thing, because of the time it takes to complete projects under way, activity on them cannot be quickly curtailed. The decline in sales while this process is under way leads to a revaluation of expansion requirements so that, in many cases, the capital expenditures currently being made are considered undesirable. No impending shortage appears after the expenditures are completed, as in the case of inventory runoff. Shrinking capital expenditures cut income payments which reduce sales, but capacity to produce is not reduced. Existing capacity will wear out only after a long period of time has elapsed; and with lowered income levels generated by decline in investment expenditures, even a shrunken capacity may appear excessive. Note that the runoff of inventories *can*, by contrast, bring a quick reduction in total inventory stock.

The depressing lack of demand for durable capital may be accentuated by deflation of credit. If financing has proceeded to an excessive extent by debt securities, financial embarrassment may become widespread. The shrinkage of markets and the onset of bankruptcies may bring asset valuations substantially below the indebtedness level. Because quick reappraisals become necessary, valuations shrink away at a rapid rate. If permitted to proceed unimpeded, a ruthless competitive process would bring asset valuations down to a profitable level in spite of the excess physical capacity. In fact, excess capacity would shortly disappear, because it would become worthless and be dismantled. The contraction would thus be brought to a culmination. But that process has the appearance of malevolence, and we are unprepared to face measures which are so harsh. Most of the ill effects of credit deflation may develop without bringing the recession to a head, for government interference is likely to obstruct the deflation process before it has gone far enough to generate culmination.

The modern prescription is government fiscal policy. If depression becomes serious enough, government expenditures would be expected to rise sufficiently to reverse the decline in total activity. If these expenditures are for public works, support will be provided to industries which have been severely depressed by shrinkage in demand for durable goods. Agreement is not universal, however, that this method would be better than reduced taxes, where consumers would be permitted to increase purchases to fit their demand schedules. Government intervention to reverse the movement of total expenditure can, in any case, be accepted as the customary influence which may be expected to bring the contraction to a culmination if deep depression occurs.

We may assume that the standard expansionary influences in the private economy will have inadequate effect. Deep concern about the inventory situation could, of course, lead to rapid runoff, foreshadowing a jolting rebound forced by necessity to produce amounts which earlier came from inventory. From what we know about past prosperities when overexpansion occurred, clearly inventories did not become particularly excessive. Prices tended to reach greater stability than in most prosperities, possibly because the large increases in capacity provided ample competition in the making of final goods. The spirit of such times precludes any great uneasiness about inventory levels in early stages of contraction. Belief in need for capital expansion on the level which has occurred makes it difficult for enterprisers to conclude that there is any significant contraction necessary. Since prices of finished goods have not been rising substantially, and the current price levels appear fully justified, inventory reductions for fear of price decline are slow to materialize. If inventory runoff does finally reach panic stages, it is only after the durable capital situation has become completely demoralized.

Other expansionary forces produce at least a moderate effect. Continued population growth adds slowly to potential demand. New discoveries continue to occur, but generally await the development of more favorable markets. Backlogs of demand are built up. The rate of completion of durable capital finally fades to virtually nothing, but existing large capacity remains a deterrent. Interest rates shrink to very low levels, but the capital demand curve shifts so far to the left that any interest rate above zero seems excessive Costs finally stabilize at low levels, but they scarcely meet out-of-pocket requirements.

UPTURN

Because decisions are made on very limited perspective in contraction, cumulative forces are even more unstable than in expansion. Day-to-day problems come to occupy the entire attention of decision makers, and important repercussions beyond the near future are largely ignored. As a result, the tendency toward culmination is powerfully imbedded in most contractions. The new philosophy of government responsibility adds the government influence as an additional factor with an expansionary bias.

The force of inventory rebound is adequately indicated above. If the rate in completing capital capacity shrinks rapidly after the contraction has about run its course, the balance between supply and demand is substantially redressed. After several months of contraction, conditioning factors—such as an improved cost position, some increases in worker and management efficiency, a rise in backlogs, an increase in technological improvements held in abeyance for favorable markets, and availability of cheap funds in the investment market—become favorable.

Exogenous forces have, at times, played a minor part in dating the upturn. Frequently, when the agricultural sector of the economy was relatively more important, large crops produced domestically, with short crops abroad, were instrumental in bringing recovery a few months earlier than could have been expected from culminating forces. At other times a large government appropriation may have exerted a similar influence. Aside from major war, however, the influence of outside forces appears to have been limited to a shift of a few months at most in dating the upturn in a normal recovery. The maturation of culminating forces marks the approximate end of contraction.

Because investment largely accounts for rise and fall in the level of activity, general overcapacity of substantial dimensions interferes with culminating forces. Conviction that little durable investment is needed effectively precludes the ending of contractionary forces. The situation is further accentuated if saturated markets have spread throughout consumer durable goods markets. Although consumer durable goods cannot be used as long without replacement as most investment capital, delay in their replacement can abnormally restrict consumer expenditure. Under these conditions, recovery comes to be dependent on government action.

FOR REFLECTION AND ANALYSIS

1. The diffiusion index has been said to identify an "unseen cycle" showing the spreading and narrowing of contraction and then the spreading and narrowing of expansion. What do you think this means?
2. Why does business cycle expansion tend to be most rapid at the beginning of the expansion phase?

3. Explain the effect of major increases in capacity at the peak of prosperity.
4. If high interest rates do not immediately discourage investment expenditure in business cycle prosperity, what is implied about equity flotations?
5. Discuss the influence of a slowing-down in the rate of new company starts at the end of expansion.
6. When consumer expenditure levels off in prosperity, why does not investment expenditure take up the slack in use of resources?
7. Why does the rise in interest rates with increasing investment expenditure in expansion imply a rightward shift of the investment demand curve?
8. Outline the importance of expenditure on durable investment in the preceding prosperity if deep depression develops.
9. Is inventory most crucial in minor or major depressions? Why?

Chapter 6

GROWTH

Economic growth is at one and the same time a most important and most elusive concept. Growth is important in our study, first, because it is the most vital of all types of economic change and, second, because it is intimately related to business cycle variations.

Growth represents a change in the general level on which economic operations are conducted. In contrast, short-term fluctuations or cyclical movements are variations about the growth level existing at the particular time. Obviously, the growth level advances as time goes on, but there is no inherent reason why cyclical movements should shift in any particular way. Growth applies both to individual industries and to total industry because over a period of time the general level of operation advances. In an expanding economy like ours, the expected levels of total operations are constantly rising and represent improvements in the standard of living. Individual industries must compete, and a few of them are always moving downward as others appropriate part of their markets. The growth of total industry represents a kind of an average of all individual industries but one which is readily misinterpreted, as pointed out later in the chapter.

As a simplifying proposition, we think of growth of total industry as the factor limiting the growth of individual industries. On the average, individual industries cannot exceed growth of the total if that total reflects practical effectiveness in use of our resources. It is helpful to think of aggregate *secular* growth in this way. We must, however, recognize the possibility that the growth of total industry may move away from secular levels for a period of years. Such a situation characterized the Great Depression of the thirties. This was more than a fluctuation or a cyclical movement.

The general level of operations in industry came to be accepted as below effective use of our resources. We therefore recognize that growth may at times experience such a departure. We call growth at these times *secondary*, to distinguish it from the more normal situation when secular growth is occurring. The distinction is useful, for secular growth lends itself to the application of a predictable framework, while secondary growth does not. We hold that growth *may* hold tolerably close to secular levels in the future, with the forecasting problems greatly simplified.

In the pages which follow, we first give more careful consideration to the definition of growth. Then, we note that responsible forces are similar to those operating on the business cycle. Next, we turn to a fuller consideration of secondary growth. In contrast, secular growth may be considered a balanced relationship, and logical component factors involved can be identified. The probable influence of these factors is analyzed in some detail. Finally, we turn to the growth of individual industries and point out the broad problems involved in that branch of forecasting.

DEFINITION OF GROWTH

Two questions are at issue in the definition of economic growth. These relate to the kind of process which represents growth and the kind of change in time to which it is related. In earlier times, with military or sociological connotations, growth was sometimes represented by the increase in human population. We might be even more justified in relating growth to changes in the stock of capital, if such data were satisfactorily available. According to present ideas, however, no *stock* figure, whether it be human population, capital stock, or whatever, represents growth as effectively as activity figures. The common practice now is to measure growth in terms of changes occurring in deflated final product. This is our best measure of aggregate economic *activity*. The advantage of activity figures is that they show changes in what is actually produced, contrasted with stock figures, which may reflect idle or ineffectively employed resources to an indeterminate extent and do not reflect productivity change. Furthermore, aggregate activity represents the results achieved by using all different types of resources, while no available measurements show changes in the combined stock of all resources.

A common practice is to call any change, no matter how short, growth or decadence. This is not to be recommended if growth is considered to represent a distinct type of change. As developed below, the long-term movement in aggregate industry or in a single industry differs distinctly from changes occurring over a brief period of time. The long-term movement is more appropriately called growth. If the movement occurs over a long period of time and is not upset by deep depression or periods of exaggerated overbuilding, we can make a case for distinguishing it as secular growth, and identify it as a balanced relationship in the sense that the total level of stocks is appropriate and that, on the average, a workable adjustment exists between various types of activity. Clearly, analysis of this kind is treacherous. Most importantly, *secular growth* must not be identified with any particular measured *secular trend*. While secular trends frequently provide the only available measurement, they illustrate growth rather than identify it. These ideas are more fully developed below.

For some purposes a net type of growth representing activity, put on a per capita basis, better reflects the kind of development to be considered. Popularly, this is what is intended when growth is treated as equivalent to rising living standards. If we are interested in improvement in economic conditions from the standpoint of the consumer, the per capita basis is the most reliable. Furthermore, this basis has been found to be the most reliable in making growth comparisons between countries. A country which experiences rapid growth in population without any increase in output per person can scarcely be credited with an economic growth as significant as that in another country which experiences a rapid rise in the standard of living.

GROWTH AND THE BUSINESS CYCLE

An important characteristic both of growth and of the business cycle is investment activity. Investment represents the sum of increases in our stock of capital and the replacement of worn-out capital. For the purposes of our analysis, we consider only business capital, eliminating capital used by consumers (except houses) and capital goods owned by the government (e.g., roads, dams, and government buildings). Actually, the measurements we use reflect business purchases of durable goods which are principally used in production of goods and services, and of inventories held to foster production.

We have shown above that investment is usually the principal factor responsible for rise in economic activity in business cycle expansion and for decline in business cycle contraction. Investment also can be considered the most important characteristic of growth. To provide for growth, an addition to capital stock is essential, which implies an increase in net investment over and above replacement requirements.

In a capitalistic economy, a net increase in the capital stock of investment goods may be considered to typify growth. To increase product for additional population, greater amounts of capital are required. To add to productiveness, improved capital is required, and the process is partially symbolized by an increase in capital stock.

Growth in capital stock does not occur at a steady rate, but varies between forward surges of investment activity in expansion and a much restricted rate of investment in contraction. This variation arises in the shifting processes of cumulation and culmination outlined in the preceding chapters. Except in the deepest of deep depressions, however, a net increase in capital stock continues to occur in contraction, albeit at a reduced rate. Variation in stock by additional investment is relatively minor compared to the total capital already in existence. The tendency is to retire old capital more rapidly in expansion than in contraction (a speeded-up obsolesence is often visualized in expansion). Irregularity in increase of capital stock is thus moderated.

Another important way of surveying this process is in terms of the uneven meshing between investment expenditures made and the funds obtained for financing them. Fluctuation in the supply of funds for financing is indicated by great variation in the interest rate cost between early and late expansion. High interest cost marks the rounding-out of financial requirements through credit extension, and low interest rates mark the paying-off of credit. Although there tends to be some accommodation of consumer expenditures for final product to the need of funds for investment, marginally the variation in financing needs for investment is achieved through credit adjustments. From the business cycle standpoint, credit availability makes it possible for enterprisers with inadequate funds to finance innovations society otherwise would not obtain.

As a result, the saving process, which undisturbed might proceed in an orderly fashion, is upset. The pressure on commercial processes to provide a greater volume of investment funds than would be forthcoming at the fairly uniform rate of expansion in consumer demand with rising income forces an abnormal pressure of capital demand on supply. Oppositely, capital demand becomes abnormally slack in contraction in relation to a forthcoming supply of saving funds. These facts are the unfortunate consequence of business cycle variations. If we visualized growth in a vacuum, we might overlook problems of this kind. The essence of the financing process then would be that some percentage—say, about 6 per cent—of the funds received in selling the total final product should be diverted to providing a net increase in the capital stock of business companies. But the process does not work in this simple way, and there is little promise than we can force it to do so in the foreseeable future.

Nevertheless, some average of a variation between about 4 and 8 per cent best represents the growth process. The fact that development is propelled like a ratchet, with reciprocating action, is no adequate basis for overlooking the average requirements involved.[1]

The conclusions reached when we look at variation in the process of product activity are even more distorting. While capital stock does tend to grow continuously, even if at an irregular rate, product arising from activity in the economy rises and falls with expansion and contraction. While activity represents our best basis for visualizing growth in the economy, the general average advancement which the economy can be expected to produce is a far better representation of growth than the up-and-down variation which occurs over the business cycle.

Not only capital stock but other stock series such as population, scientific understanding, and educational development experience a continuous advance. Rise in the level of stocks is evidence that there is a continuity in growth even though activity does not rise continuously. Direct measurement of growth is best indicated by an activity series, but continuity of the growth process is nonetheless indicated by continual advance in stocks.

STOCK / OUTPUT RATIOS

Change in stock levels in the economy is thus critical in the process of growth. An important question which arises in this con-

---

[1]The error of visualizing growth to continue at the expansion rate occurring in the business cycle is most readily understood when it is realized that capital stocks are used more and more fully as the business cycle expansion proceeds. The rate of advance involved turns on increased use of capacity. Long-term growth must rest principally on advance in capacity, rather than on increased use of capacity. See W. S. and E. S. Woytinsky, *Lessons of the Recessions* (Washington, D.C.: Public Affairs Institute, 1959), p. 10, for an apparent error of this type.

nection is the stock level required to provide a given amount of increase in activity. In analyzing this question, let us begin with the amount of stock required to produce a given amount of product. We are familiar with the idea of idle capacity and unemployment, so that, clearly, stock is not always used to the same extent. Nevertheless, there is an optimum stock level, which is usually around 10 to 20 per cent under full capacity. Some stand-by capacity will be kept for emergencies in many industries, and some industries will have too much and others too little capacity. On the average, we might think of actual capacity as falling at about optimum levels. Restricted operations in depression will be too low to reach optimum, and high operation in prosperity will lie nearer full capacity.

For the purposes of growth, we are interested in the average condition. Although there are no clearly authenticated figures, various bits of information appear to indicate that the value of private durable capital stock required in the United States at present averages about 1½ times the value of a year's production. This figure indicates that net dollar amount of durable capital (in addition to replacement) will grow half again as much as final product. If final product grows $20 billion a year, net durable capital stock will have to increase $30 billion, or an annual investment of $30 billion will be required in addition to perhaps about an equal amount for replacement.

Note that the illustration assumes that capital stock grows at the same percentage rate as activity in making final output or—what is the same thing—that the capital/output ratio remains constant. If the stock/output ratio is 1½, and if output is $500 billion, then the total capital stock will have to be $750 billion. If the stock/output ratio remains constant and output rises 4 per cent, capital stock will have to rise 4 per cent.

The relation between capital stock and output throws light on the growth process. Output varies substantially under current business cycle conditions. Growth is related to the change in capital as well as to the change in output, so that at the growth level, we should think in terms of the typical ratio. If growth is to be represented by activity in production, middle levels will have to be employed for this purpose. Activity under extremely prosperous or extremely depressed conditions is thus excluded as a direct representation of growth. At these middle levels, stock must increase proportionately with growth if the capital/output ratio remains constant.

SECULAR STAGNATION AND SECONDARY GROWTH

The above ideas appear generally acceptable at present with regard to secular growth in the United States. However, deep depression beginning about thirty years ago made popular the idea of secular stagnation, which has not been entirely dissipated even today. The principal thesis behind the secular stagnation idea is that a fundamental institutional change, intimately related to growth potentialities, arose in the American economy. The consumer was thought to have made a substantial realignment in the disposition of his disposable income in favor of saving or, rather, in his potential schedule of spending out of disposable income. He was thought to behave in this way largely because of the increasing part of total disposable income which was coming to be spent in a discretionary way.

Capital needs were also thought to be shrinking. Efficiency of the capital stock already available was increasing; new industries and the opening-up of new areas, which had accounted for a substantial proportion of past investment, appeared to be of declining importance. The rate of population growth had declined, and empirical study seemed to indicate that investment needs bore a close relation to the requirements of added population. It was thought that the potentialities of new technology for innovational projects had diminished substantially. For all of these reasons, we were thought to be faced with declining investment expenditures. With the expectation that consumers would wish to save an increasing proportion of their income, an impasse was anticipated. Without investment projects to absorb all of the savings consumer behavior would indicate at full-employment levels, inadequacy of effective demand appeared to be an inevitable problem.

The tendency toward large savings with insufficient investment outlets for them indicated unsatisfactory motivation for enterprisers. The constant tendency for savings to increase faster than investment requirements pointed to low interest rate return. But the profits required by enterprisers to induce them to take investment risks appeared to have been high in the past, and to be increasing because the promising areas of expansion seemed to be limited to luxury-type industry, where consumer demand would be less urgent and would be expected to provide for less regular sales.

These bleak forebodings gave no indication of the expanding economy we have experienced postwar. The expanding economy is related to a high level of consumer demand, rapid technological developments, the growth of new industries, and profit opportunities which enterprisers have found to possess satisfactory promise. The discrepancy is indeed great, and we do not pretend to present a satisfactory explanation here. No doubt the "cold war," with increased government expenditures and other effects, has been a factor.

Grandiose generalizations on economic growth have been notably unsuccessful, and we doubt that the theory of secular stagnation is any exception. Growth behavior in the Great Depression, which lay at the basis of the generalization, is, however, a concern which should give us pause. Growth at such a time follows a secondary slope rather than that indicated by the secular rate of change. What happens primarily is that decision makers fail to set their sights on a market target which will engender expenditures, both by consumers on consumption goods and by producers on investment goods, close to the full-employment level. The intense difficulties which are being faced are high-lighted by unfavorable profit expectations.

The fundamental reason for the onset of serious depression is overbuilding and saturated consumer markets. Naturally, with apparent excessive capacity already available, low investment programs are generated. Since consumers possess an ample stock of durable goods, their expenditures for these goods are low; the markets appear too unpromising to attract substantial investment expenditure or even promotional expenditure.

Market demand moves along an unsatisfactory level or slope for an indefinite period. The unsatisfactory general movement attained marks a secondary growth which tends to persist almost indefinitely. It is finally ended by government intervention, other exogenous forces, notably war, or the slow wearing-out of durable goods. Lack of adequate development appears reasonable to decision makers under the circumstances until dynamic outside forces appear.

Secondary growth of this kind does not eliminate the continued play of business cycle variations. In the Great Depression the expansion phase built up to a culmination in 1937, and was followed by a contraction lasting to mid-1938, even though unemployment continued abnormally large in 1936–37.

A diverse secondary growth may also appear in halcyon prosperity, when durable goods are produced so rapidly that capital comes to be overbuilt and consumers come to be oversupplied with hard goods. The situation is founded on an overoptimistic appraisal of growth needs, especially in industrial fields where growth is visualized as most promising. This kind of secondary growth precedes that which arises in deep depression. The sway of business cycle variation also accompanies secondary growth in prosperity. The 1920's illustrate such a period. Throughout the decade, there was a tendency to overproduce durable goods. However, business cycle peaks occurred in 1923 and in 1926.

Secondary growth, in the economy as a whole, is not as excessive in prosperous conditions as it is deficient in deep depression. The essential characteristic is abnormally large activity in fields where large growth is visualized; possibly, this might be partially at the expense of expansion in other areas. Labor unemployment does not appear to reach any smaller proportions than in many business cycle peaks when overbuilding does not occur. Since capital stock reaches an excessively high level, the general indication is that capacity is more than keeping up with demand.

Secondary growth may well be a phenomenon which does not induce a regular recurrence; rather, it may appear sporadically. Past variations do provide some, but not conclusive, evidence that such a movement has generally been present in our past history.[2] According to some prevailing opinions, secondary growth is unlikely to reappear in the future. No conclusive answer can be provided at the present time; therefore, we do not assume that the movement is recurrent but, rather, merely present the fact that this growth has developed at certain times in past history.

In assuming that the movement is recurrent, one prominent position designates it as a construction cycle. The position has merit in that construction is the most durable of products and has accounted for an abnormal proportion of activity in secondary growth under prosperous conditions and for an abnormal restriction of activity in secondary growth under depressed conditions. In the 1920's, for instance, overexpansion occurred in construction, and construction activity almost disappeared in the Great Depression. On the other hand, the influences of secondary growth are found in almost all durable goods. Possibly, at times, other less durable goods may be just as important in the abnormal growth. From durable goods industries the influence spreads to the entire econ-

---

[2]For further discussion, see Chapter 2; and for references, n. of that chapter, p. 27.

omy, and practically all goods and services are affected in one way or another. In fact, the causal influences may initiate in durable goods other than construction or in nondurable or service parts of the economy. Construction, after all, is provided for use in making products, or in direct satisfaction of services such as in residential building. Abnormal demand for construction services in these areas accounts for the abnormal level of construction.

Construction is closely related to growth because it represents a most important part of the activity which provides for future needs. A construction cycle therefore is somewhat analogous to the idea of secondary growth. But the construction cycle implies recurrence, which, especially for the future, appears to be in some doubt.

SECULAR GROWTH AS A BALANCED RELATIONSHIP

The ideas of secular stagnation, secondary growth, and construction cycles all imply primary dependence on demand. Secular stagnation and secondary growth in deep depressions assume that activity will fall short of reasonable use of resources, and therefore naturally are not dependent upon available supply. The construction cycle assumes that demand for construction draws whatever resources are required from the rest of the economy, so that its movement is not conceived to be essentially dependent upon available supply in the total economy.

Secular growth presents a different problem. We do not assume it to lie at the full-employment level because the business cycle produces variations in the economy which necessarily draw activity below full-employment levels. Probably, we should not conceive of growth as being at a level above actual activity most of the time. We do assume that secular growth is parallel to full-employment levels. Then, since full employment reflects the level of effective supply, if the secular-growth line has the same slope, growth is dependent upon increase in the supply of resources. This applies only to the total economy, for demand will distribute product into various industries.

We base the assumption of dependence on supply of resources on several bits of evidence. First, we visualize growth as reflecting competitive conditions. If it did not, there would be no general tendency for resources to be drawn into use. We believe that the capitalistic system does, *in the long run,* tend to make effective use of resources. If so, after some stumbling, effective supplies are drawn into use, and the growth coefficient is supply-determined. The intention is not to define away secondary growth when investment expenditures may be abnormally low, but to project secular growth as the average change over a longer period.

For competition to work in this way, it would be necessary for prices in general to move at long-term slopes which tend to produce demand adjustment. We know that in the large area of administered prices, prices tend to remain too high in contraction and too low in expansion to reflect demand conditions. In a recent study, however, the conclusion is drawn that "price flexibility does not seem to be the significant factor in the long-term price movement."[3] If the long-term movement of prices is not correlated with a degree of flexibility, plausibly areas which are nonflexible in the short run do adjust in the long run.

The growth of total industry in the past can be related to determining supply factors, as shown in the following section. The growth of major sectors of the economy or of important industries can be explained by determining factors, such as some aggregate like disposable income, other industry activity, the capital stock used in supplying the current market, price of the product, and changes in technical relations to other industries. In the short run, when activity changes are principally dependent upon demand, such functional relationships perform much less well. If the extent of use of supply on the average and over the long run was anomalous, we would not expect good conformance with explanatory variables.

In picturing past known measurements, full-employment levels may be envisioned as parallel to the growth line. In fact, we doubt that many informed persons would wish to draw a growth line for aggregate industry at any slope differing substantially from the rise in full-employment levels. Secondary growth which appears in deep depression must, of course, be considered an exception.

We must not assume that the secular growth line is important in drawing activity away from high or low business cycle levels. On the contrary, high or low levels of activity tend to maintain themselves for an indefinite time. As explained in previous chapters, a momentum is created which prevents return to a middle position as cumulative expansion or contraction continues. Maintenance of and rise (or fall) of sales stimulate (or discourage) investment,

---

[3]*Frequency of Change in Wholesale Prices: A Study of Price Flexibility,* a study prepared for the Joint Economic Committee by the Department of Labor (Washington, D.C.: U.S. Government Printing Office, 1959), p. 11.

which pushes activity further away from the growth line. Current activity is not dependent on balanced relations but upon business cycle variations which create a downturn at the end of expansion and an upturn at the end of contraction. The turning points are reactions to imbalances which have accumulated—what we have called culminating forces.

The conception that the growth line draws activity back toward it fails, furthermore, because the growth line does not exist independently of the cyclical movement. The effective resources whose use is represented by the secular growth line are brought into being or made effective by activity along the expansion and contraction phases. With a different expansion phase, for instance, the growth line accompanying it would be different. Even what effective resources are depends on the institutional setup in which the economy functions. If our economy did not permit unemployed labor, for instance, fuller use of the labor resource might be implied at the growth line; but the product of society might be no greater if the system which forced fuller use resulted in a less efficient resource allocation.

These facts in no way reduce the significance of secular growth in terms of a balanced relation to supply resources. In the world in which we live, we need to recognize the kind of balances which do exist. Since current levels of activity are in a continual state of imbalance—moving with expansion or contraction in the business cycle—the recognition of a balance which follows along with this movement provides a powerful contrast to aid in visualizing current economic conditions. The temptation to try to interpret current economic conditions as the result of balanced relations is greatly lessened.

GROWTH OF AGGREGATE INDUSTRY

The growth of aggregate industry is usually represented by gross national product, as shown in Chart 6-1. The activity covered in this measurement best represents aggregate product in the economy. It includes the work required to replace durable capital, and this involves a duplication of past activity; but replacement is not satisfactorily measured and therefore not readily subtracted from aggregate expenditures. Chiefly, growth is measured at a higher level than if replacement were subtracted. The slope is not materially different, and the growth slope is the matter of chief interest.

Gross national product, as pictured in Chart 6-1, represents

CHART 6-1

GROWTH OF DEFLATED GROSS NATIONAL PRODUCT
(1959 Prices; Straight Line Is Plotted at 3 per Cent per Year)

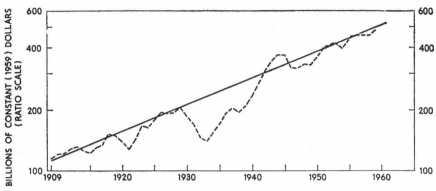

Source: Taken from *Survey of Current Business*, July, 1960.

deflated figures, i.e., the change in price level has been eliminated from the product values. Price deflation is an essential step in providing a picture of growth, for growth must be measured in real terms. Price changes would confuse the picture. A direct relation to stock figures necessary for production no longer could be made. In addition to dependence on the labor force, physical stock of capital goods, and other types of accumulation such as of knowledge, "growth" would be dependent on price changes. The amount of growth in terms of a dollar increase in product would not represent just increases for rise in the standard of living and for increased population but also for changes in the price level.

Past growth is partially indicated by the slope developed by fitting a secular trend, as shown in Chart 6-1. The secular trend, however, proves nothing in and of itself. Rather laborious efforts have frequently gone into showing that secular trends may show foolish results. Applying a straight edge to Chart 6-1, it will readily be seen that a trend fitted up to 1933 and then projected, or a trend fitted from 1933 to 1959 and then projected, would be scarcely credible. The technicalities of fitting and interpreting secular trends are not probed here but are summarized briefly in the Appendix to this chapter. The secular trend is useful only if it provides a picture which checks with a rational analysis of growth.

If changing supply factors could be neatly measured, the rational analysis of growth of aggregate product would become much clearer. Changing supply in this sense involves various types of labor, of capital, and of natural resources. Our measurements on the changing stock of capital and changing supply of natural resources are vague, and no use has been made of either of them in studying supply in relation to growth until very recently.

In 1959 the National Bureau of Economic Research published estimates of the growth of tangible capital, indicating an annual rate of more than 2 per cent compared with more than 1 per cent for labor,[4] as shown in Chart 6-2. However, we do not employ capital input estimates in analyzing growth of aggregate product. Little is known about the actual employment of the available capital stock in the production process. If we explained product growth by growth in tangible capital, implicitly we would be assuming that secularly the relative employment of capital was uniform. Our study of growth rests on the hypothesis that resource supply is used effectively in the long run; but with changing conditions, effective use might possibly imply shifting proportions of idle capital. In any case, measurements are not available on the idleness of capital over the long or short run.

Instead of relating product growth to all types of input, we rely solely on labor to represent measured input. The difference between the growth of labor input and total output is considered the second major factor determining growth of aggregate product; it is called productivity. Reliance on labor to represent input has a considerable tactical advantage, although the method is cruder than a more complete study of input factors would be. Reasonably satisfactory measurements of labor employment are available. Measurements of the actual use of labor, therefore, are contrasted with the actual product output. Figures on the actual use of other supply stocks—capital capacity and natural resource materials—are not available.

Using labor employment as the sole input measurement, the analysis of factors responsible for growth is set up as shown in Table 6-1. The number of persons employed is multiplied by hours of work (put on an annual basis) to show the number of man-hours worked each year. Gross national product divided by man-hours worked equals product per man-hour, as shown in the last column of Table 6-1. The changes in product per man-hour are taken to represent productivity because they show the changing amount of product a man-hour will obtain.

To develop the growth projections shown in Table 6-1, we

---

[4]Solomon Fabricant, *Basic Facts on Productivity Change*, Occasional Paper 63 (New York: National Bureau of Economic Research, Inc., 1959).

CHART 6–2

LABOR AND CAPITAL INPUT SHOWN SEPARATELY
(In Relation to Output)

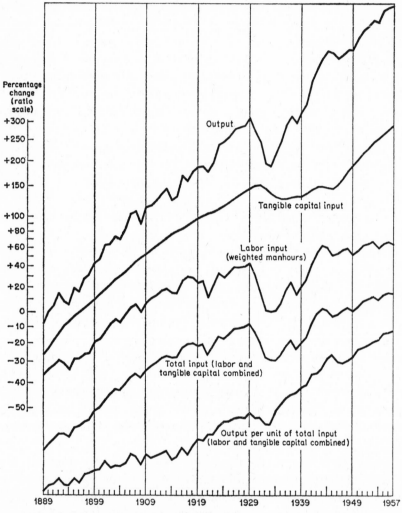

Source: Solomon Fabricant, *Basic Facts on Productivity Change,* Occasional Paper 63 (New York: National Bureau of Economic Research, Inc., 1959). Reproduced with permission.

start with labor-force estimates because these can be derived from estimates of expected population and the rates at which various age and sex groups of the population will participate in the labor force. For the near future the expected population in the relevant age groups depends upon survival of the existing population plus a very small immigration factor. Labor-force participation by sex and age groups is estimated largely on the basis of projection of past trends in the indicated percentages of participation. The percentages of the labor force in each age and sex group times the population projection in that group gives the divisional labor-force projection. The sum of the divisional figures provides the labor-force projections shown in Table 6–1.

As shown in the table, employment in the past has fallen short of the total labor force. Unemployment will occur in depressed periods, as indicated by analysis presented in the preceding chapters. But some unemployment will occur even at full employment, defined in any realistic sense, because of desire to shift jobs, layoffs for such reasons as business failures, seasonal slack, and other situations which depend on the technical way in which employment and unemployment are defined.[5] Even at the peak of World War II, some 700,000 persons were classified as unemployed.

The extent to which employment has fallen short of labor-force estimates is often called labor float. This amounted to about 4 per cent in the early fifties. The projections of employment shown in Table 6–1 are at a level 4 per cent below the labor-force projections.

The projections of hours per week and gross national product per man-hour are explained in succeeding sections. The arithmetic product of the projections of man-hours per year and gross national product per man-hour furnishes the GNP forecast.

The forecast thus obtained is at the so-called "full-employment level." Activity in recession will be below this level; therefore—in theory, at least—the forecast figures may be expected to be above a growth line cutting through the middle positions of actual activity variation. The projections of employment, hours per week, or gross national product per man-hour may be high or low, however; and actually, the GNP forecast may as a result be either high or low.

In the sense of what we have called above a net type of growth, rising employment would not be considered to produce growth because it does not provide for rising living standards. In this sense an approach to the kind of growth implied might be measured by productivity changes, as indicated in the last column of Table 6–1. Possibly, declining hours per week might be considered a reduction in the net type of growth if increased leisure is not thought of as

---

[5]For instance, persons laid off for definite periods of less than 30 days and persons waiting to be called to a new job scheduled to start within 30 days were classified as employed prior to 1957. Redefinitions changed persons in these groups to the unemployed category. The effect was to increase the level of unemployment by between 200,000 and 300,000 persons.

TABLE 6–1

Projection of the Growth of Gross National Product[a]
(All Dollar Figures in 1957 Prices)

Year	(1) Labor Force (in Millions)	(2) Employment[b] (in Millions)	(3) Hours per Week[c]	(4) Man-Hours per Year[d] (in Billions)	(5) Gross National Product (Billions of Dollars)	(6) Productivity[e] (Dollars)
1900	29.2	26.7	60.2	83.6	88.0	1.05
1910	36.0	34.0	55.1	97.4	115.8	1.19
1920	41.7	39.7	49.7	102.6	136.5	1.33
1930	49.3	45.8	45.9	109.7	178.3	1.63
1940	54.7	47.9	44.0	109.6	223.1	2.04
1950	64.6	61.5	41.0	130.8	344.8	2.64
1955	68.9	66.2	40.4	139.1	425.4	3.05
1960	72.8	69.9	39.0	141.8	492.0	3.47
1965[f]	79.9	76.7	37.5	149.6	589.4	3.94
1970[f]	87.1	83.6	36.0	156.5	701.1	4.48

[a] The principal sources of the estimates are the Department of Commerce, and J. Frederic Dewhurst and Associates, *America's Needs and Resources: A New Survey* (New York: Twentieth Century Fund, Inc., 1955). The projections, of course, are ours.

[b] Labor force and employment include the armed services. Alaska and Hawaii are not included. Their combined labor force was 300 thousand in 1960.

[c] Paid vacations are considered equivalent to a reduction in average weekly hours. Thus, one week of paid vacation amounts to a reduction of 0.8 hours per week at the present level of weekly hours.

[d] Column 2 times column 3 times 52.

[e] Column 5 divided by column 4. The projections of productivity are at the geometric rate between 1950 and 1957, 2.6 per cent per year. Productivity for 1960 is also computed that way.

[f] The figures for 1965 and 1970 represent forecasts. The employment taken for 1960 is 96 per cent of the labor force, as in the forecast years. The preliminary figure for actual GNP in 1960 is $475 billion, stated in 1957 prices.

representing rising living standards. If this were accepted as the net type of growth intended, its measurement might be obtained by dividing productivity figures by the percentage change in hours per week. Indications of the net type of growth probably are best expressed in percentages. The Productivity column in Table 6-1 or that column divided by changing hours per week can be converted to percentage changes by choosing some year as a base. The productivity projections employed in the table are 2.6 per cent per year, as explained below.

GROWTH IN THE LABOR FORCE

The labor force is dependent upon population changes 15 or 20 years earlier if migration is relatively unimportant, as has been true in the United States since the early twenties. Population growth arises from natural increase (the excess of births over deaths) and net immigration. The death rate has been represented by a fairly stable, declining function. Thus, fewer and fewer births have been required to maintain the population. The birth rate has fluctuated widely, although over the long sweep, it has shown some decline. Secular change in the labor force in the past 30 years, therefore, has been principally dependent upon the number of births 15 to 20 years earlier, with a slight upward adjustment for the declining death rate.

The number of men in the working age groups, roughly 20-65 years, is principally but not solely responsible for the size of the labor force. Its size is also dependent upon the number of women and children commercially employed and upon change in the retirement age of male workers. The proportionate number of women employed has steadily increased, but the increase has been approximately offset by rapid decrease in employment in the under-20 age groups and by a slight decrease in the rate at which males participate in the labor force.

All labor does not contribute equally to output; therefore, the possible influence of changing quality must be recognized. Unfortunately, there is no satisfactory way of measuring the influence of changing quality. Greater training and education probably do result in higher quality of work. An increased proportion of older workers may decrease quality.

The labor force is usually represented simply by the number of individuals involved. If the increased individuals added in a growing labor force do not contribute proportionately, output will increase less than proportionately to the added numbers; if they contribute more than proportionately, output will increase more than proportionately. The conclusion is that changing quality of labor is reflected in the productivity measure; for workers of higher quality are not given added weight in the measure of the labor force, but they may contribute above average output.

The extent to which the labor force is unemployed or unproductively employed will also influence the change in output. Unproductive employment, like digging and filling ditches, would be reflected in the measure of productivity in the same way as would a decline in labor quality. Unemployment will not directly influence productivity if, as is usually the case, only employed labor is counted in the productivity measurement. An increase in average unemployment will put the growth level further below productive ability.

SECULAR DECLINE IN WORKING HOURS

The total hours of labor applied to production have not increased as rapidly as the labor force because of successive reduction in working hours. The striking decline in working hours is clearly indicated in Table 6-1, when column 3 is compared with column 2. Column 3 may be accepted as representing the general change in working time, but the student should be reminded that available data on hours of work are thin for some parts of the economy, especially for agriculture. The decline which has occurred represents a choice in favor of greater leisure instead of greater production.

The irregular decline in working hours during the last hundred years represents a drop from 70 hours in 1850 to 40 hours in 1950. In that century the decline averaged three hours per decade, but a continuation of so rapid a rate is unlikely. In the past, declines in working time have usually been initiated in depression; hours are seldom fully restored when the depression ends. In the early fifties little decline occurred, since activity was running at an almost sustained prosperous level. In the 1949 and 1954 recessions, reduction in hours was only temporary because the changes were too impermanent and limited to generate a customary position.

In some parts of the economy, notably retail distribution, hours of work have been above average and have continued to decline toward more standard levels during the fifties. Some downward adjustment thus arises and will effect a slight reduction in over-all average working hours in the future. Furthermore, slow pressure toward provision of more leisure throughout most industry can be

expected to swing choices toward slightly less working time whenever opportunity offers the chance for a clear decision. The dramatic
historic decline in working hours is shown in Chart 6–3.[6] Over-all,

CHART 6-3

THE DECLINING AMERICAN WORK WEEK

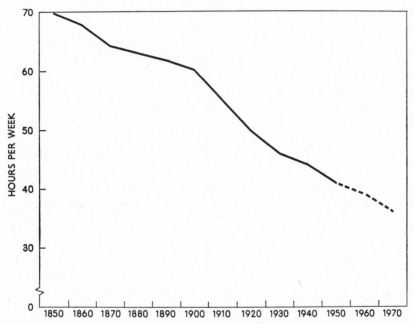

Source: For 1850 to 1950, J. Frederic Dewhurst and Associates, *America's Needs and
Resources: A New Survey* (New York: Twentieth Century Fund, Inc., 1955), p. 1073; the 1960
and 1970 figures are taken from Table 6–1.

various influences can be anticipated to produce a tapering-off of
the historic decline in working hours, as indicated by column 3 of
Table 6–1.

A 40-hour week can be expected to produce more than 80 per
cent as much output as a 50-hour week, because fatigue is less in
the former case. There is no satisfactory way of measuring what
the difference in fatigue is, however; and so far the procedure has
customarily been to let total man-hours represent the labor contribution to production. One reason for increased productivity, as
currently measured, is the reduced fatigue of shorter hours.

---

[6]A most important factor in bringing a decline in the weekly hours figure is
longer vacations. The technical method employed in computing the working hours
series is such that longer vacations show up as shorter average working hours.

RISING PRODUCTIVITY

Productivity changes result from several unlike forces. These can be classified in three groups:

1. In visualizing productivity as output relative to labor input, labor is taken as an unweighted total of man-hours applied to production and is thus uncorrected for labor quality or for the differential fatigue engendered by long hours.
2. Using output relative to labor input rather than relative to total input, efficiency changes are lumped together with changes in nonlabor input per man-hour in an inseparable total. All efficiency changes—whether due to improved application of labor, or more efficient use of raw materials, or more productive application of capital—are reflected in this measure.
3. The total output is of shifting composition.

1. The fact that changes in labor quality will influence the productivity measure was noted above. The composition of total man-hours may change, while the productivity measure merely divides output by total man-hours. If the proportion of more effective man-hours is increased, part of the increase in the productivity measure will arise from the fact that the measurement of man-hours did not increase as much as a properly weighted man-hours figure would. Of course, an increase in the proportion of less effective man-hours would create the reverse situation. Many factors may change the quality composition of man-hours. Age distribution of the population and changes in training and education are perhaps the most obvious. Their influence on the average quality of man-hours remains highly uncertain, however.

Reduced fatigue because of shorter weekly hours has an influence similar to added proportions of effective man-hours. Reduced fatigue can be expected to increase the effectiveness of the average man-hour.

2. The measurement of man-hour productivity may be influenced by a change in the raw material situation. More accessible or improved-quality raw materials will raise the productivity measurement obtained. Greater accessibility will reduce the labor input for a given amount of raw material. Higher-quality raw materials obtained with the same effort will raise productivity by increasing the total output; or they will increase the quality of output only and thus may not influence the measurement of productivity. For instance, a product may be made out of a more durable material, and the price charged may not change. The improved quality of the

product will thus not get counted in the measurement of total product. The productivity measurement in this case will be slightly understated.

In the gross national product measurement for total industry, where intermediate products are canceled out, raw materials necessarily relate to the raw materials of nature: natural resources. As more and more mineral and forest resources have been drawn from the earth, it is reasonable to assume that their condition has deteriorated or that their supply has been reduced. In isolated cases, there is evidence of this; but on the whole, it does not seem to have been important. Walnut gunstocks, for instance, have virtually disappeared, but with no important effect. Oil is a notable contrary case because, with rapid increase in its use, proved reserves have increased. The supply of oil has increased with its use, but deeper and deeper drilling has been required. More man-hours are necessary to bring a well into production. But this has been partly offset by better drilling equipment and more efficient geological practices.

The prevalent belief is that deterioration of natural resources has not been an important deterrant to rising man-hour productivity. When the use of a raw material in limited supply has increased, either new reserves have been discovered, or a satisfactory manufactured substitute has been developed. The substitute has frequently become of equal or better quality than the natural raw material and has usually come to be cheaper. There is no evidence that such practices have added to the man-hour input required.

Rising productivity in American industry frequently has been attributed to the availability of raw materials; but since the condition of raw materials has not greatly improved over time, this is incorrect. Our ample supply of raw materials is, however, one of the reasons why our productivity is higher than that of many foreign countries. Good raw materials make for high productivity and a high level of production; but if the quality and quantity of raw material resources do not increase, there is no tendency for the efficiency of production to increase.

Certainly, one of the most important reasons for the rapid increases shown in man-hour productivity is expansion in the use of capital. Except in the deepest depression the stock of capital rises continuously. The replacements and added units of equipment usually represent improved types. It is sometimes argued also that new units of industrial and commercial building are more efficient than the old. The rise and improvement in the stock of capital make an important contribution to production. Since neither the quality of labor nor the accessibility or quality of raw materials can be shown to have improved substantially, rising productivity tends to be attributed to increase and improvement of capital. When comparison is made with a restricted use of capital in industrially backward countries, efficiency of the use of capital appears impressive.

A man-hour of labor aided by modern capital produces many times what a man-hour would produce without it. The capital itself must, of course, be produced; and if this requires as many manhours as the capital saves, any increased productivity arising from capital use is illusory. That the time saved by the use of capital is not canceled by increased investment costs is indicated by known changes occurring in the economy.

When an improved machine is employed or an efficient machine is used where none was available before, output rises more rapidly than man-hours. Thus, man-hour productivity shows an increase. Does capital productivity, expressed as the output forthcoming with a given stock of capital, likewise increase? The answer to this question depends on whether new units are more efficient per dollar invested than those in the previously existing stock. Logically, it would seem that capital productivity, as well as man-hour productivity, should be rising. This would mean that the stock of capital as well as the man-hours of employment rise less rapidly than output. The evidence, however, seems to be that capital stock is increasing at about the same rate as output. (The tendency in the interwar period was for capital stock to grow less rapidly.)

3. The measurement of total industry productivity is significantly influenced by the shifting composition of total output. This is because some industries produce a higher-value product than others. Since productivity is measured by dividing gross national product (in constant dollars) by total man-hours, a shift in relative importance of various industries influences the productivity measure. Assume that total industry is made up of two industries; for every hour worked in one industry, there is a $1.00 product, and for the other a $2.00 product. Assume at the start that $50 billion is produced by each industry, or $100 billion for total industry. This would require 75 billion man-hours or average $1.33 per hour. If, now, the product of the $2.00-per-hour industry should rise to $60 billion and that of the other industry should continue at $50 billion, the total product would equal $110 billion, and the total hours worked would be 80 billion (assuming no increase in efficiency) and

would average $1.38 per hour. The declining relative importance of agriculture in American industry has produced some such influence. The hourly dollar output in agriculture, although increasing, has been substantially under the average for all other industry.

The measured increase in productivity, represented by dollar output per man-hour, has been due partly to the decline in importance of agriculture. Decline in relative importance of other

CHART 6–4

PRODUCTIVITY CHANGE IN THE PRIVATE ECONOMY
(Output per Man-Hour)
(1947-49 = 100)

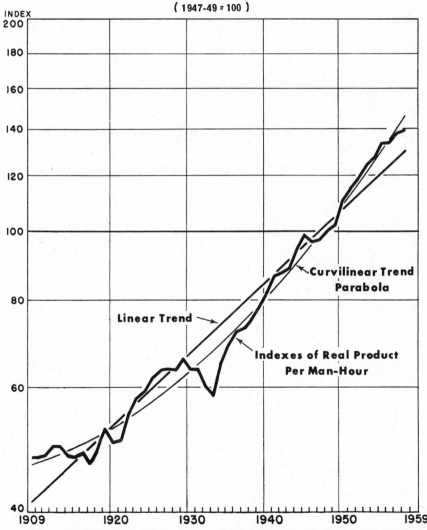

Source: U.S. Department of Labor, Bureau of Labor Statistics, *Trends in Output per Man-Hour in the Private Economy, 1909–1958,* Bulletin No. 1249 (Washington, D.C.: U.S. Government Printing Office, 1960).

"low dollar product per-man-hour" industries may also have played a part, but rises in some "high dollar product per man-hour" industries, like the automobile industry, have also been important.

In summary, changing quality of an average man-hour has had no demonstrable importance. Reduced fatigue due to shorter hours has undoubtedly contributed something to the rise shown in man-hour productivity. Labor-management relations may have had an influence, but this is indeterminate. Changes in natural resources apparently have not been important enough to have exerted a significant effect. The level and quality of our stock of capital must have been very important. The efficiency of management, if it has been increasing, could be responsible, first, for the adoption of new capital and, second, for improved practices in its use.

As figured, man-hour productivity is measured in terms of dollar of product per man-hour. The declining relative importance of agriculture is no doubt partly responsible for the rise which has occurred in dollar of product per man-hour.

Rising man-hour productivity is due to a complicated set of forces and therefore does not provide a simple logical factor in accounting for the growth of total industry. However, no more effective classification of logical factors is available for practical use at the present time. The man-hour productivity factor may be justified if the various strands of influence are qualitatively evaluated. To interpret any particular change in productivity, the factors responsible must be recognized, even though they cannot be effectively measured.

We highlight the past growth in productivity in Chart 6–4, with a measurement representing the private economy. Although substantial variations are apparent, the straight-line trend of the long-term movement is indicated at slightly more than 2 per cent (2.1 per cent per year if no adjustment is made for shifting capacity utilization).[7] Nevertheless, we assume a 2.6 per cent growth in the

---

[7] If adjustment is made for shifting capacity utilization, the growth slope is slightly higher; this is because of the influence of the Great Depression which is to pull the most recent end of the trend down when low productivity levels at that time are given full sway. For a correction to adjust for variation in employment, see John W. Kendrick, "National Productivity and Its Long-Term Projection," in *Long-Range Economic Projection*, Vol. XVI in National Bureau of Economic Research, Inc., *Studies in Income and Wealth* (Princeton: Princeton University Press, 1954).

If productivity is measured for the private economy only, as shown in Chart 6–4, the growth slope is raised to 2.3. This is because of the relative increase in the public sector, for which the figures will not indicate any increase in productivity. Recent studies appear to indicate that the early growth in man-hours was slightly less rapid than shown in Table 6–1. The 2.1 growth slope allows for these recent revisions, but they are not in a form to make satisfactory adjustments in Table 6–1.

forecast figures presented in Table 6-1. The reason for this optimistic forecast is explained in the following paragraphs.

Growth of productivity from 1950 to 1957 appeared to be at an annual percentage of approximately 2.6. It is tricky to conclude in a short period just what the growth in productivity may be, as becomes obvious by studying the shorter variations shown in Chart 6-4. Clearly, for instance, the rate of increase shown from the thirties to the early postwar is due to temporary factors and does not reflect secular growth.

For the over-all productivity measurement to maintain the past growth rate, other things being equal, shift out of agriculture will have to continue at a rapid rate. This is because shift from an industry producing a low-value product per man-hour to one producing a high-value product per man-hour has contributed to growth of productivity in the past. Viewing the rapid shrinkage in number of farm workers in the postwar period, maintenance of the past rate of shift might appear highly unlikely. But the shift has been based on increasing mechanization of farms, which enables a man to handle effectively an increasing number of acres. Continuance of this process and the plausibility of further potentialities lead us to believe that it may be expected to continue for at least another decade.

The reduction in fatigue from shorter hours certainly will be less than in the past when the work week was shrinking more rapidly. This retardation may well be offset by improved industrial engineering practices, including better plant layout and personnel relations.

Aside from improvement in technology, productivity might then be expected to continue at the rate found over the long sweep of time shown in Chart 6-4. But technology has been improving with great rapidity, and this has been supported by a satisfactory growth in the stock of capital as evidenced by the postwar level of investment, and continued development appears to be underwritten by a vastly expanded research program. American industry now spends on technical research more than 10 times the deflated prewar amount. There is every evidence that research programs will be continued, possibly expanded, in the foreseeable future. Technological development is the basis on which we forecast productivity rise at a more rapid rate than occurred in the past. Additionally, new types of power development give range for great advances.

As noted above, productivity projections are the key to the

forecast developed for gross national product. In the sixties decade the labor-force increase is projected at 1.7 per cent per year, but the decline expected in the work week brings the increase in man-hours to less than 1 per cent per year. The anticipation of a 2.6 per cent advance in productivity results in an increase of over 40 per cent for real GNP in the decade, or a geometric rate of 3.5 per cent per year. Perspective on this in relation to the slopes of various rates of growth is shown in Chart 6-5.

In looking at the growth of total industry, it is easy to confuse growth in real terms with reports currently made on current-dollar figures. This is particularly true in a period when a secular rise is occurring in average prices, as is likely to occur in the sixties. To illustrate the point, take the growth level of $492 billion of gross

CHART 6-5

THE WAY DIFFERENT RATES OF GROWTH APPEAR AGAINST REAL GROSS
NATIONAL PRODUCT

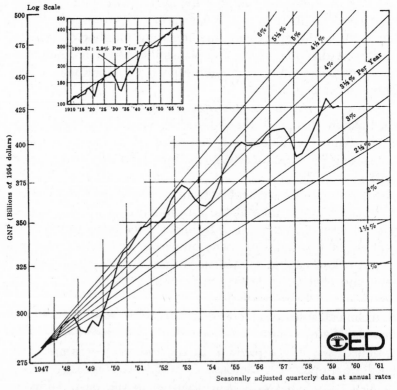

Seasonally adjusted quarterly data at annual rates

Source: *Economic Report of the President, January, 1960,* Hearings before the Joint Economic Committee, 86th Cong., 2d sess., February 1–16, 1960 (Washington, D.C.: U.S. Government Printing Office, 1960). The chart was presented by T. V. Houser, representing the Committee for Economic Development.

national product estimated for 1960 in Table 6-1. Since this is stated in 1957 prices, and since prices were advancing for the period, in actual dollars the figure will appear low. In 1960 dollars, it would come to about $522 billion. Similarly, the $701 billion shown for 1970 would come to over $743 billion in 1960 prices. Since prices in 1970 probably will be still higher, the need to correct for price changes before drawing conclusions on the indicated growth is apparent.

GROWTH OF INDIVIDUAL INDUSTRIES

The growth of individual industries varies markedly. Chart 6-6 illustrates the competitive growth of different industries in the energy market. Natural gas and oil have shown the most rapid growth in recent years. Coal, which at one time was undergoing rapid growth, until recently was in a decadent phase, experiencing decline rather than growth. Most American industries are experiencing growth. New industries frequently grow very rapidly. Most mature industries are growing more slowly than total industry.

The slow growth of mature industries has frequently led to a serious misunderstanding with regard to the growth of total industry. The growth of mature industries should not be thought to represent the growth of total industry, for new industries are likely to grow much more rapidly.

It is a curious but significant fact that total industry could grow at a constant or even accelerating rate with every individual industry growing at a decreasing rate. This fact results from the changing amounts contributed to the growth of total industry by individual industries in different stages of development. This can be shown by a simple illustration. Assume that total industry is made up of two industries, one mature and growing slowly, the other young and growing rapidly, as shown by the table below. It is clear upon examination that both industries A and B are growing at a decreasing rate. The total, however, grows 1.98 per cent from year 1 to year 2 and 2.43 per cent from year 2 to year 3.

INDUSTRY	HYPOTHETICAL PRODUCTION IN THE STATED YEAR		
	Year 1	Year 2	Year 3
A..................	100.0	101.0	102.0
B..................	1.0	2.0	3.5
Total.........		103.0	105.5

Such a mathematical relationship is logically possible, because the amount of growth of the small industry is so much greater from year 2 to year 3 than it is from year 1 to year 2 that it produces an

CHART 6–6

ENERGY CONSUMPTION IN THE UNITED STATES, BY SOURCES

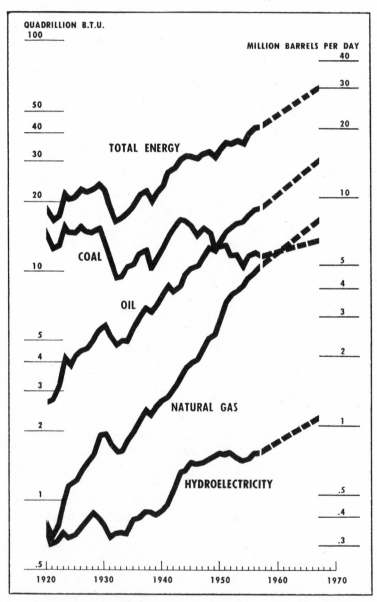

Source: Taken with permission from Frederick G. Coqueron and Others, *Future Growth of the World Petroleum Industry* (New York: Chase Manhattan Bank, 1958).

increased percentage of the total of the two industries when this is used as the base.

The growth of total industry since late in the nineteenth century has been at a constant rate of near to 3 per cent, as shown in Chart 6–1. As noted above, we forecast growth at a slightly higher rate. The rate of growth in almost all individual industries has been at a declining rate in contrast with the constant or rising rate of total industry.

Certainly, the growth of total industry cannot be represented by the separate growth of major individual industries, for the reasons given above. Obviously, this does not mean that the growth of individual industries is independent of the growth of total industry. Individual industries, in the aggregate, are completely dependent upon the increase in productive ability. With given changes in the labor force, hours of work, and productivity, there is just so much increase in output to be distributed among the individual industries. The kind of distribution does have some effect on the amount of increase to distribute, for, as noted above, productivity grows more rapidly if shifts are taking place from industries producing a low dollar value added to those producing a large dollar value added. The growth of total industry, however, sets the total growth to be distributed among individual industries.

The most important factor determining the growth of individual industries is the growth of total industry. With a given total increase in output available, the pattern of distribution among industries is fixed partly by technical considerations and partly by demand preferences and responses to relative price changes. Since consumers in our economy are free to buy in line with their preferences, no set pattern of distribution is possible. However, institutions and physical requirements establish one set of limits to the free play of choice, and joint requirements in the consumption of products and services set another. At a minimum, so much must be spent for food, housing, clothing, etc. As an example of joint requirements, corsages are required principally in connection with party dresses and services considered essential to a party, as demonstrated by World War II experience. With regard to technical considerations, any given finished product—for instance, an automobile—implies a plant and machine tools, raw materials, transportation, salesmen, and dealer service.

The shifts which can occur in the distribution of broad industry groups are thus narrowly limited. The amount of food, transportation, clothing, housing, entertainment, medical service, etc., required at any given time with a given total income is fairly closely established. The amount of output required from each broad industrial category is a function of the output of total industry. Some of these broad groups will fluctuate more widely than total industry and some less widely, but at the growth level the percentage distribution tends to remain fixed or to change according to a clearly recognized pattern. For instance, the growth of all types of transportation depends on the amount of produced goods to be transported; the amount of goods distributed is dependent upon the amount produced; and the quantity of raw materials needed depends on the fabricated products made from them. The amount of services consumers buy depends on the rise in discretionary income, which depends on the rapidity of growth in the satisfaction of desire for necessitous goods. To repeat, the growth of major industry groups is principally determined by the growth of total industry.

For minor industry groupings, total industry is much less controlling. To a considerable extent, one product may be substituted for another. For instance, the total amount of personal transportation may be narrowly fixed, but development may be in the direction of rail, air, automobile, or water. Products compete on the basis of quality, price, and adaptation to particular needs. The growth of any individual product represents the combined effect of these factors in comparison with competing products.

Practical problems center on the growth of individual products. An industry analysis is required. The broad industry group to which the product relates will be found to follow a fairly close relation to total industry; thus, the output in competition is established. At a given time the output in competition will be distributed among the competing products in an established pattern. Interest lies in determining the reason for secular changes in this pattern. For instance, as automobile transportation became cheaper in its early development, it took successively more and more transportation service away from the railroads. The growth of air travel has been based to a major extent on the quality of time saving, with which the other forms cannot readily compete. The growth of automobile transportation has been related to its close adaptation to individual needs—a personal transportation quality with which the other services find competition difficult. In many industries the race between quality and adaptation to particular needs is much closer.

In summary, the relation of a broad industry group to the growth of total industry will establish the changing output in competition. This is a necessary orientation which has been all too frequently overlooked in the past. Detailed industry analysis will then explain shifting competitive positions and can be employed to establish the secular growth line for the particular product or service.

FORECAST OF INDIVIDUAL INDUSTRIES

The growth of major expenditure divisions has generally been summarized in terms of a percentage or change in percentage of total gross national product.[8] Therefore, forecasting is most effectively developed in relation to the changes forecast for GNP. The expenditure divisions usually so forecast include consumption, residential building, other private construction and producer equipment, inventory, and government.

At the detailed industry level, a more specifically related aggregate replaces gross national product. For instance, sales of a consumer nondurable good are frequently forecast in relation to disposable income. To make use of a relationship to disposable income, the disposable income series must, of course, be forecast. This would be achieved through a forecast of GNP and of expected national income accounting relationships.

Usually, no one general industry aggregate by itself can be expected to point up the growth of a detailed industry for long.[9] There are various reasons for this. The industry growth may be related particularly to consumption by a given age group of the population, and the proportions of the total population in this age group may be shifting. Consumption of the product may be related to weather conditions; and for this reason, geographical shifts in

---

[8]See Elmer C. Bratt, *Business Forecasting* (New York: McGraw-Hill Book Co., Inc., 1958), pp. 65–90.

[9]Theoretically, a much better procedure than relating to one general industry aggregate would be to study interrelations with all other industries dependent on the given industry or on which it is dependent. A striking possibility along this line is what is called an input-output table. By use of this table an industry's output can be broken down by flow to various consuming industries and its purchases by various industries from which it buys. If the developed interrelations could be projected into the future, they might largely replace dependence on an over-all industry aggregate as an explanatory variable in forecasting, but the input-output table is not yet developed to the stage that it can be employed effectively in growth forecasting. See the author's *Business Forecasting*, pp. 94–97. Even a developed input-output table is no cure-all, however. The projected relationships will break down if they are not corrected for technological changes. Also, in case of a product in wide consumer demand a projection of consumer preferences may be more basic than the interindustry relationship.

residence of the population may be influential. The combined effect of several over-all factors may have to be considered.

In the case of durable products the existing supply of usable goods already in the hands of the public is often an important consideration. A study of the existing stock in relation to the expected potential which might be reached in the future provides a saturation analysis. Difficulties here involve the determination of what the potential stock may be expected to be and the rate at which replacement may be required in the current stock. The potential future stock depends not only on expected disposable income, but also on technological improvements in the product and on new uses found for it, as well as the development of other products which may compete. Much specific information and detailed analysis are necessary. Changing use may be illustrated in the case of automobiles. The future expansion is now more dependent on growth in multicar families than on growth of first-car owners because near-saturation has already been achieved in that respect.

The factors responsible for growth of a given product may be called explanatory variables. One method of forecasting involves setting up an econometric equation with the product of the particular industry shown on the left of the equation and the explanatory variables with assigned coefficients, as determined by past relationships, on the right. From such an equation the expected amount of product for a given future year can be determined by substituting in the equation the expected values for the explantory variables.

The setting-up of an econometric equation often has proved very helpful in providing perspective. In furnishing measurements of past relationships, understanding of the importance of various factors may be sharpened. Sometimes the equation developed can be considered an effective guide to future growth, to be qualified only to the extent that shifts in particular situations must be introduced.

So far, the more common experience has been that the econometric equation represents a background development rather than a direct basis for forecasting. The forecasts of the explanatory variables, necessary to use the equation, may prove almost as difficult as a direct growth forecast of the product. Probable shifts in the coefficients which express the importance to be assigned to the various explanatory variables may introduce a substantial area of uncertainty. Probable development of competitive products is difficult to introduce directly into the econometric equation; and usually, the practicing forecaster finds less mechanical methods better adapted to evaluate their importance.

In the few companies where forecasts are made directly with the mathematical function technique, a series of equations rather than a single comprehensive one is usually employed. Separate equations are used to derive estimates for each of the explanatory variables. The estimates obtained are inserted in a summary equation which states the relation to sales of the product of the industry being studied. A forecast for the particular product is thus developed.

After the industry forecast is obtained, each company must estimate its proportionate share, or shifts in its proportionate share, of the total sales forecast for the product. The company must evaluate its relative market, technical ability, ability to obtain financing, costs, and other efficiency factors relative to the total industry. The detailed problems differ from one company to another, and it is difficult to set up a general blueprint.

The individual company frequently faces a sales potential which is not commensurate with the total product as classified in any particular industry. Under these circumstances, a study of end uses or customer takings may provide a more effective guide. In end-use analysis, the company classifies the uses of its products and estimates the amount required for a dollar sale of each end use (often called use factors); and from forecasts of the sale involved in each use, estimates of the total demand for its products are obtained. This technique has the advantage of being specifically related to the company's market. The difficulties with the procedure relate to imponderables involved in forecasting the various uses as classified and in estimating any changes which may occur in use factors.[10]

Because of the many difficulties involved in the various methods outlined above, resort is often had to the projection of a secular trend. Although the assumptions involved in projecting a secular trend are no less complicated than those faced in the other methods, these assumptions are less immediately apparent. Looking at the past general movement and projecting it into the future involve a substantial degree of plausibility. The plausibility may, however, be misleading. The trend fitted may not cover a representative period, or the series used may not well represent the type of sales to be expected in the future. Implicitly, the projected trend assumes a continuance of the operation of past growth influences. This may be

---

[10]A more detailed analysis of sales forecasting will be found in the author's *Business Forecasting* pp. 237–87.

an incorrect assumption if (1) total activity shifts markedly, as from a deep depression to a prosperous period, or (2) prospects of the industry or company relative to the competition rapidly improve or rapidly deteriorate.

A secular trend, if carefully developed so as to project from a representative period and so as to include approximately the kind of product for which future forecasts are actually desired, may be an effective starting point. If so, the other methods outlined above almost certainly will be useful and may be indispensable in confirming or modifying the projection shown by the secular trend. In assuming implicitly that time alone explains secular growth, the secular trend provides no insight into the kind of industry relationships upon which the particular growth depends. How the growth is affected by aggregate activity and other explanatory variables certainly will help in visualizing the projected secular trend and may provide adequate reasons for modifying it. Saturation analysis, where applicable, may be helpful. For instance, the forecasts of some tobacco companies in the late twenties were based on a rapid secular trend indicated by a fitting to sales of cigarettes; but much of the growth arose from an increase in smoking by women, and projection of the secular trend a few years into the future implied more women smokers than women in the population.

Saturation or end-use analysis not only dramatizes the importance of the product in the economy, but provides a realistic appraisal of the relationships to be expected in other parts of the economy. Such a method will be more important in the analysis of some industries than in others. In the steel industry the taking of steel by other industries has long been the chief method employed in forecasting. End-use analysis in the steel industry, however, does not readily give adequate consideration to the growing competition of other materials. Thus, the best methods of growth forecasting involve the indications provided by various different methods.

APPENDIX TO CHAPTER VI

THE GROWTH CURVE SHOWN BY GOMPERTZ AND LOGISTIC EQUATIONS

Going back to the twenties, the general position on growth analysis was that a description could be effectively developed by a trend equation —the problem being one of finding the right equation. The generally accepted position now is that growth cannot be effectively identified in this way, especially for forecasting purposes. Some note on secular trend methods is warranted, however, because of their use in forecasting, as

TABLE 6-2

ASSUMPTIONS MADE BY EQUATIONS COMMONLY USED TO MEASURE THE LONG-TIME TREND*

(1) Type of Equation	(2) Equation	(3) Assumptions Made	(4) Meaning of Constants	(5) Use of Curve
1. STRAIGHT LINE	$Y = a + bx$	Growth by constant absolute amounts per year.	a represents height b represents slope	Simple method of obtaining general impression; sometimes assumptions are typical of data.
2. SECOND-DEGREE PARABOLA	$Y = a + bx + cx^2$	Difference of series changes by constant absolute amounts.	a represents height b represents average slope c represents concavity	Useful as a general method if all that can be determined is that trend has curvilinearity without change of concavity; also, size of c determines existence or nonexistence of curvilinearity under these conditions.
3. COMPOUND INTEREST CURVE	$Y = ab^x$ or $\log Y = \log a + x \log b$	Growth by a constant rate, a concave upward line.	a represents height $b - 1 =$ rate of increase or decrease	Useful when a constant rate of growth can be logically assumed.
4. PARABOLA OF LOGARITHMS	$\log Y = a + bx + cx^2$	Difference of relative changes of the series changes by constant relative amounts.	a represents height b represents average slope of relative change c represents concavity of relative change	Useful as a general method when it is shown that curvilinearity of relative change expresses the nature of the data better than curvilinearity of amount of change.
GROWTH CURVES: 5. SYMMETRICAL LOGISTIC	$Y = L/(1 + 10^{-a+bx})$	An S-curve, with upper, and lower asymptotes, and a declining relative rate of increase throughout the range of the curve; curve is symmetrical about point of inflection.	L represents upper asymptote	
6. INTEGRATION OF NORMAL PROBABILITY CURVE	No equation, use arithmetic normal probability paper	Same as symmetrical logistic.		The "growth" curves assume three general stages of growth: (1) experimentation, (2) exploitation, and (3) stability. This is the characteristic growth of consumer-goods industries over a span of 15–50 years. It may be the characteristic of total industry or basic industries over several centuries.
7. GOMPERTZ CURVE	$Y = ab^{c^x}$ or $\log Y = \log a + c^x \log b$	An S-curve, with upper and lower asymptotes, and a declining relative rate of increase throughout the range of the curve; point of inflection is reached when the level of the ordinate is 37–38% of the distance between the two asymptotes.	a represents the upper asymptote c lies between $+1$ and -1	
8. INTEGRATION OF LOGARITHMIC NORMAL PROBABILITY CURVE	No equation, use logarithmic normal probability paper	Same as Gompertz curve.		
9. NEW YORK FEDERAL RESERVE BANK CURVE	$Y = bcU/(d+x)$ or $\log Y = \log b + \log c/(d + x)$	A growth type developed to save labor in computing.		

* Equations 1, 2, 3, and 4 are ordinarily fitted by the method of least squares; this method assumes a normal distribution of the data about the trend line. The equation of the symmetrical logistic as usually written involves the use of the logarithmic base e. For common methods of computation, however, the logarithmic base 10 gives the same results more simply.

indicated above, and because their standing as an identification of growth has not been entirely discredited.

Assumptions made in some equations commonly used to measure secular trends are described in Table 6–2. Of these, equations Nos. 5–9, describing the so-called "growth curve," have attracted the widest following. While most analysts today place major emphasis on methods outlined in the body of this chapter rather than on an equation to identify growth, the growth curve still retains enough following to warrant giving it some consideration. It possesses some limited merit in describing growth, especially in the analysis of any particular consumer durable good.

Raymond Pearl and L. J. Reed, on the basis of extensive studies of population of the countries of the world and of the growth of most kinds of biological phenomena (such as various individual plants and individual animals over time), concluded that the growth curve incorporates the logical nature of population growth.[11] On the basis of these studies made forty years ago, many students came to believe that a general law of growth had been established. The term "growth curve" grew out of this belief.

Although the growth curve necessarily represents a continual decline in the geometric rate of growth, plotted on arithmetic paper it shows successive phases of slow, rapid, and again slow growth, thus: It postulates a period of slow growth, then more and more rapid absolute growth until a most rapid amount of increase is reached, then a declining amount of growth until an almost stable level is attained. In general, therefore, the growth curve can be said to assume that the industry involved passes through three stages:

1. Stage of experimentation
2. Stage of exploitation
3. Stage of stability or saturation

The second and third stages have also been considered to represent, respectively, rapid extension of competition and final maturity.

The growth of most consumer durables progresses through these three stages. This has been clearly indicated by growth of sales for automobiles, radios, and mechanical refrigerators. An indication of the relative position on the growth curve has been valuable for these goods. Recently, however, development of new durables, as illustrated by television sets, has been so rapid that the stages noted above appear vague and somewhat indefinite.

A relatively slow early development still appears to be characteristic, but changes during this early period now provide little insight into the

---

[11]The particular growth curve employed by Pearl and Reed was the logistic (see No. 5 in Table 6–2). A comprehensive description of Pearl and Reed's measurement of the trend of population will be found in Raymond Pearl, *The Biology of Population Growth* (New York: Alfred A. Knopf, Inc., 1925). For a similar curve applied to data more simply, see the description of the New York Federal Reserve Bank curve in notes by N. O. Johnson published in the *Journal of the American Statistical Association*, Vol. XXX (December, 1935), p. 717, and Vol. XXXI (December, 1936), p. 731 (No. 9 in Table 6–2).

rapidity with which production and competition will be extended in the second phase. Since the rise is now more vertical, slight variation of the angle of rise will substantially shorten or lengthen Stage 2. And the onset of the third phase appears to be better indicated by studies of market saturation (briefly described above) than by a growth curve indication of a shift to stable or mature conditions.

Another difficulty with the growth curve concept is that in an economy of rapid development like ours, an industry may not attain stability at the stage of saturation. The end of growth marks decline for many products. A better—or at least, more acceptable—product takes away part of the market.

The growth trend fitted to total industry or to raw material industries is even less helpful. Unlike consumer durable goods, where saturation is partly related to the degree to which qualified households use the durable goods, raw materials depend on degree of use rather than number of users. The point where the steel industry will reach saturation, for instance, depends on such factors as changes in the nature of demand (some industries use more steel than others), development of competitive raw materials, and changes in the quality of steel.

Aside from the use of equations to establish laws of growth, the importance of their use in studying growth is clearly established in the final section of the body of this chapter. From the point of view of application to forecasting, consideration should be given to the problem of reducing technical distortions to a minimum. The following procedures are recommended:

1. Use a technical trend shape closely approximating the general sweep of the data.
2. Fit the trend line to a period which begins and ends in the same phase of the cycle, preferably high prosperity peaks (because their difference closely approximates the growth which has occurred).
3. Use a long enough period to average out shorter movements, including several cycles, if possible.

In practice, exceptions to these procedures may occasionally be necessary, but in those cases the reasons for the exceptions should be obvious. Frequently, it will be necessary to fit to different periods and to fit by different trend equations in order to provide background information.

FOR REFLECTION AND ANALYSIS

1. Should growth be defined in terms of rising stocks or in terms of rising activity?
2. Compare the parts investment expenditure plays in the business cycle and in secular growth.
3. Develop a hypothetical illustration with assumptions as to the capital/output ratio, growth in total private output, and growth of capital stock. What are the relationships between these assumptions?
4. What is the difference between the ideas of secular stagnation and of secondary growth?
5. How does the "construction cycle" differ from secondary growth?

6. Why are real- rather than current-value figures employed in studying growth?
7. Assume you are projecting an over-all increase in productivity of 3 per cent per year for the next 10 years. (Compounded, 3 per cent per year comes to 34.4 per cent in 10 years.) Assume the labor force is to increase from 100 million to 120 million. Assume that the labor float is figured at a constant 5 per cent. Assume that hours per week, on the average, are expected to fall from 40 to 30. Assume that the productivity figure for the initial year is $3.00. What is the GNP projection?
8. What is the relation between changes in the population level and changes in the labor-force level?
9. Explain how the rise and improvement in stock of capital has come to be chosen as most important among the many factors responsible for change in productivity.
10. What does capital productivity mean as distinguished from man-hour productivity?
11. Make up an example, assuming that total industry is composed of only three industries. Assume that no change occurs in the productivity of any one of the three industries. Nevertheless, make an assumption about shift in the product mix which results in a substantial change in the measure of over-all productivity.
12. Discuss the importance of total industry in determining the growth of broad industry groups as compared to the growth of minor competing industries.
13. Explain the use of an econometric equation in forecasting the growth of individual industries.
14. Discuss end-use analysis in company forecasting.
15. Outline the strength and weakness of a secular trend as a basis for growth forecasting.
16. Explain the use of a "growth curve" in forecasting, when the curve is fitted by secular trends.

SELECTED READINGS FOR PART ONE

BURNS, A. F., and MITCHELL, W. C. *Measuring Business Cycles.* New York: National Bureau of Economic Research, Inc., 1946.
  The standard work on the National Bureau methods of measurements.
CLARK, J. M. *Strategic Factors in Business Cycles.* New York: National Bureau of Economic Research, Inc., 1934.
  An early study of the way cumulation spreads and recedes in the business cycle.
DEWHURST, J. FREDERIC, and ASSOCIATES. *America's Needs and Resources: A New Survey.* New York: Twentieth Century Fund, Inc., 1955.
  Contains a comprehensive survey of growth requirements.
"FORTUNE" EDITORS. *Markets of the Sixties.* New York: Harper & Bros., 1960.
  Important angles on the growth requirements of the sixties.

JOINT ECONOMIC COMMITTEE. *Employment, Growth, and Price Levels,* Part 2: *Historical and Comparative Rates of Production, Productivity, and Prices.* April 7–10, 1959, Hearings, 86th Cong., 1st sess. Washington, D.C.: U.S. Government Printing Office, 1959.

Contains useful information on growth, including testimony by Raymond Goldsmith and Moses Abramovitz, as well as a reprint of a National Bureau Occasional Paper on productivity.

MITCHELL, WESLEY C. *Business Cycles and Their Causes.* 3d printing. Berkeley: University of California Press, 1959.

Excerpt from Mitchell's famous 1913 Volume. A classic statement on the way business cycles are generated.

————. *Business Cycles: The Problem and Its Setting.* New York: National Bureau of Economic Research, Inc., 1927.

An outstanding all-comprehensive classic, but the presentation is cumbersome.

————. *What Happens during Business Cycles: A Progress Report.* New York: National Bureau of Economic Research, Inc., 1951.

Containing Mitchell's summary of what he had learned about the business cycle, the book throws light on the National Bureau method of measurement.

NATIONAL BUREAU OF ECONOMIC RESEARCH, INC. Conference of Universities–National Bureau Committee for Economic Research. *Conference on Business Cycles.* New York, 1951.

Presentation of several major alternatives in the study of the business cycle.

SCHUMPETER, JOSEPH A. *Business Cycles.* New York: McGraw-Hill Book Co., Inc., 1939.

This two-volume work is the classic on Schumpeter's classification of fluctuations.

PART

TWO

Theory of Business Fluctuation

Chapter 7

DEVELOPMENT OF THEORY TO EXPLAIN FLUCTUATIONS

Early in the nineteenth century, development of economic theory was new and exciting. A method which had proven to be eminently successful in the field of science was adopted. We may call this method "deductive" in that, as employed by the economists, it involved the development of conclusions about economic behavior from postulated assumptions. The method remains standard even today, and the student must have faced it in his course on economic principles. With the passing of time, however, there has arisen a substantial development in economic theory, partly because of the contribution of successive generations to theoretical ideas and more importantly because of the consideration given to statistical facts as their greater availability has increased.

The assumptions made by the economists a hundred years ago were simple, but they led to striking conclusions, the plausibility of which frequently became self-evident. As might well be suspected in light of the methods employed, the conclusions reached were not always wholly credible; indeed, some of them appeared to be in conflict with experience. A most famous case is Say's Law, which makes the essential proposition that in a developed market economy, supply is demand. Money merely greases the wheels of exchange. Any supply is exchanged for some other supply, and the market price in competition automatically adjusts in the market economy so that the movement of any supply of goods and services to the hands of those who demand it will be accomplished immediately. An oversupply of particular goods, such as of some farm product used for food, is recognized to be a temporary possibility, but no such oversupply is considered compatible with the play of free markets in the total economy. Inelastic demand cannot possibly account for excess production of all products. To grant that would

135

be tantamount to implying that unsatisfied demands do not exist. Say's Law leads to the assumption that economic change is determined by available supply, not by demand conditions.

To all intents and purposes the business cycle is defined away by Say's Law. With demand and supply in continuous adjustment the kind of cumulative movement described in Chapters 4 and 5 could not occur. The business cycle implies maladjustment between total demand and total supply, contrasted with the adjustment which may be conceived to lie at output levels providing full employment. The movement which occurs does not tend constantly toward adjustment, either, because demand, and not supply, is the predominant factor in directing its course.

The economists were loath to forswear the overwhelming conclusions deriving from plausible assumptions they had made. Any apparent phenomenon inconsistent with these conclusions was thought to represent an incorrect interpretation. This was the situation with respect to business cycle variations. But such a succinct statement does not convey the spirit of the economists' position. They were definitely interested in all aspects of economic behavior even though their appetite for empirical information was limited, which certainly was not unrelated to the scanty availability of statistical data.

Under the banking systems of the early nineteenth century the most obvious characteristic of the business cycle movement was a monetary crisis. The economists were much concerned with monetary developments, and recognized that monetary institutions might initiate undesirable economic changes under certain conditions. Particularly, the nineteenth century was beset with several serious monetary crises. No one would deny that monetary crises were worsened by ineffectiveness of banking and monetary institutions. The economists, who felt that money and banking should initiate no active influence on economic conditions, made some good points on the unsatisfactory functioning of these institutions. They did not connect monetary crises with recurrent business cycle variations; but few, if any, persons did.

THE DISSENTERS

Dissension from the position of the classical economists did arise, although its consideration was limited until near the end of the century. The position of the dissenters did not represent a clear recognition of the business cycle, but did represent questioning of the malfunctioning of money as the only basis for maladjustments between aggregate demand and aggregate supply.

Writing in 1804, Lord Lauderdale made an excellent case for looking behind the malfunctioning of money in explaining inadequacy of aggregate demand. Emphasis was placed on the derived nature of demand for capital. Capital is wanted to help provide the services or goods obtained by using it. Particularly, the demand for capital depends upon the demand for consumer goods made in the production process. The demand for consumer goods is partially determined by the distribution of income. He held that countries enjoying a wide distribution of income experience a high level of consumption expenditure.

Lauderdale was chiefly concerned with the fiscal policy being legislated at the time. He objected to plans to extinguish the national debt of Britain in about a half century and held that the funds withdrawn from the economy would reduce aggregate demand. He recognized what the logicians call "fallacy of composition," in particular that thrift for the state was not equally valid with thrift for the individual. In facing the problem of reducing government debt, he was thus led to worry about the resulting adequacy of consumer demand and to develop the rationalizations summarized in the preceding paragraph. In pursuit of the effects of a continued reduction in monetary funds the automaticity of adjustment in aggregate demand was called into question.

Thomas Robert Malthus, writing in 1820 after the Napoleonic Wars, like Lauderdale, questioned—on the examination of fiscal policy—the achievement of automatic balance between total demand and total supply. His generalizations, however, were fitted into a broader analysis of economic forces. A hundred years later, Keynes called attention to his work, and there are important parallels between their systems.[1]

Malthus was deeply concerned with the depressed conditions existing in Britain following the Napoleonic Wars. He deplored the lack of "understocked employments" (investment opportunities). This idea corresponds with what we have said above about secondary growth in deep depression.

He recognized that the government had reduced taxes with

---

[1]Keynes put Malthus "in that brave army of heretics . . . who, following their intuitions, have preferred to see the truth obscurely and imperfectly rather than to maintain error, reached indeed with clearness and consistency and by easy logic, but on hypotheses inappropriate to the facts."

the decline in war expenditure, but he felt that consumers had developed habits based on high taxes during the war which inclined them to save most of the tax reduction. Saving and consumption were thought to be rooted in established patterns, although Malthus did not identify the pattern as a schedule.

Malthus sensed that a high saving rate and low capital requirements resulted in a low national income. He pointed out that the act of saving does not insure that capital goods are wanted. Private expenditure had failed to offset the decline in government expenditures.

His prescription was to follow lines which would divert consumer funds obtained from income to expenditure rather than to saving. He was not very optimistic, but he felt that his recommended procedures would be a movement in the right direction. He advocated widening the distribution of income, encouraging imports which would add to the variety of goods and thus encourage expenditure, and the development of service industries which he felt to have a special property in adding to consumption. In the language of the Keynesian analysis presented in Chapter 9, Malthus was interested in providing measures which would increase the propensity to consume. He felt that this would lead to higher investment and ultimately raise investment expenditures.

The classical economists saw no need for special measures to induce consumption because they were convinced that for the economy as a whole the market would match demand with any available supplies. Indeed, some thirty years later, John Stuart Mill was contending that "in opposition to these palpable absurdities, it was triumphantly established by political economists, that consumption never needs encouragement." In his *Principles of Political Economy,* he took some trouble to track down the contradiction which he thought was presented. Commodities constitute the means of payment for commodities. Basically, what is wanted is not money but consumable articles for goods put up for sale. "A general over-supply, or excess of all commodities above the demand, so far as demand consists in means of payment, is thus shown to be an impossibility." Further, Mill examined the case of "absence of means in those who have the desire to consume, and the want of desire in those who have the means," but he concluded that even this could only happen in the case of misdirected production.

At the beginning of the twentieth century, John A. Hobson was saying much the same things as Sismondi and Malthus had a hundred years earlier. His inspiration was derived from a longer perspective of industrial history and turned less on generalization regarding policy requirements in a given historical period. Hobson visualized rather stable consumer expenditures out of income, but pointed to disturbances which arise from a savings proportion not meshed with a required investment proportion (relative to total product or income). There is some right proportion between saving and spending. This proportion depends on the state of technology, which determines potentialities in the use of capital, and on the need for capital in producing consumer goods. To Hobson, it was obvious that savings tended toward too high a proportion compared with investment needs. If all savings were invested, the potential supply would become excessive in relation to effective demand. The proposed specific is greater equalization of income, achieved either by higher wage rates or by graduated tax measures.

At about the same time, Alfred Marshall lent his prestige to quote approvingly Mill's position, summarized above. He did, however, qualify the position even more than Mill with respect to the extent consumers might choose to use their purchasing power. This is developed in the following section.

Perhaps there is no better statement of the dissenters with respect to the failure of the prevailing body of economic doctrine to come to grips with the problems emphasized in this section than that made by Keynes in the Great Depression:

> The completeness of the Ricardian victory is something of a curiosity and a mystery. It must have been due to a complex of suitabilities in the doctrine to the environment into which it was projected. That it reached conclusions quite different from what the ordinary uninstructed person would expect, added, I suppose, to its intellectual prestige. That its teaching, translated into practice, was austere and often unpalatable, lent it virtue. That it was adapted to carry a vast and consistent logical superstructure, gave it beauty. That it could explain much social injustice and apparent cruelty as an inevitable incident in the scheme of progress, and the attempt to change such things as likely on the whole to do more harm than good, commended it to authority. That it afforded a measure of justification to the free activities of the individual capitalists, attracted to it the support of the dominant social force behind authority.[2]

Interesting as this statement is, it clearly overstates the case. Only the classical economists provided a suitable superstructure for economic thought, so they won intellectual acceptance because of

---

[2]John Maynard Keynes, *The General Theory of Employment, Interest, and Money* (New York: Harcourt, Brace & Co., Inc., 1936), pp. 32–33.

default, if for no other reason. As for the explanation provided for phenomena arising from the business cycle, the classical explanations were scarcely more acceptable than those of the dissenters. Theories promulgated by the classicists are outlined in the following section.

On the business cycle, then, neither side won decisive approval. Ricardo, in particular, was largely ignored. He was impressed with Say's position that no causal explanation is given by simply saying that too much has been produced all around. Say had inferred erroneously from this simple idea that *partial* overproduction must be at the root of the trouble. This is *disproportionality theory*, which as Schumpeter says, sometimes got no further than citing such an illustration as an overproduction of shoes with reference to the production of coats. Ricardo tried to improve on the disproportionality theory by citing *sudden changes in the channels of trade* as the principal cause. He cited slightly more plausible cases of disproportionality, such as might arise out of foreign trade, but his analysis was vague and did not provide the basis for explaining business cycle changes. The analysis of economic instability after Ricardo is more clearly related to Adam Smith, as noted in the following section.

Both dissenters and classicists thought of explaining conditions such as a *given* prosperity or a *given* depression, not a recurrent fluctuation. The dissenters were principally concerned with what we have called a period of secondary growth. The classicists concentrated their attention on monetary crises.

THE THEORY OF COMMERCIAL CRISES

Adam Smith pointed to "overtrading," which involves buying on credit, followed by inability to pay when the credit comes due. Smith discussed this situation in only a few scattered sentences, but it provided background for the positions taken by John Stuart Mill, Alfred Marshall, and many other classical economists.

John Stuart Mill thought that general disturbances in the economy were caused by financial factors. His discussions, which are scattered through his writings, deal principally with commercial crises. Since his purpose in dealing with commercial crises was to clarify other subjects, such as the influence of credit on prices, what determines the rate of interest, and the regulation of inconvertible paper money, his analysis of commercial crises themselves is not wholly co-ordinated; but the major points he made and his influence are not difficult to summarize.

Mill thought that the difficulty which led to a commercial crisis was not excessive credit expansion by banks as such, but expectation of need for larger supplies by businessmen which produced speculation and led to higher prices. Although speculation was considered to be the usual cause, he thought a crisis might be preceded by need for unusually large foreign payments, as for instance occasioned by a high price of cotton and an unprecedented importation of food in 1847, without "an extraordinary and irrational extension" of speculative credit. In either case the abnormal demand for loans and rise in the interest rate would lead to inability of firms to meet obligations and bring on a commercial crisis. Passing note was made of the possibility of a lag in the interest rate behind the profit rate accentuating culmination of the crisis, reminiscent of the ideas of the capital theories summarized in the following chapter.

The rapid recoil in prices accompanying a commercial crisis was considered to be partially preventable by an extension of bank credit:

In the first place, a large extension of credit by bankers, though most hurtful when, credit being already in an inflated state, it can only serve to retard and aggravate the collapse, is most salutary when the collapse has come, and when credit instead of being in excess is in distressing deficiency, and increased advances by bankers, instead of being addition to the ordinary amount of floating credit, serve to replace a mass of other credit which has been suddenly destroyed.[3]

Here, then, was recognized authority for the use of clearinghouse certificates in the banking panic of 1873, noted in Chapter 12 below.

To Mill the disturbances connected with commercial crises principally produced fluctuations in prices, credit, and profit. He seemed to infer that there was a fluctuation in inventories also, but the lesson was not drawn that changes in inventory investment were caused by variations in aggregate demand. As noted above, he was convinced that aggregate supply and demand always had to be in adjustment. He spoke occasionally of particular employments being prosperous or unusually depressed, but did not apply these ideas to the aggregate economy. In fact, at the time he wrote, it was much less the fashion to speak in terms of aggregates than it is today. Even in the case of prices, no general change in level

---

[3]John Stuart Mill, *Principles of Political Economy: With Some of Their Applications to Social Philosophy* (New York: D. Appleton and Company, 1920 [from the fifth London Edition]).

was usually generalized; rather, mention was made of a similar change in many prices.

Alfred Marshall failed to see the business cycle problem clearly, not because he refused to look, but because he was looking in the wrong direction. His attention was concentrated on the economics of the transactional unit—the individual consumer and the producing firm. His conclusions on the aggregate were drawn by analogy from individual transactional units. But the business cycle arises from special conditions which develop in the aggregate economy, in what we may call macroeconomics, contrasted with microeconomics. Thus, he looked at the edges of the problem and failed to see it from the vantage point of a central position.

For instance, when he first got around to the problem of employment, near the end of his *Principles of Economics,* he argued that although the inconstancy of employment is a great evil, it appears greater than it actually is and was worse in earlier times when competition was less. Attention had come to be directed at changes in employment in large factories, but unemployment was not so clearly recognized among independent workmen or workers hired by a small employer, the typical earlier organization. Then, he argued that the *trend* of employment was upward in fast-growing industries, in contrast with stagnant conditions of medieval Europe. The issue for us here is stability, not rate of growth.

Marshall recognized disturbing elements in modern industry arising from "the rapidity of invention, the fickleness of fashion, and above all the instability of credit." He was concerned essentially with commercial and financial crises, which he associated with fluctuations in the state of confidence. Growing confidence feeds on itself until a crisis stage is reached. Then lack of confidence feeds on itself. "The commercial storm leaves its path strewn with ruin. . . . Those who saved themselves are in no mood to venture again. . . ." Warehouses are overstocked; and although this had frequently been thought to represent overproduction, Marshall insisted it was nothing but a state of commercial disorganization and that the remedy awaited a revival of confidence. He was talking in terms of individual companies or individual industries, but he noted that the situation often develops simultaneously among many various trades.

Marshall sensed that the disorganization centered in capital goods, a developing recognition we shall consider later. He noted that the greatest fluctuations in prices were in the capital goods area. He did not follow out the implications of these observations, however, because his major interest lay along other lines and because he would have soon faced contradictions with his major thesis. For him, as with Mill, fluctuations in aggregate business were essentially restricted to credit, prices, and profit.[4]

He was much interested in a solution. He thought improved competition was one possibility. For instance, he felt that the "Common Rule," by which trade unions got an agreement as regards the standard wage for work of a given class, prevented employers from profitably hiring labor which falls short of full normal efficiency and tends to check production after an inflation comes to an end. More importantly, he thought "better and more widely diffused knowledge is a remedy for that excessive confidence which causes a violent expansion of credit and rise of prices; and it is also a remedy for that excessive distrust which follows." Again, "it is conceivable that a body of able disinterested men, with a wide range of business knowledge may ultimately be able to issue predictions of trade storm and of trade weather generally, that might have an appreciable effect in rendering the employment of industry more steady and continuous." He had stated elsewhere that "the only effective remedy for unemployment is a continuous adjustment of means to ends, in such way that credit can be based on the solid foundation of fairly accurate forcasts; and that reckless inflations of credit—the chief cause of all economic malaise—may be kept within narrower limits."

EARLY PERCEPTION OF RECURRENCE OF FLUCTUATIONS

One can find some evidence in any of the writings reviewed so far in this chapter of the sensing of a recurrent movement. Quoting out of context and reading a bit into what was said, a weak case could be made for belief in a recurrent business cycle. A better

---

[4]A footnote in *Principles of Economics* is most revealing in this respect: "It is true that in times of depression the disorganization of consumption is a contributory cause to the continuance of the disorganization of credit and of production. But a remedy is not to be got by a study of consumption, as has been alleged by some hasty writers. No doubt there is good work to be done by a study of the influence of arbitrary changes in fashion on employment. But the main study needed is that of the organization of production and credit. And, though economists have not yet succeeded in bringing that study to a successful issue, the cause of their failure lies in the profound obscurity and every-changing form of the problem; it does not lie in any indifference on their part to its supreme importance. Economics from beginning to end is a study of the mutual adjustments of consumption and production; when the one is under discussion, the other is never out of mind" ([Macmillan & Co., 8th ed., London, 1920], p. 712).

interpretation is that none of these writers clearly understood the recurrent nature of the fluctuation.

With enough diligence, many writings during the nineteenth century which make definite statements regarding recurrence can be uncovered. Too much can be made of them, for they had but little influence at the time; and for each author himself, they have represented little more than an intellectual exercise. We may mention two early cases. In 1837 a gentleman, later to be called Lord Overstone, published a pamphlet in which he explained that what is called the state of trade apparently revolves in an established cycle.

John Mills read a paper before the Manchester Statistical Society in 1867 in which he made some acute observations about the recurrence of crisis in 1815, 1825, 1836–39, 1847, 1857, and 1866. Each crisis was explained in numerous pamphlets by particular accidental factors. Instead, he suggested that the fluctuations are recurrent and may be as "inevitable as the periodical tempests which clear the atmosphere of tropical regions." The principal cause, he thought, is a recurrent change in the mental mood of the trading public. Outside forces might speed up or delay the shift in phases, but his emphasis was on a credit cycle generated by a continuing rhythm in the psychology of businessmen. This is in striking contrast with the position of John Stuart Mill, who laid major emphasis on accidental outside forces to initiate changes in profit expectations.

William Stanley Jevons, an economist famous also for his value theory, had a greater influence. He began talking about periodic fluctuations as early as 1862. In his early papers, he related them to deficient or excessive harvests, noting that "great vintage years" recur every ten or eleven years. Later, when sunspot cycles were developed, he tried to connect the harvest fluctuation with the cycle in sunspots. Although he traced the business cycle to sunspots, he thought that "moods of the commercial mind" constitute "the principal part of the phenomena." These moods were thought to be controlled by "outward events," especially sunspots.

Juglar, writing in 1889, has been generally awarded the distinction of first demonstrating approximate periodicity of industrial fluctuations. Without interposing any theory or hypothesis, his analysis of the facts achieved a wide following. He traced the cause of the regularity of fluctuation to the movement of commodity prices. This scarcely provided a convincing theory, but his "great book of facts" was of major importance in explaining recurrence.

These and other writers who argued the existence of a recurrent fluctuation exerted a limited influence at the time. The ideas had a cumulative effect, however, and were much more widely heralded after the turn of the century. Largely borrowing from Juglar's summary, Tugan-Baranowsky in 1901 laid the foundation for an explanation of business fluctuations with the observation that the history of crises in England reveals a recurrent ebb and flow of economic life. He visualized the cycle as long or short according to the particular economic conditions at the time, and not regulated by mathematical law. Nonetheless, he conceived of it as a law inherent in the very nature of capitalist economy. He thought the principal force creating the cycle to be a fluctuation of loanable capital differing substantially from the growth of real productive capital. The relatively regular accumulation of loanable cash overcomes the resistance of industry to invest in depression, and its relative shortage when investment activity is high in prosperity brings the prosperity to an end. Furthermore, investment activity in the expansion creates purchasing power, raising demand; and oppositely, a decrease in investment activity in contraction cuts off demand. As to the possibility of general overproduction, Tugan faces the heart of the problem by seeing the shift in proportionality occurring over the cycle. Proportionality shifts are indicated by the much greater fluctuation in investment activity than in consumption expenditures. Investment activity rises so rapidly in expansion that productive activity outruns the power of consumption. Tugan clearly perceived the problem in macroeconomic terms. It was failure to do this that hounded the analysis of classical economists.

While we must avoid reading too much into early analysis, we can be sure that Tugan and other writers at the time were initiating a new age in business cycle thinking. Although Tugan may have been the first to tie the idea of cyclical recurrence to a clear visualization of the major cyclical forces, the contributions of several other writers, as noted below, were necessary to achieve a mature perspective on the business cycle problem.

KARL MARX

There is no doubt that Karl Marx was exerting a significant influence on rationalizations about economic fluctuations as early as the middle of the nineteenth century. He showed evidence of having understood the recurrent nature of the business cycle, as opposed to the idea of isolated, unrelated crises prevalent at the time. When profits fall below their usual level, capitalists were thought to hold their capital in money form, and thus produce a crisis. Capitalists might be unable to realize the full value of the commodities which they produce, and this was called a "realization crisis." A realization crisis might arise either from disproportionality among various lines of production or from underconsumption of the masses. In the former case the difficulty is that at the time of production, businessmen do not know precisely what the proportionate market will be for various goods. It is doubtful that Marx tied disproportionality closely to the difference in fluctuation of investment goods and consumer goods, as Tugan did later. But Marx did sense something about the importance of investment activity. He pointed out that we must distinguish simple commodity production from capitalist production. He had an idea that business fluctuations had something to do with a recurrent replacement cycle of capital, as indicated by his reflections on the influence of the life of machinery in the cotton industry.

As regards a realization crisis arising from underconsumption, Marx spoke of "restricted consumption of the masses as compared to the tendency of capitalist production to develop the productive forces in such a way that only the absolute power of consumption of the entire society would be their limit." Obviously, he was influenced by the ideas represented above of Lauderdale and Malthus. Further, he pointed out that money is the medium by which exchange is split into separate transactions representing sale and purchase. One may sell and fail to buy. But the Marxists have found difficulty in coming to agreement on the precise character of his underconsumption theory relative to business fluctuations.

"There is nowhere to be found anything approaching a complete or systematic treatment of the subject [of business cycles] in Marx's writings."[5] Marx himself made no pretense of having provided a satisfactory analysis of crises. As Sweezy puts it, "it is probably safe to say that if Marx had lived to complete his analysis of competition and credit he would have given us a thorough and systematic treatment of crises."[6] Inability to develop a satisfactory comprehensive theory fits into the state of knowledge in the period in which he lived. The fact that he did not try to formulate a theory before he could effectively fit the pieces together is a tribute to his thinking.

---

[5]Paul M. Sweezy, *The Theory of Capitalist Development* (New York: Oxford University Press, 1942), p. 133.
[6]*Ibid.*, p. 134.

INNOVATION THEORY

Arthur Speithoff's writings on the business cycle appeared shortly after those of Tugan-Baranowsky (early in the twentieth century) and were greatly influenced by them. According to Speithoff, the general impetus to expansion is provided by the areas where capital expects unusual rates of profit. These are provided by new technology and new territories. A process closely akin to what we have called, above, the doubly reinforcing character of investment is recognized as influential as the expansion proceeds: There is no counterbalancing output of finished goods as construction rises rapidly. The upswing feeds on rising demand for construction materials: iron, lumber, cement, bricks, etc. There is a pull from investment, not a push from behind by consumer demand.

He noted that later the completion rate catches up with the starting rate (to use our terminology): A feverishly increased production throws its products on the market without being met by a like consumption. About this time, investment becomes saturated. Up to then the problem had been like filling an empty bucket. But the rate of investment had been far greater than the rate of advance in consumer demand. Investment had caught up, and the bucket was full.

But Speithoff also recognized the validity of Tugan's position as to the shortage of loanable capital. This might cut off the expansion before the bucket was full because capital expenditure could not proceed without available funds. On the other hand, the boom might be intensified and extended by speculation accompanied by violent price rises, although the speculative force could not be controlling for long.

Speithoff did not accept Tugan's idea of the push of an excess of loanable funds in depression because businessmen require the stimulation of a pull exerted by investment opportunities. Likewise, he believed that savings would not cut down on prosperity, although they might intensify a depression. All of the savings freely available and more are demanded in the prosperous atmosphere of full expansion, while the exaggerated decline in investment in depression might be insufficient to absorb the savings consumers wish to make.

Speithoff clearly visualized the effect of interdependence. Fall in profit and wages reduces consumption, lowering prices, reducing production still further, which again reduces profits and wages. But contrasted with these internal forces, the production of capital proceeds by fits and starts, fed by technical changes and false estimates of future needs.

Joseph Schumpeter brilliantly built on Speithoff's theory a few years later to show more vividly how innovators supply a propelling force by adapting technical changes and how a model of the action of internal forces can be more clearly visualized. Innovation can be distinguished from technological potentialities. Innovation is the application of new technological ideas so as to introduce new techniques or new commodities, set up new forms of organization, or open up new markets. Even though technological developments might proceed at a uniform rate, innovations would not. An innovator grasps at a new opportunity and, if successful, will attract many imitators. Innovations are not isolated events, but cluster in bunches because many firms follow in the wake of a successful innovation. Schumpeter thought that breaking away from established routine essentially represents a discontinuity in development. A forward push of innovators impels a herdlike movement of followers who see tempting profit possibilities open up. Necessarily, the development is lopsided, discontinuous, and disharmonious. This represents a refinement of Tugan-Baranowsky's idea of shift in proportionality. The lopsided development necessarily leads to overbuilding and saturated markets in some areas which are difficult to adjust back to a more normal proportion. Innovations recognized as successful seldom cover all industry but fall in a limited group of industries thought to be particularly promising.

The disturbances which develop are big and force a process of adaptation. Practical realization tends to differ from the glowing expectations at the tidal wave of new development. Competition stiffens when the flow of product from the new innovations begins to come to market in large volume. Industries and companies which did not adapt with the changing times find themselves in unfavorable positions. Some of the innovations turn out to be unsuccessful, and these begin to bulk larger as optimism spreads. The errors of optimism may intensify for a time, but credit adjustments are certain to arise sooner or later.

Schumpeter did not conceive the reversing force of the cycle to be culmination of the type described in the above chapters. Rather, he thought of cyclical movements as deviations away from neighborhoods of equilibrium. Beginning with such a neighborhood position, he believed that the economic climate is most favorable for innovation; thus, a tidal wave of expansion occurs. He thought that the further activity is driven above equilibrium, the stronger is the force tending to move it back. Finally, recession is a struggling shift back to equilibrium. Usually, however, he thought that the depressive forces gain momentum in contraction to such an extent that activity plunges below the equilibrium position.

There is no force, according to Schumpeter, tending to keep activity at the depression low; and bit by bit, recuperative forces promote revival, finally bringing it back to the equilibrium neighborhood. From this point a new swarm of innovations will start a new cycle.

Schumpeter clearly visualized a macroeconomic system in which internal forces of the business system generate a recurrent fluctuation. At the start of each new cycle, however, the movement was thought to be dependent upon the strong stimulation of new developments. Minor outside forces play but a small part in his model.

Credit stimulation was not central in Schumpeter's model, as in the one explained in the following section. Nevertheless, he was certain that credit expansion played a vital part in economic change. The innovating entrepreneur would not be able to get control of the necessary resources without the kind of ordering on the economic system premitted with elastic credit. Conceptions along the simple lines of circular flow provide a satisfactory system of monetary adjustment in the neighborhood of equilibrium. But the disturbing elements of innovation introduce spontaneous and continuous change in the channels of circular flow. Innovators are floated into their places on the tide of advancing credit.

MONETARY OVERINVESTMENT

At about the same time as the development of the innovation theory, a theory dealing with substantially the same factors was argued more cogently and more categorically, and it put the relevant forces into a neat framework. We shall give the system involved only passing notice here, for it is the subject of the following chapter.

The theory is called monetary overinvestment because it looks at the disturbance which the cycle represents as the product of credit extension and contraction, and argues that investment expenditure represents the activity propelled by credit variation. This is in contrast with the innovation theory, for, in that theory, credit is considered essential in fostering progressive development, while here it is considered a disturbing and essentially an evil influence.

In monetary overinvestment theory the assumption is made that money should be entirely neutral in the sense that no changes in economic conditions should be initiated by it. Furthermore, it is asserted that nonseasonal fluctuations in economic activity originate entirely in monetary factors.

The fluctuations which occur are held to center in investment activity. Investment is financed by savings, and it is taken as a truism that interest rates act as a market price which will equilibrate the supply of savings with the investment demand for them.

Actually, however, early in expansion, voluntary savings are supplemented by credit generated by the banks. Thus, the interest rate equilibrates investment demand with artificially large savings. The interest rate is kept at a low level to accomplish this—lower than justified by the profit rate. If the credit flow could be maintained, business activity would not turn down, according to the theory. Interest rates would be kept at a low level relative to profits, and investment would be kept at a higher level than actually intended by voluntary savings.

As long as the credit funds are freely available at low interest rates, investment activity is provided a sort of subsidy in the nature of low interest rates. (Credit funds are assumed to be used only in the investment market.) If the demand for investment is highly elastic, no trouble would arise until the credit funds are cut off. But the funds are cut off sooner or later, either because of bank regulations or because of fear of inflation when resources become fully used. The cutoff of credit at that point would limit investment demand to the supply of voluntary savings. The point of equilibration with the more limited savings would be at a higher interest rate, and many investment projects would be discouraged. A downturn would be created.

This was the first neat theoretical framework provided to explain the business cycle. Furthermore, it was co-ordinate with general economic theory. In that major emphasis was placed upon a prescription for eliminating the business cycle, it also differed from most of the theories described above. The theory was not generally accepted, however, for reasons which are explained in Chapter 8.

WESLEY CLAIR MITCHELL

For most economic analysts, the work of Wesley Clair Mitchell, which began in the same period, represents a far more significant break-through. His display of business cycle facts was unprecedented, with the possible exception of Juglar's. His facts were more convincing than Juglar's because of better collection of data by the time Mitchell wrote. As Hansen says, "for the professional economist all discussion of 'crises' became at long last obsolete."[7] Long before, many had advanced the concept of the business cycle, but "it was nonetheless Mitchell who put it over." Institutional situations were given an uppermost position. Businessmen felt more at home in this new language. The discussion of business cycles was taken out of the ivory tower.

Mitchell's point was to show how oscillations or fluctuations grow out of and grow into each other. Fundamentally, he explained, there are cumulative changes in the processes of the business economy. To study them, Mitchell was determined to limit his assumptions and avoid the strait jacket of a rigid theoretical framework. He thought that traditional theory was naïvely mechanical because it lacked institutional perspective. Plausible theories multiplied abundantly, "since imaginative thinkers had no difficulty in assigning a critical role to one factor after another. . . . Occasionally a theorist would use statistical data, but as a rule their function, when called upon at all, was merely to support or illustrate a particular stage of an argument. Mitchell broke with this tradition."[8]

To study cumulative changes, he analyzed leads and lags and regularity of sequences. He realized that a clue or organizing principle must be employed. For this purpose, he hit on profits, which surely represent an important part of the motivation in business transactions. This led him to place much emphasis on the relative movement of cost prices and selling prices. For these purposes, he examined commodity prices, wage rates, interest rates, and other monetary factors. Most of the arguments given along these lines in Chapters 4 and 5 are adaptations from Mitchell. He was led to account for turning points by shifting prospects for profits, although it was not always clear that he did not mean actual changes which had already occurred in profits. He dealt with production as well as price data. He observed the cessation of inventory investment at the lower turning point. He could have carried the analysis a step further with the presentation of a theoretical model on profits, but he did not.

For Mitchell the business cycle was essentially propelled by

---

[7]Alvin H. Hansen, *Business Cycles and National Income* (New York: W. W. Norton & Co., Inc., 1951), p. 397.

[8]Arthur F. Burns (ed.), *Wesley Clair Mitchell: The Economic Scientist* (New York: National Bureau of Economic Research, Inc., 1952), p. 23.

forces within the business system. Misfortunes do not explain the end of prosperity. He did recognize that the lower turning point is not wholly generated by current business change: Technological progress, new materials, and new tastes may intervene.

Mitchell was interested from the first in finding "what features have been characteristic of all or most cycles." At first, his observations on this point were rather general. Later, however, the National Bureau of Economic Research, which he founded and headed, developed the similarity between *specific* and *reference* cycles detailed in Chapter 4. Further, he was able to announce the finding of a marked tendency toward repetition among the movements of different activities in successive business cycles.

In later work, he emphasized increasingly adaptation of analysis to go below the "money surface." This was made possible by increasing availability of monthly or quarterly series on a physical quantity basis. There is evidence that he had begun to question the use of profits as a method of summarizing and netting the effect of all economic change. In a letter written to Arthur F. Burns in 1946, he stated:

Thor virtually demolishes the notion to which I attached much importance in 1913 that unit costs encroach upon profits in late expansion, and are materially reduced in late contraction—so far as railway transportation is concerned. He leaves mere remnants of the idea, and makes me wonder whether it has much validity in other types of business. I have congratulated him warmly on this success in damaging my speculative construction.[9]

But Mitchell never got around to a sharper generalization on profits. The Keynesian and post-Keynesian work, discussed in Chapter 9, as well as other analyses, might have laid the foundation for him. Clearly, innovation and capital formation should be assigned a special role. The concept of prospective profit would have been greatly strengthened if he had applied it to investment.

Another type of theorizing, clearly indicated in earlier work, could also have been adapted without undue theorizing. This is represented by Tugan-Baranowsky's concept of disproportionality when applied to durable goods. Surely, the facts indicate clearly enough that many times overbuilding and saturation have come to be a factor.

Many of us believe that an examination of leads and lags is less helpful than Mitchell thought. In spite of the development which

[9]*Ibid.*, p. 53.

did occur in his system, the fundamental nature of his thinking did not seem to change. Hansen cryptically remarks that Mitchell's 1927 *Business Cycles*

gives one the impression that here is a vast, disorganized workshop in which many workers have thrown their tools about. The reader is unhappily not instructed which tools, if any, are of workmanlike quality. Working hypotheses are indeed needed, he tells us, to guide our selection of data and to suggest ways of analyzing and combining them, and for this purpose he seems to suggest that the different theories, if they appear at all plausible, serve almost equally well.[10]

This is merely to say that Mitchell did not develop much of a theory. If he could have done this, there is plausible doubt that he could have accomplished the Herculean task he performed along more empirical lines. Perhaps we should be thankful and not carping.

A. C. PIGOU

We may conclude this chapter with A. C. Pigou, who succeeded Alfred Marshall in the Chair of Political Economy in Cambridge University, and who is classified in the "Marshallian school." For our purposes, he can be taken to represent the matured opinion on business cycles of the classical economists.[11]

Although he seldom expressed the proposition this way, Pigou recognized the difference between macro- and microeconomic situations. Particularly, he recognized that industrial fluctuations do exist and that they are represented by variations in total production or the relative employment of the labor force. In other words, he recognized that total demand can and does move away from effective use of total resources. His position did not merely represent greater emphasis placed on the choice of consumers not to purchase, as Alfred Marshall put it. He saw that the principal variation is in investment expenditure. At first, he felt that this accelerated variation was wholly related to the businessman's forecast of the demand

---

[10]Hansen, *op. cit.*, p. 407.

[11]The ideas summarized here are taken from Pigou's *The Economics of Welfare* (London: Macmillan & Co., Ltd., 1920), and *Industrial Fluctuations* (2d ed.; London: Macmillan & Co., Ltd., 1929), the main thesis being generally the same in the two books.

There would be some merit in ending the discussion of the classical economists with D. H. Robertson who succeeded Pigou in the Cambridge Chair. We have not done this for two reasons. Several writers have taken Pigou's work as the best representation of a synthesis of pre-Keynesian business cycle thought. Robertson's major contribution merges into Keynesian thought.

for consumption goods (derived demand according to the acceleration principle); but later, he decided that some variation in investment might originate autonomously.

He felt that instability in demand which produces variation in total production arose principally from (1) price variation and (2) errors of optimism and of pessimism, about equally divided between the two. On both of these points, he was following Marshall on the ideas of commercial disorganization and lack of confidence. But the analysis was pushed much further.

The creation of bank credit was considered a major factor in price variation. Credit expansion was held to be based on profit expectations. Price movements themselves modify expectations. Credit extended is closely related to fluctuations of employment. A rise in prices operates as a levy on lenders for the benefit of businessmen.

Price changes also are not unrelated to psychological attitudes. They directly modify expectations by changing the degree of optimism or pessimism, and they condition businessmen as to expectation of price increases. Most importantly, however, waves of optimistic and pessimistic error become possible because of the irregularity of investment expenditure. Investment, with its doubly reinforcing character, as we say in this book, changes the outlook by the very fact that it has been begun; optimism is self-justifying for a time. Pigou pointed out that overoptimistic error would be found out and generate pessimism when an unusually large part of the capital came to be completed. He noted that psychological error also depends on ability of businessmen and on the nature of business organization.

In like manner, pessimistic error can cut off investment projects and justify itself. But sooner or later, this will lead to the generation of optimistic error because activity is driven to a point where the pessimistic error is discovered (capital starts are getting ahead of completions).

Pigou clearly understood the business cycle as a recurrent fluctuation, not as represented by isolated crises, a break with the classical position that fluctuations represent isolated phenomena. His position is indicated by a shift in psychological attitudes, noted above. But his analysis was farther reaching. It also recognized impulses generated by monetary and real factors. Monetary factors, in addition to interrelated influence with psychological factors, might arise from issues of paper money, gold production, or movements of international reserves. Real factors might set up impulses because of harvest variations, inventions, industrial disputes, changes in taste, or changes in foreign demand. Generally, the impulses tend to produce expansion or contraction through their effect on variations in expectations of profit. The impulses produce a business cycle because of conditions in the economy which predetermine responses. Some of these conditions are monetary and banking arrangements, the capitalistic nature of production (particularly derived demand and the replacement cycle), and other industrial conditions.

Pigou's contribution is founded on synthesis, not on originality. In Schumpeter's opinion, Pigou came nearest to accomplishing the feat of a "fairly satisfactory synthesis that . . . left no major fact unaccounted for and . . . constituted an excellent basis for further research. . . ."[12] There is little, if anything, in his theory which is actually new. His analysis gives us a blueprint of the most acceptable explanation of the business cycle at the end of World War I.

The most important contribution made since is the mechanism of saving and investment relationships explained by the Keynesians. As we shall see in Chapter 9, this advances macroeconomic analysis in general more than the explanation of recurrent business fluctuations in particular. The most telling criticism of Pigou's explanation is that it remained a postscript to his explanation of economic principles. Finally, business fluctuations were explained in a reasonably satisfactory manner, but the explanation was not co-ordinated with the general body of economic theory.

The failure to co-ordinate is most clearly understood if we look at Pigou's prescription for moderating the business cycle. This turned principally to the use of changes in wage rates and in commodity prices as countering action. Increasing such rates and prices was suggested as a principal method of moderating the excessive expansion in prosperity, and lowering them was suggested to produce the opposite effect in recession. Since prices and wage rates were considered to flow from competition in individual markets, the control of business cycle variation was thought to lie in the play of individual markets. The existence of the cycle as a macroeconomic phenomenon was recognized, but fundamental economic theory was considered to flow solely from actions taken in competitive enterprises.

Some twenty-five years later, Pigou recognized a macroeconomic

---

[12]Joseph A. Schumpeter, *History of Economic Analysis* (New York: Oxford University Press, 1954), p. 1135.

system, after Keynes had outlined the type we generally face today (see Chapter 9). His position had changed to the point that he then held manipulating demand was as important as manipulating wage rates in efforts to stabilize the business cycle.[13] With an aggregative economic theory the business cycle could be integrated with theoretical explanations of economic conditions and no longer needed to remain a postscript. Changes in transient demand could be influenced aggregatively by government action, and such action could be defended by a theoretical explanation of how total demand adjustment occurs.

FOR REFLECTION AND ANALYSIS

1. Discuss the assumptions of Say's Law with respect to the assumed influence of supply in determining business cycle changes.
2. Explain Lauderdale's position on the "fallacy of composition."
3. Connect the worry of Lauderdale and Malthus about paying off the government debt with their concern about private income and expenditure flows.
4. What did Malthus mean by saying there is some right proportion between saving and spending, and what applications did he make of the proposition in relation to current economic conditions?
5. What did the "disproportionality" theory have to do with early rationalizations about economic fluctuations?
6. Discuss the theory of "overtrading," and relate it to belief in commercial crises as the chief factor in economic fluctuation.
7. Discuss John Stuart Mill's suggestion that extension of credit would be helpful in the collapse.
8. Contrast the contribution of Juglar and his "great book of facts" with that made later by Wesley Mitchell.
9. What did Marx hold to be the two causes of a "realization crisis"?
10. What did Speithoff mean by comparing investment activity in expansion to the filling of an empty bucket?
11. Explain the innovation theory with relation to *(a)* meaning of innovation; *(b)* lopsided development; *(c)* stiffening of competition after the expansion caused by innovations; *(d)* credit as a kind of ordering on the economic system.
12. Discuss the sentence in the text stating that Pigou's analysis gives us a blueprint of the most acceptable explanation of the business cycle at the end of World War I.
13. Why was the part of Pigou's *Economics of Welfare* relating to the business cycle (called "Variability of the National Dividend") not integrated with the rest of the book? (It was left out of *Economics of Welfare* in later editions and incorporated in a separate book entitled *Industrial Fluctuations.*)

---

[13]See A. C. Pigou, *Lapses from Full Employment* (London: Macmillan & Co., Ltd., 1945); and for an excellent interpretation, see Hansen, *op. cit.*, pp. 518–20.

Chapter 8   AUSTRIAN INVESTMENT THEORY

The idea that amount or change in investment expenditure is the key factor both in growth and in business fluctuation has not been seriously challenged in this century. Growing recognition of this fact, taken together with nineteenth-centry emphasis on the instability of credit, laid a fertile basis for a business cycle theory at the turn of the century. Such a theory was formulated by the "Austrians"[1] in the last decade of the nineteenth century and the first decade of the twentieth.

The system or framework in which the ideas were organized, rather than the ideas themselves, was new. The ideas were simple and were developed principally by deductive reasoning rather than by reference to empirical facts. They relate primarily to irregularity of investment expenditure, to the relation of the time element in investment expenditure, and to resort to financing by credit. Long before, Ricardo had explained that there is a considerable lapse of time between expenditures for investment goods and the use of them in making consumer goods. Some consumer goods may flow off the lines as soon as an investment project is completed, but in the case of construction a considerable time period will elapse before its contribution to the process of production is ended. Ricardo came

---

[1]Use of the term "Austrian" refers to the fact that the development of the theory originated in Austria, although contributions also were made elsewhere. We are not interested in the ideas of any particular man, but of the general tenor of the system relating investment and credit expansion to the disturbance which might occur in the economic system. Note, however, should be taken of the background capital theory developed by Eugen Böhm-Bawerk. See Smart's translation of *The Positive Theory of Capital* (New York: G. E. Stechert & Co., reprint 1923), and for an excellent summarization the chapter on Böhm-Bawerk in Joseph A. Schumpeter's *Ten Great Economists from Marx to Keynes* (New York: Oxford University Press, 1951). For the investment theory analyzed in this chapter, F. A. Hayek's *Monetary Theory and the Trade Cycle* (New York: Harcourt, Brace & Co., Inc., 1932) may be taken as representative.

close to accepting the position that, in determining equilibrium values, the carrying charge from the time the investment good is bought to the time goods are produced with it is on a par with the quantity of labor embodied in the capital good.

In the mid-1880's, Böhm-Bawerk founded a theory of interest rates which laid the basis for the Austrian theory of investment. He laid down the principle that the net return on capital is the result of increased technical productivity of roundabout production on the one hand and the consequent postponement of the consumption of its results on the other.

The Austrian theory of investment is not today generally considered of major importance in the explanation of business fluctuations. The characteristic credit expansion involved in financing investment during expansion is, however, still recognized as significant. Furthermore, the theory is of some importance in representing the first theoretically acceptable explanation of recurrent fluctuations in aggregate economic conditions. In the explanation, certain ideas were developed to which reference is still made—notably forced saving and neutral money.

CAPITAL THEORY

The Austrian theory of investment is a fully articulated and rigidly developed system of thought. Capital is held to be a separate factor of production which involves a production period, covering the time from the production of the capital good until it is used in the creation of consumer goods. This period stretches on into the future for as long as product is produced with the capital.

Interest rate is the price of capital because that is what must be paid in carrying charges for holding the capital good until it can be utilized in the production process which it facilitates. After discounting, at the going interest rate, embodied labor for the period for which it is invested in the capital equilibrates with the value of the marginal product of labor used in other types of production. Capital goods which render products at future dates may involve a substantial productivity advantage, in making possible considerably greater output with the same investment of labor than could be obtained without the aid of capital. The interest rate is the price which must be paid for provision of the advantage possessed by capital goods. The interest rate discount is crucial in determining the marginal position of capital goods.

Although the brief, simple message of these two paragraphs

omits refinements and details, we believe it carries the essential points in Austrian capital theory. The theory has been frequently challenged by other economists, especially by Professor Frank H. Knight of the University of Chicago.[2] The contention in essence is that capital must be conceived as a perpetual flow of monetary value, once the investment has been made, not as an inventory of plant and equipment items which are slowly wearing out. Under these circumstances, the "period of production" of existing capital becomes meaningless. Once the investment has been made in an expanding society, with rises occurring in net investment, no net dissaving is possible for society as a whole. The capital value has been forever committed. Knight recognizes that shift from one use to another requires time and may create temporary disturbance, but the stock of durable capital is not reduced in typical recessions.

NATURE OF INVESTMENT

For our purposes the nature of total existing capital stock is not particularly at issue. What is at issue is current investment made. Replacement of capital and net additions to total capital stock only are involved. The problem is simplified if the idea of a period of production is discarded and replaced by the idea that investment necessitates a roundabout process of production.[3] Whenever currently employed resources are diverted to capital uses, a commitment is made to a roundabout process of production. The degree of roundaboutness is marked by the time required to obtain a return from the resources used and can be contrasted with various choices down to the use of resources to make product immediately available for final consumption. The question turns on choice between making goods and services immediately available and making goods involving various degrees of roundaboutness in the sense that time necessarily elapses between commitment of resources and output of products which may be made with the capital.

---

[2]For an excellent summary and major references, see Raymond J. Saulnier, *Contemporary Monetary Theory,* Studies in History, Economics, and Public Law, No. 443 (New York: Columbia University Press, 1938), pp. 261–75.

[3]Knight has insisted that in the case of replacement the period of production is zero because capital value already is in existence; that in the case of addition to stock the period is infinity because in a growing society the investment is forever committed. He also has made the point that the time factor is only one of many determining the cost of capital goods. For instance, higher productivity, which is the particular claim for capitalistic methods of production, is not always determined by the length of life of the good. Highly productive equipment with a life of fifteen years or less has been growing more rapidly than construction with a much longer life.

In this connection the Austrian theory faces a most fertile application of the disproportionality theory. Resources may be devoted either to currently consumable products or to roundabout production. The crux of the theory turns on the explanation of forces which direct production to currently consumable products or to those involving various degrees of roundaboutness. Demand is held to determine the proportionality, with profits equalized at the margin in view of the difference in prices.

THE INFLUENCE OF CREDIT EXTENSION

The distinctive character of capital goods is their durability, the fact that their service becomes available only after a period of time. The price which must be paid for such delay in use is the interest rate. The Austrians explain the interest rate by the loanable funds theory—by the intersection of the schedule describing

CHART 8-1

MONETARY OVERINVESTMENT THEORY

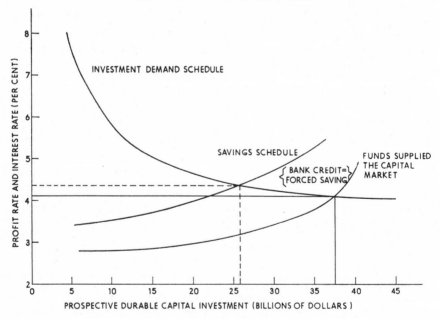

the supply of loanable funds with the schedule describing the demand for funds. Generally, the only demand for funds they recognize is the demand for durable business capital—an investment demand schedule for durable investment with the interest rate price on the vertical axis and the amount which would be invested on the horizontal axis. The schedule is visualized as quite elastic, with substantial investment increments accompanying slight declines in the interest rate. (See Chart 8-1.)

The appropriate supply of loanable funds is thought to be voluntary savings, as distinguished from funds derived from the extension of credit, and the schedule is thought to slope upward from left to right because individuals are expected to save more at higher interest rates.

When credit is added to voluntary savings, the loanable funds are increased. The schedule of loanable funds is shifted to the right; its intersection with the schedule describing the investment demand for funds is at a lower interest rate, as shown in the hypothetical diagram in Chart 8-1.

Credit expansion is interpreted as a process by which the price (interest rate) of capital goods is made artificially low. The value of a capital good depends upon the required time discount, which is set by the going interest rate. If the interest rate is assumed to remain at 3 per cent for 15 years, the product derivable in the fifteenth year would currently be discounted 36 per cent. But if the interest rate is assumed to remain at 5 per cent for 15 years, the discount would be 52 per cent.[4] For purposes of argument, we may assume that the current costs of the labor and materials going into the capital good are comparable with the costs of labor and materials directly fabricated for immediate consumption. Then, the discounts represent the relative costs of roundabout production. The advantage of the lower interest rate is obvious. With a lesser discount, the current worth of the capital is much higher.

Even though the value of capital goods must be discounted for the period that their use in making product is delayed, they are often more desirable than products for immediate consumption because of the higher productivity they provide. Their relative desirability, however, depends on the necessary discount. At the slighter discounts (low interest rates), they are desired to a greater degree and involve a disproportionate bid for current resources.

Thus, production comes to involve a disproportionate amount of capital goods when credit is extended; and thereby, interest rates are kept low. The production involved is at equilibrium but at an

---

[4]With constant interest rates prospected, the formula is $(1 + r)^{-n}$. If the life is 15 years and equal usufruct is expected each year, the sum of discounted values for 15 years at 3 per cent would represent about 80 per cent of the cost, and at 5 per cent less than 70 per cent.

interest rate determined on a supply-of-funds curve shifted to the right by bank provision of credit. Sooner or later the credit supplied will be reduced or eliminated altogether.

At that time a recession will occur unless consumers should all at once increase their saving to make up for the difference involved arising from less credit extension. Such action is so unlikely that it may be disregarded. The purpose of the theory is merely to show how such a disturbance arises. Bank credit extension, however, obviously will slow down or cease in most expansions. Credit is cut off to avoid inflation as full employment is reached. A rapid decline in the degree of credit extension will cut down on investment. Clearly, this would lead to cumulative recessionary forces.

FORCED SAVING

The idea of forced saving was recognized a century before the Austrians wrote, e.g., by Jeremy Bentham. Bentham was thinking principally of the effect of the creation of paper money by governments to raise revenue. The added money could be expected to advance prices and force "frugality" on the populace to offset added government expenditure.

We still talk of forced saving in that way. If the government should add to the stock of money as a means of meeting expenditures, savings might be forced from individuals. This would occur if the government spending based on added stock of money faced a fully employed economy. For no additional real product could be obtained if, for illustration, we may be permitted to assume that the limit of available real product is reached when full employment is achieved. The government expenditure from added money supply would bid resources away from the private economy by driving up prices. The loss in real purchasing power suffered by individuals would represent a saving forced from the private economy to pay for government expenditures financed by printing money. Note that this would not be the result if there were an ample supply of unused resources. The additional money might buy product made with unused resources, and the real product available for the private economy would remain undiminished (or would be increased in accordance with the multiplier principle).

As applied by the Austrians, forced saving relates to the competitive advantage investment goods are thought to achieve with the extension of credit. As noted above, according to the theory, interest rates are made artificially low, and this means that capital goods appear cheap in relation to consumer goods. Thus, resources are bid away from consumer good industries. In the process, commodity prices are driven up. Wage earners can buy less at the higher prices, for there is nothing in the Austrian system which would indicate that wage rates would rise. With the same wages, consumers can buy less, since prices have risen; and the savings thus forced out of consumers pay for the investment financed by credit.

The Austrian framework may well be contrasted with the relation between saving and investment in income and product accounts.[5] These accounts represent past history, not what is anticipated at a future time; but presumably, the Austrian theory also intends to show what actually happens.

The Austrian theory visualizes saving and investment as equal, but leans toward attributing any increase in investment to increases in saving (because of the central position given to credit expansion). The theoretical framework accepted today, on the other hand, assigns saving a more passive role. Saving is generated by rising investment, which is to some extent independent of changes in the interest rate (because the investment demand curve shifts to the right).

The higher rate of investment may be based (1) wholly on increases in total output, (2) partly on increases in output and partly on increases in price, or (3) wholly on increases in price. The Austrian theory assumes the third case. It is thought that prices are pushed up in driving resources from the production of consumer goods to the production of capital goods. But if unused resources exist in the economy to any substantial extent, they may make advancing investment possible without any increase in prices.

Rising investment always increases income in terms of actual dollars. The increased income augments consumer expenditure because of the stability of the consumption function. Whether this adds to real expenditure of consumers depends on the extent of rise in prices.

Price rises are not likely to be great enough to prevent any increase in the real expenditure of consumers. Some capacity is constantly becoming available in a growing economy. In late prosperity, chances are that the rate of increase in capacity will be accelerated. If that is accompanied with a fair increase in productivity, prices are unlikely to absorb all of the increased expenditure consumers may make with rising income.

---

[5]See a description of the American income and product accounts in Chapter 15.

The conclusion is that forced saving has a much narrower meaning than the Austrians thought. Only when production is at capacity limits will all of the increase in investment expenditure be drawn from resources which otherwise would be available for consumer expenditure. If wage rises lag behind price increases, some of the increase in investment in peak prosperity may represent a draft of resources from the consumption sector. To the extent that this occurs, forced saving as conceived by the Austrians will arise.

Some workers are frequently faced with reduced real income because their wage rates rise less rapidly than the prices of things they buy. This is because their wage rates are less flexible than prices. We might say that they experience forced saving in the *social* sense, but in the individual sense the idea would lead to awkward conclusions. Certainly, the individual gains no title to "forced" savings. The social effect may at times be that savings are forced from some individuals but not from others. If the workers with inflexible wage rates face falling prices for the things they buy, there is no significant sense in which we could say they experience forced *dissaving*.[6]

Forced saving cannot be given the sweeping application the Austrian theory implies. It becomes most nearly applicable under conditions of full employment.

CLARIFICATION PROVIDED BY THE AUSTRIAN INVESTMENT THEORY

The Austrian investment theory is to be credited with a rigorous demonstration that overextension of investment depends on credit financing. The close tying-together of credit overextension and wide fluctuation of investment is certainly a step forward from the positions reached by the classical economists in the nineteenth century.

Furthermore, the theory shows that a general defection in demand can arise because of disproportionate advance in investment financed by credit extension. Historically, this must have exerted an important influence in leading economists to renounce Say's Law of Markets as it applies to conditions at the business cycle downturn.

---

[6]If they do not increase their real expenditures, however, they may add to contractionary conditions by contributing to an advance in savings when investment is declining. If they are induced to spend more because of the low prices in relation to their incomes, the performance would be somewhat comparable to the so-called "Pigou effect," where real expenditures are expected to increase with the advance in real value of asset holdings.

The holding that overextension of credit lasts to the very peak of the business cycle appears to check with current statistical measurements. Consumer savings as a proportion of disposable income do tend to increase in the expansion, but not fast enough to supplant the need for credit. The early underconsumptionists were thus wrong in holding that savings made in the expansion do not find sufficient investment outlets.

NEUTRAL MONEY

Neutral money implies that real changes are the only ones which really matter and that money is merely a veil which should not be permitted to produce hampering effects. The Austrians see the problem in these terms and offer a solution: Maintain the structure of production at the proportion between the demand for consumer goods and the demand for producer goods as determined by voluntary saving and spending. Credit is, of course, visualized as the disturber which prevents the achievement of a neutral money balance. It keeps the interest rate at a level lower than otherwise possible and thus, at the schedule relationship, provides a competitive advantage for producer goods which involves a discounting of future product.

Credit extension is therefore thought to provide the basis for a disproportionality or maladjustment between consumer and producer goods. This maladjustment is said to depend on extension of credit. Money might be considered neutral if the credit extension which leads to disproportionality between consumer and producer goods could be avoided.

The neutral position of the Austrians as indicated by these statements shows that the central problem emphasized is disproportionality, not merely credit extension or even rise in prices. Some credit extension, such as that necessitated by changes in the proportion of total trade transacted in money rather than in barter terms, is not considered disturbing. The neutral money ideas point to rising prices as a disturbance only to the extent that resources are shifted from consumer to producer goods industries. No commitment with respect to other price rises is involved. Since credit is assumed extended primarily in the building of producer goods, presumably no general price increase is necessarily implied.

The bidding of resources away from consumer goods industries assumes full-employment conditions. The possibility that unused resources may be employed, the likely condition at the initiation of expansion, is ignored.

The importance of credit in growth is not carefully investigated. As Schumpeter has pointed out (in innovation theory), credit is often essential to an innovator in financing the projects he is willing to develop. Thus, there may be a very real conflict between the growth foregone and the maladjustment avoided in preventing credit extension.

Neutral money ideas of the Austrians in accordance with these facts are not particularly appealing at the present time. Possibly, some undeveloped idea of neutral money might appear more fruitful. The problems of comparing our present monetary economy with a barter economy are almost insuperable, however. Does an efficient banking system have an important influence on economic development? If the kind of competitive economy in which we live depends on monetary transactions, could its outcome possibly be duplicated in a barter economy? Price changes are only a part of the effects generated over the business cycle, and we believe it almost inconceivable that a system could be developed which would eliminate these without touching nonmonetary influences.

By neutral money, one may mean merely the elimination of general price changes. Certainly, there would be no intention of eliminating *all* price changes, either up or down, if competition is advocated. The problems of preventing variation in the level of any general price index depend on the technicalities in its construction, the degree of its representativeness in reflecting prices in the general economy, and the relation of problems in preventing price rises to those of reducing fluctuation in real activity. These questions will be discussed in Chapters 16 and 21–24.

WEAKNESS OF THE THEORY

The Austrian theory does not wholly escape from the old idea of isolated crises: Emphasis is placed on how credit extension and capital expansion can develop into a position where the aggregative market is unsustainable. Explanation of the contraction and upturn is little more than an afterthought. Even more fundamentally, there are four basic flaws, reviewed in the following paragraphs.

As soon as any credit is extended which influences the interest rate, resources are said to be shifted from consumer to producer goods. Thus, full employment is implied at the very bottom of the recession. Otherwise, capital expansion could draw on unused resources. The argument proceeds from analysis of an equilibrium condition under full employment when credit injections are made.

Shifting conditions over the business cycle cannot be explained along an investment demand curve, a supply-of-funds curve, or an intersection of these curves at fixed levels. They must be explained by shifts in these curves. Otherwise, the level of investment would not increase with rising interest rates. Such shifts represent the only possible way of explaining the rise in investment with marked increases in interest rates from the upturn in the spring of 1958 to mid-expansion in 1959. An even more exaggerated case is the evaluation of companies represented by the manyfold rise in stock prices from June, 1932, to the mid-1950's.

The businessman is assumed to have complete knowledge of future interest rates and of future use of the capital he installs. This is unrealistic. Even though major advances have been made in long-term forecasting in recent years, the long-term outlook visualized by businessmen remains very shadowy.

The theory completely rules out demand for capital induced by change in sales, and there is clear evidence that businessmen are motivated to invest because of rise in sales. Instead, demand for capital is held completely dependent on interest rate price. From this rigidly employed construct, the conclusion is reached that capital expansion typically occurs with declining consumer product sales. The theory does not justify this extreme unrealism.

FOR REFLECTION AND ANALYSIS

1. Explain the Austrian idea of the forces which direct production to currently consumable products instead of those involving various degrees of roundaboutness.
2. How do low interest rates involve a lower discount in the value of capital goods from the time of commitment to the time of use? Explain why the lower discount encourages investment expenditure.
3. Why does a reduced rate of credit extension theoretically reduce favorability in spending for investments compared with spending for currently usable consumer goods?
4. Note cases where the idea of forced saving becomes meaningful.
5. To what extent does the Austrian idea of neutral money involve disproportionality in production?
6. Who was right about the inadequacy of savings or oversufficiency of savings in business cycle expansion?
7. Criticize the Austrian theory on the following counts: (a) assumption of full employment, (b) shifting of investment demand curve and supply-of-funds schedule, (c) perfect long-term forecasting, and (d) relation of investment to sales of final goods.

Chapter

9

KEYNESIAN THEORY

This chapter deals with Keynesian theory and its application to the business cycle.[1] The Keynesian theory has established the most successful aggregative theory of the economy. It is founded on income and product relationships. These relationships were seen more clearly than ever before. Subsequent success of the system has been due to an important extent to the development of national income accounting, which has made possible the quantification of indicated relationships.

Although our attention generally is centered on the business cycle in this book, we appropriately face first the general aggregative system in this chapter. The aggregative system of the Keynesian theory is its most important contribution. Aggregative economics, the consideration of which has been principally forced by the business cycle, was placed in a key position in economic theory by the Keynesian analysis. The change is indeed significant, in spite of the fact that even now, integration with traditional economics of the firm can scarcely be declared complete.

EXPLANATION OF EQUILIBRIUM IN THE AGGREGATE ECONOMY

Various efforts were made prior to the Keynesian system to provide a statement of the equilibrium of the total economy. These can be classified into three types:

1. Systems far in advance of theory and of measurement at the time of invention, such as Quesnay's *Tableau Oeconomique*.

---

[1]The Keynesian theory was stated by John Maynard Keynes in *The General Theory of Employment, Interest, and Money* (New York: Harcourt, Brace & Co., Inc., 1936), and in subsequent articles.

2. Systems which offered no basis for a breakdown of the total into its component parts, such as Fisher's equation of exchange.
3. Unqualified acceptance of Say's Law of Markets on a deductive basis.

The first two exerted no material influence on the theory of business fluctuations and can be almost ignored in any effort to explain the relation between aggregative change and economic theory. By the thirties, Say's Law of Markets was generally rejected in explanations of the Great Depression, and co-ordination between the facts of aggregative change and economic theory had completely broken down.

Under these conditions, a crying need existed for a consistent explanation of aggregate economic equilibrium. The Keynesian theory appeared tailored for this purpose.

Much has been made of the fact that demand, rather than supply, became controlling in the system. This, however, was inevitable with renunciation of Say's Law. Furthermore, with the striking exception of Austrian investment theory, demand clearly was controlling in generally accepted explanations of the business cycle. Nevertheless, discovery of a system which established equilibrium with demand controlling was something of a novelty.

The Keynesian equilibrium represents rather simple relations between three schedules:

1. The liquidity preference schedule (in conjunction with exogenously determined quantity of money) as an explanation of the interest rate.
2. The marginal efficiency of capital schedule as an explanation of demand for investment.
3. The propensity to consume schedule as an explanation of consumer demand.

These schedules relate to consumption and investment, which, for the purposes of a simplified theory, are taken to encompass total expenditure. The concepts related to each are summarized in Chart 9-1.

The liquidity preference schedule shows the amount of money the public will desire to hold at various interest rates in relation to the existing quantity of money. Motives for holding money are (1) to satisfy transactional needs, (2) to provide for precautionary requirements, and (3) to satisfy speculative demands. It is thought that the amount of money which the public wishes to hold will bear little relation to the prevaling interest rate as regards the first

CHART 9-1

OUTLINE OF KEYNES'S GENERAL THEORY*

			Average
		PROPENSITY TO CONSUME	
			Marginal (to Derive Multiplier)
	CONSUMPTION		
		SIZE OF INCOME	
TOTAL EFFECTIVE DEMAND or TOTAL EMPLOYMENT or TOTAL INCOME			Liquidity Preference (Transactional, Precautionary, and Speculative Motives)
		RATE OF INTEREST	
	INVESTMENT		Quantity of Money
			Expectations of Profit Yields on Investment Projects
		MARGINAL EFFICIENCY OF CAPITAL	
			Supply Price or Replacement Cost

*Adapted from Dudley Dillard, *The Economics of John Maynard Keynes: The Theory of a Monetary Economy* (New York: Prentice-Hall, Inc., 1948), p. 49. Reproduced with permission of Prentice-Hall. Inc.

two motives. Starting with a relatively constant amount required for these motives, the additional money added to the public holding for speculative purposes will increase very rapidly with low interest rates, but will virtually disappear if the interest rate rises enough.

The liquidity preference theory had an obvious appeal under the depressed conditions of the time because of observed hoarding. In more prosperous times, its significance is somewhat less clear. Surely, the demand for funds by borrowers has something to do with the interest rate as well as the supply holders are willing to put on the market. Also, the amount of cash balances is not unrelated to the level of income, so that the amount of money held must be interpreted in light of the income level; the interest rate thus comes to be partially dependent upon the position in the business cycle, with which the income level moves.[2]

There is a sense, however, in which the liquidity preference theory has substantial importance. If we think not of holding or loaning funds as simple alternatives, but rather of choices between various uses, the influence on interest rates is more readily seen. Assume that funds are put into gold bars and locked in vaults; supply available to users of funds will be reduced and the interest rate increased. Assume, on the other hand, that all idle funds are quickly used to bid for high-grade bonds. As bond prices are driven up, their yield is forced down in relation to their face value; thus, the interest rate declines. There are many other possibilities. Demand deposits may be held, increasing the lending ability of commercial banks, and interest rates would be lower than if funds were used to hoard gold bars. Bonds may be sold for fear of inflation, and the funds released may be used to bid up stock prices. Interest rates would be driven up, but the yield on stocks would be driven down (unless the fear of inflation created an extremely expansionary situation).

Leaving the subject at this juncture, we have done no more than direct attention to a few points which are of interest in business cycle analysis. For our purposes, it is unnecessary to go further. With modifications which most analysts make, the liquidity prefer-

---

[2]The position now generally taken is that the holding of money for transactional needs and for precautionary purposes is not independent of the level of income. See Alvin H. Hansen, *Monetary and Fiscal Policy* (New York: McGraw-Hill Book Co., Inc., 1949), pp. 66 ff. Liquidity preference is accepted to depend partly on the level of income. A mutual dependence must be recognized. Since the volume of money is not perfectly correlated with the income level, it is correct to say that there is some interaction between liquidity preference, interest rates, and income.

ence theory and the loanable funds theory (which relates a demand-for-funds schedule to a supply-of-funds schedule) converge.[3] To develop the Keynesian aggregative theory, it is necessary only to assume that the interest rate has been determined. In other words, the first step in the Keynesian theory is to establish the interest rate. Any effort to defend a particular interest rate theory appears unnecessary for the development of the major concepts presented on equilibrium in the aggregative economy.

CHART 9–2

MARGINAL EFFICIENCY OF CAPITAL SCHEDULES

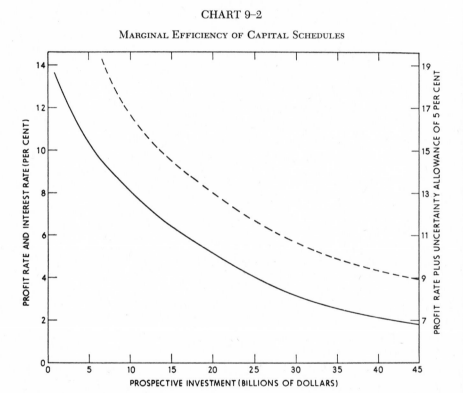

PROSPECTIVE INVESTMENT (BILLIONS OF DOLLARS)

If we may assume that the current interest rate has been ascertained, the next step is to set it against the rate businessmen are willing to pay for money to be used in investment. This rate is established by what Keynes called the "marginal efficiency of capital," an investment demand schedule, sloping down to the right in accordance with the marginal rate businessmen are willing to pay

[3]See Joan Robinson, "The Rate of Interest," *Econometrica*, April 1951, pp. 92–111; Sidney Weintraub, *An Approach to the Theory of Income Distribution* (Philadelphia: Chilton Co., 1958), pp. 149–68; J. R. Hicks, *Value and Capital* (2d ed.; New York and London: Oxford University Press, 1946), pp. 153 ff.

for investment funds. Such an investment demand curve is pictured in Chart 9–2. If the marginal efficiency of capital schedule is fairly elastic, as pictured in Chart 9–2, investment rises substantially as the interest rate declines and vice versa.

The idea represented in this schedule is clear. There are always some investment projects which will pay high returns, but these are limited. Hence, the prospective amount of investment rises at lower and lower expected marginal rates of return.

The vertical axis on Chart 9–2 represents the expected rate of return as well as the interest rate. The interest rate can be thought of as the rate which must be paid to borrow money to finance investment projects. Scaled expected rates of return are indicated by the vertical position of the marginal efficiency of capital at various points along the plotted line. The rate of return may not be expected to remain the same throughout the life of the capital; and to avoid the details of such a problem, we may think in terms of the average expected rate during the life of the capital. The problem of changing interest rates over time may be avoided, too, in our simple model by assuming that the necessary funds are currently borrowed for a long enough period that successive refunding operations will be unnecessary. With annual depreciation charges, obviously the level of the debt might be reduced year by year until fully repaid at the end of the period of expected life.

What Chart 9–2 shows is the hypothetical investment expenditure a given interest rate can be expected to call forth. In the upper reaches of the marginal efficiency of capital curve, the rate of return is so high that the relevant investment projects would be implemented even at extremely high interest rates. At the point where the current interest rate cuts the curve, the expected return and cost of funds are equal, and this will mark the feasible limit of investment projects.

As we have shown in preceding chapters, investment is the principal driving force bringing advances in the level of business activity in expansion and reductions in the level in contraction. The Keynesian theory demonstrates the principle in a neat and simple way and, in fact, has played a major part in high-lighting this influence. The way that is done is demonstrated in Chart 9–3. First, we must establish a principle about consumer expenditure behavior, especially since it represents the major part of total expenditures in the economy. As repeatedly emphasized in the above chapters, overwhelming evidence exists that consumers, except under unusual circumstances, spend a reasonably stable proportion of their disposable income (in recent American experience the percentage of disposable income spent has not deviated far from 93 per cent and

CHART 9–3

KEYNESIAN INCOME DETERMINATION*
(With Figures in Billions of Dollars)

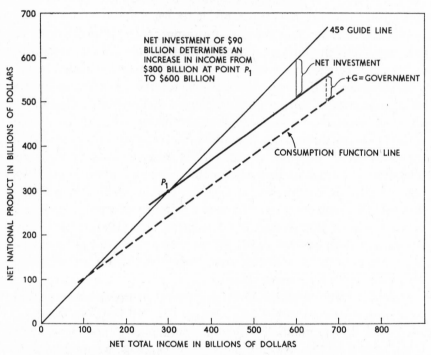

*The aggregate expenditure represented is net national product, or gross national product minus capital consumption allowances. Thus, net investment is represented (with replacement eliminated). Government expenditures as represented include only those for goods and services. The consumption line is so drawn that it shows an increase of $70 billion for every increase of $100 billion in net national product. The multiplier, therefore, is 10/3 or 3 1/3.

of net national product not far from 70 per cent).[4] This, we have said, establishes an inertia in total expenditures, so that only limited fluctuation will occur from one quarter to another. The Keynesian theory was the first to dramatize that fact. For the purpose, the

---

[4]Total income, rather than disposable income, is used as the comparison on Chart 9–3. The figures are net of capital consumption allowances; for, the way the chart works, net investment is compared to net saving. From 1950 to 1959, consumer expenditures fell between 70 and 73 per cent of net national product, except for the three Korean War years, 1951–53, when the percentage was slightly under 70. The consumption function line is drawn on Chart 9–3 so that it rises $70 billion for every rise of $100 billion in net national product, representing a multiplier of 3⅓.

concept of propensity to consume was devised. The idea is that each consumer has a propensity that makes his expenditures out of a given level of disposable income reasonably predictable.

Totaling all consumer expenditures and comparing the resulting aggregate with total disposable income, we may similarly speak of a consumption function. This is shown as the sloping line on Chart 9-3, which rises less steeply than the 45° line. Looking at the consumption function line, it is obvious that, as it is drawn, the higher income becomes the less fully consumer expenditure accounts for enough sales to support the current expenditure level. Partly, this hypothesis is supported by the generalization made earlier in this book to the effect that a consumer expenditure lag tends to occur, that consumers tend to spend a smaller and smaller proportion of current income as expansion rises. This fact is more evident in relation to personal income in the United States at the present time because, with graduated income taxes, an increasing proportion of personal income is channeled off into taxes before consumers obtain it as disposable income. The hypothesis is also supported by the fact that, as we know, with rising income, investment expenditure tends to rise disproportionately.

Expenditures in addition to those made by consumers at any income level include those made for investment, by the government, and those involved in net exports of goods and services. The latter are small, and for purposes of illustrating the equilibrium represented by the Keynesian theory, we may ignore them. On the chart, we assume that government expenditures represent a constant amount, regardless of the level of income, and that they are shown by the line labeled +G. (Although this is not in accord with fiscal policy advocated by Keynes, it simplifies the demonstration by leaving only one type of expenditure, investment, as the determinant.) Above the consumption function +G line, we have left only investment for addition.

In accordance with the Keynesian theory, the amount of investment expenditure is determined on the marginal efficiency of investment schedule by the point where the interest rate coincides with the marginal expected rate of return, as shown on Chart 9-2. If the indicated amount of investment expenditure is added vertically above the consumption function +G line, as shown in Chart 9-3, it may be moved along rightward on the chart until the scaled line representing the amount of investment just reaches the 45° guide line. At that point, it will determine the equilibrium between income and expenditure. Thus, income and expenditure are in balance because, at any point on the 45° guide line, the horizontal and vertical distances are equal on the chart.

Equilibrium, then, is seen to depend on a balance between saving and investment. If consumers spent all they received, if the government maintained a balanced budget, and if no investment expenditures were made, equilibrium would be achieved at the point marked P_1 on the chart. Since at least some net investment is to be expected, such an equilibrium is very unlikely.

If some net investment prevails, it, and not saving, determines the equilibrium. Expected saving would be represented by the vertical distance between the consumption function +G line and the 45° guide line; but if it is not spent on investment, expenditure is not raised above the +G line. On the other hand, investment represents expenditure in addition to the consumption function +G line, and therefore does add to total expenditure. Looked at in this way, investment may be said to determine income. If savings would not otherwise have been forthcoming in the economy, investment could be financed by credit. Conversely, if part of the income received was not engaged in investment expenditure, its actual effect would be merely to reduce the total level of expenditure. Total expenditure would fall back to the point on the 45° guide line where the total investment expenditure made would establish the equilibrium. Thus, investment expenditure can be said to be an active factor, contrasted with saving as a passive factor.

The total expenditure level is determined by the amount of investment. This conclusion rests on the assumption of a stable marginal propensity to consume, representing the proportion of an increase in income spent by various consuming units in the society. This stability is generalized as a consumption function for the entire economy. In Chart 9–3 the function is represented by a single line, indicating that the amount of consumer expenditure is determined by the level of income. If this is assumed to be true, and also if government is considered to represent simply a constant additional amount of expenditure, only investment expenditure remains undetermined at any income level. Therefore, investment expenditure will determine the total expenditure level. Other parts of total expenditure are assumed to react in a predetermined fashion to whatever income level is attained. Since the expenditure level will determine the equilibrium point on the 45° guide line, the total expenditure level determines the total income level.

A given increase in investment expenditure adds considerably more to total expenditure than the added dollar amount of investment expenditure. This is because the consumption function slopes upward to the right. If, for every $10 billion increase in income, consumer expenditure increases $5 billion, the upward slope of the consumption function line would be such that, at a vertical increase of $5 billion in investment, total income would increase $10 billion. This is said to represent a multiplier of 2.[5] With such a consumption function line, any given increase in investment will generate twice as much income.

As indicated above, consumer expenditure has been increasing about 70 per cent as much as net national product in recent years in the United States. Under these circumstances, an increase of $3 billion in investment might be said to increase total income $10 billion. This is a multiplier of 10/3, or more than 3.

Clearly, Keynesian equilibrium involves no relation to full-employment conditions. The particular investment demand might be far less than enough to produce a satisfactory level of full employment. There are no forces indicated on Chart 9-3 which provide any tendency for investment to increase enough to produce full employment. The secular stagnation idea noted in Chapter 6 presupposes an income equilibrium. Thus, the Keynesian theory develops equilibrium in the aggregative economy without the implication of full employment involved in Say's Law of Markets.

In the above illustrations, we have assumed government expenditure to be a completely autonomous factor. This is because the +G line is carried as parallel to the consumption function line. With only slight complication the unreality of the assumption can be eliminated. Under recommended fiscal policy, government expenditures would be larger at lower levels of income, and a deficit would be created at such a time. Such an assumption would introduce two complications into a diagram like that shown in Chart 9-3. A deficit would mean that the government would absorb some of the savings arising in the household economy. Less investment would then be required to balance out expenditure at any consumer saving level. Total expenditure, represented by the consumption

---

[5]The student should not be troubled if he is accustomed to an algebraic expression of the multiplier. As a quick computing device, it is sometimes easier to find the multiplier from the equation 1/[1−(marginal propensity to consume)]. The advantage of seeing the multiplier on the chart is the visual picture of its determination by the slope of the consumption function line.

function +G line, would slope upward less than under the assumption of constant government expenditure; therefore, the total multiplier would be reduced.

We would scarcely be satisfied with a government expenditure function which recognized no other realism than higher government expenditures at low income levels. It is true that to some extent, government expenditures do tend to rise automatically in recession because of the payment of unemployment benefits. But there are many other realistic influences. The primary difficulty with a generalization as simple as high government expenditures at reduced income levels is that the Keynesian income equilibrium makes no pretense of tracing the business cycle movement separately. Rising income traces all types of forces which may produce higher income, including growth. Government expenditures tend to increase as the economy grows, so we can scarcely obtain a realistic picture by showing government expenditures contracting at higher levels of income.[6]

GENERALIZATIONS ON THE BUSINESS CYCLE

The position of Keynes on the business cycle is not fully reflected in his explanation of equilibrium in the aggregative economy. In *The General Theory of Employment, Interest, and Money,* he states: "Since we claim to have shown in the preceding chapters what determines the volume of employment at any time, it follows, if we are right, that our theory must be capable of explaining the phenomena of the Trade Cycle."

However, the contribution of the explained equilibrium was more in the direction of bringing the phenomena of the business cycle within the fold of general economic explanations than to explain the business cycle specifically. In his brief notes on the business cycle, he does employ the framework of the propensity to consume, the state of liquidity preference, and the marginal efficiency of capital. But his explanations are in terms of fluctuations in these schedules, particularly in the marginal efficiency of capital, rather than in movements along them. Not only the cycle itself, but crises accompanying the downturn, may probably be explained

---

[6]One practice is to group government expenditures with investment and add "G + I" to the consumption function. We shall not follow this line because (1) government expenditures tend toward greater regularity than investment expenditures, and (2) government expenditures could not be determined by the interest rate related to marginal efficiency of capital, as developed earlier in this section.

by shifts in marginal efficiency of capital. "A sudden collapse in the marginal efficiency of capital" may explain the crisis:

The later stages of the boom are characterized by optimistic expectations as to the future yield of capital-goods sufficiently strong to offset their growing abundance and their rising costs of production and, probably, a rise in the interest rate also. It is of the nature of organized investment markets, under the influence of purchasers largely ignorant of what they are buying and of speculators who are more concerned with forecasting the next shift of market sentiment than with a reasonable estimate of the future yield of capital-assets, that, when disillusion falls upon an over-optimistic and over-bought market, it should fall with sudden and even catastrophic force.[7]

While recent data provide little evidence that catastrophic leftward shifts do occur at cyclical downturns, crises of the type characterized by many downturns in the nineteenth century have not troubled us in recent times. The foresight of businessmen no doubt has improved somewhat, but change in the banking system is a more striking difference. We therefore would judge that catastrophic shift in the investment demand curve has played a smaller part in developing crises than Keynes's statement indicates.

Emphasis on the influence of fluctuation in the marginal efficiency of capital in explaining the business cycle is currently accepted, as shown by the importance assigned to shift in the investment demand curve in Chapter 5 and elsewhere in this book. Businessmen raise their sights on investment potentials to a point in expansion that is not sustainable, and conversely in contraction.

The shift in demand Keynes visualized over the business cycle is principally in the marginal efficiency of capital, although some shift in liquidity preference and in propensity to consume is recognized. We may take the position that his liquidity preference schedule is not critical in the business cycle explanation. A more catholic explanation of the interest rate would not do violence to his explanation. The marginal efficiency of capital schedule shifts over the business cycle, and the interest rate therefore is not a critical factor in determination of the immediate level of investment.

However, if the propensity to consume (or on an aggregative basis, the consumption function) is quite stable, the current amount of investment expenditure would largely determine the level of total income and total expenditure. This fact can be seen by looking back on Chart 9–3. The consumption function is taken as given;

---

[7]*The General Theory, op. cit.,* pp. 315-16.

changes in income and expenditure relate to movements along that schedule rather than to shifts in it. Adding investment vertically to the point where the consumption function +G cuts the 45° guide line determines the total income and expenditure levels.

The investment which may be inserted on Chart 9-3 not only adds to expenditure in such a way as to produce a multiplier effect on consumption (is added to the rising consumption function line), but is equal to whatever savings current activity generates. This is because the distance above the consumption function +G line represents an amount over and above expenditure by the consumer and government sectors—i.e., saving.

The Keynesian theory thus can be attributed with the accomplishment of having integrated the relationship between saving and investment with the level of total economic activity. This is the primary basis for saying that it establishes the dependence of the level of activity on effective demand. Any planned saving which is not invested merely results in a decrease in total expenditure as the actual effects work themselves out. Any investment expenditure over and above planned saving raises expenditure levels and thus similarly raises income levels; additional saving is generated to accommodate the expenditure level. These relations are readily traced by assuming different investment levels on Chart 9-3.

In the Keynesian theory, however, changed conditions are not traced through cumulative adjustments. Rather, the effects of changed conditions are traced merely to the new equilibrium level. The method used to do this in Chart 9-3 is called comparative statics because it traces conditions from one static equilibrium point to another. In an effort to follow the course of the adjustment process, a "period analysis" method has been developed; this breaks the adjustment down into short, successive periods to show the time path of the adjustment. This method is employed in the analysis of the following chapter. Keynes's analysis is not cast in these terms. Limited to the method of comparative statics, his analysis of the mechanics of saving and investment can show only changes from one equilibrium point to another, and not the cumulative adjustment in cyclical expansion and contraction.

Perhaps the reason for this is the emphasis placed on shifts in the marginal efficiency of capital. If the focus of cumulation over the business cycle lies in this change, reasoning with respect to cyclical adjustment of saving and investment, as it could be demonstrated on Chart 9-3, is of little avail.

Certain other reflections of Keynes on the business cycle may be summarized briefly. As we have indicated above, the rightward shift of the investment demand curve in the period of expansion is clearly visualized. Increasing interest rates may bring disappointment of expectations because rightward shift of the investment demand curve cannot forever offset the contractionary effect of such increases.

Keynes hints at an exciting theory with respect to the length of the business cycle: "The interval of time . . . may be a somewhat stable function of the average durability of capital in a given epoch." The durability must be related to the normal rate of growth because such problems as the time when overbuilding may be reached in expansion depends on the rate of growth. "The second stable time-factor is due to the carrying-costs of surplus stocks which force their absorption within a certain period, neither very short nor very long." But neither Keynes nor any of his followers has followed up his lead with respect to the durability of capital nor connected it up with "surplus stocks" (inventories). *The General Theory* provides no more than a hurried observation.

Inventory investment is given a very important place in the explanation of business cycle generation in *The General Theory*. The earlier influence of agricultural inventories is clearly indicated. When harvests are particularly bountiful, it is natural to believe that an increased quantity of agricultural products will be carried over into later years. The proceeds add to the income of the farmer, whereas the investment involves no drain on the income-expenditure relationship. The opposite effect is produced with a poor harvest. Since agriculture represented so large a part of total activity in earlier times, the indicated influences were of major importance. "Thus it is natural that we should find the upward turning-point to be marked by bountiful harvests and the downward turning-point by deficient harvests." In this analysis, ignoring the characteristic movement of agricultural prices with changes in quantity of production due to low price elasticity no doubt reduces or eliminates the validity of the point. (The decline in agricultural prices with bountiful harvests may actually reduce farm income.) Clearly, the general effect of inventory investment is identified. The process described is precisely what we have called the doubly reinforcing nature of investment in Chapter 4.

Inventory investment in other industry in more recent times is stated to be important "in causing oscillations." No doubt, more emphasis would have been placed on the point if Keynes had not been so intent on demonstrating the nature of secular stagnation. This led him on a false scent. An accumulation of stocks after the boom is broken is pointed to. Frequently, inventory stocks do continue to accumulate early in recession, albeit at a reduced rate, so that inventory investment is declining. Businessmen are driven to effect additional inventory cuts because of the unfavorable movement of sales. A further conclusion, however, is all wrong. Because of the unfavorable anticipations noted, it is held that inventory stocks are reduced, causing a "damping-down of the subsequent rate of recovery." Actually, recovery does not tend to get under way until the inventory correction is virtually complete. A powerful culminating force tends to be built up as that occurs, resulting in a rapid rate of early recovery. Of course, if attention is concentrated on recessions into deep depression, such as 1929–33, our description is scarcely more characteristic than Keynes's. No doubt, this is the emphasis intended, in view of his preoccupation with secular stagnation.

STAGNATION

The General Theory deals much more with deep depression or stagnation than with the business cycle. In fact, what we think of as the business cycle in the present business era often is slurred over as "minor oscillations within the main movement of the trade cycle" or ignored entirely. In Keynes's connotations the trade cycle refers to a much more serious affair, including deep depression. This part of the Keynesian thinking is germane to our purpose because we are facing the problems presented by all types of economic fluctuation.

The Keynesian stagnation thesis goes back at least to 1919 with the publication of *Economic Consequences of the Peace*.[8] The stagnation thesis is stated rather clearly in that document. The story may be summarized as follows: Laissez-faire capitalism came to an end with the outbreak of World War I. The future could be expected to differ from the past in many important respects. No great new conquests of food and raw material supplies would occur. Population growth would be more moderate. The rate of technological advance would recede. With all this the rate of bourgeois saving could be expected to persist because of ingrown habits. The result-

---

[8]London: Harcourt, Brace and Company, Inc., 1920.

ing saving would perform no function because the spirit of private enterprise was flagging, and investment opportunities were vanishing. The bourgeoisie were continuing to bake cakes in order not to eat them (to save instead of consuming), and the persistence of the habit was going to make conditions much worse than they needed to be.

Keynes and his followers in the thirties and later were telling the same story, with some elaborations growing out of the Great Depression experience. The evidence on slackened population growth was clearer, and data seemed to indicate that past investment activity was closely tied to population growth. Slower emigration and settlement of new land masses literally represented disappearance of the frontier and, with it, the capital investment required to settle new communities. The automobile appeared to mark the last great stimulator of new industry development. As discretionary income was increasing, it appeared that the new markets cultivated would comprise less stable demand because there would be lack of urgency for buying. Much of the productivity advance then occurring was possible with very modest capital outlays, so that even the growth to be expected would not stimulate much investment expenditure. The bleak picture thus revealed slackened demand, reduced investment to satisfy any modest increase in demand which might be expected, and increased risk in providing whatever small amount of capital investment might appear desirable. To recognize the seriousness of the projection, we must remember the strategic position of investment expenditure in stimulating business cycle expansion.

The clinching theoretical argument, though, was that savings habits would persist together with reduced investment outlets. The result could be no other than a persistently low level of aggregate expenditure, induced by a constant tendency for current expenditures to fall short of the income payments to which they relate. The theoretical framework introduced earlier in this chapter explains the mechanism by which expenditure levels are thereby kept relatively low.

The accusation frequently is made that the secular stagnation conclusion arises from the fact that the reasoning is largely about a stationary process.[9] The capital stock in the economy is held constant, production functions are not assumed to change, and employ-

---

[9]See Joseph A. Schumpeter, *Ten Great Economists from Marx to Keynes* (New York: Oxford University Press, 1951), pp. 282–84.

ment is taken to remain approximately proportional to output. Thus, the phenomena which dominate the capitalist process are excluded from consideration. For our purposes, we do not have to face such major philosophical considerations as would be involved in deciding the degree to which the assumptions are question-begging. The institutional potentialities for investment described in the above paragraphs fail to correspond with the probable outlook for the foreseeable future.

The expectation of secular stagnation colors the Keynesian theory. With so unfavorable a secular outlook, a moral is constantly sought—methods by which stabilization measures can be invoked. This situation can be illustrated by conclusions stated on interest rate control measures. Since no reasonable prospect of full employment exists, experiments should be made with keeping interest rates low rather than raising them, in order to "prevent disappointment of expectations which may lead to a slump." If the interest rates are kept low, a better chance is provided for expanding investment expenditure and for justifying the current position of the marginal efficiency of capital schedule. To assume that the schedule is necessarily shifted too far to the right is taken to be dangerously and unnecessarily defeatist.

This undercutting of the traditional position of interest rate control is founded on the assumption of an unsatisfactory secular outlook. If that assumption comes to appear inappropriate—as is actually the case in the early sixties—the conclusions are changed. If interest rate control is postponed, the time when investment expenditures must be discouraged is merely put off. The longer strict measures of credit control are put off, the greater is the possibility that invoking them will initiate more powerful contractionary forces. Furthermore, with the way our economy is now working, uncontrolled credit expansion cannot be counteranced in view of inflationary dangers. The fact that interest rate changes are effective in controlling credit only after a lag because of shifts in the marginal efficiency of capital schedule does not cancel their importance. Delayed effects make control measures less potent but do not necessarily make them undesirable.

LIMITATIONS

Keynesian theory paints with a broad brush. The strokes are made with relatively few major economic aggregates—total income, total expenditure, consumer expenditure, investment expenditure, and the money supply. Some theorizing may be involved with respect to distribution of these aggregates, such as the effect on the consumption function of shifting income distribution. Major conclusions, however, are founded on three basic "laws" which are applied to the above aggregates. These are propensity to consume, liquidity preference, and the marginal efficiency of capital. Generally speaking, these laws are based on forces which are expected to behave in such a way as to make the laws persist.

The fact that the schedules are assumed to shift over the business cycle provides sufficient flexibility in short-period fluctuations that realistic and characteristic changes can be represented. By the same token, however, the laws no longer provide neat solutions. The implied business cycle process under these conditions could well be as we have described it in Chapters 4–5. We should recognize, of course, that the business cycle could be more closely articulated by use of period analysis, which Keynes himself never accepted. The closer articulation is obtained at the expense of accepting greater stability in the laws of relationship. The methodology of period analysis is taken up in the following chapter.

Over the longer span, growth depends on positions assumed for the major schedules. The Keynesian theory proposes that these positions are such as to produce secular stagnation. The argument is founded on particular institutional changes occurring in the economy, as outlined above. These changes do not appear to correspond with the present outlook; therefore, we may hold equally well, employing the same framework, that secular stagnation is not imminent.

Great doubt remains as to the effectiveness of an aggregate investment demand function until we have established more with regard to the character of individual-business, investment demand functions. From what we know about the decision-making process concerning investment expenditure in individual companies, it is difficult to believe that the interest rate plays much of a part in most cases. What this may amount to is that the investment demand curve of such individual companies is practically vertical—that the businessman does not consider the interest rate to be an important factor in making decisions to invest (see Chart 9–2). There certainly are exceptions. In the case of most public utilities, it has been traditional to estimate long-term growth of sales and to give consideration to revenue rates government bodies might permit in planning capital expansion. Clearly, the interest rate becomes an important factor in making investment decisions in such cases. For most other businesses, it would appear that the cost of money is much less important than expected sales, than cost saving possible in capital replacement, and than expansion necessary to maintain or increase the company's market share (and possibly many other factors such as current willingness to take chances on untried ideas).

Certainly, the individual company does not in any case think in terms of a current market rate of interest, but rather in terms of a supply-of-funds schedule. Investment action likely to be taken depends on the part of this supply of funds obtainable from plowed-in profits, from flotation of bond issues, or from flotation of equity issues. For many small companies the first of these sources may be the only one available because the cost of the other sources is prohibitive. For others, there may be a reluctance to go into debt. For more, probably there is an unwillingness to float stock issues because problems of maintaining control of the company may become complicated. When we learn more about the source of funds for individual companies, we may discover a great deal about problems of obtaining capital that Keynes at least vaguely sensed in his liquidity preference schedule. What businessmen will invest may depend to an important extent on how they can get the funds. (This, of course, is far different from the summary criterion of the interest rate which must be paid).

Possibly, the investment demand schedule of most businessmen actually is quite elastic. Rapid shifting over the business cycle gives it the appearance of being vertical. In recession, the shift may be so far to the left that very little investment expenditure will be made at any interest rate. In expansion, the shift to the right may be so great that a large amount of investment expenditure is forthcoming even at very high interest rates. Such possibilities are perfectly consistent with an elastic investment demand schedule in relation to interest rates. (The fact can be visualized by drawing a chart showing very elastic but widely shifting investment demand schedules.) Over the short period an increase in interest rates tends to be correlated with the same forces which drive the investment demand curve to the right, so that an elastic curve would not result in a quick cutting-off of investment projects when interest rates rise.

If the facts turn out to be similar to the situation described in the preceding paragraph, a change in interest rates would not determine shifting amounts of investment over the business cycle, even though the demand curve is elastic. Whatever additional information on the investment demand curves of individual businesses may reveal, the investment demand curve is not likely to provide an effective method of organizing information on change in investment expenditure over the business cycle, at least not in the near future. With increasing business interest in long-term planning based on long-term forecasts, the time may come when the investment demand curve becomes much more critical than it is now. Plausible expectations on the future use of capital and on the economic climate in which it will function would make a study of the investment demand schedule a rewarding technique.[10]

FOR REFLECTION AND ANALYSIS

1. Explain how the Keynesian theory arrives at the conclusion that investment expenditure determines the level of income in the total economy.
2. What happens if planned savings are less than planned investment? More than planned investment? Which is the active factor?
3. Apparently, what was Keynes's position on the shift of the investment demand curve over the business cycle?
4. If we accept the idea that there are cyclical shifts in the investment demand curve but hold that the consumption function line is reasonably stable under peacetime conditions, what does the Keynesian theory imply about the importance of the amount of investment?
5. What is meant by saying that Chart 9–3 represents comparative statics rather than cumulative adjustment?
6. Do inventory stocks typically dampen the subsequent rate of recovery after a recession?
7. Do the proceeds of building inventory stocks of agricultural crops necessarily add to the incomes of farmers (without farm price supports)?
8. Is capitalism hounded with the bourgeoisie baking cakes in order not to eat them?
9. What does the anticipation that productivity advances can be made with very little additional capital imply about the capital/output ratio?
10. Why does the argument about keeping interest rates low to prevent the disappointment of expectations which may lead to a slump probably ignore any important rightward shift in the investment demand curve?
11. Speculate about the relation between the idea that the rate of interest determines the level of investment and the idea that the chief relation is to a supply-of-funds schedule.
12. Draw a chart showing very elastic but widely shifting investment demand schedules. Might the conclusions drawn from such a model be about the same as from a vertical investment demand schedule?

---

[10]Substantial shifts in the investment demand functions of individual companies would remain because of changing competitive conditions and because of new innovational discoveries. In reasoning about the outlook of individual companies, some shift in investment demand appears inevitable. Since the shifts will be correlated with the business cycle, they will also show up in the aggregate investment demand curve.

Chapter 10 : MULTIPLIER-ACCELERATOR MODELS

In the preceding chapter, we examined the Keynesian model, which shows how changes in total income and total expenditure levels are determined by change in investment expenditure. The method employed is called "comparative statics" because it traces change from one equilibrium level to another. We can scarcely hope to obtain a blueprint of the business cycle by this procedure, for its path is generated by cumulative change; and obviously, the path followed does not represent equilibrium in any significant sense. A closer approach to realistic short-period fluctuation would be provided if the expected changes were traced beyond an equilibrium point and before another equilibrium was reached.

The method designed to do that is called period analysis. Changes are estimated from one spending "period" to another. The changes are initiated by disturbance at the first equilibrium point. The path followed may be in the direction of equilibrium, but with clear recognition that the new equilibrium will not be attained at once.

The period sometimes is considered strictly arbitrary, such as a figurative "day," or it may be taken as a "spending period." The meaning of "spending period" is best discussed separately with respect to the multiplier and the accelerator. No satisfactory statistical measurement of the length in calendar time is available in either case. A year is the time period most frequently suggested as plausible, and we shall speak of the period as a year in length in the initial presentation. This is purely a matter of convenience, and it is not our intention to draw inferences from any assumed length of period.

THE MULTIPLIER

The multiplier relates to the increase in consumer expenditure which can be expected to arise with an increase in income. It is most readily visualized as the steepness of the rise in the consumption function line, as shown in Chart 9-3 (page 174). The consumption function line on that chart has a slope of .7, which, as explained in the preceding chapter, amounts to a multiplier of 3⅓. That is, for an increase in expenditure of $1 billion, a total increase in income (or expenditure) of $3.33 billion is to be expected, although the remaining part of that total amount of increase in expenditure is spread over many following periods.

If consumer expenditure had been compared with consumer disposable income, instead of with total income, the consumption function line would have had a much steeper slope, something over .9.[1] From the point of view of the multiplier effect in the total economy, the consumption function shown on Chart 9-3 is more appropriate, for part of the consumer income is channeled into "leakages" such as higher income taxes and larger undistributed corporate profits.

The multiplier reaction is not instantaneous in the real world. By tracing the reaction through periods, some approach to short-period effects is indicated. A period represents the average interval of time for dollars of income received by households to circulate and to be received by households a second time. The income period thus described is made up of an expenditure lag, running from the time income is received until it is spent, and a production lag, running for the time it takes businesses to produce goods to replace those they have sold. The production period is usually thought to comprise the major part of the income period. In summary, the income period represents the time it takes consumers to spend income and for businesses to pay out income a second time in reaction to the sales made in the first expenditure of income. In other words, it is the time from one receipt of income to another as traced through the circular flow of income between producers and consumers.

The idea of following economic change by period analysis is to assume a disturbance in the circular flow of income and trace its effects in the following periods. This disturbance takes the form of an "injection" of additional expenditure into the system. An injection might actually initiate from any expenditure additional to

---

[1] A rough indication of these differences is indicated by the fact that consumer expenditure is about 70 per cent of net national product, and over 90 per cent of disposable income. This assumes the average and marginal propensities are about equal in a limited range covering income levels.

that covered in the circular flow as previously operating. This might come from speeded-up operation to produce for inventories which may have been depleted by exceptionally high rates of consumer purchase, from expenditure on durable investment, or from increased government expenditure. Let us assume a single injection of $1 billion as a one-shot affair. If it is made at the end of period 0, the expenditure lag and production lag both first arise in period 1, and we can trace the effect through successive full income periods. If we assume a 60 per cent[2] consumer expenditure through successive periods, the increases in expenditure over period 0 would be as follows:

Period	Consumer Expenditure Induced by Injection in Period 0 (Millions of Dollars)
1	600
2	360
3	216
4	130
5	78
6	47
7	28

These figures are obtained merely by taking 60 per cent of the amount in the preceding period to find the induced amount for the given period, on the assumption that the consumption function is represented by a straight line with a 60 per cent slope. The induced effect may be considered insignificant beyond period 7. (By period 10, it comes to only $6 million.) If no other disturbance arose in the circular flow after that, for all practical purposes, we could assume that income would have fallen back to the level in period 0.

A second case worth illustrating is the effect produced not by a single injection but by a permanent rise in the expenditure stream. Let us assume that investment rises permanently by $1 billion. Then the rise in consumer expenditure would be projected to follow the pattern shown below:

Period	Consumer Expenditure Induced by Higher Investment Level (Billions of Dollars)
1	0.600
2	0.960
3	1.176
4	1.306
5	1.383
6	1.430
7	1.458
8	1.475
9	1.485
10	1.491

---

[2]We slant the consumption function at 60 per cent on the assumption that the marginal rate is somewhat below average. Actually, consumer expenditures do tend to decline slightly as a percentage of gross national product in expansion.

The figures are obtained by adding series (as shown above for a single injection) for successive injections beginning in periods 0, 1, 2, 3, etc. At the limit, they will reach $1.5 billion, so that, for all practical purposes, the multiplier effect of a higher level of investment has been spent well before the tenth period is reached.[3]

These illustrations show the successive consumer responding effects of an increase in the circular flow of income. In the case of a single injection, the influence on succeeding periods is founded on the fact that it will take time for saving to erode the higher level of expenditure once created, assuming that no secondary effects arise to expand income further. Equilibrium is finally reached when income has fallen back to the beginning level. In the case of a permanently higher level of investment, the influence of succeeding periods is founded on the fact that as consumers spend the higher income received, total expenditures will be advanced. In this case the final equilibrium is the point where the rising consumption function line indicates a higher consumer expenditure commensurate with the advanced level of investment. (See Chart 9–3, page 174.)

Needless to say, many plausible forces are ignored at this phase of generalization. One of these is the investment reaction. We shall consider this reaction, first, as an isolated phenomenon. Then, we shall examine the interaction between the multiplier and the accelerator.

THE ACCELERATOR EFFECT

The accelerator represents the investment expenditure induced by an increase in consumption expenditure and thus, to some extent, rounds out the supplementary effects involved in the multiplier analysis of the preceding section. In general, the multiplier identifiies the induced consumer expenditure effects, and the accelerator identifies the induced investment expenditure effects.

The accelerator relates to the fact that an increase in product expenditure, if it starts with full-capacity operation, necessarily involves an increase in capacity. If we assume that the marginal requirement for capital capacity is similar to that for capacity now in operation, the accelerator can be indicated by the capital/output ratio which is descriptive of current requirements.

---

[3]The multiplier is 2.5, but $1 billion expenditure is involved in period 0, before consumer re-expenditure develops; so, for the purposes of the cumulative effect, the amount involved is $1.5 billion. This also is the figure which applies in the preceding illustration involving only one injection, but in that case the expenditures add up to that figure rather than building up to it. That the multiplier is 2.5 is easily seen. Using the method of Chart 9–3, $1 billion investment would represent 40 per cent of the total income increase (40 per cent above the 60 per cent slope of the consumption function line); the total, therefore, would be $2.5 billion.

The size of the capital/output ratio is dependent upon the length of the period, for the numerator of the fraction is a stock concept, independent of time, while the denominator is a flow concept, increasing as the length of the period increases. If we take a year, which is the time unit often employed in making investment plans, as the length of the period, present American experience indicates a capital/output ratio of between 1.5 and 2.0.[4] Too much should not be made of such a figure, for (1) the amount of capital required to produce output varies greatly between industries, and (2) available estimates of the stock of capital are crude. With so wide a variation in the capital/output ratio between industries, a change in the industry mix can produce an important change in the total industry average. Because of the crudity of current measurements, substantial revision might arise with better data.

The period is defined as "the normal time taken for output to adjust itself to a change in demand, so that at the end of one period induced investment in working capital and induced disinvestment in stocks are just about balancing."[5] The capital obtained for expansion is spent during the period, and any runoff in inventories forced by demand conditions is restored. Increased capacity in reaction to an indicated rise in demand is assumed to occur within the period.

The accelerator is an important factor in individual-industry expansion. In other words, decisions to invest are often founded on a rise in sales. It is logical, although, as we shall see later, probably not comprehensive enough, to hold that capital investment demand in any industry is made up of (1) that induced by a rise in sales and (2) that required to replace worn-out capital. Viewed on these simple assumptions, great variation in investment expenditure can be readily illustrated. Table 10–1 shows such an illustration for a cloth manufacturing industry. The following assumptions are made: The average life of the looms is 20 years; thus, one twentieth of the stock will wear out each year. The capital/output ratio in terms of

---

[4]*Fortune* magazine, on the basis of Machinery and Allied Products Institute data, and comparing private business capital with total product, including government, has arrived at an estimate of 1.5. See Gilbert Burck and Sanford S. Parker, "Another Big Decade for Capital Goods," *Fortune,* December, 1956. Including a much wider group of durable goods as capital, a ratio of approximately 2 might be obtained.

If the length of the period were a month, the denominator of the capital output ratio would be one twelfth as much, and the ratio would equal 18.

[5]J. R. Hicks, *A Contribution to the Theory of the Trade Cycle* (London: Oxford University Press, 1950), pp. 53–54.

number of looms and of millions of yards of cloth is 1. (Compare column 1 with column 2.) All looms are operating at full capacity in the first year considered. There is no piling of cloth inventories.

TABLE 10-1

HYPOTHETICAL ILLUSTRATION OF INDUCED DEMAND FOR LOOMS

Year	(1) Assumed Cloth Consumption (Unit = 1,000,000 Yards)	(2) Total Looms in Use	(3) Looms to Be Replaced*	(4) Demand for Looms Induced by a Rise in Sales	(5) Gross Investment Demand
1........	1,000	1,000	Unknown	Unknown	Unknown
2........	1,000	1,000	50	None	50
3........	1,200	1,200	50	200	250
4........	1,320	1,320	50	120	170
5........	1,200	1,200	50	−120	− 70

*The replacement is computed on the basis of the looms in use in the first year. None of the loom produced in years 1–5 is assumed to need replacement. While this is not a strictly accurate actuarial assumption, it is simple and does not distort the illustration.

Table 10-1 shows that the accelerator tends to produce an unstable demand for investment expenditures. The variation in cloth demand assumed is 20 per cent or less, but variation in the demand for looms is manyfold.

TABLE 10-2

HYPOTHETICAL ILLUSTRATION OF INDUCED DEMAND FOR INVENTORIES
(In Billions of Dollars)

Year	(1) Assumed Total Business Sales (Monthly)	(2) Total Business Inventories	(3) Inventory Investment (Addition to Inventories)
1.............	60	90	Unknown
2.............	62	93	3
3.............	66	99	6
4.............	66	99	0
5.............	64	96	−3
6.............	68	102	6

A more important illustration is the induced demand for inventories, for it is clear that change in sales is the chief guide in making decisions to invest in inventories. Furthermore, investment in inventories represents a major part of the variation in total expenditures over the business cycle. Total book value of business inventories, as now reported, is running about $90 billion. Total business sales are at about $60 billion a month.[6] The capital/output ratio, thus, on a monthly basis, is 1.5. Table 10–2 shows the variation which may arise in inventory investment with variations in business sales of well under 10 per cent.

The accelerator principle illustrates the variation in demand for consumer durable goods which arises because of fluctuation in the adequacy of consumer stocks of these goods. Table 10–3 provides such an illustration with relation to automobiles. The life of the automobile is assumed to be 10 years, represented by 10,000 miles of use each year. In this case, perhaps, we should speak of the automobile population/consumption service ratio (column 2 over column 1 in Table 10–3) instead of the capital/output ratio. That ratio is 1 in this case if we take the automobile consumption unit to be 10,000 miles. If we assume no change in business inventories of automobiles, we may get a substantial variation in the demand for automobiles, as shown in column 5 of Table 10–3, even though automobile consumption varies less than 10 per cent.

TABLE 10–3

HYPOTHETICAL ILLUSTRATION OF INDUCED DEMAND FOR AUTOMOBILES

Year	(1) Assumed Automobile Consumption (Unit = 10,000 Miles)	(2) Total Automobiles in Use	(3) Automobiles to Be Replaced*	(4) Induced New Demand for Automobiles	(5) Total New Automobile Demand
1......	40,000,000	40,000,000	Unknown	Unknown	Unknown
2......	40,000,000	40,000,000	4,000,000	None	4,000,000
3......	43,000,000	43,000,000	4,000,000	3,000,000	7,000,000
4......	44,000,000	44,000,000	4,000,000	1,000,000	5,000,000

*As in the loom illustration in Table 10–1, the replacement is computed on the basis of the automobiles in use the first year. None of the automobiles produced in years 1–4 are assumed to need replacement. In this connection, see Ragnar Frisch, "The Interrelation between Capital Production and Consumer Taking," *Journal of Political Economy*, Vol. XXXIX (October, 1931), pp. 646–54.

Before turning to an analysis of interaction between the multiplier and accelerator, we may usefully examine the evidence on the extent to which the accelerator is a main-spring of change in the aggregate economy. Table 10–4 shows the postwar changes which have occurred in yearly gross national product, together with plant and equipment expenditures. Substracting business depreciation charges, some approach to an estimate of net investment is ob-

---

[6]These figures are currently reported in the *Survey of Current Business*. In the January, 1961 issue, for instance, manufacturing and trade inventories were reported at $93 billion and sales at $60 billion for November, 1960.

tained in column 3. If we assume a capital/output ratio of 1, a theoretical approximation of what the net investment should be according to the accelerator principle is shown in column 2. Although the figures in columns 2 and 3 are similar in some years, the comparison is not close in many others. This is especially noticeable in the recession year of 1954 and in some years of rapid advance in gross national product—notably 1950, 1951, and 1955. In all of those years, there were special influences at work which partially explain the deviation. In 1954, capital expansion was exceptional because businessmen were forced to wait until after the Korean War to obtain desired capital materials. The great advances in activity in 1950 and 1951 are also related to the Korean War. In 1955 an exceptional rise occurred in consumer demand for durable goods.

TABLE 10–4

ACCELERATOR PRINCIPLE APPLIED TO THE TOTAL ECONOMY*
(In Billions of 1954 Dollars)

Year	(1) Gross National Product	(2) Changes in Gross National Product	(3) Net Investment	(4) Business Depreciation	(5) Gross Plant and Equipment Investment
1946.....	283		12	14	26
1947.....	282	− 1	17	15	32
1948.....	293	11	18	16	34
1949.....	293	0	3	18	21
1950.....	318	25	14	19	33
1951.....	342	24	15	20	35
1952.....	354	12	14	21	35
1953.....	369	15	14	23	37
1954.....	363	− 6	10	25	35
1955.....	393	30	12	26	38
1956.....	401	8	14	27	41
1957.....	408	7	12	29	41
1958.....	399	− 9	5	30	35

*These figures are taken from *U.S. Income and Output; A Supplement to the Survey of Current Business* (Washington, D.C.; U.S. Government Printing Office, 1958) and the July, 1959, *Survey of Current Business*. The Business Depreciation column represents the sum of corporate and noncorporate depreciation charges. deflated by the average of nonresidential construction and producers' durable equipment implicit price deflators. Such a price deflation is crude, but perhaps makes little difference in the illustration. (Most accidental damage to fixed business capital and capital outlays charged to current expense are excluded from column 4, but this does not materially change the result.) While the major part of durable business investment is included in plant and equipment, shown in column 5, a larger investment total could be employed, including residential housing, etc. Theoretically, column 1 should represent net national product.

The differences between columns 2 and 3 are great enough, however, to make us realize that the accelerator does not automatically identify all of the forces responsible for inducements to make net investment expenditures. Particularly, net investment is indicated in every year in Table 10–4, although in four years, gross national product failed to increase. In those years, one might argue that net investment was due to a reasonably high level of sales rather than to an increase in sales, but in that case the accelerator principle no longer applies.

In line with earlier suggestions on the probable level of the capital/output ratio, question may be raised as to the ratio of 1 implicitly assumed in Table 10–4. Actually, the Net Investment column comes to a total of $148 billion for the twelve years 1947–58, compared with $116 billion to which the yearly differences in gross national product total in these years. But if the years in which gross national product declined or failed to rise are omitted from the Net Investment column, the total net investment is slighly less than the sum of yearly differences. Clearly, differences of actual levels of gross national product provide a better comparison than could be obtained by multiplying gross national product by a multiple representing a higher capital/output ratio. This, of course, does not prove that the capital/output ratio is 1; it may merely indicate that other important investment incentives are involved.

We may well recognize the rigidity of assumptions which are involved if the accelerator is considered the sole determinant of investment. Differences in the interest rate are considered immaterial; presumably, they would be offset by shift in the investment demand curve. Any change in prices merely represents conditions already allowed for in incentives determined by the accelerator. The accelerator does not change; or if it does, its changes can be predetermined.

These assumptions become most implausible when applied to total industry. Very likely, the accelerator will fluctuate because of change in industry mix and because of innovational changes in the need for capital. Nevertheless, applying the accelerator to total industry provides rewarding lessons. The consumption function has importance as it reflects consumer reactions in the total economy. The multiplier, founded on the consumption function, provides useful insights when contrasted with the accelerator.

MULTIPLIER-ACCELERATOR INTERACTION

Keynesian theory is sometimes said to trace all economic change to investment. Experience appears to indicate that sales conditions are at least a partial explanation of investment made. If such is the case, not only is the level of consumption expenditures dependent upon the level of investment, but the level of investment is at least partially dependent upon consumption expenditure, since it represents the major part of sales. Such an idea tallies with recognized interaction in the economy.

TABLE 10–5

INTERACTION OF ACCELERATION AND MULTIPLIER PRINCIPLES: ONE INJECTION[a]
(In Billions of Dollars)

Period	(1) Consumption Expenditure	(2) Consumer Respending	(3) Induced Investment (Accelerator Equals 2.5)	(4) Total Output
1.............	120.0	.....	......	120.0
2.............	130.0	10.0[b]	......	130.0
3.............	128.0	8.0[c]	25.0[d]	153.0
4.............	146.4	26.4[e]	57.5[f]	203.9
5.............	187.1	67.1[g]	127.3[h]	314.4

[a]Column 2 is equal to 80 per cent of the increase from period 1 to the preceding period in column 4 thus, 26.4 in period 4 is equal to 0.8 (153 − 120). Column 3 is equal to 2.5 times the change in column 4 in the two preceding periods. Column 1 is equal to 120 plus column 2. Column 4 is equal to column 1 plus column 3.
[b]The injection is assumed to be a transfer payment, such as a "soldiers' bonus," amounting to $12.5 billion and paid at the end of period 1. Being a transfer payment, it does not enter as part of product. Eighty per cent, or $10 billion, adds to consumer expenditure in period 2.
[c]Eightyper cent of the $10 billion increase in expenditure in period 2 becomes expenditure in period 3.
[d]Output increases $10 billion between periods 1 and 2. Since the accelerator is 2.5, investment is increased 2.5 times the increase in output.
[e]The $26.4 billion is the sum of 80 per cent of $25 billion and 80 per cent of $8 billion.
[f]Output increases $23.0 billion from period 2 to period 3. Since the accelerator is 2.5, investment is increased 2.5 times the increase in output.
[g]The $67.1 billion is the sum of 80 per cent of $57.5 billion and 80 per cent of $26.4 billion.
[h]The $127.3 billion equals 2.5 times $203.9 billion − $153.0 billion.

If a model depicting interaction is to be set up, working rules must be established. A common method is to use period analysis. The consumption expenditure of a given period can be considered induced by income in the preceding period. Investment expenditure may be assumed induced by the change occurring in output or sales in the two preceding periods. An illustration along these lines is shown in Table 10–5. The disturbance or injection which starts the induced expenditure going is assumed to be $12.5 billion in transfer payments at the end of period 1. Such payments are unrelated to current output, so they do not get counted in the table. We make the assumption that consumers spend 80 per cent of additional income, so consumer expenditure is increased $10 billion in the second period. After passing through the circular flow of income and expenditure, 80 per cent, or $8 billion, is assumed spent in the third period, and so on. But in the third period the accelerator provides an additional effect, since output rose by $10 billion in period 2. In this example, we assume an accelerator of 2.5, so induced investment amounts to $25 billion in the third period. From here on the intereffects mount, and output rises at a rapid rate. In fact, it is obvious that the rise in dollar amounts in a few more periods would be so fast that the result might be considered representative of hyperinflation.

The system illustrated is explosive. This fact is dependent upon the sizes assumed for the multiplier and accelerator coefficients. For an explosive system to arise, the accelerator must be large in relation to marginal consumption expenditure. The accelerator assumed in Table 10–5 is large in this sense; and mathematically speaking, it is in the explosive area.

Models can be developed which illustrate the generation of cycles by assuming a smaller accelerator. If small enough, the indicated variations in output will shortly disappear, and output will settle down at an equilibrium level. Properly chosen, a cycle of uniform amplitude may be generated. With a larger accelerator, cycles of increasing amplitude will appear; and finally, if the accelerator is made large enough, the system will be explosive, as shown in Table 10–5.[7]

A cycle may remain within the bounds of close to constant amplitude, even though the accelerator is large enough to be explosive, if upper and lower boundaries are assumed to be operative, because of limits in the economic system. Full employment is conceived to set an upper limit. This is shown by a series establishing full-employment use of resources in the first period and rising in successive periods in accordance with growth potentialities, as indicated by the responsible forces outlined in Chapter 6 (see column 5 of Table 10–6).

The lower limit is set by two principlal forces, which are considered effectual even with a large accelerator. Zero is the lower limit

---

[7] It is not our purpose to develop the mathematics of these models. According to the systems developed, different criteria can be established for the cases indicated in the text. Paul A. Samuelson shows a regularly recurring cycle of constant amplitude to arise if the accelerator is precisely equal to the reciprocal of the rate of consumption expenditure ("Interactions between the Multiplier Analysis and the Principle of Acceleration." *Review of Economic Statistics*, May, 1939; reprinted in *Readings in Business Cycle Theory* [Homewood, Ill.: Richard D. Irwin, Inc., 1944], pp. 261–69). J. R. Hicks shows an accelerator of 1 to be the dividing line between diminishing and increasing amplitude, while the size of the accelerator required to produce substantial dampening or substantial increases in amplitude will depend on the marginal rate of saving (see *A Contribution to the Theory of the Trade Cycle* [London: Oxford University Press, 1950], p. 71).

of net investment in durable capital, except for the extent to which the existing stock wears out or becomes obsolete. (The upward thrust is less limited because it is represented by a positive amount of investment expenditure.) Secondly, some expenditures move independently of the income level or, at least, of change in the income level. This applies to some private investment expenditure and to most government expenditure,[8] indicated by column 1 in Table 10-6.

That all changes in expenditure cannot be encompassed in induced consumption and induced investment has become increasingly recognized. Some investment certainly is "autonomous," although the term in hard to define positively. Negatively, the term implies investment expenditure not induced by current changes in sales. Investment made on hopes for the long-run future, like the transcontinental railroads, is a case in point. The building of clubs and provision of better facilities for employees are others. An intermediate, difficult case is investment induced by the level of sales, rather than by change in them. It is sometimes said that by looking *backward* instead of *forward,* all profitable investments have been related to increasing sales. But even this is not entirely true. "Modernization" investment, making it possible to reduce costs or improve products, is not necessarily related to rising sales, and most persons believe that such investment is a rising proportion of total investments.

Also, there are other expenditures in the economy which must be recognized—most significantly, government expenditures. In modern national income accounts, government investment is not segregated from other types of government expenditures, and the system has merit.[9] Foreign expenditures—net exports of goods and services—are essentially autonomous. In the model shown in Table 10-6, we assume all of these factors—autonomous private investment, government expenditure, and net foreign sales—are included in column 1, designated as Autonomous Investment.

The marginal rate of consumption expenditure is assumed to

---

[8]The system described in the remainder of this section is essentially Hicksian. However, most of the ideas were anticipated before Hicks worked out his system, and we are trying to summarize the useful idea as now generally visualized rather than to explain the beliefs of a particular scholar. Hicks's system is described in *A Contribution to the Theory of the Trade Cycle.* Notably, Hicks includes government investment as part of the autonomous total.

[9]Much government research is as truly investment as are durable products. For contrast with the private economy, government savings are most usefully considered government surpluses.

be .6. This is slightly less than the proportion that consumer expenditures now represent of total net national product in the United States. The accelerator is set at 1.5. Exception might be taken to so high an accelerator on the basis of the slight evidence presented at the end of the preceding section. In the illustration presented there, an accelerator of 1 provided a better "fit" than an accelerator of 1.5. Reworking the computations shown in Table 10–6 by substituting an accelerator of 1 instead of 1.5 defeats our purpose, for the full-employment ceiling is never reached in that case, and total income shortly becomes approximately stable.

TABLE 10–6

MULTIPLIER-ACCELERATOR MODEL*

WITH AUTONOMOUS INVESTMENT AND CEILING AND TROUGH BOUNDARIES

(In Billions of Constant Dollars)

Period	(1) Autonomous Investment	(2) Induced Net Investment (Accelerator = 1.5)	(3) Induced Consumption Expenditure (Marginal Consumption = .6)	(4) Total Net Expenditure	(5) Full-Employment Net Expenditure
0	120.0	......	180.0	300.0	400.0
1	144.8	......	180.0	324.8	416.0
2	129.8	37.2	194.9	361.9	433.0
3	135.0	55.7	217.1	407.8	450.0
4	140.4	68.9	244.7	454.0	467.9
5	146.0†	69.3†	272.4†	486.7†	486.7
6	151.8	49.1	292.0	492.9	506.1
7	157.9	9.3	295.7	462.9	526.4
8	164.2	− 40.0	277.7	401.9	547.4
9	170.8	− 40.0	241.1	371.9	569.3
10	177.6	− 40.0	223.1	360.7	592.1
11	184.7	− 16.8	216.4	384.3	615.8
12	192.1	35.4	230.6	458.1	640.4
13	199.8	110.7	274.9	585.4	666.0
14	207.8†	191.0†	351.2†	692.6†	692.6
15	216.2†	160.8†	415.6†	720.3†	720.3
16	224.8	41.6	432.2	698.6	749.2
17	233.8	− 32.6	419.2	620.4	779.1
18	243.2	− 40.0	372.2	575.4	810.3
19	252.8	− 40.0	345.2	558.0	842.7
20	262.9	− 26.1	334.8	571.6	876.4

*Full-employment ceiling is assumed to be $Y = 400 (1.04^n)$, with n representing the period. Autonomous investment also is assumed to grow 4 per cent per period. Capital replacement requirements are assumed to be $40 billion for each of the periods shown. Column 2 is equal to 1.5 times the increase between the two preceding periods in column 4. Column 3 is equal to 60 per cent of the preceding figure in column 4. Column 4 is equal to the sum of columns 1, 2, and 3.

†In periods 5, 14, and 15, total demand adds to more than the full-employment level, so total expenditure is given at the full-employment level. What the distribution of demand is under these conditions is not indicated. Replacement requirements are assumed limited to $40 billion in these years. The stock of capital is not assumed to make the 1.5 accelerator inoperative in period 6 forward and in period 16 forward.

An accelerator of 1 may much better represent the facts. This would account for the relative stability we now experience, as contrasted with the great instability shown in the model of Table 10-6. Under these conditions, the accelerator as such would lose much of its importance as a generator of the business cycle, although that would not imply any diminution in the importance of investment. Since this section attempts to show the potential of the multiplier-accelerator interaction, and since we do not really know what the size of the accelerator is, we have used an accelerator of 1.5 in the illustration.

Table 10-6 illustrates the achievement of two ceilings. The assumed accelerator is very powerful, and it will be seen that induced investment reaches rather fantastic levels at the second ceiling. The limitation of resources, as indicated by the full-employment levels, makes any such rise impossible. This is because the model assumes constant prices. Prices, of course, could be bid up to any extent and induced investment might rise merrily along. Monetary control no doubt would prevent that in our country, but we shall point out in the final section of this chapter that ignoring any price rise adds unrealism to the model.

The way the accelerator and marginal consumption expenditure constants operate is precisely similar to that illustrated in Table 10-6. A one-shot injection of $20 billion in the nature of autonomous investment is assumed to arise in period 1. This, taken together with a normal increase of 4 per cent in antonomous investment, induces an additional consumption expenditure of $14.9 billion in period 2, representing 60 per cent of the increase in consumer expenditure in period 1. (The total induced consumption in period 2 is 60 per cent of the total income in period 1, for the marginal and average consumption rates are assumed to be the same in the model.) Since the rise in income is $24.8 billion in period 1, induced investment is 1.5 times that amount, or $37.2 billion in period 2. Similarly, the figures shown are generated for each period.

The troughs are supported by a continuous rise in autonomous investment and by the flattening-out of induced investment at the limit of depreciation, which is assumed to be $40 billion. Some questions are raised in the last section of the chapter regarding these assumptions. Attention may be called to the assumed length of the contraction, which covers nearly as many periods as the expansion. Our American experience does not fit that pattern; but since the investment considered is durable investment, and that is most typical of disturbed secondary growth situations, the pattern may be fairly typical of the kind of experience to which overexpansion of durable capital is most closely related. Contractions tend to be long when moving into deep depressions. Furthermore, the period is set by the time required for output to adjust itself to a change in demand, and that time may differ in different phases of the cycle.[10] Hicks notes that the period may be shortened in calendar time in the recession because of urgency felt for reducing inventories.

THE CAPITAL/OUTPUT RATIO AS A PARAMETER

We may sense that the accelerator is overplayed in the multiplier-accelerator models. This is both because, actually, the degree to which investment is generated by change in the level of sales is uncertain and because the accelerator is artificial when applied to the total economy. There is a growing tendency to make less rigid assumptions about the influence of the accelerator than are implied in Table 10-6. An attractive possibility is to think of the capital/output ratio as an important explanatory variable in the study of economic change.[11]

When capital stock is high relative to output, only the theorists who are guided most rigidly by the investment demand curve would hold that substantial inducements are offered for investment. The reason such theorists might hold investment to be encouraged is that interest rates are likely to be low under these conditions. With far more capacity than can be put into use, most analysts would hold that investment incentives are weak. In the opposite situation, with capacity generally inadequate, only the high interest rates likely to prevail at such a time would be a discouraging factor.

The general financial situation is also a dependent factor. The strength of prices tends to be related to the degree to which re-

---

[10]Alice John Vandermeulen and Daniel Carlson Vandermeulen, in *National Income Analysis by Sector Accounts* (Englewood Cliffs, N.J.: Prentice-Hall, Inc., 1956), p. 85, state: "The income period is analytical rather than chronological in nature. It is measured not by the passage of a fixed amount of time but rather by the occurrence of certain events. In this respect the income period is closer to an inning in baseball, which is measured by the occurrence of three outs for each team, than it is to the quarter in football, which is measured by the lapse of fifteen minutes on a stop watch."

[11]The most complete system cast in these terms will be found in James S. Duesenberry, *Business Cycles and Economic Growth* (New York: McGraw-Hill Book Co., Inc., 1958). The emphasis of V. Lewis Bassie on the critical importance of the total stock of goods implies a similar point of view; see his *Economic Forecasting* (New York: McGraw-Hill Book Co., Inc., 1958).

sources are fully employed. With much capacity looking for markets, prices are not readily bid up and are vulnerable to contractionary factors. Oppositely, when capacity is very limited, prices tend to be strong. We may note that the contrasting multiplier-accelerator model assumes constant prices, and provides no insight into changes in financial strength or weakness.

We may conclude that high levels of the capital/output ratio are deflationary and low levels inflationary. Generally, the ratio moves inversely with the business cycle. As output rises more rapidly than the stock of capital in the expansion, investment is encouraged. It is not until fairly late in expansion that any real pressure on capacity generally is likely to be indicated, and the National Bureau of Economic Research measurements point to that part of the cycle as the time when durable capital expenditure tends to rise most rapidly. As the recession gets under way, excess capacity may not appear to be too great in most lines; and capital demand may continue at a high, though reduced, rate. This experience is especially noticeable after periods when materials required in the capital industries have become short. Many businessmen may reason that projects should be pushed while materials are available. The recession of 1953 is a particularly good illustration, but the tendency appears to have been present in the early part of many recessions. As output drops further, the capital/output ratio rises to an area which engenders contractionary attitudes.

A major problem lies in the difficulties of measuring the stock of capital. The very statistical problem of assigning deflated dollar values to all parts of the stock in order to add up and obtain a significant total is manifest, although perhaps not insurmountable. If, in addition, the rates of obsolescence vary greatly over time, prospectively no capital stock total may be of much value in current economic analysis.

Even though precise measurements of changes in capital stock are still questionable, a reasonable basis exists for theorizing on what happens to the capital/output ratio over the business cycle. An illustrative model is shown in Chart 10-1. The capital/output ratio rises to a peak at the bottom of recession because in recession the total level of capital stock tends to continue to rise, even though the rate of rise is reduced, while output declines. In expansion the ratio declines because of the rapid rise in output; but often, capacity does rise rapidly at the end of prosperity, and therefore prosperity peaks are marked on Chart 10-1 at points early in the rise of the ratio.

Let us assume that the total stock of capital needed is 50 per cent more than a year's output. Then, the horizontal 1.5 line on Chart 10–1 represents a position of equilibrium between capital stock and output. Competitive distress which arises at the high levels of the ratio in recession is dissipated when rising output early in the expansion phase pushes the ratio down. As output is pushed higher and the ratio declines to below equilibrium levels, demand appears very favorable. A rise in the ratio late in prosperity, even though the ratio still lies below equilibrium levels, reduces demand favorability.

CHART 10–1

MODEL OF CAPITAL/OUTPUT BEHAVIOR

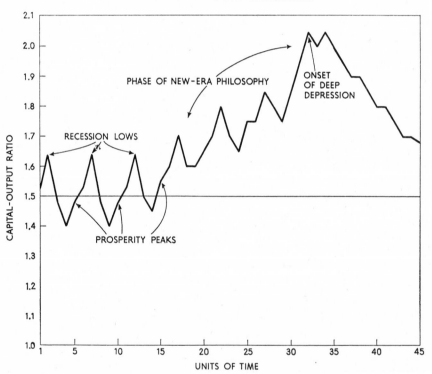

We may argue that although no tendency exists for the ratio to settle down at equilibrium levels, substantial departure tends to set up some corrective forces under usual competitive conditions, typified by the movement of the ratio in the left-hand part of Chart 10–1. The high levels of the ratio in recession retard increase in capital stock. The low levels to which the ratio is driven as expansion gets well under way encourage a more rapid advance in accessions to capital stock. The capital/output ratio, therefore, can be considered to provide a stabilizing force.

If the future comes to appear so promising that fear of overbuilding generally disappears, the situation illustrated in the right-hand part of Chart 10-1 might materialize. With a New Era philosophy, capital stock might grow out of proportion to demand needs. Extravagant anticipations of future demand might make the unused capacity showing up in recession seem less disturbing. Advances in the capital/output ratio come to suffer less interruption, and the level of the ratio comes to reach higher and higher levels in successive cycles.

Assuming that capital requirements in relation to output have not advanced from the 1.5 level, the time will come when little need is seen for additional capital. The ratio may finally rise to frightening proportions in a recession, as pictured at the peak point on Chart 10-1. As investment is reduced, total output declines, and the ratio appears even more excessive. Waiting for enough capital to wear out to bring the ratio back to normal proportions becomes a long, drawn-out process. This may be unduly extended because restrictions are likely to be set up which dissuade businessmen from scrapping less efficient capital. Unless fiscal policy is called upon to force higher expenditures, an extended decline in the capital/output ratio may follow. This would differ from the optimism induced by the declines shown in the ratio at the left-hand side of the chart. There, the decline is accounted for by rising output. The extended decline pictured at the right-hand side of the chart would be accounted for by a slow reduction in capital stock.

MULTIPLIER-ACCELERATOR GROWTH MODELS

In this section, we deal with a growth model founded on the multiplier-accelerator relationship.[12] A key concept is warranted rate of growth. This is defined as the growth which results when sufficient investments are made to balance savings generated by saving tendencies in the economy. The problem posed is how stable and sustainable the warranted rate of growth is and how closely it corresponds with the "natural" rate of growth, which is equivalent to

---

[12]Attention should be called particularly to R. F. Harrod, *Towards a Dynamic Economics* (London: Macmillan & Co., Ltd., 1948); and Evsey D. Domar, *Essays in the Theory of Economic Growth* (New York: Oxford University Press, 1957). No effort is made in this section to report on what these or numerous other authors writing on the subject have said. We are trying only to state the general idea involved.

the idea employed as the foundation for growth measurement in Chapter 6—involving expected changes in the labor force, labor hours, and productivity.

The warranted rate of growth varies directly with proportionate saving and inversely with the accelerator.[13] The greater savings are, the greater is the provision made for growth. As we saw in the preceding chapter, however, savings must be employed in adding to capital to become effective. Therefore, they are related to investment made at the same time. If we assume that all net investment expenditure depends on providing facilities for additional product and is exactly financed by the saving called forth by a given level of income, we adduce that warranted growth depends on the ratio of the savings rate to the accelerator.

As an illustration, in 1957, net saving in the United States, as measured by the national economic accounts, was $35 billion. Net national product was $403 billion; therefore, the net savings rate was about 9 per cent. If we assume that the accelerator is 2, the warranted rate of growth is 4.5 per cent.

Recognizing the crudity of the figures on which these estimates are based, we can scarcely hope to determine the warranted rate of growth very precisely. Possibly, the accelerator is as low as 1.5, in which case the warranted rate of growth would be 6 per cent. $(9 \div 1.5.)$

If warranted growth is greater than the natural rate of growth, savings may be excessive in relation to the investment demand for them. This means that savings are higher than needed investment. Too high a warranted rate of growth tends toward secular stagnation. Savings not balanced by investment outlets reflect a decline in product expenditures, as explained in the preceding chapter.

If warranted growth is less than the natural rate of growth, savings are insufficient to satisfy investment requirements. This means that savings are not great enough for needed investment. Investment expansion then depends partially on credit, which is inflationary. The resort to credit in the United States in the present period of history would indicate that the warranted rate of growth is too low, with inflationary implications.

---

[13]Harrod holds that the accelerator applies to *all* durable goods, including those held by consumers. Since the national accounts are not kept in that way, the argument becomes awkward, and we assume that the application is to business capital only.

Since saving is the complement of expenditure, saving tendencies will be described by the slope of the expenditure line (e.g., the consumption function line). The multiplier, therefore, is appropriately used to describe saving tendencies.

On the other hand, if the "natural" rate of growth is between 3 and 4 per cent, as we have indicated in Chapter 6, the above figures relating to current estimates on the saving rate and the size of the accelerator would appear to indicate that the warranted rate is too high. Since credit extension and its inflationary implications are observable, the inflationary argument appears more impressive.

"The target of policy should be to bring the warranted rate as near as possible to the natural rate."[14] Such an accomplishment, were it possible to achieve, would not be expected to eliminate the rather moderate type of cyclical fluctuation we have been experiencing in the United States in the postwar period. It would, however, eliminate excessively great discrepancies between the savings which would be made to provide for durable assets and the expenditure to be expected for these assets in accordance with the accelerator principle. Thus, "this is a dynamised version of the stagnation thesis."[15] Balance is visualized between the rate of saving and the investment required for growth, rather than between the static amount of planned saving and the amount of investment.

The model does not deny the existence of autonomous investment; but if some of the investment is autonomous, the saving rate must be adjusted for it before being balanced against the accelerator. In a growing society, income will increase, so that the saving rate will be related to an increasing amount of income. If the economy is growing at a constant percentage rate, and if the accelerator remains constant, capital required according to the principle of providing for an advancing level of sales will represent an increasing amount of investment. To maintain a steady advance under these conditions, autonomous investment would have to grow at a stable rate. Otherwise, the increasing amount of saving would not balance the increasing capital requirement indicated by the accelerator. For instance, if autonomous investment remained at a constant level, accelerator investment would have to grow still faster to keep up with the advancing amount of savings. If autonomous investment were dependent upon the investment demand curve (marginal efficiency of capital), as is sometimes suggested, it probably would not grow at a stable rate.

Of course, these ideas are founded on the assumption that the accelerator expresses *the response made in investment expenditure*

---

[14]R. F. Harrod, "Domar and Dynamic Economics," *Economic Journal,* September, 1959, p. 455.
[15]*Ibid.*

to provide capacity for increases in output. No one will question that additional output will technically require increases in capital, if we start with operations at approximately full-capacity levels. If, however, the relation is no more than a *technical* coefficient stating the increase in capital required for additional output, the process is more reliably described by an investment demand curve than by the accelerator. Nevertheless, an increase in sales does play a part in investment decisions, which is the same as saying that the accelerator does represent a response coefficient, at least to some extent.

Response, as used in the above paragraph, refers to whether rising sales represent all of the influences which induce businessmen to make expenditures in durable investment. As a practical matter, all analysts would answer in the negative. To provide perspective, we list here some of the other influences. The limited meaning of such a list should first be made clear. The question relates to what drives businessmen to invest at a *particular time,* not what will drive them to invest sooner or later. The latter idea is closely related to what we call a technical coefficient in the preceding paragraph, not to the investment called forth by given conditions, but to the amount technically necessary to achieve growth.

If operations were fully rational in a certain world, the interest rate would call forth investment at any given time as described by the investment demand curve (see Chart 9–2, page 172). This situation, as pointed out elsewhere, is most closely approached in public utilities and in housing. Rising sales have frequently been considered *the* alternative inducing factor, but a moment's thought will indicate that many other influences should be recognized. For one thing, rising sales are surely less effective in calling forth investment expenditure if accompanied by low profits than if accompanied by high profits. As confidence is achieved in high prosperity, sales may come to rise slowly, but a *high level of sales* may for a time appear to call forth as much investment expenditure as rising sales appeared to earlier in the expansion. Certainly, when the level of sales is down in depression, investment expenditure will be down, even the part that may have been called autonomous (as far as the private economy is concerned). Investment expenditures are also often made to reduce costs (modernization), to provide a better-quality product, because other companies are making investments (to maintain the company's relative position in the industry), to provide better working conditions for employees, to follow regional shifts in the market, or to diversify the company's product. We do not pretend that this list is exhaustive; but clearly, to consider rising sales, capital replacement, and autonomous factors as a complete explanation of the forces leading to current investment is an oversimplification.

LIMITATIONS

Although the multiplier-accelerator model provides stimulating intellectual insights, no quantitative application at the present time appears promising. The accelerator varies widely between industries, and any very precise expectation for a near-future period will lack reliability. This is especially true in light of inadequacy of measures of total capital stock, which, if satisfactorily available, would give us some background as to past movements in the capital/output ratio. Furthermore, the accelerator is greatly influenced by the shifting extent to which total capital capacity is employed in making output, but no real knowledge is available as to the degree of the influence. To answer this last point by asserting that the accelerator operates only under conditions of full use of capacity is wholly unsatisfactory. *Some* inducement must have been provided when output increased, even though the capacity limit had not been reached.

Additionally, what full-capacity use involves is very vague. The penumbra of stand-by capacity is looked at differently at one time than at another. Finally, the full use of capacity is not reached simultaneously in all industries. In fact, there are *always* some industries with unused capacity. The idea of the accelerator applied to *total* industry does have its disadvantages.

In addition to these points, five major difficulties may be reviewed. In the first place, we are justified in feeling that change in sales is made to carry too much weight as an explanation of investment incentives. Substantial evidence, illustrated by Table 10–4, appears to indicate that the level of sales in actual practice may provide about as important an investment inducement as change in sales. Also, much investment appears to be founded on the "need for modernization" at the present time, rather than on total industry expansion. To say that this merely represents a part of the investment required to replace capital consumption does not explain its increasing importance. Generally, there is a vague and indeterminate part of investment called autonomous, which makes the development of a sharp model difficult, to say the least.

Along the same line, how may we visualize the growth or advance in autonomous investment? From the practical point of view, to say that we do not know so we will assume exponential growth, equal to that in the total economy, is no answer. All analysts now seem to agree that depression of any major variety *will* bring sharp drops in autonomous investment.

Second, the assumption that current change is entirely represented by deflated values is suspect. Of course, no one believes that no monetary changes occur, and the use of deflated values is primarily to indicate that changes may be induced without any monetary shifts at all. No fault can be found with such an expository device. Problems do arise, however, when attempts are made to provide subsequent allowance for monetary changes. It seems reasonable to conclude that allowance cannot be made by modifying conclusions already achieved by deflated-value models. The model must be entirely reconstructed, with allowance made for monetary changes in the process of its development. The interaction of changes in commodity prices and of profits is so integral a part of economic change that it cannot be analyzed more or less as an afterthought. No such reconstruction of the multiplier-accelerator models has been made, at least none that has come to our attention.

Third, the very definition of the period to a large extent makes the multiplier-accelerator model inapplicable to the typical American business cycle. The business cycle—as we are now experiencing it, at least—largely represents a process of adaptation to the current situation. Most important in this adaptation is the inventory adjustment which becomes necessary because of the limited accuracy involved in setting production schedules. But the very definition of the period assumes the inventory adjustment to have been achieved before the end of a period. As noted earlier in the chapter, Hicks holds that the period represents the "normal time taken for output to adjust itself to a change in demand." It is that adjustment and readjustment of output to demand that is constantly going on in the business cycle, especially in the recession. Constant efforts are made to cut back inventories in line with the changed demand situation. This is an integral part of the contraction as we are now experiencing it. Actually, investment is *not* limited to the degree to which capital wears out or becomes obsolete. It is principally influenced by the degree to which inventory investment becomes negative, which later may set up a powerful culminating force.

Fourth, in line with the failure to reflect the process of adaptation, the multiplier-accelerator models principally represent the changes which may occur in durable investment. Durable investment becomes the central maladjustment in extravagant growth situations—secondary growth in halcyon prosperity and secondary growth in deep depression. We have experienced deep depression in the past and may do so in the future. There is no guaranty that overbuilding of capital and saturated markets of consumer durables, with the aftermath of a long period of working off excess capital, will be avoided. But there is no certainty, either, that it will occur. The application of the growth models is somewhat limited if they apply only to the development of deep depressions.

Fifth, the accelerator is likely to lose in importance as careful long-range planning develops. The investment demand curve is more applicable if confident long-range forecasts are available. Some possibility exists that the multiplier-accelerator models best represent a fading era. Such a prospect is favorable. We would be well advised, however, to guard ourselves against being carried away with wishful thinking.

FOR REFLECTION AND ANALYSIS

1. Why is period analysis better adapted to the study of business fluctuations than comparative statics?
2. It is sometimes said that the accelerator principle means more when applied to individual industries than when applied to total industry. Discuss.
3. Discuss the definition of a period in period analysis.
4. Discuss the relation between a dampened, uniform, and explosive cycle in multiplier-accelerator interaction and the sizes of the accelerator and consumption function constants.
5. Make observations on the validity of ceiling and trough boundaries in the multiplier-accelerator interaction model.
6. Why does the capital/output ratio move inversely with the business cycle?
7. Explain the conflict of ideas between the message of Chart 10–1 and the position that the level of capital investment will be determined by the height of the interest rate.
8. What problems arise if the warranted rate of growth is high relative to the natural rate of growth?
9. What is meant by saying that multiplier-accelerator growth models represent a dynamized version of the stagnation thesis?
10. What consideration is given to autonomous investment in multiplier-accelerator growth models?
11. What relation is there between the accelerator and the extent to which total capital capacity is employed in making output?
12. What would you say about the influence of commodity price changes in current economic conditions in relation to the changes in economic conditions indicated by Table 10–6?
13. How does the multiplier-accelerator model conflict with the idea that the business cycle principally represents a process of adaptation to the current economic situation?

Chapter

11

THEORY BASED ON

BUSINESS INVENTORIES

Until recently, little attention has been given to inventory theories. Nevertheless, there are two reasons why we should heed these theories: (1) As shown below, a substantial part of the change in activity over the business cycle is accounted for by inventory investment. (2) Inventories bear the major brunt of adaptation to shifting business prospects. While the process of adaptation will be treated more exhaustively at the end of the chapter, we may note here that it is receiving increasing emphasis, for several reasons. Fundamentally, the business cycle can be attributed to the process of adaptation to change. Correctly or incorrectly, the belief is now expressed that durable investment will proceed at a more stable rate than in the past. Advances which have been made in long-range planning and forecasting provide some basis for this belief. If cyclical variations in durable investment could be further reduced, the chief area left where business decisions are made to adapt to the shifting outlook would relate to inventories.

EMPIRICAL INFORMATION ON INVENTORIES

Chart 11-1 provides a visual impression of the close co-ordination between changes in total activity and nonfarm inventory investment in the postwar. (A similar picture is shown if total business inventory investment is charted, but farm investment is omitted because it does not reflect business adaptation.) Clearly, inventory investment is a major factor. This fact is most apparent in recessions. Going from the peak rise in gross national product to the point of most rapid decline for the 1952-53 and the 1956-58 periods, as shown on Chart 11-1, inventory investment accounts for about 60 per cent of the change.

A more usual method is to show the proportion of decline in

gross national product from the peak level to the trough level accounted for by inventory investment (the peak or trough usually occurs later than the point of maximum change). On this basis the relative declines for the three postwar recessions are as shown in the following tabulation:

Quarter and Year	(1) Decline in Gross National Product (Billions of 1954 Dollars)	(2) Decline in Nonfarm Inventory Investment (Billions of 1954 Dollars)	(3) Percentage (2)/(1)
IV–1948 to II–1949.............	7.0	7.6	109
II–1953 to II–1954.............	13.7	7.5	55
III–1957 to I–1958.............	19.6	8.6	44

CHART 11-1

GROSS NATIONAL PRODUCT AND NONFARM INVENTORY CHANGES COMPARED

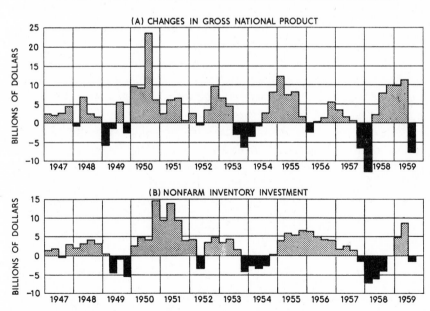

However figured, inventory investment accounts for nothing like a similar proportion of the expansion. Only about 10 per cent of the increase in gross national product from the 1949 trough to the 1953 peak or from the 1954 trough to the 1957 peak is accounted for

by inventory investment. A significant fact is that although inventory investment accounts for an important part of the recession, it accounts for a very minor part of the expansion. Consumer purchases and durable investment are the major part of most expansions. Although declines do occur in other areas of expenditure in recession, only in inventory investment is it correct to say that for every two steps forward there follows about a step backward.

The experience of the twenties, as summarized by Abramovitz,[1] corroborates these results. In deflated figures, as indicated by the sample studied and computed on an annual rather than on a quarterly basis, he shows that for five business cycles, 1919-38, about a fourth of the expansion and about half of the contraction are accounted for by inventory investment. The exact size of his estimates should not be emphasized, but that they are of the same general order of magnitude as in the postwar period is important.

The model presented below emphasizes the influence of inventory investment in both expansions and contractions. In terms of what has occurred historically, the evidence is most significant with respect to recessions. What happens to markets for consumer durables is most revealing in that respect. In the 1957-58 recession the *output index* for major consumer durables shows a decline of 17 per cent, whereas the *measurement of consumer expenditures* for durable goods shows a decline of only 7 per cent. Automobile *output* declined about 30 per cent, but *consumer expenditures* only about half as much. The difference is accounted for by inventory shrinkage. For instance, business inventories of motor vehicles and parts shrank over 20 per cent in the 1957-58 recession. Inventories are readjusted at the various stages of distribution—including those of manufacturers, warehousemen, wholesalers, and retailers. A substantial part of the total decline in production is accounted for by runoff of inventories at various stages of distribution, rather than by shrinkage in final sales. To show complete rather than sample facts along these lines would require the development of more consistent classifications for various types of products between production and inventories at various stages of distribution and final sales.

IMPORTANT INVENTORY TYPES

Table 11-1 shows the broad distribution of inventory stocks at the approximate peak following the 1957 downtown. Although the

[1]Moses Abramovitz, *Inventories and Business Cycles, with Special Reference to Manufacturers' Inventories* (New York: National Bureau of Economic Research, Inc., 1950).

final sales of durable goods are only about half those of nondurables, the maintained inventory stocks are greater. Furthermore, the cyclical variation in durable stocks is much greater than in nondurable stocks. Durable stocks do not advance much more than nondurables in late expansion (although they did in 1952–53 because of the Korean War), but they fall much more in recessions. The greater variability of durable stocks is attributed to the volatility of durable markets. Sales are cut off much more sharply than for nondurable goods in recession, and there is a strong motivation to bring inventory stocks quickly into line.

TABLE 11–1

BROAD DISTRIBUTION OF BUSINESS INVENTORY STOCKS
In Billions of Dollars, as of January, 1958

Stage of Distribution	Durable Goods	Nondurable Goods	Total
Manufacturing............	30.6	22.3	52.9
Retailing.................	11.3	13.1	24.4
Wholesaling.............	6.6	6.0	12.6
Total...................	48.5	41.4	89.9

Over half of the inventory stocks represented in Table 11–1 are in manufacturers' hands, and these inventories vary more than those at later stages in distribution. In 1958, for instance, manufacturers' inventories declined over 7 per cent, while the inventories of retailers and wholesalers combined declined only a little over 4 per cent. (Note that the percentage effect of inventory investment is much greater than that shown here for inventory stocks.) A large part of the instability created by shifting inventories is centered in durable stocks in the hands of manufacturers.

Inventory change varies somewhat from one business cycle to another, depending on (1) differences in movement of sales and (2) extent of the formation of new companies or the introduction of new products. For instance, the relatively small decline in inventories of nondurable consumer goods in postwar recessions is related particularly to the resistance disposable income has shown to cyclical declines. The second point is well illustrated by a surge in inventory stocks during the Korean War, paced especially by the introduction of new types of defense products.

There is a chance that we may miss or exaggerate regularities in inventory change by dealing with changes as aggregative as those shown in Table 11-1. The relative size of inventories required varies significantly between one product and another. (This is substantially the same point as the long-recognized fact that turnover figures vary among different types of business.) Changes in the product mix could thus result in important changes in the size of total inventory stocks.

Another possibility is that greater uniformity of inventory change may be shown by industry groups than by broad aggregates. This possibility has been high-lighted by Moses Abramovitz in his monumental work published in 1950.[2] Classification can be made as to technical conditions of various industries—whether the inventory is supply-dominated or demand-dominated, and whether the inventory represents a raw material or a finished product. While such classifications are certainly significant, the information derived in using them has not to date provided a satisfactory base from which to project models of inventory change in the total economy. With one exception, noted below, we shall not pursue in this chapter the use of classification by technical conditions.

In the analysis of current economic change, classification of inventory stocks by stage of fabrication has thrown light on the difficult question as to whether inventory accumulation is planned or unplanned. Manufacturing inventories are classified according to whether they represent (1) purchased materials, (2) goods in process, or (3) finished goods. These classifications, fortunately for our purposes, are made according to the way the good appears to the individual manufacturer. (Some items may be raw materials for certain manufacturers and, at the same time, finished goods for others.) Inventory stocks are divided about equally among the three groups, although we may usefully note that finished good inventories actually are somewhat more than a third of the total. Roughly, we may hold that changes in stocks of raw materials and of goods in process are about as planned, but that stocks of finished goods tend to swing away from desired levels because businessmen try to maintain reasonably stable production schedules, permitting adaptation to current demand by shifting levels of inventory stocks of finished goods. If raw materials are purchased on long contracts and require long periods of shipment in transit, adaptation to desired levels will be impossible, and to that extent the principle is quite inaccurate. However, no possibility now exists of obtaining a

---

[2] *Ibid.*

separate measurement of such inventories. Classification by stage of distribution has not as yet lent itself to effective use in the development of theoretical models, but the classification is found especially helpful in forecasting, as noted in Chapter 18.

The businessman's most important guide in deciding on needed inventory levels is the level of sales. Thus, the stock/output ratio is a most important criterion. The marginal ratio required is not quite equal to the average ratio. The ratio of inventories to output was only about three fourths as high in 1947–58 as in 1920–29.[3] It would appear also that the typical increase in inventories required in a business cycle expansion is relatively less than the increase occurring in sales. Exceptions will, of course, be found in expansions where (1) an abnormal number of new companies is being formed and (2) the shift to new types of products is unusual. A basic stock of inventories must be established for each new company; similarly, a basic stock must be established for each new type of product.

What this means is that the stock/output ratio tends to decline over time, whether secular growth or business cycle expansion is represented. A constant ratio thus is not an effective standard. A better device to represent requirements is a scatter diagram, as represented for manufacturers of durable goods in Chart 11–2. In this and other cases, there appears to be an approximately linear relationship between inventory stocks and sales, but a decline in the ratio is indicated with time.

Because businessmen tend to permit inventory variation to bear the brunt of adaptation of production schedules to change in sales, inventory stocks tend to lag after changes in sales. This conclusion is adequately verified by actual statistical data. The logic of the lag is readily explained. As sales begin to rise less and less or to decline, inventory stocks are permitted to continue to rise so that production schedules will not immediately have to be adapted to a precise forecast of sales. Similarly, as sales begin to decline less and less at the end of a contraction, production schedules are not precisely forecast, and a continued decline in inventory stocks is tolerated.

The lag in inventory stocks contrasts with coincident timing of inventory investment with sales. Although inventory stocks tend to continue to rise after a downturn in sales, the rise tends to slacken, inasmuch as such is the movement occurring in sales. Since inventory investment is measured by the change in inventory stocks (with

---

[3]See *Survey of Current Business*, April, 1959, p. 8.

appropriate adjustments to make prices comparable), inventory investment tends to decline as soon as sales decline, or to advance as the rate of sales expansion slackens. Similarly, at the upturn, inventory investment tends to rise concomitantly with the rise in sales.

CHART 11-2

RISE OF INVENTORY STOCKS IN RELATION TO SALES
(For Durable Goods in the Hands of Manufacturers)

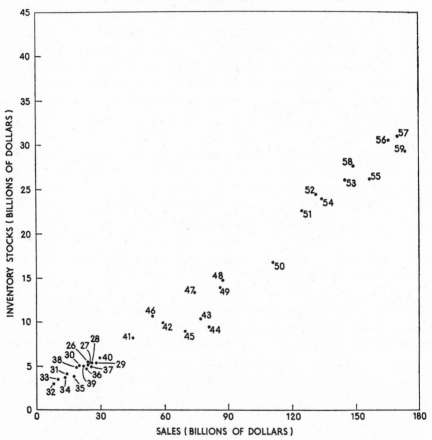

MODEL INDICATING THE EFFECT OF PLANNED CHANGE IN SALES AND PLANNED CHANGE IN INVENTORIES

As indicated in the preceding chapter, the accelerator much better describes expenditure reaction in the case of inventories than in the case of durable investment. This is because, at least theoretically, inventories can be quickly brought into line with sales, since they can be run off quickly or built up quickly. Such is not true of durable investment. As sales decline in contraction, capacity becomes excessive in relation to current sales; and as sales rise in expansion, capacity increases may not be made rapidly enough to keep up with the cyclical advance.

Furthermore, inventory needs are logically related to current sales, while durable investment is more logically related to sales in the more distant future. What is implied is that current sales are more clearly the standard of motivation in the case of inventories than in the case of durable investment. The application of such a standard probably is not practically represented in the model presented in Table 10-2 (page 193). In that model, the reader may remember, inventory stock is assumed to represent a constant proportion of sales. This implies that businessmen are able to keep inventories in constant adjustment with sales. (We might assume that the desired adjustment is some decline in the stock/sales ratio over time, as noted in the preceding section, but the principle would be the same.) The fact of the matter is that businessmen probably are quite powerless to keep inventory stocks at the desired levels at all times.

The problem can be illustrated by manufacturers who do not make goods to order. Decision must be made on the amount of production in advance of acutal sale. It is convenient to think of a plan established for an advance period. This is what has been done in the model set up in Table 11-2, which is described below.

Current production rates are not dependent upon advance plans if goods are produced on order only after actual sales are made. Some companies produce goods only on order, and many others produce some goods on special orders. We are unable to state how extensive such practices are, but our impression is that they represent but a small proportion of total manufacturing activity. It is true that practically all manufacturers of durable goods and some of nondurable goods follow the practice of accepting new orders in advance of actual production.[4] We know from experience, however, that order backlogs in these industries do not prevent rapid shifts in the rate of manufacturing activity. The "firmness" of such orders may frequently be in considerable doubt, for orders may not specify a date of shipment, but may be delayed indefinitely. Such orders should be clearly distinguished from goods uniquely made to order.

---

[4]In the Department of Commerce *Industry Survey*, described in Chapter 17, new orders are reported for the following nondurable goods industries: textile mill products, leather and products, paper and allied products, and printing and publishing.

Most of the new orders so reported refer to standard-type goods made on regular-line operation.

Similarly to the operation of a manufacturer, retailers and wholesalers must formulate plans which will establish the flow of goods expected for a limited future period. The plans usually must be made in advance of actual consumer sales in retail stores or actual purchases of retailers from wholesalers. In other words, plans are dependent upon forecasts of sales which will be effected in a future period. (Frequently, the forecasts are merely implicit assumptions that the rate of sale, seasonally corrected, will equal the recently prevailing rate.) If the plans are too high, unintended inventory accumulation will occur. If they are too low, undesired inventory runoff will result. It should not be thought that businessmen set their inventory plans with sharpness; but there will be acceptable ranges within which they would wish to keep inventory levels.

To illustrate the force of advance planning in a model, it will be convenient to assume a sharp visualization of inventory needs. This assumption is made in the model presented in Table 11–2.[5] To provide a maximum degree of contrast for the student, we start with the beginning levels employed in Table 10–6 (page 200). The assumptions from that point forward, however, are very different. We highlight here changes which arise to meet current sales levels and to maintain a desirable inventory level. The model can be understood most simply if it is considered to apply to manufacturers selling for a market unfixed by advance order. While that is too restrictive to represent total activity in the entire economy, the idea is clearer if initially put in that focus.

Autonomous investment is conceived to involve exactly the same coverage as in Table 10–6. Except for the introduction of a $20 billion injection in period 1, however, the similarity ends at that point. In Table 11–2 a $20 billion higher level of investment is assumed

[5]The ideas on which the model is based are principally those of Metzler, Nurkse, Bassie, and Lewis. See Lloyd A. Metzler, "The Nature and Stability of Inventory Cycles," *Review of Economic Statistics,* August, 1941; "Factors Governing the Length of Inventory Cycles," *Review of Economic Statistics,* February, 1947; and "Business Cycles and the Modern Theory of Employment," *American Economic Review,* June, 1946; Ragnar Nurkse, "The Cyclical Pattern of Inventory Investment," *Quarterly Journal of Economics,* August, 1952; V. Lewis Bassie, *Economic Forecasting* (New York: McGraw-Hill Book Co., Inc., 1958), pp. 662–70; John P. Lewis, *Business Conditions Analysis* (New York: McGraw-Hill Book Co., Inc., 1959), pp. 486–88. The student should clearly understand that we are not trying to explain what these authors believe, but rather to explain significant ideas which they helped to originate. Particularly, note should be made of the fact that we talk principally of "planned" levels.

TABLE 11-2

FAILURE OF PLANNED INVENTORY AND PLANNED SALES LEVELS TO CORRESPOND WITH ACTUAL SALES LEVELS*

(ELASTICITY OF EXPECTATIONS: .75)

(In Billions of Dollars)

Period	(1) Planned Sales to Consumers	(2) Planned Inventory Investment	(3) Actual Inventory Investment (in Addition to Amounts Shown in Column 2)	(4) Actual Sales to Consumers	(5) Other Expenditures	(6) Gross National Product	Period
0	180.00	......	......	180.00	120.00	300.00	0
1	180.00	......	−12.00	192.00	140.00	320.00	1
2	201.00	+12.00	−10.80	211.80	140.00	353.00	2
3	226.65	+10.80	+0.18	226.47(H)	140.00	377.45(H)	3
4	237.47(H)	−0.18	+11.10	226.37	140.00	377.29	4
5	226.45	−11.10	+13.24(H)	213.21	140.00	355.35	5
6	203.34	−13.24	+5.28	198.06	140.00	330.10	6
7	186.70(L)	−5.28	−6.15	192.85(L)	140.00	321.42(L)	7
8	188.94	+6.15	−12.11(L)	201.05	140.00	335.09	8
9	207.20	+12.11	+8.39	215.59	140.00	359.31	9
10	226.50	+8.39	+1.57	224.93(H)	140.00	374.89(H)	10
11	231.94(H)	−1.57	+9.72	222.22	140.00	370.37	11
12	220.19	−9.72	+9.91(H)	210.28	140.00	350.47	12
13	201.32	−9.91	+2.47	198.85	140.00	331.41	13
14	190.28(L)	−2.47	−6.41	196.69(L)	140.00	327.81(L)	14
15	195.07	+6.41	−9.82(L)	204.89	140.00	341.48	15
16	211.04	+9.82	−5.48	216.52	140.00	360.86	16
17	225.24	+5.48	+2.81	222.43(H)	140.00	370.72(H)	17
18	226.86(H)	+2.81	+8.43(H)	218.43	140.00	364.05	18
19	215.43	−8.43	+7.23	208.20	140.00	347.00	19
20	200.53	−7.23	+0.55	199.98	140.00	333.30	20
21	193.81(L)	−0.55	−6.14	199.95(L)	140.00	333.26(L)	21
22	199.94	+6.14	−7.71(L)	207.65	140.00	346.08	22
23	213.43	+7.71	−3.25	216.68	140.00	361.14	23
24	223.45	+3.25	−3.43	220.02(H)	140.00	366.70	24

*It is assumed that inventories are in adjustment with sales in period 0. In period 1 an injection of $20 billion in investment is made. Business anticipatory reaction to the change is assumed to be as follows: (1) Any change in inventory investment is planned to be made up in the following period, i.e., the figures in column 2 are the same as in column 3, but with signs reversed and lagged one period; (2) production schedules are set to increase the production of consumer goods by three fourths of the increase in the preceding period, i.e., the difference between succeeding figures in column 4 times three fourths equals the excess of the figure in the next period in column 1 over the figure in column 4. The consumption function is assumed to have a slope of .6, i.e., column 4 is 60 per cent of column 6. The sum of columns 1, 2, and 5 equals column 6. Column 3 is column 1 minus column 4. The letter H marks a cyclical high and the letter L a cyclical low. Note that the plans in columns 1 and 2 are assumed to be carried out for the period for which they are set up.

to arise and to continue indefinitely. Autonomous investment is not assumed to advance secularly, as in Table 10–6. This change in assumption is made in order not to complicate decisions made on the inventory process by changing levels of autonomous investment. Also, no consumption lag is assumed in Table 11–2; that is, sales to consumers are assumed to represent 60 per cent of gross national product in the *same period,* not after a lag of one period according to the method employed in Table 10–6. Again, the reason for the change in assumption is to highlight decisions made on needed inventories and to avoid complicating the illustration by assuming a consumption lag.

With such a simplification of assumptions, it is possible to hypothesize that in period 0, inventories are at appropriate levels and that any change from those levels is undesired (except to allow for the slight increase in autonomous investment). To implement that hypothesis, is it assumed that for any change which is found to occur in inventories, as measured in column 3, an adjustment is made in the following period to re-establish the level existing before the change occurred; in other words, the same amount with the sign reversed is introduced in column 2 in the following period.

It is also assumed that businessmen react to a change in sales made to consumers, as shown in column 4, by changing production schedules in the following period to the extent of 75 per cent of the change which has occurred in the two preceding periods. For instance, in column 4 the change in consumer sales from period 0 to period 1 is $12 billion; three fourths of $12 billion is $9 billion, and $9 billion added to the $192 billion shown in colunm 4 at period 1 is $201 billion, which amount appears in row 2 of column 1, showing planned sales to consumers.

With these two assumptions—that businessmen are induced to raise or lower production schedules on the basis of changes which have been occurring in consumer sales and in accordance with undesired changes in inventory levels—a cycle is generated as shown in the following periods illustrated in Table 11–2. A peak is reached in gross national product in period 3, a low in period 7, another peak in period 10, another low in period 14, etc. In this particular model the cycle in inventory investment generally lags one period after that in gross national product, although the conclusion derived should be merely that the cycles in inventory investment and in activity are approximately timed together. (Variation in elasticity of expectations or in slope of the consumption function may eliminate the lag; see footnote 7, below.)

Obviously, the level of inventory stock shows a lag, as it does in the real world; the lag can be read from the table by noting that inventory investment continues to be positive after the peak in gross national product and to be negative after the trough in GNP.

The cycle is produced by the failure of businessmen to anticipate correctly the multiplier effect of their own actions in increasing production; the higher level of production creates more income, which adds further to consumer expenditures in expansion. By assuming that 60 per cent of the added gross national product winds up in consumer expenditures, it may be seen that an additional factor properly should be taken into account in making production plans if a cyclical movement is to be avoided. Similarly, in the contraction, since in the model consumers are assumed to reduce their expenditures by the extent of 60 per cent of the decline in gross national product, production plans would have to be cut back to allow for that.

Why do the expansion and contraction level off in the model and finally turn around? The attempt to make up for inventory deficiency in the expansion is partially successful. Although inventory stocks continue to decline, the rate of decline is reduced as the expansion continues. Sooner, or later, this leads to a reversal because the slower rate of inventory accumulation reduces the rise in consumer expenditure; and finally, some inventory accumulation actually occurs. When that happens, gross national product has started a decline. This produces a decline in consumer sales, which makes the planned inventory reduction inadequate. As the reduced inventory investment catches up with the lower level of consumer sales, it overshoots as in expansion and leads to an upturn.

We do not have to assume that the businessman will react exactly as the constants indicate in Table 11-2. The fact is, however, that to prevent the cycle, he would have to allow precisely for the .6 marginal propensity of consumers to spend out of the increased product which is assumed to become available in any given period. He could readily adjust his production schedules to do that if the problem really were that simple. As noted below, it is not so simple, and the unanticipated spending of increased income which becomes available stands for a wide variety of unpredicted factors.

A cyclical movement is displayed in the model whether we assume businessmen plan production schedules to allow for an advance in sales of 75 per cent of the recent increase in sales or some other reasonable figure. If it is assumed that businessmen plan for only the current level of consumer sales, instead of an increase founded on advances which have been occurring, a substantial cycle will occur only at first, after which the variation will become so slight that it may be ignored. Starting with the same figures as shown in Table 11–2, the cycle rises to a peak not far below that shown in period 3 in the table; but only a slow decline occurs to period 10, and after that the GNP column approaches a stable level.

If we assume that businessmen run their production schedules as high, or as low, as would be indicated by a continuation of the full amount of the recent increase in consumer sales, or of the recent decrease in such sales, the amplitude of the cycle will rapidly increase. Starting with the same figures as shown in Table 11–2, the peaks and troughs in gross national product will be dated exactly as shown; but by period 17, GNP will reach nearly $440 billion and by period 20 fall to nearly $245 billion. Similarly, the amplitude of the cycle will increase, although to a lesser extent, if businessmen are assumed to set production schedules to provide for a continuation of 90 per cent of the change which has been occurring in consumer sales; by period 17, GNP will reach about $401 billion and by period 20 decline to about $298 billion.

On the other hand, if businessmen are assumed to set production schedules to provide for a continuation of only 50 per cent of the change which has been occurring in consumer sales, the cycle will dampen out after period 20 to correspond closely with the result noted earlier when businessmen are assumed merely to continue production schedules at the current rate.

The failure of production plans to correspond closely with actual sales to consumers has frequently been called an "output lag."[6] In this sense what is implied is merely that production plans do not react immediately to changes occurring in final sales. As long as the anticipatory character of the lag is emphasized, there can be no quarrel with the terminology. Care must be taken not to interpret the concept as connoting the technical time required to readjust the production process. If that were the assumption, it would seem that, aside from the difference in mechanical problems among industries, the most significant delay would arise in connection with

---

[6]The concept is generally attributed to Erik Lundberg, *Studies in the Theory of Economic Expansion* (London: P. S. King, 1937), chap. ix.

an approach to full-capacity operation. But this influence is not at all emphasized. Table 11-2 bears no relation to the rate at which capacity is operated. Early in the expansion, there is no question that the businessman could promptly bring the production rate up to consumer demands in most industries if the latent demand were fully understood.

The oversimplification involved in the model presented in Table 11-2 should be clearly recognized. Explicit reference to the accelerator has been avoided by assuming that inventories are in balance in period 0 and that efforts are constantly made to bring them back to that *level*. For this reason a model which might greatly change the level of gross national product would be inappropriate. The assumption that businessmen make production plans in conformity with the full amount of change of consumer sales is not illustrated,[7] since the rising amplitude of the cycle involved implies substantial changes in the total level of inventories. Disregard of the accelerator would be more serious if the illustration assumed a secular rise in gross national product. Lack of explicit recognition of the accelerator does not mean that the relation of inventories to sales is ignored. On the contrary, it is assumed that efforts are constantly made to bring inventories back to the assumed equilibrium relation with sales in period 0.

Since the model of Table 11-2 is set to move about a horizontal path, it could not be considered a growth model. Growth implications have been intentionally excluded in order to high-light adaptation to current demand conditions. Hence, all durable investment is considered autonomous and is taken to remain at a horizontal level.

This means that the model is geared to changes occurring in consumer demand only. Anticipation of changes in need for inventory investment in connection with durable investment requirements may actually be just as important. Fluctuation is greater in durable investment areas, technological change is more apparent, and shifting inventory needs may be more difficult to anticipate. Indeed, as simple a relation as the 60 per cent marginal consumption function would be truly unrealistic in anticipating durable investment demand.

---

[7]If the reader prefers, the term "elasticity of expectations" may be employed to convey the meaning involved in such expressions. For the phrase in the text, the elasticity would be unity. See J. R. Hicks, *Value and Capital* (2d ed.; New York and London: Oxford University Press, 1946), pp. 205–12.

Even in the case of consumer goods, the major difficulty in anticipating inventory needs at key times is probably missed in the model illustrated. In real life, changes in inventory investment become most crucial at business cycle turning points. The great difficulty at those times, as emphasized earlier in the chapter, is the reevaluation of inventory needs at successive stages of distribution, rather than failure to anticipate the induced effect of inventory actions on consumer spending.

Finally, we may recognize that business expectations may be founded on other factors than actual change in sales, particularly on changes which have been occurring or are anticipated in prices. Surely, for agriculture, change in prices is a far more important indicator than change in the quantity of sales, partly because of prevailing atomistic competition and partly because of the long period of time over which production plans must be made.

If these, and perhaps other, complicating factors were introduced in the model, a more realistic representation would be obtained. The greater complications, however, would introduce many uncertainties, and clear conclusions would be more difficult to develop. In any case, no such model is available, but we may hope that progress will be made toward setting it up. In the meantime, without a better foundation, we may assume that the general characteristics of the problem are established in Table 11-2. By following columns 1 and 4, it can be seen that planned sales are uniformly higher than actual sales during contractions, and uniformly lower in expansions. (Slight differences in turning points are ignored in these statements.) The same story is told by column 2. During contractions, planned inventory investment is negative; and during expansions, planned inventory investment is positive. The picture painted is inability of businessmen to get inventory stocks high enough in relation to sales in expansion until the peak is reached or to get inventory stocks low enough in relation to sales in contraction until the trough is reached.

Some evidence that these changes do represent what actually happens is provided by recorded statistical data which indicate that inventory stocks do not rise as rapidly as sales in expansion and do not decline as rapidly in contraction. Of course, since stocks represent assets, compared to sales which reflect current activity, a very large change in current inventory investment would be required to keep in exact step with a rapid change in sales levels.

Care should be exercised to avoid overstressing this model just because it tallies with some statistical facts. For it is not influenced by many of the leveling forces which appear near the peak or trough, as described in Chapters 4 and 5; therefore, important statistical forces do not appear to be represented. The model as shown in Table 11–2 is completely independent of forces which may be exerted by approach to full capacity. For this reason, consideration is not given to the leveling influence of such factors as losses of advantage available earlier in the expansion in adding product with little added overhead cost. As another illustration, we may note the importance sometimes attained by the shifting relation between completion and starting rates in construction activity.

UNSATISFACTORY FULFILLMENT OF PLANS IN PLANT AND EQUIPMENT

The fulfillment of plans is frequently unsatisfactory for all forms of investment. It will be helpful to show how lack of fulfillment in inventories differs from that in durable capital. The differences relate primarily to (1) the length of time for which a commitment is involved and (2) the length of period required for any given commitment to be finalized. Obviously, the time involved in both of these situations is shorter for inventory. The difference in time is narrowest in some short-lived equipment; and in these cases, cyclical behavior tends to approach that characteristic of inventories. It is well known that the behavior of short-lived capital equipment usually varies like inventory investment. When it does not, it is because of urgency of demand, as in 1953–54.

We may take up the second of these points first. In cases where considerable time is required from planning to completion, opportunity is offered for major changes to arise in the outlook for sales. If sales have declined, it may well be that the project never would have been started if the later expectations had prevailed, or at least the project might have been set up on a smaller scale. Under these circumstances, work may be continued only because of the amount already invested. Thus, on the revised plans, overfulfillment is being achieved. It is awkward to consider these changes to occur within a period for the economy as a whole because the average demand adjustment in other areas would involve much less time. Similarly, if sales have risen, it may well be that larger or more projects would have been started, given the expectations prevailing at the later date.

Possibly, some revision of Table 10–6 could be made to incorporate the kind of assumption required regarding unsatisfactory fulfillment of plans. The needed research for such a model has not been developed. The point we wish to make here is that such a model would differ substantially from that shown in Table 11-2. The difference is founded partly on the fact that lack of fulfillment could not be as conveniently set up in neatly cut-off periods, as explained in the preceding paragraph. It is also dependent upon the fact that the changing supply situation is not as readily corrected as in the case of inventories.

In a significant sense, both durable capital formation and inventory investment may be said to relate to a kind of "inventory." In the former, it is an inventory of productive capacity. Once established, this cannot be sold currently (at least not by the entire economy), but can be used up only by letting it wear out. This may take a long period of time.

Neither can durable capital be expanded as rapidly as an inventory of goods. Let us assume that inventory stocks should grow 2.5 per cent per year from the present business inventory stock of $100 billion. In a substantial recession, inventory deficiency might reach $12.5 billion. To make up for the deficiency, then, we may assume $15 billion is required in a year. On a GNP level of $500 billion, this represents only 3 per cent and conceivably could be obtained without great difficulty.

Assume, on the other hand, that durable capital should grow at 3 per cent per year from a base of $750 billion capital stock, and that a 10 per cent deficiency is recognized; the 13 per cent comes to nearly $100 billion and would represent an almost impossible requirement to make up in a year if gross national product were about $500 billion. Recognizing the doubly reinforcing character of investment, the deficiency would be enough to keep activity at maximum levels for several years. If, under these circumstances, the high demand situation, created by efforts to increase investment stock, induces businessmen to overshoot on investment requirements by, say, $100 billion, a long, slow, and painful process of working off the excess would be required.

This, taken together with the fact that the criterion for a satisfactory level of durable investment is much less clearly the current sales level than for a satisfactory level of inventory stock, points up the major difference between the behavior of the two types of investment. Durable investment can get further out of hand because

the demand situation is disturbed for a longer period and because
the criterion of satisfactory relationship to sales may become dulled
in the optimistic atmosphere of prosperity, only to become pain-
fully clear as depressed conditions develop.

Actually, the difficulty would be less if the level of current sales
as a criterion for needed durable investment came to be repudiated,
and if its place were taken by the investment demand curve. Under
these conditions, however, much more satisfactory long-term forecasts of demand would be required than are now available.

A lengthy period is involved in commitments for durable investment. This, of course, relates to the length of life of such goods. The
true logic of the situation is that the criterion of adequacy of investment should relate to the future level of sales rather than to the
present level.

In summary, we can see that in the case of durable investment,
market difficulties are just as dependent upon over- and underac-
cumulation as in the case of inventory stock. The difference is that
a much longer and more painful process of adaptation is involved.
These facts can be clarified by recognizing that durable investment
is more closely related to growth than is inventory investment. Inventory investment is required to provide a smooth flow from current production to current consumption. Durable capital formation
is required to provide for future needs.

CYCLICAL PROCESS OF ADAPTATION AS REPRESENTED BY
FLUCTUATION IN INVENTORY INVESTMENT

A perusal of the literature shows a wide recognition of the idea
of a cycle of adaptation centered on inventories. It is characterized
by "waves of adaptation," noted by Schumpeter and referred to by
Metzler.[8] Keynes's long interest in the variation of inventories as
an influence in business fluctuation was clearly evidenced by his
reference in *The General Theory of Employment, Interest, and
Money* to the importance of inventory investment in causing oscillations, as noted in Chapter 9. Such ideas appear consistent with
the modern theories of decision making, which explain that "notions
of adaptive and satisficing behavior, drawn largely from psychology,

---

[8]Metzler, "Business Cycles and the Modern Theory of Employment," p. 290; and
Joseph A. Schumpeter, *Business Cycles,* Vol. I (New York: McGraw-Hill Book Co.,
Inc., 1939), p. 180.

are challenging sharply the classical picture of the maximizing entrepreneur."[9]

The idea that the business cycle has essentially become an inventory cycle is a parallel characterization. The principal purpose of inventory investment, at least as depicted by current American business attitudes, is to provide needed changes in inventory stocks to service sales. Naturally, goods are sold if available. On the other hand, if sales are overestimated, inventories are permitted to rise to a greater extent than the level of sales would require. Thus, inventories bear the brunt of the failure of production changes to accord with changing sales. The process is exaggerated by the obvious fact that when inventories become too low businessmen struggle to raise them, and thereby add to total economic activity; or when inventories become too high, businessmen struggle to reduce them, and thus cut down on total economic activity.

The usual experience has been about as follows: Production scheduling follows fairly simple rules, dependent upon recent shipment rates, inventory requirements, employment commitments, and any more direct anticipatory information, such as reports of salesmen. In the course of many weeks or months a short-trend projection of past shipments, adjusted for any need to add to or cut down on shop inventories of finished goods, provides a satisfactory basis for setting the production schedule. As the cyclical peak is approached, inventory requirements have been achieved as needed; demand no longer rises fast enough to thwart efforts to build up stocks. Because the trend of sales is leveling off, projection of recent rates tends to be too high. Small additions tend constantly to be made to inventories. This is looked on as desirable, because for a long time unsuccessful efforts were being made to increase inventories, because the prosperous atmosphere lulls a lack of concern, and because inventory requirements are looked on in terms of an

---

[9]Herbert A. Simon, "Theories of Decision-Making in Economics and Behavioral Science," *American Economic Review,* June, 1959, p. 279. In the quotation, "satisficing" is a coined word. Its meaning is clarified by the following quotations:

"If we seek to explain business behavior in the terms of [aspiration levels], we must expect the firm's goals to be not maximizing profit, but attaining a certain level or rate of profit, holding a certain share of the market or a certain level of sales. Firms would try to 'satisfice' rather than to maximize.

". . . Economic man is a *satisficing* animal whose problem solving is based on search activity to meet certain aspiration levels rather than a *maximizing* animal whose problem solving involves finding the best alternatives in terms of specified criteria."

acceptable range, not an exact point. With sales actually leveling off, however, the time comes when the inventory stock begins to exceed the upper limit of the acceptable range. The production schedule is cut, but not drastically. If the timing is similar in many other concerns, reduction in production schedules alone will induce reduced sales in the total economy. Thus, the inventory stock will continue to increase. After this experience is repeated for a few scheduling periods, rising inventory stocks appear threatening, and drastic cuts are made in the production schedule, producing large negative inventory investment.

As frantic efforts are put forth to bring inventory stocks into line with sales, general cumulative contractionary forces are set up in the economy, and total activity is forced down. For a time, negative inventory investment fails to accomplish its purpose, for the decline in sales more than matches the change in inventory stock. Drastic enough action is finally taken, however, and inventory stocks are clearly being brought into line. As this is recognized, little more negative inventory investment is required, so that higher production rates become necessary to maintain the same level of sales. The higher production rates induce further activity because of the income effect; thus, recovery is under way.

Since the war, increasing attention has been given to the control of inventories. The interest of businessmen in this problem no doubt stems from the hope of producing more effective production-planning techniques, and not principally from the point of view of stabilizing general business activity. If true, a rather exciting potentiality is pointed up. If inventory adaptation is the principal business cycle force, and if businessmen are to find effective methods of inventory stabilization, the business cycle problem might appear to be well on the road to effective control.

The control of inventories must stem from relatively detailed levels. The businessman must face the adequacy of specific inventory, not of an amorphous aggregate. True, he must avoid getting down to detailed individual items when there is an almost infinite number of items stocked, but the concrete level to which the control must be carried forces the problem far below the aggregative level on which our analysis is sighted in this book.

The control of individual inventories is greatly abetted by various systems, involving criteria such as reorder points, lot sizes, and lead time. Defining these criteria or explaining their use is outside our purpose,[10] but we should point out that considerable improvement in their use has been achieved since the war. Fundamentally, the problem can be viewed as a series of "stock points," each fed by one or more operations and drained by other operations. Unfortunately, the flow through the stock point is seldom steady. Ordinarily, the principal unsteadiness is pushed back from demand.

Generally, therefore, no mechanical control procedure will work in establishing the needs at stock points unless it is integrated with a forecast of demand. Problems in forecasting demand, obviously, vary greatly between different products and different points in distribution. It is important to note that *demand* of the final buyer and not actual *sales,* represents the needed forecast.[11] The inventory it is desirable to hold at a stock point relates to the *final* sales which are being made or would be made if sufficient supply were available. Potential sales may be more than present supplies can meet, but desired inventory is set by that demand. Any increases in stocks at later points in distribution should not, however, be permitted to raise inventory levels.

The ability to forecast sales or demand satisfactorily must be judged against our understanding of the economic process. As indicated earlier in the chapter, especially in the case of consumer goods, inventory flows at later stages in the distribution process must be understood.

In the case of investment goods a very fluctuating and dynamic demand is involved, and simple forecasts founded on trend projection or on assumed stability are certain to break down at critical points. In fact, a good case could be made that the fluctuation of inventory investment in this area is due to the high variability of the product demand to which it is related.

Furthermore, apparent inventory requirements are induced by the force of cumulative factors in cyclical expansion or contraction. The lesson of Table 11-2 is that the very act of trying to accumulate inventories of consumer goods increases the need for inventory of consumer goods. A similar demonstration could be developed for efforts to accumulate inventories of investment goods. Additionally, there are cumulative and culminating forces, outlined in Chapters

---

[10]An excellent statement and analysis of relation to production planning will be found in John F. Magee, *Production Planning and Inventory Control* (New York: McGraw-Hill Book Co., Inc., 1958). See also Robert G. Brown, *Statistical Forecasting for Inventory Control* (New York: McGraw-Hill Book Co., Inc., 1959).

[11]This point is well stated by Magee, *op. cit.,* p. 106: "Sales represent demand as filtered by the manufacturing and distribution system."

4 and 5, such as shifting relations in construction activity between completion and starting rates, with resulting changes in the level of demand and thus modification of inventory requirements.

To conclude, the exciting idea that we are about to "lick" the business cycle by inventory stabilization is premature, to say the least. Sales forecasts have shown substantial improvement, but the precision with which it would appear that demand must be forecast to avoid cyclical variation has scarcely been approached. Particularly, if sales begin to decline sharply, are businessmen likely to plan confidently, so that sharp decline in inventory investment will be avoided? If not, the major disruptive influence produced by inventory runoff in recession will be likely to persist.

There is no call, however, for discouragement. The progress now being made with aggregative models can be expected in time to improve our understanding enough that the cyclical variation of inventory investment will be at least moderated.[12] Especially, the possibility of obtaining much additional information more promptly by use of electronic calculators will aid in identifying demand changes which are clearly understood.

Seasonal demand provides the basis for a simple model where many companies have effectively employed inventory variation to smooth out production schedules. These are unquestionably cases where activity has been made more stable by recognition of the potentialities of inventory investment to offset undesirable fluctuations in demand. There are more companies, however, which have found the use of inventory variation impractical as a method of offsetting seasonal variation in demand. Aside from technical reasons, such as deterioration in storage or great bulkiness, lack of regularity of seasonal demand is a frequent reason.

If we can make the forecast of demand as obvious for business cycle changes as it is for the most regular seasonal variation, there is no doubt that inventories might be voluntarily accumulated in recession, thereby reducing the impact that a decline in sales might have on activity. Under these circumstances, what happens in seasonal stabilization would become a valid example of potential achievement. Particularly applicable would be readily storable raw materials. For the price of many such raw materials sinks to rela-

---

[12]A summary of some of the important aggregative models will be found in Thomson M. Whitin, *The Theory of Inventory Management* (Princeton: Princeton University Press, 1953), pp. 140–61.

tively low levels, and they could be stored against the need in prosperity when the price rises to high levels.

The situation may be contrasted with what now happens when inventory stocks continue to rise in early recession. No need for any such inventory is foreseen in the planned future, and effective action is taken to initiate a substantial inventory runoff. Such action is, of course, decidedly contractionary.

FOR REFLECTION AND ANALYSIS

1. Why does inventory investment account for much more of the decline in gross national product in a recession than of the rise in GNP in an expansion?
2. Does the manufacturer typically try to adjust for a greater decline than occurs in the final demand for his goods when a recession occurs?
3. Why is the level of sales so important a criterion for the businessman in deciding on needed inventory stocks?
4. Why would the businessman have to take into consideration the changes in expenditures induced by changes in investment on consumer expenditure if he were to keep his inventory stock in adjustment with current sales? Would this be difficult?
5. Compare the problems of judging the unsatisfactory fullment of plans for investment in inventories with those for investment in producers' equipment.
6. Is inventory adaptation the principal business cycle force?
7. What are the chances that businessmen will shortly find effective methods of inventory stabilization?

SELECTED READINGS FOR PART TWO

ABRAMOVITZ, MOSES. *Inventories and Business Cycles, with Special Reference to Manufacturers' Inventories.* New York: National Bureau of Economic Research, Inc., 1950.

A comprehensive study on the yearly movement of manufacturers' inventories.

AMERICAN ECONOMIC ASSOCIATION, COMMITTEE OF. *Readings in Business Cycle Theory.* Homewood, Ill.: Richard D. Irwin, Inc., 1944.

Many especially useful articles, including Kondratieff on long waves, Clark on the acceleration principle, Samuelson on the interaction of multiplier and accelerator, and Ezekiel on the Cobweb Theorem.

HABERLER, GOTTFRIED VON. *Prosperity and Depression.* Rev. ed. Geneva: League of Nations, 1939.

This is the standard work on pre-Keynesian business cycle theory.

HANSEN, ALVIN H. *A Guide to Keynes.* New York: McGraw-Hill Book Co., Inc., 1953.

A very useful statement of many of the implications of Keynesian ideas.

————. *Business Cycles and National Income.* New York: W. W. Norton & Co., Inc., 1951.
  This book contains classic descriptions of various business cycle theories.

HARROD, R. F. "Domar and Dynamic Economics," *Economic Journal,* September, 1959, pp. 451–64.
  A most lucid statement on the multiplier-accelerator growth model.

HICKS, J. R. *A Contribution to the Theory of the Trade Cycle.* London: Oxford University Press, 1950.
  A classic on the multiplier-accelerator model.

JOINT ECONOMIC COMMITTEE. *Staff Report on Employment, Growth, and Price Levels, December 24, 1959.* 86th Cong., 1st sess. Washingington, D.C.: U.S. Government Printing Office, 1960.
  Although some of the conclusions may be controversial, important light is thrown on the postwar recessions.

KEYNES, JOHN MAYNARD. *The General Theory of Employment, Interest, and Money.* New York: Harcourt, Brace & Co., Inc., 1936.
  In addition to the famous general theory contained in Keynes's book, a chapter considers "The Trade Cycle" and comes to some conclusions summarized in Chapter 9.

MATTHEWS, R. C. O. *The Business Cycle.* Chicago: University of Chicago Press, 1959.
  A good summary of most of the modern ideas.

METZLER, LLOYD A. "The Nature and Stability of Inventory Cycles," *Review of Economic Statistics,* August, 1941, pp. 113–29.
  Original statement of the central idea involved in Table 11–2.

NATIONAL PLANNING ASSOCIATION. *Long-Range Projections for Economic Growth: The American Economy in 1970.* Planning Pamphlet No. 107. Washington, D.C., 1959.
  Long-term aggregative forecasts.

NURKSE, RAGNAR. "The Cyclical Pattern of Inventory Investment," *Quarterly Journal of Economics,* August, 1952, pp. 385–408.
  Illustrates how interesting conclusions can be drawn by developing assumptions in quantitative models.

SAULNIER, RAYMOND J. *Contemporary Monetary Theory.* Studies in History, Economics, and Public Law, No. 443. New York: Columbia University Press, 1938.
  Especially useful for summarizations of theories by Hawtrey and Hayek.

SCHUMPETER, JOSEPH A. *History of Economic Analysis.* New York: Oxford University Press, 1954.
  Unusually fertile interpretations of various economic ideas.

————. *The Theory of Economic Development.* Cambridge, Mass.: Harvard University Press, 1949.
  The classic statement of innovation theory; originally published in German in 1911 and translated in 1934.

TAYLOR, OVERTON H. *A History of Economic Thought.* New York: McGraw-Hill Book Co., Inc., 1960.

This book includes valuable insights on the relation of the general stream of economic thought to modern employment theory.

WHITIN, THOMSON M. *The Theory of Inventory Management.* Princeton: Princeton University Press, 1953.

Contains a summarization of several inventory models.

PART

THREE

History of Business Fluctuations

Chapter 12

BUSINESS FLUCTUATIONS BEFORE THE GREAT DEPRESSION

In all honesty, we believe in business fluctuations because we have experienced them. Theories are but rationalizations to aid in explaining how fluctuations take place or to provide a basis in formulating forecasting models. The ideal would be to demonstrate in this series of chapters how history verifies effective theory.

The history chapters cannot be said to measure up to any such ideal, but they do demonstrate that there are instances where some of the theoretical formulations, presented in the preceding chapters, do provide effective descriptions of actual conditions. They also bring out cases where the historical movement is contrary to what certain theories imply. Frankly, however, our factual knowledge is insufficient to trace the intricate interrelations that business cycle theories postulate, especially in the earlier periods.

Therefore, this series of chapters must be looked on as providing illustrations of the variety of economic fluctuations rather than as establishing verifications of theories of fluctuations, much as we might like to see the latter. Clearly, the record of historical experience does aid our understanding of the effectiveness of various theories, but neat generalizations as to what the record indicates regarding them would be too forced to be of great value. The history chapters do lay some foundation for drawing conclusions on one's own and even for setting up some personal rationalizations. This contrasts with a restriction to rationalizations made by others, which is about where the matter stands without some dipping into history.

EARLIER VARIATIONS

The business cycle as we know it today is limited roughly to the last two hundred years. Business variations occurred earlier in the world's history, but they were more or less limited to the influence of outside forces. The weakness or complete absence of internal forces in earlier times is principally accounted for by three factors:

1. Relatively small importance of capitalistic production.
2. Slow economic growth and narrow margin above elemental wants.
3. Restricted markets, so that economic changes did not spread rapidly through the economy.

1. As we have learned, the wide variation in investment is a major factor in the business cycle. Investment has been much more important in the last two hundred years than earlier because it is dependent upon capitalistic production. Much capital has come to be employed in production, and this makes a large volume of investment necessary. Particularly, durable capital investment is subject to wide fluctuations in demand because of changes in the market for the products capital stock will produce. This influence is most simply explained by the accelerator. The accelerator traces investment demand to changes in product demand, and an increase in the accelerator in expansion makes for a continued advance in investment demand even though the growth of product demand slackens. These influences could not have been great when investment played a minor role in the economy.

Aside from limited invention and enterprise, many primitive societies could not have achieved a substantial investment flow because of the lack of credit facilities. Primitive peoples tended to have a high liquidity preference; what little savings they were able to accumulate they held in jewels or hoarded coins, and they were willing to part with them only at onerous interest rates. Without an elastic credit system, businesses could not garner together the funds necessary to permit a large expansion of investment.

2. The economic growth of earlier economies was much less than we experience today, and the standard of living was much lower. These two factors taken in combination must have kept propensity to consume very high. With a slow growth in the standard of living, expenditure lag could not have been important; the principal reason average propensity to consume declines in prosperity is lag in consumer expenditure behind advances in discretionary income to new high levels. The low standard of living meant that little more than the most elemental wants could be satisfied for the bulk of the population. While "elemental wants" appear greater when the standard of living reaches higher levels, living standards have changed so much more than have ideas about

elemental wants that a greater variation in propensity to consume has become possible.

If propensity to consume varied but little in earlier times, the variation in consumer expenditure was small. Consumer respending of income received in preceding periods almost completely supported disposable income at all times. Because investment was unimportant, it could not have produced significant variations. All expenditure tended to maintain itself.

3. When outside forces disturbed the flow of goods and services in earlier times, the effects were not readily carried along to other economic activities because of the limited influence of the market. Markets were principally local, with a large degree of self-sufficiency within small areas. Restricted use of money limited the market. Prices were generally fixed by decree instead of fluctuating toward a position of market adjustment. A change in the supply or demand situation in one area of the economy had little opportunity to spread to other areas. Disturbances thus tended to be localized. The business cycle is a characteristic of the aggregate economy. Disturbances in localized activities are more likely to offset each other than are disturbances which readily spread.

Prices set by custom or decree encouraged little inventory investment, for a strong stimulus to inventory accumulation is a rise in prices. Some inventory accumulation might occur because weather conditions made for varied crop yields, but aggregate economic activity was little affected. The larger crop was produced with about the same labor, so that inventory investment did not lead to increased activity in the way the creation of industrial facilities does.

With little variation in expenditures by consumers or producers and a minimum spreading of their influences through the business system, internal forces played a minor role. Exogenous factors may have been even more influential than they are today, for man lived more at the mercy of cosmic forces. Plagues, fires, and other accidental disturbances were important. War was important, although it could not cut so deeply into customary expenditure patterns as does present-day all-out war, because at no time was expenditure far above the requirements for elemental wants. Government controls and expenditure, although burdensome, may have been less uncertain than they are today. New inventions and new industries were less important. Foreign conditions were generally less disturbing, because industry was localized. On the whole, however, outside forces were probably even more important than they are to us.

A self-generating cyclical movement depends upon variation in internal forces; therefore, exogenous factors led to isolated disturbances rather than to cumulative expansions or contractions. Variation in internal forces was not completely absent at all times and places prior to two hundred years ago. Such variation was perhaps at a minimum under the feudal system of the Middle Ages. Down through the ages, there have been instances of prices fluctuating in the market, and that might induce a price-inventory-accumulation spiral. At times, economic progress was rapid enough that some expenditure lag may have occurred. Under these conditions, rudimentary business cycles may have been encountered at various times in the world's history.

During the last 200 years the strength of internal forces has greatly increased. It is probable, therefore, that characteristics of the business cycle have changed, but the following pages show pronounced similarity over the last 150 years.

AMERICAN INDEPENDENCE TO THE CIVIL WAR

By the last quarter of the eighteenth century, English business activity clearly displayed business cycle fluctuations. Because the United States depended significantly on foreign trade, the British business cycle tended to be superimposed upon our activity. The pattern is disturbed, though, because of our heavy dependence on agriculture, which does not conform closely with business cycle fluctuations. Trade effects of the ending of war resulted in depression to about 1787.

Trade revived in the late 1780's and remained prosperous to the mid-1790's. Stimulation was provided by the formation of the federal government, demonstrating financial strength, including establishment of the First Bank of the United States.

Conditions remained generally prosperous until after the War of 1812, although recessions occurred in 1797–98, 1802–03, and 1807–08, timed fairly closely with British business fluctuations. The principal stimulation in the period came from the sale of goods to European warring powers.

After the War of 1812, beginning in 1815, business was depressed by the reopening of our markets to relatively efficient European producers. Business conditions were greatly confused by financial disturbance, since state banks were issuing paper money without specie backing. This financial situation arose from the termination at the outbreak of the war of the First Bank of the United States, while adjustment to the control of the Second Bank, established shortly after the end of the war, was drawn-out and disturbed. Prices, although lower than during the war, were fairly stable until 1818, and foreign trade was at greatly expanded levels. Deflationary financial policies were adopted by the government in 1819, and prices and foreign trade fell substantially. Business conditions remained moderately depressed through 1823.

The period 1824-34 was prosperous, marked by stable prices, rising foreign trade, an eightfold increase in immigration, and a doubling of the population in urban areas. Canal building represented a first great surge of investment. Very minor recessions were scarcely noticed. Land purchases were encouraged after 1832 by the deposit of government funds in private banks of the West. Public land sales rose from 2.5 million acres in 1832 to 20 million acres in 1836. Recognizing that the exaggerated purchase of these lands was fostered by the ready availability of local bank currency at banks holding newly created federal bank deposits, President Jackson issued his famous Specie Circular in 1836, requiring that payment for government lands be made in specie. This started a major deflationary trend. Total bank deposits declined from $190 million in 1837 to less than $80 million in 1843.

Most of the statistical facts needed to describe the impact of this depression are unavailable—unemployment, manufacturing production, and the like. Qualitative reports, however, indicate that serious declines occurred in expenditures and that unemployment increased. Imports dropped from $180 million in 1836 to substantially less than $100 million in 1843, perhaps to a lower level than that reached in the early 1820's. Foreign trade represents our best indication of the decline occurring in expenditures.

Commodity prices held almost stable until 1839. This is related to the spirit of the times, such that great efforts were made to support speculative positions. Ultimately, the support was unsuccessful, and prices broke sharply from 1839 to 1843.

We suggest that the contraction of 1837-43 is comparable with the two most serious ones our country has experienced—1873-79 and 1929-33. It was preceded by a wave of great investment in canals. When completed, most of these proved to be unprofitable. Apparently, no new investment potentialities of similar importance lurked on the horizon in 1836. In somewhat the same way, a large, unsustainable investment in railroads preceded 1873 and in construction preceded 1929. Uncontrolled speculation in land in the early 1830's may be contrasted with speculation in railroads preceding 1873 and in the stock market preceding 1929. Efforts to bolster speculative positions early in the contraction were similar to the experiences after 1873 and after 1929. All three of these contractions are notable for their length and for the relative stability preceding them.

According to the National Bureau of Economic Research *Business Annals*,[1] the rest of the 1840's (after 1843) was marked by quickly recurring recessions—three, in fact, by 1848. There was a net outflow of capital, instead of investment flowing to the United States. Perhaps the fact that business remained depressed after the 1937 recession until World War II was well along could be thought of as a contrasting situation.

A burst of rapid growth occurred in the 1850's. It may have been sparked by gold discovery in California, which increased gold production from an annual rate of about $1 million to over $50 million. The sweep of improved conditions began in 1849. Foreign trade more than doubled by 1860. Railroad mileage rose from 7,000 to 30,000 miles. National wealth is estimated to have tripled. Urban population nearly doubled.

Advance was most dramatic in the first half of the decade. Prices rose about 15 per cent from 1849 to 1855. A recession occurred in 1854–55. From that time, railroad construction slackened substantially. Prices leveled off and trended downward from 1857 to the beginning of the Civil War, when the lower levels of 1849 again ruled.

A second recession occurred in 1857–58, and another was threatening in 1861 at the outbreak of war. Some evidence was developing that overexpansion had occurred in relation to current needs, such as in railroad development; and it is sometimes held that the country was headed for a period of more depressed conditions. The Civil War precluded any such outcome.

In these early periods, not much can be done in representing aggregate fluctuations quantitatively because of inadequacy of available data. Beginning at the Civil War or a little later, with some risk, we may draw pictures of aggregate fluctuations, as illustrated in Charts 12–1 and 12–2. Although the dating of turning points on

---

[1]For a picture of what is shown by these annals for various countries from 1890–1925, see Chart 25–1, p. 553 and reference there cited.

INDEXES OF UNITED STATES BUSINESS CONDITIONS, 1875–1951*

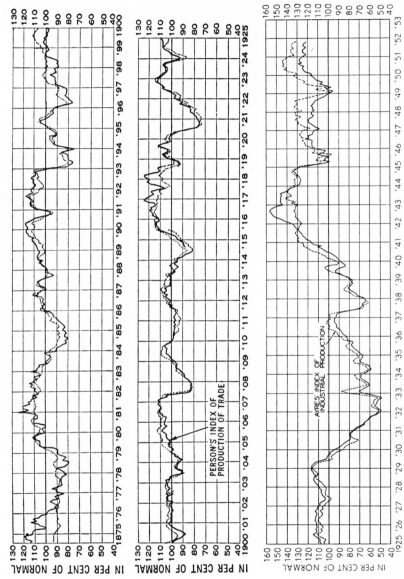

*Ayres' Index in recent years represents an adjustment of the Federal Reserve Board Index of Industrial Production. Persons' Index is kept up to date by Barron's. The difference between the showing of the indexes in the seventies is due to the price element in Ayres' Index at this early period.

For description of Ayres' Index, see Leonard P. Ayres, *Turning Points in Business Cycles* (New York: Macmillan Co., 1939). For recent years a personal request sent to the Cleveland Trust Company is required. For description of Persons' Index, see Warren M. Persons, *Forecasting Business Cycles* (New York: John Wiley & Sons, Inc., 1931); Edwin Frickey, *Barron's Index of Business 1899* (New York: Barron's, 1943).

CHART 12-2

FRICKEY'S STANDARD PATTERN OF SHORT-TERM FLUCTUATIONS IN AMERICAN BUSINESS ACTIVITY, 1866–1914

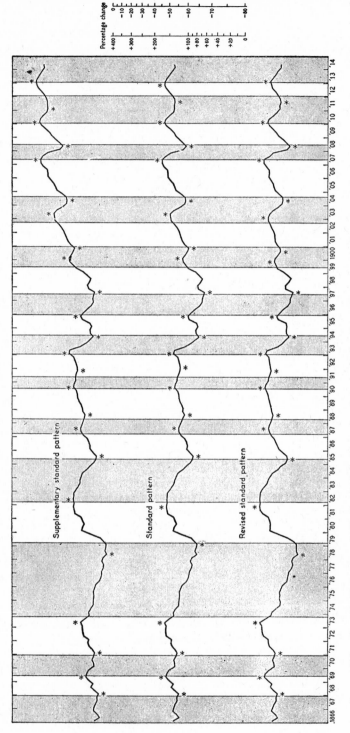

Source: Taken from A. F. Burns and W. C. Mitchell, *Measuring Business Cycles* (New York: National Bureau of Economic Research, Inc., 1946), p. 112. Reproduced with permission.

NOTE: Shaded areas represent "reference contractions" as measured by the National Bureau of Economic Research, white areas "reference expansions." (See description in Chapter 4, especially Chart 4–1.) Asterisks identify peaks and troughs.

these charts may be fairly satisfactory, the amplitude of fluctuation shown cannot be readily defended because the data used to represent it are quite limited, especially in the earlier periods. Also, note should be taken of the fact that effort is made to show fluctuation about growth, rather than growth itself.

CIVIL WAR TO END OF NINETEENTH CENTURY[2]

The fact that war produces urgent demand and drives up total expenditures accounts for its economic effects and the problems to which it inevitably leads. The period from 1861 to 1865 represents the first major disturbance of this sort in the American economy growing out of *domestic* war.[3] For the first time, internal revenue became a major factor in financing the federal government. Although federal government receipts rose about sixfold, expenditures rose about twentyfold, and the deficit rose to nearly $1 billion, contrasting with an earlier maximum deficit of about $30 million in 1847. Federal government debt rose from about $65 million to about $2.7 billion, representing a far greater percentage increase than has occurred in more recent wars.

A doubling occurred in prices, in money in circulation, and in bank deposits. A large part of the money in circulation, at one time nearly half, was represented by "greenbacks" (United States notes not redeemable in gold at par).

Unlike our experience in the two world wars of the twentieth century, prices declined after the end of the war. The postwar experience is related to a large increase in taxation and to substantial government surpluses. The years 1866 and 1867 were depressed, compared with prosperous conditions following in the wake of the recent world wars.

In spite of unfavorable government fiscal policy, rapid development was under way. After 1866, railroad building accelerated. By the time of the downturn into serious depression in 1873, railroad mileage had doubled and had reached approximately a third of the ultimate later achieved in the twentieth century. As currently observed in the 1870's depression, the railroads represented "a large mileage connecting nothing in particular." But the nature of such

---

[2]A most useful study of this period is Rendigs Fels, *American Business Cycles, 1865–1897* (Chapel Hill: University of North Carolina Press, 1959).

[3]In contrast, the War of 1812 produced an increase in War Department expenditures from about $2 million to about $20 million, instead of from about $20 million to about $1 billion, as occurred in the Civil War.

innovation was to provide transportation out into the wilderness; and as it was provided, many new communities were springing up. Residential building was proceeding at a booming rate. Immigration was mounting, and another flurry in urban development was under way. Only the rail lines west of the Mississippi were truly unpromising; this was partly because of difficulty in bridging the river.

A general consensus recognizes overdevelopment to have been achieved by the downturn in 1873. Obviously, capital expansion was not excessive in relation to the ultimate growth of the country, but probably it exceeded current needs. For instance, grain and cotton production had risen rapidly, and farm product prices dropped dramatically in 1870 and continued to trend downward thereafter.

The downturn in 1873 was set off by financing difficulties. These were not founded on basic market instability. Security prices had been fluctuating along a horizontal level until a few months before the downturn, commodity prices had not risen substantially at any time after the war, and bank loans were not excessive. It is true, however, that by the autumn of 1873, important financial houses were engaged to an abnormal extent in financing capital expansion with short-term funds. Notably, Jay & Cooke Co., famous for responsibility in government financing during the Civil War, failed in September, 1873,·because of inability to cover short-term loans used as interim financing in building the Northern Pacific Railroad. Following on the heels of similar fiascoes, a severe monetary crisis was created. Before the crisis, however, indications were clear that the railroad companies were overextended; twenty-five railroads had defaulted on their bonds before September in 1873.

One factor in the crisis involved technical conditions of the National Banking System, which tended to concentrate the banking reserves of country banks in deposits in New York banks, and involved a dependence on government bond reserves, while the bonds tended to be paid off in prosperity. Both of these conditions were unfavorable in September, 1873, with the government running a surplus and country banks needing funds to finance the movement of crops. However, the situation was little worse than in autumns of preceding years. Funds for moving crops provided a problem only because seasonal difficulties came to a head in the autumn. The government surplus was less in 1873 than in the preceding years, but continuing surpluses had reduced the volume of government bonds available for reserves.

More important was the reduced availability of European investment funds. This was at least partly due to the indication of clouded prospects for the railroads.

The ensuing panic was brief. The New York banks used clearinghouse certificates, based on pooled reserves of the banks, to make current payments. These were issued so freely that cash payments were partially suspended for only a few days, and in two months the reserve ratio of New York banks again exceeded the legal minimum. No doubt, a short interruption was induced by the panic in some business activity, notably in the movement of farm crops, and we can surmise that confidence was shocked. At the maximum the panic itself could have been no more than a minor influence.

The long contraction, lasting until 1879 and exceeding in length any other in American history, undoubtedly was deeper seated. Three factors were of major importance: (1) overdevelopment when the contraction began, (2) procrastination and disagreement on policy, and (3) contractionary governmental action.

The evidence of overexpansion is emphasized above. Extensive freight rate wars among the railroads in 1876 provide additional evidence that overbuilding had occurred.

All through the contraction, there was evidence of failure to come to grips with the problem of adjustment. In January, 1875, the Resumption Act was passed, calling for redemption of greenbacks in gold four years later and calling for a 20 per cent decrease in outstanding greenbacks before that date. In a way, this was legislating a long period of uncertainty. In the meantime, many inflationary bills were proposed, some of which were passed.

Effective actions were instituted in 1877 to prepare for the implementation of the Resumption Act. Two more years of falling prices were thus assured. Legislation was proposed, and occasionally passed, to regulate the railroads and railroad rates. This legislation tended to scare off investors.

Fels holds that, in terms of output, the contraction was singularly mild.[4] If true, it does not follow that the depression lacked seriousness. So long a mild decline, in the face of the great growth potential which existed, might be considered a perilous depression.

The slow, steady decline in prices and slow, steady increase in business failures are ample testimony that usual culminating forces

---

[4]*Op. cit.*, p. 107. Note that the decline in Persons' Index of Industrial Production and Trade, from 1875 to 1877, is wholly accounted for by decline in bank clearings in seven cities, which may have been largely financial. Beginning in 1877, pig iron production is included; this series showed no decline in 1877, but did in 1878. The bank clearings series also continued to decline in 1878. See Chart 12–1, p. 245.

posited in business cycle theory were ineffective. Factors other than those ordinarily experienced in short recessions must be considered responsible.

A substantial degree of railroad capital expansion got under way in 1877. Under these circumstances, the mystery is that the contraction continued for two more years. Significant declines continued in residential building. Immigration fell every year during the contraction until, in 1878, it was only a third of the 1873 figure.

The renewed railroad activity finally sparked a recovery in 1879. Resumption of paying greenbacks in gold eliminated the contractionary force of the preparatory efforts and inspired confidence of investors. A contributory factor was abnormal increases in farm income resulting from large crops here and shortages abroad.

Railroads were expanded at a rapid rate all during the 1880's. Their growth was exceptionally rapid until 1882. The expansion represented principally the completion of main lines started before the 1870's depression. Immigration surged from less than 150,000 in 1878 to nearly 800,000 in 1882, about two thirds of the maximum rate attained in the twentieth century; it then receded rapidly until 1886.

The downturn in 1882 appears to be related to the completion of railroad projects, with industrial activity rounding off and starting a slow decline. No major new railroads were being started. By the spring of 1884 the slow, unspectacular recession had lasted two years. At that time the overextension of a large brokerage firm, Grant and Ward, set off a financial crisis in Wall Street. The issue of clearinghouse certificates, as in 1873, quickly brought financial forces under control. The downswing accelerated, although unfavorable agricultural conditions were about as influential as the delayed financial panic.[5]

Corn production had increased substantially, and prices had halved. Some of the increased farm production was in remote regions so that relatively constant transportation costs reduced the farm value to a vanishing point and corn became a common fuel in Kansas.

By the spring of 1885 the contraction had lasted three years. The length warrants the designation of deep depression. Except for the length and delayed financial crisis, however, there is little that differentiates the contraction from an ordinary recession. After so long

---

[5]Possibly the panic is also related to the tendency of businessmen to maintain output and build up inventories earlier in the recession. See Fels, *op. cit.*, p. 129.

a decline, the typical culminating forces presumably were less responsible for the upturn than in most recessions.

As the upturn occurred in May, 1885, security prices had stabilized following the crisis, commodity prices were steady, residential construction was rising, government expenditures were increasing slightly, monetary influences had become slightly favorable, and foreign trade relations were beginning to improve. Business activity advanced only slowly until railroad reorganizations were completed later in 1885, and new construction plans were being implemented. By the second half of 1886, railroad construction was proceeding at a rapid rate.

The railroad activity in 1886 and 1887 was largely done by existing companies in building feeder lines. Taken by increase in mileage alone, railroad expansion reached an all-time peak in 1887; but because of other types of railroad investment expenditure, only a slight, gradual decline occurred in total railroad investment after 1887. Housing construction declined somewhat, farm crops were poor, and agricultural exports dropped substantially in 1888. Passage of the Interstate Commerce Act in April, 1887, no doubt was a temporary dampening factor on railroad investment.

A minor recession developed from 1887 to 1888. Perhaps the typical inventory culmination experienced in the twentieth century was a major factor, although inventory investment data are not available. Activity in the new steel industry showed its first substantial decline in 1888. Bottlenecks had been reached in 1887, producing some delay in railroad construction. These facts are similar to those developing in twentieth-century recessions.

The expansion from 1888 to 1890 showed no spectacular advance in any particular line of activity, although durable production was clearly rising rapidly, as indicated by the outstanding advance in steel production. A notable characteristic of the expansion was the movement of prices, which declined in 1889 and did not advance much from then until the downturn. Perhaps this was the result of monetary forces, inasmuch as money in circulation increased scarcely at all in 1889. Interest rates also declined and remained below the 1887 peak until 1891.

The 1890 downturn was marked by British recall of American funds. A factor in the recall of funds, no doubt, was passage of the Sherman Silver Purchase Act, which provided a basis for questioning the soundness of our currency. The movement was brought to a climax by failure of famous London investment bankers, notably

Baring Brothers, who found recall of American funds necessary as an outgrowth of the collapse of investments made in the Argentine. An important source of American investment funds was thus removed.

These influences were short-lived. After a sharp decline in the early part of 1891, steel production shot up to reach the 1890 peak late in the year. The crisis of the London investment companies subsided. Passage of the McKinley Tariff Act late in 1890 provided some trade protection.

The short contraction, therefore, appears to have been ended largely by exogenous factors. One factor, a rapid rise in agricultural prices, may have been related to an unusual type of inventory runoff. Crop shortages abroad led to heavy exports of farm products and drove up prices; but American crops were also short in 1890, so that substantial increases in farm income arose from the runoff of inventories of farm products. The 1891 crop prospects were good.

Expansion occurred in the United States from 1891 to 1893 in the face of continued depression abroad. Railroad and housing investment rose substantially in 1892; but, as Fels notes, there was no sign of exuberance. In spite of depressed conditions abroad, large increases in food exports occurred in 1892 as an accompaniment of bountiful harvests, but farm prices were driven back to the much lower prerecession levels. Even though exports increased, gold was being withdrawn because of continued fear that we would leave the gold standard. Foreign investment funds were not forthcoming to sustain the investment market.

Exports declined dramatically in 1893 with continued foreign depression and lower farm crop levels. This, taken together with the fact that foreign investment funds were not available in sufficient quantity to keep investment activity rising, accounts for the downturn which occurred early in 1893.

Only weeks after the downturn occurred, the contraction was speeded up by the development of panics, set off by the failure of the Reading Railway. The spectacular Reading failure was merely representative of many others in railroads, iron and steel companies, and banks. Fels characterizes the problems of these companies as (1) overindebtedness and (2) excessive inventory accumulation growing out of attempts to maintain high cartel prices.[6] Substantial inventory liquidation occurred in the recession.

---

[6]*Op. cit.*, p. 185.

The financial situation grew steadily worse. Gold exports became exceptionally large because of doubt regarding the stability of our currency. This was partially responsible for widespread reduction of credit by the banks. Some stock prices dropped fantastically. By the summer of 1893, culminating forces were slowing down the contraction and setting in motion the forces which led to revival in mid-1894. The contraction had brought falling prices, leading to an increase in exports and to reduced imports because our income had fallen. Low security prices were beginning to attract foreign buyers, and high interest rates were attracting foreign money. The continued loss of gold assured that a special session of Congress would repeal the Sherman Silver Purchase Act, promising foreign investors that the silver bloc would not drive the country off the gold standard.

The high failure rate slowed down in the summer of 1893 but did not end. A substantial number of new companies, however, was starting up. The following months to mid-1894 may be characterized as a transitional period. Perhaps the upturn would be dated late in 1893, with the onset of the powerful culmination noted above, except for paralyzing strikes in the spring of 1894, high-lighted by the famous coal strike. The march of Coxey's army of unemployed on Washington was also indicative of the spirit of the times.

With the end of major strikes, business activity improved, and the expansion phase was under way. If any embarrassing inventories were still overhanging the market, they must have been absorbed during the strike period. The ensuing expansion was a faltering one, with the peak attained late in 1895, a year and a half after the trough, and scarcely reaching the previous high level of activity. This is one of those rare cases in American history when recovery to reasonably full activity was not achieved (1937 is the only other clear case). Probably, the expansion which did occur was largely sparked by inventory investment rather than by durable investment.

The federal government was running a deficit from 1894 to the end of the decade for the first time since the Civil War; but for the time being, it was more contractionary than expansionary. Great difficulty was being experienced by the Treasury in maintaining required gold reserves. Fear of the soundness of our money had not yet ended, and required government borrowing was made difficult.

The disturbances involved in failures and strikes of the preceding contraction presumably remained to haunt the anticipatory attitudes of decision makers in the expansion. The agricultural situation was on the whole depressive. With large corn crops, prices sank to all-time lows in 1895 and 1896. Similarly, cotton prices sank to an all-time low in 1894 and, after a recovery in 1895, began declining again with renewed increase in cotton production. The low peak level in 1895, then, is attributed to the disturbed monetary, financial, and labor situations, and to a generally unsatisfactory agricultural market. Furthermore, it is sometimes thought that, with railroads representing a receding field for investment, capital formation had run out of steam.

The following downturn is related to a threat of war which occurred in December, 1895. On the recommendation of the President, we were intervening in a boundary dispute in Venezuela. Unless the British yielded to our position, war appeared imminent. Panic broke out in the stock market, and a rash of failures developed. The British were conciliatory, but currency embarrassment persisted. That embarrassment was accentuated by Bryan's campaign on the "cross-of-gold" slogan. The election of McKinley was generally considered as irrevocable acceptance of sound money, and recovery began by mid-1897.

BEGINNING OF THE CENTURY THROUGH WORLD WAR I

From this point forward, for seven years, a much broader-based investment expansion arose. Steel production doubled without experiencing substantial intervening declines like those which occurred in 1893 and 1896. Cement production tripled. Electric energy production rose by leaps and bounds.

This was the beginning of a period of rising prices which was to last until after World War I. The rise in prices to 1904 was over a fourth. This rise was sparked partly by a resurgence of gold production. It is anomalous that, during the long period when worries were general about soundness of the currency, prices were in a long, sweeping decline; but when the soundness at last seemed assured, rapid price increases occurred.

Two minor recessions developed: in 1900, and from 1903 to 1904. The first may have been related to decrease in government expenditures following the Spanish-American War, and the second to financial security manipulation. In any case, stock prices dropped 40 per cent from mid-1902 to the end of 1903, but activity declined little in either period. Of course, with long-term expansion occurring so rapidly, a leveling-off clearly marked a recession. The major influence in both cases appears to have been culmination of internal forces within the business system.

The expansion from 1904 to 1907 was of major proportions. Steel production almost doubled, even though production in 1904 was only slightly below earlier peaks. The output of consumer durable goods rose by over 40 per cent in current prices, of semidurables over 30 per cent, and of perishables over 20 per cent. Immigration rose 50 per cent to all-time peak levels. Electric power production much more than doubled. Although growth in the use of electric power was most notable, expansion spread widely through much of industry, including many types of capital formation and of consumer goods.

Prices rose, especially in 1907. Credit experienced expansion, partially indicated by about 30 per cent increase in bank loans and in deposits. Also, trust companies, often unrestricted by the banking laws, branched out into commercial banking and added to credit even more rapidly. Their inadequate reserves were a major factor in the bank panic which was experienced in the last quarter of 1907.

The panic was set off by failure of the Knickerbocker Trust Company. The now familiar clearinghouse certificates kept financial operations under reasonable control in the face of inadequate bank reserves. Actually, the downturn occurred at mid-year, although the rate of contraction speeded up with the banking panic at the end of the year.

The decline was very rapid in the first half of 1908. This is usually explained by the financial panic at the end of 1907. Growing out of the recession, the inadequacies of the National Banking System became the leading problem of the day. Congressional investigations, reflected in the famous reports of the Aldrich Committee, provided studies which set the framework for later development of the Federal Reserve System.

We suspect, however, that inventory deflation was just as important. Banking statistics show a reduction of only 3 per cent in credit for the year 1908 as a whole, but most of the deflation occurred late in 1907 and cannot be segregated from earlier rises in that year. There were evidences of serious disturbance before the panic developed. Cotton consumption (by producing mills) had declined substantially by the time of the downturn in mid-1907, and prices of metals and metal products were declining by then.[7]

---

[7]Many businessmen could remember the difficult experience of 1893, when over-indebtedness and excessive inventory accumulation had gotten them into trouble. After the long advance with rising prices, many inventory stocks must have been on the high side. Possibly, 1907 is the first clear case of the modern "inventory recession." Note, however, the above discussion of some earlier recessions. See, for instance, remark about the 1887–88 recession on p. 251.

In any case, the recession was sharp and short, which is the typical behavior when inventory runoff represents the principal contraction. After a long and substantial rise, with sharp advances in the final months of expansion, experience teaches us that some overaccumulation of inventory is to be expected. No substantial decline occurred in expenditures for durable investment; and if it had, the contraction would have been longer.

The expansion, beginning in June, 1908, lasted only a year and a half, but it was vigorous. Consumer expenditures rose, with a growing demand about comparable with the two earlier expansions. Steel production more than doubled from the bottom of the recession, but reached levels only about 10 per cent above 1907. Electric power production continued its rapid advance. Cement production peaked preceding levels by 50 per cent. Most types of capital formation experienced satisfactory, but not unusual, advance.

Prices were continuing to rise as in earlier years, with the rise accelerating late in the expansion. Furthermore, prices increased for three months after the downturn in 1910. The decline in activity was minor, and it leveled off after a few months. It was unusual in that, after leveling off, activity remained approximately stable for two years.

The experience does not well fit typical business cycle behavior. If an induced inventory runoff occurred, it should have led to a culmination, not to stability at the cycle trough. If overexpansion were recognized, this should have led to a dwindling-away of investment projects, inducing a continued decline in activity. Consumer expenditures, including durables, continued to rise, so they do not provide an explanation.

The fact is that the period was one in which there were numerous restrictive governmental actions. An act was passed conferring on the Interstate Commerce Commission power to suspend freight rate advances and to institute rate reductions. This power was used early in 1911. Trust prosecutions were being pressed, including cases against the American Tobacco Company and the Standard Oil Company. The general apathy existent in business, even though the level was reasonably satisfactory, was reflected in the stock market, where the volume of transactions was extremely low.

Expansion began with the opening of 1912. Commodity prices had begun to increase almost a year before, and the uptrend continued through the short ensuing expansion. The economy surged forward to virtual capacity levels by the end of the year and then turned downward. Interest rates rose to higher levels than had appeared since the seventies, aside from panic periods. Steel industry operations came about as near capacity as they have reached in any nonwar periods.

The high interest rates appear to have been contractionary. Residential construction turned slightly downward; and so did the purchase of business motor vehicles, which had been doubling yearly. The purchase of railway equipment, which had zoomed upward from 1911, leveled off.

Again, we have no evidence of substantial deflationary effects of culminating inventory levels or of overexpansion of durable products. Total activity declined only slightly until early 1914. The volatile steel industry dropped about a third by the end of 1913, a proportion in keeping with a mild recession. Prices no more than leveled off until 1914.

Early in 1914, months before the war began, exports declined with the onset of foreign depression, producing a negative trade balance for the first time since 1910. The decline in activity speeded up, and prices began moving noticeably lower for the first time in the recession. With the outbreak of war in Europe at midyear, financial difficulties arose, largely because of European recall of funds, and activity continued to decline until the end of the year. By that time, our exports had speeded up, and the initial stages of stimulation from European war spending were being felt.

If we look at the business cycle experience after the 1908 upturn in terms of periods of expansion versus periods of contraction, the picture appears quite unfavorable. Thirteen months of expansion are followed by 24 months of contraction, and then 12 months of expansion are followed by 23 months of contraction: netted, 25 months of expansion compared with 47 months of contraction. This contrasts unfavorably with the common experience of long expansions and short contractions. One interpretation is that serious economic difficulties were headed off by the occurrence of war. We disagree. Rather, the above facts indicate that operations were continuing close to capacity levels until the initial effects of the war were felt. The theory that deep depression was imminent appears to overemphasize the instability of the economy. We might better conclude that some evidence was appearing that the cyclical movement seemed to be virtually damped out. Even if we play up the decline which arose early in 1914 because of foreign business contraction, the answer is not changed a great deal. Depression had lasted abroad only briefly before war broke out. The burden of proof is on those who contend that the foreign developments otherwise would have grown into a deep depression.

The war produced the usual expansionary expenditure effects. During the years 1914–16, our defense expenditures rose not at all. Our exports, however, more than doubled. Although our crude material imports were stimulated enough that total imports increased, the export increase was far greater; and the trade balance rose to over $3 billion, as compared with a previous maximum of only a fifth as much. Both output and prices were driven up. Manufacturing production rose over a third to a level not exceeded during the war. Wholesale prices rose in about the same proportion. Steel *capacity* was driven up about 20 per cent.

After we entered the war in April, 1917, government expenditures rose rapidly, reaching a maximum early in 1919, after the war ended. Figured for the two years, federal government expenditures rose about twenty-five times, while receipts rose about fivefold. By 1918 the deficit came to $13 billion, and the debt had been driven up twentyfold.

Activity shrank somewhat with urgent war demands removed, and the National Bureau of Economic Research marks a trough in the spring of 1919. About all that was occurring, however, was withdrawal of resources driven into use by the war, plus dislocations which arose with demobilization and with shift of resources to peacetime use.

THE TWENTIES

Prices continued their ascent. By mid-1920 the wholesale price index was registering a level 100 per cent above that of six years earlier, and nearly 25 per cent above that at the end of the war a year and a half earlier. The expectation of price increases became widespread. This led to a rapid increase in inventory accumulation, at least in the later stages of the expansion. Residential building rose dramatically in 1919, in view of the housing shortage, but declined substantially in 1920 with the extremely high interest rates then prevailing. Business equipment expenditures rose scarcely at all, and nonresidental private construction expenditures advanced less than might have been expected. Public construction expenditures in constant prices dropped two thirds from 1918 to 1920, in view of virtual elimination of military construction.

The 1920–21 recession was marked by inventory runoff. With a high inventory accumulation, declining prices, and a short-term interest rate of about 8 per cent by mid-1920, an urge to deplete inventories was inevitable. The leveling-off of prices was induced by a shift in federal government finances from a large deficit in the first half of 1919 to a balanced budget in 1920, and by lower food prices with the rest of the world getting back into full production. Both of these factors are related to shift in the foreign trade balance, which, with slight exaggeration, can be said to have halved yearly from $4 billion in 1919 to $400 million in 1923. The decline in exports is related to greater self-sufficiency of foreign countries, especially European, and to the elimination of foreign credits provided by the federal government.

By mid-1920, businessmen generally became anxious to reduce inventories. The forces of inventory runoff, as explained in Chapter 11, boiled to a culmination by a year later. Commodity prices had declined over 40 per cent. Industrial production was down nearly a third. Steel production in July dropped to the lowest level since 1904.

Because of the technical nature of inventory culmination, industrial production snapped back quickly; and before the end of 1922, it had reached new high levels. Average wholesale prices, however, showed no rise. Prices fluctuated in the following years, but were to end the dynamic decade at the same level, about 40 per cent above prewar.

The stability of prices is indicative of the apparent calm of the period. Work stoppages because of strikes, etc., dropped steadily and became inconsequential. Wage rates, with a few exceptions like the building trades, remained virtually stable. Federal government expenditures held at a little more or a little less than $3 billion every year from 1922, and a federal budget surplus always was achieved. Even foreign trade appeared stable, with merchandise exports holding between $4 billion and $5 billion after 1920, although the trade balance did fluctuate with business cycle changes. Death rates changed little, and birth rates steadily declined. Immigration came under rigid control and leveled off at 300,000 a year after the middle of the decade.

As will be more fully explained below, business cycle fluctuations appeared to be relatively unimportant. The standard of living was rising at an exceptionally rapid rate early in the decade. This appears to be related to a technological awakening growing out of experiences during the war.

The two most dramatic stimulants leveled off well before the period was over. Automobile production doubled from its 1920 high to 1923, but later only slightly exceeded that high. Residential building tripled from 1920 to 1926 and then slid off. Nonresidential private construction, which represented the third most dramatic influence, did continue to rise to 1929, but most of the steam was gone after 1926. Within these three important durable goods areas, some rapid expansions occurred in the late twenties, while other divisions of the aggregates declined. Notably, there was a rapid late rise in office building and apartment house construction, resulting in obvious overbuilding. Even in the parts of these aggregates which leveled off near the end of the prosperous period, overexpansion was recognized when depression began. Expansion was principally sustained in the latter part of the prosperity by advance in various types of producer equipment, in chemicals, and in newer types of consumer durables, e.g., radios.

Consumer expenditures were advancing almost as rapidly in the late as in the early twenties, nearly 5 per cent per year. The most rapid advance shifted from durables in the first part of the period to services in the last part. One may speculate that the rising service expenditures arose from limited additional penetration of goods markets with rising inflexibility of prices, the increased maintenance cost of a growing stock of consumer durables, and a feeling of wealth which accompanied the growing speculative attitude.

At the 1929 peak level, stock prices averaged three times as high as the peak preceding the 1924 recession and more than twice as high as two or three years before. This tremendous upsurge was financed by credit—some $8 billion of brokers' loans and perhaps nearly as much in personal loans made by banks to individuals. The capital gains shown by current prices were an important stimulant of consumer expenditures in the late twenties. Added to this was an unprecedented growth of consumer credit, which rose with the advance in personal income; instalment debt rose from $1 billion in the early twenties to over $3 billion in 1929. The remarkable thing is that other short-term loans increased scarcely at all, commodity prices moved along a horizontal trend, wage rates were stable, and interest rates had remained stable at historically reasonable rates (about 4 per cent) until the rapid stock market credit expansion beginning in 1928.

The explanation is that there came about an almost universal conviction that we had emerged into a New Era. There would be "no more depressions." A great growth potential lay ahead. The high stock prices were discounting it.

As we have said, the recessions which occurred were minor and only slightly interrupted the advance of the twenties. There were two of them—from 1923 to 1924 and from 1926 to 1927. The 1923–24 recession may be ranked as comparable with the 1957–58 one, while that occurring in 1926–27 is milder than any which has occurred since except for the scarcely noticeable decline at the end of World War II.[8]

Measured on a yearly basis, total consumer expenditures as an aggregate did not decline in either recession. Consumer durable expenditures did decline slightly in 1927. In each recession the major declines were primarily in inventory investment and secondarily in producer durables.

The 1923–24 recession represents what has come to be called an "inventory recession," since a decrease in inventory investment accounted for the major part of the decline in gross national product. However, even among the forces we can measure, other influences should be noted.

The output of most nondurable goods, for instance, had leveled off well before the peak. This, of course, tended to lead to a reversal in inventory stocking (see Chapter 11), but the leveling must be explained. Partly, general leveling was due to approach to capacity levels; and partly, it was because funds were harder to obtain, as indicated by slight rises in interest rates. Stock prices receded before the downturn occurred in mid–1923, and this might be taken as indicative of a questioning of the general outlook. Commodity prices also began to decline slightly before the business cycle downturn.

Even though inventories lay at the center of the movement, most expenditure groups and economic processes were affected. The advance of most consumer expenditures slackened, and likewise did private, nonresidential construction. As noted above, expenditures for producer equipment declined. In a period with less obvious demand potential, its influence would have come closer to that of inventories.

Wholesale and consumer prices dropped. Short-term interest rates halved. Industrial production dropped about 20 per cent and factory employment about 15.

As activity leveled off at the end of the rapid expansion from

---

[8]See, for instance, Geoffrey H. Moore, *Measuring Recessions,* Occasional Paper 61 (New York: National Bureau of Economic Research, Inc., 1958).

1921 to 1923, many inventory stocks looked too large. The inventory runoff which followed reached a typical rapid culmination. A minor favorable factor was occurrence of the first advance in export of crude foodstuffs since 1919 and at substantially improved prices. The recession was disturbing only in industrial centers; and compared with the preceding one, it seemed like a minor annoyance.

The early rise in 1924 was as rapid as that which occurred in 1921; but it soon leveled because, with the milder recession, activity was closer to capacity levels. As peak levels were reached, expansion in the principal strategic areas—automobiles and private construction—had reached an approximate summit. Notably, these areas held near the high level until the onset of the Great Depression, but the further advance in activity as a whole was spreading into many other areas.

Downturn occurring late in 1926 was scarcely noticeable. At the worst, industrial production was down only about 6 per cent, and only 2 per cent except for a few months late in 1927. These months marked a substantial decline in automobile production, with Ford out of production to change models.

Wholesale prices peaked late in 1925 and were off 3 per cent in 1926, with the decline continuing to mid-1927. The rise in industrial production had leveled off for nearly a year before the downturn. Under these circumstances, little incentive remained to add to inventories, and inventory investment dropped to approximately zero and held there for two years. The decline in inventory investment was mild enough that no sharp upturn was induced by its culmination—as, for instance, occurred in 1924. Elsewhere, no more than leveling occurred except for automobiles and for a slight reduction in expenditures for business equipment.

Early in 1928 the coming boom in producer equipment was indicated by sharp rises in new orders for machine tools, foundry equipment, and electric hoists. Automobile production was reattaining peak levels. The experience is more like the mid-twentieth-century conception of "rolling readjustment"—that new types of demand are forthcoming when old ones run out—than the classic type of business cycle. Perhaps the chief distinction between this and a typical business cycle is an almost complete absence of lack of confidence. As construction expenditures failed to gain, their place in the advance in demand was taken by consumer expenditures for goods and services and by increased expenditures for business equipment. Generally, inventories were not getting out of hand, although there were exceptions such as the exuberance evidenced in automobile production in 1929.

New-era confidence called forth demand, like continued high construction expenditure or automobile production in excess of retail sales. In retrospect, this can be seen to have gotten the economy in trouble, but who can say that unwavering confidence might not have sustained demand indefinitely? That would be true, however, only if the problems to be faced had been solely those of lopsided expansion.

With the difficulties compounded by the financial ones which arose, no such simple solution appears comprehensible. Nonetheless, the paradoxical fact is that to a large extent the new-era faith is traceable to the ascribed achievements of monetary control. The Federal Reserve monetary control did not become effective until after the 1921 recession because, in the preceding expansion, the Federal Reserve was saddled with support of the Victory Loan bond market. Without arguing about the timing, we cannot question the fact that the Federal Reserve took the right steps for stabilization in open-market sales and purchases and in the setting of rediscount rates (see Chapter 23 for fuller explanation of these measures) in the contractions and expansions in the 1923–24 and 1927–28 experiences.[9] Granted the faith in these measures generally prevalent in the twenties, we cannot deny that they had an influence in smoothing out the recessions which occurred.

Financial control was not maintained, however. It is true that, except for declines in 1924 and 1926–27, the commodity price level was kept stable. Most notably, commodity prices moved generally downward after an initial weak advance following the 1927 recession. Currency and demand deposits rose only about 25 per cent from 1922 to 1929, while industrial production rose twice as much. Payments, as represented by bank debits, however, doubled. This was achieved by a 50 per cent increase in use of the money supply (turnover rate). Speed-up in the use of money was almost entirely concentrated in the expansion from 1927 to 1929. If we must point

---

[9] See E. A. Goldenweiser, *American Monetary Policy* (New York: McGraw-Hill Book Co., Inc., 1951), pp. 137–50; New York Clearing House Association, *The Federal Reserve Re-examined* (New York, 1953), pp. 56–58 and 84–85. The Federal Reserve is sometimes taken to task for not taking sufficiently contractionary open-market actions in 1925–26. See, for instance, Maurice W. Lee, *Economic Fluctuations: Growth and Stability* (Homewood, Ill.: Richard D. Irwin, Inc., 1959), pp. 167–70. We may question, nevertheless, whether expansion in 1925 to 1926 appeared excessive enough at the time to warrant contractionary policy.

a moral, a control of the money supply will not necessarily restrict spending because the rate of its use may be speeded up.

A tightening of money conditions began in mid-1928 with a continuance of the rapid expansion of brokers' loans which started in the 1927 recession and with return of a rapid expansion of private security loans and instalment credit which was under way before the 1927 recession. The result was an exaggerated overextension of credit in these areas, in spite of effective credit control in productive transactions. This got us into trouble. (Later, public demands arose for qualitative credit control.)

FOR REFLECTION AND ANALYSIS

1. Discuss the distinction between business cycles and the kind of economic variation ordinarily experienced over two hundred years ago.
2. Contrast the depressions beginning in 1836 and in 1873.
3. Discuss the influence of railroad investment decade by decade for five decades beginning with the 1850's.
4. How did American business conditions relate to those in the rest of the world in the early 1890's?
5. Outline growth in America for the ten years beginning with 1897.
6. What do you think the failure of the Knickerbocker Trust Company had to do with the 1907–08 recession?
7. How do you explain the relative brevity of expansion periods from 1908 to World War I?
8. Why do you think that foreign trade virtually halved every year from 1919 to 1923?
9. Explain the nature of inventory culmination such as occurred at the peak in 1920 and the trough in 1921.
10. Explain the paradoxical position that, in terms of most standard measures, the twenties ranked high as a period of stability, while great instability was developing within the economy.
11. Contrast the three recessions which occurred in the twenties.

Chapter 13

THE GREAT DEPRESSION

AND WORLD WAR II

The Great Depression was partly a heritage of the twenties and partly dependent on the environment developing in the depression. As in the case of individual persons, the relative importance of inheritance and environment can never be finally determined. About all that we can do is to point out influential forces of both types and identify some of the more obvious known effects. Before turning to a summary of the legacy of the twenties, we look briefly at the comparable influence of the preceding prosperity on earlier deep depressions.

EFFECT OF PRECEDING PROSPERITY ON DEEP DEPRESSIONS

There are important contrasts between the precedents of the depression of the 1930's and those of the 1830's and 1870's. These relate to durable investment, speculation, and credit exuberance on the one side and to the apparent stability of preceding prosperity on the other.

Important canal building began in 1817 and, encouraged by the success of the Erie Canal, surged forward to a high peak in the middle 1830's. In later phases, more and more canals were proving financially unsuccessful; and at the time of precipitous drop in this kind of activity about 1836, little promise for future investment remained. The rapid investment had been encouraged by state subsidies, which also helped to draw foreign investment funds into the private investment projects. Added to the burst of investment in canals were the building of toll roads and the building of steamboats. These activities declined at about the same time as that in canal building. The federal government did not engage in public works expansion during the ensuing depression, in accordance with a policy set by Andrew Jackson as early as 1829.[1] Not only did the rise in investment end in the mid-1830's, but no basis remained for sustaining anywhere near the then existing levels.

As explained in the preceding chapter, vast increases in the sale of public lands, especially in 1835 and 1836, financed by issue of state bank currency, were eliminated and followed by currency deflation as a result of the Specie Circular. Commodity prices, which had risen a fourth from 1834 to 1839, declined rapidly in 1840. Because of the support of speculative positions, prices on the average continued to rise long after the decline in activity.

Although the period from 1824 to 1834 was one of rapid advance, prosperity had all of the appearances of reasonable stability. Commodity prices were stable, or actually showed a greater tendency to fall than to rise. However, the great wave of land speculation in 1835 and 1836 was accompanied by credit expansion.

Turning to the 1870's, it is clear that a rush of railroad investment preceded the downturn in 1873. Like canal building in the earlier experience, railroad building was supported by government subsidies, in this case by federal government land grants, and heavily financed by a large flow of foreign investment. Investment could not be sustained after 1873 because foreign funds became generally unavailable and because conviction arose that the railroads were overbuilt. This conviction was founded principally on unsatisfactory financial results as many lines came into operation.

Speculation was marked in the principles espoused by the major financiers, such as Jay Gould and Jim Fisk, whose purpose was not essentially to provide effective railroad facilities, but to maximize security profits in issue flotations. It is difficult to estimate how much of the provided investment funds flowed into underwriting profits, but they must have been substantial and gave the investment expansion a significant speculative tinge. Sharp rises in steel and coal prices in 1872 are also indicative of a speculative fervor. As in the 1830's, note should be taken of the fact that speculative developments occurred late in the expansion. While the traditional type of credit expansion did not arise, two types of credit disturbance created a similar effect.

Bank credit is commonly used to provide temporary financing by investment banking firms. Largely because of a lag in the flow of regular investment funds, this practice became exaggerated in

---

[1]See Norman J. Silberling, *The Dynamics of Business* (New York: McGraw-Hill Book Co., Inc., 1943), pp. 217–18.

1873. The result was a large volume of "undigested" securities, which, when long-term financing faltered, led to a banking crisis. The effect was disturbing but not especially protracted, except to the extent that it may have led to lack of confidence in the railroads. However, another influence, the inconvertibility of the greenbacks, remained troublesome throughout the contraction. Furthermore, what looked to many persons like credit irresponsibility, a constant flood of bills on silver, ceased only shortly before the upturn in 1879.

The preceding prosperous period did have the major earmarks of stability, even though it represented a period of rapid growth. Commodity prices declined from the Civil War to 1871 and then approximately leveled until 1873. Security prices remained substantially stable. The federal government maintained a considerable surplus throughout the generally prosperous period.

The decade of the 1920's also was recognized as a stable period even though it was one of rapid growth. Commodity prices, wage rates, labor relations, immigration, and many other social and economic factors showed little variation, even though advance in the standard of living was moving at a rapid pace. In fact, those of us who can remember the period will testify that economic movement seemed dull by contrast with post-World War II. Even security prices were not as variable as one might think. Short-term interest rates were fairly stable from 1925 to early 1928, although they began a rapid ascent in mid-1928. The price of high-grade bonds was not significantly lower in 1929 than in 1925 or 1926. The price of common stocks rose rapidly for only four years, 1925–29.

LEGACY OF THE TWENTIES

Overexpansion. As in the preceding prosperity periods described above, disturbances were transmitted to the following depression because of overexpansion of durable goods, overextension of credit, and speculation. As a result of the new place taken by consumer durables in the twenties, the overinvestment category must be extended to encompass not only overinvestment in the traditional sense, but consumer durable goods as well.

Automobiles represent the most important case of overexpansion of consumer durables. Three fourths of American families had cars in 1929, compared with a third at the start of the decade. The result is far from absolute saturation, but a point had been reached where additional market penetration was difficult. Furthermore, half of the automobiles on the road had been built after the middle of the decade, so that the yearly number of cars scrapped leveled off at just under three million. With the 1929 production rate of close to five million cars, this left nearly two million to be absorbed by expanding markets. Considerably less had been so absorbed in the two preceding years. In fact, the trouble was plain to see in 1929—secondhand cars were stacked on dealers' lots to an alarming extent. (Most new buyers began with secondhand cars.) Automobile production averaged only a third of the 1929 rate in the years 1931–33.

The story on radios is somewhat similar, although, of course, the industry was smaller and the impact on the economy less. The proportionate decline in radio production was about the same. New types of consumer durables, like the mechanical refrigerator, were not being priced for a mass market and could lend little assistance in taking up the slack.

TABLE 13–1

DECLINING RATE OF POPULATION INCREASE

Year	Population Increase (In Millions)	Year	Population Increase (In Millions)
1924	2.16	1929	1.27
1925	1.72	1930	1.31
1926	1.57	1931	0.96
1927	1.65	1932	0.80
1928	1.46	1933	0.74

Residential building was a tragic case. The advance in available housing units had substantially exceeded that in families.[2] Perhaps this was partly due to the slackened population growth, as shown in Table 13–1, although the decline in family growth was much less rapid than in population. (The rapid slackening of population growth does indicate that the growth potential for housing was due to fall markedly.) More disasterous than the excessive growth in total housing supply was its distribution. More and more of the units could not be rented or sold at existing rates. For instance, middle-class apartments in the New York area had so greatly exceeded demand that many new units were lying idle.

The fact that residential building activity had been declining since 1926 was not of much help. A nonsustainable type of market

---

[2]Lowell J. Chawner, *Residential Building*, Housing Monograph Series, No. 1 (Washington, D.C.: National Resources Committee, 1939), p. 16.

had been developed in residential housing even with allowance for the three-year slackening. Limited down payments attracted buyers, and practically no amortization payment was required. Terms so attractive must have provided a temporary support for the market. At the same time, outstanding mortgages were left in a highly vulnerable position. With even minor declines in housing prices, equities would vanish. Mortgage holders later faced a perplexing situation, and a powerful debt-deflation force arose. Construction of houses averaged only a fifth of the 1929 rate in the years 1932–34.

Nonresidential construction rose in 1929 after three years of approximately horizontal movement. One way of indicating the appearance of overbuilding in this area is to compare the amount of construction with the amount of equipment. Private, nonresidential construction came to less than 70 per cent of the dollar amount of business equipment installed in the first five years of the twenties; while in the last five years, it came to over 80 per cent. (The figure is 70 per cent for 1957.)

Much more important is overexpansion in certain types of nonresidential construction. Some were declining in the late twenties; and it does not appear that significant overbuilding was occurring in these areas—agriculture, iron and steel, stores and restaurants, recreational and religious buildings, and hospitals. A striking increase, however, occurred in certain types of industrial structures and in office buildings. It is easy to point to city after city where office buildings had exceeded any foreseeable need. The contrasting change over time for some building types is shown in Table 13–2.

In the nondurable areas, inventories were generally at a reasonable level, which evidenced no important oversupply. The experience of the early twenties had generated an almost fanatical urge to avoid overstocking of inventories. Agriculture was an exception. As a result of the war, crop acreage, especially for wheat, had become overexpanded throughout the Western world. Readjustments had not been made by 1929. It became more and more difficult to obtain export markets for our farm products. In 1929, our wheat stocks doubled, even though the harvested crop declined substantially. Wheat stocks were also building up in the rest of the world, especially in Canada. For wheat, both exports and domestic consumption were declining.

Credit Overextension. Reference is made above to the mortgage financing of residential housing. Outstanding mortgages had about doubled from the mid-twenties and by 1929 were relatively extended even in comparison with 1959 levels, when reasonable amortization requirements were in force, satisfactory mortgage guaranties existed, and house ownership was spread wider.[3] Foreclosures from 1932 to 1935 were at about four times the level prevailing in the mid-twenties. Even the foreclosures in the mid-twenties were high by modern standards, about twice the number occurring in the fifties when the stock of houses was nearly twice as great.

TABLE 13–2

New Construction for Selected Years

(In Billions of 1947–49 Dollars)

Year	Total Private	Residential Housing[a]	Industrial	Warehouses and Office Buildings[b]	Stores, Restaurants, and Garages	Public Utility	Total Public
1915.....	9.1	4.6	0.8	(c)	(c)	1.5	2.4
1920.....	8.8	3.4	1.8	0.5	0.6	1.1	1.8
1925.....	18.9	11.5	1.1	0.7	1.3	2.2	3.6
1926.....	20.1	11.6	1.5	0.7	1.5	2.4	3.7
1929.....	16.4	7.3	2.1	1.1	1.1	2.7	4.4
1930.....	12.0	4.3	1.3	0.6	0.7	2.7	5.4
1932.....	4.3	1.7	0.2	0.3	0.3	1.0	4.6
1933.....	3.2	1.2	0.5	0.1	0.3	0.5	3.5
1940.....	10.1	5.9	0.9	0.2	0.6	1.4	6.6
1950.....	21.3	13.0	1.0	0.4	0.8	3.0	6.7
1956.....	24.9	13.6	2.3	1.3	1.4	3.4	10.0

Source: *Construction Volume and Costs, 1915–1956: Statistical Supplement to the Construction Review* (Washington, D.C.: U.S. Government Printing Office, 1958).
aExcludes farm and public.
bIncludes also loft buildings.
cData not available separately for this category.

The receipt in the twenties of payments from other governments on debts incurred in relation to World War I was a "fair weather" policy. Until 1928, it worked with the assistance of funds made available by our large foreign investment. Difficulties began to arise in mid-1928 and became more and more intense in 1929 because the high New York call-loan rate, an outgrowth of the stock

[3]The records, which no doubt lack complete coverage, show $21 billion outstanding on one- to four-family nonfarm homes in 1929 (Federal Home Loan Bank Administration, *Statistical Supplement to the Federal Home Loan Bank Review* [Washington, D.C.: U.S. Government Printing Office, 1947]), while the contrasting figure at mid-1959 was $125 billion, or six times the 1929 level. To put the figures in relative proportion, we use the fact that gross national product was nearly five times as great. The 1959 mortgage levels were 2½ times the 1951 levels.

market speculation, drew short-term funds to New York. As a result, foreign countries found increasing difficulty in making foreign trade payments even before the depression began. As the depression got under way, our foreign investments declined, and foreign trade shrank about two thirds. The foreign debt payments became an impossible burden; and President Hoover made his famous moratorium proposal in 1931, forgiving for a year foreign debt payments to the federal government. Unfortunately, the decision was made too late to be of much help. Although not understood at the time, our Allies were depending on reparation payments to provide the funds required for war-debt payments, and the Germanic countries were depending on short-term loans from our Allies to provide the funds for reparation payments. The increasing level of short-term loans to the Germanic countries led to a European monetary crisis in 1931. The psychological effect of this crisis was an important factor in extending the length of the depression.

Consumer instalment credit reached about $3 billion and all other consumer credit about an equal amount in 1929. Credit extension had risen with disposable income. As disposable income declined, consumer credit was contracted, and this added a contractionary factor. The nearly $2 billion decline in instalment credit represented approximately 6 per cent of the decline in disposable income in the depression. Instalment credit has risen to much higher levels in the fifties, and has become three times as high in relation to disposable income. However, we are now more accustomed to its use, and the holding of liquid assets by individuals has increased about in proportion.

Brokers' loans rose more than $7 billion in the twenties and declined even more to mid-1932. Other stock market credit approximately duplicated this performance. Thus, by far the greatest amount of credit deflation in the depression developed in the stock market.

Speculation. The principal speculation was in the stock market. It reflected faith in the future, related to belief in a New Era, and definitely was not founded on fear of inflation. Thus, it represented an act of faith and not of fear. It made for excessive ease in obtaining equity funds. A dramatic shift to equity financing occurred. From a fifth of total domestic capital flotations in 1926, equity flotations rose to nearly two thirds in 1929. The fact that equity funds were so readily obtained and that their use was not accompanied by effective long-term forecasting led to overdevelopment. Easily available investment funds and optimistic appraisals encouraged investment projects.

THE DOWNTURN

Business activity leveled off in the summer of 1929. It was directly related to the marketing difficulties being faced by the automobile industry. The major areas in the Industrial Production Index which experienced a downturn in the spring or early summer were transportation equipment, textiles, nonferrous metals, and rubber, all of which are closely related to the volume of automobile production. In a sense, then, we can say that faltering automobile markets account for the downturn in August, 1929. Partly because recession was already under way in several foreign countries, our foreign trade balance had begun to show substantial declines before midyear.

Furthermore, the leveling of activity must have had some effect on the stock market which, with a large ownership on thin margins and at high interest rates (the rate on call loans reached 9 per cent in March), was patently vulnerable. The stock market peak attained on September 3 was not exceeded. It was nearly reached a week later and again in two weeks; but from then on, all of the high points were lower than the early September figure. Once it became clear that the market would not go higher, the "bears" took over for a field day. From the middle of October the stock market averages kept falling. By Saturday, October 26, it became obvious that no sustained recovery would occur. "Gunning" for weak-margined stocks became a common trading practice. The market continued to decline, at first at an accelerated pace, until the averages registered a 45 per cent decline from the high levels in mid-November.

With the perspective now available, it is clear that a business contraction would inevitably follow; but in the new-era optimism then existing, no such outcome seemed apparent. In Wall Street, assistance was rallied to support the price of stocks which might endanger certain banks whose liquidity had come to depend on loans on these stocks. President Hoover followed the direct approach and called successive conferences with businessmen to assure the maintenance of wage rates and of investment programs.

Looked at in the colder light of history, a contraction was irrevocably under way. The particular influences which operated to level activity in the summer and those which operated to prick the credit bubble in the stock market were merely incidental. The vulnerability of activity is more fundamentally indicated by the existing overexpansion, credit overextension, and speculative activity indicated above. With the unbalances which had developed by late 1929, a culmination within a limited time was inevitable.

THE CONTRACTION

From the downturn in August, 1929, industrial production rose only once until late in 1932. The single rise, which occurred in the spring of 1931, was slight in amount and lasted only briefly, possibly because of the European monetary crisis which was unfolding (discussed below).

The decline in expenditures speeded up as the contraction continued, which may be characteristic of what has happened in deep depressions. Obviously, this means that for a protracted period, no tendency arose for culminating forces to become ascendant.

The structure of the decline is indicated in Table 13-3. Most remarkably, the consumer area continuously accounted for well over

TABLE 13-3

CHANGING EXPENDITURES DURING THE CONTRACTION*
(Changes from Preceding Year in Billions of Dollars)

Explanation	1930	1931	1932	1933
Personal consumption expenditures....	− 8.0†	− 9.7	−12.0	−2.9
Residential construction.............	− 1.5	− 0.5	− 1.0	−0.1
Other private construction..........	− 1.0	− 1.7	− 1.2	−0.3
Producer equipment.................	− 1.4	− 1.4	− 1.2	.....
Inventory investment...............	− 2.1	− 0.9	− 1.3	+1.0
Net exports.......................	....	− 0.5	......	.....
Government expenditures............	+ 0.7	‡	− 1.1	−0.1
Gross national product*.............	−13.3	−14.8	−17.8	−2.5

*The sum of the component expenditure changes differs slightly from the change in gross national product in 1931 and in 1933 because of rounding errors.

†Note should be taken of the fact that of this $8 billion, only a quarter was in consumer durables, another quarter was in services ($1 billion in brokerage charges and interest, and investment counseling alone), and nearly half in consumer nondurables.

‡Actually, the federal government increased nonproduct expenditures by $1 billion in 1931 by an increase in transfer payments, principally because of payments to veterans on their bonus bonds. Of course, this does not show in the table, since transfer payments do not count as part of gross national product.

half of the declining expenditures. That area is usually expected to be the least vulnerable in the economy. If a depression is to attain serious proportions, a substantial decline in consumer expenditures ultimately would have to occur. We may justifiably be surprised, however, to find that consumption expenditure experienced so violent an initial decline. The explanation lies in a reaction to the high plateau of spending attained and to the force of contracting debt in reducing expenditures. Forced contraction of debt accounted for the disposition of a substantial amount of currently received disposable income. Thus, personal saving is estimated to have amounted to well over $3 billion in 1930 (presumably related to the unusual extent of debt payment.)

If it is true that the high level of consumer expenditures in the late twenties was related to belief in the New Era and to actual and unrealized capital gains, plausibly expenditures had deviated markedly from basic propensities to consume. In other words, a considerable part of the total consumer income realized, including that obtained from capital gains as well as that obtained from productive activity, was discretionary and not closely tied to well-established living standards. With the disappearance of capital gains, which were in the order of billions of dollars in 1928 and 1929, consumption was adjusted downward to a level commensurate with the receipt of productive income. By 1930, unemployment accounted for some decline in consumer expenditures, but wage rates were well maintained, and income was paid out in proportion to the continued level of employment.

The most notable decline in investment in 1930 occurred in residential housing. On the basis of the above arguments, this might have been expected because the purchase of new housing is related to consumer standards of living. Also, housing had been overexpanded in the preceding prosperity.

A large decline in inventory investment is inevitable in any recession, as explained in Chapter 11. As shown in Table 13-3, the decline in inventory investment was substantial in 1930; but compared to what happened in the recessions in the twenties, it was indeed minor. It was considerably less than in 1924 and only twice as great as in the very mild recession in 1927. The decline in investment in equipment in 1930 was greater than in the recessions of the twenties, but no greater than would be expected in most relatively mild recessions (much less than in 1938).

For this particular period to represent deep depression at low levels of secondary growth, it was necessary for expenditure for construction and the more durable types of business equipment to fall to very low levels. Low levels of residential construction were definitely related to preceding overexpansion.

The decline in nonresidential construction was less sharp in 1930. No doubt, some types of construction were less overbuilt than housing, but many were in about as serious a "fix," as explained in connection with Table 13-2 above. Slow reaction to the decline in many nonresidential types is due to the long lead time necessary in planning them. Even though overoptimism may have been well realized before the end of 1930, the only prudent course appeared to be completion of operations already well under way.

The severe decline in construction, amounting to nearly 90 per cent from the high peak in the twenties to the low in 1933, is just as closely related to shrinking consumer expenditure as to preceding overexpansion of building activity. The 10 per cent decrease in consumer expenditures in 1930 made the excess of productive facilities manifest. As efforts were made from that point to bring capital stocks into a reasonable relationship with current markets, capital formation dwindled away. The multiplier reaction in further reducing consumer expenditures made the overcapacity look successively worse. The operating rate of the existing capital stock was further reduced. The processes of culmination, by which the contraction is usually reversed, were thus thwarted.

The Outcropping of Contingencies. The unfolding of events is closely related to the depth and length of the 1929–33 contraction. An exhaustive treatment is beyond the limits of this book, but it is important for us to examine the most influential contingencies which developed.[4]

Perhaps the most catastrophic effect was created by the European monetary crisis. Industrial production showed a slight rise in the spring of 1931. We may reasonably conclude that the cumulative forces of contraction had weakened. However, as pointed out above, culminating forces were relatively impotent. It would seem that sentiment had come to represent an unusually critical factor in determing the business outlook. As the European monetary problems became more intense, confidence was shaken in this country.

Germany and Austria had built up larger and larger debit balances in the short-term loan market. In fact, the payment of reparations had been fully covered by these loans. With sharp declines in foreign trade, increasing difficulties were faced in maintaining large external credits. The Austrian Creditanstalt Bank faced insolvency in May, but the Bank for International Settlements saved the situation by providing a loan through the Austrian government.

---

[4]For complete references, see William W. Shirley, *The World Depression 1929–: A List of Books and Pamphlets in the New York Public Library* (New York: New York Public Library, 1934); Dixon Wecter, *The Age of the Great Depression* (New York: Macmillan Co., 1948); and J. K. Galbraith, *The Great Crash* (Boston: Houghton Mifflin Co., 1955).

A rush to recall loans resulted, with the French able to withdraw most of their funds. When the Darmstädter Bank failed in Germany, emergency measures had to be taken to protect German credit. A "stand-still agreement" was entered into, whereby no recall of short-term loans from Germany should be required for six months. The agreement fell heavily on England, for English short-term loans were the chief ones remaining in Germany. As a safety measure, other centers began to recall funds which had been loaned in London. Gold flowed out of England so rapidly that on September 21, 1931, the Bank of England suspended gold payments.

The results apparently were disastrous in America. Hoarding was precipitated, as indicated by the fact that the holdings of large-denomination currency and of gold coin nearly doubled, while bank deposits declined; and bank debits, indicative of payments actually made, fell a third. Hoarding tightened money conditions. The rate on bankers' acceptances, which was less than 1 per cent before September, rose to over 3 per cent in November.

The same attitude that induced the general public to hoard led the monetary authorities to tighten monetary policy to protect reserves, in reaction to the pressure created by hoarding. The New York rediscount rate was raised from 1½ per cent in September to 3½ per cent in October. Excess reserves of New York City member banks were drawn down, and a slight increase in borrowing from the Federal Reserve was required. That monetary policy obviously was wrong.[5] Measures which are effective in offsetting inflationary levels of activity are not the ones to employ to offset the monetary effects of hoarding.

The Federal Reserve is sometimes criticized for not buying government bonds in support of the long-term capital market at this time. Under the circumstances, stock flotations had been virtually eliminated before the European crisis, but bond flotations were as large in early 1931 as they had been in 1929. By late 1931, they also had fallen to small amounts. If open-market purchases of govern-

---

[5]Lest this statement appear uncharitable, we point out explicitly that the Federal Reserve lacked needed freedom until the passage of the Glass-Steagall Act early in 1932, which authorized the banks to use government bonds as collateral in the place of gold. Gold was flowing out of the country late in 1931 in anticipation of possible monetary difficulties in the United States. Furthermore, in 1931, our merchandise exports were declining more rapidly than our merchandise imports. But these facts do not excuse the failure of the Federal Reserve to buy government bills and notes in the open market late in 1931. Such measures were taken early in 1932, when, no doubt they helped to provide a stabilizing influence, but that was too late to create the maximum effect.

ment bonds had been made, long-term interest rates would have been kept lower. The yield on government bonds rose from 3.2 per cent in the summer to over 4 per cent early in 1932, the highest rate prevailing since the early twenties. We doubt, however, that flotations would have remained high if the long-term interest rate had been kept down. Visualization of need for capital expansion at any interest cost was vanishing.

Some capital building, maintenance of wage rates, and maintained dividend payments were thought of by many companies as temporary support measures in 1930. With industrial demand growing still worse in the summer of 1931, temporary support measures could no longer be afforded. Average hourly earnings in manufacturing declined 7 per cent in 1931, although they were down only 2 per cent in 1930. Total wages and salaries were down 15 per cent, twice as much as in the preceding year. More employment was not induced by cutting wage rates under the circumstances, and drop in consumer expenditures was accelerated.

With the contraction lasting so long, measures taken by various countries to obtain temporary domestic relief at the expense of imports came to compound the difficulties. An illustration is the Smoot-Hawley Tariff of 1930, which raised American duties on imports. For a limited time, such measures gave each country an export advantage. As the depression lasted, however, "beggar my neighbor" policies universally reduced the level of foreign trade, with an unfavorable effect on everyone. Since many other countries are more dependent on foreign trade than we are, the induced effect on their domestic economies was even more detrimental. The European monetary crisis was directly caused by the fading-away of foreign trade.

United States foreign trade dropped to a third of its 1929 level by 1932. A very important repercussion was the bankrupting of underdeveloped countries which depended on the sale of raw material exports to capitalistic countries, especially to the United States. With industrial activity falling to such low levels, the use of raw materials was drastically curtailed.

The most influential developments early in the contraction centered around successive stock market declines, especially in view of the credit deflation induced by those declines and the resulting conversion of capital gains into capital losses. The following rapid credit deflation left insolvency and bankruptcy in its wake.

Although about three fourth of the stock market credit was paid off by the end of 1930, the timing of loan deflation was important in 1930 and later, and the attitudes acquired persisted after the deflation was complete and continued to exert a depressive influence. Stock prices had a seasonal appearance in 1930 and 1931, with a rise in the spring, a decline at midyear, some rise in early summer, and then a tapering-off with an accelerated decline at the end of the year. The lows of late 1929 were not broken until a year later. By that time, all efforts at support of stocks, whose decline in price might embarrass certain financial institutions, were eliminated. Bank suspensions increased substantially at the end of 1930, but there is no evidence that sound institutions were hard-pressed or that hoarding gained major momentum.

In early 1931, stock prices rose less than they did early in 1930, even though industrial production was rising slightly. The monetary crisis developing in Europe soon brought a renewal of the stock market decline, and bank suspensions again increased at midyear. At the end of 1931, when the full effects of the European crisis were being felt, stock prices hit much lower levels; and runs developed on banks, with bank suspensions exceeding the high level of the year before. A much larger proportion were member banks of the Federal Reserve System, indicating that failures were spreading to sounder institutions.

Stocks continued a general decline until mid-1932, when all-time lows were reached. Runs on banks were still just as common, but the number of suspensions was only half as large as in the preceding year. Member banks of the Federal Reserve System represented as high a proportion of the suspensions as in the preceding year.

Stock prices doubled from the low in June, 1932, to September, 1932, largely as a technical reaction from the extreme lows; but it is true that industrial activity had finally leveled off. The technical rise to September was followed by some selling by speculators, producing a renewed decline in stock prices. Possibly, the relatively slight decline occurring from September to the end of the year had some influence on the initiation of bank holidays.

There was a close connection between decline in stock prices and bank liquidity because of the involvement of the banks in security loans. With each decline in the stock market, bank suspensions increased. This effect, however, became far less pronounced after 1931. The bank holidays beginning in Nevada on the last day of October, 1932, cannot be accounted for by reduced liquidity arising from declines in the stock market. The stock market was not breaking to new lows, and the number of banks failing in the fourth quarter of 1932 was only a third of the number a year earlier. The failing banks were smaller.

The immediate factor responsible for bank holidays in Nevada and other Western states was a rash of foreclosures on farm mortgages. By the mid-twenties, farm land values had dropped a third, and they dropped even more from 1929 to 1932. Before the 1929–33 contraction, $11 billion in farm mortgages had been pared by only 10 per cent; but by 1932 a long process of further paring was under way.

Orders suspending all banks in Louisiana and in Michigan in the first half of February, 1933, started the principal "conflagration." The basic causes of these state-wide suspensions are obscure, but certainly they were related to the confused sentiment at the time. As explained above, little tendency had existed for the contraction to attain maturity; therefore, there was no effective development of culminating forces. Under these circumstances, outbreaks of depressive sentiment were more probable than their avoidance.

After the Michigan closings, it was merely a matter of time before the effects spread, and much of the country became engulfed. To meet payrolls in Michigan, it was necessary for the large corporations to call on their accounts in banks located in cities in adjoining states. With the anticipation that the adjoining states might have to call holidays, a safety measure taken by many corporations was to close out their accounts in the cities involved, moving them to New York. The combined effect of such fund withdrawals forced the declaration of additional state-wide suspensions. The movement came to be called "one-way banking." Funds moving out of a state under universal suspension found no means of returning.

THE 1933 UPTURN

The trough of the depression is sometimes characterized as "double-bottomed," because the stock market hit bottom in June, 1932, and after that date industrial production leveled, then began rising in the fall. We think the characterization essentially incorrect, not because production began falling again after its abortive rise in the fall, but because culmination had appeared only in the stock market. The stock market culmination was far too weak to turn the trick. The strategic factor had become sentiment, and this remained decidedly pessimistic until March, 1933.

Two major factors are responsible for the upturn at that date.

A national bank holiday was called shortly after President Roosevelt took office; and the soundness of banks, as they reopened, was implicitly guaranteed by the government. The Reconstruction Finance Corporation loaned huge sums to banks which were insolvent, but which appeared to have basically sound assets. Movement was begun immediately to provide guaranty of bank deposits, and a formal act making such provision was passed in June.

The second, and probably more important, influence was the reassurance by the incoming federal administration that prices would be increased. Businessmen generally were convinced. The obvious course indicated was to accumulate inventories against the anticipated price rise. The course was followed so universally that, actually, little inventory accumulation occurred. Rather, the activity generated by production for inventory induced rising consumption expenditures which absorbed most of the goods produced for inventory, along the lines of the models described in Chapter 11. As a result, industrial production rose at the most rapid rate shown in the historical record—60 per cent in the four months from March, 1933, to July, 1933.

THE EXPANSION, 1933-37

The ensuing expansion lasted over four years, the longest uninterrupted by business cycle recessions in recorded American history. The growth was horizontal, as evidenced by the fact that the 1937 peak was at approximately the 1929 GNP level (in deflated prices—since actual prices were lower, the actual GNP value was lower). This is an illustration of secondary growth in deep depression. It is not unrelated to the growth occurring in the preceding prosperity, which may also be called secondary; but over-all, that growth is not necessarily greater or less than the secular growth which might have been expected in any prosperity. The prosperity secondary growth, however, is marked by the diversion of an excessive proportion of resources to durable investment, to the production of consumer durables, and by unsustainable attitudes. Such attitudes in the twenties were marked by speculation and expenditure rates abnormally dependent on incomes derived from speculation. The low output of durable goods in the thirties can be explained as a reaction from these attitudes, as a response to embarrassment following credit overextension, and by inaction resulting from realization of overexpansion.

In other words, the 1933-37 expansion was a heritage of the

preceding prosperity almost as much as the contraction phase was. Capacity appeared oversufficient, and there was little need to add to it. Not only was this representative with respect to incentives to invest, but it no doubt largely accounted for the New Deal attitude with regard to business. Why should efforts be directed at the encouragement of business investment when such efforts were bound to be unsuccessful in view of the overcapacity in existence?

Our contention is that philosophy of this kind best explains what happened. Consumers were reluctant to increase their standards of living. Businessmen found little or no inducement to add to capital. Most of the technological improvements introduced represented minor adjustments in evening out over-all capacity or were pointed at cost reductions, so that the secular stagnation theories, which were then germinating, emphasized inability on the part of the economy to add to capacity.

Perhaps the expansion provides a useful background for the study of a stationary state. We must grant that the adjustment to such a state was a jolting one and that short-period variation was exceptionally marked. The market target looked to by businessmen, though, clearly was representative of stationary conditions. In general, consumers made little effort to increase living standards, no doubt in response to recognition of the high level of unemployment which was but a part of the whole complex. The movement of markets into new types of goods was surprisingly limited.

Since the cyclical expansion started from the extremely depressed level of 1933, obviously the advance was substantial in reaching the predepression level by 1937. Carefully interpreted, Table 13–4 will guide us in showing what happened. It is constructed on the same principle as Table 13–3, showing the year-by-year increase in activity in each major expenditure division. We are handicapped by lack of half-yearly data in picturing the early expansion.

The rise was so rapid in the latter part of the first half of 1933 and in the last half of 1935 that the annual data hide the fact that industrial production was at the same level in mid-1933 as in mid-1935. In this two-year period the National Recovery Administration was in effect. The NRA code authorities in every major industry set up an established principle to avoid adding to excess capacity. Hence, no businessman was permitted to add to capacity if already existing capacity in the industry was sufficient to satisfy market needs. In almost all cases, existing capacity was adequate. Since investment is the principal dynamic influence sparking expansion, the

NRA codes provided effective warranty that no net advance would occur.[6]

After the demise of the National Recovery Administration in mid-1935, recovery was rapid. More than half of the rising expenditure each year is accounted for by personal consumption expenditures, as typically occurs in expansion; but by 1937, these expenditures were not high enough to provide for more than the 1929 standard of living.[7] It is easy enough to say that the rise in consumption expenditures is dependent upon the rise in income; and historically speaking, that undoubtedly is a significant explanation. In 1936, consumer expenditures were nearly 95 per cent of disposable income, which is about in line with the American consumption func-

TABLE 13-4

CHANGING EXPENDITURES DURING THE EXPANSION*

(Changes from Preceding Year in Billions of Dollars)

Explanation	1933	1934	1935	1936	1937	1938
Consumption expenditures...	−2.9	+5.5	+4.4	+ 6.3	+4.7	−2.7
Residential construction.....	−0.1	+0.1	+0.4	+ 0.6	+0.3	+0.1
Other private construction...	−0.3	+0.1	+0.2	+ 0.4	+0.8	−0.5
Producer equipment........	.....	+0.7	+0.8	+ 1.0	+0.9	−1.5
Inventory investment.......	+1.0	+0.5	+2.0	+ 0.1	+1.2†	−3.1
Net exports...............	.....	+0.2	−0.5	......	+0.2	+1.0
Government expenditures...	−0.1	+1.8	+0.2	+ 1.8	−0.1	+1.1
Gross national product*.....	−2.5	+9.0	+7.5	+10.2	+8.1	−5.6

*The sum of component expenditure changes differs slightly from the change in gross national product in 1933, 1934, and 1937 because of rounding errors.

†This high figure is the result of a build-up in farm inventories, while nonfarm business inventories declined by $0.4 billion for the year as a whole. Farm inventories rose $0.5 billion, after declining over $1 billion in 1936. The reason was that farmers held their crops over because of a decline in farm prices. This influence was not expansionary and should be subtracted from the increase in total gross national product expenditures to determine the expansionary influence, netting only $6.5 billion instead of $8.1 billion.

tion. It is very possible, however, that the thinking of consumers was not typically geared to a rising standard of living. Although never stated so explicitly, the thinking of the business enterpriser at the time necessarily reduces to that proposition. For if businessmen generally had been convinced that consumers would buy in-

[6]Some analysts logically take the position that, in view of the existing overcapacity, little expansion would have been undertaken, anyway. The textual point is not completely invalid, however, because modernization and cost-reducing investments were often turned down by code authorities. We knew personally of several cases at the time.

[7]Per capita consumption expenditures in 1937, in 1954 dollars, were $1,025 and in 1929 were $1,050. Employment in 1937 was no greater than in 1929, while consumption expenditures were slightly higher.

creased product, all they had to do was produce it, and the income so generated would have been spent. The rapid rise in industrial activity in the second quarter of 1933 illustrates the outcome. But when businessmen did step up production and accumulate inventory late in the expansion, they got into trouble.

Nevertheless, most weight must be placed on the unsatisfactory advance in investment expenditure. The earliest recovery expenditures of this type are typically for inventory, maintenance and repair, and some needed equipment. Scarcely any inventory build-up occurred until the end of the NRA period. (The positive figures in Table 13–4 indicate reduced rate of inventory runoff in 1933 and 1934.) Our figures on maintenance and repair are inadequate; but we may assume that a rise of satisfactory proportions occurred from 1934 to 1936, although not in the second half of 1933. The early rise in equipment expenditures was the most expansionary of all investment.

For more durable equipment and plant expenditures, the National Recovery Administration provided an effective stumbling block until mid-1935, and after that the tone it set continued to sustain a defeatist attitude for many enterprisers. Undoubtedly, the prestige of businessmen had fallen, and they became less sure of themselves. Moreover, activity unquestionably continued to remain well below capacity in most lines. With a closer approach to capacity in 1937, construction did pick up substantially.

On the slow advance in residential construction before 1936, we must remember the heritage of an oversupply of housing, and we must again note the consumers' indifferent state of mind. In 1936 an unusual increase in income, as noted below, did add some stimulus.

In all durable expenditure groups an overhang of legal difficulties engendered a degree of vacillation in adding further to capital stocks. A large number of railroads remained in indeterminate bankruptcy proceedings. To a lesser degree, such situations existed in other industries. Some houses and many farms remained in default on mortgages without a legal settlement having been achieved. As an illustration, many of us remember the destitute squatters who were not readily evicted from illegal lodgings in our urban centers.

The increase in government expenditures in 1934 is principally accounted for by federal grants-in-aid to penurious state and local governments. Grants-in-aid remained at about the same level in 1935, but government expenditures provided no further boost. By

1936 the state-aid program was cut back, but payment of veterans' compensation certificates much more than made up for the difference. A balanced budget in 1937 developed from the ending of temporary payments to veterans and from cutback in government construction programs.

The payment of the veterans' certificates in 1936 was a notable event. It was timed, not intentionally, with the replacement cycle for shorter-lived durables, notably automobiles. The average life of an automobile at that time was about seven years. Passenger car production rose briefly early in 1937 to the levels prevailing in the late twenties. The increase in consumer expenditures for nondurables and services actually was more than for durables; and no doubt, the cash windfall helped in these areas. Some of the nondurable purchases also were of the restocking variety. The rising service expenditures were related to increasing consumer confidence and approach to reattainment of former living standards.

Payment of the veterans' "bonus" was of the single-injection type. As the effect of a single injection wears off, income reapproaches the level existing before it was made. Thus, as we moved into 1937, the tendency was for the business expansion to flatten out.

Because of the low levels attained, one would not expect bottleneck situations; but actually, some had developed. Notably in the rubber factories in Ohio, skilled labor became very scarce, and lively bidding developed for the available supply. With so much unemployment, managements had become lax in the maintenance of training programs.

Other leveling factors included the slightly reduced government construction program; an increase in Social Security taxes imposed in January, 1937; large payments of dividends in December, 1936, because of the new undistributed profits tax; contractionary monetary policy initiated by the Federal Reserve; weakening of commodity prices with a continued rise in wage costs; and discontinuance in adding to the stocks of nonfarm inventories. No further elaboration on some of these factors is necessary to indicate that they produced a contractionary effect. We present some brief notes below to clarify the others.

The large dividends paid in December, 1936, to avoid tax penalties had some of the characteristics of a single injection. Further dividend payments at such a level certainly would not occur for a year and perhaps not even them.

Excess reserves of member banks had become so large that the monetary authorities began to fear an inflationary effect. They added 100 per cent to required reserves in successive steps from August, 1936, to May, 1937. The effect was largely psychological, but it did lead to some selling of bank securities by commercial banks and to a tightening on loan policy in major cities.

Raw material prices, especially agricultural, dropped drastically. A major increase had occurred in world supplies. Britain discontinued stockpiling of raw materials in March, 1937, which had been pursued as a defense measure. In April, President Roosevelt announced at a press conference that some prices were too high, which came as a shock to the business community because the general belief was that government policy was to manipulate prices back to the 1926 level. These events led to a reappraisal of the relatively large inventory stocks which had been accumulated. Labor unions were riding high, and wage rates were driven up one cent per hour per month on a base of about 60 cents per hour in the winter of 1936–37. The average hourly rate in manufacturing rose from 62 cents in November to 71 cents in June. With leveling prices, shrinking profit margins tended to occur, and profit expectations became depressive.

1937 DOWNTURN AND CONTRACTION, 1937-38

Except for inventories, the factors noted were not powerful enough to develop rapid culmination. The downturn is dated in May; and by that time, most of the depressive factors were operative. But their contractionary influence was limited. Industrial production was not significantly lower in August than it had been in May. A summer lull had been expected, since there was an increasing tendency to close down for vacations in the summer. The generally expressed sentiment was that a strong upsurge of demand would occur in the fall. When September rolled around, no such upsurge was in evidence; on the contrary, activity began to shrink rapidly. The evidence on inventory levels was incontestable. They had been increasing more rapidly than sales, and with horizontal or declining prices a runoff was indicated. Clearly, this was a conclusion deduced privately by most businessmen, and each one found it surprising that almost all others had reached a similar conclusion.

The net result was much as shown in Table 11–2 (page 221). The harder businessmen tried to deplete inventories, the more sales fell; and thereby, at first, inventory stocks continued to rise because of deliveries on minimum contracts already made. Soon, however, drastic enough measures were taken to cut the stocks down to size, even allowing for the reduced level of sales. By 1938, activity was leveling off, and little further contraction was experienced. In the autumn of 1937, however, a decline of 25 per cent occurred in industrial production, the most rapid rate in the historical record.

Culmination was speeded up by the very fact that durable investment had risen so little in the preceding expansion. The full play of the rapid culmination in inventories was felt in the movement of total activity. Temporary support was not provided by the completion of unwanted durable capital.

We may plausibly ask why activity did not rise rapidly early in 1938 instead of leveling off. The answer lies in the weakness of basic demand. As explained above, consumer urges to buy scarcely exceeded the living standards set a decade earlier. Nothing in the recession changed the basic evaluation for long-term capital investment. The major part of the decline had lasted only a few months, and drastic pinches in inventory requirements had not developed. Principally, what had happened was a lowering of desired inventory stocks because the inflationary potential and profit expectations had shrunk.

1938 UPTURN AND EXPANSION TO SEPTEMBER, 1939

Most types of industrial production did not begin to rise until mid-1938, although some lines, notably rubber and textiles, which had overdepleted inventories in the autumn, snapped back with some immediate inventory accumulation early in 1938. Inventory accumulation would have been typical throughout industry if a more normal growth stimulation had been present.

The upturn is dated at June, 1938. Data are too unsatisfactory to state dogmatically that recovery would have gotten under way without the counterpoise of exgenous forces. In any case, sentiment reversed itself about midyear, as indicated by a rise in stock prices. Government stabilization shifted to public works. In June, Congress passed a $4 billion public works and unemployment relief bill. In May the undistributed profits tax had been modified fundamentally and appeared less oppressive to businessmen. The whole government emphasis on reform measures was reduced.

The rise in activity was rapid from June to the end of the year. It was fairly general and particularly notable in residential construction and in the manufacture of rubber products. In the rubber factories, difficulty had been faced in getting production schedules up to desired levels before the recession because of an insufficiency of skilled workers.

While satisfactory recovery was obtained in the second half of 1938, the year 1939 was disappointing. Industrial production did not rise significantly before war broke out in Europe that September. In fact, stagnation was almost universal throughout manufacturing. Little or no advance was occurring in investment, except for a very modest rise in producer equipment. Little change was occurring in consumer expenditures. Government stimulation by fiscal policy had faded out, with government expenditures on the decline. And yet, unemployment was still over nine million, or about 17 per cent of the labor force.

WOULD SECULAR GROWTH HAVE REAPPEARED WITHOUT WAR?

The inevitable question is whether the depression would have continued if war had not occurred. Some insight can be obtained by looking at the behavior of decision makers at the time. For the period up to the 1937 recession, we merely summarize the story told above. The growth outlook, for producers and consumers alike, had become limited. The appearance of overbuilding tended to be clinching.

What happened, however, is closely tied to the unfolding of current events. Current chance happenings show how the long expansion from 1933 to 1937 was generated. The National Recovery Administration was permitted to cripple advance for most of the first half of the expansion. The advance was very rapid in 1936 to 1937, but loaded with a "single shot in the arm" force, and this aided in developing typical culminating mechanisms. The most important of such mechanisms involved was inventory building, and we cannot condemn the motivation which produced it, given the limited understanding available to enterprisers at the time.

If it is true that demands were reappearing on a widened scale and that the expansion would have carried to full-employment levels except for the overpowering of culminating forces, the answer to the main question of this section is that depression continued not because of the absence of growth potentialities, but because of the transient nature of advance in demand in the business cycle. However explained, the 1937 "submerged" peak, with seven to eight million persons still unemployed, is disappointing. After the following recession, predisposition was established to make a harsh judgment on any further untoward events.

The rapidity of the recession in the fall of 1937 is closely tied to the inventory deflation which was involved. We cannot improve on the explanation given above on the leveling in the first half of 1938. The rate of expansion in the second half of 1938 was fully satisfactory.

We are brought then to the disappointing performance in the first three quarters of 1939. Prices were not rising, no rapid increases were occurring in demand, the memory of unwanted inventory in 1937 was vivid, and therefore a cautious inventory action is entirely explicable. The very slow increase in producer expenditure for equipment was disappointing, but understandable, in view of the rapid accumulation in that area from 1935 to 1937 and of the fact that no earth-shaking technological improvements had appeared. With due recognition of the rapid advance in plant and other construction in the twenties and of the low level of sales in 1938, we could scarcely have expected rapid investment in plants. While the advance in consumer expenditures was slight (about 4 per cent from the first to the third quarter), it was well distributed among various products and services, and was remarkable in view of the level of disposable income. Personal saving was cut down substantially from the first to the second and third quarters, and dropped to only about 3 per cent of disposable income. Maintenance of the higher level of residential construction achieved late in 1938 indicated at least a weak vote from the consumer in favor of improved accommodations.

What we have said sums up to little more than that the behavior of spending was not unusual in view of the low level of growth along which the economy was moving. It is possible that a major advance might have shortly gotten under way even if the war had not occurred, and such an advance might have brought activity back to secular growth levels without any powerful exogenous force. The major question, however, is still open. It does not help much to give the Hicksian accelerator-multiplier model answer: In time, durable capital would have worn out and would have required replacement.

Looking at the problem historically, possibly in the sense of Mr. Macawber, something always has turned up. The 1840's provide a useful contrast. For years, it seemed that strong recovery would not get under way. Finally, gold was discovered in California. Was the vibrant expansion in the early 1850's wholly due to that? If the internal forces in the business system reach a phlegmatic state, does this in itself set up obscure influences which are largely responsible for the generation of what we call exogenous forces? Did World War II have its roots in the Great Depression? These are unanswered riddles of economic change.

The standard answer for ending a deep depression is fiscal policy, as we explain in Part Five. Looking back to 1939, however, it seems clear that in spite of the continued high level of the stock of investment capital in relation to product demand, investment in cost-reducing and modernization equipment would have been very profitable. It may well be that encouragement of research and technological development would have been as effective in restoring full employment as a full-dress program of government spending.

WORLD WAR II

From the time war broke out in Europe until we entered, our physical product rose 10 per cent in World War I and a third in World War II. Since both wars intensely stimulated demand, the difference is largely accounted for by the extent to which resources were idle at the outset. The difference in price rise is remarkable, being scarcely a third as much in the forties as in the first war. With an ample supply of resources to call on, demand drove up prices less in the forties. Since exports were rising less in the second war, perhaps demand was actually stimulated less in the early phases.

Compared with a business cycle expansion after a sharp inventory recession, the war rise was not particularly impressive. From the business cycle trough in 1921 to the peak two years later, industrial production rose 60 per cent; while from September, 1939, to December, 1941, it rose only 50 per cent. Unemployment at nine million persons in 1939 was much greater than in 1921. Unemployment still averaged eight million in 1940.

Table 13–5 will give us some perspective on the changes taking place in major types of expenditure. Gross national product rose less in 1940 than in 1936. Looking down the 1940 column, one sees little clue to developing war activity. Furthermore, the government deficit was less than $1 billion that year compared with $2 billion in 1939.

After the German invasion of western Europe in the spring of 1940, defense appropriations were greatly stepped up, but actual defense expenditures were of little importance until late in the year. Even then, and during most of 1941, the only pinch on the civilian economy was on items related to scarce materials, principally steel and rubber. The steel plants were driven to capacity operations by the end of 1940. A scheme permitting quick write-off for tax purposes was put into effect to encourage private industry to add to capacity in the areas of greatest defense needs. Table 13–5 shows that no very spectacular investment spending actually was forthcoming.

The economy remained generally depressed through most of 1941, with unemployment averaging 5½ million. Consumer expenditures rose more than in the two preceding years, as Table 13–5 indicates, but wholly in nondurables and services. In the spring, consumer expenditures for durables had reached their war maximum, slightly above the 1929 level. From then on, the materials and plant capacity to make consumer durables were increasingly diverted to the making of war product, until slight reconversion was permitted by 1944.

TABLE 13–5

CHANGING EXPENDITURES DURING THE WAR*
(Changes from Preceding Year in Billions of Dollars)

Explanation	1939	1940	1941	1942	1943	1944	1945
Consumption expenditures...	+3.0	+4.3	+10.0	+ 7.8	+10.8	+ 9.3	+13.8
Residential construction.....	+0.7	+0.3	+ 0.5	- 1.8	- 0.8	- 0.1	+ 4.5
Other private construction...	+0.1	+0.4	+ 0.6	- 1.1†	- 0.6†	+ 0.5	+ 0.9
Producer equipment.........	+0.6	+1.3	+ 1.4	- 2.6†	- 0.3†	+ 1.4	+ 1.7
Inventory investment.......	+1.1	+1.8	+ 2.3	- 2.7†	- 2.6†	- 0.2†	+ 9.9
Net exports...............	-0.2	+0.6	- 0.4	- 1.3†	- 2.0†	+ 0.1†	- 3.2
Federal government expenditures.................	-0.1	+1.0	+10.7	+35.1	+29.2	+ 7.8	- 2.9
State and local government expenditures...........	+0.7	-0.2	- 0.1	- 0.1	- 0.3	+ 0.1	+ 1.8
Gross national product*.....	+5.9	+9.5	+25.0	+33.3	+33.4	+18.9	+26.5

*The sum of component expenditure changes differs slightly from the change in gross national product in 1941 because of rounding errors.
†Amounts which would normally have been counted under these cells are included in federal government expenditure because the government took control of investment in prosecution of the war.

By the time we actively entered the war in December, 1941, the over-all economy was operating near full tilt. In some sectors, as noted above, this had been achieved a year earlier. Throughout the period of our participation the problem of a diverted demand distribution was as much of a pinch on civilian activity as was the high level of forced draft. This fact is only partially indicated by the disproportionate rise in industrial production, which more than doubled, compared with a rise of less than 75 per cent in total physical product. More critically, the expansion of weapon-induced industrial production was relatively much greater than that of other manufacturing activity. It drew not only from other types of industrial production, but also from potential civilian products in the same industrial classifications.

Even as a rough measure of critical demand, industrial production provides a revealing picture. The peak in industrial production was reached in November, 1943, long before the war ended. This fact is related to a type of culmination, much like that which occurs in the business cycle. Early in the war, calls could be made for defense production anywhere because needed supply was universally short. By the time of the peak in industrial production, this was no longer true. In fact, supplies were readily and quickly built up wherever specifications were clear. Shortages arose with respect to new weapons which were just leaving the drawing board stage. These facts are functions of the rapid changes taking place in the technology of war, so that many of last year's weapons had constantly become out of date. In a vague way, too, it was related to the scale at which we had pitched our war effort to begin with, although such a thesis is too complicated to pursue here. Surely, that thesis would not be valid if our efforts had not continued to achieve some measure of success, for then we might have materially reevaluated the war contribution expected of the civilian economy.[8]

An early leveling of the economy is also indicated by the fact that the number of persons attached to the armed services reached an approximate peak sometime in 1944. Unemployment increased from 700,000 in 1944 to a million in 1945. By 1944, to an increasing extent, some resources were being kept idle and not released for civilian activity. The problem was not simple, and on the whole the decisions made were sound. Certain materials had reached a supply sufficient to permit their use in civilian production; but in desired civilian activity, they would have had to be combined with complementary materials which were still short. Furthermore, supplies which were plentiful one day might be short the next, as an outgrowth of technical change in weapons. Regional problems also led to some difficulty, for manufacturers in one area might be able to call on unemployed labor, while in other areas, labor was still tight; neat decisions were required to avoid the appearance of giving a head start to certain companies whose executives were aiding in the direction of the War Production Board.

The degree of forced draft had reached major proportions after we entered the war. The total labor force rose from 56 million in

---

[8]See Bureau of the Budget, Committee on Records of the War Administration, *The United States at War*, Historical Reports on War Administration, No. 1 (Washington, D.C.: U.S. Government Printing Office, 1947). Dr. Clarence H. Danhof played a vital part in the preparation of this book.

1940 to 66 million in 1944. Some seven or eight million of these would not have entered the labor force according to the prevailing labor participation rates in various divisions of the American population in 1940. The labor force dropped back to 61 million by 1946.

Table 13-5 very poorly reflects the forced draft situation. To begin with, it is virtually impossible to obtain a meaningful total when product distributions are shifting so rapidly and are complicated by relatively artificial pricing in the expanding government sector. For this reason, the total changes in activity shown do not well reflect changing demand. We did not use constant price units in that table because of vagueness in year-to-year change in prices of goods bought by the government.[9] The fact clearly revealed by Table 13-5 is the predominant influence of the federal government as well as the continued rise in consumer purchases. Even in constant dollars, consumer purchases rose every year except 1942, when a major cutback was made in consumer durables.

The investment classifications are unreliable in Table 13-5. The government stepped up investment expenditures, and these are buried in the tremendous rises shown for the federal government. Even today, the amounts involved have not been entirely disentangled. We do know that government construction expenditures rose dramatically in 1942 and were cut back thereafter, but good information is not available on the amount of government money spent for producer equipment. Inventory accumulation in the hands of government agencies must have been large. Presumably, these government expenditures more than offset the declines the table shows in private investment.

War Financing. The way a war is financed has a major impact on the postwar period, and World War II was no exception, as we shall see in the following chapter. On the whole the financial operation was reasonably successful in this case. Over half of the federal government expenditures were financed by taxes, and a third were from funds borrowed from nonbank investors, essentially a subtraction from the current income flow. Wholesale prices rose only 12½ per cent from Pearl Harbor to VJ day. They had risen substantially more in the year 1941.

Bills were successively submitted to raise taxes with advances in war expenditures, although there was a lag in Congressional

---

[9]The information is provided conveniently in constant prices in *U.S. Income and Output: A Supplement to the Survey of Current Business* (Washington, D.C.: U.S. Government Printing Office, 1958), pp. 118–19.

action, and the liquidity situation could have been kept under better control with prompter decisions. On the other hand, some increase in "take-home" pay was necessary to induce the movement of resources into war production, especially in the early phases of the war. Taxes scaled at too high a level might have had a crippling effect.

Consumer expenditure was kept down in various ways, many of which were unplanned. Perhaps most important was a change in the social structure arising from the draft of ten million men. Life at home no longer was the same. Furthermore, patriotic impulses were sensitively touched. Even aside from these influences the effective stoppage of the flow of critical items (gasoline, for example) essential for a rounded social life reduced the urge to consume many others.

A key factor thus was involved in the War Production Board orders on allocation of materials and limitation of production of various types of goods. While these orders were issued essentially for the purpose of assuring a sufficient supply of materials and plant capacity for war production, they had the effect of limiting items critically needed in rounded consumer expenditure.

Certainly, rationing and price controls under the operation of the Office of Price Administration exerted an influence. Rations were placed principally on food, which fortunately was produced in increasing supply and with a decreasing labor force. The abundance of farm production has been a continual embarrassment in peacetime, but is a great boon in war time, especially when large food supplies must be provided Allies whose domestic sources have been reduced and to vastly increased armed services. Meat was a problem; and at times, rationing did not work too well, because the supplies did not build up as rapidly as in the case of grain crops.

The effectiveness of price control has remained a continual argument. We believe it to have been reasonably effective, because the majority of civilians did not wish to buy beyond the allotment the price controls logically implied. The reasons for such restraint have been explained in the above paragraphs. The price control, however, was effective in keeping the minority reasonably well in line when overwhelming sentiment favored it. We are convinced that the guidance of public opinion was essential to the success of price control and rationing.

The Federal Reserve willingly subordinated monetary policy to successful financing of the war. Interest rates were kept low, partly by monetary management and partly by the major elimination of civilian demand for investment funds, an outgrowth of limitation and material controls. Excess reserves of member banks were built up to unprecedented levels in 1941 and 1942. They were permitted to decline substantially by 1945 with the tremendous build-up of commercial bank holdings of government securities (from $20 billion to $80 billion), but remained large enough for maneuverability. The government bill rate rose from 3 to 3¾ per cent, with the reserve banks absorbing $12 billion, but the rate on long-term government bonds held close to 2½ per cent. The rate of return on industrial bonds declined somewhat. Credit ease was effectively manipulated. Stock prices tended to rise after 1942, but the future looked uncertain enough that they did not reattain the relatively low 1936 level until mid-1945.

One important effect was a vast increase in personal savings. These grew to a fourth of disposable income in 1943 and 1944, compared with a typical peacetime percentage of 7 or a little less. The result was an increase in liquid assets—including principally currency, deposits, and government bonds—of $100 billion. Additionally, business holdings of liquid assets increased $50 billion.

Another effect was the coercion to maintain credit ease which the monetary authorities found themselves inheriting from the war. With taxes paying only a little over half of the cost of the war, the federal government debt had risen more than $200 billion. In the light of current postwar decisions, its management appeared most feasible to the administration under a system of easy credit. In the next chapter, we shall see that these situations played vital parts in the following years.

FOR REFLECTION AND ANALYSIS

1. Contrast the prosperity period preceding the depressions beginning in 1836, 1873, and 1929.
2. Critically appraise the influence of conditions in the twenties on the development of serious depression.
3. How did stock market declines play a part in the downturn and contraction, beginning in 1929?
4. How did the National Recovery Administration influence the 1933–37 recovery?
5. Why was the standard of living not higher in 1937 than in 1929?
6. What part did consumer expenditures play in (a) the 1929–33 decline and (b) the 1933–37 expansion?
7. Comment on changes in government expenditure in the Great Depression.

8. How could a business cycle downturn occur at the depressed level of activity in 1937?
9. Why did the contraction culminate faster in 1937–38 than in 1929–33?
10. Comment on the sizable proportion of GNP increase accounted for by consumer expenditures in 1940 and 1941.
11. Did the business cycle peak in 1943 or 1945?
12. Discuss the financial arrangements employed in financing World War II.

POSTWAR GROWTH

AND RECESSIONS

The major lesson of recent economic history is that universal efforts to increase liquid assets result in an over-all decline, while universal intentions to spend such assets result in their increase. In the early thirties, frantic efforts were made to pay off debts and accumulate monetary funds. The result was a 30 per cent decline in bank deposits from 1929 to 1933. In the postwar the predominant tendency has been to use monetary funds to purchase product, and liquid assets have risen 70 per cent from 1946 to 1960. The total to 1959 is broken down by type in Table 14-1.

The reason for such enigmatic behavior is clear from an analysis of aggregative activity. Widespread failure to spend feeds on itself, in accordance with the multiplier principle, and credit which financed the higher level of activity is liquidated. (Liquid assets are credit manifestations of financial institutions—as, for instance, the bank deposit created by short-term borrowing.) Widespread increases in spending, on the other hand, force the setting-up of credit in the financing process. (How much credit must be set up has been a perennial argument in economics.)

The liquid assets do shift between various groups in the economy in accordance with urges to spend. While the holdings of individuals rose steadily from 1946 to 1949, those of unincorporated business declined. Total demand deposits increased by two thirds from 1949 to 1959, while the holdings of individuals remained practically constant. Business, rather than individuals, needed more deposits to care for rising transactions in that period.

The large rise in liquid assets in the postwar was closely related to advancing prices and interest rates. While the creation of liquid assets reflects an aggregation of individual choices, it is subject to some degree of governmental control. The desirability of control

TABLE 14-1
LIQUID ASSETS OF NONFINANCIAL SECTORS, 1939–59
(In Billions of Dollars)

Year	(1) Total Liquid Assets	(2) Money Supply	(3) Time Deposits	(4) Savings and Loan Shares	(5) Mutual Savings Deposits	(6) Credit Union Shares	(7) Postal Savings Deposits	(8) Policy Reserve in Life Insurance Companies	(9) U.S. Savings Bonds	(10) Total as a Percentage of Gross National Product
1939	95.4	36.2	15.3	4.1	10.5	0.2	1.3	25.8	2.0	105.7
1940	104.6	42.3	15.8	4.3	10.7	0.2	1.3	27.2	2.8	104.0
1941	115.7	48.6	15.9	4.7	10.5	0.3	1.4	28.9	5.4	92.0
1942	140.7	62.9	16.4	4.9	10.6	0.3	1.4	30.8	13.4	88.4
1943	175.8	79.6	19.2	5.5	11.7	0.3	1.8	33.0	24.7	91.3
1944	208.7	90.4	24.1	6.3	13.4	0.4	2.3	35.6	36.2	98.7
1945	240.0	102.3	30.1	7.4	15.3	0.4	2.9	38.7	42.9	112.4
1946	258.8	110.0	33.8	8.5	16.9	0.4	3.3	41.7	44.2	122.8
1947	271.4	113.6	35.2	9.8	17.8	0.5	3.4	44.9	46.2	115.8
1948	276.7	111.6	35.8	11.0	18.4	0.6	3.3	48.2	47.8	106.7
1949	283.8	111.2	36.1	12.5	19.3	0.7	3.2	51.5	49.3	110.0
1950	296.2	117.7	36.3	14.0	20.0	0.8	2.9	54.9	49.6	104.1
1951	310.8	124.5	37.6	16.1	20.9	1.1	2.7	58.5	49.1	94.5
1952	327.2	129.0	40.7	19.2	22.6	1.4	2.5	62.6	49.2	94.3
1953	341.6	130.7	43.7	22.8	24.4	1.7	2.4	66.7	49.4	93.5
1954	359.9	134.4	46.8	27.3	26.4	2.0	2.1	70.9	50.0	99.1
1955	376.9	138.2	48.4	32.2	28.2	2.4	1.9	75.4	50.2	94.8
1956	391.7	139.7	50.6	37.1	30.0	2.9	1.6	79.7	50.1	93.4
1957	405.3	138.6	56.1	41.9	31.7	3.4	1.3	84.1	48.2	91.6
1958	430.5	144.2	63.2	47.9	34.0	3.8	1.1	88.6	47.7	97.5
June, 1959	433.7	139.0	65.4	51.4	34.6	4.1	1.1	91.1	47.0	90.4

Source: John G. Gurley, "Liquidity and Financial Institutions in the Postwar Economy," Study Paper No. 14, *Study of Employment, Growth, and Price Levels for Consideration by Joint Economic Committee, Congress of the United States* (Washington, D.C.: U.S. Government Printing Office, 1960).

measures must be evaluated in the light of evolving economic conditions and therefore is discussed below in connection with the consideration of particular periods.

RECONVERSION TO PEACE

As the war was ending, the major question on reconversion of the economy was: To what extent will the prewar depression return? The answer frequently given was that the economy would move back to depression levels. The most famous postwar forecast which gave direct recognition to changes in expenditure levels was the one made by Hagen and Kirkpatrick in reflection of the prevailing attitude in various federal government departments. In indicating the quarterly change in activity, the forecast represented a good performance, but it was pitched at so low a level that unemployment was greatly overestimated.[1] Hagen later confessed: "The egregiously erroneous conclusion was drawn that the economic climate of the transition would be dominantly deflationary. . . . I was bemused by my preconception of a deflationary period during the reconversion interval."[2]

The economic analysts who made gloomy postwar forecasts were those who were impressed by the secular stagnation doctrine. Since they could be so wrong on the postwar period, it seems fair to say that they could have been quite wrong on the prewar period. We suggest that there is no closed case indicating that forces internal to the business system could not have generated prosperity if war had been avoided.

We do see, though, that an important shift had occurred in attitudes. The predominant motivation before the war was the acquisition of cash funds. Shortages of supply of product were virtually unknown. The predominant motivation after the war was procurement of goods. Shortages of goods were almost universal. They had existed during most of the war, and deferred demand was widespread. Liquid funds were in unprecedented supply.

Unsatisfied demand was almost universal. This leads to prosperous rather than to depressed activity. Time required for reconversion was an important question, and estimated unemployment was related to delay in getting peacetime plants set up. In some

---

[1] See the writer's "A Reconsideration of the Postwar Forecasts," *Journal of Business of the University of Chicago*, April, 1953.

[2] Everett E. Hagen, "The Reconversion Period: Reflections of a Forecaster," *Review of Economic Statistics*, May, 1947.

cases, reconversion actually was unnecessary or performed momentarily, as in the case of most nondurable goods. The market would absorb supplies of practically anything, like the urgent demand of the armed services early in the war. Where supplies were short, much employment was created by appointing co-ordinators whose job it was to obtain goods in short supply.

If you look back to Table 4–1 (page 48), you will see that the National Bureau of Economic Research dates a downturn at February, 1945. This is the point, well before the war was ended, at which drastic decline in government expenditures began. Because of that, and because civilian activity was still restrained from getting immediately under way, indicators show a drop at that date. We would argue, however, that the National Bureau rules which require dating reference points at the end of horizontal movements does not work too well in this case. As noted in the preceding chapter, the peak of war production was reached late in 1943, and the peak in total draft of labor some time early in 1944. The culminating factors involved were related to the technicalities of war and therefore do not help too much in the analysis of peacetime variation. For most purposes, we may ignore that downturn at any of these dates.

The National Bureau dates the upturn at October, 1945, almost immediately after the end of the Japanese war. As the above analysis indicates, civilian demand flooded the market from that point on. While we have no argument with the dating of an upturn in the autumn of 1945, we doubt its peacetime significance, since the downturn itself is related to culmination of war activity, and whatever decline did occur was due to disruption caused by withdrawal of war demand or the withdrawal of the forced draft on resources. This "business cycle" fluctuation, therefore, is given no further consideration.

As Table 14–3 (page 306) shows, federal government activity was cut back with abandon. By the end of 1946 the cutback amounted to nearly $70 billion. This represented a third of total product. It is indeed remarkable that expenditures in the private economy rose almost fast enough to offset the decline. Private expenditures rose rapidly in every area, as can be seen by looking down the 1946 column in Table 14–3.

The rapid rise in civilian expenditures in 1946 was fed by inflation. The fires of inflation were dependent on high liquidity, deferred demand, and a continued policy of easy credit. The Federal

Reserve, rather unwillingly, continued to support the government bond market by buying government securities when necessary. Excess reserves of member banks doubled from early 1945 to 1946, and bank loans rose rapidly at the expense of holdings of government securities by member banks.

Wartime controls of prices and wages were not dropped neatly, and their elimination was inflationary to an indeterminate extent. At first, wage rates were freed of control so long as any rise did not require price advances. The unions generally argued that price advances were unnecessary to support the wage increases they desired to achieve, and the door was swung open on sharp labor-management clashes. The steel industry was virtually closed down by a strike in January, 1946, and this was highly inflationary in view of the urgent demand existing for steel. In mid-February, the administration outlined its wage-price policy more fully, to the effect that wage rate increases of 33 per cent from January, 1941, would be granted automatically and price increases when necessary to meet the higher costs. Inevitably, this ruling recognized the need for an increase in steel prices, since they had not advanced during the war. A wave of price increases was set off, as shown by the wholesale price line in Chart 14-1.

By June the increase represented 5 per cent, and the Congress was not impressed with the price control performance. Enactment of a measure to replace expiring price control was unsatisfactory to President Truman, and he vetoed the bill. Price advances amounted to over 10 per cent in early July, and in desperation the President signed a bill not differing substantially from the June measure, except that rollbacks for some recent advances were enacted. The rollback idea did not work; and by executive order, all price controls except rent were terminated in October. By December, wholesale prices were a third higher than they had been at the end of the war, but further rises were minor up to the time of the Korean War. Perhaps the price advance would have been no more, or even less, if the entire control mechanism had been dismantled at the war end. However, we do not believe that would have represented the wisest answer. A slow dismantling of controls appears to have been indicated, but it should have proceeded in an orderly fashion. Unplanned, *ad hoc* decisions surely exaggerated the price increase. Retreat from depression forecasts was responsible. If the true degree of demand urgency had been forecast, a slow release of the control brakes could have been put into effect.

Condemnation of lack of credit control by monetary authorities and lack of contractionary measures through fiscal policy has become common in recent years. If taxes had been maintained at the war rates, instead of being rapidly reduced, a large part of the liquid funds in the economy would have been eliminated. The process, however, would have produced recession, and this outcome would have been unsatisfactory. Any such proposal would have been a shock because of the pervasive conviction that removal of war expenditures would, of itself, initiate deep depression.

CHART 14-1

PRICE RISE IN THE 1946–48 PROSPERITY

(February, 1946 = 100)

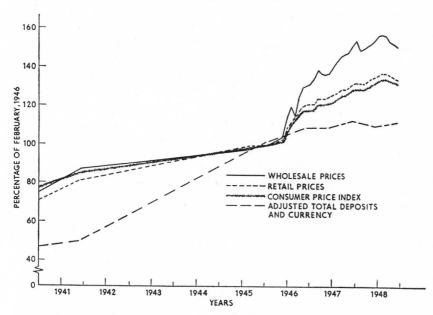

Inflation could have been avoided to an indeterminate extent by stricter monetary controls. Holding down bank loans would have slowed the expansion of inventories. Increase in interest rates in line with the market demand for investment funds would have reduced profit expectations available in pursuing investment projects. How much inflation would have thereby been reduced cannot be readily guessed. The holding of liquid assets by individuals and businesses in itself could have financed substantial inventory build-up. In the case of durable investment, needed expansion to meet current demand appeared to be the principal drive accounting

TABLE 14-2

POSTWAR ADVANCE IN EXPENDITURES

(In Billions of 1954 Dollars)

Explanation	1940	1944	1945	1946	1947	1948	1949	1950	1953	1957	1959
Gross national product	205.8	317.9	314.0	282.8	282.3	293.1	292.7	318.1	369.0	408.6	428.0
Personal expenditures	144.6	160.2	171.4	192.3	195.6	199.3	204.3	216.8	235.1	271.3	289.3
Residential construction*	7.3	1.4	1.8	7.3	9.6	11.4	11.2	15.5	13.6	15.3	19.4
Other construction*	6.3	3.4	4.8	10.0	10.3	11.2	11.1	11.9	14.0	16.5	15.0
Producer equipment	10.9	9.2	12.7	16.1	21.7	22.8	19.8	21.3	22.5	24.6	21.3
Inventory investment	4.5	− 1.7	− 2.4	9.0	0.1	4.4	− 3.6	7.2	0.5	1.6	5.2
Net exports	1.1	− 6.7	− 5.6	3.8	− 8.0	2.0	2.6	0.2	− 0.9	3.8	− 2.4
Federal government	13.1	138.4	117.1	28.2	19.4	22.9	25.3	21.6	58.8	43.2	43.6
State and local government	18.0	13.8	14.0	15.8	17.8	19.2	21.9	23.5	25.5	32.3	36.6

Source: Department of Commerce, as of the 1959 revisions.

*Farm residences are included with other construction.

for capital expenditures. What this means is that any interest cost, within reasonable limits, was assumed to be readily covered in prices the market would sustain in view of the urgency of demand.

In writing history, we should avoid getting too far away from the facts in pointing out "what could have been." In summary, however, we may say that the most promising procedure for keeping down inflationary price rises would have required a planned removal of price and wage controls and a satisfactory forecast of demand potentialities. Lacking these, any lengthy discussion of the evils of lax fiscal and monetary controls would be irresponsible. We do not mean to say that fiscal and monetary policy could not have played a part in the process. But they would have required planning in relation to the withdrawal of controls and realistic assumptions on civilian demand.

POSTWAR GROWTH

In the view of the urgency of civilian demand, a simple projection of postwar growth might appear readily possible, but it is not. Without any question, output was moving along a much higher level than prewar. This, however, indicates no more than that prosperous, rather than depressed, conditions were enjoyed.

To reflect growth, we must examine physical product, for a change in the price level does not indicate a higher or lower standard of living. Table 14-2 shows that deflated gross national product did not get back to the 1944 war peak until 1950, six years later. Certainly, this period represented upward rather than horizontal growth. There are three reasons for the horizontal appearance: (1) The war marked an abnormal advance in production, so that even with rapid growth the postwar product would have involved some retrenchment. (2) The reconversion necessitated a very great product redistribution. (3) A rapid price advance occurred. The price advance was not uniform among different products, and the measurement of violent price changes is not reliable.

The fact that some decline from the high wartime levels had to be expected presents something of a problem in interpreting empirical data. The degree to which war overexpansion occurred cannot be precisely measured, and the prewar levels were far below secular levels, so that no satisfactory base from which to measure postwar growth is available.

At best, the adding-together of very unlike products to measure total product cannot provide precise results. The make-up changed rapidly, as shown in Table 14-2. With violent price changes, error in price measurements for different types of product might indicate significant modifications of the total.

Little hope, therefore, can be held for an effective empirical measurement of growth for the latter half of the forties. The rise which occurred in consumer expenditures from 1946 to 1949, nevertheless, is not entirely lacking in significance. It amounted to 6 per cent per year, in spite of the fact that 1949 was a recession year. In this same period, expenditures for producer equipment rose over 7 per cent per year, and construction rose even more; but short-period expenditures for investment are unreliable as an indication of growth. Even government expenditures advanced. Gross national product, in deflated terms, rose more than 3 per cent per year. The slower advance in total product is accounted for by a major shift occurring in inventory investment. Artificially adjusting inventory investment to zero, the increase in deflated gross national product would be over 8 per cent per year. Recognizing that 1949 was a recession year and that the changes occurring in inventory investment resulted from conditions in transient demand, very satisfactory growth appears to have occurred in the first three postwar years.

With the Korean War breaking out in 1950, it is difficult, again, to estimate growth in the economy because of the rapid build-up in government product. Some idea of the growth may be obtained, however, by measuring change from the 1948 peak to the 1956-57 (July, 1956-June, 1957) peak. The advance averaged 4 per cent per year. This is a more rapid advance than shown by longer-run growth. The percentage increase in gross national product from 1910 to 1956-57, for instance, is 280, or 3 per cent per year.[3] The long-term measure is likely to be more accurate because it is less influenced by minor variations appearing in particular years. Precise differences between these percentages have no reliability, but we may reasonably conclude that the rate of growth was accelerated in the fifties. The most plausible explanation of accelerated growth is technological improvement, as explained in Chapter 6.

The postwar period was marked by certain artificial, expansionary forces. In the early years, activity was driven up by excessive

---

[3]The measurements given in this paragraph are derived from *U.S. Income and Output: A Supplement to the Survey of Current Business* (Washington, D.C.: U.S. Government Printing Office, 1958), pp. 118-25 and 138. From the 1953-54 peak to the 1956-57 peak represents an advance of only 3 per cent per year, for 1953-54 was abnormally high because of the Korean War.

liquidity and by deferred demand. As these influences were declining, the outbreak of the Korean War created a renewed surge in demand, but it left less liquidity (in relation to the higher prices) and less deferred demand in its wake. With less artificial expansion of demand in 1955–57, unemployment was a third higher than in 1948 and a half again as much as in 1952–53.

Certain inflationary forces were constantly present. A rapid advance occurred in population growth, and this assured an expanded area of demand even if the rise in living standards should lag. The recessions which occurred obviously were moderated by automatic stabilizers, and the maintenance of consumer demand encouraged the holding of prices. Depreciation charges universally added to the cost of product, first because of accelerated defense amortization, then because of liberalization of the tax code to permit faster depreciation write-offs, and finally because the rise in cost of capital goods carried forward for a long time a steady increase in the dollar amount of depreciation write-offs. With the established farm program, the rapid increase in farm production was not permitted to bring substantial cuts in the price of agricultural produce, and thus a contractionary effect was avoided, while government stock-piling of agricultural commodities added a constant support. Government expenditures, although not uniformly rising, were much higher than prewar, except for 1947, and thus provided a minimum buttress supporting demand. The shift in employment to "white-collar" workers who normally would be classified as overhead represented a similar development.

Contrasted with the thirties, advance was exceptional, representing 75 per cent to the end of the forties and nearly 140 per cent to the end of the fifties. This, of course, is a measure of shift from depressed to prosperous conditions rather than a measure of growth.

EARLY POSTWAR EXPANSION AND 1949 RECESSION

The rapid cutback in federal government expenditures is shown in Table 14–3. In current-dollar terms, in which the figures are stated in the table, no over-all gross national product decrease occurred in 1945 and only a negligible one in 1946. The result is partially due to rising prices, but rising prices will sustain a market condition as well as physical output. About half of the over $50 billion decline in government expenditures in 1946 was offset by a rise in consumer expenditures and the other half by a rise in business expenditures. This marks the powerful influence of deferred demand and of abnormally high liquid assets. In ordinary peacetime conditions, major expenditure groups rise and fall together. The tremendous extent to which expenditure gains in the private economy were compensating for expenditure losses in the government economy sparked the imagination. It is too much to say that the idea of "rolling readjustment" was born at this date, but an important background was established for its plausibility, to which the post-Korean developments lent reassurance.

The year 1947 was one of difficult decision. With rapid price rises and urgent private demand, expansion of the economy was not significantly in doubt after 1946 was well under way. By early 1947, however, prices were showing less strength, and a runoff of inventories was beginning.

TABLE 14–3

CHANGING EXPENDITURES EARLY IN THE POSTWAR*

(Changes from Preceding Year in Billions of Dollars)

Explanation	1945	1946	1947	1948	1949	1950
Personal expenditure........	+11.9	+25.4	+18.3	+12.9	+2.9	+13.8
Residential construction†.....	+ 0.3	+ 3.7	+ 2.7	+ 2.6	−0.5	+ 4.5
Other construction†..........	+ 0.8	+ 3.6	+ 1.4	+ 1.6	−0.1	+ 0.9
Producer equipment.........	+ 2.3	+ 3.0	+ 6.0	+ 2.2	−1.7	+ 1.7
Inventory investment........	− 0.1	+ 7.5	− 6.9	+ 5.2	−7.8	+ 9.9
Net exports................	+ 0.5	+ 6.3	+ 4.1	− 5.5	+0.3	− 3.2
Federal government.........	−14.2	−54.2	− 4.9	+ 3.6	+2.9	− 2.9
State and local government...	+ 0.6	+ 1.8	+ 2.8	+ 2.5	+2.7	+ 1.8
Gross national product*......	+ 2.2	− 2.9	+23.6	+25.1	−1.3	+26.5

* Expenditures do not add precisely to total gross national product in 1945 and 1947 because of errors in rounding.
† Farm residences are included with other construction.

Nearly half of the rise in gross national product in the first half of 1947 is accounted for by net exports, but aid and gold funds were being exhausted in making payments for our exports. The major source of increases in activity seemed certain to recede. The picture changed, however, when Secretary Marshall proposed that we provide funds in a European recovery program sufficient to re-establish normal trade. Instantaneous favorable response led to continued high net exports for the rest of the year.

With large liquid assets and deferred demand, consumers were spending approximately all of the disposable income received. An increase in veterans' benefits in the third quarter sparked a continued high rate of expenditures. By the fourth quarter an additional spurt occurred in residential housing. Unemployment fell to the lowest level since the war. Prices were again showing substantial advances in a buoyant market.

Early in 1948, however, it was obvious that many prices were passing peak levels. Wheat, which had more than tripled in price from prewar, dropped 25 per cent by midyear. This was an omen, indicating that the bloom was gone from foreign demand. Food had been the shortest commodity in the war-torn countries; and with the international sources of supply re-established, dependence on our supplies was fading. By mid-1948, total net exports were barely a third of the high level reached a year earlier. Prices in some commodity groups passed their peak levels in January, including foods, hides and leather, and chemicals. Many others reached peaks by midyear. A modest inventory accumulation was under way, after discontinuance in 1947. Price-wise, it was justified by accumulators of important metals and of building materials. Zinc and copper prices rose substantially during the year but hit peak levels before the year end. By that time, need for caution was universally recognized.

After mid-1948, expenditures tapered off on a physical quantity basis. Some continued rise occurred in inventory investment in critical materials and in government expenditures. Other groups, in deflated terms, did not rise. As for durable investment, the fact that expenditures, in deflated terms, had been leveling off no doubt meant that the completion rate was catching up with the starting rate.

Much has been made of the leveling which was occurring in consumer expenditures. This was most obvious in nondurables. Presumably, deferred demand had been made up most conspicuously in that area. Expenditures for consumer durables were rising less than in the preceding year. This occurred in spite of the fact that personal taxes were cut 15 per cent early in 1948, as a result of lowered income tax rates. Either the lowered income taxes brought a price increase under the expansionary conditions, or individuals largely chose not to spend the increase made available in disposable income. In either case the net effect was a return of the personal saving rate to the normal level of about 7 per cent. Since physical expenditures did not increase much and prices did, both influences may have been involved.

Inventory investment does not appear to have been dependent on the leveling of consumer expenditures. The greater rise in consumer expenditures in 1947 resulted in no inventory investment, while a fair inventory investment did occur throughout 1948.

It is not likely that other investment reacted adversely to slackened consumer buying. The very advanced rate of expenditure for producer equipment must have largely exhausted deferred demand. In deflated terms, such expenditures were only slightly higher in 1955–57, when consumer expenditures were a third greater. On a deflated basis, nonresidential construction little more than leveled off in the recession in 1949.

In line with the weakening of the doubly reinforcing influence of investment, the supply situation generally appeared easier, as indicated by prices. On the average, wholesale prices hit their peak in August, three months before the downturn. Price rises which continued later in the year were spotty. Rising imports and declining exports were deflationary throughout the year. All of these factors played a part in rounding out the expansion, but spreading of the belief that prices were actually "topping out" was the most influential in leading to culmination.

Not only did practically all commodity prices pass their highs by the end of the year, but it was becoming increasingly clear that tighter monetary policies were to be expected. Consumer credit controls were revived after a lapse of nearly a year. Member bank reserve requirements were raised three times in 1948. The Federal Reserve had bought $10 billion of government bonds to support the government bond market in the year beginning with December, 1947. Even with this unprecedented maneuver, bond prices were slipping. Government bond prices were at war levels at the end of 1948, after having risen about four points. The Reserve Bank holdings were being pared even before the end of 1948, however, and it was clear that the Federal Reserve might be expected to reassert monetary control.

Inventory investment fell from $6 billion in 1948 to −$5 billion in 1949. The $11 billion decline was more than the total drop in gross national product. Actually, though, the decline in nonfarm inventory investment was less than $9 billion, equaling the drop in GNP. With falling farm product prices, farmers were selling part of their inventories, which accounted for $2 billion of the $11 billion drop in GNP. Since a runoff in farm inventories does not directly curtail activity, the $2 billion less significantly reflects contraction.

Other expenditure streams moved oppositely enough to cancel each other out. Government expenditures rose $5 billion, largely because of a rise in defense expenditures from the extreme lows which had been reached (and unrelated to the exigencies of the recession). Net exports reacted by about $1 billion from the lows of 1948 because our prices of the goods bought were falling in the recession. Producer equipment expenditures declined some $3 billion, as they would be expected to do in recession. The fact that inventory investment accounted for the total decline in gross national product is, therefore, something of a coincidence.

Neither can it be said that the inventory decline in relation to price expectations, by itself, accounts for the recession, although it does most powerfully mark the culmination. The downturn was also related to leveling of expansion, marked by approach to full use of resources, by sharp decline in net exports (from 1947 to 1948), and by the leveling of durable investment and of consumer expenditures.

The fact that consumer expenditures experienced no net decline and, in deflated terms, actually rose in most of the recession is worth noting. The result is partly dependent on automatic stabilizers which had become more powerful than in earlier recessions, on the reduction of the personal income tax in the spring of 1948, and on the rise in service expenditures with continued increases in service prices (although even in deflated terms, service expenditures continued to rise somewhat). Also, the high level of holdings of liquid funds, even after discounting for advance in prices, must have had some influence. Recognition must be given, of course, to the fact that consumer expenditures tend to fluctuate less than investment, and that a leveling-off may mark a recession in an economy experiencing rapid growth.

Increase in inventory investment from the low of the recession in the fourth quarter of 1949 accounted for nearly all of the rise in gross national product to the first quarter of 1950. This is characteristic of typical culmination of inventory runoff, which was discussed in earlier chapters. The advance involved sparked recovery, and the typical rapid advance of early expansion was in evidence from the first to the second quarter of 1950, most notably in business equipment. The rapid early advance in residential construction was unusual. By early 1950, both gross national product and industrial production exceeded all earlier levels, even though the upturn occurred in October, 1949.

THE 1950-53 EXPANSION AND THE 1953-54 RECESSION

The whole character of the expansion was changed with our entry into the Korean War in June. The third quarter of 1950 and the first quarter of 1951 were marked by a surge of consumption expenditure unparalleled except at the end of World War II. The buying frenzy was related to fear of war shortages. In deflated terms, consumption expenditure fell after the third quarter of 1950 because of the extreme high attained in spending for durables. Expenditures for less storable goods and services rose about as rapidly later as in the 1946–48 expansion.

Although the Korean incident occurred in June, 1950, the rise in defense expenditures was only getting under way at the end of the year. In fact, for the full year, government expenditures were less in 1950 than in 1949, as shown by Table 14–4. The table reveals, however, that the rise in government expenditures was the predominant influence in 1951. According to the official figures, that rise principally represented increases in physical product. The large dollar increase in personal expenditures in 1951, on the other hand, almost wholly represented increase in prices.

TABLE 14–4

CHANGING EXPENDITURES IN RELATION TO KOREAN WAR*

(Changes from Preceding Year in Billions of Dollars)

Explanation	1950	1951	1952	1953	1954	1955
Personal expenditure................	+13.8	+14.8	+10.0	+12.8	+ 5.4	+18.9
Residential construction†..........	+ 4.5	− 1.6	+ 0.2	+ 1.0	+ 1.6	+ 3.3
Other construction†................	+ 0.9	+ 2.2	+ 0.4	+ 1.1	+ 0.5	+ 1.9
Producer equipment................	+ 1.7	+ 2.4	+ 0.0	+ 1.0	− 1.5	+ 2.3
Inventory investment..............	+ 9.9	+ 3.4	− 7.1	− 2.7	− 2.1	+ 7.4
Net exports......................	− 3.2	+ 1.8	− 1.1	− 1.7	+ 1.4	+ 0.1
Federal government...............	− 2.9	+19.5	+14.1	+ 5.1	−10.5	− 2.2
State and local government........	+ 1.8	+ 2.0	+ 1.5	+ 1.7	+ 2.8	+ 2.6
Gross national product*..........	+26.5	+44.4	+18.0	+18.4	− 2.3	+34.4

*Expenditures do not add precisely to total gross national product in 1954 and 1955 because of errors in rounding.
†Farm residences are included with other construction.

In 1952 the increase in all prices was smaller. In physical terms, increase in defense expenditure represented a greater amount than the total increase in gross national product. As indicated in Table 14–4, the major negative factor was a reduced rate of inventory accumulation. The very rapid rate of inventory accumulation in 1950–51 was necessary for servicing the build-up in defense expenditures, especially in view of the development of new weapons. Inventory accumulation was not necessary at the same rate once the basic stocks were established for the new production.

Only a little over half of the $10 billion increase in personal expenditure in 1952 represented physical product, but price inflation was far less than in 1951, when price rises accounted for virtually all of the increase. Personal saving was close to the normal rate, a little less than 8 per cent in both 1951 and 1952.

Unemployment had reached even lower levels than in 1948. Why did the price rise abate in 1952? Successive increases in income tax rates reduced the proportion of disposable income available out of personal income. Rapid increases in consumer buying from mid-1950 to early 1951 encouraged an increase in prices and induced producers to increase inventories in view of the abnormally high level of buying, which they were able to accomplish when consumer buying slackened before major increases occurred in defense spending. Consumers could spend about a normal proportion of their income against an ample supply of goods in view of the early business inventory build-up and because of the fact that the level of war spending was not pitched high enough to pinch production of consumer goods much below the level of consumer purchases. Even in the case of durable goods, which had been cut back by allocation orders, little market pressure was visible.[4]

There were market pressures in the investment area, but allocation orders kept them under control, except for residential housing. Mortgage credit controls were imposed late in 1950 and account for the drop in residential building in 1951; but the controls were partially relaxed in September, 1951. Virtually no increase occurred in construction and equipment expenditures in the private economy in 1952, as Table 14-4 shows. Such expenditures were permitted to remain at high levels, while urgency for still higher levels was moderated by backed-up inventories in many lines, and by controlled prices paid by the government on what came to be a major proportion of many types of investment. Because of allocation, supplies could not have been increased by bidding up prices in any case. Many of the price ceilings which the Office of Price Stabilization was asked to enforce were actually above market quotations.

While the major purpose in this book is to evaluate given economic conditions, we may well point out that the unfolding of economic activity in the Korean War would not likely be precisely

---

[4]See *Economic Report of the President, January, 1952* (Washington, D.C.: U.S. Government Printing Office, 1952), p. 20. In one quarter, the first of 1951, durable goods expenditure, especially furniture and household equipment, rose substantially, and personal saving dropped to 4 per cent. The market pressure in that quarter quickly subsided, and personal saving was up to 9 per cent in the next quarter.

duplicated in another case, and we could not expect the controls employed to provide a satisfactory blueprint. It will be seen, for instance, that consumer "scare" buying at the outbreak of war was responsible for many unexpected developments.

Tax increases actually were great enough that a $6 billion surplus was achieved in 1951, and there was only a $4 billion deficit in 1952. No doubt, this was possible partly because we were accustomed to higher tax rates in World War II. Measures restraining credit expansion must be assigned an important place in keeping inflation under control. As we found ourselves in another military engagement, the inflationary credit arrangements inherited from World War II became increasingly outdated. Reserve requirements were marked up early in 1951. A program of voluntary "credit restraint" was worked out, but the inflation potential appeared too great to rely entirely on moral sausion.

A major issue was support of the government bond market. After the large Federal Reserve purchase of government bonds in 1948, it had been possible to dispose of a substantial part of them in 1949 in a rising bond market, because of more plentiful credit in the recession. The disposal was continued in 1950, but at falling bond prices. The Treasury was worried because it appeared that bond prices shortly would be driven below par, and necessary government borrowing might be made difficult. A Treasury–Federal Reserve Accord was reached in March, 1951, which involved exchange of long-term bonds overhanging the market for a higher-rate non-marketable issue (exchangeable before the due date with five-year notes), precautionary measures to be taken to maintain an orderly bond market when the provisions of the exchange offering were made public, and reduction of purchase by the Federal Reserve of short-term government securities to permit the money market to adjust to a position at which banks would depend on borrowing from the Federal Reserve.[5] As a result, the Federal Reserve was able to discontinue additional purchases of long-term government bonds, except for brief periods. Some additional Federal Reserve purchases of short-term government securities were found necessary, but at a slackened rate after 1951. Thus, after 1951 the traditional function was restored to the money market, and it must have played an important part in keeping the inflation within bounds.

---

[5] See Federal Reserve System, *Thirty-Eighth Annual Report of the Board of Governors, 1951* (Washington, D.C., 1952), pp. 98–101 and 3–8.

Short-term interest rates rose substantially during the rest of the expansion phase. Government bond prices fell significantly.

Defense expenditures advanced slowly in the last year of the war, which ended in mid-1953. Release of resources to the private economy was beginning in mid-1952. Residential construction increased with the complete suspension of mortgage credit controls in September of 1952. Expenditures for business equipment also rose with the elimination of controls by the summer of 1952. The first substantial increases in consumer durable expenditures since early 1951 were experienced with the release of materials. Personal saving, however, remained in the reasonable range of around 8 per cent of disposable income.

These advances little more than offset weaknesses in demand for food and clothing, which had faced little restriction during the war. The prices of both textiles and foods had been declining since early in 1951 and were down by 15 and 8 per cent, respectively, in mid-1953. That demand readjustment was not limited solely to consumer soft-good lines is indicated by the sharp decline in zinc and lead prices in the first half of 1952.

Defense expenditures were rising only imperceptibly early in 1953 and began to decline very slowly when the Korean truce was signed at mid-year. The contrast with the cutback after World War II is marked. Little more than leveling of defense expenditures, however, sparked a culmination of the phase of expansion in 1953. The downturn is marked at July. Expansionary and contractionary demands were about balancing each other in the private economy, and businessmen began to question continued inventory accumulation. As stated by the Council of Economic Advisers, "business requirements for additions to inventories had been fairly well met by the beginning of the year, when it became clear that quicker deliveries could be counted on. The reshaping of the defense program also affected inventories, which here and there became redundant in relation to the reduced military production rates in prospect."[6]

The ensuing decline involved little more than shrinkage in inventory investment and a slow cutback in defense expenditures. By happy circumstance, textile and food demand stabilized at about the time of the downturn in 1953, and prices in these areas were approximately stable until the upturn in August, 1954. Zinc and lead prices experienced but little further decline. That demand generally

---

[6]*Economic Report of the President, January, 1954* (Washington, D.C.: U.S. Government Printing Office, 1954), pp. 21–22.

had stabilized is indicated by the fact that the over-all wholesale Price Index, which had peaked in early 1952, showed no additional decline after the downturn got under way.

The areas where early rises occurred in civilian demand—consumer durables, residential building, and business equipment—little more than leveled off. The inference is that enough deferred demand had accumulated during the Korean war to sustain the achieved rate of activity, but that uncertainties induced by the recession developed enough hesitation in demand that no advance occurred while the recession lasted. For instance, as the recession began, declines occurred in some building prices, notably lumber, which may have induced delays in starting residential construction.

From the peak in the second quarter of 1953 to the trough in the second quarters of 1954, defense expenditures declined $9 billion, nonfarm business inventory investment over $7 billion, and gross national product $10 billion. Obviously, defense expenditures and inventory investment more than accounted for the total expenditure decline in the recession. Furthermore, to a considerable extent, the shrinkage in inventory investment was related to diminishing defense expenditure, although such inventories had been substantially deflated as early as 1952. Other areas of expenditure more than made up for the $6 billion excess of decline in defense and inventories over grosss national product.

The situation gave birth to the idea of "rolling readjustment"— that as inventory and defense expenditures declined, the vacated demands were nearly replaced by others in the economy. Surely, the 1953–54 recession was not wholly typical of earlier ones in our history. The demand for consumer durables scarcely slackened. Even more significantly, durable investment, notably business equipment, experienced only a slight decline. To some persons, it looked like a new kind of readjustment, such that fading demands in one area would be met by rising demands in others. The thesis that the old-type business cycle was gone began to spread.

Before permitting this heady wine to reform our thinking, it is advisable to consider certain facts. Consumer expenditures experienced no decline, partly as a result of more powerful automatic stabilizers, but the proportionate effect of automatic stabilizers is still in doubt. For one thing, the increased payments from social insurance funds to a considerable extent were accounted for by growth in old-age and survivors' insurance benefits, as well as by added unemployment benefits. And failure of consumer expenditures to decline in the postwar is by no means unique. Some measurements indicate that little, if any, such decline occurred in the recessions of the twenties. Furthermore, sustained demand for durable goods, both consumer and producer, was partly due to the building-up of a demand backlog during the war. Certain contingencies, such as shift in agricultural demand so that the market began to stabilize about the time of the business cycle downturn, were a minor factor of strength. Also, net exports tended to stabilize after declining substantially to mid-1952.

The recovery was facilitated by government policy. Member bank reserve requirements were reduced in July, 1953, at the date of the downturn. The federal administration allowed the temporary increases in income taxes on persons and excess profits taxes to lapse in January, 1954. Excise taxes were cut. These were important measures in developing a relatively smooth shift in expenditures from defense to demands in the private economy. It must be admitted that a rise in Social Security contributions which became effective in January, 1954, is to be reckoned as a partial offset of the tax cuts.

THE 1954-57 EXPANSION AND THE 1957-58 RECESSION

Defense expenditures were leveling out by mid-1954 at about three fourths of the Korean War peak. Most durables, both producer and consumer, were beginning to show slight increases. The market forces are to some extent indicated by change in lumber prices, which began to rise abruptly in mid-1954. Clearly, there was little need to wait longer to buy new houses. Residential construction was rising rapidly by midyear. Recovery was sparked by a rise in demand for durable goods, especially in reflection of consumer demands accumulated during the Korean war. This included residential housing as well as what is commonly classified as consumer durables.

The early rise in residential construction is particularly notable. Elimination of rent controls in many states put the cost of new housing on a more competitive basis. Contractors, sensing a large potential volume, were willing to sell at lower profits. Home mortgages became more attractive to lenders with the lower interest rates prevailing in the recession, and the more favorable terms found a ready response from builders and home purchasers.

Business cycle upturn is indicated at August, 1954. Inventory runoff was continuing at about the rate in effect since the beginning of the year. Since no abrupt decline had occurred in any area of final demand, inventory readjustments were only slowly spreading throughout the economy. Presumably, some time was required to recognize the new level of inventory needs which would be appropriate after shifts in demand had been made from the defense to the civilian economy. With little inventory culmination, the initial upturn was not sharp. The Industrial Production Index approximately leveled off until the end of the year.

By November the inventory runoff was ending, and the increase of activity was speeding up. The change in inventory investment from the third quarter of 1954 to the second quarter of 1955 amounted to $5.5 billion, and it contributed the typical inventory culmination influence, although it was occurring after the expansion phase had already gotten under way.

The year 1955 was one of rapid expansion of durable goods. Residential construction remained at a high, unprecedented level throughout the year. The same can be said for automobiles, except that output was rising in the first part of the year. Nonresidential construction and business equipment also were moving to new postwar highs. With construction and other durables spurting ahead, as they did in 1955, the dollar output per worker (productivity) was rising rapidly. This is because the large dollar output per man in making durable products is accentuated when it comes to represent an increased proportion of the total.

The proportion of durables in total output was no more than maintained in 1956. Residential construction and consumer durable expenditures were declining slightly, but were approximately balanced by some increase in nonresidential construction and business equipment expenditures. Service and nondurable expenditures were rising about as rapidly as in the previous year. Thus, dollar output per worker did not gain by a shifting distribution of output as it had the year before, and the productivity measure showed a much smaller rise. Gross national product, which rose by 10 per cent (stated in current dollars) in 1955, rose only half as much in 1956. The tendency described is common in the expansion phase, but was accentuated in 1955 by the early rapid rise in residential construction and in automobiles.

Total activity was leveling off in the first half of 1957. The decline in residential construction was continuing, and expenditures for consumer durables were no longer rising. The purchase of business equipment was tapering off. Among civilian durables, only nonresidential construction was continuing to advance; and even in that area, activity was leveling out after the beginning of the year. The slowing of automobile production was related to an approach to market saturation and to increasing import of foreign cars. The sliding-off of residential building was induced by increased unattractiveness of FHA and VA loans, where the maximum interest rate permitted had fallen behind the rising interest rates prevailing in the money market. Also, the urgency of housing demand had slackened, as evidenced by continued decline in housing even after the extension early in 1956 of allowable maturities to thirty years on FHA and VA mortgages. Producer equipment purchases had experienced no substantial decline since the rise began early in 1950, and some reaction was overdue in that area.

Wholesale prices rose substantially in 1956. These rises were related to the rapidity with which durable projects had been started and to the approach to capacity levels. With less deferred demand and fewer controls, unemployment fell to 4 per cent at the peak of activity, compared with 3 per cent in 1948 and with 2 per cent in 1953.

Wholesale prices ceased rising in the first half of 1957. This reflected the leveling-out which was occurring in investment; demand induced by what we have called double reinforcement was vanishing. Inventory investment fell nearly to zero. The slackening increase, or decrease, in durable investment indicated that the completion rate was catching up with the starting rate. This fact is even better indicated when the change in detailed investment projects is studied.

The leveling wholesale prices were paired with rising costs. The rising costs were made up of continued advances in wage costs, rising prices of some raw materials, and higher depreciation charges as new, more expensive investment projects were put into operation. Profit prospects were becoming increasingly unfavorable.

Some sectors, including government and foreign trade, were pushing expenditures upward instead of downward, but their influence was of less consequence. Government expenditures had held at the post-Korean War low reached in 1954 until late in 1956. The rise in government expenditures in the first part of 1957 was concentrated in defense. Net exports rose in this period as a result of special circumstances—petroleum exports because of temporary disruption of traffic through the Suez Canal, cotton to rebuild foreign stocks as our export price came down to world levels, wheat because of poor European harvests and special-program shipments to Asia, and steel products because of the possibility of rapid delivery demanded by booming European activity at the time. Farm prices rose, on an average, with higher livestock prices accompanying reduced meat supplies flowing to the market (increased exports of wheat and cotton merely reduced stocks and had little influence on crop prices under the price support system).

At the downturn in July, 1957, both defense expenditures and net exports turned unfavorable. Concerned with the continued rise in consumer prices, the federal administration canceled several defense contracts. The special influences supporting exports were fading, and net exports began to decline. No areas of activity were continuing to rise except consumer services and state and local government expenditures, and even in these the principal part of the rise represented price rather than quantity increases.

The downturn represented a slow rounding-off. Inventory investment had been on a modest scale since the beginning of the year, and little urge arose to deflate inventories until the sales picture began to show substantial deterioration. The minor inventory accumulation was slowing, however.

Government action in slowing down the defense program was matched with restrictive monetary action. Federal Reserve holdings of government securities were reduced in the first half of 1957, and the rediscount rate at Federal Reserve banks was raised in August. Possibly, these contractionary fiscal and monetary policies may have hastened the date of the downturn, but the position in the civilian economy surely was approaching a culmination of the expansion. The diffusion index of profits was declining, fewer and fewer companies were reporting increases in durable investment,[7] FHA and VA mortgage financing of residential construction was facing increasing difficulties, and increasing evidence was appearing that a wide group of consumer durables was approaching market saturation. Evidence on substantial completion of business equipment programs in various industries was particularly impressive.

As the recession got under way, negative inventory investment came to play an increasing part. A substantial inventory runoff was taking place before the cyclical upturn occurred in April, 1958. The turnaround in activity was not sharp, but was principally related to declining inventory runoff. Increases were occurring in govern-

---

[7]Geoffrey H. Moore, "The 1957–58 Business Contraction: New Model or Old?" *American Economic Review, Papers and Proceedings*, May, 1959, pp. 292–308.

ment expenditures and in consumer expenditures for services, the latter representing a continuing expansionary bias.

Fiscal and monetary policies had turned expansionary in the fall of 1957, following the successful launching of the first Sputnik by the Soviet Union. Defense expenditures began to show slight increases, more because of fears generated by the "cold war" than by planned contracyclical policy. Late in 1957 and early in 1958, expansionary open-market operations, reductions in rediscount rates, and reductions in reserve requirements were put into effect. The monetary authorities were encouraging credit ease when the expansion phase began in the spring of 1958. On the other hand, there were no tax reductions, as occurred in 1948 and in 1954.

Although short, the decline in the recession was greater than in 1949 or in 1954. In terms of industrial production the decline was nearly 15 per cent, contrasted with about 10 per cent in each of the earlier cases. The slighter decline in 1949 was due to the continued existence of widespread urgent demand and in 1954 to ready absorption in the civilian economy of many of the resources released by the ending of the war.

The 1949 recession was more closely related to a price readjustment than were the other two recessions. Measured in constant prices, the 1957–58 recession was somewhat more severe than the 1949 one, because a slight rise in prices better maintained the value of product. The principal difference in price behavior, however, was in farm products and foods. In fact, the difference in price movement in 1953–54 is completely accounted for by the fact that farm prices happened to be falling during that recession. In 1953–54, as well as in 1957–58, prices other than farm products and foods remained horizontal. In both 1949 and 1953–54, farm prices were in a phase of decline, while in 1957–58, they happened to be rising. Too much can be made of the uniqueness of rising prices in 1957–58, but it does appear that prices were tending to decline less in recession than in prewar times.

The 1957–58 recession, lasting nine months, was slightly shorter than either of the two earlier ones. We may surmise that the brevity of the recession is due to the sharp rise which occurred in profits early in 1958. The behavior of profits can be described by a mathematical cusp, with a sharp drop from the downturn in activity to the end of the first quarter of 1958 and then an equally sharp rise.

The sharp rise which occurred in profits reflected various influences. The strength of demand was indicated by the tendency of finished goods prices to rise all during the recession. On the other hand, raw material prices, which had been rising during the recession, turned downward early in 1958, strengthening profit positions. Corrective measures had been taken on inventory expansion as early as the first quarter of 1957. By the first quarter of 1958, when the maximum runoff was occurring, it became obvious that needed inventory correction was limited in extent. Plans were being formulated for aggressive action.

EXPANSION TO 1960

By the end of the third quarter of 1958 the GNP peak attained in mid-1957 had been reached again. This was less than the usual time required in earlier recessions. The principal expenditure streams accounting for the rise were consumer services and nondurable goods, residential building, government expenditure, and decline in inventory runoff. There was a strong growth factor in consumer services, involving increased rents, expanded medical care, more life insurance coverage, and automobile repair. A large part of the increased expenditures for nondurables went for food. The rise in residential building marked an increase in statutory interest rates in government-assisted programs, so that private lenders were stimulated to invest and a government program of supplying increased mortgage funds through the Federal National Mortgage Association (FNMA, often called "Fannie May"). The declining inventory runoff developed from the culmination of rapid inventory contraction and from the reassurance provided many businessmen by rising profits. Government expenditures were increasing because of the great state and local needs and because of the needs which became obvious in the defense space program.

As the expansion continued, activity began to rise in all sectors except exports. New demands and replacement needs were developing in consumer durables, and expenditures were reaching new highs. Similarly, residential building was matching the highest levels ever attained. Nonresidential construction also was approaching new postwar highs. The rise in business equipment lagged because of widespread completion of programs in the preceding prosperity; but by 1959, rising expenditures were also occurring in this area. Net exports were falling until the second half of 1959. Not only were our imports rising to new high levels, but the recession had hit most of our foreign customers; and with the leveling of their activity, purchases from us were increasing only slowly.

Inventory investment was moving erratically with the onset of the longest steel strike in history in the summer of 1959. To limit short supplies, should a strike occur, inventories had been built up at a high rate in the second quarter. When the strike materialized, inventory investment fell to negative levels in the third quarter, and gross national product declined. The incident illustrates the principle that an exogenous factor may interrupt an expansion or contraction phase which is under way, but it seldom establishes a turning point.

After the strike ended, inventory rebuilding matched the high level reached preceding the strike. Since the increased expenditure, generated by advance in inventory investment, paid out income which had already been anticipated by temporary financial arrangements during the strike, the induced effect was less than a similar inventory investment would produce in a typical business cycle expansion. Recognition by businessmen of the temporary effect kept them from reaching an optimistic appraisal. In the summer of 1960, investment plans already formulated were being carried out, but they were not being extended.[8]

As a result, inventory investment fell back to low levels. An inventory change representative of a business cycle downturn had occurred. But price and expenditure changes were not responsible, as they usually are. Many indicators, of the type developed in Chapter 17, pointed to a downturn.

Another novel situation developing in 1959 was the extremely high level reached by interest rates. Unquestionably, the demand for investment funds was so great that resort to credit extension was called for, and the Federal Reserve was attempting to keep the flow of credit in check because of its inflationary impact. In pursuance of a policy of greater restraint, Federal Reserve banks in March, May, and September raised the rediscount rate charged to member banks from 2½ to 4 per cent, paralleling the rise in the interest rate on three-month Treasury bills. Operations influencing reserve funds were so conducted that the money supply, including demand deposits and currency, increased by only .5 per cent, compared with 4 per cent in 1958.

The rise in interest rates did, therefore, to a substantial extent, reflect a greater demand for investment funds than obtainable with-

---

[8]As measured by the National Industrial Conference Board, fewer companies were reporting greater investment spending than a year earlier by the second quarter of 1960. Investment appropriations had been declining since mid-1959.

out advancing interest rates. By the end of the year, however, it was clear that other forces also were at work. As a result of the steel strike, inventory investment, which was substantial in the first half, was eliminated in the second half. Domestic durable investment was curtailed in the fourth quarter because of diminished supplies of steel. Advances in credit requirements, such as in the financing of housing mortgages or of consumer credit, did not equal these declines. Savings were about as great as ever. Yet, interest rates were rising to the highest levels since the twenties. Commercial paper which was quoted at 1½ per cent in early 1958 ran to nearly 5 per cent. The yield on long-term government bonds was up from 3 to over 5 per cent in some cases. More than supply and demand for investment funds was involved.

The key is provided by the rise occurring in the stock market. Because of conviction that inflation would impair the value of the dollar, investment funds were used to an inordinate extent to bid up stock prices. The yield on common stocks declined from 4½ per cent to 3 per cent, while that on government bonds rose from not much over 3 per cent to well over 4. This situation was largely reversed by the summer of 1960.

THE CHANGING ECONOMIC PICTURE IN THE FIFTIES

Despite the resurgence of fear of inflation in the 1957–59 period the inflation potential had steadily declined, as shown in the last column of Table 14–1 (page 297). The Federal Reserve had been following a policy of credit restraint when it felt this to be desirable, ever since the Treasury–Federal Reserve Accord in 1951. Before that, equilibrium was achieved by price inflation; this was made possible by greatly expanded liquid assets. It was dictated by centering control policy on maintenance of high employment rather than on prevention of inflation.

When interest rates were permitted again to function effectively in the money market, liquid assets came to rise less rapidly than gross national product. Holding down the expansion of liquid assets slowed the monetary inflation.[9] Higher interest rates, after some delay, choked down some investment expenditures.

Aside from the more aggressive monetary policy, business cycle

---

[9]See John G. Gurley, "Liquidity and Financial Institutions in the Postwar Period," Study Paper No. 14, *Study of Employment, Growth, and Price Levels for Consideration by Joint Economic Committee, Congress of the United States* (Washington, D.C.: U.S. Government Printing Office, 1960).

peaks were coming to put less pressure on marginal resources. The urgency of demand had receded. In 1948, deferred demand was so great that resources were pushed into use to an abnormal extent. The same happened again with the drain on the private economy because of the waging of the Korean War from 1951 to 1953. In 1957 the prosperity peaked off with an unemployment of about 4 per cent instead of 2 per cent and 3 per cent in the earlier expansion peaks.

The stock of capital had increased relative to output. The extent of the increase was not entirely clear, partly because of the difficulty and lack of basic studies in measuring capital stock, and partly because of uncertainty with regard to the part of current capital expenditures which represented replacement. If the rate of obsolescence had increased significantly, the stock/output ratio had not increased as much as some analysts were saying. Fears were expressed that capital stock had become so large as to endanger the avoidance of deep depression.

Some increase in the stock/output ratio had been desirable. Capital stock was abnormally depleted because of limited capital formation during the Great Depression and during the war. The growth potential of the sixties appeared great because of technological developments and because of expected acceleration in growth of the labor force. With that prospect, a capital stock/output ratio on the high side was not necessarily dangerous. We had to hope that improved long-term forecasting would lead decision makers to keep the amount of capital stock within reasonable bounds.

FOR REFLECTION AND ANALYSIS

1. Explain the influence of gloomy postwar forecasts on postwar inflationary developments.
2. How could it be that little or no real recession occurred when government expenditures were cut back ruthlessly?
3. Should prices have been permitted to rise so much in 1946?
4. Gross national product, on a deflated basis, barely reached the war levels in 1950. Does this indicate lack of growth?
5. How are we to account for the 1948 recession?
6. Why did inventory investment rise much more rapidly in the first part of 1950 than in the first part of 1938?
7. Why did the voluntary "credit restraint" become less necessary after the Accord between the Treasury and Federal Reserve in 1951?
8. Compare the drastic decline in government expenditures at the end of World War II with the mild retraction at the end of the Korean War and the differing induced recessionary effects occurring at the two times.

9. Discuss the idea of "rolling readjustment."
10. Discuss the indications in the private economy that a culmination of the expansion phase was being approached in the early part of 1957.
11. Contrast the three postwar recessions.

SELECTED READINGS FOR PART THREE

CHANDLER, LESTER V. *Inflation in the United States: 1940–1948.* New York: Harper & Bros., 1951.
    Throws light on the postwar inflationary influences.

CREAMER, DANIEL AND OTHERS. *Capital in Manufacturing and Mining: Its Formation and Financing.* Princeton: Princeton University Press, 1960.
    Excellent on capital-output relations in manufacturing and mining.

FELS, RENDIGS. *American Business Cycles, 1865–1897.* Chapel Hill: University of North Carolina Press, 1959.
    A searching historical study, with generalizations founded on the application of theoretical models.

GALBRAITH, J. K. *The Great Crash.* Boston: Houghton Mifflin Co., 1955.
    An interestingly written and integrated discussion.

HICKMAN, BERT G. "An Interpretation of Price Movements since the End of World War II," in *The Relationship of Prices to Economic Stability and Growth: Compendium of Papers Submitted by Panelists Appearing before the Joint Economic Committee, March 31, 1958,* pp. 143–210. 85th Cong., 2d sess. Washington, D.C.: U.S. Government Printing Office, 1958.
    An interpretative and historical study of price influences.

HULTGREN, THOR. *Changes in Labor Cost during Cycles in Production and Business.* Occasional Paper 74. New York: National Bureau of Economic Research, Inc., 1960.
    A basic study of man-hours and labor cost per unit of product over business cycles from 1933 to 1958.

MOORE, GEOFFREY H. *Measuring Recessions.* Occasional Paper 61. New York: National Bureau of Economic Research, Inc., 1958.
    Measures on the duration and amplitude of fluctuations since the mid-1920's.

ROOSE, KENNETH D. *The Economics of Recession and Revival: An Interpretation of 1937–38.* New Haven: Yale University Press, 1954.
    A careful development of the effective forces in the recession named.

SHIRLEY, WILLIAM W. *The World Depression 1929–: A List of Books and Pamphlets in the New York Public Library.* New York: New York Public Library, 1934.
    A comprehensive list of references to timely discussion.

ULMER, MELVILLE J. *Capital in Transportation, Communications, and Public Utilities: Its Formation and Financing.* Princeton: Princeton University Press, 1960.
    A fundamental study of capital formation from 1870–1950.

WECTER, DIXON. *The Age of the Great Depression.* New York: Macmillan Co., 1948.

A careful study.

NOTE: Two of the best sources for following current historical developments are the February Annual Review Number of the *Survey of Current Business* and the *Economic Report of the President* (Washington, D.C.: U.S. Government Printing Office), issued in January of each year.

PART
FOUR

Indicators and Forecasting

INDICATORS OF GENERAL

BUSINESS ACTIVITY

Many possible indicators of general business activity exist; and as a matter of historical fact, many different ones have been employed in the past.[1] For our purposes, three are important enough in current usage to warrant consideration—gross national product, industrial production, and employment. The first of these is most important to us, for it offers the most comprehensive representation and the greatest promise of displaying the interrelationships which exist within the economy.[2]

INCOME AND PRODUCT

In the short run the problem of first importance is to measure total demand and the output it calls forth. Total demand is best measured by the total of final expenditures made in the economy. By final, we mean that the one making the expenditure is the "last buyer"; the product is not resold in trade. The product under consideration includes both goods and services, for in our economy, much of the demand is for services as well as for goods. A measure, made to order for this purpose, is gross national product, generally identified as GNP. It is a comprehensive measure indicating changes

---

[1] No effort is made here to provide a catalogue. Several of the more notable ones, which are omitted here, are briefly described in the fourth edition of this book (Homewood, Ill.: Richard D. Irwin, Inc., 1953), pp. 359–64.

[2] A "break-through" which will provide a far more effective analysis of interrelationships can be expected within the next ten years. In fact, before 1965 the Department of Commerce expects to provide at least some integration of income and product with input-output and perhaps with flow of funds. Integration with flow-of-fund statements (often called money flows) is most important from our point of view, and it would show the relation between movement of funds through the capital market and into investment expenditures counted as final product. Perhaps it is too much to expect that this integration will be available by 1965. For an extended discussion of the advantages of integration, see National Bureau of Economic Research, Inc., *The National Economic Accounts of the United States: Review, Appraisal and Recommendations,* General Series 64 (New York, 1958).

in the demand of final buyers. Activity is geared to final demand. Its aggregate indicates the total activity called forth in the economy.

If the demand of buyers who resell the product—either in its present form or after further fabrication—were included, obviously a great deal of duplication would be involved. Such intermediate demands, as well as the final-product demand, would add up to much more than the total value of products. Nevertheless, contributions at earlier stages of production are represented in final-product demand, since the sum of all the value added in earlier stages— extraction, processing, distribution—is represented in the value of final product. If an automobile company buys wheels from a parts manufacturer, for instance, the component cost represents a part of the value of the final automobile.

In our analysis, it is important to classify total final expenditures. This it is possible to do with gross national product. In 1957, for instance, as shown below in Table 15–1, GNP totaled $442.8 billion. Of this, $285 billion, or more than 64 per cent, represented consumer expenditures. Another $87 billion, or nearly $20 per cent, represented government expenditures. About 1 per cent represented net exports; and the other 15 per cent came from business expendi-

TABLE 15–1

NATIONAL INCOME AND PRODUCT ACCOUNT FOR 1957[a]

(In Billions of Dollars)

National Income		Final Expenditure or Product	
Compensation of employees....	255.5	For personal consumption.........	285.2
Proprietors' income...........	44.5	For gross private domestic investment	66.1
Corporate profits[b]............	41.7	For net exports..................	5.0
Rental Income[c]...............	11.9	For government goods and services..	86.5
Net interest[c].................	13.4		
Total national income........(367.0)			
Nonincome Charges			
Indirect business taxes........	38.2		
Capital consumption allowances.	37.4		
Other charges and adjustments[d].	0.2		
Total charges and adjustments..(	75.8)		
Gross National Product........	442.8	Gross National Product...........	442.8

[a]Information given here was taken from *Survey of Current Business*, July, 1960.

[b]The corporate profit figure here reported has been corrected for inventory valuation adjustment, so that the total will come to gross national product. Inventory valuation adjustment came to −$1.5 billion in 1957.

[c]Rent and interest available to persons only is included. Government interest paid to persons is not included. See text section on "Variety of Aggregate Measures Provided" (p. 343).

[d]Includes business transfer payments (principally corporate gifts to nonprofit institutions and consumer bad debts) of $1.8 billion in 1957; current surplus of government enterprises minus subsidies (not segregated—the surplus is like a profit, and the subsidy represents business receipt but not final product) of −$1.0 billion in 1957; and statistical discrepancy (arises because the two sides of the account are computed from largely independent figures) of −$0.6 billion in 1957.

CHART 15-1

GROSS NATIONAL PRODUCT: TOTAL FINAL EXPENDITURES AND MAJOR DIVISIONS

(Annually, 1929–38; Quarterly with Seasonal Adjustment since 1939)

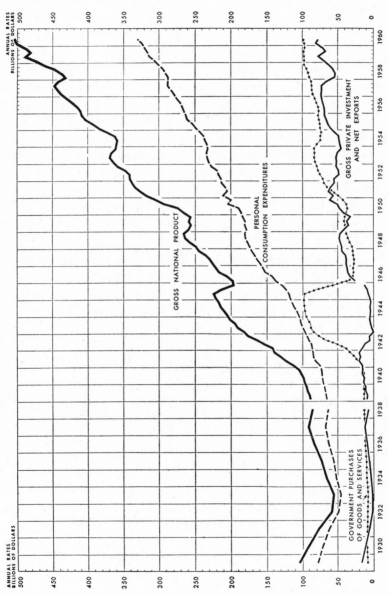

Source: Board of Governors of the Federal Reserve System, *Historical Supplement to Federal Reserve Chart Book on Financial and Business Statistics* (Washington, D.C., September, 1960).

tures on equipment, construction, and inventories. All of these groups can be subclassified. The parts of total final expenditure can thus be indicated; and, what is more important to us, the changes in these parts show where the movements in activity are concentrated at any time. Movement of the total and parts is shown in Chart 15-1.

Final expenditure and final product are considered to be equivalent because the product bought, stated in current prices, would be the same as the expenditure made. The utility of final-product figures in studying economic change is enhanced by employing a double-entry bookkeeping procedure. The funds received in the sale of final products are traced to the income flows they produce or to other kinds of business charges they support. All of the final-product expenditures received in the sale of final products must be accounted for.

This representation is usefully idealized as a circular flow, but we should recognize that the flow is not an exact replica of what happens in the real world. The difference merely is that, for many of the final products considered, the businessman from whose hands the product passes into final sale actually pays only a part of the income and other business charges which account for allocation of the funds. He pays out a substantial part for semifinished products to businessmen at earlier stages in the process, who in turn pay out income and provide for essential business charges.

This is the reason we employ the value-added concept. Each businessman allocates from his receipts, in accordance with the value he adds to the product, final income and essential business charges. Our model, then, represents a net aggregation of the disposal of funds at successive points in the flow of the product from its initiation to its final sale.

The measurements indicate the amount of income and business charges allocated from final sale of product. As shown in Table 15-1, in 1957, compensation of employees came to $255.5 billion, or 58 per cent of the total. Other income streams amounted to 25 per cent. Note that all of these incomes are appropriately called final income because they are income attributable to persons; for instance, interest or rental income paid to businesses merely adds to gross income receipts and gets counted in final income only to the extent that it affects profits.

Other than final income, the essential business charges which must be counted here principally represent indirect taxes and capital consumption allowances. These came to over $75 billion and accounted for approximately all of the 17 per cent remaining after the final-income flows noted above.

The circular flow identified represents income-expenditure-output. Let us start with final output, and note again that the funds derived in the sale of it are employed to pay final income and to provide for other essential business charges. The income flows back in various ways as expenditures. Some of the income is paid back directly as personal consumption expenditures. Some is withheld by corporations as undistributed profits and used in investment expenditure. Some is saved out of consumers' disposable income (this concept is identified more clearly on page 344) and spent on business investment. A considerable amount represents personal and business taxes, and goes ultimately for government expenditure.

Half of the essential business charges represent indirect taxes and also provide for government expenditures. Most of the rest represent capital consumption allowances, having been set aside to replace capital which is wearing out, and thus to be used at some time or other in making investment expenditures.

We must note immediately that there is a certain vagueness in all of this, for in each case the funds provided are not necessarily spent in the particular time period represented—personal monetary funds could be increased or reduced (liquidity preference) instead of going for investment expenditure, and similarly with respect to monetary funds held by corporations, and the difference between government receipts and expenditures. We identify this vagueness more clearly below and indicate the kind of information we must have (and do not have) to understand fully what is happening in each case.

For the time being, we merely take the circular flow at face value and recognize that the *total* of the expenditures provided for out of income and essential business charges must equal expenditure in the particular time period. This is a tautology, as is also the earlier statement that the funds received in the sale of final product must be employed in providing for final income and other essential business charges. What we are saying is that we are dealing only with a past, chopped-off time period. When this information comes to us, it is an historical record. As such, it adds to a certain GNP total and does not explain changes in gross national product to the next time period. We use the device of stating changes between chopped-off time periods to aid in interpreting economic change; but the circular flow, as we have been able to develop it quantitatively, truly relates to only one time period.

In that one time period, it does help us interpret past history. To continue the story, the *total* of final income and other essential business charges can be interpreted to provide the funds used in making final expenditures for product, even though a fixed formula will not describe the extent to which any income or other charge always applies to expenditures. This fact is important because it is in the shifting use of funds to make expenditures that a change occurs in the level of gross national product. Although not represented, we may visualize the funds spent to apply to a new level of expenditure and thus conceive a flow instead of a flat picture of the past. The new level of receipts for the sale of final product would in turn be spent on final income and other essential business charges in the new time period.

Monentarily, let us go back to the static concept to recognize one essential regularity that it identifies. For any past period, total saving and investment are equal, simply because of the way we define our terms. Balance is achieved in Table 15-1, for instance, because all of the income on the left-hand side flows into expenditure on the right. This means, among other relationships, that the saving on the left is used for investment expenditure on the right. In some cases, like part of undistributed profits, investment may be said to flow directly from the income shown. In these cases, saving obviously equals investment. Where saving represents a residual income after direct expenditures are made, it must be balanced by the remaining investment because the two sides of the account total to the same amount.

When we remove the assumption that we are dealing merely with relationships in a past, fixed time period, the situation is modified. We can see this by looking at successive time periods in the past. Total gross national product almost invariably changes from one time period to another. Usually, investment is the principal expenditure sector responsible for the change. Consumption expenditure tends to follow along a fairly stable consumption function and therefore is likely to introduce a change in total expenditure to a minimum extent. Excepting rapid change in policy, as illustrated either by beginning or ending of war, government expenditure tends to follow a fairly stable movement.

For reasons discussed earlier, investment may rise or fall rapidly. When it does, total expenditure is likely to rise or fall accordingly. The increase in product flowing from investment expenditure increases allocations on the income side. If the period involved is reasonably long, the income generated by the increased investment expenditure no doubt will generate additional consumer expenditure; but axiomatically, enough saving will be generated to pay for the added investment expenditure. One possibility is that the income payment may have come so late in the period that consumers have not had time to spend the income received. If made earlier in the period, and if consumers have a very high spending (consuming) propensity, total income and expenditures will be driven up rapidly. If consumers actually spend all of the increased income received, added durable investment expenditure will be balanced against reduced inventories, but it is more likely that consumers will not spend all of the added income immediately. In any case, all of the added receipts from sales will be allocated, and the total allocation must equal the total sales of product.

If investment is rising, the extra funds may come from credit expansion or from expenditure of past accumulation of liquid funds. Unfortunately, there is no way to trace change in credit through the national economic accounts, although work now in process may make that very desirable development possible in a few years.[3] Credit adds to savings funds; but in itself, it is counted neither as final-product expenditure nor as income allocations made with the funds obtained from such expenditure in the period in which it was obtained. After the credit expansion has developed product expenditure, the increase will of course show up both as an increase in expenditure and as an increase in income which was paid out in making expenditure.

The mechanics of the change is that, if a net addition of credit is employed to add to investment, total expenditure is increased. The credit extension adds to the total money flow which may be divided into direct expenditures and savings. In the income and product accounts a rise in investment equal to the amount of credit added leads to a like rise in savings. If credit is paid off and investment curtailed, gross national product is reduced. The savings and direct expenditure which otherwise would have occurred in the income and product accounts are reduced by the amount of credit reduction.

When there is better integration of income and product accounts

---

[3]The Federal Reserve quarterly survey of the flow of funds, saving, and investment represents an initial start. See "A Quarterly Presentation of Flow of Funds, Saving, and Investment," *Federal Reserve Bulletin*, August, 1959. See further the discussion in Appendix B to this chapter and especially Table 15–5 presented there. The reader should be warned, however, that there are unavoidable discrepancies between the Department of Commerce and Federal Reserve definitions at the present time, and that the flow-of-funds accounts do not have to be consistent with a net product total.

with credit flows, this whole process will be clearer. Nevertheless, it is easy to exaggerate the extent to which our present problems will be cleared up. Part of the advance or decline is often traceable not to change in bank credit, but to change in velocity of money or to change in the use of "near-money" instruments. Integration of what these changes do to gross national product is even more difficult than of what added bank credit does.

Furthermore, the assumption that credit changes apply only to investment expenditures is an unjustified oversimplification at the present time. Consumer credit adds directly to consumer expenditure, especially for durables, in expansion. Contraction of such credit during recession tends to reduce consumer expenditure.

Thus, while the processes of economic change will be clarified significantly when we learn how credit changes relate to product and income changes, the improvement may not be as revolutionary as it would seem at first blush. The importance of the changes which occur can be developed by studying the forces which are largely responsible for changes in each type of product expenditure, according to the methods we followed in Chapters 13 and 14. Furthermore, much can be gleaned about credit influences by a direct reading of monetary factors, such as measurements of changes in bank credit, consumer credit, the money supply and all liquid assets held in nonfinancial sectors, and interest rates. While the precise effect on product expenditures usually will be in doubt, important insights can often be developed.[4]

SUMMARY ON FINAL EXPENDITURES IN THE ACCOUNT

Table 15–1 contrasts final expenditures with final income and other essential business charges for the year 1957. The final expenditures by consumers for private consumption, by business for investment goods, by government for goods and services, and by foreigners for our net exports (in 1957, $26 billion of exports minus $21 billion of imports) adds to total final product, as explained above. We call it "gross" national product because the investment expenditure is gross of accruing needs for replacement. Since replacement, at least theoretically, merely keeps the total capital stock intact, net national product would be obtained if replacement were subtracted out. The gross figure is usually employed because no good estimate can be had on the need for replacements and because speeded-up re-

---

[4]See, for instance, John A. Gorman, "Financing the Expansion of GNP in the Current Cyclical Move," *Survey of Current Business*, May, 1960.

placement adds to current product activity at times and slowed-up replacement reduces it at others.

Consumer expenditures are available yearly for ninety divisions, and this detail provides the background for many marketing analyses. Quarterly, they are reported according to durable, nondurable, and service divisions, which percentage-wise represent 15, 50, and 35. Ten finer subsidivisions are now available quarterly, including, for instance, automobiles, household durables, and clothing.

Investment includes private construction, business equipment, and change in inventories. Private construction is about equally divided between residential and all other. For each, finer subdivisions are available monthly. Note should be made of the fact that another third of total construction is publicly financed and is included in government expenditures. Investment represents a strategic expenditure in relation to economic fluctuation, and variation in the major types is pictured in Chart 15-2.

Business equipment expenditures run to about 50 per cent more than private, nonresidential construction. Currently, no complete breakdown is available on this type of investment. Various miscellaneous figures are available on particular types, as reported by trade associations and some government sources, and attention is called to such information in Chapter 17. One of the difficulties faced here is lack of a satisfactory count of government purchases of equipment-type goods in the defense program, even as an historical record. Another is the fact that breakdowns are principally by kind of equipment, rather than by purchasing industry.[5] Much remains to be done to provide satisfactory detail on business equipment.

Inventory investment, or change in business inventories, represents an extremely small proportion of final product. Its major importance to us is dependent upon the fact that it varies so widely. As noted repeatedly in the above chapters, because of this fact it usually represents a major part of the decline in expenditures in recession. Due to the way accounting records are kept on inventory stocks, most of them have to be corrected for price changes since the inventories were accumulated, to give change in inventory stocks a significant meaning. The total inventory stocks, as shown on most business records, add up similar items at different prices because

---

[5] It is true, however, that the combined plant and equipment total, as reported in Department of Commerce–Securities and Exchange Commission survey, is broken down by purchasing industry. See Chapter 17.

CHART 15-2

PRIVATE INVESTMENT BY MAJOR TYPES

(Annually, 1929–38; Quarterly since 1938)

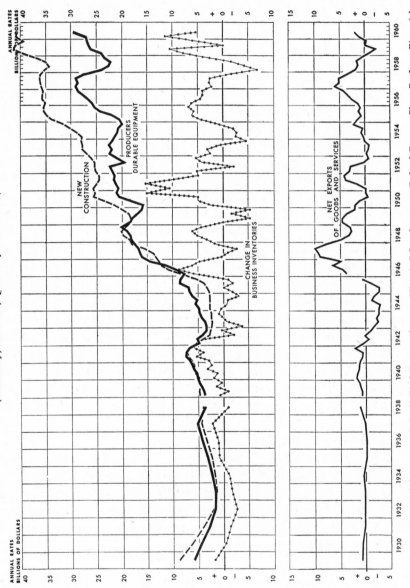

Source: Board of Governors of the Federal Reserve System, *Historical Supplement to Federal Reserve Chart Book on Financial and Business Statistics* (Washington, D.C., September, 1960).

they were accumulated at different times (in accordance with the first-in, first-out method of inventory count). Putting the items on a current price basis is called inventory valuation adjustment, and is required before the change in stocks will give us a significant measure of final expenditure.

Actually, even then, final expenditure is measured only in a special sense—it is final for the period. If an inventory increase is reflected, the added inventories are thought of as purchased by the holder, even though in later periods they will be subject to further sale. This is necessary to get counted product which increases activity in the given period. On the other hand, if a decrease in inventories occurs, the amount is subtracted from final sales because, to this extent, the final sales did not create activity in the given period.

Business inventory investment is divided into farm and nonfarm. The classification is important because farm inventories frequently do not imply double reinforcement. An exceptionally good farm crop may result in inventory accumulation, but it is due to better yields rather than to any significant addition of labor. The better yields are largely dependent on vagaries of the weather. With the current type of government support program, higher inventories of farm products have little market effect. A breakdown of nonfarm inventory investment would be highly desirable, but so far the only classification published is between durable and nondurable commodities, and this is available only after considerable delay.

A monthly classification along important lines, especially for manufacturing industries, is provided for inventory stocks. This is our best source of information for locating the distribution of inventory change; but it must be used carefully, for no valuation adjustment has been applied to correct for different pricing within any inventory stock. A classification on inventory stocks of manufacturers which has been recently developed relates to purchased materials, goods in process, and finished goods (according to each company's own classification) and is helpful in forecasting, as we shall note in Chapter 18.

Net export of goods and services (which may be either positive or negative) is included as a part of final product because it increases (or reduces) our activity. If we send goods abroad, activity is required in producing them, but the imports must be netted out because they add to sales but do not require activity on our part. In our country, foreign trade is relatively much less important than in most countries, but it cannot be ignored. It is particularly important in a small part of total industry which depends to a major extent on foreign sales. It is not to be considered important only as a limiting influence in the interrelation with some specific industries, however, because the small net total for the whole economy shows a wide variation. Fortunately, the net export figure is not as sensitively related to business cycle movements as is inventory change; so, although the changes frequently push the cyclical movement higher or lower, they have a less violent effect than inventory investment.

The last of the final product groups to be considered is government purchases of goods and services.[6] This is shown quarterly by national defense, other federal, and state and local. These are significant divisions because of differences in behavior. National defense, which represents nearly half of total government expenditure for goods and services, moves with defense needs and shows little cyclical or contracyclical variation. State and local represents most of the rest, and is dependent largely on budgetary requirements which tend to move along a fairly steady trend; it also bears little relation to cyclical movements. Federal other than defense, which comes to less than 10 per cent of the total, is largely bound by budgetary considerations, but does permit some leeway for contracyclical action, especially in relation to construction expenditures.

Much has been done recently to classify, on a yearly basis, government expenditures by type of function. This includes eight divisions—national defense, general government, international affairs, welfare (health and education), veterans' services, commerce and housing, agriculture, and natural resources. Although about half is in the one division—national defense—following the movement of expenditures by these various functions will provide greater leverage in understanding the kinds of influences which govern changes. This classification includes transfer expenditures which are

---

[6]Criticisms have been made of the Department of Commerce method (which we follow) of making this measurement. The goods bought by the government are final product under the conditions that the government is the final buyer. But the labor services purchased by the government are in a special category. We may argue, for instance, that part of these are intermediate services that business would buy and include as a cost of production if the government did not furnish them. Such points have merit, but they do not point to a practicable operation. No one has been able to segregate intermediate services of the government in any satisfactory way. On the other hand, counting all services of the government as product automatically provides a balance between the product involved and the income paid because the same figures are used on both sides of the account. For our purposes the exact level of gross national product developed is not of major importance. We are concerned, rather, with the *change* in that level. The crude procedures which would have to be employed in estimating government intermediate product probably would not be sensitive enough to show significant change in the amount of intermediate product to be subtracted from one time period to another.

not included as an integral part of gross national product. The handling of those expenditures in the accounts is discussed in the fourth following section (page 343).

SUMMARY ON FINAL INCOME IN THE ACCOUNT

We call "final" what is known as national "factor" income to differentiate it, like the product expenditures from which it is allocated, from intermediate types of income. It is final in a significant sense, in that it includes only income to which persons are entitled for services performed. By the nature of the account shown in Table 15-1, only income in payment for services can be included, for it is allocated in the production process.

The largest part of the allocation is compensation of employees, and about 95 per cent of this represents wages and salaries. Nearly 40 per cent of these go to distributive and service industries, about a third to manufacturing, and about a sixth to government. In addition to wages and salaries, employer contributions for social insurance and pension funds are included in the compensation total.

Proprietors' (nonincorporated business) income represents about 10 per cent of gross national product. This is divided between farmers, who get a third, and business and professional men, who get two thirds.

Corporate profits comes to a similar amount, with half going for taxes and the other half divided between dividends and undistributed profits. Corporate profits and a large part of proprietors' income represent a residual type of return, with all other claimants entitled to an earlier share. Therefore, these income streams are subject to wide fluctuations. For instance, profits dropped 15 per cent in 1958, with profits taxes and undistributed profits sharing the brunt.

Rent and interest complete the types of income payments included in the allocations of receipts from the sale of final product, as shown in Table 15-1. Rent and interest together comprise about 5 per cent of gross national product. They are the most stable of the income streams, although two influences have made these streams increase recently. Rental payments have doubled since World War II with scrapping of rent controls. Interest payments have doubled since the Korean War with a gradual rise in interest rates following release from artificial controls. We may remind the student that these payments relate only to the interest and rent paid to persons. Government interest, which is not considered paid in relation to a currently rendered service, is not included even when paid to persons, as explained on page 343.

SUMMARY OF NONINCOME CHARGES INCLUDED IN THE ALLOCATION

Nearly all of the essential nonfactor expenses that business must meet out of receipts from the sale of final product are indirect business taxes and capital consumption allowances. Together, these represent about 17 per cent of gross national product. Thus, national income amounts to less than 85 per cent of GNP.

The indirect business taxes, like income taxes, could have been included in income, but it is thought more nearly correct to say that indirect business taxes represent a cost rather than a subtraction from profits (the question, really, is one of tax shifting; if profits taxes were thought in effect to become costs and to add to the price of the product, they should be included under nonincome charges rather than income). In an economic sense, half of the taxes classified as "indirect business" might properly be called personal taxes. More than half of the amount collected comes from sales or excise taxes and most of the rest from property taxes.

Capital consumption allowances arise because we measure gross, rather than net, product. In practice, capital consumption allowances represent an important part of saving and are a most significant factor in corporate investment. To a major extent, corporations depend upon their own operations to generate a supply of investment funds, and consumption allowances provide three fourths of that supply. Whether or not capital consumption allowances come anywhere near representing actual replacement requirements, there is no reason to believe that they are spent at the same rate as capital stock depreciates. There are good reasons to believe that variations in replacement tend to correspond with those in additions to capital stock. Generally, if times are good for one type of investment, they may be considered good for the other.

The other types of business charges and adjustments required to make the allocation side of the account add to gross national product are briefly described in the footnote of Table 15-1. They are small in amount, and it is not necessary for us to go into great detail about them. They are unlikely to account for materially significant variations.

QUESTIONABLE INFLUENCE OF MAINTENANCE AND REPAIR EXPENDITURE

In using gross national product to represent fluctuations in total activity, we assume that the major relevant fluctuations are highlighted. Expenditures for maintenance and repair represent a type of variation in which this principle probably does not hold. Maintenance and repair are considered business costs to be charged to current revenue. Their fluctuations should thus be reflected by an inverse pattern in profits. This fact does not help too much in providing a current interpretation, for (1) the variation in profits is dependent upon so many other factors, and (2) some of the current changes in profits are poorly estimated. Until 1960, maintenance and repair expenditures were reported only on a yearly basis and then by use of inadequate information. Current surveys on maintenance and repair expenditures were started in 1960, and better information is now expected. This should aid in making current interpretations of final product expenditures. For instance, many persons now believe that maintenance and repair tend to be speeded up in the early part of recessions of the kind we have been experiencing postwar. Householders turn to painting their homes and making other repairs when they are laid off or their hours of work are reduced. Also, it is thought that corporations tend to catch up on maintenance and repair as activity slackens, partly to avoid unnecessary employee layoffs.

VARIETY OF AGGREGATE MEASURES PROVIDED

So far, we have directed our attention to gross national product, net national product, and national income. The analysis has been focused on GNP, for it best represents current activity. Net national product, equaling GNP minus capital consumption allowances, is less important partly because of the uncertainty regarding the representativeness of the measurement of capital consumption. The meaning of national income is most clearly indicated in Table 15-1 as far as our use of it in studying economic change is concerned, for that table shows how it represents an allocation of GNP.

By introducing supplementary information, two other very useful aggregates become available—personal income and disposable income. Personal income represents income persons actually receive, except that taxes are not subtracted, contrasted with income earned by them in production, as shown in national income. To make the personal income measurement, the parts which do not currently flow to persons—corporate profits paid in taxes and those retained for use in the business, plus business contributions for social insurance—are subtracted. Income not derived from providing current services (in making final product) must be added—net interest paid by the government (net because interest paid to the government is subtracted), and transfer payments made by the government and by business.

It should be clear why the additions are not included in national income. Interest paid by the government, which netted $6 billion in 1957, is largely in service of war debt and is not closely related to current product or activity. Transfer payments are not in payment of services currently provided by persons. (Transfer payments made by business are an essential cost of doing business and therefore are included in gross national product, but obviously are not payments to individuals for services currently rendered by individuals and therefore are not included in national income.)

It is possible to classify personal income more effectively than disposable income, and this is its particular advantage. Not only can employee compensation be classified by type of industry making payments, but transfer payments can be classified with respect to the program under which the payments are made.

Disposable income equals personal income less personal taxes.

CHART 15–3

CONSUMPTION FUNCTION—EMPIRICAL REPRESENTATION

(In Constant Dollars)

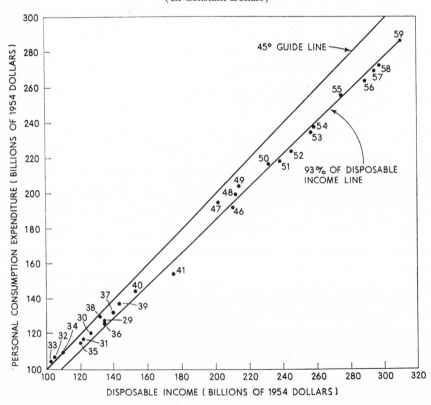

This is a most useful concept because it reflects the amount that individuals have to spend. The importance of such a measurement is indicated by the consumption function concept. The extent to which consumers spend disposable income, when price variations are eliminated, is shown by Chart 15–3. Since taxes paid cannot be readily classified by type of income payment, significant classifications of disposable income are not available. For classificatory purposes, indications shown by personal income classifications are usually employed. Because the most useful aggregates for our purposes are gross national product and disposable income, we show the accounting differences between the two concepts in Table 15–2.

TABLE 15–2

ACCOUNTING RELATIONSHIP BETWEEN GROSS NATIONAL PRODUCT AND DISPOSABLE INCOME, 1957*

(In Billions of Dollars)

Gross national product.........................				442.8
Minus:	1.	Tax payments......................		114.7
		Sales and other indirect taxes......	38.2	
		Personal income taxes............	42.6	
		Corporate profits taxes†..........	19.4	
		Contribution for social insurance...	14.5	
	2.	Income retained by producers........		47.2
		Capital consumption allowances...	37.5	
		Undistributed profits.............	9.7	
	3.	Surpluses of government enterprises‡...		.....
Plus:	1.	Subsidies and government interest.....		7.2
		Subsidies‡......................	1.0	
		Government interest.............	6.2	
	2.	Government transfer payments.......		20.1
	3.	Statistical discrepancy..............		0.6
Disposable income.............................				308.8

*Data taken from *Survey of Current Business*, July, 1960. Similar figures for more recent years can be obtained from successive July issues.

†The corporate profits taxes subtracted have been adjusted for an inventory valuation adjustment of −$1.5 billion. Corporate profits are entered into the accounts only after this adjustment.

‡By Department of Commerce methods, subsidies and surpluses of government enterprises are not segregated; therefore, we have not tried to show the figures separately. The two categories are entered at the appropriate places in the adjustment and the difference between the two entered as correction under subsidies.

USE OF FUNDS MADE AVAILABLE BY PERSONAL SAVING

Just as it is important to know the distribution of consumer expenditures in interpreting current behavior, it is helpful to know about the flow of savings funds.[7] The total personal saving is dis-

[7]The distribution described here was developed by the Securities and Exchange Commission, and it is being perfected by the Federal Reserve in connection with the flow-of-funds system now being made available. A reconciliation with the personal saving estimate arising in the income and product accounts is presented by the Department of Commerce. See, for instance, *Survey of Current Business*, July, 1960, p. 26.

tributed to show (1) amount spent on nonfarm homes; (2) increases in various types of financial assets, including currency and bank deposits and different kinds of securities; and (3) changes in debt to corporations and financial intermediaries by important types, including consumer debt and mortgage debt.

An important problem which arises in the interpretation of personal saving is that it includes savings made by noncorporate businesses and nonprofit corporations. This introduces a difficult confusion, for it is hardly appropriate to assume that saving inducements are the same for persons as for these other groups. Fortunately, the new flow-of-funds estimates, now being made by the Federal Reserve, show unincorporated business savings separately. This makes possible a more reliable analysis of the total flow of personal savings and rationalization of the responses resulting from flows into various types of financial instruments.

MEASUREMENT OF GOVERNMENT SURPLUS OR DEFICIT

The government surplus or deficit is another type of saving (or negative saving in case of deficits) which has created considerable confusion. The typical figure reported in the press is the balance indicated by what we may call the "administrative" budget. This balance shows receipts and expenditures as they appear in official government reports. Notably, the official figures for the federal government are those reported in the *Daily Treasury Statement*. Table 15–3 shows the discrepancy between the balance shown by those

TABLE 15–3

FEDERAL GOVERNMENT BUDGET BY ADMINISTRATIVE BALANCE AND NATIONAL ACCOUNT BALANCE

(In Billions of Dollars for Fiscal Years)

Fiscal Year	(1) Administrative Budget Surplus (+) or Deficit (−)	(2) National Account Budget Surplus (+) or Deficit (−)	Difference Column 2 − Column 1
1952........	− 4.0	−1.0	+3.0
1953........	− 9.5	−6.4	+3.1
1954........	− 3.1	−8.6	−5.5
1955........	− 4.2	−1.1	+3.1
1956........	+ 1.7	+6.8	+5.1
1957........	+ 1.6	+4.4	+2.8
1958........	− 2.8	−4.9	−2.1
1959........	−12.4	−4.8	+7.6

Source: *U.S. Income and Output; A Supplement to the Survey of Current Business* (Washington, D.C.: U.S. Government Printing Office, 1958), pp. 178–79; *Survey of Current Business*, July, 1960, p. 23.

figures and by the national economic accounts for 1952–59 fiscal years (1957, for instance, represents the year July, 1957, to June, 1958). The differences in the balance from the administrative budget and from the national account budget are material. Clearly, a need exists for a wise choice between the two.

To what the differences are due in the federal budget is shown in Table 15–4. We do not wish to emphasize the technical account-

TABLE 15–4

RECONCILIATION BETWEEN FEDERAL ADMINISTRATIVE AND NATIONAL ACCOUNT BUDGETS

(For Fiscal Year 1956, in Billions of Dollars)

Receipts

Administrative Budget Receipts......................			68.2
Less:	Intragovernmental transactions...............	2.7	
Plus:	Trust fund receipts[a]........................	11.7	
Equals:	Consolidated cash receipts...................		77.2
Plus:	Various adjustments[b].......................	0.2	
	Adjustments for timing[c].....................	0.3	
Less:	Adjustments for capital transactions[d].........	1.4	
Equals:			
National Income Account Receipts...................			76.3

Expenditures

Administrative Budget Expenditures.................			66.5
Less:	Intragovernmental transactions...............	2.7	
	Accrued interest and other cash expenditures....	0.9	
Plus:	Trust fund expenditures[a].....................	9.4	
	Government-sponsored enterprise expenditures..	0.3	
Equals:	Consolidated cash expenditures...............		72.6
Plus:	Various adjustments[b].......................	0.0	
	Adjustments for timing[c].....................	−1.3	
Less:	Adjustments for capital transactions[d].........	1.8	
Equals:			
National Income Account Expenditures...............			69.5

Addendum

Budget balance:		
	Administrative budget...........................	+1.7
	Consolidated cash budget........................	+4.6
	National income account budget..................	+6.8

Source: *Survey of Current Business*, July, 1959, p. 26.

[a]Trust funds cover old-age and survivors' insurance, federal-aid highways, unemployment insurance, federal employees' retirement, federal disability insurance, railroad retirement, veterans' life insurance, and other. They are not included in the budget because they are not available for general purposes of the government.

[b]Adjustments here are for exclusion of District of Columbia expenditures, and inclusion of government contributions to retirement and life insurance funds, employee contributions to retirement funds, and interest received plus other earnings and proceeds of government sales.

[c]Timing adjustments relate to excess of taxes included in national income accounts over cash collections, accrued interest on savings bonds and Treasury bills, Commodity Credit Corporation loans, increase in clearing account, and other.

[d]Capital transactions include realization on loans and investments, sale or purchase of land or other existing assets, recoveries and refunds, trust and deposit fund expenditures, redemption of International Monetary Fund notes, and Federal National Mortgage Association operations.

ing detail necessary to reconcile the different types of budgets. The interested individual can learn a great deal about the accounting required by a careful study of the table. Without extensive analysis, however, we may clearly deduce that the administrative budget does not provide the correct economic picture. To cover all of the government influence, we must recognize differences in receipts and expenditures of various funds which the government holds in trust for later payment to individuals or to divisional governmental units, correct for distortion in receipts of expenditures resulting from capital transactions, and adjust for other transactions which fail to reflect the government influence on current activity. These adjustments are made to develop the national account budget; therefore, it excels the administrative budget in a study of the economic situation.[8]

Generally, the national account budget has shown a smaller deficit or a greater surplus than the administrative budget because trust fund receipts have exceeded trust fund expenditures. This is due to the newness of the programs; and after the liabilities they entail are fully matured (as when the full component of those in the old-age insurance program reach retirement), the difference will largely disappear. In the meantime, under particular conditions, the national account budget may show the greater deficit, as in 1954, when actual money receipts from corporate profits taxes did not match accrued liabilities.

In the case of state and local governments the administrative budget is adjusted in accordance with the same principle. In these cases the major adjustments relate to elimination of capital transactions and of overlap with expenditure and receipts covered in the federal government account. Since federal government grants-in-aid are added to the receipts shown by the administrative budget, the national account budget for state and local governments has also shown a smaller deficit than the administrative budget.

DEFLATED PRODUCT AND INCOME MEASURES

The current demand condition over the short period is better reflected for many purposes by the current amount of dollar expenditure or of dollar income than by deflated figures. This is because dollar expenditures or dollar incomes influence demand by inducing a change in price as well as by generating the exchange

---

[8]In addition, as shown in Table 15–4, an adjustment is made for timing. This is because the national accounts are carried on an accrual basis, in common with typical business accounting.

of a given quantity of product. The separate influence of price and quantity may, however, frequently provide useful insights, and the current publication of gross national product and its major components on a quarterly deflated basis is a welcome innovation.

Over the long period the deflated figures have more meaning than current dollar figures. Growth is related to changes in living or at least expenditure standards. The government and business sectors may appropriately be incorporated in such a concept, so that the rising expenditures need not necessarily accrue to the benefit of individuals. But the idea that growth also relates to price changes is artificial. The deflated gross national product figures are universally used when growth is being analyzed.

We may reasonably expect that long-term relationships between income and expenditure are most usefully compared in fixed buying power dollars. For that reason, Chart 15-3 shows the consumption function as depicted by data since 1929 in deflated dollar figures. Even though the deflation of these figures is far from perfect, the general stability of the spending (consuming) tendency is clearly represented. The years 1942–45 are not shown, for the war produced abnormally large savings. The 93 per cent of disposable income line is drawn in to guide the reader in visualizing the approximate propensity indicated.

INDUSTRIAL PRODUCTION

Our measurement of industrial production follows a different approach from that in measurement of income and product. The Federal Reserve, in developing the industrial production measurement, begins with quantity instead of dollar figures. The quantity measurements are weighted and combined to form a single index to represent the total group. As revised in 1959, electric and gas utilities are included in the Index, as has become the practice in most other countries. The weight attributed to utilities is only 5 per cent; and, although it introduces some unfamiliarity into the American measure, it does not change the result greatly. Principally, it adds slightly to the stability of the Index and increases the advance made in the thirty years 1929–59 from 163 per cent to 174 per cent. The growth of utilities has been greater and the movement more stable than in manufacturing and mining, which are the other components of the Index.

The major importance of the Industrial Production Index for our purposes is its sensitivity and its timeliness. Economic change in the short period shows up most clearly in manufacturing and mining; therefore, the Industrial Production Index is a better indicator of the immediate conditions prevailing than income or product data. It is available monthly instead of quarterly, so that keeping up with current conditions is facilitated. Nevertheless, as shown on Chart 15–4, except for abnormal conditions like those existing in World War II, the broad fluctuations of the two types of measurement are similar. Industrial production, however, has grown more rapidly. The advance in deflated gross national product since 1929 is 134 per cent instead of 174 per cent.

CHART 15–4

RELATION OF INDUSTRIAL PRODUCTION TO DEFLATED GROSS NATIONAL PRODUCT

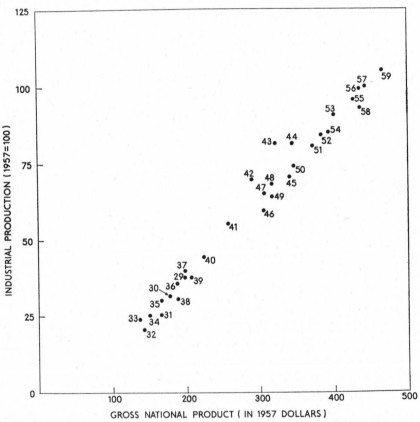

Movement in divisions of the Industrial Production Index is shown in Chart 15–5. The wide fluctuation in production of durables is clearly indicated. A significant advantage possessed by the Industrial Production Index is the representation provided on various types of durables. The current measures shown on equipment pro-

CHART 15-5

INDUSTRIAL PRODUCTION, BY MAJOR DIVISIONS
Federal Reserve Indexes, Adjusted for Seasonal Variation
1957 = 100

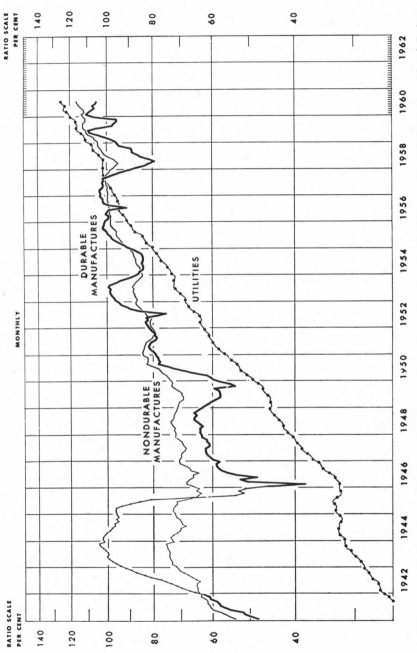

Source: Board of Governors of the Federal Reserve System, *Historical Supplement to Federal Reserve Chart Book on Financial and Business Statistics* (Washington, D.C., September, 1960).

duction are very important, since equipment production represents an important part of expenditure changes in sharp cyclical movements (not shown separately in the chart).

EMPLOYMENT AND UNEMPLOYMENT

Employment is an important indicator of general business activity because of its social impact and because labor, being the scarcest of major resources, provides an indication of the approach of capacity operation. Over-all productivity is variable and difficult to predict over the short period; therefore, employment does not move in as close conformity with gross national product or industrial production as might be expected. Labor force, representing the sum of employment and unemployment, is not entirely dependent upon the movement of activity. When activity is high, the demand for employment increases, and more persons may be drawn into the labor force. On the other hand, secondary family workers may be drawn into the labor force in recession if the main breadwinner is disemployed or put on short time. As yet, we are not entirely certain whether the tendency for the labor force to increase is greatest under prosperous or under depressed conditions.

The labor force, as currently measured by a Department of Labor survey, roughly represents those who are able to work and wishing to work.[9] It includes all of those person who are employed and who are classified as unemployed in accordance with criteria

CHART 15-6

Labor-Force Participation

LABOR FORCE PER THOUSAND IN SAME POPULATION GROUP

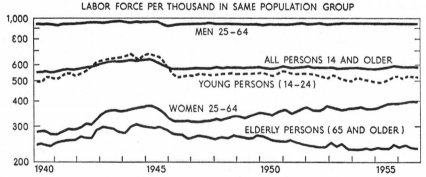

Source: Joint Economic Committee, *Employment, Growth, and Price Levels,* Part 3: *Historical and Comparative Rates of Labor Force, Employment, and Unemployment,* Hearings, April 25–28, 1959 (Washington, D.C.: U.S. Government Printing Office, 1959).

---

[9]A more precise definition will be found in various issues of *Monthly Report on the Labor Force,* published by the Department of Labor; or see the writer's *Business Forecasting* (New York: McGraw-Hill Book Co., Inc., 1958), pp. 27–28.

which have met the test of experience. Under the forced draft conditions of war the labor force will increase substantially. Otherwise, except for seasonal variation, as indicated by Chart 15–6, it is principally dependent upon the participation rate of various age and sex groups, which tends to remain fairly stable. The general movement of the labor force for thirty years is shown in Chart 15–7.

Employment, of course, traces the same general picture of economic fluctuation as industrial production or gross national product, and unemployment traces an inverse picture. When major interest lies in the extent to which employment is offered to those who need it, as it usually does in questions of social welfare, employment and unemployment are the central indicators. But because of temporary variations in output per man, the amount of production or output may not be clearly revealed by labor-force measures. On public policy questions, it may nonetheless become essential to estimate the relation between the two measures.

Near expansion peaks, figures on unemployment become strategic in indicating output and price conditions. Since labor is generally our most limited resource, unemployment is most indicative of the approach of bottlenecks as full-capacity operations are approached. It is our clearest indication of the basic strength of prices, as explained in the following chapter.

Prospective secular growth is vitally dependent on the level of employment, as explained in Chapter 6. For this purpose, we do not need to be concerned about the birth rate if growth is not to be projected more than 15 or 20 years. Labor participation rates are applied to surviving numbers in each age-sex population group. It is generally expected that the labor participation rate of women will continue to increase, with slight declines in the male groups and more marked declines in the younger age groups. The over-all participation rate is expected to remain fairly stable. Having obtained an estimate of future labor force by this method, employment is estimated for secular growth purposes by applying a labor float percentage. Around 3 or 4 per cent is usually recommended.

APPENDIX A FOR CHAPTER 15: SOURCES OF DATA

The most important source for information discussed in this chapter is the *Survey of Current Business*. Every few years a supplement is published providing basic income and product data, extensive supplementary information, and professional explanations. The two most recent supplements are *National Income: 1954 Edition* and *U.S. Income and Output*, published in 1959. The next edition of this supplement is expected in the early sixties and may, for the first time, contain some integrated input-output data. Each July the *Survey of Current Business* brings all

CHART 15-7

LABOR FORCE, EMPLOYMENT, AND UNEMPLOYMENT

Bureau of the Census Estimates 1940–June, 1959
Bureau of Labor Statistics Estimates 1929–39 and July, 1959

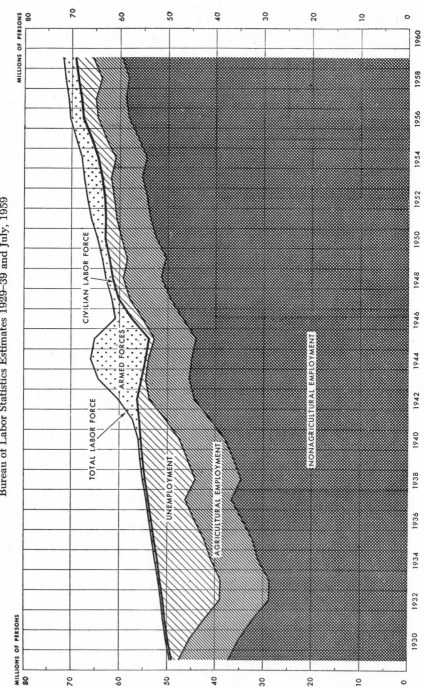

Source: Board of Governors of the Federal Reserve System, *Historical Supplement to Federal Reserve Chart Book on Financial and Business Statistics* (Washington, D.C., September, 1960).

of the income and product tables up to date. The February issue provides the previous year's major totals on a preliminary basis for the first time. These are the sources from which income and product data were derived in this chapter.

The monthly issues supply a well-rounded list of tables which include most of the varied information an analyst needs in regard to current conditions. These tables, among many other types of data, include the most recent income and product data, industrial production figures, and employment and unemployment.

An extended catalogue of references to data is not intended, and we need go little further than citing the *Survey of Current Business*. Three other monthly publications will be mentioned: (1) *Federal Reserve Bulletin*, especially useful for monetary and banking data; (2) *Monthly Labor Review*, useful for price and labor data; and (3) *Economic Indicators*, prepared by the Joint Economic Committee of Congress, and noted for a discriminating inclusion of important data.

Three annual sources are especially useful: (1) *Statistical Abstract of the United States*, prepared by the Department of Commerce, covers the most comprehensive range of useful data. (2) *The Economic Almanac*, prepared by the National Industrial Conference Board and published by the Thomas Y. Crowell Company of New York, is especially prepared to provide broad information needed in studying economic change. (3) The *Economic Report of the President*, prepared by the Council of Economic Advisers, contains a useful statistical appendix.

The Federal Reserve publishes a monthly *Federal Reserve Chart Book on Financial and Business Statistics*, which is the most useful chart book generally available. The *Historical Supplement*, published in September, is most noteworthy in providing background pictures. We may note that some of the charts from that Supplement are reproduced in this book. The fact that they are reproduced here and in most books written along similar topics testifies to their general applicability.

APPENDIX B FOR CHAPTER 15: FLOW-OF-FUND STATEMENTS AND INPUT-OUTPUT TABLES

Since reference is made in this chapter to two other ways of organizing aggregative data, a brief, elementary explanation may be in order. A succinct statement made by the National Accounts Review Committee provides as concise an explanation of these accounts as is available:

Flow-of-funds statements cover all money and credit transactions in the economy; they thus deal with financial as well as income and product transactions. They provide information on the extension of bank credit, the purchase of securities, and other changes in the assets and liabilities of the different sectors of the economy, as well as on the payments and receipts of income. In contrast with input-output tables, flow-of-funds statements divide the economy into institutional sectors—corporations, unincorporated enterprisers, banks, insurance companies, and so forth—rather than into processing industries. Flow-of-funds statements thus are intended to show the financial transactions of various groups in the economy, rather than physical transformation relationships.[10]

---

[10]Joint Economic Committee, *The National Economic Accounts of the United States* (Washington, D.C.: U.S. Government Printing Office, 1957), pp. 132–33.

TABLE 15-5. SUMMARY OF FLOW-OF-FUNDS ACCOUNTS FOR 1959

(In Billions of Dollars)

Transaction category	Consumer and non-profit U	Consumer S	Farm[1] U	Farm S	Non-corporate[1] U	Non-corporate S	Corporate U	Corporate S	Federal U	Federal S	State and local U	State and local S	Commercial banking[3] U	Commercial banking S	Savings institutions[4] U	Savings institutions S	Insurance[5] U	Insurance S	Finance n.e.c.[6] U	Finance n.e.c. S	Rest-of-world U	Rest-of-world S	All sectors U	All sectors S	Discrepancy[7] U	Natl. saving and investment[2,8]	Code
Gross saving[2,9]		74.0		4.1		8.2		34.8		-4.5		-4.4		1.5		.9		1.2		-.5		102.5		117.8	[11]2.3	115.2	A
Capital Consumption[12]		43.4		4.1		8.2		23.3																79.0		79.0	B
Net saving (A−B)		30.6		*				11.4		-4.5		-4.4		1.5		.9		1.2		-.5		2.5		38.7		36.1	C
Gross investment (E+J)[2]	76.2		4.1		8.2		30.7		-4.5		-3.9		2.4		.7		1.6		-.1		1.8		117.1		-1.6	113.7	D
Private capital expenditures (net of sales)[13]	65.6		5.4		11.4		32.3																115.4			115.4	E
Consumer durable goods[12]	43.4																						43.4			43.4	F
Nonfarm resident.constr.[14]	18.5				1.9		1.9																22.3			22.3	G
Plant and equipment[15]	3.7		4.9		8.9		25.5																43.8			43.8	H
Change in inventories[16]			.5		.6		4.8																5.9			5.9	I
Net financial invest. (K−L)	10.6		-1.3		-3.2		-1.6		-4.5		-3.9		2.0		.7		1.2		-.1		1.8		1.6		-1.6	[16]-1.8	J
Net acquis. of finan. assets[17]	31.3		-.4		*		13.4		6.3		3.1		4.6		10.0		9.9		4.6		5.8		88.7			4.0	K
Net increase in liab.[17]		20.7		.9		3.2		15.0		10.8		6.9		2.6		9.4		8.8		4.7		4.0		87.1		5.8	L
Gold and Treas. currency[18]									*	*			-1.0								1.1		.1	1.1	-.1	-.1	M
Dem. dep. and currency[19]			-.4		-.3		.2		.7		.5			1.1	-.2		.1		.1		-1.0		1.7	1.1	-.6	-.1	N
Fixed-value redeem. claims	9.6								*	-2.0	-.4		1.2	1.2	-.2	8.4			-1.0		-1.0		7.6	7.6		1.0	O
Time deposits[20]	4.1									-.2	-.4		1.2	1.2	-.1	1.2							2.2	2.2		1.0	P
Savings shares[21]	7.3														-.1	7.2							7.2	7.2			Q
U.S. savings bonds[22]	-1.8								-1.8	-1.8													-1.8	-1.8			R
Saving through life insur.[23]	3.7									.1		1.8					3.7	3.6					3.7	3.7			S
Saving through pen. funds[24]	7.9									.9							7.9	5.2					7.9	7.9			T
Credit and equity mkt.instr.	15.3	20.6	2.0		.4	4.8	5.5	11.6	3.8	10.7	2.9	5.1	5.6		10.6	.9	9.8		4.5	4.7	3.1	.8	61.5	61.4	-.1	-2.3	U
Federal obligations[25]	9.4						4.4			11.3	1.0		-7.1		.6		.2		.1		2.8		11.3	11.3		-2.8	V
State and local obligations	2.5											4.9	-.2		*		1.4		.2				4.7	4.7			W
Corp. and foreign bonds	.1						3.3				1.2				-1		3.5		1.0	.5	.4	.5	4.4	4.7		-.2	X
Corporate stock	1.1	13.2					2.3										1.3		1.8	1.0			4.4	4.4			Y
1- to 4-family mortgages	1.5					1.4	.1		1.6				1.3		8.2		1.9		*				13.3	13.3			Z
Other mortgages	1.8				.4		.8		.6				1.1		1.8		1.0						5.8	5.8			a
Consumer credit[26]		6.3											2.4		1.8				1.9				6.3	6.3			b
Security credit[26]	-.2					2.7	.3	2.5												*			6.3	7.9		*	c
Bank loans n.e.c.[27]	.4	.7	.7	.9	.4			3.4	-1.6			.2	7.9		*			.5		1.3	*	.2	7.9	7.9		.2	d
Other loans[28]	-.5	.2				-.6				-.6			-.6			.8	.5		1.0		-.1	*	2.8	2.7		.1	e
Trade credit	.1			1.1		[29]2.6	6.8	3.3		.1								.1					6.9	6.9			f
Proprietors' net invest. in noncorporate business[1]	-6.1			-1.1		-5.0																	-6.1	-6.1		.8	g
Misc. financial trans.[30]					*		1.3	.1	1.8	1.0		.2	-1	-.9	-1		-.4		-.4	1.3	2.4	3.2	5.4	4.6	-.8		h
Sector discrepancies (A−D)[31]	-2.2						4.1			-.6					-.2		-.4				-.8		.7			1.5	i

Details may not add to totals because of rounding.

° Less than $50 millions.

NOTE: U = uses of funds; S = sources of funds. Financial uses of funds represent net acquisitions of assets; financial sources of funds, net changes in liabilities.

[1]Net saving of, and consumer investment in, unincorporated business.

[2]For government sectors, saving is excess of all nonfinancial receipts overall nonfinancial outlays; investment excludes, government purchases of tangible assets. Government current outlays include, and government (and national) investment excludes, government purchases of tangible assets.

[3]Consolidated account for monetary authorities (Federal Reserve System, ESF, and Treasury currency accounts) and commercial banks in United States (excluding territories and possessions).

[4]Mutual savings banks, savings and loan associations, and credit unions.

[5]Life and nonlife insurance companies and private pension plans.

[6]Finance companies, open-end investment companies, security brokers and dealers, banks in U.S. territories and possessions, and U.S. agencies of foreign banks.

[7]For discussion, see p. 857 of the Federal Reserve Bulletin for August, 1959.

[8]Totals for domestic sectors; financial entries are net uses plus items in discrepancy column. For comparison with national saving and investment in national income accounts of Department of Commerce, see p. 842 of the Bulletin for August, 1959.

[9]For content of sector saving, see Tables 1 and 4 and pp. 833 and 849 of the Bulletin for August, 1959.

[10]Rest-of-world surplus on current transactions with United States.

[11]Discrepancy between total nonfinancial sources and uses of funds (line A minus line E in "all sectors" column).

[12]Depreciation, accidental damage to fixed capital, and capital outlays charged to current account.

[13]Transactions in land excluded from sector investment for statistical reasons. Such transactions, when recorded as capital flows, affect sector allocation of investment but not the national total.

[14]For consumers, one- to four-family dwellings and other private residential construction. Investment of nonfarm business sectors includes work in process on one- to four-family dwellings and other private residential construction.

[15]After inventory valuation adjustment.

[16]Financial component of national investment equals net lending to rest of world; financial flows among domestic sectors cancel out in national total. (Discrepancies in financial transactions attributed entirely to domestic transactions.) Differs from U.S. "net foreign investment" (net exports minus net unilateral transfers in national income accounts) by discrepancy in rest-of-world account, which equals "errors and omissions" in Department of Commerce balance-of-payments statement for the United States.

[17]"Liabilities" cover equity as well as debt claims.

[18]For description, see p. 852 of the Bulletin for August, 1959.

[19]Demand deposit liabilities of banking system are net of Federal Reserve float and cash items in process of collection as reported by commercial banks. Sum of sector holdings (partly on holder-record basis) differs from liability total mainly because of mail float (checks in transit from drawers to drawees).

[20]At commercial and mutual savings banks and Postal Savings System.

[21]Shares in savings and loan associations and credit unions.

[22]Consumer-held only; includes net interest accruals. Savings bonds held by other sectors included in federal obligations category.

[23]Private and federal government life insurance. Estimated as equal to changes in reserves against life insurance policies and supplementary contracts and in policy dividend accumulations.

[24]Private pension plans and railroad and government employee retirement funds. Estimated as equal to changes in reserves of pension plans administered by life insurance companies and in assets of other private plans and of railroad and government employee retirement funds.

[25]Excludes federal debt held by federal agencies, consumer-held savings bonds, special notes issued to IMF, and currency items in public debt; includes federal agency debt and accrued interest on Treasury bills and on savings bonds (other than consumer-held).

[26]Loans from banks for purchasing or carrying securities and customer debit and net free credit balances on books of security brokers and dealers.

[27]Mainly commercial, industrial, and agricultural loans (other than open-market paper and CCC-guaranteed loans); includes loans to foreign banks, loans to individuals (other than consumer credit), and other loans. Gross of valuation reserves. Loans to domestic commercial banks excluded in consolidated banking statement.

[28]Mainly federal government loans (other than mortgages), CCC-guaranteed loans, open-market paper, finance company loans to business, and policy loans on life insurance.

[29]Trade debt net of trade credit.

[30]For coverage, see p. 856 of the Bulletin for August, 1959.

[31]Saving and investment are equal in concept but may differ statistically because of discrepancies. See p. 857 of the Bulletin for August, 1959.

Flow-of-funds statements are now published quarterly in the *Federal Reserve Bulletin*. The publication began in the August, 1959, issue. Table 15–5 shows the flow of funds for 1959 as indicated by the Federal Reserve report. This report provides a beginning in showing the interactions of financial and nonfinancial developments. It is important for us to see how the report differs from income and product. (1) Financial sectors, including commercial banks, saving institutions, insurance, and other finance, are represented directly. This makes it possible to reflect credit flows. (2) A detailed statement of source and use of funds is provided by major sectors, including consumer, farm, noncorporate nonfinancial, corporate nonfinancial, federal government, state and local government, commercial banking, nonbank financial, and rest of world. (3) The holdings of principal financial assets and liabilities are shown by sector. (4) Funds raised in each sector are shown as well as funds advanced by each sector. Thus, gross flows are shown in both directions. (5) The flow-of-funds statements are not founded on any principle like summation to final product which characterized national income accounting. Therefore, any totals shown for the total economy are less meaningful.

Input-output tables involve even more detail than the other accounts. It is necessary to have a Census of Manufactures year to provide a satisfactory table, and no comprehensive account after 1947 was available until 1960. The table is shown by industries, and for most purposes a great many are required to avoid a large, unmanageable "all other" group. Industries are listed in columns of the table to identify purchasing activity. The same list is shown in rows to identify producing activity. Thus, the purchases of an industry, broken down by industry producing, are shown in the columns. The sales of an industry, broken down by industry purchasing, are shown in the rows. Much is made of the percentage distribution of the columns, called flow coefficients. They are often interpreted as the standard technical requirements for production in an industry. An input-output table is thus a complete "from whom to whom" breakdown of áll commodity (and sometimes service) flows within the nation. It can be adapted on a more abbreviated basis for use in individual companies or industries (especially for marketing analysis). The use of input-output analysis often has been called mathematical programming.

An input-output table may depict either a "closed" system or an "open" system. In a closed system, all industries are assumed to be completely interdependent, and their inputs and outputs to be functionally related. Consumer households might be considered to constitute one industry having consumer goods and services as input and to be represented by labor as product. In the open system, some industries do not have to be functionally related to all others, even though a relation is recognized. An input-output table does not necessarily have to cover the whole economy. Much duplication arises in the table; therefore, the gross total shown by the table has little meaning (for example, many industries provide only intermediate product).

The difference between flow-of-funds statements and input-output tables has been most effectively stated by the National Accounts Review Committee:

Neither in theory nor in practice is there a close relationship between flow-of-funds statements and input-output tables. Indeed these two aspects of a comprehensive national accounting system are about as far removed conceptually and statistically as is possible within that system. The flow-of-funds statement emphasizes financial flows and collects all its data on an enterprise basis. Input-output tables omit financial transactions altogether, concentrate on flows of goods and services among producers, and must be derived from very detailed data collected on a plant and preferably even on a process basis.[11]

FOR REFLECTION AND ANALYSIS

1. In what sense do gross national product and national income measure total output and the demand it calls forth?
2. What is meant by the value-added concept?
3. How does the extension of credit enter in income and expenditure measurements?
4. Why is the equality of income and expenditure in our present framework of estimation a static concept?
5. What is the difference between replacements of worn-out capital and consumption allowances as far as timing is concerned?
6. Why does not Table 15-1 include all rent and interest payments?
7. What is meant by nonincome charges?
8. Explain the subtractions and additions required in moving from GNP to disposable income.
9. What are the major reasons why the administrative surplus or deficit of the federal government differs from the national account figures?
10. May undeflated GNP figures, under certain circumstances, provide more insight on economic conditions than deflated figures?
11. Why does the movement of industrial production differ from that of GNP?
12. Why may an increase in employment not always bring forth a commensurate increase in product?

---

[11]National Bureau of Economic Research, Inc., *op. cit.,* p. 238.

Chapter	MEANING AND
16	FORECASTING OF
	AVERAGE PRICES

This chapter parallels the preceding one. There, we talked of indicators of general business activity, where the emphasis was on the physical volume of change. At times, we found that total value is the most relevant measure; but when we departed from that position, we turned to the measure of physical volume, never to the measurement of price. Price represents a measure of the rate of exchange, not of activity.

Study of over-all prices is a modern proclivity. In the nineteenth century, reference was usually made to prices of individual commodities. We are still interested in the prices of individual commodities, but principally in relation to particular industries. Interest in over-all prices grew with the realization of the importance of over-all economic change. While over-all price measures do not provide a satisfactory representation of activity, they do throw important light on demand and changes arising in supply conditions.

Every businessman is cognizant of the demand implications of price. To him, high or rising prices represent a favorable market, while low or declining prices represent an unfavorable one. It is true that he thinks in terms of individual prices of a limited range of commodities of particular interest to him, but his argument parallels the one we make. Most prices scatter along a similar path. The path represents the general measure with which we are concerned, so that the combined reasoning of businessmen about the demand indications of prices reflects an important interpretation of over-all average.

Depending on the situation, price changes may more clearly reflect changes in supply conditions than in demand. Rising activity early in business cycle expansion may more clearly reflect a shift in supply than in demand conditions because of culmination of inventory investment. The temporary pinch may push up prices, even though demand is still relatively low. If preceded by an extreme contraction, prices may have been driven down to out-of-pocket costs, and any increase in demand in the expansion may induce businessmen to put up the price because of the cost of providing additional supply. This contrasts with a minor recession, when the basic price structure may not have declined at all, and with expansion, when businessmen may sometimes compete for the increase in demand by a reduction in price.

As the expansion gets under way, prices are moved principally by demand until capacity operations are approached. Under capacity operations, limited supply accelerates the rise in prices. Later on in prosperity, a contrary supply shift often occurs. Investment projects started earlier at a rapid rate are completed. Frequently, the increase in capacity is great enough that supplies appear reasonably abundant and prices weaken.

Decline in prices in recession is closely geared to anticipatory attitudes. When contraction is being forced rapidly by inventory runoff, the experience is that quoted prices decline substantially less than activity. When much durable capital remains to be completed and a general feeling has developed that a great deal of overbuilding has occurred, activity is supported by completion of investment projects started earlier, while the pessimistic atmosphere is conducive to price declines.

Prices reflect anticipatory attitudes at all times, but no doubt the anticipatory influence is accentuated in recession. As long as activity is expanding, administered prices do not promptly adjust to anticipatory expectation if current prices are reasonably favorable in relation to costs. When activity begins to decline, much rationalization may arise in the administered price area. If it is felt that the decline in activity is only temporary, prices may be well maintained. If, however, fading demand appears impressive, price cuts may be severe.

In this chapter, we are talking primarily about commodity prices, secondarily about service prices, and to an insignificant extent about other market "prices." These other market prices include wage rates, interest rates, and any rate of exchange determined by demand and supply relationships. Commodity prices are important to us because they most clearly reflect demand conditions and most clearly point to the degree to which pressure is being applied when there is approach to capacity operations. Competitive conditions tend to be more controlling in the determination of commodity than of other prices.

THE AGGREGATE SUPPLY FUNCTION

As demand rises and activity increases, there is a tendency for producers to advance the price at which supply will be made available. When capacity operations are approached, the price required by producers rises sharply. What will happen to prices when demand falls and producers are called on to supply smaller quantities is less clear. As noted in the above paragraphs, anticipation apparently plays a major role with respect to changing prices if demand begins to fall.

These conclusions might or might not be as effectively developed microcosmically with respect to individual commodities and individual firms as they are when the general movement of the total economy is visualized. Without doubt, however, the analysis is enriched when placed in juxtaposition with what is known about the typical fluctuation of total activity, as we have tried to show in brief summary above. Nevertheless, it is clear enough that we have advanced little further than obvious reflections from known empirical facts. A rounded theory has not yet been fully developed, but the nature of economic fluctuation in activity will have to be taken into consideration in any such theory.

An important advantage of thinking in terms of an aggregate supply function is that tightness or ease of money relates to over-all conditions. At a point far under capacity rates of operation, pressure is not likely to be put on the money supply; therefore, the supply curve can usually be explained by a simple relation to changing demand. Pressure *could* be put on the money supply early in expansion, and price rises might be reduced. The result, no doubt, would be a slowing of the rise in demand, so that the failure of prices to increase might be largely accounted for by the fact that activity increased little.

As capacity is approached, money controls are likely to be tightened. Price is influenced by credit limitations as well as by physical limitations of capacity. Again, depending on the conditions, the tightening of monetary policy may restrict demand as an alternative to rising prices. The actual outturn depends on the anticipatory effect which accompanies the change. High enough anticipations might largely offset credit control. Anticipations will be largely guided by characteristic economic fluctuations, explained in the opening paragraphs of this chapter.

STRUCTURE OF PRICES

Prices, representative of different parts of the economy, have not moved uniformly over time. In the thirty years from 1929 to 1959, most wholesale price groups advanced in the neighborhood of 100 per cent. At more detailed levels, less similarity of movement is found. Competition arose principally at the more detailed levels, where products are bid against each other in the same market group. Over the long run, differences in the rate of productivity advance largely account for different price movements.

The long-term price changes of some major groups have deviated markedly from the general pattern. Consumer prices advanced only 70 per cent from 1929 to 1959. A similarly restricted advance occurred in the price of crude materials. A major factor accounting for the limited advance in consumer prices is that house rents rose only 31 per cent. Rental rates are heavily influenced by traditional factors and adapt slowly to changing conditions. The restricted rise in crude material prices is accounted for by technological advance in producing materials and by the fact that the pricing of crude materials antedates the added margins in the distribution process which have increased disproportionately over time.

Since the 1948 recession, most price groups have increased about a fifth. In a few cases the advance has been substantially less—in apparel, household appliances, crude materials, most chemical products, electricity, gas, and most miscellaneous products. In all of these cases, improved technology largely accounts for the restricted price increase. In a few other cases, price rises have been well above average—public transportation, medical care, machinery, and most other durable goods. Rising costs in public transportation account for a doubling of prices in scarcely more than a decade. In the other cases the rising prices relate to a large expansion in demand, together with limited technological improvement. Nondurable goods prices scarcely increased in this period, while durable goods prices rose nearly 50 per cent. The explanation lies in the much greater increase in demand for durable goods, more restricted productivity advance, and the fact that quality improvements are not readily given consideration in pricing durable products. The price of farm products was held down after the late forties by increased availability, and this exerted a heavy influence on the price of many nondurable products.

In the shorter period, some discrepancy in price movements reflects cyclical maladjustments. A careful study of Chart 16-1 will convince the reader that prices of the materials shown reflect cycli-

CHART 16–1

Wholesale Prices of Selected Materials

(Monthly Averages: High, Low, and December)

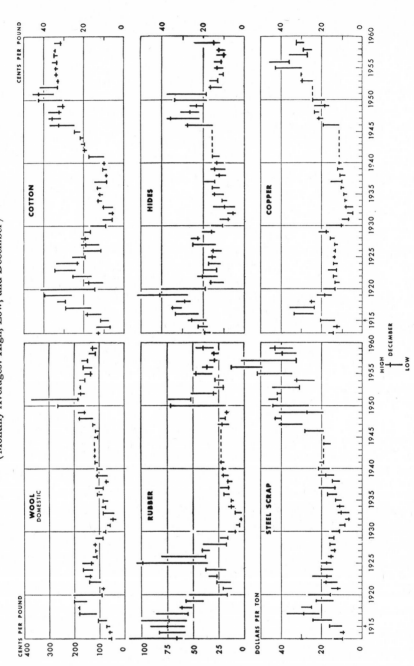

Source: Board of Governors of the Federal Reserve System, *Historical Supplement to Federal Reserve Chart Book on Financial and Business Statistics* (Washington, D.C., September, 1960).

cal fluctuations. Other materials add substantially to the list of cyclically sensitive materials—for instance, zinc, lead, lumber, and many farm products. Such prices have advanced inordinately in expansion and fallen disproportionately in contraction. The reason is readily identified. The markets for these materials are highly competitive, and the materials are produced—in the short run, at least—under conditions of increasing cost. The meaning is clear. Prices which predominantly take on the character of costs in most business operations exert a contractionary influence near the end of expansion and an expansionary influence near the end of recession.

This price influence is readily overemphasized under current conditions. As for agricultural commodities, price support under the government program keeps change in demand from exerting an important influence on price, but agricultural prices before the advent of such control were the least consistent of the raw material prices in relation to the business cycle because of weather-determined variations in supply. For the other sensitive commodities, it is not clear that any important change has occurred in the sharpness of competition or in the rapidity of increase in cost of production when demand rises substantially. But the development of man-made substitutes has brought about substantial inroads into the markets for many of the older types of raw materials. Their relative importance on the total economic situation therefore has been reduced.

The structure of prices for final goods and services that is now most influential on cyclical conditions relates to the extent to which price changes respond directly to changes in demand or only indirectly by following the general price movement. At the one extreme, there are products in highly competitive "bid and ask" markets, which appear to initiate changes in general prices. Next, manufactured and some other commodities are usually sold at what we call administered prices, or prices established by the producer. Lewis says that "they are the result of conscious, deliberative group-thinking processes, processes which in the larger corporate organizations often are rather ponderous; decisions are neither lightly arrived at nor lightly changed."[1] Third in order of flexibility are services, which are priced at customary levels but slowly adapt to the general price levels which come to prevail. Finally, we may note public service rates set by the government.

---

[1]John P. Lewis, *Business Conditions Analysis* (New York: McGraw-Hill Book Co., Inc., 1959), p. 122.

If we assume that "bid and ask" prices arrived at on open markets establish demand conditions, it is clear that when demand is rising, administered prices lag behind and usually are set at levels below those which demand would warrant; and when demand is falling, they are above the levels open markets would establish. Over the full business cycle, then, administered prices may not differ greatly on average from open-market competitive levels. If open-market prices were the controlling factor in the general price movement, administered prices might be visualized as drawn to them. Unfortunately for this argument, apparently commodities sold in the open market are now shrinking in importance. Cost-push factors (rising wage demands) may bring administered prices closer to the level warranted by the demand situation in expansion. If recession is looked on largely as a short-run supply distortion (too much inventory) and not as a shift in underlying demand, administered prices may be well maintained when open-market prices exert but a minor depressive influence. With rising prices in expansion and little or no decline in recession, an upward price bias will prevail.

If prices in general rise rapidly over a short period of time, as they did after World War II, the inflationary bias may be accentuated by the movement of service prices. These prices lag so far behind open-market requirements that they may frequently be rising after the recession gets under way in response to the general price advance occurring earlier. At least, we have many price changes which this explanation appears to fit in the postwar period, e.g., substantial rises in medical care expenses in the 1948 and in the 1957–58 recessions. The rise in government-controlled rates tends to lag even more. Not only do these prices tend to catch up with general advances after they occur in business cycle expansions, but they may advance because of underpricing which existed even before the rapid inflation began. (We may cite the postwar increase in the rate paid for such services as domestic help or local transportation in major urban centers.)

THE MAJOR PRICE MEASURES

The various price averages which are currently published have not been developed in response to a carefully developed program in the analysis of economic change. Practically every average, however, throws some light on changing economic conditions. A possible approach, therefore, would be to study each available average with respect to its contribution to an understanding of economic conditions. Unfortunately, much more detail would be required than is practicable in this book.

For our purposes, we shall consider five price indexes—Spot-Market Prices of Basic Commodities, Wholesale Price Index, Wholesale Price Index of Commodities Other than Farm Products and Foods, Consumer Price Index, and GNP Implicit Price Deflator. Four of these indexes are pictured on Chart 16–2.

CHART 16–2

POSTWAR MOVEMENT OF FOUR PRICE INDEXES

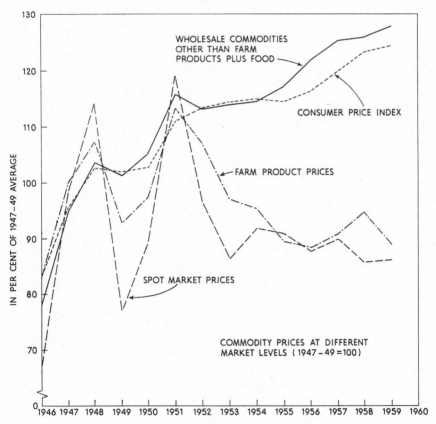

The Spot-Market Prices of Basic Commodities Index measures the change in price of twenty-two basic commodities sold on the open market. It represents the best indication we have of prices warranted by demand conditions. In nearly all cases, any substantial increase in supply can be obtained only at rapidly rising costs, so that the sensitivity to demand conditions is accentuated. Because of this, and because the commodities included represent the total demand picture to a decreasing extent (as explained above), the

Index can scarcely be considered to reflect the average of all prices warranted by changing demand.

The Wholesale Price Index is a comprehensive monthly measure of the change in prices at primary market levels, reflective of the first commercial transaction for each commodity. About two thousand items are represented. (A weekly Index is reported which is based on fewer items.) Note should be taken of the fact that this Index in most cases actually will not represent the wholesale stage of distribution, since it is ordinarily taken where the first commercial transaction occurs. The comprehensive Wholesale Price Index is of limited value because it represents too many diverse primary transactions and is not necessarily indicative of prices at later stages of distribution.

The Wholesale Price Index of Commodities Other than Farm Products and Foods is more homogeneous because the other commodities are mostly representative of administered pricing and because they reflect a more homogeneous supply situation. The prices of farm products are not administered in the same sense. Their supply is dependent upon yearly crop yields or longer cycles (such as in the development of meat animals). The "other" commodities do not reflect all administered prices, for many retail prices are administered; but we have no other index which so well represents the movement of administered prices. In any case, the measurement of administered prices is most complicated because the actual selling price involves many agreements other than just a quoted unit price. Price extras or discounts are representative of a maze of complications which still are not effectively measured.

The Consumer Price Index is our best measure of the final prices paid by the consumer. It is representative of most products the consumer buys, including services (such as medical care and rent) as well as commodities (notably food and apparel). The comparable movement of transportation, rent, food, and apparel is shown in Chart 16–3.

The Consumer Price Index can be more simply interpreted than the Wholesale Price Index because it reflects only prices of products going to final consumers, while the Wholesale Price Index includes also commodities going to business and government. On the other hand, the Consumer Price Index covers a whole series of successive margins added onto prices at primary markets. Because these margins tend to be fairly stable, the Consumer Price Index may be expected to be less variable than the Wholesale Price Index under most conditions. This result is not very apparent in recent price

CONSUMER PRICES, BY MAJOR TYPES

Bureau of Labor Statistics Indexes, 1947–49 = 100
Monthly except Where Otherwise Indicated

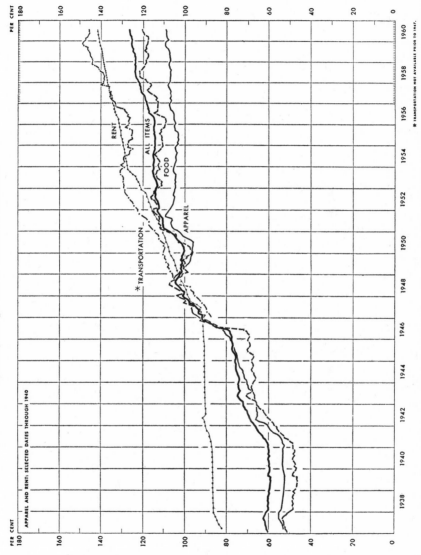

Source: Board of Governors of the Federal Reserve System, *Historical Supplement to Federal Reserve Chart Book on Financial and Business Statistics* (Washington, D.C., September, 1960).

movements because the Consumer Price Index has been almost constantly reflecting lagged adjustment to earlier rapid rises in price levels.

Finally, we should note that the Consumer Price Index actually was not constructed to reflect the price paid by all consumers, but rather to reflect the price paid by families of city wage earners and clerical workers. Although it does not too well reflect prices paid in distinctly farm areas, it represents, as far as we know, the general change in consumer prices as well as a broader index might.

The GNP Implicit Price Deflator is our best comprehensive measure of all final product prices. This Index is computed by the Department of Commerce in the process of presenting income and product measures. In deriving the measure, about two hundred product groups were separately deflated by price indexes computed to represent each separate group. The deflated product groups were then added up and divided into total gross national product; the result, therefore, is called an "implicit" price index.[2] As in the Consumer Price Index, a whole series of margins (markups) is represented. Since these should be expected to be fairly stable, the Index might be thought to fluctuate less than the Wholesale Price Index. As indicated above, however, because of continual lagged adjustment to the higher level of general prices in the postwar period, the Index has been rising about as rapidly as wholesale prices.

FORECASTING PRICES: BASIC FACTORS

The movement of average prices is most closely related to the change in activity. Therefore, this section is closely dependent upon Chapters 17 and 18, which develop the methodology used in activity forecasts. The movement of prices depends secondarily upon other factors than activity, notably on credit supply. To a major extent, however, the credit influence affects activity, and any change in price principally flows from the change in activity.

The extent to which rises in activity will induce price increases depends materially on the supply situation. If supply is universally overabundant, no price increase may occur, even if activity rises rapidly. It depends partly on what happened to prices previously and what is expected to happen in the near future. If prices had been cut to a point where they scarcely more than met out-of-pocket costs, a rise in activity would surely increase them, even though

---

[2]By this method, the separate prices have variable quantity weights, contrasting with constant weights in the price indexes computed by the Bureau of Labor Statistics.

there was no supply shortage anywhere. Such low prices, however, are characteristic of deep depression.

Even following the more typical business cycle recession, prices may show some advance when operations are far short of capacity levels. This situation would occur only if still higher prices were anticipated. Current price changes depend not only on present demand-supply relationships, but also upon expected developments. The present situation would be given by far the greatest weight; however, expectation of some increase in prices might generate a slight price increase in the present.

Anticipatory expectations assume importance as the expansion proceeds and even more importantly when recession develops. Since administered prices which tend to lag behind prices dictated by demand in business cycle expansion are assuming an increasingly important role, a developing possibility exists that the potentialities will be sensed by labor unions and that wage demands will be recognized which bring administered prices closer to levels warranted by demand conditions.

As recession develops, the depressed level of sales may be looked on as a supply distortion, arising from overaccumulation of inventory. If the fundamental demand situation is considered sound, prices may be cut only to a minor extent. Such action may be warranted by recognition of the facts we have pointed out above: that price changes over the business cycle are coming to correlate with activity changes to a decreasing extent.

Anticipatory attitudes thus tend to produce an inflationary bias. This does not mean that prices will always rise; but barring pernicious secondary deviation from secular growth, that may be the general tendency. Prices may rise early in expansion largely because the inflationary bias is sensed. Later, the requirement of drawing somewhat less effective resources into use to satisfy demand warrants price increases, and pressure from labor demands may drive up administered prices to match more nearly the levels warranted by demand than occurred in expansions before the Great Depression.

The best method to employ in judging the presence of situations described in the above paragraphs is contrast with the recent past. As an illustration, consider the probabilities in the early sixties. The conditions described were present in the fifties and can be expected to continue to prevail. An important difference which appears probable, however, is a reduction in lagged price increases as we move farther away from the times when rapid over-all price increases occurred (after World War II and in the Korean War). A way of estimating the reduction of inflationary impact implied is to study the change which has been occurring in lagging prices, notably services such as rent or medical care. The slowing-down of the rate of increase in such prices which has been occurring can be safely projected into the future, barring the development of a new, over-all rapid rise in prices.

There is another general anti-inflationary possibility which should not be ignored. A shift has been occurring with regard to objectives emphasized in reaching for economic stability. Increasing emphasis has been placed on preventing inflation and less on main-tenance of full employment. This development must be watched. If it goes far enough, stable or declining prices will obviously be anticipated, and the likely developments suggested above will not occur. The student is referred to Part Five for an analysis of the kind of measures likely to be employed in efforts to approach economic stability.

The forecasting procedures suggested in this section are qualita-tive. They could be quantified by development of a mathematical model, but our understanding is not clear-cut enough to make that worth while. More quantitative, and less analytical, methods are available. These are described in the following section. As a mini-mum, they are useful as a supplement to the analytical methods proposed here. Some of the vagueness of the proposed qualitative indications is eliminated by appraising the quantitative figures which the following methods suggest.

FORECASTING PRICES: QUANTITATIVE METHODS

A simple trend projection provides a fair price forecast at most times. The method is most effective if only a limited recent period, a few months at most, is followed in making the projection. The method may be considered quite reliable if accompanied by a satisfactory qualitative appraisal, such as suggested in the preceding section. For instance, if capacity operations are being widely ap-proached and an acceleration is appearing in price rises, the trend projection may be rationalized. Thereafter, contractionary influences should be watched for in the investment areas—signs of declining inventory investment or of the speeding-up of the completion rate in durable investment. These are the forces which can be expected to slow down the advance in prices sooner or later.

Obviously, a trend projection will not perform well in forecast-ing turning points. The turning points for prices correspond closely with those for activity (if average prices turn down at all during the business cycle), and the best procedure is to employ the techniques used in forecasting the turning points in activity. These techniques are described in Chapter 18.

A diffusion index of prices (proportion of price series which is rising at any time) would appear to provide an important forecasting method.[3] Clearly, price changes spread because of competitive relations in industry and because of the possibility of substitution of one product for another. Unfortunately, the use of diffusion indexes in prices remains very limited. A measure of the percentage of the two thousand price series included in the Wholesale Price Index which are rising, for example, would provide useful background in evaluating the potentialities of this method.

What we call analysis of the market situation in the following chapter appears to offer important insights into prospective prices. What this amounts to with regard to price forecasting is a comparison with data on orders, sales, and inventories. Prices reflect the favorable or unfavorable developments which show up in these measures. Other things being equal, rapidly rising orders would tend to indicate rising prices. Or increasing inventory stocks would indicate that, at least to some extent, price rises which are occurring may be geared to transient demand forces.

REAPPRAISAL OF THE PRICE PROBLEM

Analysis of the meaning of over-all prices is a new development. It stands in marked contrast with the supply-demand meaning usually attributed to individual prices. Economists universally recognize that the demand curve slopes downward moving from left to right. Involved is the assumption that over-all demand situations do not change. The burden of this chapter has been to show how an analysis of the over-all price movements throws light on changes in demand.

Efforts to build a demand function by developing a scheduled relationship between output and price are rated as unpromising, however. It is true that over-all prices are principally guided by the changes in activity, but the character of the relationship is

---

[3]Recent published information is not available on price diffusion indexes. Informal estimates of private scholars seem to indicate that the price diffusion index did not lead in the 1957–58 recession, perhaps because of the insensitiveness which had developed. A duration-of-run index, which is a current adaptation of a diffusion index, for wholesale prices is shown for 1920–55 in Milton Lipton, *Cyclical Diffusion: A New Tool for Business Analysis*, Technical Paper No. 5 (New York: National Industrial Conference Board, Inc., 1956), pp. 19–20. For a description of duration-of-run indexes, see the following chapter.

determined by the nature of demand forces at different points in the business cycle or as induced by other types of economic change. For that reason, we have indicated above that the adjustment of over-all prices to the demand situation depends on particular economic conditions. Possibly, simpler and more mathematical generalizations will be available when we learn more about the problem.

Starting with an over-all supply function appears to offer greater promise. Since most prices are now administered, rises in prices tend to average less than warranted in times when activity is expanding. Under these circumstances, costs are likely to exert some continual upward pressure, even before capacity levels are approached. When capacity levels are approached, costs will tend to drive prices up much faster. Near the cyclical peak, however, the supply function becomes more complicated. A rapid completion of capacity, for instance, may drive down the prices at which producers are willing to provide the same supply. In recession the problem becomes even more difficult. We have generalized above that, because of confidence in the soundness of fundamental demand and of the inflexibility of costs, businessmen may be willing to sell at little if any reduction in prices as activity declines. (In the event of the development of deep depression, this conclusion obviously would not be implied.)

Crude as many of our generalizations are, they are unavoidable. Consideration of the influence of over-all prices cannot be by-passed. Much of the analysis of current economic change is best made in terms of change in the current dollar value of production. A certain indefiniteness necessarily is involved until we provide some indication of the part price change plays in the total current-value change. Quantity changes can be estimated only by use of the process of price deflation.

Price changes are tied to the basic character of business fluctuation. Activity changes represent important effects, but they cannot be well understood unless the accompanying price changes can be made apparent. This fact explains the efforts to provide generalizations in this chapter.

Strange as it may seem, sustained attention has only recently been given to the forecasting of over-all prices. The yield of such forecasts is likely to be mediocre for some time to come. Present methods should be considered tentative; but actually, they may be superior to any procedures which are now available for direct forecasting of short-period changes in *physical quantity* of product. Our recommendation is to derive the short-term forecast of physical quantity by dividing a value forecast by a price forecast. This subject is further developed in Chapter 18.

APPENDIX FOR CHAPTER 16: CURRENT AVERAGE PRICE MEASURES

Four of the five price measures briefly described in the body of this chapter are computed by the Bureau of Labor Statistics, the most important source for price measures at the present time. In addition to the measures noted, several other important price measures are provided by that Bureau. The Consumer Price Index is reported by 13 major subgroups (apparel; dairy products; fruit and vegetables; meat, poultry, and fish; gas and electricity; house furnishings; rent; medical care; personal care; reading and recreation; private transportation; public transportation; and other), as well as several other subdivisions. Eight of these are combined to form three main subgroups—food, housing, and transportation. Actually, prices are collected on about 300 items. The prices are collected from 20 large cities and from 26 medium-sized cities, for which separate indexes are computed.

The GNP Implicit Price Deflator is reported by the Department of Commerce for each major expenditure division (except inventory investment and net exports, which are too unreliable for separate publication); by goods output, broken down into durable and nondurable, services, and construction; by seven major consumer expenditure groups; and by purchaser under each of the durable goods, nondurable goods, services, and construction product groups. Detailed subgroup deflators are published by construction and producer durable equipment. No deflators are published for factor prices. The only income group deflated is disposable income, and the deflator for consumer expenditures is employed to provide that deflation.

Since the implicit price index times gross national product in constant prices (quantity) necessarily equals GNP in current prices, it is interesting to show the relative influence of price and quantity on the postwar cyclical movements, as indicated by this method:

Time Period	Price Percentage over Period	Quantity Percentage over Period	Current Price GNP Percentage over Period
1945–4th Q, 1948	131.6	94.7	124.6
4th Q, 1948–4th Q, 1949	98.0	98.6	96.6
4th Q, 1949–3rd Q, 1953	113.1	126.3	142.8
3rd Q, 1953–3rd Q, 1954	100.8	97.8	98.6
3rd Q, 1954–3rd Q, 1957	109.1	113.5	123.8
3rd Q, 1957–2nd Q, 1958	101.5	96.0	97.4

Many divisions of the Wholesale Price Index, besides the Wholesale Price of Commodities Other than Farm Products and Foods, are reported. These include a division between durable and nondurable commodities, by stage of processing (crude materials for further processing, intermediate materials, supplies and components, and finished goods), and by 15 major commodity groups (farm products; processed foods; chemicals and allied products; fuel, power, and lighting materials; furniture and other household durables; hides, skins, and leather products; lumber and wood products; machinery and motive products; metals and metal products; structural nonmetallic minerals; pulp, paper, and allied products; rubber products; textile products and apparel; tobacco manufactures and bottled beverages; and miscellaneous), each of which is further subdivided.

The twenty-two commodities included in the Daily Index of Spot-Market Prices are burlap, butter, cocoa beans, copper scrap, corn, cotton, cottonseed oil, hides, hogs, lard, lead scrap, print cloth, rosin, rubber, steel scrap, steers, sugar, tallow, tin, wheat, wool tops, and zinc. Indexes of this sort are frequently called "sensitive," because they promptly reflect changes in demand. Several others are computed by private agencies. An Index of Commodity Futures, which is reported hourly and daily by Dow-Jones & Company, Inc., satisfies a similar purpose.

Several other commodity price indexes have a wide distribution. The Department of Agriculture reports on Prices Received by Farmers, Prices Paid by Farmers, and a Parity Ratio which is obtained by dividing the former by the latter. Many other price indexes are currently published, a large proportion of which are developed by private concerns. The most important ones are described in Arthur H. Cole, *Measures of Business Change* (Homewood, Ill.: Richard D. Irwin, Inc., 1952), pp. 119–75.

Most of the indexes referred to above are currently reported in the *Survey of Current Business;* however, for the GNP Implicit Price Deflator group, the sources noted in Appendix A for Chapter 15 should be used.

Fuller descriptions are readily available. For the GNP Implicit Price Deflator, see sources noted in Appendix A for Chapter 15. For the Consumer Price Index, see Bureau of Labor Statistics *Bulletin 1140* and *Bulletin 1165*. For the Spot-Market Price Index, see *Monthly Labor Review,* September, 1952. For the Wholesale Price Index, see *Monthly Labor Review,* February, 1952.

FOR REFLECTION AND ANALYSIS

1. Is there any point in trying to explain the movement of average prices instead of trying to explain the movement of each individual price?
2. Do you believe that open-market prices have been having decreasing importance in the American economy?
3. What difference in causal factors do you see in the prices which rise or fall most in the long run as compared to those which rise or fall most in the short run?
4. In studying economic change, why is the "other" price index more important than the comprehensive wholesale price index?
5. Why is the consumer price index less variable than the wholesale price index?
6. What is meant by an "implicit" price index?
7. What distinction can be made between price changes which respond directly to changes in demand and those which respond indirectly by following the general price movement?
8. What is the likelihood of an upward price bias in the next decade?

Chapter 17

FORESHADOWING STATISTICS

The future does not represent a break with the past. Rather, changes are largely determined by present conditions. If we knew enough about how these changes take place, we could forecast the future. Any effective forecast recognizes this fact. The assumptions made represent the pattern of economic change which it is desired to forecast. The implementation of the assumptions provides a technique for projecting the pattern of change.

The eternal dream of those who must peer into the future is of a warning signal which will foretell coming events. Foreshadowing statistics represent the closest approach. They provide an advanced reading of what is expected to follow in the series to be forecast. In this chapter, we shall consider the series to be forecast to be general business activity unless some other data are specified.

Surely, consideration must be given to why foreshadowing statistics lead. Too frequently in the past, belief in leads has rested solely on what historical data actually revealed. Empirical evidence should not be disregarded, but we need as a minimum to assure ourselves that the indicated lead is reasonable. This is particularly true in view of the distinctly limited period for which any statistical data are available. If a very long record showed a consistent lead, we might argue that only an obvious change in conditions would eliminate the lead. The empirical evidence is never so strong, and we must lean less heavily on it.

Until recently, lead series rested almost wholly on empirical analysis, because the theory of foreshadowing statistics had been developed to a minimum extent. The procedure essentially was to examine all recorded statistical series to find which, if any, had led in the past. This has been more rewarding than one might surmise offhand. The tendency of many series to lead has showed up. Furthermore, as developed below, the tendency of many other series to move coincidentally or to lag has been revealed, and this is valuable information. Starting with the fact that a given series has led, useful rationalized explanations have been developed, and much of the advance which has occurred in the theory of foreshadowing statistics rests on the clues provided by empirical analysis.

Expectation of lead can be developed from theory as well as from facts. First, there are processes which can be expected to show turns before the implied activity. These represent advance commitments, contracts, orders, financing arrangements, or budgets, which will be discussed more fully below. Second, surveys may be conducted to indicate what decision makers actually plan to do. Figures so developed are far less conclusive than might be expected. Decision makers are generally attuned to a program of adaptation to current conditions. Although we can assign logical precedence to certain processes, we can be no more sure that they will lead than that the leads shown by empirical evidence will hold in the future.

In summary, empirical leads must be checked against the logical forces which might corroborate them. And theoretical formulations as to what leads should appear must be checked against empirical evidence. Only by cross-checking between empiricism and theory can progress be expected. In the past, most progress has been achieved through explanation of leads empirically determined. As we advance more rapidly in the analysis of foreshadowing statistics, we may expect to find initially established theoretical formulations more frequently verified by factual evidence.

THE FORECASTING OF TURNING POINTS

Foreshadowing statistics are most useful in forecasting turning points, where most other forecasting techniques tend to break down. If leads are shown by foreshadowing statistics, a later turning point is indicated. The utility of such an indication depends on the consistency with which the lead can be expected to occur and the time uniformity of the lead. According to our best information at present, mechanical conclusions will not be dependable. This is partly due to the fact that no fixed relation can be established with the foreshadowing statistic.

Furthermore, minor exogenous forces may divert the timing, especially in case of flat-topped peaks. For instance, new orders for durable goods might rise past the time of downturn of total business activity if belated price increases were generated by strike settlements late in expansion. The dating of the downturn in general business activity may be diverted by many exogenous factors. An early decline might be produced because cool summer weather restricted the sale of air-conditioning equipment, if other exogenous factors did not cancel this effect.

Clearly, the forces accompanying any particular business situation must be carefully examined. If foreshadowing statistics are established because of reliable performance in the past and because this performance has been satisfactorily explained, clear identification of specific irregular forces present at any given time should provide the essential leverage to identify the current significance of the movement. If, for instance, irregular forces are driving the foreshadowing statistic down, the decline shown in the series should be discounted before being considered the harbinger of a downturn. Needless to say, such analyses can be approximate at best; therefore, foreshadowing statistics seldom provide an infallible antecedent of a downturn. They are most usefully employed in connection with other techniques, discussed in Chapter 18.

To a less dependable degree, foreshadowing statistics do provide some evidence on the degree of movement in activity to be expected, when a turning point is not in prospect. Rapidly rising orders, for instance, may indicate that activity in prospect will rise more rapidly than if orders were rising less rapidly. Our experience along this line is meager, however, and such conclusions should be drawn cautiously. Perhaps better results will be achieved by relating the change indicated by the foreshadowing statistic to particular types of activity and organizing the prospective type of activity along with other types in a GNP model, as outlined in Chapter 18.

EMPIRICALLY DEVELOPED DATA: 1. THE HARVARD INDEX CHART

There are many illustrations of the early use of lead series. One of the most notable is the Brookmire "United States Barometer Chart," a comparison of banking funds, security prices, and business activity, developed early in the century.[1] A common lead indicator used in the early days was bond prices, which tended more clearly to turn down at about mid-expansion than they do now.

The first thorough empirical analysis of timing differences be-

---

[1]See Ray Vance, *Business and Investment Forecasting* (New York: Harper & Bros., 1925); or C. O. Hardy and G. V. Cox, *Forecasting Business Conditions* (New York: Macmillan Co., 1928), pp. 55–56.

tween various statistical series was made by the Harvard Committee on Economic Research in 1918 and 1919, under the leadership of Warren M. Persons. Timing relationships were developed from visual inspection and from correlation analysis. The final summarization of timing differences was made in three indexes representing what was considered to be the best evidence on leading, coincident, and lagging series. The relation between these three indexes is shown in Charts 17–1 and 17–2, for 1875 to 1939, when the analysis was discontinued. It will be noted that the leading series was called (A) Speculation; the coincident series, (B) Business; and the lagging series, (C) Money. Thus, the device may be appropriately labeled the "three-markets chart," representing respectively the stock market, the commodity market, and the money market.[2] Thus, it is fair to say that although the study was empirical, the three indexes came to represent three economic processes, if somewhat vaguely. Thus, a logical summarization was made of the empirical results.

CHART 17–1

THE PREWAR HARVARD INDEX CHART

Adjusted Indexes of (A) Average Stock Prices and New York Bank Clearings, (B) Wholesale Commodity Prices and Outside Bank Clearings, and (C) Rates on 60–90-Day Commercial Paper: Bimonthly, 1875–1902. Adjusted Indexes of (A) Speculation, (B) Business, and (C) Money: Bimonthly, 1903–13.

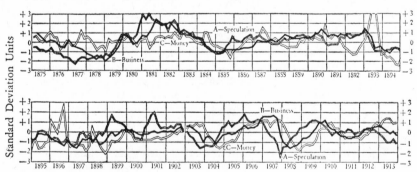

Source: Reproduced with permission from J. L. Snider, *Business Statistics* (2d ed.; New York: McGraw-Hill Book Co., Inc., 1932), facing p. 422.

Clinching evidence of the relationship involved appeared to have been developed for the test period from 1875 to 1913. The move-

---

[2]Perhaps the B curve would have had a wider foundation than commodity prices if more quantity and value-activity data had been available in the test period. Note, for instance, that it came to be represented by bank debits from 1933 to 1939. But we might also speculate that the indexes would have been founded on the wider series described in the following section if data had been available.

ment of the three curves on the Index Chart indicated the phase of the cycle current at any time and forecast the phase immediately ahead. For instance:

The sharp decline in curve A, speculation, which began in November,

CHART 17–2

THE POSTWAR HARVARD INDEX CHART

(As Revised at the End of 1928)

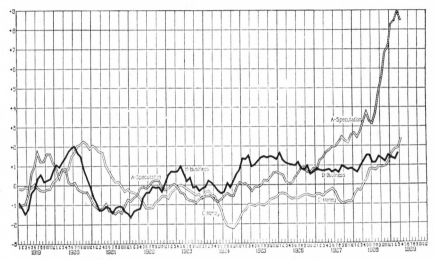

Source: Reproduced with permission from J. L. Snider, *Business Statistics* (2d ed.; New York: McGraw-Hill Book Co., Inc., 1932), p. 422.

HARVARD INDEX OF GENERAL ECONOMIC CONDITIONS

(Monthly, January, 1933–September, 1939)

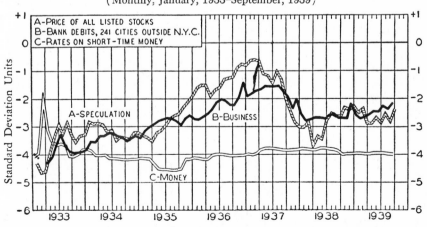

Source: Reproduced with permission from *Review of Economic Statistics,* November, 1939, p. 149.

1906, accompanied by high money rates, clearly anticipated by ten months the sharp break in commodity prices and business activity which was inaugurated in the fall of 1907. Again, the recovery of business, which began in the early summer of 1908, was preceded by a reversal in the trends of curves A and C, the upward movement of speculation and the downward movement of money rates which began at the very end of 1907 providing a substantial basis for the forecast that within a period of from six to ten months business would begin to recover from the depression. Throughout the remainder of the period the same general relations continued to hold.[3]

Except for the 1921 recession, pictured at the beginning of the first panel in Chart 17-2, the Index Chart gave very poor forecast indications. The most widely employed explanation is that the new banking system and Federal Reserve open-market operations changed the behavior of the money market and that speculation accompanying the New Era of the twenties distorted the stock market. We are sure that these arguments are substantially sound. In the fifties, for instance, we can show that the order of lags claimed reappeared, although the lags were shorter.[4] Because of irregularities of the recent series, however, any substantial forecasting leverage is questionable.

An interesting question is posed. If the Harvard Index Chart has been discredited, is the deficiency centered (1) on the use of empirically developed timing relationships or (2) on the generalizations developed regarding the relationships between the three markets? The statistical analysis made in 1918-19 was thorough; but as time passed, many new series became available. Since the method came to emphasize the relationship between speculation, business, and money, as indicated by successive revisions, new data which did not reflect this classification were ignored. Although we would insist that a basic truth was incorporated in the three-markets relationship, its importance had faded partly because of changing monetary and other institutional factors and partly because of the abnormality of the times. Proof was not provided that other timing relationships are sterile.

---

[3]H. B. Vanderblue, *Problems in Business Economics* (A. W. Shaw Co., 1924), pp. 34–35. The general analysis of the method is particularly well developed in a pamphlet by the Harvard Committee on Economic Research entitled *The Harvard Index of General Business Conditions: Its Interpretation* (Cambridge, Mass., 1923).

[4]See Elmer C. Bratt, *Business Forecasting* (New York: McGraw-Hill Book Co., Inc., 1958), pp. 160–61.

EMPIRICALLY DEVELOPED DATA: 2. STATISTICAL INDICATORS

Interest in timing relationships has been revived in recent years. This has stemmed from careful studies of scholars at the National Bureau of Economic Research.[5] Careful empirical studies have been made of the timing of various statistical series. Common-sense criteria (length and uniformity of timing relationship to reference dates, other indications of conformance to the business cycle, limited influence of erratic movements, smallness and regularity of seasonal movements, breadth of activities covered, and stability and economic significance of the covered activities) were employed to isolate eight leading series, eight coincident series, and five lagging series. Culled from some thousand series, the results provide the best available evidence on timing differences. The thirteen leading and lagging series are described in Table 17-1.

Before examining the logical reasons why the series included in

---

[5]See particularly Geoffrey H. Moore, *Statistical Indicators of Cyclical Revivals and Recessions,* Occasional Paper 31 (New York: National Bureau of Economic Research, Inc., 1950); and Wesley C. Mitchell, *What Happens during Business Cycles: A Progress Report* (New York: National Bureau of Economic Research, Inc., 1951). Notably, two business services which center on timing relationships indicated in these studies have been formed in recent years: (1) Statistical Indicator Associates of Great Barrington, Massachusetts; and (2) W. A. Beckett Associates, Ltd., Toronto, Canada.

While this book was in press in 1961, the NBER announced a new publication in which a changed list of statistical indicators is to be presented. The total number of series will be increased to 26, as follows: Leading—(1) business failure liabilities, (2) common stock prices (Standard and Poor's), (3) new orders of durable goods manufacturers, (4) housing starts, (5) commercial and industrial building contracts, (6) average workweek in manufacturing, (7) net change in number of operating businesses, (8) industrial raw materials price index, (9) gross accession rate in manufacturing, (10) layoff rate in manufacturing, (11) corporate profits after taxes, (12) change in business inventories; Roughly Coincident—(13) employment in nonagricultural establishments, (14) unemployment rate, (15) bank debits outside New York City, (16) industrial production index, (17) gross national product in current dollars, (18) deflated gross national product, (19) wholesale price index excluding farm products and foods, (20) personal income, (21) retail sales; Laggers—(22) consumer instalment debt, (23) manufacturer's inventories, (24) bank interest rates on business loans, (25) plant and equipment expenditures, and (26) wage and salary cost per unit of manufacturing output. Despite the extensive change in the actual series employed, most of the processes represented are similar. The principal differences are: (a) profits after taxes now are used, and these move from the coincident to the leading group; (b) layoff rate in manufacturing and change in business inventories are added to the leading group; (c) personal income and retail sales are moved from the laggers to the coincident group; (d) plant and equipment expenditures and wage and salary cost per unit of manufacturing output are added to the laggers group. Some of the changes made are implicit in the following discussion, and the rationale given there applies rather well to the new series. See Geoffrey H. Moore (ed.), *Business Cycle Indicators* (2 vols.; Princeton: Princeton University Press, 1961). Volume I will explain the factors accounting for the characteristic behavior of the series, and Volume II will provide seasonally adjusted data for more than fifty economic indicators.

TABLE 17-1

TIMING OF SELECTED BUSINESS INDICATORS*

LEAD SERIES	PEAKS			TROUGHS		
	Total No.	No. Leading	Av. Lead (Months)	Total No.	No. Leading	Av. Lead (Months)
1. Liabilities of Business Failures, inverted, Dun's.	14	11	10.5	16	14	7.5
2. Industrial Common Stock Prices, Dow-Jones Index.	11	8	6.0	11	8	7.2
3. New orders, selected durable goods†	25	21	6.9	30	24	4.7
4. Residential Building Contracts, floor space, F. W. Dodge.	5	4	6.2	6	5	4.5
5. Commercial and Industrial Building Contracts, floor space, F. W. Dodge.	5	4	5.2	6	4	1.7
6. Average Weekly Hours in Manufacturing, BLS.	4	3	3.8	5	3	2.6
7. New Incorporations, number, Dun's.	20	12	2.5	20	15	3.5
8. Index of Spot Market Prices, BLS.	11	7	2.6	11	8	3.2

LAG SERIES	PEAKS			TROUGHS		
	Total No.	No. Lagging	Av. Lag (Months)	Total No.	No. Lagging	Av. Lag, (Months)
1. Personal Income, Commerce.	4	3	4.0	5	1	−0.2
2. Index of Retail Sales, Commerce.	5	4	3.8	6	3	1.8
3. Consumer Installment Credit, FRB.	2	2	5.0	2	2	3.5
4. Bank Rates on Business Loans, Quarterly, FRB.	5	3	5.5	6	5	4.8
5. Manufacturers' Inventories, current prices, Commerce.	2	2	6.5	2	2	7.5

*Adapted from table on pp. 64–65 in Geoffrey H. Moore, *Statistical Indicators of Cyclical Revivals and Recessions*, Occasional Paper 31 (New York: National Bureau of Economic Research Inc., 1950). The cycles on which these summaries are based carry only to 1938. In several cases the historical data for testing timing is filled out with earlier series.

†Five series for 5½ cycles are used. The series are new orders for southern pine lumber, oak flooring, architectural terra cotta, fabricated structural steel, and machine tools and forging machinery. Note that the number of peaks or troughs obtained depends upon counting 5 different series in each cycle.

Table 17-1 should lead or lag, we may usefully note the eight co-incident series. These include (1) employment in nonagricultural establishments, (2) unemployment (inverted), (3) bank debits outside New York City, (4) freight car loadings, (5) Industrial Production Index, (6) gross national product, (7) nonfood wholesale prices, and (8) corporate profits. The tendency for all of these series to be approximately coincident should be reasonably clear. Employment certainly is closely related to activity generated, and similarly with regard to unemployment since the labor force does not vary with activity. Bank debits outside New York City represent payments other than in transfer of assets, and tend to reflect a very comprehensive measure of activity. Freight car loadings, portraying the transportation of goods, should reflect the variation in activity after allowance is made for the declining percentage of freight carried by the railroads. Industrial production is our most sensitive measure of activity. Gross national product, although less sensitive, is the best comprehensive measure. As developed in the preceding chapter, wholesale prices other than foods and farm products should conform with the movement of activity, except for the possibility that declines may be virtually absent in future recessions. Corporate profits, which represent the most effective measure of inducement of commercial decision makers, may well be expected to move with the activity generated. Clearly, the moral is that none of these eight prominent indicators can be turned to for a forecast of business activity. They reflect the current pace and cannot be expected to foreshadow the movement.

The logic behind the early movement in leading series is equally clear. If the competitive situation becomes increasingly formidable as the prosperity peak is approached, in line with the arguments presented in Chapter 5, an early increase in failures is to be expected. Similarly, if the competitive situation improves before the upturn, a decrease in failures is to be expected. Thus, although failures move inversely, they may be expected to lead. Obversely, new incorporations (representing the formation of new businesses) should lead because of shift in the competitive situation. Stock prices should lead simply because they reflect the weighted average of expectations of major owners, who possess a detailed understanding of the outlook of many businesses.

Weekly hours is considered our most reliable leading series. Leads tend to be somewhat longer at the peaks than at the troughs. An inducement to reduce hours at the peak is the elimination of overtime hours, and no corresponding influence is found at the trough. Numbers of employees are dropped or added with reluctance. Hence, slight changes in demand are adjusted to by shifts in working time. Studying changes on the individual plant level, it is found that decisions on hours are made by foremen and supervisors at the local plant to provide short-term adjustment to current work loads. Employment policies leading to longer-term adjustments are determined at a higher managerial level. This throws light on the smoother and less sensitive movement of total employment that occurs in working hours. Changes in working hours lead more consistently in manufacturing than in nonmanufacturing, largely because manufacturing is more sensitively related to the business cycle.[6]

Spot-market prices tend to lead because the commodities included are sold in highly competitive markets. Supply tends to become somewhat more abundant just before the downturn, and competitive pressure is reduced. Before the upturn, highly competitive prices tend to strengthen slightly as competitive unfavorability is lessened with the leveling of activity. New orders and contracts represent antecedent steps in the decision process and are discussed in the second following section (page 397).

The lag series included by Moore, as shown in Table 17-1, represent the broad processes of income payments and spending, interest rates, and total inventory accumulation. Generally, the lags represented are less well established statistically than are the leads discussed above, not only because of considerable variability but also because of the shortness of the test periods employed.

Reclassification by the National Bureau of Economic Research in 1961 shifts the first two laggers shown in Table 17-1—personal income and retail sales—to the roughly coincident group. As shown in the table, earlier evidence indicated but a short lag for these series and more recent movements offset that slight tendency. (See footnote 5 on page 383.)

Instalment credit tends to move with changes in income payments. Lag at the downturn is based on action of groups whose income is still rising. The lag at the upturn is related to the fact that small increases in income are unlikely to instill confidence that rising income will continue. Generally, in fact, consumers are not

---

[6]See Gerhard Bry, *The Average Workweek as an Economic Indicator,* Occasional Paper 69 (New York: National Bureau of Economic Research, Inc., 1959).

likely to spend the increased income received in the initial month
or two.

Lag in short-term interest rates has been more generally accepted than any other lag included in this list. The banks have a
superabundance of reserves at the trough, and there is no great
demand for loans; so interest rates, which have adjusted to the
demand situation tardily, continue to decline. As the peak of activity is passed, the need for loans may become even greater,
because the downturn generates illiquidity, because excess reserves
are small, and because bankers become more conservative. Therefore, interest rates continue to rise. Newer conceptions on credit
control make these relations less automatic than they formerly were,
but some lag is likely to continue to occur in interest rates.

Inventory investment moves promptly; it may even lead the
business cycle movement. This happens because inventories are
added to less rapidly in late expansion and are reduced less rapidly
in late contraction. The actual level of inventories, however, is
seldom reduced until contraction is under way and is seldom increased until expansion is under way. In fact, in minor contractions
inventories may be quite depressive without the total level of inventories declining (if preceded by rapid rises in stocks).

Although lagging series obviously do not reveal advanced indications, they are important in the use of foreshadowing statistics.
A continued rise in any of these series clearly is not a good indication
that a downturn is not to be expected, and a continued decline is
not a good indication that there will be no upturn. When lagging
movements paralleling the change in leading and coincident series
do appear, a turn is confirmed if allowance can be made for
erratic movements. Chart 17–3 shows a recent picture of the
twenty-one statistical indicators discussed.

Modern statistical indicators belong to the same family of forecasting techniques as the Harvard Index Chart. They are more
useful, however, for they represent conclusions derived from recent
data, and they are readily applied to any timing differences which
do exist. Although the Harvard Index Chart was founded on a
comprehensive empirical analysis of statistical series, it came to
represent the relation between speculation, business, and money,
which relation was partially outdated by institutional changes.
Modern statistical indicators have not become closely tied to any
particular institutional pattern.

This is because the leading, coincident, and lagging series in

CHART 17–3

REPRESENTATIVE LEADING, COINCIDENT, AND LAGGING INDICATORS

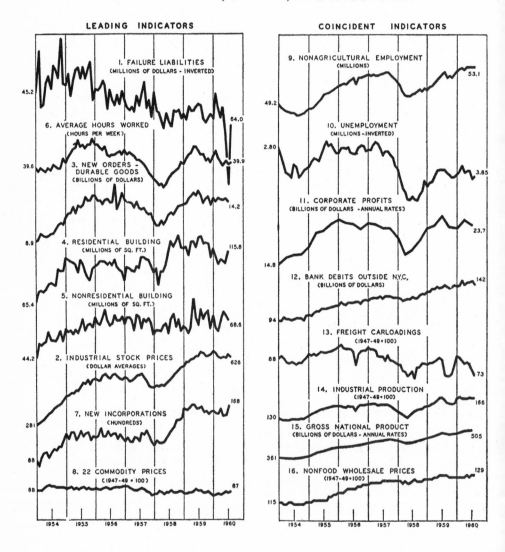

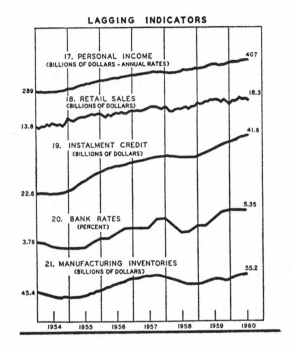

LAGGING INDICATORS

17. PERSONAL INCOME
(BILLIONS OF DOLLARS - ANNUAL RATES)   407

289

18. RETAIL SALES
(BILLIONS OF DOLLARS)   18.3

13.8   41.6

19. INSTALMENT CREDIT
(BILLIONS OF DOLLARS)

22.6   5.35

20. BANK RATES
(PERCENT)

3.76

21. MANUFACTURING INVENTORIES
(BILLIONS OF DOLLARS)   55.2

45.4

1954 1955 1956 1957 1958 1959 1960

Explanatory Notes

Original sources of data are: Dept. of Commerce-indicators 3, 10, 11, 15, 17, 18, and 21; Dept. of Labor-6, 8, and 16; Dow Jones & Co.-2; Dun & Bradstreet-1 and 7; the Federal Reserve-9, 12, 13, 14, 19, and 20; F. W. Dodge Corporation-4 and 5. Unemployment and failures are inverted; they rise when business falls and vice versa.

The most recent data are often our own estimates. These estimates are indicated in the table by a dagger (†).

All series are seasonally adjusted except indicator 2 (industrial stock prices) and indicator 20 (bank rates).

Only indicators 8, 13, 14, and 16 are indexes. Indicators 6, 9, and 16 are on an arithmetic scale because monthly percentage changes are too small to be seen on a ratio scale. All others are on a ratio scale; thus, equal vertical distances measured in the same direction anywhere on the charts represent equal percentage changes.

Source: Chart furnished by Statistical Indicator Associates, Great Barrington, Massachusetts, Reproduced with permission from the weekly report regularly sent to subscribers.

the new analysis of statistical indicators have never been divorced from the historical record. In general, each series is considered separately, rather than as a part of an average of leading, coincident, or lagging series.

Under this program, there is less possibility of formalizing a relationship which identifies outdated institutional relations. Furthermore, each separate series can be studied with respect to its own irregular components. If, for instance, specific information indicates that the irregular component of a specific series has induced an unusual rise, the rise may be discounted in analyzing timing relationships. This is less successfully accomplished when each of the leading, coincident, and lagging groups is presented only as an average, for particular movements tend to become unidentifiable.

THE DIFFUSION INDEX

The diffusion index was introduced in Chapter 5 as a device to reveal the spread of rising activity early in expansion, the spread of declining activity later in the expansion, the accelerated spread of declining activity early in the contraction, and the spread of rising activity late in the contraction. We found this useful in explaining the operation of cumulative and culminative forces over the cycle. Our purpose here is to examine the use of diffusion indexes in forecasting, rather than to explain cyclical movements.

The diffusion index, it will be remembered, represents the percentage of the items in a total group which is rising at any given time. The "total group" may or may not be an economically significant total. A diffusion may be made of the profits of all of the companies engaging in manufacturing activity, or of the output of these companies, or of the prices of the goods sold by these companies, etc. The total might be all companies in a given industry or in all industry instead of relating to all manufacturing. It might relate to other processes such as durable investment or inventory investment, and show the number of companies with rises in these areas. The student may readily add to the examples.

More frequently, the diffusion index relates to "indicators of activity" rather than to an economically significant total. A measure which is frequently published relates to the twenty-one indicators discussed in the preceding section. Obviously, these indicators all pertain to general economic conditions, but do not comprise an economically significant group.

Possibly even more useful is a diffusion index computed from a comprehensive group of several hundred series, as illustrated in Chart 17–4. The advantage of a large group arises from the fact that if many indicator series are assembled, surely a few will provide

CHART 17–4

DIFFUSION INDEX AND THE MOVEMENT OF BUSINESS ACTIVITY

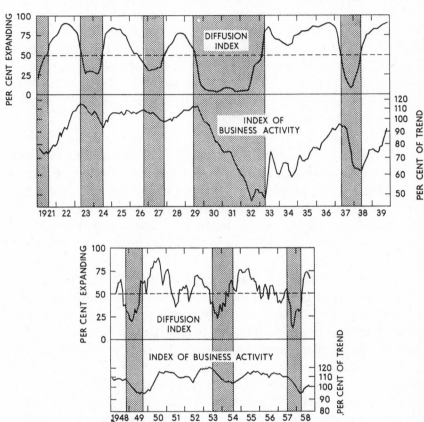

NOTE: Shaded areas represent contractions of business cycles, white areas expansions, according to National Bureau of Economic Research chronology.

Diffusion index plotted on arithmetic scale; index of business activity plotted on ratio scale.

Source: Diffusion index, 1948–58, based on 213 to 279 economic series, is from Julius Shiskin. *An Experiment with New Measures of Recession and Recovery* (Bureau of the Census, mimeographed, November, 1958), pp. 37–39. The 1921–39 index is not only based on a different sample of series than the later index, but is constructed in such a way that more of the minor fluctuations are ironed out. Index of Business Activity is published by the Cleveland Trust Company and is adjusted for long-run trend.

Reproduced, with permission, from paper by Geoffrey H. Moore, "The 1957–58 Business Contraction: New Model or Old?" *American Economic Review*, Papers and Proceedings, May, 1959, p. 298.

an early indication of the turning point. There are good reasons why this should be so in any given business cycle, and the series which leads in a particular business cycle may not usually lead. The diffusion index makes it possible to take advantage of such irregular leads, for what is counted is merely the proportionate number of series which is rising, regardless of what any series may typically do in cyclical movements.

Actually, the lead is increased somewhat if only leading series are combined in the index, as illustrated in Chart 17–5. Because fewer series are available for a total comprised only of leading indicators, irregularity is increased, and this about cancels the advantage of using only leading series. Some advantage is achieved, nevertheless, in comparing diffusion indexes for leading, coincident, and lagging indicators. This method is often employed to summarize the comparable movement of the three groups of indicators discussed in the preceding section.

For forecasting purposes, the choice between diffusion indexes made from diverse statistical indicators rather than from the parts of an economically significant total group is not obvious. What we wish is the series which provides the clearest advance indication. As we shall see in the following chapter, no forecast can rest wholly on statistical foundations. If leads were satisfactorily explained, the indicated diffusion could be logically organized with other analytical arguments.

To provide current forecasts, some substitute must be made for the percentage of the series included which are expanding, because it is never possible at any current moment to know what series are still expanding. A *duration-of-run* index, illustrated in Chart 17–6, provides an excellent current substitute. Essentially what is counted in a duration-of-run index is the cumulated total of continued rises of the component series. In other words, the number of months each of the series has been rising is counted. Some limit must be set for the number used for any series because some series vary so little that a very large number of months of rise would be shown for them. The maximum to be used for any one series is commonly set at six. The sum of the total number of months of rise (with a limit of six for each series) for all of the series put together supplies the figure for the duration-of-run index for any particular month. The index can be kept up to date because the number of rising months is counted down to the present. Frequently, the total obtained is divided by the number of series used. The average duration of run obtained might rise to about four, out of a possible six, for most computations when expansion is spreading rapidly, and fall to as low as −4 when contraction is spreading rapidly.

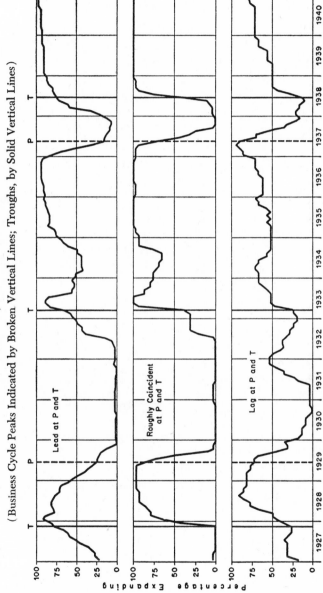

CHART 17-5

DIFFUSION INDEXES, THREE GROUPS OF SERIES

(Business Cycle Peaks Indicated by Broken Vertical Lines; Troughs, by Solid Vertical Lines)

Source: Taken with permission from Geoffrey H. Moore, *Statistical Indicators of Cyclical Revivals and Recessions*, Occasional Paper 31 (New York: National Bureau of Economic Research, Inc., 1950).

CHART 17–6

DIFFUSION INDEXES COMPARED WITH A DURATION-OF-RUN INDEX

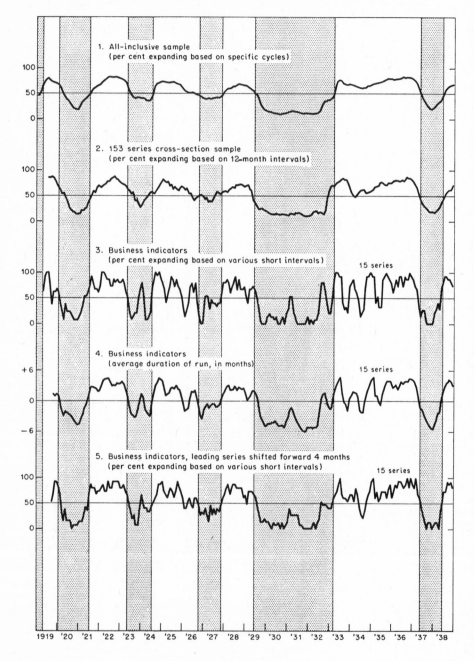

CHART 17–6 *(Continued)*

SIMILAR COMPUTATIONS FOR 1947-55

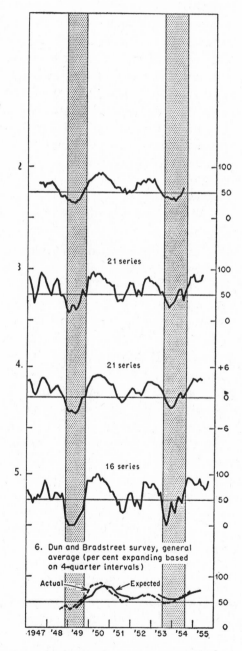

Source: Taken with permission from Geoffrey H. Moore, "Diffusion Indexes: A Comment," *The American Statistician*, October, 1955.

NOTE: Shaded areas represent contractions of general business cycles; unshaded areas, expansions.

Returning to consideration of diffusion indexes computed on the basis of the percentage of series rising, we may point to an "idealized" picture of what we might expect if the facts perfectly bore out the theory of diffusion indexes. Assume that the aggregate of the total items in the group used for computing the diffusion index fluctuates in a perfect sine curve. At mid-expansion of the aggregate, three fourths of the series would be rising, and the diffusion index would hit its peak. It would then decline, reaching the point where just half of the series are rising at the time the aggregate curve hits its peak. It would continue to decline, reaching bottom at the point where only a fourth of the series were still rising, just as the aggregate curve is halfway down the contraction. When the aggregate curve reaches its trough, it would have rereached the point where half of the series were rising. A careful study of Chart 17-4 will convince the reader that, with a large number of series, factual experience sometimes approaches this idealized picture.

More frequently, especially when dependence is placed on the limited amount of currently available information, the picture traced deviates widely from the idealized. This is because the widening and shrinking of the cumulation in the business cycle phases sometimes does not proceed smoothly. For instance, the expansion of 1949-53 did not widen and shrink according to the idealized pattern because of the outbreak of the Korean War. A duration-of-run index of the component industries represented in the Industrial Production Index rose to a peak before the end of 1950 and fell to well under zero in 1951, only to hit a new high below the 1950 one late in 1952. The answer is simple. Rapid spreading of the expansion occurred in 1950 because of "scare" buying by consumers. Later, consumer expenditures leveled off, and war expenditures expanded among a more restricted number of industries. Intelligent use of the diffusion index requires some understanding of the developing cumulation occurring in any particular business cycle.[7]

Note has often been made of the fact that diffusion is correlated with rate of change. The forecaster, however, will find the diffusion index much more valuable than a measure of the rate of change of the aggregate of the total items in the group used for computing the diffusion index. The theory we are relying on depends on the spreading of cumulative cyclical movements among different groups.

---

[7]The reader will find a picture of the industrial production duration-of-run index in Milton Lipton, *Cyclical Diffusion: A New Tool for Business Analysis,* Technical Paper No. 5 (New York: National Industrial Conference Board, Inc., 1956), p. 14.

Usually, a wider spreading may mean sharper change in the total, and narrowing may indicate slower change. The exceptions, however, can be very important. For instance, industrial production was rising as rapidly from July to November in 1952 as from February to August of 1950, but the spreading of the movement throughout the economy (rise in the diffusion index) was less. Furthermore, changes in the aggregate do not high-light effectively the spreading of the movement which the forecaster needs to visualize.

SERIES WHICH REPRESENT EARLY STAGES IN THE DECISION PROCESS

Certain series logically should precede activity involved in production. Contracts and orders represent the most familiar measures of this kind. Three of the lead series in Moore's Statistical Indicators, discussed above, are orders or contracts. New orders for durable goods tend to lead business cycle reference dates. This is partly because orders are usually registered in advance of the activity they set in motion, especially in the case of durable manufactured goods. Construction contracts represent a similar situation. Once the contract has been let, any particular project tends to flow forward according to a predetermined pattern. In both orders and contracts (which are really another kind of order), variation tends to be large, and a considerable increase or decrease one month may not be followed by a rise or fall in activity in a later month because the movement may be smoothed out by opposite movement of orders in the immediately following months. Furthermore, many kinds of orders are open to delay in execution or even may be open to later cancellation.

Nevertheless, data on orders and contracts are valuable in forecasting if used in conjunction with other information. Wide variations do not occur without reason, although reasons frequently are difficult to uncover. Construction contracts, for instance, may show a large rise because of the addition of a few large projects. It may be possible to develop a probable judgment as to whether more large projects will be forthcoming in the following month. If the orders are delayed, it will likely be that the large rise which occurred was founded on erratic influences.

Many new types of anticipatory data are now becoming available. The National Industrial Conference Board conducts a continuing quarterly survey of the capital appropriations among the one thousand largest manufacturing companies in the United States.

Capital appropriation, in the sense of the survey, constitutes authority to incur obligations for new plant and equipment. Each quarter, estimates are shown of backlog of budgeted appropriations; appropriations newly approved in the quarter; the amount committed, spent, and canceled in the quarter; and the backlog at the end of the quarter. This survey was first reported at the end of 1956, but it is already proving its worth.

In June, 1957, for instance, the statement was made that "these findings *now* point strongly in the direction of a leveling out of capital expenditures by large manufacturing companies in the months ahead. In the *two* previous reports, which highlighted declines in appropriation approvals, the emphasis was on the slowdown of the capital goods boom."[8] It will be noted that these statements preceded the downturn in July, when the Federal Reserve and many government officials failed to recognize the turn in business.

The survey did not provide such important evidence on the ending of the contraction running from July, 1957, to April, 1958, but it did clearly indicate that expansion was under way by the third quarter of 1958, by providing information on advance in appropriations in fifteen manufacturing industries and by indicating a substantial rise in the diffusion index of appropriations among covered manufacturing companies, computed on the basis of change from the previous year. The problem of seasonal changes has added to the difficulty of interpreting the survey results, but the record is now long enough that some seasonal adjustments are being made. It is readily seen that appropriations have led actual expenditures for new plant and equipment (defined as actual costs chargeable to fixed asset accounts). Chart 17–7 shows the lead in appropriations as well as in changes in backlogs of accumulated appropriations not yet spent.

Many other types of anticipatory data are being investigated. One illustration is unpublished data on financial commitments by investment houses on housing mortgages. Another is a study which is now under way to survey architects on plans being drawn for new building. Such ideas are imaginative, but have yet to be proved to be of significant value in forecasting. Their present interest to us is that they represent early stages in the investment process.

---

[8]"Capital Appropriations Stabilize," *Conference Board Business Record*, June, 1957.

CHART 17-7

Capital Appropriations in Relation to Expenditures

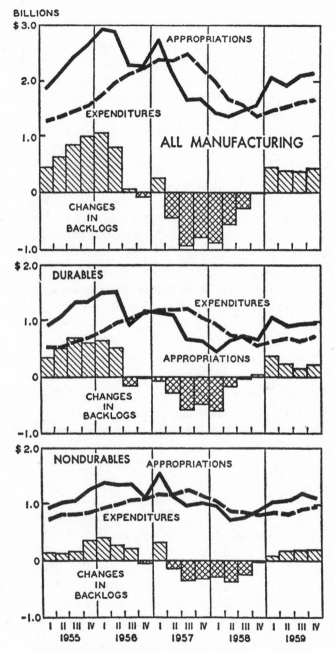

BILLIONS
$3.0

APPROPRIATIONS

2.0

EXPENDITURES

1.0

ALL MANUFACTURING

0

CHANGES
IN
BACKLOGS

-1.0

$2.0   DURABLES

EXPENDITURES

1.0

APPROPRIATIONS

0

CHANGES
IN
BACKLOGS

-1.0

$2.0   NONDURABLES   APPROPRIATIONS

1.0

EXPENDITURES

0

CHANGES
IN
BACKLOGS

-1.0

I   II III IV   I   II III IV   I   II III IV   I   II III IV   I   II III IV
1955   1956   1957   1958   1959

NOTE: Seasonally adjusted.
Based upon five hundred respondents. Changes in backlogs obtained
by subtracting seasonally adjusted expenditures and cancellations from
adjusted new appropriations. Seasonal adjustment factors are preliminary.
Source: *Conference Board Business Record,* April, 1960. Reproduced
with permission of the National Industrial Conference Board, Inc.

DIRECT MEASURES OF BUSINESS EXPECTATIONS

Since the war, more and more emphasis has been placed on the use of surveys which ask decision makers about their anticipations or expectations. The most useful relate to expenditures businessmen plan to make because, to some extent, programs are set beforehand, with commitments already made.

For forecasting purposes, plant and equipment anticipations have been given increasing attention. Two surveys are publicly released—one made co-operatively by the Department of Commerce and the Securities and Exchange Commission, and the other by the McGraw-Hill Department of Economics. The former survey is made quarterly and is comprised of a satisfactory sample of manufacturing, mining, transportation, public utility, and commercial companies.[9] Chart 17–8 shows that from 1955 the short-period surveys have been reasonably close, although generally somewhat high. The fact that these anticipations are high is largely a function of the conditions of the time; over the full period of the surveys since they were begun in 1947 the anticipatory figures are about equally divided between high and low. Annual estimates also generally have been reasonably close to the outturn, except for 1947, 1950, and 1955.

The present forecasting practice is to use the plant and equipment anticipations derived from this survey as the first estimate of projected values. Without more intimate information than most forecasters have, it would be hard to find a better initial estimate.

However, the forecaster should attempt to improve on this figure in his more final estimates. In the first place, the past reveals a distinct tendency for the business anticipatory figures to be too high in recession and too low in expansion. For instance, the 1955 anticipation showed an increase of $1 billion compared with an actual increase of $7 billion, while the 1958 anticipation estimated a decline of $13 billion compared with an actual decline of $18 billion. Too great a tendency remains to use current levels as future estimates.

Actually, the forecaster should conceive of the survey figure not as his forecast, but as that of the businessman. Unfortunately, not enough is known of the extent to which the survey report made is a plan representing commitments or a forecast founded on an analysis of the prospects of the economy as a whole or merely a figure

---

[9]For a technical description of the methods used in making this survey, see Bureau of the Budget, Office of Statistical Standards, *An Appraisal of the OBE-SEC Estimates of Plant and Equipment Expenditures, 1947–58*, Statistical Evaluation Report No. 1 (Washington, D.C., October, 1959), pp. 70–118.

CHART 17–8

EXPEDITURES FOR NEW PLANT AND EQUIPMENT

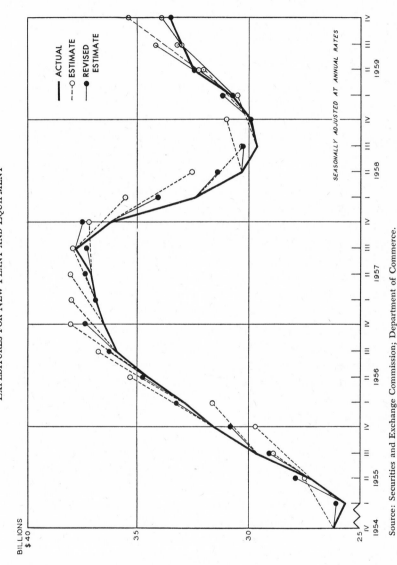

BILLIONS
$40

ACTUAL
ESTIMATE
REVISED
ESTIMATE

SEASONALLY ADJUSTED AT ANNUAL RATES

Source: Securities and Exchange Commission; Department of Commerce.

representing something close to current expenditure levels.[10] The forecaster must rationalize about this from past experience. For instance, as shown in Chart 17–8, anticipations were high in 1956. This was because the rapid rise in capital expenditures in 1955, yet early in the expansion, led to exaggerated anticipations. By watching the way the survey results turn out, the forecaster can draw inferences regarding the biases inherent in the conclusion businessmen are drawing.

The McGraw-Hill survey ordinarily is used for checking. Only annual anticipations are asked for in that survey, so that it must be used to check the full-year anticipation. Only reasonably large companies are surveyed, and we believe that such companies do more planning than small companies, so that the sample has its advantages. This is true especially since the government survey does not show separately the results derived from large and small companies. The McGraw-Hill survey also is useful in that it develops information on modernization versus expansion expenditures, construction versus equipment, and the relation of operating rates to capacity as estimated by each particular company. This information provides insights not available in the government survey.

Also, co-ordinate sales anticipations are asked for in both of those surveys. The forecast of sales, unlike that of capital expenditure, depends upon expectations of economic conditions in the general economy rather than upon commitments and financing arrangements made by the company. It is true that capital expansion depends to some extent on expected sales, and it is therefore helpful that the question on sales expectations is asked. The sales forecasts have generally moved in the same direction as the actual changes which were later found to occur in sales.[11] Understanding that businessmen are generally correct in their sales forecasts is helpful, as indicated in Chapter 18. However, the forecaster must develop his own general business forecast, and not depend on what business companies expect the prospects to be.

There are many other surveys of expectations of businessmen on sales prospects. Note may be made of the Dun and Bradstreet Surveys of Businessmen's Sales Expectations. Examined in terms of actual changes indicated, most such surveys appear to give ludicrous

---

[10]With a more extended analysis, one can summarize extensive studies which do provide a closer approach to an answer to the questions asked. See particularly Murray F. Foss and Vito Natrella, "Investment Plans and Realization: Reasons for Differences in Individual Cases," *Survey of Current Business*, June, 1957. A more general summary of this problem will be found in Bratt, *op. cit.*, pp. 323–29.

[11]See Bratt, *op. cit.*, p. 330.

conclusions. However, if these surveys are thrown into diffusion index measures, they appear to indicate that, broadly considered, businessmen do make reasonably satisfactory forecasts.[12] Knowing that forecasts of most companies derive from an inadequate background of changes in the total economy, the forecaster must be willing to set a substantial discount on the forecasts indicated for a broad group of companies.

Many other business surveys on business expectations could be mentioned; but for the time being, most of them are of doubtful value to the forecaster. The surveys of inventory investment, however, are worth considering. So far, the most important such survey is that conducted by *Fortune* magazine. The forecaster should be cautious enough not to accept the survey results as valid, but they do give some indication of business thinking. On inventories, the fact is that businessmen generally are guided by past sales. Their forecasts may be nearly correct except at turning points. It is at the turning points, however, where inventory investment attains major importance. The forecaster must use his best analysis of turning points in general business conditions to develop a plausible position on inventory anticipations.

The *Fortune* Survey of Homebuilding may also be noted. This is probably the best of the many surveys which have been started on residential building, and it is the only one which has been regularly continued. Evidently, the contractor is particularly impressed by the current level of his activity in this survey; but if added to an analytical study of residential housing potentialities, it should provide needed realistic appraisal.[13]

INFERENTIAL INDICATORS

Before the new fashion of direct surveys developed some ten years ago, principal reliance was placed on inferential indicators to indicate business thinking. Most of the series in the above sections on "Statistical Indicators" and "Series which Represent Early Stages in the Decision Process" may be considered inferential indicators. For instance, new orders represent an inferential indicator

---

[12]See Millard Hasty, "The Dun and Bradstreet Surveys of Businessmen's Expectations," in *Proceedings of the Business and Economic Statistics Section* (Washington, D.C., American Statistical Association, 1955), pp. 93–123.

[13]For a description of *Fortune* Surveys of Inventories and Homebuilding, see Board of Governors of the Federal Reserve System, "An Appraisal of Data and Research on Businessmen's Expectations about Outlook and Operating Variables," *Report of Consultant Committee on General Business Expectations* (Washington, D.C., September, 1955), pp. 84–92.

in that the decisions reflected in recorded data on orders indicate the attitude of businessmen.

Other series which have been considered important inferential indicators may be mentioned. Money turnover is indicative of attitudes with regard to the urgency of making purchases. A measure popularized by Leonard Ayres is the spread between low-and high-grade bonds. The differential represents an evaluation of the risk premium over the nearly "pure" interest rate. It shows the anticipation related to more speculative securities compared with the well-established ones. Thus, it may be held to represent the differential prospects of the type of business most likely to add to the total level of activity.

The trouble with money turnover and bond price differentials as measures of business expectations is that the vague kind of anticipations involved are not spelled out. For instance, the critical importance of business anticipations in the determination of bond prices was indicated by their fall in 1959 and their rise in early 1960. If inferential indicators come to play an important part in the formulation of forecasts, it will be necessary to provide a more definitive explanation of the way anticipations operate.

CONSUMER ANTICIPATIONS

The major background relating to surveys of consumer spending was developed by the Survey Research Center of the University of Michigan, until recently financed by the Federal Reserve.[14] The work is continuing, for the time being under sponsorship of the Ford Foundation. Although several instances can be cited when the survey by the Survey Research Center appeared to provide substantially better forecasting indications on consumer actions than other data,[15] the information has never become important enough to be considered other than supplementary in adjusting conclusions derived from general business analysis.

A very interesting new survey of "Consumer Buying Plans" is now being conducted by the National Industrial Conference Board

---

[14]In 1959, with the interviewing work farmed out to the Census Bureau, the Federal Reserve began a new, experimental quarterly survey of consumer intentions to buy selected durable goods. A quarterly sample of 15,000 to 20,000 households is being employed. See, e.g., "Quarterly Survey of Consumer Buying Intentions," *Federal Reserve Bulletin,* September, 1960.

[15]See Board of Governors of the Federal Reserve System, "Consumer Survey Statistics," *Report of Consultant Committee on Consumer Survey Statistics* (Washington, D.C., July, 1955). A brief review will be found in Bratt, *op. cit.,* pp. 333–36.

through continuing daily telephone interviews.[16] Contrasted with an annual survey of 3,000 persons and interim, twice-a-year surveys half that size made at Michigan, the Conference Board survey calls about 5,000 individual a month. Generally, buying plans are requested for the next six months, which appears to be more in focus with consumer buying perspective than a year (questions on taking vacations relate to the full year). The results have proved most useful for the following month or two. Questions are asked about plans to buy various specific durables (including homes) as well as clothing. Any plans involved are given perspective by asking related questions on employment and financial status. Also, questions as to whether the present is a good time to buy tend to show the extent to which buying plans are geared to personal decisions rather than to general business expectations.

Biases are unavoidable in any household survey; and obviously, the limitation of the Conference Board survey to the telephone subscriber universe is one. Allowance must be made for the fact that nonsubscribers are not represented, but we can expect the results to suffer much less than those of the *Literary Digest* poll of voters in 1936. The telephone is now more universal, and a household lacking a telephone is unlikely to consume as much as a household possessing one.

We cannot expect consumers to show expertness in forecasting general business conditions; therefore, what the forecaster should look for in a consumer survey is what consumers are likely to do if general business conditions do not change, or if they change in accordance with some type of naïve projection which appears to be generally accepted at the time. The short range of the Conference Board survey gives the forecaster some chance to think in these terms. An important part of what we can hope to learn is how adequate the consumer considers his stock of durable goods. The Conference Board survey appears to have given good results with respect to the types of durable goods which are likely to be in the greatest demand.

THE INDUSTRY SURVEY

The "Industry Survey," conducted by the Department of Commerce, obtains monthly figures on sales and inventories in manufacturing and trade, and in some cases on new and unfilled orders.

---

[16]For a brief, but fuller statement, contrasting the NICB survey with earlier ones, see *Conference Board Business Record*, November, 1958.

These data, together with price information, provide the basis for analyzing the market situation. To a considerable degree, a direct analysis of market data can be said to be an alternative to using sales anticipations data in forecasting. The market data reflect an evolving picture.

Frequently, the businessman draws inferences on the demand picture from price changes alone. The conclusion is clearer if related to other series in the market situation. For instance, if inventories are low and rising relative to sales, any price rise may not reflect rising final demand. Orders data are given important weight in durable industries. Rising orders might, however, merely reflect temporary market adjustments, as in cases where rapid ordering arises to beat a price rise. Leverage is given in the analysis if all of the market series are related.

Important possibilities are available in drawing inferences on the prospects for total economic activity from separate analyses of the market situation in different industries. The market picture is clearer at the concrete industry levels because much blunting occurs when somewhat diverse market situations are added together. For instance, orders may be rising in one industry and declining in another, so that the total of the two shows no change, but the total market effect is scarcely zero. The separately determined sales prospects in the various industries can be combined to show the over-all effect, but at the individual-industry level the market series come closer to showing real market forces.

Unfortunately, the Department of Commerce's Industry Survey does not get close enough to detailed industry levels to represent actual market changes very accurately. Data are available for sales and inventory stocks for several major manufacturing divisions of durable and nondurable goods industries. In some of the durable industry groups, orders data are available. Price data are not directly comparable and must be rationalized to a degree to provide effective comparisons. For one who has intimate knowledge of characteristics and practices of each of these major groups, the analysis is better than if conducted at the total manufacturing level.

Retail and wholesale industry data are available only by durable and nondurable product divisions. For retail, one may extend the analysis substantially by using the Federal Reserve figures on department store sales and stocks classifications.

Actually, analysis of this kind has not been generally emphasized. Each businessman, however, studies the market situation in his particular industry. Sales anticipation figures tend to summarize the results.

The inventory stock data available in the Industry Survey are particularly important because inventory investment shown in income and product accounts is not broken down by industry. A rough indication of the industrial breakdown of inventory investment can be judged by taking the change in inventory stocks held in the different major manufacturing industries. (We must not, of course, lose sight of the fact that the inventory stocks of most commodities are stated in prices of the different times at which the accumulation occurred.)

The breakdown of manufacturing inventory stocks by durable and nondurable products into purchased materials, goods in process, and finished goods has important forecasting significance. These classifications are not set up according to any absolute standard, but in relation to the way commodities fit into the picture in each particular company, and this is to our advantage. The bulk of changes in raw material inventories ordinarily proceeds according to intention. This is not true of finished goods. The manufacturer sets his production schedule according to an implicit or explicit forecast of sales. If the forecast is too high, finished goods inventories accumulate. If it is too low, these inventories are run down. In so far as raw material inventory accumulations are according to plan, their change may be used as a guide to determine whether or not the movement of inventories of finished goods was planned or unplanned.

FOR REFLECTION AND ANALYSIS

1. What criteria do you use to test the reliability of leading series?
2. Contrast the Harvard Index Chart with a modern diffusion index.
3. Should foreshadowing statistics be limited to series which represent early stages of the decision process?
4. Would you expect to find manufacturers' sales forecasts more or less accurate than plant and equipment forecasts?
5. What hope do you see for surveys of inventory anticipations?
6. What do you think of the theory that it is better to watch the actions of a decision maker than to ask him what he expects to do?
7. Why is it held that a six-month range on consumer buying plans is better than a year?
8. Do new orders data, as the term is used in this chapter, refer to made-to-order goods?
9. What rationale lies behind each of the leading indicators of the National Bureau of Economic Research?

Chapter	SHORT-TERM FORECASTING
18	OF AGGREGATE INDUSTRY

In this chapter, we deal with the forecasting of comprehensive, nonseasonal changes of aggregate industry. While this principally involves business cycle changes, the more comprehensive title is to be preferred to "business cycle forecasting." Sidewise or even inverse movements during business cycle expansion and contraction need to be anticipated. The aggregative techniques now employed provide some basis for forecasting these movements.

The methodology presented in the preceding chapter on foreshadowing statistics is invoked to throw light on certain aspects of the aggregative outlook. We take the position that a more comprehensive framework than statistical indicators must provide the foundation for aggregative forecasting. In this chapter, we consider the major frameworks employed to provide that foundation, and examine the way all available outlook information is woven into the analysis made possible.

FAVORABLE AND UNFAVORABLE FACTORS

The immemorial method of inclusive recognition of all factors in aggregative industry forecasting involves an assembly of the favorable and unfavorable factors in the outlook. One advantage of this method is that new, critical factors are readily brought into the analysis. Similarly, since the method is not tied to any particular theory, any kind of influence or evidence is readily introduced. Thus, all influences pertinent to the forecast *could be* recognized.

Unfortunately, however, there is no way to check for inclusiveness. All evidence found can be classified, but only exhaustiveness of the search for information can assure us that coverage is complete. No form has been developed, and perhaps cannot be, to show all of the needed information which one may know of in advance of the search for "straws in the wind."

The principle determining what is to be considered favorable or unfavorable may be vague. Surely, those using this method have often been more influenced by their sense of right and wrong than by any clear analysis of what the business impact of given factors may be. Higher tariffs provide one example. The economist, convinced that they are harmful, has sometimes listed them as unfavorable, but it is more likely that they will temporarily add to expansionary influences. Horizontal or rising wage rates provide another example. What their influence may be is most likely dependent upon the particular cyclical condition faced. For instance, if profit margins are shrinking late in the expansion because of increased intensity of competition, higher wage rates are likely, on the whole, to be contractionary. If, on the other hand, prices warranted by the competitive situation are generally above the administered prices set on the market, rising wage rates are likely to be expansionary. The forecaster should not confuse a favorable outlook with what is good or an unfavorable one with what is bad. Advancing business may not always be "good," at least for some interested parties. Presumably, the purpose of the model is to indicate the movement of general activity, not whether that movement is good in some meritorious or laudable sense.

Even though the classification may represent a thorough search for evidence and may be analytically clear, generally it will not be convertible into quantitative figures. The listed factors are qualitative and cannot be added together. At times, one list may clearly be more impressive than the other; but if this is so, the general outlook is so unobscured to everyone that the formality of drawing up lists of favorable and unfavorable factors has availed little.

Nevertheless, we do not conclude that the method is without value. Although it does not check with an aggregate, and thus fails to generate evidence on whether or not all pertinent information is counted, it does often uncover obscure information on detailed areas which might well be overlooked by other methods. Methods which add activity figures to obtain an inclusive total may fail to recognize critical, current circumstances. For instance, an important rounding-off in retail markets occurred in the spring of 1951; but in many of the models discussed later in this chapter, this factor was not observed because consumer expenditures were estimated by relatively formalized procedures. As a check on coverage of current contingencies a listing of favorable-unfavorable factors is not matched in other methods.

What is more important, the favorable-unfavorable method has fertile applications to particular types of outlook analyses. Notably, it has proved invaluable in guiding the framework of analysis in judging the likelihood of a turning point. The GNP model is weak in this respect. Factors indicating a turning point, contrasted with factors indicating a continuation of the current cumulative movement, have been found very useful in giving the forecaster perspective. The most important evidence employed is taken from the methods explained in the preceding chapter on foreshadowing statistics. The method is developed more fully below.

NATIONAL INCOME AND EXPENDITURE MODEL

Following the development of gross national product measurements during World War II, the GNP model was quickly assigned a central position in short-term aggregate forecasting. The reason is that GNP provided a total in which all types of economic activity are represented. Since it is broken down into expenditure divisions, the influence of each sector in bringing about past changes in total economic activity is indicated. Furthermore, since changes in different types of expenditures can be compared for any time period, inferences can be drawn as to the interrelated influences which are involved.

Contrast with methods available earlier indicates the striking advance in methodology which had been achieved. The principal earlier advance related to development of methods involving "historical comparison," as typified by the part of Chapter 17 on foreshadowing statistics concerning prewar developments. This was an improvement over a listing of favorable and unfavorable factors when that method proceeded on the basis of a static analysis of what was favorable or unfavorable. But the new method provided evidence which was symptomatic of changes which were occurring, and provided only limited analytical potentialities. One could present changes which were analogical to those which had occurred in earlier movements, possibly modified by arguments regarding the irregularity of current movements; but even this qualification was frequently forsworn. The argument often was that if we deviated from the statistical showing, we were likely to lose our objectivity and to be swayed by wishful thinking.

The GNP model establishes the basis for a structural analysis of expenditure patterns. Expenditures do reflect activity in a realistic sense, for activity is induced by expenditure. The symptomatic indicators founded on historical comparison provide an indication of economic change but provided little basis for further analysis. The evidence so obtained involves little more than empirical facts.

In giving us a total of final sales, gross national product provides the basis for a much richer analysis of the influences which can be expected to produce economic change. We can, if we like, at any time project the average expenditure relations which have occurred in the past under similar conditions. This is essentially what statistical indicators symptomatically provide. But we can do much better. We can take into consideration actual changes expected to occur in particular expenditure streams. And we can estimate the effect a change in one type of expenditure is likely to have on others comprised by GNP. The analysis of interrelated effects is a most important advantage of the GNP model. Furthermore, as we shall see, evidence derived from any other forecasting technique can be integrated in the model.

The "Naïve" Model. Before illustrating the model more specifically, we may note that it is most helpful when a turning point is not imminent. Other than near turning points, a study of recent changes is a useful way to start. If a turning point is to be expected, we must put initial emphasis on other techniques and introduce the conclusions so developed into the model at an early stage, as explained below.

Let us consider first the simpler case when a turning point is not imminent. Assume that inference, founded on techniques set forth below, has led to the conclusion that no turning point is impending. We may then illustrate the initial guidance which can be obtained by projecting the recent path of each major expenditure division.

In Table 18–1, we compare actual expenditures in the fourth quarter of 1958 and in the first quarter of 1959 with an extension of the advance in expenditures which had been occurring. Certainly, this is no way to make a rational forecast, but it provides a quantitative representation of the general inclination of movement. In every case where the difference between the actual levels in the fourth quarter of 1958 or in the first quarter of 1959 varies substantially from the columns showing the preceding quarter "plus change," the deviation can be readily explained (with the possible exception of net exports in the fourth quarter). Residential construction was

TABLE 18–1

GROSS NATIONAL PRODUCT AMOUNT-OF-CHANGE PROJECTION MODEL

Figures in Billions of Dollars, Seasonally Adjusted, at Annual Rates

Explanation	(1) Second Quarter 1958	(2) Third Quarter 1958	(3) Third Quarter Plus Change	(4) Fourth Quarter 1958	(5) Difference	(6) Fourth Quarter Plus Change	(7) First Quarter 1959	(8) Difference
Gross National Product	*434.5*	*444.0*	*453.5*	*457.1*	+3.6	*470.2*	*470.4*	+0.2
Private Investment	*52.6*	*55.8*	*59.0*	*61.5*	+2.5	*67.2*	*69.0*	+1.8
Residential construction	16.9	18.0	19.1	19.9	+0.8	21.8	21.9	+0.1
Nonresidential construction	17.7	17.4	17.1	17.4	+0.3	17.4	17.8	+0.4
Producer equipment	22.6	22.2	21.8	23.2	+1.4	24.2	23.9	−0.3
Inventory Change	− 5.8	− 3.4	− 1.0	0.8	+1.8	5.0	6.3	+1.3
Net exports	1.2	1.6	2.0	0.2	−1.8	− 1.2	− 0.9	+0.3
Exports	22.3	23.1	23.9	22.7	−1.2	22.3	21.5	−0.8
Imports	21.1	21.5	21.9	22.5	+0.6	23.5	22.4	−1.1
Government Purchases	*91.0*	*93.9*	*96.8*	*96.3*	−0.5	*98.7*	*97.4*	−1.3
National defense, less sales	43.8	44.2	44.6	44.7	+0.1	45.2	45.5	+0.3
Other federal	7.5	8.9	10.3	9.4	−0.9	9.9	8.3	−1.6
State and local	39.7	40.8	41.9	42.2	+0.3	43.6	43.6	.....
Personal Expenditures	*290.9*	*294.4*	*297.9*	*299.1*	+1.2	*303.8*	*304.0*	+0.2
Durable	36.7	37.1	37.5	39.8	+2.3	42.5	41.3	−1.2
Nondurable	141.5	143.1	144.7	143.6	−1.1	144.1	145.3	+1.2
Services	112.7	114.2	115.7	115.7	.....	117.2	117.4	+0.2

Explanation	(1)	(2)	(3)	(4)	(5)	(6)	(7)	(8)
Gross National Product	434.5	444.0	453.5	457.1	+3.6	470.2	470.4	+0.2
Total of detail	434.5	444.1	453.7	456.9	+3.2	469.7	470.4	+0.7

NOTE: Rounding errors appear in the table, as found in the published data; in building any actual model, the analyst must face rounding errors. To aid in understanding them, the actual gross national product shown in the table is contrasted with the total of the detail:

moving up faster than the projected path, but increased loan commitments by the Federal National Mortgage Association ("Fannie May") partly explain the acceleration. The positive difference for producer equipment in the fourth quarter is accounted for by the fact that rises in this area were delayed until after the second quarter. With an actual decline in the third quarter, the naïve method of following preceding changes projects a still further decline, but such was not to be expected with the advance getting under way in general activity.

Although the differences shown for inventory investment are large in both quarters represented in Table 18-1, the projections are in the right direction and, in view of the volatility of this kind of expenditure, actually are not too bad. As for the fourth quarter, when inventory investment rose to a small positive figure, the situation which developed might well have been anticipated. A continuation of inventory runoff (which negative inventory investment in the Third Quarter plus Change column implies) would appear to be an unlikely continuation in view of the rapid recovery in general activity which had been occurring after the second quarter.

The irregularity of movement in "other federal government expenditure" explains the large differences in that row. It is also related to increasing expenditures during the recession, which were cut back after the fourth quarter. If the rounding-off of these expenditures had occurred more smoothly or closer to the business cycle upturn, the recorded difference between behavior and projection would not have occurred.

A similar point can be made with regard to consumer nondurable expenditures. A rapid rise from the second to the third quarter produced a substantial advance in the "Third Quarter plus Change" column, but the recorded rise in the fourth quarter was small. As a result the Fourth Quarter plus Change column shows little advance, but the first quarter experienced a rapid rise. The naïve projection does not follow the quarter-to-quarter zigzag, although over the two quarters the actual change closely matches the general movement which was occurring.

Again, a large amount in the Difference column following the 1958 fourth-quarter figure for net exports illustrates the fact that reversals of movement will not be anticipated when we merely project the recent path of change. The reversal of the rise which had been occurring in exports was founded on the fact that recovery had been less rapid in foreign countries, so that their demand for our exports had not kept pace, and on the increased desire of foreign governments to build up gold holdings. Acceleration in the rise of imports was due to increased demand for raw materials, with rapid business improvement in our country and increasing imports of fabricated products such as foreign automobiles.

While the above paragraphs represent rationalizations about past history, they illustrate an important method of uncovering deviations which may be expected from the naïve projections. All of the points made above were more or less obvious in the third quarter of 1958. They were well covered in the business literature published at the time. Forecasting may be simplified if attention is focused on probable deviations from projections of changes which have been occurring in the various expenditure streams.

Cases of Irregular Variation. Although the suggested procedure is helpful enough of the time to be employed as a continuing procedure, recognition of situations in which it is inapplicable is important. Note has already been taken of the fact that little is to be gained from naïve extrapolations in visualizing prospects when a turning point is imminent. Turning points are taken up later as a special case. Other cases of inapplicability are also readily visualized. Without question, the effectiveness of projecting past changes is more limited in the second two quarters of 1959 than in the quarters illustrated in Table 18-1, because of interruptions arising from the steel strike. Whenever the movement of gross national product is temporarily reversed, past changes provide limited perspective, even though the situation is too temporary to be considered a turning point. We may note that, other than at turning points, the third quarter of 1959 is the only time in the postwar when a reversal occurred. Abnormal leveling did occur at other times, notably in the second quarter of 1952.

Before examining the third quarter of 1959 and the second quarter of 1952, we may point to other cases where projections of past changes should be heavily discounted. The rate of cumulative change in the general movements can be expected to deviate from linearity for various reasons, and the forecaster should look for such situations. We cannot hope to catalogue the types which may develop; but as an illustration, we may note the tendency for activity to rise most rapidly fairly early in expansion, which implies later deceleration. A very important factor here is prospective change in prices because the deceleration might be partially or wholly negated by sharp price rises. Finally, any particular expenditure stream may level off or reverse itself for reasons developing within the particular area, even though no such movement appears in aggregate gross national product. Clearly, a thorough analysis of conditions in each expenditure division is more necessary than one might conclude from the ready rationalizations of deviations from projected change late in 1958 and early in 1959.

Turning to the third quarter of 1959, gross national product declined 1.3 per cent, in contrast with earlier and later rises. Since the decline was specifically related to the steel strike, no one expected to see it continue after settlement, so projection of the decline to the following quarter would have been meaningless. Gross national product rose in the fourth quarter to bring the aggregate back to the second-quarter level. Most of the expenditure streams declined, however, and even more than a projection of the movement from the second to the third quarter would have indicated. This is partly because, in several areas, expansion continued in the third quarter, consuming inventory in the process; but by the fourth quarter, shortage of inventory curtailed production. This differentiates decline in the third quarter of 1959 from a cyclical recession. The major decline in activity was related to an inventory cutback which far more than accounted for the decline in activity, while other expenditure streams did not show a "sympathetic" contraction, as almost always occurs in a cyclical recession. The difference was that the inventory contraction was "unplanned" or "undesired." While a naïve model does not help much in these circumstances, neither could principal conclusions about most expenditure streams be derived from exclusive consideration of demand factors in each area. Shortage of materials and contractionary influences produced by the strike had to be given consideration. The GNP model therefore was useful in making a forecast during and after the strike period.

The leveling of gross national product in the second quarter of 1952 resulted from rapid rises in defense expenditures and in automobile sales, together with a steel strike. As in 1959, the steel strike brought declines in inventories which failed to induce declines in other expenditures. Similarly, rise in inventory investment in the fourth quarter of 1952 did not bring rises in most expenditure streams.

Use of Current Price Figures in the Model. The position taken in this book is that the short-term forecasting model is initially best set up in current prices rather than in deflated prices. Projection of the recent path of movement in the various expenditure streams is much less consistent if deflated figures are used. The reason is that the expenditure values represent the market situation, and the strength of mechanical projections shown above rests on the fact that they carry forward the market movement which has been in progress.

The market values are important in identifying market forces at turning points. For instance, prices frequently weaken at the peak of the cycle with rapid capacity completions and the leveling of various types of demand. Prices in such a case may be more important evidence on the direction of movement than changes in activity. Similarly, at the trough of the cycle, any strengthening of prices has frequently been more indicative of an upturn than rises in physical activity.

Several reasons have been given for the contrary position. First, what we are really interested in is real changes, not only in production but also in employment. This is true, but the fact has nothing to do with how effective the figures are in forecasting. Furthermore, employment figures are not readily developed from production figures at any current moment of time because of the erratic movement of "productivity" figures.

Second, various relationships between variables used in GNP-model forecasting are best put in physical terms, like stock-flow relationships or activity in relation to capacity. Although we believe that the emphasis on physical terms in relationships may readily be exaggerated, we agree in principle. The argument provides reason for using deflated figures in part of the analysis, not for their sole use. If the established relations are held to be "normal," the tendency is to assign any deviation to exogenous forces.[1] Actually, however, current market forces can become deceptive, leading perhaps to redundant production, and carry relationships away from what the forecaster has held to be normal. In this case the factor of value represented by prices would play an important part.

Finally, it is argued that the change in prices is most significantly developed by relating to deflated-value changes. It is true that changes in activity represent an important "explanatory variable" in forecasting prices. This does not mean, however, that activity stated in constant prices will perform better in this respect than will activity stated in current prices. And even if it does, the key point is whether forecasts are most effectively made in quantity or value terms.

---

[1] See V. Lewis Bassie, *Economic Forecasting* (New York: McGraw-Hill Book Co., Inc., 1958), pp. 511–17.

Emphasis on the current-value model is relative, however. Perhaps we are most impressed with the empirical evidence—that more meaningful naïve projections can be made with gross national product in current prices. Possibly, experience may demonstrate that most useful results flow from a combination of three models— GNP in current prices, the movement of prices themselves, and deflated GNP. Conceivably, interrelations between these three models may provide important insights.[2]

The Forecasting of Turning Points. The forecaster must be constantly on the alert for the development of turning points. This is especially true if the GNP model is the central forecasting technique, for that model does not show the unfolding of turning points effectively. Possibly, the techniques outlined in the following section may uncover the turn of total activity separately in each of the major expenditure streams where it is in evidence, but the analysis of particular expenditure streams does not readily disclose changes in direction of total activity. Change in direction is principally a function of the aggregate economy; and to a considerable extent, what happens in individual expenditure streams is the result of change in movement of the total.

A useful method involves a running record of evidence indicating the weakening or likely reversal of the cumulative movement. Such a record is helpful both in expansions and in contractions, but is more readily illustrated in the former and probably more helpful in view of the fact that the process of "maturing" stretches out over a longer period. We shall illustrate the developing indications of reversal in the expansion only.

For this purpose, we borrow from indicator analysis and from the analysis of evolving forces in business cycle theory. As for the former, we look to leading series, orders and other commitments, appropriations or financing arrangements, and diffusion indexes. For the latter, we appeal to the induced effects which can be expected from typical prosperity developments.

We may illustrate the method by its application to the evolving business situation in the fall of 1956. The imminence of a downturn was indicated by the following factors:

1. Diffusion indexes were in a general decline, and we visualized that such a decline would have been in evidence on profits if satisfactory computations had been available.
2. New orders for key durable goods were declining, and the new

---

[2]See Table 18–3 near the end of this chapter.

NICB survey was showing a leveling or decline in capital appropriations.

3. The average weekly hours per worker in manufacturing were beginning to decline.

4. A leveling-out was occurring in construction starts, indicating, after earlier rapid rises, that the completion rate was about to mount relative to starts and to bring added capacity at a time when impetus of increased expenditures was missing.

5. Wide evidence of approaching temporary saturation for a wide group of consumer durables was impressive, and timed with abnormal increases in certain consumer service costs, such as rising public utility rates and the adoption of new taxes in local communities.

6. Checking through optimistic forecasts, no substantial contrary evidence could be found except for the listing of favorable factors given below.

The check list of favorable factors was:

1. Rising government expenditures (actually, when the downturn occurred in mid-1957, the "stretch-out," which had been quickly implemented in government defense work, became a negative factor).

2. Large research expenditures could be expected to maintain the rapid pace of technological development.

3. Universal optimism existed with respect to potential growth. One indication was the rise in number of persons who would enter adult life in the late sixties.

Like all lists of favorable and unfavorable factors, no precise quantitative balancing was possible; but clearly, the evidence was pessimistic, however the balance might be struck. Note should be taken of the fact that this conclusion, unlike a less specific listing of favorable and unfavorable factors, did not represent generally apparent information.

It is true, however, that a majority of the forecasters in business organizations recognized this picture in the fall of 1956. As a result, inventory investment fell to low levels in the first quarter of 1957. In spite of that development, activity remained on a high, although horizontal, level. Business forecasts tended to shift to the favorable side by the end of the first quarter, and inventory investment rose to more normal levels in the second quarter. Needless to say, this action confused the picture, but it did not neutralize the contractionary forces indicated in the above list.

A method of this kind can point to the probability of a downturn, but does not point to any effective methodology of dating the turn. The studied timing of relationships in economic indicators is only of limited help because of the irregularity shown by past averages.[3] Most important in this connection is recognition of particular current conditions which might be expected to influence the lead in any given situation, but the required methodology is vague and not readily summarized.

A more important method of dating the downturn relates to the timing pattern developing in the induced effects evolving in the expansionary movement. An illustration is the moderating effect which follows after the surge in expenditure induced by a single-shot injection, such as payment of the veterans' compensation certificates in 1936.

In early 1957 the increasing pressure resulting from capacity completions helped set a pattern for the downturn. While models on the induced effects which are of major importance in any particular expansion do make possible the development of a timing picture, work of this kind is not sufficiently developed for effective simple summarization.

In studying the running record of evidence indicating weakening of cumulative advance, attention must be focused on the nature of culmination which may develop. Central attention in this connection must be placed on the inventory situation because of its inevitable crucial importance. A possibility, although usually remote, is that contractionary forces arise principally from realization that inventory stocks are fully adequate or excessive. More frequently, the decline in inventory investment starts from other factors, such as belief that consumer sales are leveling off, that growth potentialities are growing more limited, or that financial and monetary factors are injurious. Or developments may grow out of the shifting competitive picture. For instance, new companies and new industry, which account for an important part of the normal inventory increase, may be rapidly shrinking and thus hobble expansionary influences. Because of reduced profit margins or a slow shift to unfavorability in the market picture, businesses may increasingly decide to invest less, which strikes at a sensitive type of inventory accumulation (that related to investment needs).

As an illustration, we may cite early 1960. Businessmen were confessing to increasing confusion with respect to the business picture. Economic indicators were generally experiencing a slow decline

---

[3]The most important evidence along these lines is that shown by Geoffrey Moore. See references to his work in the preceding chapter.

by the end of the first quarter. In reading the running record of evidence on the cumulative movement, factors pointed increasingly to the possibility of a turning point. Decline in inventory investment arose because essential restocking had been completed. Efforts to avoid inventory distortion appeared unusually prevalent. At the same time, no great momentum had developed in most expenditure streams. The leveling influence of the strike period persisted in most types of expenditure. It is interesting to note that a similar flattening effect followed the 1952 strike. It was difficult to visualize a downturn at that time, however, because no strong culminating influences, such as described in the preceding paragraph, could be spotted. If the reaction to inventory restocking after the strike had been less constrained or had involved as much expenditure as in 1960, on the other hand, it is easy to understand how culminating forces could have become overpowering.

In the above paragraphs, we have dealt entirely with the upper, rather than the lower, turning point. We have noted that a running record of forces tending to weaken cumulative forces in the contraction is of limited value in most cases because of the shortness of the movement. Attention is best concentrated on spotting the kind of forces which may lead to a culmination. The simplest kind of case arises when the inventory runoff proceeds so fast that when it ends, the increase in inventory investment forced as a result brings a pickup in activity. This development may be illustrated by the change from the fourth quarter of 1949 to the first quarter of 1950. An $8.8 billion rise in gross national product was almost wholly accounted for by an increase in inventory investment, which rose from −$5.3 billion to +$2.5 billion.

Having estimated the quarter in which the turning point will occur, the forecaster must then judge the amount by which gross national product will change. Emphasis on initial decision regarding change in total GNP at turning points is founded on the focusing of culminating forces in which a model of the shift in phase can be visualized. This model remains too undeveloped to generalize in simple form. For the present the best procedure is first to establish the nature of the principal culminating forces and then to trace a quantitative model of the way in which they can be expected to work. We have explained in the history chapters a range of influences which have led to slight modification in general conceptions regarding the adequacy of inventory stocks. In 1957, for instance, a major factor was the increased rate at which capacity was being completed. The added capacity made possible prompter increases in the supply of finished goods, and therefore diminished somewhat the volume of finished stocks required. Production schedules were reduced slightly to avoid further increases in inventory stocks. The slight curtailment in the rate of production induced minor declines in expenditure. This led to further cuts in production schedules, carrying forward the contractionary effect, and soon brought decisions at later stages of distribution to trim inventories to the modified sales picture, which apparently demonstrated the need for still further cuts in inventory stocks held by manufacturers. Since mild action taken in the early stage of this process failed to bring inventory stocks to the expected levels, the point was finally reached at which manufacturers decided to take much more drastic action, at which time production schedules were cut enough to accelerate the decline in total GNP.

Whatever the major forces tending to weaken the cumulative movement may be, it appears that most of the time the model illustrating the turning point can concentrate on the effect generated on inventory investment. How this effect develops, however, would seem to depend a good deal on what the weakening forces are and how they spread. This is the reason for our decision not to try to sharpen this model by presenting a simple quantitative construct.

Surely, various divisional expenditure streams play a part in the behavior which leads to a turning point, notably inventory investment as set out in the above paragraphs. Whatever information can be picked up by studying inventory investment directly is of course essential, but the inventory change is intimately related to induced expenditure effects as production schedules are shifted, and therefore cannot be readily picked up separately from the total GNP movement. Usually, there are some expenditure streams which are rising when a downturn appears imminent. This often applies to government expenditures. Integrating such changes in the turning-point model is of first importance, although timely information is not always available. In 1957, government expenditures were increasing, and plans were set according to that pattern until the time of the downturn. In complete ignorance of the change taking place in the business cycle phase, the federal government initiated a "stretch-out" policy in defense expenditures to combat inflation just as the downturn began. It is too much to expect the forecaster to pick up this kind of exogenous change long enough in advance to help significantly in the turning-point model.

First Revision of the GNP Model. Whether we start with a model involving a naïve projection of rate of change, as illustrated in Table 18-1, or with a turning-point model, the next step is to draw on direct estimates of each of the expenditure divisions as a basis for revising the first-model figures. The revision may not always be most effectively achieved in precisely the same way. For instance, we have noted above that much of the time the divisional expenditure estimates which will prove least satisfactory may be much improved by offhand judgments regarding widely accepted information.

The forecast, however, will be on a firmer foundation if careful studies are made of each of the major expenditure divisions. The forecasting of each of these divisions is worthy of much more attention than we can give it here; and in the following paragraphs, we can do no more than note the most crucial considerations in each expenditure group.[4]

Other than when the forecaster must follow a devious course in anticipating inventory investment, such as in the development of the turning-point model, the basis for estimation is recent changes in sales, market analysis, and survey reports. Typically, changes in inventory stock reflect recent movements in sales, and this is a firm basis for projecting stock except for new companies or new products or for sales which are concentrated in standard products where efficiency in use of inventories will make possible slower increases in stock.

An illustration of the exaggeration in increase in inventory stock is provided by the Korean War, when new types of war "hardware" necessitated rapid increases in inventory stock. A firmer basis for projecting the relationship to recent sales will be forthcoming if some study of co-ordinate changes in prices and orders is made for important industry divisions. Such market analysis may be simplified by use of outlook reports. Especially notable in this connection is the current information supplied by the National Association of Purchasing Agents in its weekly *Bulletin.* Surveys of inventory anticipations, such as the one conducted by *Fortune,* are worth noting, but must still be considered supplemental.

When inventory changes become critical, the most important

---

[4]Much useful literature is available. For orderly attention to each of the expenditure divisions, see especially John P. Lewis, *Business Conditions Analysis* (New York: McGraw-Hill Book Co., Inc., 1959), pp. 168–282 and 389–519; Bassie, *op. cit.,* pp. 147–488.

problem faced by the forecaster is differentiating between planned and unplanned changes in inventory stocks. The most useful information for following this difference is the classification of manufacturing inventories by stage of fabrication—purchased materials, goods in process, and finished goods. When finished goods stocks are moving positively with purchased material stocks, usually we may assume that changes in stocks are as planned. But if they move oppositely, the movement should be investigated to see if we may not plausibly assume that finished goods stocks are acting as a buffer for inexact setting of production schedules—either declining because sales are rising faster than planned or rising because sales are lower than planned.

The forecaster should recognize that change in inventory stocks must be converted to inventory investment to reflect directly the influence produced on activity. For this purpose the change in inventory stocks must be corrected to allow for the fact that many inventory stocks cover the same commodities at the different prices at which they were bought in the past (what is the same thing, must be adjusted for differences in inventory valuation). A fair procedure the forecaster can employ is to relate the inventory change to the recent movement of nonfarm prices. The correlation with a three-month cumulation of price changes is shown in Chart 18-1. The past three-month cumulation of price changes can be computed at any time; by dubbing in a point which lies on the approximate relationship with inventory valuation adjustment in Chart 18-1, the analyst can estimate the correction necessary to convert the change in inventory stock to a price-corrected inventory investment figure. The forecaster can often improve on the relationship in particular cases by arguing about likely past effects present in the inventory stocks. For instance, the zero correction in the last quarter of 1953 and in the first quarter of 1954 followed from a large accumulation of stocks in 1951 and 1952 with generally declining prices. When prices are rising, a downward correction must be made in the change in inventory stocks to allow for valuation adjustment, and conversely when prices are falling.

The outlook for residential building is dependent upon changes in household formation; the movement of rents compared to down payments and monthly charges in buying a new house; the house vacancy rate especially in areas where activity is likely to change most rapidly; and the level of interest rates and changes occurring in disposable income. The problem is complicated, and we can provide only some brief notes. Information is being rapidly improved, and chances are that a much better basis for short-term forecasting will soon be available. The rate of household formation plus the rate of demolition of houses plus the increase in ownership and use of vacation homes provide the basis for housing demand.

CHART 18-1

INVENTORY VALUATION ADJUSTMENT AND CHANGE IN PRICES

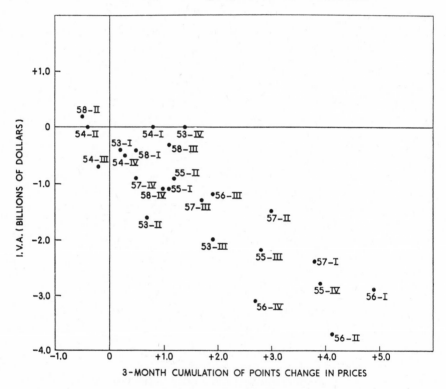

NOTE: The wholesale price index for other than farm products and foods, on a 1947–49 base, is used in computing the three-month cumulation in points of price change.

The urgency of these demand factors depends on the vacancy rate, demand obviously being greater when few vacant houses are available. Low interest rates (in so far as they are effective in the rate established on housing mortgages) encourage housing construction and improve the advantage of buying new houses compared to renting old ones. Except in periods of forced rent controls, the rent-price relationship and vacancy rate can both be used to check demand-supply relationships.

To an increasing extent, residential housing expenditure is influenced by increases in disposable income, especially for additions or alterations and for vacation cottages. Precise relationships between residential housing and these explanatory variables have not been dependably established, but the generalizations here presented provide statements regarding direction of influence of the explanatory variables. With some experience, the plus and minus indications thus given can provide the forecaster a crude basis for estimating the approximate change to be expected in housing expenditures. The result may be checked against anticipation surveys, notably the Homebuilding Survey conducted by *Fortune.* Such surveys must be used with caution, with special attention given to biases contractors may follow in making such reports.

The most dependable figures to use in estimating nonresidential construction and producer equipment expenditures are the results obtained in the surveys of plant and equipment. As shown in Chart 17–8 (page 401), the Department of Commerce and Securities and Exchange Commission combined survey has given good indications in the past. It would be foolish, however, to accept that survey figure without qualifications regarding the probable reliability under the particular conditions prevailing in the forecast period. If a downturn is expected, cancellation or delay of some equipment projects is to be expected. On the other hand, acceleration in the rise of sales in expansion may frequently add to equipment purchases. At times, especially when the economy is operating near peak prosperity, some delay in receipt of materials may properly be anticipated and tend to reduce the actual rate of expenditure as compared to the survey figure. In most cases, businessmen probably assume financing conditions existing at the time when the survey questions were answered, so that if a change in financing conditions is estimated by the forecaster, he should make some adjustment. Again, this is a case where experience in forecasting helps a great deal in judging the size of adjustments to be made. In any case, these adjustments ordinarily should be minor, since the record shows that the survey figure has usually come close to the actual outturn.

The plant and equipment figure represents a slightly different content than the GNP nonresidential construction and producer equipment categories.[5] Ordinarily, it is not worth while to attempt a reconciliation for the small difference, but rather to apply the percentage change shown in the survey figure to the combined total

---

[5]The difference is explained in *U.S. Income and Output: A Supplement to the Survey of Current Business* (Washington, D.C.: U.S. Government Printing Office, 1959), pp. 82–84.

of nonresidential construction and producer equipment. In some of the adjustment cases noted above, more correction is required for the latter than for the former category. For instance, in case of an expected downturn, unanticipated in the survey, the full percentage change in the survey figure may be applied to nonresidential construction to estimate expected change, but it may be reduced somewhat before applying to producer equipment to allow for expected cancellations and delays.

In the goods and services covered by the summary figure "net exports," the merchandise trade balance is usually most important, and we shall limit our attention to that. Merchandise imports will move with changes in our gross national product, but usually at a slightly greater percentage. A better understanding of prospective imports can be obtained by looking at the types which have been experiencing recent increases or decreases and facing the question of the likely continuation of these changes. As an illustration, the observer would have noted in the spring of 1960 that, with the large increase in sale of domestically made small cars, foreign-car imports would not maintain the past increase. Theoretically, the same kind of analysis should be conducted with respect to the principal countries which take our exports in order to estimate the likely change in exports. A short-cut method which usually will give fair results is to assume that our exports will correlate positively with the movement of business conditions in the countries which account for the principal part of our exports.

Government expenditures should be forecast separately for the three divisions—defense, other federal, and state and local. It is usually best to examine the defense budget, to the extent that it is publicly available, to get an understanding of the different expenditure trends within the total.[6] Usually, however, the total maintains the momentum which developed in the recent past, and a reasonable forecast would be obtained by making that assumption. In fact, sudden reversals often represent quick changes in policy, such as the "stretch-out" beginning in mid-1957, and a speed-up started later in that year to meet the challenge of the Russian Sputnik. No satisfactory method is available for forecasting a quick change in policy.

Other federal expenditures for goods and services are reasonably well set out in advance in budget statements, although at times

---

[6]Budget figures are usually translated into income and product terms in the February issue of the *Survey of Current Business*.

allowance must be made for the practice of filling out expenditures at the end of the fiscal year by obtaining deficiency appropriations. The budget figures do not satisfactorily reveal a zigzag movement which frequently appears in the quarterly figures (since the data are seasonally corrected, presumably the zigzag is not principally due to seasonal factors). Unless the budget figures indicate rising or falling expenditures, the inference is that any quarterly forecast differing substantially from the outturn is likely to balance out in the following quarters.

State and local budget data are not readily assembled, and possibly are not very reliable in any case. For much of the postwar period, forecasts a few quarters in advance could be made adequately by a simple extension of recent advances. That trend should be modified by general knowledge concerning the adequacy of financing additional expenditures, major road-building programs, and the extent of need felt for other types of construction, such as school building. Many times, tax funds cannot be readily increased. At other times, new measures like sales taxes or wage taxes spread rapidly and make for rapid increases in revenue, but revenues quickly rise to practiceable limits. Early in the postwar, additional funds were readily obtained by flotation of bond issues, but the major parts of the funds easily obtainable from that source were quickly borrowed and spent.

The likely state and local expenditure changes in the road-building program can often be estimated from information of the availability of federal grants-in-aid. Other construction, notably for school building, can be estimated from publicized information on work under way in some areas.

In addition to purchases of goods and services, which are included in the government sector of gross national product, forecasts are needed for transfer payments and government interest paid to round out estimates of personal income (the forecast of which is considered below). Transfer payments have been steadily rising because of increasing old-age benefits and of some upward trend in the other types. Unemployment benefits vary inversely with the fluctuation in GNP. Government interest payments vary with the level of the debt and adjust with a lag to changes in interest rates.

Personal consumption expenditures are divided into durable, nondurable, and service. Durable expenditures have usually fluctuated with the business cycle, but the other two types have been less affected. In automobiles, as well as most other major consumer durables, replacement demand has come to represent well over half of the total current market. Scrappage of old cars has varied independently of total activity in recent years. In 1955, when the sale of new cars rose dramatically, scrappage declined slightly. In 1956, when sales of new cars dropped a fourth, scrappage increased. And in 1957, when sales increased slightly, scrappage declined. Then, in 1958, when sales declined nearly a third with the recession, scrappage increased. In each of these years except 1958, sales were substantially in excess of scrappage, so that the stock of cars was increasing. But the movement of scrappage inverse to sales tended to be stabilizing. Relatively more old cars were kept in use in years of large sales and relatively fewer in years of smaller sales. If it had been the other way around and total automobile demand had remained the same, new-car sales would have fluctuated even more.

The demand for consumer durables was not closely correlated with the rise in gross national product or disposable income either in the 1950-53 or in the 1954-57 expansion. While the timing of replacement of old units may have been unusual in the second case, still the forecaster should not expect the demand for consumer durables to be guided by the degree of rise in GNP. It does appear safe to assume that the demand for consumer durables always will decline in recession.

Forecast of the demand for consumer durables in expansion must rest more on the direct market for these goods than was often recognized in the past. Replacement demand is very important in this connection. More information than we now have is needed on condition of the stock of major durables. Much may be done with market analysis; but for this purpose the analyst needs intimate information on prevailing trade-in rates, together with a better knowledge of inventories; therefore he can best employ conclusions made available by anlysts in the consumer durable goods industries. Some appeal can be made to the National Industrial Conference Board's Buying-Plan Survey to find what consumers say their plans are. Some weight may also be given to rising total expenditures, even though recent experience provides little support for that method. Care in watching for major *market developments* in durable industries is highly desirable.

The movement of consumer nondurable goods is much more closely tied to changes in disposable income, with respect to both rises in expansion or leveling-off in contraction. Allowance must be made for a slow, secular decline in the proportion of disposable income spent in this group. The analysis is sharpened if separate consideration is given to the two major types of expenditure involved—food and beverages and clothing and shoes. Together, these groups account for roughly three fourths of the total group and frequently are responsible for an important part of a zigzag movement in the quarterly figures. For instance, food expenditures remained on a horizontal plane in the last three quarters of 1958, while clothing expenditures jumped sharply from the second to the third quarter, with the result that the nondurable goods total experienced a disproportionate part of its rise in the first three quarters of the year. The particular market movements taking place, especially in clothing, need to be studied separately.

The forecaster can expect consumer nondurable goods expenditures to move with disposable income, although a correction should be made for a slightly slower growth. By this simple assumption, he will obtain a reasonable projection of the average change during the following year. The actual quarterly change is likely to be less regular and principally dependent upon the market developments which are occurring in the major products in the group.

Service expenditures almost entirely account for the resistance of consumer expenditures to the leveling or slackening of advance of disposable income in recession. Expenditure for durable commodities drops and for nondurable commodities reacts fully as much as disposable income. Service expenditures experience only a slight slackening in recessions such as we have experienced in the postwar. Since the war, they have risen more rapidly than disposable income, but the excess in any expansion year has been limited; if disposable income is increasing 5 or 6 per cent, services may rise as much as 7 or 8. In contrast, consumer durable commodity expenditures may rise as much as a fourth, as in 1955, or may even decline later in the prosperity, as in 1956. While nondurable commodity expenditures do not decline under prosperous conditions, the rate of advance may drop substantially, as in 1952, when it fell to 5 per cent after an advance of 10 per cent in 1951.

If a turning point is not in prospect, consumer service expenditures can be forecast with reasonable success by extending the rate of advance of the preceding year. If a turning point is in prospect, a slight modification is desirable, since the rate of advance during a recession year is likely to be slightly diminished. If a closer approximation of the advance in service expenditures is necessary, a more careful analysis must be made of expenditures on housing, household operation (these two account for about half of the total), transportation, and other.

The use the forecaster will make of direct estimates of expenditures in the various divisions, here recommended, depends on whether he is revising the "naïve amount of change projection" model or the turning-point model, and upon how thorough a forecasting job he finds to be necessary. As a minimum in revising the former, he may avoid involving himself in much more analysis than suggested as obvious in adjusting Table 18–1, presented early in the chapter. If reversals have occurred, such as in the third quarter of 1959, the extension of amount of change will be much less reliable, and procedures such as recommended in the following paragraph for revising the turning-point model should be used.

In the turning-point model, chief emphasis is placed in the beginning on change estimated in total gross national product. In fact, until direct estimates are made of various expenditure divisions, many of the cells of the GNP table will not be filled in. Besides the total, some information will have been developed on the process expected to be most influential in setting off a culmination (for instance, increasing completion of capital capacity in 1957) and the assumed induced actions to bring inventories into line. If the developing culmination visualized in the turning-point model is missed in the direct estimates of expenditure divisions, the sum of these estimates may vary substantially from total GNP as developed in the turning-point model. The check thus provided is useful, but may require a great amount of additional work to attain a reconciliation. A re-examination of the expenditure divisions, in the light of expected culminating influences, may uncover potentialities missed in the first examination. If not, a careful reappraisal of the assumed culminating forces will be required. If the two approaches then do not begin to provide consistent results, they will be brought into line by the methods suggested in the following subsection.

The question of thoroughness of the forecasting job is an important one. Our approach, at most times, is to estimate minimum changes on the theory that the most important information required is that on timing of turning points and direction of change. If more precise estimates of the amount of change are required, much more careful work will be necessary in making direct estimates of the various expenditure divisions. Even when such estimates are developed, the resulting GNP model is likely to be less reliable as to precise amount of change than the simpler work is with regard to the direction of change only. For many applications, the price paid for the efforts to develop the likely amount of change will be excessive.

Second Revision of the GNP Model. After the direct estimates of expenditure in each division of activity are entered into the model, careful studies must be made of likely induced effects of the changes in various expenditure divisions on the other expenditure divisions. One method of handling this problem is to check with relationships between the various expenditures which, on the average, have held in the past. Principally, these have related to the concept of the Keynesian multiplier.

A common version of this relates to the extent to which gross national product is seen to vary with changes in nonconsumption expenditures.[7] Chart 18-2 shows that there is a fairly good relationship between changes in nonconsumption expenditures and changes in GNP (with farm inventory investment excluded, since it does not induce other expenditure). To check on the forecast model, we recommend plotting the paired point indicated for the forecast change in nonconsumption expenditures and forecast change in GNP (with farm inventory investment eliminated) on such a chart. Assumption that any point should fall on the plotted regression line is not warranted, but the position of the point provides the basis for initiating a revision if the point does not fall on the regression line. No simple mechanical rule for doing this is satisfactory, but we can illustrate the problem. The year 1947 falls far above the regression line because of the great initial postwar expansion founded on deferred demand rather than on demand induced by investment expenditure. The year 1951 falls below the line because the nonconsumption expenditures were for war, and consumer expenditures were unusually phlegmatic following their exceptional rise in the latter half of 1950. The high level of the plotted point for 1957 reflects the fact that investment was leveling from the beginning of the year because of the oncoming recession, while consumption expenditure continued to rise until the end of the year, due to consumption lag.

The forecaster is faced with analyzing the forthcoming period to ascertain if some such factors as those illustrated in the preceding paragraph are likely if the point plotted for the forecast period departs from the regression line. If no such arguments appear valid,

---

[7] See Bassie, *op. cit.,* p. 457.

or if they appear too unimportant to account for the total divergence, the forecaster is faced with readjusting the relative changes projected for consumption and nonconsumption expenditures. Whether to lower the one which is high or reduce the one which is low depends on which rests on the more solid foundation.

CHART 18–2

APPARENT CHANGES INDUCED IN GROSS NATIONAL PRODUCT
BY CHANGES IN NONCONSUMPTION EXPENDITURE

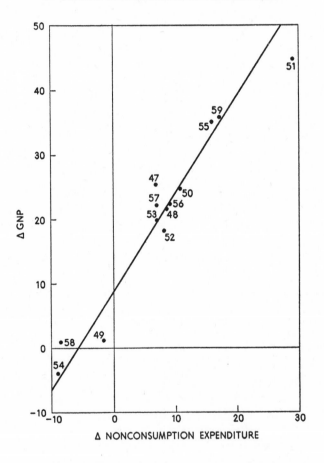

There is another possibility. We know that inducements to spend develop between other areas and in certain change relationships. For instance, a rapid increase in investment in new companies or in new products will induce rapid inventory increases, as it did in 1951. Such a relation does not explain consumption-nonconsumption relations, but is important in explaining relations within the investment area. Returning to the consumption-nonconsumption relationship, a considerable difference in inducement arises in relation to what is happening to the starting and completion rates in durable investment projects. While this influence has been taken account of in the recorded figures of the past, only when the problem is clearly recognized is it likely to be given consideration in a forecast. A rapid rise in inventory investment or in starting durable investment projects will improve the demand picture and lead to self-induced investment as well as to induced consumer demand. Under such circumstances, the forecaster may wisely add to expected investment demand. On the other hand, when investment demand is not increasing as fast as it was when a greater number of investment projects were being started a year or two before, investment demand may be wisely minimized.

The above analysis does not provide a simple mechanical adjustment in developing the second revision of the model. This is because many factors must be taken into consideration; and for doing this, we have not found a satisfactory formula. Each situation must be examined in the light of developments that appear in the picture. For the present, we cannot safely go much beyond a presentation of the kind of problems which arise when the various expenditure streams are to be subjected to readjustment on the basis of relations found to exist between them.

Projection of Income. The forecaster cannot wisely ignore probable levels of the income allocation which balances expenditures on the GNP side of the account. This is partly because the forecast expenditures appear more plausible if the income payments made from them are explained, but more importantly because income-expenditure relations provide important checks.

Table 18–2 shows the change in major income items in the fourth quarter of 1958 and the first quarter of 1959 to balance the expenditure figures shown in Table 18–1. The relationships appearing in that table are inherent in the nature of the national economic accounts. Table 18–2 is set up on the basis of change from the preceding quarter rather than on the basis of the total income level, because change in income is the important question for the forecaster. The expenditure forecasts take on added meaning if the resulting income changes are indicated.

We must by-pass the independent problem of making income forecasts, for that would take us too far afield. Suffice it to say that available methods are perhaps cruder than those employed in making expenditure forecasts.[8] Even though the income magnitudes may often not be forecast explicitly, the expenditure forecasts are continuously checked with the implied incomes. This provides the third and final revision procedure.

TABLE 18–2

INCOME CHANGES WHICH BALANCE EXPENDITURE CHANGES[a]

Figures Show Changes in Billions of Dollars, Seasonally Adjusted, at Annual Rates
Quarter Changes Shown Are in 1958 and 1959

Explanation	Fourth Quarter Change from Third Quarter	First Quarter Change from Fourth Quarter
Wages and salaries...............................	+ 2.8	+ 5.9
Dividends..	− 0.6	+ 0.8
Interest[b]...	+ 0.3	+ 0.2
Rent[b]..	......	+ 0.1
Unincorporated enterprises.........................	+ 0.6	− 0.5
Transfers minus employee contributions[c]..........	− 0.2	− 1.0
Personal Income.................................	+ 2.9	+ 5.5
Less: Personal taxes..........................	+ 0.5	+ 1.1
Disposable Income...............................	+ 2.4	+ 4.6
Personal Income.................................	+ 2.9	+ 5.5
Less: Government interest[d]....................	......	+ 0.2
Transfers.............................	− 0.3	− 0.4
Plus: Corporate profits in excess of dividends....	+ 6.1	+ 1.2
Contributions for social insurance.........	+ 0.2	+ 2.0
Wage accruals[e].........................	+ 1.3	......
National Income................................	+10.8	+ 8.9
Plus: Capital consumption allowance............	+ 0.5	+ 0.8
Indirect business taxes....................	+ 0.8	+ 0.8
Business transfers........................	......	......
Government enterprise surplus, less subsidies	......	+ 0.2
Statistical discrepancy..................	+ 1.0	+ 2.6
Gross National Product..........................	+13.1	+13.3

[a]Expenditures, as included in gross national product, are presented in Table 18–1.
[b]Only nongovernment interest payments to individuals and rent payments to individuals are included.
[c]In our presentation, we have included also "other labor income" in this item.
[d]Net of interest received by governments.
[e]In addition to wage disbursements.

Third Revision of the GNP Model. The relationship of figures on the income side of the account to expenditures completes the patterns to which the forecaster subjects his expenditure estimates. Increase in consumer expenditures for nondurable goods and serv-

---

[8]Some start is provided by Lewis, *op. cit.*, pp. 497–510; Bassie, *op. cit.*, pp. 460–88; and Elmer C. Bratt, *Business Forecasting* (New York: McGraw-Hill Book Co., Inc., 1958), pp. 188–91.

ices can be expected to absorb all or slightly more than the increase in disposable income in recession and a major part of it under more prosperous conditions. If the forecast percentage deviates substantially from the recent record, efforts to justify it will be useful.

Under present conditions, disposable income lies close to 70 per cent of gross national product in prosperity and one or two percentage points higher in recession. Some of the components of the income total can be checked against expenditure figures to develop consistency. As illustrations, consumer expenditures for durable goods bear some relation to the amount of personal saving. Producer equipment expenditures bear some relation to retained corporate profits.

Important relations on the income side can be usefully studied. These include relations between personal taxes and personal income, indirect taxes (much of which represents sales taxes) and personal income, corporate taxes and corporate profits, and the movement of manufacturing wage and salary disbursements in relation to the total of other wage and salary disbursements. Scatter diagrams help to reveal the degree of relation to be expected.

The desirability of placing the results obtained by study of these relationships in an orderly tabular framework to systematize the setting-up of reconciliations required in making the final revision should be emphasized. Care is needed, however, to keep the framework flexible so that the adjustments are founded on an understanding of the forces of change, rather than on a mere formal juggling. Otherwise, we shall have little more than a forcing of assumed changes to meet preconceived relations, which admittedly are not well established. No magic exists whereby uncertainties of the future can be made certain. Mechanical devices should aid in making plausible and flexible assumptions, not in forcing assumptions into a set groove. For these reasons, we do not illustrate a mechanical method of recording the reconciliation of the forecast.

Relating the Model to Expected Price Changes. While we argue that the GNP forecasting model can be operated most effectively if left in terms of actual prices, the sharpening provided by putting it into quantity terms usually leads the forecaster to estimate quantity changes at some stage in the analysis. A basic table for this purpose is that of implicit price deflators. The change in those deflators from the end of 1958 to the first quarter of 1959 is shown in Table 18-3. The price measures are not available for a few of the categories shown in Table 18-1, but sufficient detail is shown for illustrative purposes. The actual price change is very close to the naïve projection of the change from the preceding quarter for the more inclusive measures—gross national product, total government purchases, and total personal consumption. This is because the divergent movements tend to average out in the totals. As a result, price change can ordinarily be projected into the future satisfactorily by a short-trend projection.

There are three cases where this cannot be done: (1) when a turning point is in prospect, (2) when the economy approaches full-capacity operation very quickly, and (3) when anticipations experience rapid shifts. To face the first case, the forecaster must turn to the turning-point model, outlined above. Generalization as to the needed method of analysis in this case is of little avail, and each situation must be faced with consideration given to the strategic forces operating at the time. We can conclude, however, that the price decline is likely to be greater and more regular when the driving force in recession is related to an excessive durable capital/output ratio rather than to inventory correction.

The other two cases point to an acceleration of the price change which has been occurring. Increases in operating rates in several key industries are published information and give a clue to pending shortages. Even more important is rapid shrinkage of unemployment as low levels of unemployment are reached. Public policy may moderate the price change to some extent in these circumstances, but policy similar to that used in the recent past is unlikely to change the prospects greatly. Anticipatory influences may have a greater effect. If private investment projects are being started at a rapid rate, while completions are being achieved at a much lesser rate, anticipations are likely to be very optimistic, with prices advancing rapidly. If the rise in private investment and government expenditure has slackened off substantially, even though it still is at a high rate, prices may level off. An illustration is what happened in 1952 and 1953, following a very rapid upsweep in investment and in government expeditures in the two preceding years. Prices rose rapidly in 1951, but scarcely at all in 1952 and 1953, when investment and government expenditure were advancing much more slowly. The position of the plotted points for these years in Chart 18-2 (on page 432) illustrates the shifting relationship in the expenditure distribution.

Space does not permit further elaboration on the development of a price model. The background material on price forecasting is presented in Chapter 16, and ideas introduced there should bring the problem into better focus. Price forecasting in connection with the GNP model is an application of broader ideas on average prices.

We do not develop tables to show a forecast of deflated output, for the mechanics vary with specific situations which have not been effectively classified into categories which would indicate particular mechanical methods. To obtain the deflated product forecast, having given the price forecast as illustrated in Table 18–3, the price forecast of course is divided into the GNP expenditure forecast. (We may note, however, that a trend projection, as shown in Table 18–3, is unlikely to work near business cycle turning points.)

TABLE 18–3

PRICE FORECASTING: AMOUNT-OF-CHANGE PROJECTION MODEL*

1954 = 100

Explanation	(1) Third Quarter 1958	(2) Fourth Quarter 1958	(3) Fourth Quarter Plus Change	(4) First Quarter 1959	(5 Differ- ence
Price Index for:					
Gross national product	110.7	111.3	111.9	111.8	−0.1
Residential construction	110.8	111.9	113.0	113.6	+0.6
Nonresidential construction	115.9	117.5	119.1	118.6	−0.5
Producer equipment	119.3	119.7	120.1	120.8	+0.7
Exports	103.7	104.3	104.9	105.2	+0.3
Imports	98.4	97.4	96.4	96.6	+0.2
Government purchases	119.0	119.4	119.8	119.7	−0.1
Federal government	119.7	119.9	120.1	119.8	−0.3
State and local government	117.9	118.9	119.9	120.4	−0.5
Personal consumption expenditures	107.1	107.5	107.9	107.9	.....
Durable	105.2	106.0	106.8	106.4	−0.4
Nondurable	105.8	106.0	106.2	106.4	+0.2
Services	109.3	109.7	110.5	110.5	.....

*The information needed for computation of this table is currently provided by the Office of Business Economics of the Department of Commerce, and is published in the *Survey of Current Business.*

Adaptability of the GNP Model to the Use of Any Forecasting Information. It is a mistake to think of the GNP model as technical and obscure. It represents the most direct approach possible to the aggregation of total economic activity. In no sense can it be considered a narrow approach when employed by a forecaster alerted to the use of all pertinent information.

Most of the current information on the economic outlook relates to the major expenditure divisions into which gross national product is divided, or to subdivisions of them, even down to information on individual companies. Information considered in the preceding chapter on foreshadowing statistics provides indications with respect to turning points. Prospective turning points certainly cannot be disregarded in the GNP model. We have suggested that any pertinent information on the turning point should be developed in a turning-point model.

Whatever is high-lighted in the favorable-unfavorable listing can be considered in the GNP model. In fact, the dollar expenditure impact of the factor considered may be developed in some cases. If measurement of expenditure effects is not possible, the principal application of the information will be the light it throws on how current facts should be interpreted. We have pointed out in this chapter many ways in which understanding can be developed by pursuing such interpretations at specific times.

The Need for Reforecasting. Even a short-period forecast must be constantly subject to revision. New conditions may arise which the assumptions could not reveal, or the techniques for implementing the assumptions may have been faulty, or the assumptions employed may be found to have been less plausible than others.

There are two important reasons for making forecasting a continuous process. Its value turns on its dependability, which may be greatly increased if modifications can be made, should the picture change. Planning, which represents the application of forecasts, usually is kept flexible, so that adjustments can be made for unforeseen circumstances. Outdated forecasts poorly match up with planning needs. A warning is needed, however, with respect to insignificant revisions. If conflicting changes cancel each other, or if the revision is minor, release of the information on revision to the planner may be only confusing.

The second reason for keeping the forecast constantly subject to examination is the aid it provides the forecaster in the development of sound methods. The forecaster should never put himself in the position of defending a forecast he would not make today, as has often happened. If he has made mistakes, the sooner he corrects them, the more progress he can make in adapting his procedures.

INDUSTRIAL PRODUCTION MODEL

Although industrial production represents something less than 40 per cent of final expenditures in the economy, it covers most of those expenditures which move sensitively with the business cycle. Less than half of the total value of products included in the Industrial Production Index represent final products (46.75 per cent of the 1957 values, to be exact). The rest of the groups in the Index represent materials.

Covering final products only, the model is illustrated on an abbreviated basis in Table 18-4. Industry divisions in greater detail are available, but not currently published. On the basis shown in Table 18-4, a model can readily be developed from data released monthly in the *Federal Reserve Bulletin*. Separate estimates of the industry detail can be combined to provide a forecast of the over-all indexes by multiplying by the weight column and dividing the sum of the weighted figures so obtained by the total weights.

A method of relating divisional groups to the total of final products included is thus made possible. One of the advantages of the GNP model is thus duplicated. Preference for this or the GNP model turns partly on familiarity with the current situation in the divisional groups represented. Many persons in industry are more familiar with the groups in Table 18-4, although they may be well acquainted with only a few of the industries closely allied with their own businesses. Economists are likely to be more familiar with the group division in the GNP table. As illustrated in column 6 of Table 18-4, the naïve projection tends to develop poorer projections than the GNP projection.

A distinct advantage of the GNP model is that it relates to a comprehensive aggregate. If attention is restricted to the industrial production model, one can never be sure of changes initiating in other parts of the economy. Notably, inventory investment, construction activity, government expenditure, and export activity are not high-lighted.

Possibly, the industrial production model might be used to supplement the GNP model. It is true, of course, that the categories provided in Table 18-4 could be readily employed as further detail in the relevant divisions of the GNP model. On the other hand, the materials component of the Industrial Production Index may provide even more important supplementary information. The materials data are not included in Table 18-4, for we are trying to illustrate a model including final-product relationships which can be aggregated as an alternate to gross national product.

The materials account for more than half of the value of products included in the Industrial Production Index and give information

TABLE 18–4

INDUSTRIAL PRODUCTION FORECASTING MODEL*

Restricted to Final Products, Seasonally Adjusted
1957 = 100

Explanation	(1) Value Weight (1957 Basis)	(2) November-December, 1958	(3) January-February, 1959	(4) Column 3 Plus Change	(5) March-April, 1959	(6) Difference
Final Products Index†	*42.6*	*101*	*102*	*103*	*105*	*+ 2*
Consumer Goods†	*30.4*	*105*	*107*	*109*	*109*	*....*
Automobiles	2.0	101	96	89	106	+17
Automobile parts and allied products	1.3	106	112	118	110	– 8
Appliances	1.3	117	110	103	111	+ 8
TV and home radios	0.5	85	94	103	94	– 9
Furniture and rugs	1.2	110	114	118	116	– 2
Miscellaneous home goods	1.5	105	107	109	109	....
Apparel, including shoes	5.2	108	110	112	116	+ 4
Processed foods	8.1	103	104	105	106	+ 1
Beverages and tobacco	2.3	108	106	104	109	+ 5
Drugs, soaps, and toiletries	2.7	105	107	109	110	+ 1
Newspapers, magazines, and books	1.5	97	103	109	105	– 4
Fuel oil and gasoline	1.2	103	105	107	106	– 1
Electricity	1.6	114	114	114	113	– 1
Equipment	*12.2*	*89*	*91*	*93*	*95*	*+ 2*
Industrial	7.3	86	88	90	91	+ 1
Commercial	2.5	94	96	98	99	+ 1
Freight and passenger	1.8	96	95	94	96	+ 2
Farm	0.6	93	100	107	116	+ 7

*The information as presented here is available in each of the monthly issues of the *Federal Reserve Bulletin*. The weight column makes it possible to combine the component products index to obtain over-all indexes (indicated by italics).

†Excluded are defense equipment and gas because current values were not available at the time represented. The weight factor for defense equipment was 3.46 and for gas 0.69. To obtain an over-all index built up from components, after multiplying by the given weights and adding, division must be made by the particular weight sum, e.g., by 42.6, to get the "final products index." The weights could, of course, be converted to add to 100 per cent, but then they would not conform with published Federal Reserve figures.

not available in the GNP model. A study of the changes shown, therefore, must be of major value in directing attention to what is happening with respect to purchase of materials. The output of materials has risen above the final sale of goods and construction activity in each postwar expansion and fallen below in each postwar contraction. The difference is attributable to a combination of changing inventory investment and changing relative use of materials in the types of output rising most rapidly or falling most rapidly. Much has yet to be learned to segregate the output of materials accounted for by these factors. The development of such information, however, promises to provide powerful tools which may be used in forecasting economic change.[9]

FOR REFLECTION AND ANALYSIS

1. Contrast short-term forecasting depending on a GNP model with the methods of an unfavorable-favorable factors model.
2. Do you think a GNP model should be in current or in deflated prices?
3. What is meant by a turning-point model?
4. What do you think of using inventory anticipations obtained from a survey of businessmen as the revised estimate of inventory change in the GNP model?
5. Why does a naïve model perform poorly at turning points?
6. Explain the idea of building a forecasting model which employs minimum changes.
7. How should the GNP model be related to comparable price changes?
8. What is the use of income projections in a GNP model?
9. What type of information can be co-ordinated in a GNP model?
10. Emphasize the strength and weakness of an industrial production model for short-term forecasting.

---

[9]There are many difficulties—e.g., the degree to which the Federal Reserve Index provides full coverage of materials is unknown. On the other hand, there are many other possible relationships on which divisions of the Index throw light: comparable movements of business equipment and of consumer goods, output and expenditures of consumer goods, and relation of materials production to construction treated separately. See Clayton Gehman, "Output Measures in Economic Analysis," *American Statistical Association Proceedings of the Business and Economic Statistics Section* (Washington, D.C., 1958), pp. 34–47; and "Industrial Production in Current Analysis," a processed paper privately distributed by the Federal Reserve in October, 1960.

Chapter 19

USE OF DYNAMIC

Chapter

ECONOMICS IN SOLVING

19

BUSINESS PROBLEMS

Basically, the problem of any business is (1) to understand what profitable sales can be made and (2) to make adequate provision for handling these sales. These problems are unique with any business. Entrepreneurship appertains to the solution of the multifarious unique problems businesses face.

Forecasting perspective is the principal contribution of dynamic economics to their solution. Forecasting is a major support in understanding what profitable sales will be. Planning for sales is the central problem, however, and forecasting cannot substitute for planning. Rather, forecasting can make planning more logical, more clearcut, and better organized. This is because plans unrelated to an expectation of the level of sales are necessarily vague.

Since the future is uncertain, planning is necessarily an adaptive process. Forecasting cannot eliminate the need for adaptation to an uncertain future, but it can reduce the adaptation required. The planned tolerances are lowered and made less vague. Tighter controls become possible. The budgeting which accompanies developed sales forecasting permits the introduction of a co-ordination and integration of management functions of a new and exciting character. Without eliminating the maintenance of useful flexibility, the forecast can bring into fruition co-operative action toward a common goal which has been made as explicit and plausible as our understanding of dynamic change will permit.

SALES FORECASTING

The core around which the new planning techniques center is sales forecasting. The techniques devised have been principally founded on the operations in the company in which the forecast need became apparent. The usual operation has arisen to serve as a selling aid in the sales department. The most common need recognized has been a criterion against which selling effort could be judged, but in many cases the forecast has been used as a basis for setting selling quotas to be employed as a foundation for paying commissions. The usual method of forecasting for this purpose has pointed to what the salesmen may have uncovered with regard to demand. Aggregating the forecasts made by salesmen is called a "sales force composite method." In recognition of the weaknesses of salesmen in making forecasts, the method has been commonly supplanted by reports co-ordinated by district sales managers or co-ordinated with other forecasting methods, detailed below.

A somewhat more sophisticated method, originally developed principally from sales information, involves estimates of the amount of product which will be absorbed by various industries or involves a classification of purchasers consuming the product, often called "end-use analysis." When published information is available on production of the consuming industries, this analysis has come to be conducted in the central office, and usually has replaced or supplemented the information directly provided from sales offices in the field.

Other methods of central office forecasting have been developed. One derives directly from opinion of the major executives, and is called "jury of executive opinion." It varies from independent sales estimates made by major executives to a co-ordination by the major officers of a flow of information from others.

Usually, "jury of executive opinion" forecasting rests heavily on market analysis for the industry, with major reliance on relationships between sales, inventories, prices, and order data. In some cases, analytical background work is fed to the officers by a forecasting office. Since the major officers of a company necessarily are finally responsible, the most sophisticated forecasting technique could be designated as determined by executive opinion. Whatever methods are employed, the executives, formally or informally, accept or modify the conclusions reached before the forecast is used in planning. Rather more lackadaisically, especially in small companies, the major officers may initiate the market analysis themselves.

To an increasing extent, forecasts of the industry or the industries of which the company forms an integral part provide an important basis for the sales forecast. The industry forecasts are developed by analytical divisions in the central office, sometimes assisted by consultants or associations outside the company. A final step in this analysis involves an estimate of the company's penetration in the total industry market.

To an increasing extent, it has become clear that the outlook for each individual industry is tied in a considerable degree to the condition of the aggregate of all industry. This conclusion could have been developed the other way around—since we know that the business cycle influence permeates most business activity, we could expect that the forecasting of individual industries would be abetted by total-industry forecasting. The development of sales forecasting through company or industry data, however, is readily understandable. As indicated above, forecasting typically arose in subservience of the sales function; and naturally, the specific market was one of the first sources looked to for a forecast.

Furthermore, some types of activity within industry appear to be largely unrelated to general business conditions for an extended time. Aside from agriculture and similar extractive activities, two major situations are now involved: (1) industries related to demand which is growing so rapidly that supply is continuously insufficient, and (2) companies whose sales are predominantly to the government, notably those making defense products. These are readily recognized as special cases.

General business forecasts are often employed by correlating industry data with some over-all aggregate, such as disposable income. Truly, the best relation is seldom a simple correlation because the influence of the total economy on the particular industry usually varies in different phases of the business cycle. Space does not permit delving into the intricacies of the over-all relationships;[1] but it is important to point out that the dependence is involved not only in forecasting, but also in understanding the feeling of helplessness which comes over the business community when over-all influences become preponderant, as at times of rapid inventory runoff in recession.

THE USE OF BUDGETS

The precision of budgets as management tools is greatly sharpened by use of sales forecasts. At a sophisticated level, sales budgets are developed to high-light the influence of sales as opposed to actual production. The part played in current activity of the com-

---

[1]See the author's *Business Forecasting* (New York: McGraw-Hill Book Co., Inc., 1958), pp. 237–87.

pany by inventory building thus comes to be underlined. The forced emphasis on the part of the current movement accounted for by sales helps to clarify the influence of inventory accumulation when it becomes critical. A functioning in which sales are the active factor, with inventory accumulation the inactive one, comes to be recognized as sound, with inventory in the active role recognized as unsound. The sales budget is a management tool and usually is of only limited aid to the public in interpreting the business operation. But management tools are of major significance in improving business performance.

The cash budget similarly is of notable aid in the control of financial needs. The flow of cash funds into and out of the hands of a company is an intricate process and must be organized in an orderly fashion to provide the best results. Involved are not only the payments for supplies and wages and the flow of payments for sales of the company's products, but also a maze of influences involving nonoperating receipts and payments (such as rents), sale or purchase of capital assets, and financing and credit operations. Many small companies have faced insolvency because care was not taken to match cash receipts and cash disbursements at the times at which critical relations would occur.

Only recently have many companies come to economize on cash holdings, so that the excess cash could be placed in temporary investment when holdings were overample and arrangements could be made to obtain seasonal lines of credit when a large cash drain would briefly bring the cash holding below a prudent minimum. The key figure necessary to develop a cash budget is a sales forecast. Payment for wages and materials in the production process accounts for the major part of the cash outflow at most times, and payment for sales the major part of the inflow. These flows are determined by sales.

VISUALIZATION OF INVENTORY NEEDS IN THE SALES BUDGET

Special emphasis should be placed on improved visualization of inventory needs because of the importance of inventory movements at critical times. The idea is that the businessman obtains a sharper visualization of inventory needs and can thus set his inventory requirements with smaller tolerances; and he can change his inventory stocks more confidently and with less hesitation.

In the first place, production needs for inventory are clearly segregated from needs to satisfy shipments made in filling orders. When the border line between production for meeting sales and for maintenance of satisfactory inventory levels is hazy, the tendency is for inventory stocks to drift to undesirable positions. While expenditures are rising rapidly in the business cycle upswing, the tendency is for inventory stocks to fall even though sales are rising, so that at later stages in the business cycle expansion, rises in inventory stocks are accepted with quiescence even though the stocks have become large enough to be unstabilizing. A vigilant check made constantly of desirable inventory levels would be effective in tempering the degree of insufficiency or redundancy which now develops in inventory stocks.

In the second place, a sales forecast which gives clear consideration to the influence of movements in total economic activity will alert the businessman to the induced effects arising from important changes in nonconsumption expenditures, including broad shifts in inventory investment. If the businessman realized that a part of the sales decline to which he is trying to adjust his inventories in recession is caused by the fact that universal declines in inventory investment are reducing final expenditures in the economy, he would be able to explain to himself his difficulty in getting inventories into line even with repeated decisions to cut production schedules. In this connection, we may note that the sales budget procedures so far developed fall short of needed adaptation to *all* of the induced effects to which a manufacturer is subjected.

At critical times, it is important that the manufacturer differentiate between *sales* and *final demand*. As contractionary conditions appear to bring desirable cuts in inventory, reductions are made not only at the manufacturing stage but also at later stages in distribution. Therefore, a large part of the reduction in manufacturing sales is accounted for by cuts in inventory at the wholesale and retail stages of distribution. This is illustrated by final sales in the 1957–58 recession and is shown in Table 19–1. The development of an accounting technique which would correct the sales budget for changes in later distribution stages would further sharpen the visualization of inventory needs. This is especially true in view of the relative importance of inventory stocks in the hands of manufacturers.

The conclusion is that a powerful technique has been made available which not only tightens business decisions to provide a more efficient operation but will substantially improve the businessman's understanding of the economic changes which he faces. For the first time, some hope can be held out that panic proportions may be avoided in inventory runoff occurring in recession. This is because inventory stocks may be kept under better control as the prosperity matures, and the businessman may better understand the feedback on expenditure which is initiated by the inventory runoff he frantically forces to keep in adjustment with declining sales (expenditures).

TABLE 19-1

PRODUCTION AND FINAL SALE IN THE 1957–58 RECESSION*

Illustrated by Durable Goods in the Civilian Economy

Explanation	Third Quarter 1957	Second Quarter 1958
Final sale to civilian economy of final-type durable goods.	$74.0 billion	$56.5 billion
Amount of final sale currently produced..............	$75.0 billion	$50.0 billion

*Department of Commerce income and product data.

LONG-TERM CAPITAL BUDGETS

Capital budgets can be neither very effective nor reasonably consistent in planning unless they are founded on long-term forecasts. The use of durable capital stretches into the long-term future and obviously depends little upon current needs except as these are indicative of future ones. The need for capital in the years ahead is the rationally important question in capital budgets. No stable policy on growth is possible as long as the planning of projects depends on the vacillation of current demand because current demand over short-term fluctuations is dependent upon so many transient factors.

Long-term forecasting inevitably appeals to growth of the total economy. Growth of the total economy rests on increases which will occur in available supply. As explained in Chapter 6, a reasonable basis is available for forecasting the requirements of a full-employment economy, which is in conformity with the growth in total available supply. In the case of individual industries, growth rests on advancing demand, which is not readily bounded until the changes in total supply are known. Thus, budgeting for capital expansion is clarified by working out a relation to changes in aggregate economic conditions.

As contrasted with decisions regarding the initiation of capital projects founded on the current outlook at any given time, long-term capital budgeting has many distinct advantages. Understanding is developed as a long-term plan is evolved. Financing can be simplified because possibilities can be visualized long in advance. More orderly planning and purchasing are possible with the head start provided. Various potentialities can be more thoroughly studied. Less liability of the need for hurried projects to face imminent shortages is likely to be faced. Some cost benefit is available because, with advance understanding of needs, advantage can be taken of times of low cost. When investment plans turn wholly on indications of current demand, plant capacity tends to be completed just as the downturn is occurring, when competitive pressures on capacity are the greatest. When long-term plans are based on growth potentialities, periods of completion should be better distributed.

We should clearly recognize that firms usually cannot afford to delay investment when demand is rising. With long-term budget plans, investment schedules fixed long in advance are unnecessary and, in fact, usually undesirable. The broad plans written into the capital budget can be pared off as the times warrant. Actual capital appropriations can flow through just as flexible a framework as if no long-term plans had been made. Management need not be tied to any greater rigidity than when plans are set out without the background of a long-term budget. The long-term budget provides needed information and desirable continuity without any necessity of holding to a prejudged arbitrary program.

ADAPTATION TO NEW ACTIVITIES OR PRODUCTS

Careful long-term plans aid in adapting strategy on new fields of endeavor. Lines of decreasing profitability are more clearly indicated. Long-term plans provide background for any changes in company structure which might appear challenging at the moment.

Short-term forecasting is also helpful in maintaining perspective in the consideration of changes. Because of the large fluctuations they experience, some activities are high and profitable at the prosperity peak, but low and unprofitable in depression. An understanding of cyclical conditions may make it possible to take advantage of knowledge of this type by the purchase of assets in cyclically depressed areas. If coupled with an analysis of long-term growth potentials, some understanding of the current cyclical conditions should improve the chances of making favorable decisions on questions with respect to reshuffling the company's activity. Perspective is improved for the long run, and short-run variations appear less deceiving.

ADJUSTMENT TO DYNAMIC MOVEMENTS IN THE TOTAL ECONOMY

Whatever improvement can be made in forecasts will aid in bringing company decisions into focus. We have shown above that an important side effect is improvement made possible in company co-ordination and execution. The executives of the company are bound together in a co-operative effort in which the sales forecast is the catalytic agent. Chances are improved that standards of operation will be more uniformly maintained. For instance, differences in standards for approval of the average capital project in recession and under prosperous conditions may be reduced. The needed level of inventory stock may become subjected to rather similar criteria, whatever the general business cycle position may be.

A better understanding of inventory needs and capital requirements, made possible by forecasting, has been shown to emerge from prepared strategies and controls. The developed strategies and controls have other applications. A notable case is dynamic pricing. This means, in essence, pricing on the basis of the potential, rather than the past, market. In such cases as commodities whose cost curve does not decline with rising demand or whose demand has already been saturated, dynamic and traditional pricing may lead to the same results. In other cases the demand may be such that price reductions are not indicated even if great efficiencies are possible with a larger market. A possibility is that buying may—for the time being, at least—be largely on "snob" appeal. The major cases for the application of dynamic pricing are exciting new products which can be produced with improving efficiencies as the demand grows. This is one way that businesses can partially underwrite their own markets.

FOR REFLECTION AND ANALYSIS

1. What is the relation between forecasting and planning?
2. How do forecasts developed at the "grass roots" differ from those evolved in the central office? Are there possibilities of developing a method which will put together the strength of each?
3. What is meant by a sales budget?
4. Why should production need for inventories be segregated from needs to satisfy shipments?

5. How does Table 11-2 (page 221) indicate that businessmen ignore induced effects in planning for inventories?
6. Why would the businessman increase perspective by distinguishing between sales and final demand?
7. Do long-term budget plans imply investment schedules fixed long in advance?
8. How does dynamic pricing help businessmen to underwrite their own markets?

	APPLICATION OF DYNAMIC
Chapter	ECONOMICS TO THE
20	OUTLOOK OF INDIVIDUALS

This chapter deals with economic well-being of the individual and how an understanding of prospective changes in aggregative economic conditions is helpful in this respect. Sole final equity in what happens in the economy is that of individuals—behavior in the economy is important only if consequential to them.

The study of the economic aspects of individual relations has usually related to what we may call "normative" aspects, for considerations have centered on equity. Unquestionably, any individual has a large stake in equitable adjustment between himself and his fellows. He may have an even larger stake in what happens to the total economy.

The criterion of equity relates to how total income is divided among different individuals. The individual's interest in economic behavior relates to stability and total amount of income. Needless to say, individual interests vary widely with respect to the behavior criteria. Two extremes may be noted if the existence of many in-between positions are recognized. At one limit, income is highly stable, employment is assured, and the rate of pay is considered satisfactory. This may be illustrated by some individuals in government service. At the other limit, we find highly unstable income and rates of pay which are scarcely satisfactory, or satisfactory only because of future promise. Illustrations are many types of day laborers or persons initially entering the labor force in cyclically unstable industries.

Personal interests at the two extremes are almost opposite. For the first extreme, price inflation would be very disruptive, but there is little to worry about with respect to the growth or stability of total income. For the other, price inflation is likely to be favorable, and improved stability and growth in the total economy would be of vital importance. With many gradations of interests, the difficulty of generalizing on the effects of total economic activity on individuals is clear. Something could be done with respect to classifying by individual types the differences in impact of possible economic changes. Such a classification would be complicated and would require many assumptions.

CHART 20–1

RISE IN AVERAGE DISPOSABLE INCOME AND WAGE AND SALARY INCOME

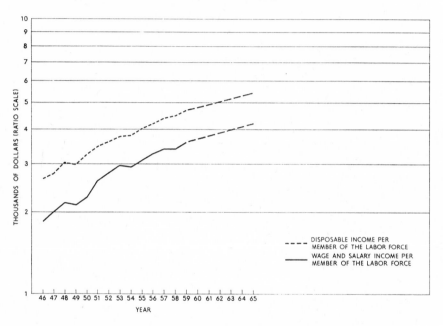

Source: Table 20–1.

For our purposes, it is perhaps more effective to illustrate how one might relate his own situation to changes in the total economy. Chart 20–1 shows the changes in wages and salaries per member of the labor force and disposable income per member of the labor force since 1946, with projections to 1965. Largely because of increased unemployment, the wage and salary ratio declined in each recession, and the disposable income ratio declined in the first two. Any individual may relate his disposable income experience to this picture. Not only his comparable income level but the comparable fluctuations are worth noting. If no disemployment has been experienced, the contrast may be relatively favorable, with possibly no declines occurring in recessions. Some indication is given in Table 20–1 comparing the plotted figures with average annual earnings per employee in banking. The level is almost the same as the total per capita disposable income, but no declines occur in recessions because division is by employed persons rather than by the labor force. The level is relatively favorable, since there is a disproportionate number of salaried employees in banking. For a few individuals, whose disposable income is critically dependent upon profits, disposable income may drop to or below the wage or salary level in recession.

TABLE 20–1

AGGREGATIVE AND INDIVIDUAL-INDUSTRY PER CAPITA CHANGES IN INCOME*

(In Thousands of Current Dollars)

Year	(1) Wages and Salaries per Member of Labor Force	(2) Disposable Income per Member of Labor Force	(3) Wages and Salaries per Full-Time Employee in Banking
1946.......	1.83	2.63	2.65
1947.......	2.00	2.75	2.86
1948.......	2.15	3.01	3.04
1949.......	2.11	2.98	3.17
1950.......	2.26	3.21	3.34
1951.......	2.59	3.45	3.46
1952.......	2.77	3.58	3.60
1953.......	2.94	3.75	3.73
1954.......	2.90	3.79	3.85
1955.......	3.06	3.98	3.97
1956.......	3.23	4.16	4.15
1957.......	3.37	4.36	4.31
1958.......	3.36	4.44	4.48
1959.......	3.59	4.65	4.67
1965.......	4.20†	5.37†	5.46†

Source: Department of Commerce income and product data.
*Note should be taken of the difference in aggregates represented in the three columns of the table. In the first column, only wage and salary disbursements, which usually represent less than 70 per cent of personal income, are included; in the second column, disposable income, which usually represents less than 90 per cent of personal income, is included; and in column 3, the denominator of the ratio covers only working persons, and this partly accounts for its relatively high level.
†The assumptions in the 1965 projections are a 2.5 per cent increase per year in productivity, a reduction in the average work week from 40 to 37 hours per week, and a 9 per cent increase in average prices from 1959 to 1965. Without the price increase the 1965 projections would be, respectively, 3.85, 4.93, and 5.01.

INCREASING STABILITY OF INCOME

Aside from the possibility that the business cycle movement may have been dampened since the war, there are two groups of forces which have made the income of workers increasingly stable: (1) unemployment insurance and graduated income taxes, and (2) a structural shift to an increasing proportion of salaried workers.

The government has increased the stability of disposable income by varying the proportionate tax directly with the level of income and by providing partial compensation if and when involuntary unemployment occurs. The graduated income tax cuts down on the relative amount of disposable income the individual can retain if his personal income rises under prosperous conditions, and it increases the relative amount retained if his personal income falls in recession. Unemployment compensation works only as a partial offset for loss of income when he is disemployed.

These income-stabilizing influences are not only effective in shifts over the business cycle. Some individuals experience a reduction in personal income even in years of increasing prosperity, and they find reduced tax rates a partial offset. Unemployment insurance benefits amounted to $1.4 billion in the prosperous year 1956. Most individuals, however, find that tax rates are lower in depressed years and that risk of unemployment increases. For instance, personal taxes represented 12.2 per cent of total personal income in 1957, but only 11.9 per cent in 1958. Unemployment benefits doubled, rising from $1.8 billion in 1957 to $3.9 billion in 1958.

Salaried workers represent an increasing proportion of the total, especially since the war. The number of "white-collar" workers has increased a third, while the number of manual workers has remained stationary. Since salaried workers are less subject to disemployment, depression layoffs now are generally less of a worry for individuals. Of course, this is no help for those who remain day laborers, but it is an important item for individuals to consider in adjusting themselves to the shifting economy. The individual may find it desirable to train for a salaried position, rather than to move passively into the day-laborer class. The trend away from day laborers can be expected to continue, with increasing proportions of the labor force in the skilled and "white-collar" classifications.

ADVANCING STANDARDS OF LIVING

Most individuals experience rising income in the first half or so of adult life and, after the zenith is reached, some decline in financial responsibility. While this is an important consideration with respect to any individual's economic planning, it has little to do with his relation to changing aggregative economic conditions. Unless he lives in an unprogressive economy, a relatively steady advance in the standard of living is superimposed on the life cycle of income. If we think of a "generation" as twenty years, the way things are now moving, the next generation will consume a third more at the same age bracket. This means that an individual now entering adult life should expect to reach at his zenith, not the income of colleagues twenty years his senior, but a third more. Most individuals are likely to feel that terms such as these are overoptimistic. But the advance is indicated by growth of our economy.

The individual may feel guilty if he plans to change his consumption habits to conform to so high an income level. If he can expect to experience normal promotion, however, only planning for so great an advance is realistic. Planning by indivduals for future expenditure levels indicated by the natural growth of our economy not only would make for a better lifetime distribution of potential living standards, but would tend to dispel the fallacious conclusion that we live in an economy of plenty. This is because the increasing demand which higher growth potentials make possible would be more readily visualized. The demand which new generations will evidence would influence expenditure patterns more promptly.

There is a possible catch to all of this. If war expenditures greatly increase, much less would be available for advancing the standards of individuals. This is not necessarily the outcome of large increases in government expenditures in general. Very possibly, the advancing standards we most desire could best be met by the government providing a substantially increased part in services, recreation facilities, and other public works. Those persons most shocked by this proposal should feel the greatest need to plan individually how they themselves will, in their lifetimes, spend the great increase in income which they can confidently look forward to.

A note on the methodology used in developing the growth conclusion is in order. Forecasts for as long as twenty years should be avoided whenever feasible, but the period is convenient for individuals who may wish to think in terms of the income levels they can expect to attain. The one-third increase in standards of living postulates an average yearly rise of 2.5 per cent in productivity and a reduction of 20 per cent in hours of work during the twenty years. If working hours were not to decline at all, the increase in standard of living would approximate two thirds instead of one third.

PROVISION FOR PERSONAL CONTINGENCIES

Greater provision is being made on a comprehensive basis than ever before to meet the cost of possible needs for expenses of medical care and of old age, at least on standards which would appear acceptable to us. These include systems of insuring for a major part of hospitalization and unusual medical expenses as well as automatic old-age annuity programs. Most of the health programs are private but co-operative in nature and have come to be taken for granted by most employees. The systems can be expected to undergo further expansion, especially in taking care of the expense of long illness. The annuity programs include the comprehensive government Old Age and Survivors' Insurance program and mushrooming programs of employer contributions to pension funds.

These programs, and further expansion of them to be expected in the near future, involve a major change in individual responsibilities. To an almost vanishing extent is the indivdual expected to have to provide for health and retirement expenses out of his "take-home" pay. He is relieved of technicalities involved in estimating probable needs for important nonrecurrent expenses and for old age. He can more wholeheartedly devote his attention to his job, his avocations, and his chosen leisure activities.

EFFECT OF INFLATION ON INDIVIDUALS

Rising prices for commodities and services are important to individuals, both in relation to current activities and in relation to savings. In these connections, there is some divergence of individual interests. As every businessman recognizes with respect to the products he sells, rising prices are taken to represent strong demand conditions. Any worker who is particularly exposed to unemployment or to reduced employment when aggregate demand lies well under full-employment requirements and begins to fall would find his short-run interest to favor rising prices. As outlined above, the description relates particularly to the day laborers, but they represent a declining proportion in the labor force.

On the other hand, individuals whose rate of pay changes slowly, if at all, are hurt by rising prices. In fact, most of those who are already employed will not receive wage increases immediately, so that any price increase is injurious, at least to a minor extent. Also, those persons whose income depends substantially on the level of profits will no doubt obtain immediate benefits from price increases, but may not on the average over a longer period. If prices advance too rapidly, a later reaction may more than wipe out all of the temporary increase. If the price increase is in reaction to past or anticipated rises in costs, even temporary price increases may be small or nonexistent. Enterprisers usually are opposed to over-all advances in commodity prices, which would indicate they do not believe them to be basically favorable to higher profits.

Those persons who receive rent income on realty or interest income on debt securities most certainly stand to lose from inflation. The amount of funds received increases slowly or not at all, while the purchasing power of the dollars in which they are paid declines.

A general decline in commodity prices will be helpful to rent and interest recipients and to employees with a fixed, assured income, at least for a limited time. If the decline should go far enough, property may be vacated, or interest may not be paid because of liquidation. For all other income receivers, declining prices are unfavorable.[1]

In all of this analysis, we have taken price change as given, in order to trace the direct effects on individuals. No pretense has been made of examining the forces governing the behavior of prices or of evaluating measures which might be taken to make prices behave differently than they do now. Nor have we examined theoretical interrelations between price variation and physical activity movements, because that would be out of place in this chapter.

THE PINCH OF FORCED SAVING

Rising prices may pinch off expenditure for those persons whose income does not increase. If they continue to receive no more than the same amount of dollar income, real income will have declined. The income groups which suffer a loss in real income when prices rise may be forced to reduce consumption. In no meaningful sense can these individuals be said to increase their savings, forced or otherwise. Rather, they likely will be forced to reduce their savings, perhaps to the vanishing point. In a social sense, however, if resources are bid away from consumers by investment spending, we might say that savings are forced involuntarily out of the hands of income recipients whose pay rate does not increase. This phe-

---

[1]Professor G. L. Bach of Carnegie Institute of Technology has shown that, in spite of a doubling of the consumer price index from 1939 to 1952, the proportion of national income going to compensation of employees actually rose, that going to unincorporated business ended up at about the same proportion, and corporate profits before taxes just about returned to the 1939 proportion. Other factors than inflation accounted for the stability. However, by more minor classifications, such as we have considered, inflation tended to be much more overriding. See G. L. Bach, *Inflation: A Study in Economics, Ethics, and Politics* (Providence, R.I.: Brown University Press, 1958), pp. 23–26; and the background study by G. L. Bach and Albert Ando, "The Redistributitional Effects of Inflation," *Review of Economics and Statistics*, February, 1957.

nomenon may arise when resource capacity is fully engaged or when expenditures rise too fast to absorb enough unused resources to provide for the advance. "Forced saving" does not convey a legal title to anyone.

PLANNING A SAVINGS PROGRAM

Individuals in the United States, on the average, save in the order of 7 per cent of their disposable income, usually slightly less in a recession and slightly more in an expansion. Almost all of the saving comes from families (spending units) in the top 20 per cent bracket of income. Much positive saving does occur in lower income brackets, but it is offset by negative saving by other families in the same brackets. Some negative saving occurs even among top incomes, and the Michigan Survey Research Center estimated that less than half of the family units receiving the top fifth of the country's income had positive saving in 1946.

Although most of the individuals who save are in the high income groups, there are enough exceptions that analysis of savings programs should not be confined to those groups. Furthermore, for older persons who no longer work, a savings program is of vital importance, even though negative saving occurs. Their income depends on "accumulated" savings, i.e., their ownership of assets.

The basic saving made by almost any individual is "contractual," predetermined by agreements already made, including part of the payment on ordinary life insurance or on house mortgages or on instalment credit. Also, there are old-age annuity programs, including payments regularly made into Social Security. Bond savings by payroll deductions or payments made on Christmas savings clubs are essentially contractual. The relative amounts involved vary from individual to individual; but for the majority of individuals, keeping expenditure down to meet the requirements is usually difficult. When income is rising rapidly, most individuals will have some funds left over for discretionary saving, because contractual savings are not likely to rise similarly, at least not immediately. Some individuals regularly provide discretionary savings, especially many of those in the higher income brackets.

The largest part of discretionary saving goes into liquid assets, including increases in deposit accounts. Most of the savings currently made by those who provide discretionary savings only because of a quick rise in income fall in this category. Later, the deposit accounts may be drawn down as the individual makes a selection of securities or property which will provide some return on his investment. The largest category of contractual saving is monthly amortization payments on mortgages by home owners.

A savings plan is particularly needed by those individuals who have discretionary saving to use in buying assets. Something also is to be gained by individuals whose regular saving has all been contractual. For instance, a re-examination of the types of insurance carried may be useful. The savings feature incorporated in some types of life insurance is of a highly conservative type; and if related insurance has risen to large figures, the individual may find that part of the saving involved could better flow into securities carrying a greater risk but providing opportunity for profit from appreciation.

Reasons for saving are an individual matter, but any person would find it profitable to ask himself what his savings are for. The common reasons for discretionary savings are to provide for emergencies or particular future needs, such as expenses of college education for the children; to lay the basis for a higher living standard at a later date; or to build up an estate for heirs (possibly to assure family control of certain assets). Each individual must decide what the reasons are.

In a savings program, various types of assets are chosen. The major features may be classified as follows: (1) safety of principal, (2) rate of return, and (3) potential capital gains or losses involved. Various types of assets can be classified to show the extent to which they excel in these and other features, such as danger of illiquidity. For instance, currency as an asset is entirely safe, and there is no danger of illiquidity; but no return is available from holding it, and, measured in current dollars, no capital gains or losses can occur. Other assets, such as life insurance, savings bonds, bank savings accounts, mortgage securities, corporate bonds, common stocks, private businesses, or real estate can be similarly classified.[2] All of these relations between types of assets and the features of these assets should be tailored by the individual to the reasons for which he is saving. On reflection, most of the features desirable for particular savings programs will be obvious.

For the most effective program a still finer classification is desirable. For instance, the individual needs to decide on the type of common stock investment which is most adaptable to his needs.

---

[2]This subject is simply developed by Sherman J. Maisel, *Fluctuations, Growth, and Forecasting: The Principles of Dynamic Economics* (New York: John Wiley & Sons, Inc., 1957), pp. 529–33.

Some stocks have great danger of illiquidity compared to the majority, some pay a low rate of return (in terms of dividends), and some offer unusual appreciation possibilities. The features are varied, and the individual must choose between them. One possibility is the use of professional management of savings funds if the individual is able to generate a sizable amount of savings. For most individuals the best plan is to invest in "mutual funds," which provide professional investment of small individual savings.

A major problem in a savings program is satisfactory diversification. Safety lies in not "putting all of the eggs in one basket." Diversification is very difficult for small investors. They have such small amounts available for investment that wide diversification is impractical because of brokerage fees and time required to develop a program. Their best bet in this respect is provided by mutual funds. For others, either a careful study is required, or professional management should be sought in making investment choices.

ADVANTAGES TO BE DERIVED FROM A KNOWLEDGE OF ECONOMIC CHANGE

Finally, we should round out this chapter with an explicit statement of the advantage an individual may derive from a knowledge of economic change. This relates to his investment program, his expenditure plans, his understanding of the standard of living he enjoys, and the potential improvement which can be made in his public choices.

Knowledge of cyclical fluctuations offers a substantial advantage in developing a program of security purchases. This relates particularly to common stocks, for their prices vary greatly between the upper phases of expansion and the trough of contraction. Knowledge of cyclical fluctuations does not lend major assistance in choosing the *right* stocks to buy in order that appreciation possibilities may be maximized; this problem is discussed briefly below in connection with advantages to be derived from a knowledge of growth prospects. Furthermore, advantage of the variation in common stock prices can be taken only after careful scrutiny. The fact that stock prices usually lead change in business activity over the business cycle means that the successful investor must take early action. He needs some understanding of prospects as well as of the current situation.

Investment in equities is particularly advantageous in a growing economy. An uncommonly large number of profitable opportunities are available. Implicitly, we are assuming that on the whole, prices are likely to be slanting upward; this is because of the optimistic climate that accompanies such a situation. If, instead, prices are in a deflationary trend, debt securities may be more attractive.

We must remember that a growing economy is comprised not only of an unusually large number of promising securities but also of an unusually large number of unpromising ones. This is because the new is replacing the old. Many companies will not keep up, and several cannot, because of the peculiar inflexibility of their capital plant, which may be tied to products with a fading demand (but note the surprising adaptability of some companies to the sale of products where the demand has been growing, as illustrated by anthracite coal companies; sometimes, tax profitability of loss carryover has played a part in adaptation to innovative possibilities).

Mere knowledge that the total economy is growing offers only modest, if any, advantages to the investor. Any preponderant advantage necessitates understanding of shifting structures involved within the over-all growth. The dynamic changes must be differentiated from the relatively static or decadent. This is a large order and involves a considerable understanding of differentiated growth in individual industries. But even such an understanding is not enough to provide the basis for truly successful investments. New companies mushroom in the growing industries, as described by innovation theory (see Chapter 7). Some will be successful, and some will not. Furthermore, the growing industries frequently follow a tortuous path in their early development stages; witness, for instance, the movement of uranium stocks in the fifties. Adequate diversification, however, may offset a large part of the losses which accrue from owning stocks involved in these faltering developments.

Individuals can profit significantly by establishing flexibility in expenditure plans, especially in relation to durable goods. The prices of such goods are advantageous in special sales in recessionary periods. Achieved savings depend not only on an understanding of the occurrence of a recession but as well on the time of its probable continuance. Also, little will be gained if the individual is deceived into buying at lower prices which represent no more than inferior quality.

Some potentialities are offered in buying durable goods in the light of an understanding of long-term inflationary developments. These can be illustrated by the profitability of buying residential properties in many communities prior to World War II. The possible advantages cannot be denied. Nevertheless, major prospective difficulties must not be ignored. Aside from the difficulties of forecasting inflationary changes in the light of our limited understanding at the present time, consideration must be given to style and technological developments. The newspapers frequently report stories of persons who buy automobiles years in advance of actual use. It is hard to believe that such purchases prove to be economical. To a lesser degree, the same may be said of the purchase of residential properties. If technological changes in the building of houses should accelerate in the future, the advantages of price advances attained in the past may present an illusory picture.

Advantages in planning living standards over the lifetime cycle are noted earlier in the chapter. The application at that point is made in very general terms. Perhaps the gain would be greater if considerations were more specific. For instance, an individual might take into account the growth of his company and industry in relation to the aggregate economy. This would involve the working-out of forecasts more specific than those of total industry.

In planning his standard of living, the individual may gain a great deal by evaluating the economic hazards he faces. His saving and expenditure plans may be made with much greater assurance if he comes to understand what the *changing* pattern of public or company provision for personal contingencies comes to. Changing programs of this kind are briefly noted earlier in the chapter. The traditional pattern of saving-expenditure division of income after allowance has been made for contractual saving may be hopelessly outdated.

Lastly, we may note the contribution the individual makes to public welfare by having attained an intelligent assessment of economic issues. Public participation in economic affairs is assuredly increasing. Even for his own good, the individual can well afford to become informed on economic issues so that he may wisely participate in public choices. In our democratic society, his choice counts as much as that of any other person. For instance, he must help decide on the part fiscal policy or the avoidance of inflation (taken up in Part Five) should play in public decisions. In the aggregate, such choices will be determining forces on the stability of his job, the effectiveness of his savings, and the development of his standard of living.

Not only will the individual himself profit by applying an understanding of economic change in the management of his affairs, but a general improvement along this line will make for more rational behavior. For instance, a vital part of the Keynesian argument on secular stagnation related to "baking cakes in order not eat them." Consumer education would help in encouraging the individual to take action which is in the interest of the economy as a whole, because this would be in his interest also. Particularly, the level of the consumption function line would come to be more rationally determined by the consumer's understanding of the worth of investment which he might come to own with his savings. The simple way by which this development might be expected to arise is outlined in the preceding paragraphs. Notably, if the individual saw that promise for investment was indeed limited, he would save less and spend more, or vice versa. We do not expect miracles to happen, but this is the direction to which a wider understanding of economic change points.

THE INDIVIDUAL'S INTEREST IN PEACE

We would be remiss in summarizing the individual's relation to aggregative influences if we failed to note the tremendous stake he has in the maintenance of peace. The disturbance to the economic system arising from all-out war of the type which has developed in the world pervades all aspects of the individual's life. No definitive conclusions are possible if one tries to speculate on what would have happened if the two world wars could have been avoided; but needless to say, the effect on individuals would have been fundamentally different. For instance, there is no reason to believe that inflationary periods like those following the wars would have been experienced.

The impact of any future world war can be expected to be far greater than any in the past. Much of what we have said about the influence of total economic change on the individual is drab compared with what would have to be said if we were to assume another world war. The individual's concern in preventing such a war is so uniform throughout the world that his failure to give more thought to it is a tragedy. In totalitarian and democratic governments alike the psychological reaction of the individual is highly respected. While concern of war transcends economic considerations, nevertheless it represents the most devastating aggregative economic effect with which the individual must be concerned.

FOR REFLECTION AND ANALYSIS

1. Why is an analysis of the aggregate economy important with respect to the outlook of individuals?
2. Why has the income of individuals become increasingly stable?
3. Should an individual plan his expenditures years in advance?
4. What is the effect of inflation on individuals?
5. Outline the reasons why a savings program is desirable.

SELECTED READINGS FOR PART FOUR

BASSIE, V. LEWIS. *Economic Forecasting.* New York: McGraw-Hill Book Co., Inc., 1958.
    A comprehensive development on short-term aggregative economic forecasting.

BOWMAN, MARY JEAN (ed.). *Expectations, Uncertainty, and Business Behavior.* New York: Social Science Research Council, 1958.
    Papers delivered at a conference on anticipations. They are highly stimulating; and after careful editing, they provide insights even for the nonexpert.

BRATT, ELMER C. *Business Forecasting.* New York: McGraw-Hill Book Co., Inc., 1958.
    A handbook on methodology and applications of both short-term and long-term economic and business forecasting.

BROWN, ROBERT G. *Statistical Forecasting for Inventory Control.* New York: McGraw-Hill Book Co., Inc., 1959.
    Carries the Magee study listed below a step further into forecasting models.

BUREAU OF THE BUDGET, OFFICE OF STATISTICAL STANDARDS. *An Appraisal of OBE-SEC Estimates of Plant and Equipment Expenditures, 1947–1958.* Statistical Evaluation Report No. 1. Washington, D.C., October, 1959.
    An objective evaluation of the very important government survey on plant and equipment anticipations.

DUESENBERRY, JAMES S. *Business Cycles and Economic Growth.* New York: McGraw-Hill Book Co., Inc., 1958.
    Although the book is tough going for the nonexpert, it lays an important groundwork for generalizations on average prices.

GRAHAM, BENJAMIN. *The Intelligent Investor.* 2d rev. ed. New York: Harper & Bros., 1959.
    Discusses approaches to investment, security selection, and a famous "central-value" method of buying and selling securities.

LEWIS, JOHN P. *Business Conditions Analysis.* New York: McGraw-Hill Book Co., Inc., 1959.
    A comprehensive analysis of short-term economic forecasting with an analytical development of responsible forces.

MAGEE, JOHN F. *Production Planning and Inventory Control.* New York: McGraw-Hill Book Co., Inc., 1958.

Helps to visualize the way inventory investment influences short-term fluctuations.

MAISEL, SHERMAN J. *Fluctuations, Growth, and Forecasting: The Principles of Dynamic Economics.* New York: John Wiley & Sons, Inc., 1957.

Includes practical applications on decisions of businesses and persons.

NATIONAL BUREAU OF ECONOMIC RESEARCH, INC., COMMITTEE FOR THE REVIEW OF THE NATIONAL ACCOUNTS. *The National Economic Accounts of the United States.* Washington, D.C.: U.S. Government Printing Office, 1958.

The most penetrating study available on needed national economic accounts.

————, CONFERENCE OF. *Short-Term Economic Forecasting: Studies in Income and Wealth,* Vol. XVII. Princeton: Princeton University Press, 1955.

Although somewhat out of date, the papers in this volume still throw useful light on short-term forecasting.

————, CONFERENCE OF THE UNIVERSITIES–NATIONAL BUREAU COMMITTEE FOR ECONOMIC RESEARCH. *The Quality and Economic Significance of Anticipations Data.* Princeton: Princeton University Press, 1960.

Useful papers on forecasts and expectations.

TERBORGH, GEORGE. *Business Investment Policy: A MAPI Study and Manual.* Washington, D.C.: Machinery and Allied Products Institute, 1958.

A practical guide which has had some influence on decisions regarding modernization investment.

PART FIVE

Problem of Maintaining Reasonable Stability

Chapter 21   STABILIZATION GOALS

    The plan of centering attention on behavior and behavior patterns, so far followed in this book, must now be forsworn. Stabilizing policy, by its very nature, implies the focusing of attention on efforts to change the course of events rather than merely on understanding that course. The position here is to recognize what we know about the unstable behavior of aggregative activity and ask ourselves what we can do about it.

GOVERNMENT PROGRAMS

    We are looking for methods of countering undesirable variation in aggregative activity. In this connection, we shall limit our attention to those measures which are under the aegis of responsible governmental authority. Earlier chapters have given some consideration to the stabilizing potentialities of better long-term forecasting, improved inventory control, and dynamic pricing, as these procedures are developing in private companies.[1] Although aids in stabilizing activity may flow from developed procedure along the indicated lines, they are best analyzed as a part of changing behavior in the private economy. Companies engage in them because it is in their own interest to do so; therefore, they may not be considered purely from the point of view of tendencies to add to stability. Furthermore, the guidance of stabilizing measures should be by responsible authority. Otherwise, the accusation of fascism may be

---

[1]Further consideration of the stabilizing possibilities of investment decisions will be found in National Bureau of Economic Research, Conference of the Universities–National Bureau Committee on Economic Research, *Regularization of Business Investment* (Princeton: Princeton University Press, 1954). Two types of accounting reforms proposed by some students because of expected stabilizing effects are reviewed in the third edition of this book (Homewood, Ill.: Richard D. Irwin, Inc., 1948), pp. 479–82.

warranted. As noted in Chapter 24, gains may be made when private companies co-operate in national programs to improve stability.

Government programs to provide greater stability relate principally to fiscal and monetary measures. Fiscal measures represent induced variation in taxes and/or government spending in order to counter fluctuations in total expenditures in the economy. Monetary measures represent changes made in cost and/or supply of credit, and possibly in other credit arrangements, which are expected to exert an influence on total expenditures in the economy.

EMPHASIS ON GOALS

For a clear visualization of government stabilization programs the goals implicitly assumed must be identified. A clear recognition of what the goals are is certain to lead to value judgments as to their relative importance. These judgments must be tempered, however, by recognizing that there is a substantial conflict between them. The areas of conflict are analyzed in the following section.

Stabilization goals relate to the inducement of changes in total expenditure in the economy. There are two major reasons for wishing to change total expenditure. One is to raise physical activity so as to provide fuller employment when resources remain idle to an extent thought excessive. Countering involuntary idleness is thought desirable both because of the hardship placed on unemployed persons and because of the deprivation of product which otherwise would be available. The other reason for wishing to change total expenditure is to prevent or moderate commodity price increases, especially when resources are quite fully employed.

The goals set for stabilization policy, therefore, are principally the reduction of unemployment and the avoidance of inflation. More positively, the goal is sometimes said to be the provision of stable growth. Stable growth may be considered unsatisfactory, however, if it is at a level which leaves unemployment larger than considered necessary.

For that reason, emphasis has recently shifted to maximizing economic growth. That goal has come into particular prominence because of the arms race in the world. If growth could be speeded up, an increase in military expenditures would be less onerous. Our growth has often been looked on as unsatisfactory when posited against higher rates in other countries whose military establishments have been advancing rapidly and which are often characterized as potential enemies.

Although questions have been raised as to whether the need is not merely to shift a larger amount of resources to public use, the preponderant opinion would appear to be that growth maximization is a highly important goal. The fact is, however, that the desirability of one goal cannot be stated in isolation from the consideration of other goals. This is because goals conflict with each other.

Few persons would accept any one stabilization goal, whatever the precise meaning may be, to transcend all other goals. Seldom, if ever, may a neat statement be made of the extent to which other goals must be given precedence; but many are kept in mind, such as equity among individuals, desirable allocation of resources, efficiency and continuity of governmental operation, national defense, maintenance of essential services, etc. The extent of conflict between stabilization and other goals is not readily summarized, but possible clashes may be visualized. For instance, a public works project might be started to counter inactivity in a recession; but before completion, it might be found to add unduly to expenditures in a prosperous economy. Interruption of the project might be tantamount to destroying much of the work already finished.

The emphasis on one goal or another is a value judgment. Value judgments cannot be uniquely reached by pursuit of economic analysis. Any citizen is entitled to formulate his own. It is improper for the economist or any other professional to dictate on value judgments. In our form of democratic government the majority opinion prevails.

CONFLICT OF GOALS

Goals will be visualized most clearly if those for the long run are distinguished from those for the short run. This is because the exigencies of the short run bring changes which most persons would agree to be undesirable if continued indefinitely. Let us turn first to the short-run problems.

In the short run, we face what has been called the "unemployment-inflation dilemma." If conditions are rendered inflationary enough, full employment will be achieved. This is partly because, if no holds are barred, purchasing power can be made sufficient to absorb a volume of output pressing on available resources. Inasmuch as we are assuming that the provision of purchasing power has been achieved by indirect controls (by shotgun measures), purchasing power will be in excess supply in some sectors of the economy, but may be adequate on average to absorb available resources. Furthermore, if any doubt remains as to the use of buying power to a sufficient extent to employ all resources, the development of anticipatory influences should dissipate it. If price rises are great enough, the inducement to convert money funds into consumption goods or asset ownership is irresistible.

On the other hand, inflation can unquestionably be avoided by keeping demand low enough that the supply of resources greatly overbalances market demand. Under these conditions, competition would keep prices from rising; and in view of the difficulty faced in making a precise adjustment, necessary tolerances would no doubt force a decline in prices. The level of activity which would avoid change in average prices is unknown, but many of us believe that reasonably safe outside limits can be set. We have suggested that labor unemployment of 10 per cent or more will usually make average prices fall and of 5 per cent or less make them rise.

Such absolutes are unsatisfactory. The inflationary choice holds the economy at urgent demand levels. The noninflationary choice holds it at depressed demand levels. While limits are established, these propositions fall far short of satisfactory goals.

To provide an approach to more realistic goals, knowledge of behavior must be taken into consideration. We must recognize, in the first place, that some increase in average prices is usually unavoidable under satisfactory business cycle expansions. Historically, with few exceptions, average prices have risen in expansion. Furthermore, average prices should rise in accordance with the logic of the situation. In an economy growing as rapidly as ours, the dominant influence will be areas of increasing demand. In some cases, like new consumer durable goods, the tendency may well be for prices to fall with the achievement of greater efficiencies as large-scale markets materialize. More frequently, the rising demand is matched with some price increase. This serves to draw resources into the growing industries. The rising prices lead to added investment demand for facilities in the growing areas. In summary, price flexibility is essential to permit effective reshuffling of resources in a competitive economy. With a rapid upsweep in demand, which is required in a business cycle expansion in our economy, the areas drawing resources predominate; therefore, a general tendency for price advances is to be expected.

If we tried to prevent these price increases by designed economic control, it is reasonable to believe that recovery would be impeded. Probably, most persons would agree that we do not wish to slow down the rate of recovery in expansions, at least until late, high-prosperity stages are reached. Except as the accompaniment of major increases in demand generated by war, the rise in wholesale prices in business cycle expansion seldom has exceeded 5 per cent per year. It was 4 per cent in 1923, slightly over 5 per cent in 1925, and less than 2 per cent in 1928. The only relevant postwar year is 1956, when the increase was 3 per cent (all earlier recoveries were obscured by war effects).[2] Uniformly, prices rose less earlier in recovery, e.g., about .5 per cent in 1954, and less than the maximum rate in the later part of almost every recovery. The smaller rise early in recovery is due to less full use of resources and late in recovery to the completion of new facilities and added efficiencies in the use of labor in the new capacity rapidly being put into use.[3]

Once reasonably full recovery has been achieved, price increases tend to be snubbed. This is not generally thought to be very expensive in loss of employment, for rising demand at that stage is drawing against only small additional resources. Control agencies are likely to proceed cautiously, however, for they may be fearful of hurrying a downturn.

Prices have usually begun to decline near the downturn. This is first accounted for by stepped-up additions to capacity and later by fading demand. With a few exceptions—notably in 1958—wholesale prices have followed this pattern. While the price declines may not have been great enough fully to offset the increases in expansion phases, they were usually great enough to allay widespread fears of secular inflation.

PRICE BEHAVIOR IN THE 1957-58 RECESSION

The simplest way to face the current fear of secular inflation is to review briefly the 1958 case. Actually, wholesale prices did level off and decline slightly after the downturn in mid-1957, but they rose by the time of the upturn in April, 1958. Thereafter, they remained level for two years. The rise which occurred during the

---

[2]Attention may be called to 1959, although it also scarcely represents a situation comparable to most earlier recoveries because earlier than usual measures were taken to tighten credit. Average wholesale prices did not rise perceptibly over 1958 (but excluding farm products, they rose nearly 2 per cent), although the 1958 average was nearly 1.5 per cent over 1958.

[3]Emphasis must be placed on the selective influence. Over-all, the advance in output per man-hour is slowing down in late recovery because there is no longer a shift to durable product industries with their large use of capital and high dollar product per employee, and because some efficiencies tend to decline in the prosperity atmosphere. The over-all slowdown in the rise of productivity tends to pinch costs but does not add to demand.

recession was adventitious in the sense that it was wholly accounted for by rise in prices of agricultural commodities. For policy purposes, therefore, we must face the fact that prices merely level off during the recession.

What should be done depends on why prices failed to decline in 1957–58. One theory is that failure was due to the changing wage and price structure in the economy, with union and corporate power holding prices up. Another view is that structural changes may not have been very influential, and that administered prices were held up because there was little fear that high-level demand was any more than temporarily interrupted. Reasons are that the mildness of postwar recessions tended to be projected and that great growth potential was anticipated for the following decade.

It will be seen that different reasons bring us to different conclusions regarding the likelihood of a horizontal price movement in recessions in the future. For instance, if visualization of a great growth potential in the sixties was largely influential, prices might be expected to decline in a future recession when long-term prospects might be viewed less optimistically.

Until our explanations become more convincing, avoidance of too rigid a prescription may be the wisest policy. Many studies of inflationary dangers and of the influence of changing market structure are in progress. We can at least hope that they will narrow the explanations. Future history may be most important, for the direct extrapolations may fail to materialize.

Possibly, if the pattern of price declines in recession fails to return, the importance of price increases in expansion will fade. Although restrictive monetary policy is at least partially responsible for the failure of average wholesale prices to increase after the 1958 upturn, the failure may be partly due to a reduced need for rising prices in generating a shift of resources to areas of rising demand when the movement is not preceded by falling prices.

THE "CREEPING INFLATION" ARGUMENT

Arguments on "creeping inflation" have become confused, because distinction between long-term price increases and increases in business cycle expansion has not been clearly made. Progress is likely to be impeded and unemployment kept unjustifiably large, as noted above, if competitive forces are not allowed substantial play in drawing resources to areas of greatest demand in the expansion phase. If it is found that competitive forces do not produce long-term price increases, fears of inflation may be somewhat allayed. The idea, for instance, that expectation of higher prices makes buyers speed up their purchases may be important in the short run but is rather vague in the long run, since long-run price anticipations do not play too great a role in business thinking. The fact that long-run inflation redounds to the benefit of the "doers" is more a judgment on equity than a description of motivational influences.

At first blush, it might seem that the more inflationary the financial situation is made, the higher will be the rate of long-term growth. This is because resources would be constantly urged into use. The services of labor, and to a lesser extent of other resources, are irretrievably lost if disemployed. While this is true, it must be balanced against the provision for enough slack to permit flexibility in the use of resources. The cost of disemploying resources is not readily balanced against the cost of using resources ineffectively because so little flexibility exists that they tend to be frozen in current use. The general principle is that growth will be maximized if fluctuation is minimized up to the extent that it does not substantially reduce flexibility in the economy. The implied criterion is something we must learn about by experience, but most persons believe that perhaps even less fluctuation than that which has occurred in the postwar is required.

If long-term price rises came to be anticipated, growth might actually be reduced. This is because the cost of borrowing funds would greatly increase, and it is possible that the demand for investment would be lessened if it had to be fully financed by equities. Take housing, for instance. High interest rates reduce the demand for it.

The historical evidence on the influence of long-term price increases is not as clear as often supposed. Possibly, the reason why growth has been less rapid in periods when prices were in a declining trend is that the depressions with accompanying price declines were so long that they made prices fall on the average over the long run. The more common interpretation is that because of declining prices, the depressions were long. We believe that the former explanation is the more valid one, but there is no conclusive evidence as to which is the correct interpretation.

CONCLUSION

The conclusion is that conflict of goals is most important beyond the range in which operational effects are most clearly understood.

No doubt anti-inflationary goals conflict with full-employment goals to the extent that all resources could be drawn into use, at least for a limited time, if highly inflationary conditions were forced. But the final outcome of any such policy is in considerable doubt.

If control is more modestly kept within the limits of our understanding, dangerous inflation can be avoided in connection with a policy of moderating cyclical fluctuations. Some price rises may have to be permitted in business cycle expansion; and it is possible that this may create a mild long-term inflation, especially if the effectiveness of antirecession policy is widely accepted and if the growth potential is great. Because of this situation, some reshuffling may occur in policy emphasis. Determination to prevent recessions may not be pursued to such an extent that what is considered to be substantial inflation appears imminent. On the other hand, there may be an increasing emphasis on speeding up the rate of growth in near-future years, and whatever inflation develops from price rises in expansion may be condoned if it is felt that this is in the interest of speeding up growth.

Stabilizing schemes cover a wide range of possibilities. Control may be indirect, in the sense that it applies to general market conditions; or it may be direct, in the sense that it interferes with particular market adjustments. Specific price controls are representative of direct controls, and are considered in Chapter 24. Fiscal and monetary controls, studied in the two following chapters, are generally of the indirect type. If any faith is placed in the competitive process, avoidance of direct controls is distinctly advantageous. In contrast, indirect controls provide only general market pressures, leaving individual markets to attain levels reached by competitive adjustment.

FOR REFLECTION AND ANALYSIS

1. To what extent should stabilization policy be centered in the government?
2. Should stabilization goals be set by professional experts?
3. If the policies required to minimize unemployment do not wholly correspond with those required to prevent inflation, how will we decide what to do?
4. Explain the "unemployment-inflation dilemma."
5. Should all rises in average prices be prevented?
6. Speculate on the relation between "creeping inflation" and growth.

Chapter 22   FISCAL POLICY

Fiscal policy refers to tax and expenditure measures taken by the government to foster stability of the aggregate economy. The idea is based on macroeconomic theory. Although fiscal policy is usually accepted to represent only one objective of public finance, its importance has been enhanced by recognition that the income level at which equilibrium is achieved in the aggregate economy depends on the volume of nonconsumption expenditure (see Chapter 9). Tax equity and government efficiency are still considered important but no longer monopolize the field. Government finance may also be used to promote stability.

AUTOMATIC STABILIZERS

Fiscal policy controls may be automatic or discretionary. There are several automatic stabilizers. The graduated income tax brings disposable income to a successively lower percentage of personal income as activity rises, and to a successively higher percentage as activity declines. For instance, the percentage was about 87.5 at the business cycle peak in early 1957 and 89 at the trough in the spring of 1958. Change in the tax bite added to disposable income relative to personal income.

Personal income declines less in recession than gross national product because of the rise in government transfer payments. Unemployment insurance benefits rose from $1.5 billion early in 1957 to nearly $5 billion in the summer of 1958. Also, more persons drop out of the labor force in depressed periods, leading to an increase in the payment of old-age benefits.

Since profits change rapidly, corporate income taxes vary with the cycle. They dropped from $22 billion at the peak in 1957 to $16 billion at the trough in the spring of 1958. Thus, they accounted for a substantial reduction in taxes uncorrelated with any change in government expenditure.

Farm price supports keep farm prices at reasonably high levels, and thus tend to sustain agricultural income. In 1948–49, for instance, the acquisition of farm products by the Commodity Credit Corporation increased $2 billion by the end of 1949. Farm income was thus supported, even though it actually declined over 20 per cent while income in the rest of the economy declined scarcely at all. Without price floors the same output would have sold at lower prices, so that farm income would have fallen still more than it did. In 1958, however, price supports had no effect. Support holdings declined because farm prices strengthened during the recession, as a result of improved demand and supply relationships in agriculture. Perhaps too much has been made of farm price supports as an automatic stabilizer.[1]

Other fiscal policy, including expenditures for public works and changes in established tax rates, require administrative decision and thus are discretionary. Likewise, all monetary controls depend upon discretionary judgments. Discretionary fiscal policy is discussed later in the chapter.

EFFECTIVENESS AND ACCEPTABILITY

Any control measure must be examined for effectiveness. Automatic stabilizers rate high on that scale, for they come into play at the right time and appear to interfere less with private incentives than discretionary measures. On the other hand, by their very nature (in that they relate to flexibility of taxes and to minimum supports for certain income flows), they can be no more than partial offsets. Furthermore, their effectiveness declines with time, and they may fade out entirely if the depression lasts long enough. How long depends partly on the institutional situation at the time. Personal income taxes would quickly fail as a recession support if the income tax rates should return to the pre-World War II levels, for individual income payments would soon fall below the high levels at which

---

[1]Although the most important cases have been noted, for other reasons tax yields may vary directly with national income, and government expenditures other than for unemployment benefits may vary inversely with national income. In private industry, notably in automobile and steel companies, a plan called "supplementary unemployment benefits" has recently been devised. The SUB plans provide for the building up of funds by the companies in prosperous times and the payment of them to workers when they are unemployed. Semiautomatic stabilizers may be extended by "formula plans," as explained below.

the tax rates apply. The corporate income tax is a stabilizer of consequence because of the high rates in effect. Taxable income shrinks rapidly in depression, and very limited support to expenditures could be provided after early phases of a recession if the rates were low. The effectiveness of unemployment benefits is dependent upon laws regarding the number of weeks in a year for which payments will be made, and upon adequacy of unemployment reserves accumulated. When the benefits run out, legislation is likely to extend them, as it did in 1958, but discretionary action is required.

Discretionary policy is limited in its effectiveness because of various lags relative to the time it becomes effective, the ways private motivation is influenced, and the extent to which measures can be discontinued when no longer useful. The lags relate to the time required for administrators to realize measures are needed and the time it takes these measures to become effective after they are applied. Lag resulting from poor forecasting has been important in the American experience. At the peak in mid-1957 a stretch-out was ordered in defense spending, and the Federal Reserve marked up rediscount rates after the downturn. It is fair to say that the government seldom has sighted turning points until after they occurred. In the case of government spending, problems of drawing up contracts and working out other mechanical problems, such as assembly of resources at the site of operations, frequently result in long delays. Delays in the time required for monetary measures to take hold are less clearly visualized. They are more closely related to changes occurring in private motivation.

The introduction of measures to foster stabilization produces wide and complicated anticipatory repercussions. The very announcement of a program of increased public expenditure may be reassuring under certain circumstances and induce businessmen to spend more freely. Similarly, the announcement of changes in monetary policy is often intended to produce "moral suasion," in that commercial banks are expected to take a cue from announced changes. Such influences tend to reduce the lags which may grow out of motivational effects.

Some businessmen may feel that increased government spending introduces a note of uncertainty or that it is competitive with private industry, and may therefore delay expansionary decisions until effects of increased government spending are actually apparent on their markets. Anti-inflationary monetary measures may lead businessmen to hurry rather than delay business expenditure because they may feel that further tightening is indicated by the action taken.

Discretionary government expenditures are not much more readily cut off when no longer effective than they are started when needed. This is because the time taken to complete projects is unlikely to mesh neatly with the times when resources become effectively employed, and political pressures to continue expenditures often are irresistible in view of the affirmations of selfish interests. About all we can hope to do is choose types of projects which are finished quickly, so that discontinuance is made feasible. Because of unsatisfactory forecasts, measures may be continued longer than desirable.

Control measures are limited by the extent to which they are acceptable. Lack of acceptability may turn on conflict with other goals, or it may turn on the revolutionary character of the proposal. Opposition to public works often derives from the feeling that it is not the most efficient allocation of resources, in view of the nature of consumer wants. Or the redistribution effect implicit in graduated income taxes may be considered undesirable; therefore, that part of the bases for automatic stabilization may face opposition. Measures "underwriting consumer expenditure," described later in the chapter, are opposed both because they may be felt to conflict with incentives to work and because it may be felt that they lead to revolutionary changes in social organization. Measures cannot be adopted without regard for general psychological reactions, although some opposition can be expected for any policies which mark changes from the past.

DEVELOPMENT OF THE IDEA OF FISCAL POLICY

Public responsibility for the total level of economic activity in our kind of an economy is a twentieth-century idea. The idea of fiscal policy is even more recent, scarcely antedating the Great Depression of the thirties. The principal idea involved in the early phases can be described as "priming the pump," involving an initial government expenditure which was expected to get increasing levels of private expenditure under way. That the idea is, at least to some extent, fallacious is indicated by the fact that a one-shot injection without the introduction of other accompanying influences results in a steady *decline* in activity after the first period.[2] However, a

---

[2]See pp. 190-91. Also, an historical illustration of how a one-shot injection tended to create a culmination is represented on p. 284.

slow increase in public expenditures over a few periods probably would set up side effects which might generate a cumulative expansion.[3] Many of the ideas on priming the pump can be inferred to have assumed the development of such side effects.

In its most "advanced" form the idea of fiscal policy can be characterized as "functional" finance.[4] The idea is that the primary purpose of government expenditures is to generate enough income to underwrite full employment, and that the primary purpose of taxation is to avoid inflation. Whenever employment is below the accepted standard, government expenditures would be increased or, when over-full, government expenditures would be decreased. When price inflation is generated, taxes would be increased; and when prices fall more than desired, they would be decreased. The sole reason for government expenditures becomes the maintenance of full employment, and the sole reason for taxation the avoidance of inflation. All other reasons for government expenditures or taxation become purely incidental. This concept of fiscal policy is not generally acceptable because (1) it appears to slur over many government functions and responsibilities, (2) it might lead to a different form of economic organization, and (3) it is not wholly clear that it would work. If the last point is applied to a period of all-out war, expenditures obviously would be above the standards set, and taxation would have to be pushed to much higher levels than have been found workable in the past. On the second point an unanswered question is whether or not we would experience a rapid encroachment of the government on the private economy.

A third idea represents countercyclical measures. This is now the most generally accepted position on fiscal policy. The idea is that when private expenditures are unsatisfactorily low, government expenditures will be stepped up, and/or taxes will be cut; when they are unsatisfactorily high, the reverse action will be taken. Generally, although not universally, the accepted position is that the needed action may or may not be symmetrical over the business cycle. Activity may, or may not, be high enough in prosperity that surpluses should balance recession deficits. On the other hand, there is an increasing acceptance of the idea that the economy is now inflationary enough that prosperity surpluses may be expected to more than offset recession deficits.

The multiplier is emphasized in contracyclical policy. As seen

---

[3] See pp. 55-56.

[4] See A. P. Lerner, *The Economics of Control* (New York: Macmillan Co., 1944); and "Functional Finance and the Federal Debt," *Social Research*, February, 1943.

in Chart 22-1, increases in nonconsumption expenditures usually are paired with much greater increases in gross national product. This is because consumer expenditures rise at a fairly steady proportionate rate in relation to rising income, as explained in Chapter 10. Since consumer expenditure tends to rise more or less passively with changes in total income, increases in government expenditures can be expected to generate a multiplied activity. Conversely, decreases in government expenditure can be expected to generate a multiplied decline. The multiplier effect is smaller in case of changes in taxes, since consumption expenditure rather than nonconsumption expenditure is principally affected.

CHART 22–1

CHANGE IN GROSS NATIONAL PRODUCT AND CHANGE IN NONCONSUMPTION
FINAL EXPENDITURES

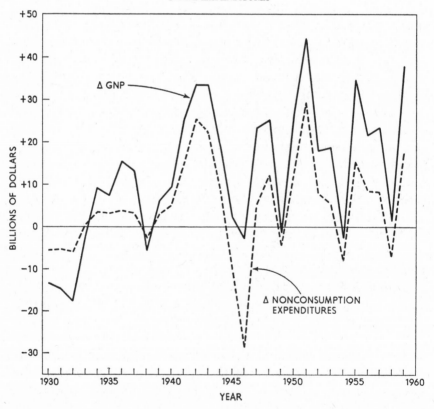

BALANCED BUDGET MULTIPLIER

A fourth possible conception of fiscal policy is represented by commensurate changes in expenditures and taxes, but scarcely anyone really favors it. The reason is that the changes required to produce any substantial effect are very large. If we assume that, in the private economy, some of the income will be saved and that the government runs a balanced budget (no surplus or deficit), obviously the higher rate of government spending will be more expansionary than if some of the government income were kept in the private economy. How much more depends on any difference in the rate of spending funds received from the government as compared to funds received in the private economy. Little reason appears for expecting a difference in the groups selling goods to the government or to the private economy. Wages and salaries perhaps are spent as rapidly, whichever their source. The higher the rate of private spending, the less will be the effectiveness of the balanced budget multiplier.

Gross savings in the private economy are running close to 20 per cent of gross private expenditure.[5] If this percentage were to hold and the balanced budget multiplier were fully effective, as described in the above paragraph, to add $2 billion in expenditure, the government budget would have to be increased $10 billion. In other words, a $2 billion deficit would be as effective in increasing activity as a $10 billion increase in expenditures when the budget was kept balanced, with the given assumptions.

FORMULA FLEXIBILITY

As we shall see, most of the stabilization effect attributable to fiscal policy in the postwar can be traced to the operation of automatic stabilizers. This being true, attention is certain to be directed to possibilities of extending the operation of these stabilizers. If we stop to think about the changes in taxes and changes in expenditures involved in automatic stabilizers, the conclusion we reach is that the processes which make them work were set up for other reasons than to provide stabilization. For instance, the high corporate income tax was not established to add to stability, nor would it be retained if there were no other reasons for doing so. Extension of automatic stabilizers does not appear very promising.[6]

Procedures, however, can be set up which come close to being automatic in their operation. Measures which are indicative of activity can be set to trigger changes in fiscal policy. A common

---

[5]In 1958, $68 billion out of $349 billion.
[6]The growth of supplementary unemployment benefits in private industry is an exception. See n. 1.

proposal is to apply a rule, such as a given reduction in income tax rates for every million increase in seasonally corrected unemployment figures. If rising activity is to be countered, increases in income tax rates also would be required to counter decreases in unemployment. Such a scheme has been denominated "formula flexibility."

A major problem in this connection is the delegation of authority to the executive department of the government to such an extent that formula flexibility can become operative. The most closely guarded responsibility of the legislative branch of governments is the setting of government tax and expenditure rates. Deliberation is the very nature of the legislative branch of the government, and decisions by formula flexibility in that branch are inconceivable. Delegation of authority to the executive branch to change expenditure or tax rates is nearly incredible. The time may come when such delegation would be agreed to in accordance with mutually accepted formulas, if the legislative branch of the government were permitted to retain substantial safeguards. For instance, if the need for improved stabilization were clearly understood by legislators, they might agree to a formula plan, with the proviso that changes could be vetoed after a full hearing was given to the responsible executive agency.

For the time being, a more promising procedure would appear to be the use of authority executive departments already possess—the right to speed up or slow down expenditures under appropriate authority now available. If the executive department cannot arrive at effective decisions with respect to such authority, doubt may be expressed as to whether it could conduct an effective plan of formula adjustment, unless action were mandatory. And Congress is unlikely to delegate purely mandatory action.

DISCRETIONARY FISCAL POLICY

Since instability occurs fundamentally because of inability to foresee the future adequately, the conclusion that stability could be produced automatically would be surprising. Since we have not been surprised in that way, we need to face squarely the problems of implementing discretionary policy.

"Crash" programs on changing tax rates and/or changing government expenditures are involved. As to the former, changing rates in the federal personal income tax program represent the chief measure. The idea is to reduce these rates so as to release to consumers a greater amount of disposable income when total expenditure is expected to be inadequate to support a satisfactory level of activity and to raise them in the opposite situation. To the extent that income taxes are withheld by employers, the change in disposable income would be almost immediate. With these taxes now accounting for half of total federal government receipts and nearly 10 per cent of gross national product, great maneuverability is at least theoretically possible. At the lower levels of the income tax prevailing before the war, the possible fiscal policy influence was much more limited, especially for expansionary effects, unless subsidies (negative income tax rates) could be resorted to after income taxes were reduced to zero.

A famous application of crash programs operating on income tax rates is the "underwriting of consumer expenditure."[7] This proposal is much closer to a policy of functional finance than to one of countering cyclical fluctuations in expenditure. The idea is to set income taxes at such a level that consumer expenditures will add or subtract from total gross national product a sufficient amount to keep total activity at full-employment, but not inflationary, levels. If gross national product falls or tends to fall below full-employment levels (usually defined to allow for a reasonable labor float), tax rates would be reduced. If full employment continues to be endangered as all or a significant part of the income tax rates reach zero, scaled subsidies would be paid in the tax-vacated brackets of income. The sponsors of the program recognize that saving rates might increase somewhat as income tax rates are reduced or subsidies are paid; therefore, the quantitative effect of tax reduction would have to be somewhat greater than the increase expected for consumption expenditure.

In the underwriting of consumer expenditure the possibility of expenditures so high as to induce overfull employment is recognized. Under these circumstances, the proposal is to increase income tax rates, thereby discouraging consumer expenditure. Theoretically, there is no question that total expenditures could thereby be reduced if the policy were followed ruthlessly. If acceptable, therefore, full employment could be maintained. The scheme of underwriting consumer expenditure, however, faces a noninflationary goal much less effectively than a full-employment one. It is possible that

---

[7]See J. H. G. Pierson, *Full Employment and Free Enterprise* (Washington, D.C.: American Council of Public Affairs, 1947); P. J. Strayer, "Stabilization of Personal Incomes: A Limited Fiscal Policy," *American Economic Review*, December, 1950.

substantial inflation would be induced at all times because of the key importance attached to maintenance of adequate consumer expenditure, whatever the cost.

Crash programs involving changes in income tax rates could, of course, be applied much less comprehensively. Additions could be made to the effect produced by automatic stabilizers without introducing the inflationary difficulties likely to be met in efforts to replace these stabilizers by an underwriting of consumer expenditure. Problems involved in implementing such a program are discussed in the following section.

Instead of attempting to reduce taxes when total expenditures are too low to maintain full employment, government expenditures may be increased. Such a program avoids the "leakage" involved in saving part of the increase effected in disposable income through reductions in income tax rates. A smaller total dollar amount would therefore be required to produce an equal influence on activity. Many problems, nevertheless, point to almost insurmountable difficulties in contriving a discretionary expenditure program to offset minor recessions, as explained in the following section. We should note that only public works programs are effectively available for this purpose. And the major part of this limited type of expenditure arises in state and local government operations, which are not amenable to adaptation in short recessions. The federal government expenditures for construction come to only $3 billion or $4 billion, less than 1 per cent of total gross national product. Possibly, we might double the amount by adding federal grants-in-aid to state and local governments, but the total would not reach 2 per cent of gross national product.

Another, more radical, possibility should not be ignored. Large additional payments could be made to expenditures in relief of unemployed persons. At the extreme of matching the proposal for underwriting consumer expenditure, such expenditures could be increased enough to offset any reduction in income suffered by disemployed persons. It would likely be even less acceptable than underwriting consumer expenditure by tax changes, and certainly compares unfavorably with increased public works on a merit scale graduated according to product bought by government expenditures.

PROBLEMS FACED IN DISCRETIONARY POLICY

The most universal problem is that of forecasting. Expenditure changes cannot be countered if their occurrence is not understood prospectively. Unused resources resulting from past declines in expenditure are lost forever. On the other hand, the damage done by price inflation which has already occurred is irremediable. The forecasting effectiveness of the government, as indicated by expenditure decisions, is very low. Possibly, we may expect it to become somewhat better in the future. With the forecasting record as poor as it has been in the past, only mediocre achievement can be hoped for from discretionary policy in minor recessions.

Timing faces even more critical problems. It is simplest in the case of tax programs. Especially in the case of tax withholding, an immediate effect can be produced on disposable income by changing tax rates. However, what we may call a "political" lag is involved here. Even if the forecast of GNP changes is adequate by the most informed governmental advisers, the lag in acceptance of need for changing the tax rate is likely to be so long as to cancel most, if not all, of the possible effect in a short recession. In high prosperity when increase in rates may be desirable, the lag is likely to be even longer because of the unpopularity faced in increasing income tax rates.

More lags are involved in timing government expenditures. A lag may be faced in finding acceptable programs. The answer to this is a shelf of public works to be held in waiting for reduced levels of activity. Successes in building up such a shelf have been far from spectacular. The reason is that demand for public expenditures varies with changed economic conditions, just as happens with demand in the private economy. Effective additions to the shelf are impeded by what is currently felt to be necessary, and further public expenditures usually appear marginal. Not only is it difficult to add to desirable public expenditures in recession, but it is difficult to reduce them in prosperity.

Once an expenditure program is decided upon, a lag is faced in getting it started. For public works, this is likely to involve several months or perhaps as long as a minor recession lasts after it is recognized. If the technical requirements have been established in a shelf of public works, the lag is reduced somewhat; but there are still substantial lags in assembly of resources, including manpower, required in execution of the project and in contracting for work by private firms which is usually required.

Timing problems are also faced in closing out the crash program. Tax rates, once reduced, are raised with reluctance by the legislative branch of the government. Many types of public works take a long time to complete; and usually, it is uneconomical to stop them in a half-finished state. A distinction may be made between "heavy" and "light" public works, on the basis of the time required for completion. Roads and airfields are notable illustrations of the light type; but even in these cases, completion dates are unlikely to correspond neatly with the requirements of effective public policy.

Regional problems are serious in fiscal policy programs. Tax programs fail to mesh with regional needs. It would scarcely be practical to vary reduction in income tax rates with regional unemployment. But since a recession strikes the country unevenly, the result of reducing income tax rates would be to increase disposable income to new high levels in some communities, while disposable income in cyclically sensitive areas (such as steel towns) would remain depressed.

The problem is even more serious in public works programs. Needed works are principally concentrated in nonindustrial and sparsely populated areas. The brunt of unemployment is concentrated in industrial areas. If attention is centered on light public works, the contrast is somewhat less exaggerated, since roads and airfields are needed in thickly populated areas, but probably even in this case less, relative to unemployment, than in more remote regions. An almost insurmountable difficulty is faced in attempting to move industrial workers out to regions where such works as dams are most needed.

Finally, we may note how the effects of fiscal policy programs are influenced by behavior in the private economy. Partly because of knowledge of empirical reactions, we have been able to establish crude working models of the economy in earlier chapters. Much more exacting requirements are faced when we try to state what the behavior will be when various adjustments have been imposed by government authority. About the best we can hope to do is to follow through the outcome of various assumptions about behavior reactions. While disciplined thinking along these lines is of some limited assistance in visualizing the fiscal policy problem, it involves far too much theoretical conjecture for use in this book.[8]

Aside from typical behavior patterns, psychological reactions to policy decisions play a part. Anticipatory decisions are certain to be affected somewhat when fiscal policy action is announced. If the

---

[8]For an excellent analysis, see Richard A. Musgrave, *The Theory of Public Finance* (New York: McGraw-Hill Book Co., Inc., 1959), pp. 407–500.

policy decisions involve measures to increase total expenditure, decision makers in the private economy may immediately decide to
increase spending. Until the likely influence of fiscal policy is clearly
understood, however, many decision makers may fear its effect and
play a waiting game. To the extent that this does not happen,
psychological reaction may reduce the lags discussed above. On the
other hand, if policy decisions involve measures to decrease total
expenditure, decision makers in the private economy are likely to
decrease spending fairly promptly. Anticipations in reaction to fiscal
policy decisions, therefore, are likely to reduce the lag growing out
of the slowness of the machinery which puts fiscal policy into effect.

SELECTIVE EXPENDITURE AND TAX PROGRAMS

We have considered the fiscal policy problem above as though
any change in government expenditure or government receipts has
about the same impact as any other. While that position is decidedly
incorrect, the broad outlines of the problem are most readily seen
when uncomplicated by selective differences between types of expenditures and receipts. Furthermore, with limited knowledge of
reaction patterns to various expenditure and tax programs, our understanding of the possible achievement of selective programs does
not go far beyond the limited conclusions already drawn. Clearly,
some distinction can be made between light and heavy public works
programs on the basis of time required to get the programs into
operation and the time required to complete them. Involved is an
important basis for distinguishing between action which would be
necessary in a deep depression and the maximum action which
would be feasible in minor recessions.

Another significant classification of government expenditures is
between those made for goods and those made for services or transfers, especially in case of wages paid for services. This is because,
with wage payments, some saving is to be expected. On the other
hand, payments made for goods represent entirely amounts going
for production which reflects activity. All of this activity might not
occur in the given time period, however, for some of the funds might
be spent in the purchase of materials which were already stocked.
In the case of unemployment benefit transfers, payments presumably are made to individuals in great enough need that little or no
savings are possible. Most of the increase in payments to individuals
would be of that type, since little basis is likely to be available for
speeded-up wage payments. On net, then, difference in the fiscal

policy effect is not likely to be great between goods and personal payments.

Taxes may be classified as heavy or light, depending on their influence on private expenditures. Heavy taxes, which tend to reduce expenditures most effectively, are usually thought to include personal and corporate income taxes. To a considerable extent, however, income taxes may be paid out of income which otherwise would be saved. Any increase in corporate income taxes may reduce dividend payments or investment from retained profits. What would happen with a reduction in corporate income taxes is less clear. To the extent that such taxes are passed through to market prices, price reductions might occur which would tend to be deflationary. Furthermore, even in the absence of price changes, investment might not be increased. Expenditures like research, which have grown partly because a large part (at the present about half) of their cost otherwise would be paid in taxes, might be decreased.

Increases in sales taxes, under certain conditions, do not appear to reduce consumer expenditure much, if at all.[9] They may actually result in an increase in prices great enough to offset them. Then, if wage contracts contain escalator clauses, increases in sales taxes may produce automatic wage increases by raising the cost-of-living index. To an extent not fully understood, some tax increases may actually be inflationary.

It is possible that forced borrowing from consumers, by mandatory deduction from wages for the purchase of savings bonds, might be more deflationary than sales taxes. If most of the borrowed funds otherwise would have been spent, and if sales taxes are offset by price increases, the purchase of savings bonds will be the more deflationary. Thus, there is no magic in a government deficit. To a limited extent a government deficit might be less inflationary than a government surplus.

This conclusion presupposes that we know how heavy or how light various taxes are, as well as the impact of different types of borrowing. The latter is a better assumption than the former. The terse statements in the above paragraphs no doubt leave an unduly disparaging impression as to our ability to distinguish between light and heavy taxes. The fact of the matter is that the characteristic influences of each type of tax remain somewhat vague from the point

---

[9] A decrease in sales taxes would always have an inflationary effect, however. This is because either a reduction in prices to the consumer or an increase in profits to the producer would be expansionary.

of view of both theory and experience. The differences are not too important, partly because, from practical points of view, the choice of fiscal policy may not fall between such extremes as income and sales taxes. If it does, in recession the taxes might be equally inflationary. Reduced personal income taxes no doubt would increase consumer purchases. Reduced sales taxes probably would either increase consumer purchases or bring the businessman to increase prices, which would also be inflationary.

METHODS OF FINANCING

In financing, the government can provide different effects in accordance with the type of investor. From that point of view, investors can be classified into three types:

1. The government may borrow from consumers and other nonbank investors under deficit conditions and pay off these investors under surplus conditions. To the extent that consumers loan funds to the government that they would otherwise have spent, the stepped-up government expenditures would not be expansionary. No such neat balance is ordinarily possible except in war, but this is the least expansionary type of borrowing under most conditions. Paying off nonbank investors may not be deflationary if consumers use all of the funds received on current expenditures. This is unlikely; but if the funds are made available for private investment, they substitute for a draft on credit in a period of expansion. The resulting ease in the credit market would partially offset the contractionary effect of reduced government spending.

2. The government may borrow from commercial banks and buy back the government securities when excess funds are available. Borrowing from the banks does not draw the needed funds from private saving but from credit creation. Depending on what counter monetary measures may be taken, this is about as inflationary as credit extension in the private economy. Without any countering action, reserve balances of the commercial banks will be drawn down, and the supply of money wil be increased. Repurchase of government securities when a surplus is available will increase bank liquidity, and would confuse monetary policy if pursued in prosperity. The sale and purchase of securities to the banks is like Federal Reserve open-market operations, discussed in the following chapter, except that in the latter operation, credit is not extended for use in increasing government expenditures when securities are sold to the banks.

3. An uncomplicating expansionary and contractionary influence is produced if funds are obtained directly from the Federal Reserve when needed and returned when surpluses are available. When the funds are obtained, no tightening of credit is produced as occurs when the funds come from commercial banks, but savings are added to by the amount obtained from the Federal Reserve. When the loans are repaid, they offset current savings in the economy without easing credit conditions. The operation is the modern equivalent of obtaining funds by printing money or reducing funds by destroying money. The amount of loans permitted by this procedure is set by law at $5 billion, and it has not been used to any significant extent except during World War II.

The choice of financing methods should take into consideration not only the mechanical factors described above, but also the best inferences which can be made on behavior reactions to be expected when a particular financing technique is employed and the incentives it may be desirable to encourage under the particular conditions faced. Behavior reactions to various financing arrangements unfortunately are predicted no more readily than for the fiscal measures themselves. As to incentives, if funds must be obtained under prosperous conditions, nonbank investors should be encouraged to make loans because some curtailment of private expenditure could be expected to result. Unless such investors can be convinced that making loans will not be flagrantly opposed to their own interest in view of price inflation which may be in progress, however, little success may be anticipated. If conditions are so depressed that private expenditures should not be discouraged, borrowing from the banks may be the more desirable. If surpluses are achieved under prosperous conditions, repayment of funds borrowed from individuals may encourage expenditure and partly offset the contractionary effect. If repaid to the banks, credit will be eased and might encourage more business spending.

No financing method is perfect. We should recognize, nevertheless, that fiscal policy seldom will require extreme contractionary or extreme expansionary measures. The former would be appropriate only when the avoidance of inflation became of paramount importance. In that case, the extreme measure of drawing funds into the Federal Reserve would be warranted. In deep depression, if an all-out public works program should materialize, loans could expediently be obtained from the Federal Reserve. In mild recessions or moderate prosperities, such extreme measures would appear unnecessary.

SUPPORT OF MINOR RECESSIONS VERSUS MAJOR DEPRESSIONS

Most of the above analysis is pointed at the kind of aggregate fluctuation we have experienced in the postwar. If a major depression should occur, full use of discretionary policy would be desirable without qualification. The weaknesses of fallibility in forecasting, poor timing and indeterminate lags, and even regional distortions would fade into the background. The one overriding consideration would be the development of increase in activity. The problem of what is to be done when massive expenditure is no longer required would have to be overlooked, with the hope that it could be faced effectively when recovery got well under way.

While there is little disagreement on what would have to be done in a deep depression, a decided difference of opinion exists on *when* the problem of a deep depression should be attacked. One school holds that early doses of discretionary policy are necessary to assure that a deep depression will not develop. The strong point behind this position is that no assured method exists for distinguishing between the onset of a minor recession and a deep depression shortly after the downturn occurs.[10] The argument is that a period of grace —a "breathing space"—is available before total expenditures have declined a great deal. During that time the expenditures required to end the downswing are thought to be small compared to those which would be necessary later on, after nonconsumption expenditures had declined substantially. The exponent of this view may recognize that culminating forces do arise to turn activity into a recession and still point correctly to the fact that a much larger program would be entailed to turn activity around later *if* it came about that a deep depression was unfolding.

An opposite position turns on the argument that a "wringer application" is desirable, so that maladjustments requiring correction will not be perpetuated. In the most extreme form, this argument is blown up into a type of natural law by which various maladjustments arise under prosperous conditions, and which inevitably lead to readjustments at reduced levels of activity.

---

[10]A promising possibility is the degree of excess capacity in existence, but this is scarcely dependable at the present time because of the unsatisfactory state of capital stock measurements. For evidence along this line, see particularly V. Lewis Bassie, *Economic Forecasting* (New York: McGraw-Hill Book Co., Inc., 1958), pp. 681–92.

Extensive empirical work, with less developed theoretical defense, will be found in Geoffrey H. Moore, *Measuring Recessions,* Occasional Paper 61 (New York: National Bureau of Economic Research, Inc., 1958).

The truth surely lies somewhere between these two extremes. Maladjustments do arise in business cycle expansion in the sense of the threat of narrowing profit margins, some personal inefficiency because of overoptimism, and demand reaching levels which are fed by transient forces, while cumulative forces sooner or later are reversed by a culmination. But this is no more than a notation of what behavior patterns now tend to be according to our best information. As emphasized earlier in the chapter, what the behavior would be if control factors were introduced can only be projected on the basis of various assumptions regarding behavior patterns which would be met if various controls were introduced. Possibly, the readjustments might develop in a prosperous, as well as in a depressed, climate.

If the "early dose" school is represented by "trigger-happy" stabilizers, inflation may be aggravated, as explained in Chapter 21. If guided by careful analysis of changes arising in aggregative expenditures examined in the light of problems faced in discretionary policy and of recent history summarized in the following section, possible achievement in attempting to counter declines before recession gets under way falls far short of the ideal. The use of early doses to avoid a depression still has to prove itself.

The difference in control needed in a minor recession contrasted with a deep depression is not in doubt. Recognizing the practical problems which must be faced in attempting to iron out business fluctuations, we must admit that discretionary policy is of little assistance in minor recessions. As for deep depressions, discretionary policy is unquestionably necessary. *When* we should decide to take action to counter a deep depression is still an unsettled argument.

POSTWAR EXPERIENCE WITH FISCAL POLICY

Chart 22-2 traces the movement of federal government receipts, expenditures, and the different surplus or deficit with variations in gross national product. The supporting influence of deficits is very apparent in the recessions of 1949, 1953-54, and 1957-58. As gross national product declined in these recessions, deficits developed, largely because of automatic stabilizers. The deficits obviously moderated the recessions, but the precise degree of the influence is not measurable.

The surpluses arising in the postwar period prior to the 1949 recession were a moderating influence; but unquestionably, they were unplanned. They arose because defense expenditures were cut back faster than income taxes. The surplus in 1950–51 resulted from the rapid increase in personal income and in profits before war expenditure got into full swing. The minor deficits from the latter part of 1951 to the cyclical downturn in mid-1953 were caused by a slightly faster advance in defense expenditures than rise in taxes with higher rates. Increase in the deficits from late 1953 to early 1954 was largely the result of the operation of automatic stabilizers in the recession.

CHART 22–2

RELATION BETWEEN FEDERAL GOVERNMENT RECEIPTS AND
EXPENDITURES AND GROSS NATIONAL PRODUCT

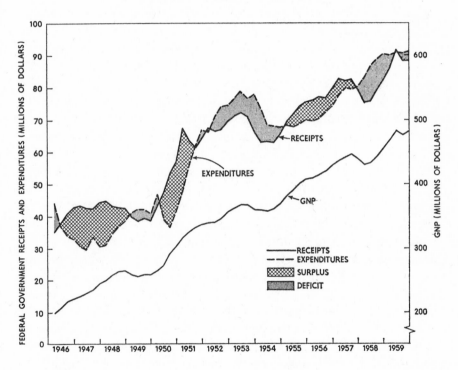

The rapid rise in activity in 1955 and slight further rise in 1956 and early 1957 account for the surpluses achieved in view of the operation of automatic stabilizers. The failure of the surplus to increase after early 1956 is due to the rise which was under way in defense expenditures and the leveling which occurred in corporate profits after a rapid advance in 1955 (corporate profits taxes account for about a fourth of total government receipts in good years).

Deficits beginning late in 1957 and rising to nearly as high a level as in 1953 were accounted for by the operation of automatic stabilizers. Most important in 1957 was the drop in profits taxes as profits fell in the recession. The deficit did not fade as rapidly as in 1954 because defense expenditures were increasing instead of declining as in the earlier case. The shift to a surplus was interrupted in the third quarter of 1959 with the cut in profits produced by the steel strike.

In all of this history, there is little evidence of effective operation of discretionary policy. True, in two instances, reduction in tax rates alleviated recession. The first is the controversial personal tax cut, passed over President Truman's veto in the spring of 1948. Since it accounted for nearly a quarter of the decline in the surplus shown in Chart 22-2, it was an important factor in moderating the recession But was it discretionary policy in any realistic sense? Speaking of the taking of this action in an over-all economic environment of inflation, McConnell holds that it "stands as a classic example of inappropriate fiscal policy in the late 1940's."[11] Basically, McConnell's complaint is that the change to recession was unforeseen.

The second instance is the tax cut which occurred in the 1953–54 recession. This was made in response to cuts in defense expenditure rather than as fiscal policy. No income tax cuts were made in the 1957–58 recession, although widespread arguments for a cut were voiced by late 1957, when the recession was half over.

The stretch-out of defense expenditures in mid-1957 is a notable example of poor discretionary fiscal policy, although it may be defended on McConnell's argument of what should be done in an inflationary environment. Coming exactly at the downturn, it contributed to the decline. By the second quarter of 1958, when the recession was ending, defense expenditure was being speeded up, but in response to the launching of the Sputnik rather than as a fiscal policy measure. Federal expenditures for highways were speeded up by about $1 billion in 1958, but this was only partially because of deference to the recession; the major factor was maturation of the road-building program. History provides little evidence of our ability to plan discretionary fiscal policy successfully.

Combined state and local receipts and expenditures provide scanty evidence of decisions made for fiscal policy control. Except for very slight surpluses during the Korean War, small deficits occurred all during the fifties. Because these government expenditures have been insensitive to declines in gross national product in the

---

[11]C. R. McConnell, *Elementary Economics* (New York: McGraw-Hill Book Co., Inc., 1960), p. 279.

postwar period while receipts slowed, a minor support, never as much as $1 billion, has occurred in recessions. The effect of state and local budgets, however, has been swamped by the federal budget, as shown in Chart 22–3. The relative unimportance of the state and local budgets in fiscal policy is noteworthy because, for instance, they account for more than three quarters of public construction expenditure.

CHART 22–3

CHANGE IN GOVERNMENT SURPLUS AND CHANGE IN GROSS NATIONAL PRODUCT

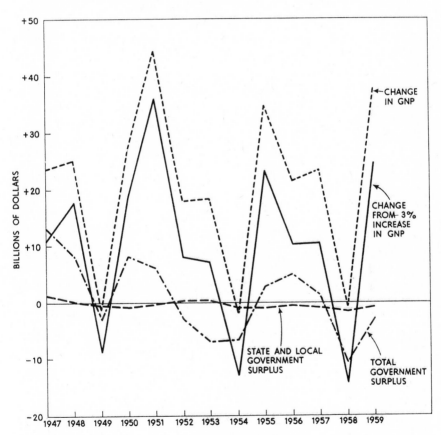

In Chart 22–3, we show that the balance between total government receipts and surpluses has correlated with changes in gross national product about half of the time. Positive correlation is a rough criterion of the effectiveness of fiscal policy. The approximate 50 per cent success is principally accounted for by automatic stabilizers. Furthermore, as the literature now is widely emphasizing, measures of this kind are very crude because they do not take cognizance of the wide differences between different kinds of taxes and expenditures. And as indicated above, our knowledge of the selective effect of such differences is too undeveloped to make a simple evaluation possible.

EVALUATION

As Musgrave says, "the possibility of preventive action remains limited as yet. The problem of stabilization is still primarily one of remedial adjustments aimed at preventing further destabilization and restoring equilibrium".[12] Neither analysis nor experience warrants the belief that fiscal policy can provide much more stabilizing influence than is automatically available because of income taxes and unemployment benefits.

A major difficulty in drawing conclusions about the potentialities of discretionary fiscal policy turns on our inability to spot behavior patterns which we can confidently expect to hold up when discretionary changes are made. Along the same line is the question of what the influence of specified changes will be on incentives. If we had more than hypothetical answers to these questions, it is possible that some of the other difficulties would disappear. Delay in implementing programs is largely based on uncertainty regarding the effect which would be produced if policy changes were made.

We should clearly recognize that increased activity in recession does represent an increase in the efficiency with which resources are used.[13] The economy gains when resources which otherwise would remain idle are put to effective use.

Finally, fiscal policy should clearly be recognized as an institutional matter. Particularly, the problem in underdeveloped countries differs from ours. There, the difficulty is especially that of transferring resources to capital formation without producing inflation. Certainly, underemployment exists in underdeveloped countries but fundamentally because real wage rates are so low that leisure is preferred. The problem is not unemployment in the same sense as it is ours in depressed periods. Our problem could become similar if *capital* instead of *labor* should become the relatively short resource. Then, unemployment might arise not because of current inadequacy of market demand but because not enough capital resources were available for all workers to be engaged. The fiscal prob-

---

[12]*Op. cit.*, p. 502.
[13]See Musgrave, *op. cit.*, esp. pp. 519–20.

lems we face turn on the fact that *labor* is our relatively short resource. Unemployment can occur in the labor resource even though it is always in relatively short supply. This is because of the transientness of demand, which is controlling in the short run. But at such a time, capital is even less fully employed.

FOR REFLECTION AND ANALYSIS

1. Contrast the relative advantages of automatic and discretionary policy.
2. Why is there a difference between effectiveness and acceptability of policy action?
3. Could taxation avoid inflation if all other considerations regarding taxes were disregarded?
4. Would the balanced budget multiplier work if no gross savings occurred in the private economy?
5. If you were a Congressman, would you delegate authority to set tax rates?
6. Does the scheme of "underwriting consumer expenditure" provide adequate safeguards against inflation?
7. Point out the advantages of "light" compared with "heavy" public works in countering minor recessions.
8. Is it easier to distinguish between heavy and light public works or between heavy and light taxes?
9. Under certain circumstances, is it possible that a government deficit might be less inflationary than a government surplus?
10. What do you think of financing fiscal policy by drafts on the Federal Reserve?
11. Contrast the "early dose" school with the "wringer application" school.
12. How effective has fiscal policy been in the postwar recessions?
13. Why does the promise of fiscal policy rest with the federal government?
14. What does the success of fiscal policy have to do with behavior patterns?

Chapter 23

MONETARY POLICY

Monetary control as a national policy dates well back into the nineteenth century, but was not developed in the United States in these early years because the National Banking System was not conducive to the development of a national monetary policy. In Britain, where there was an early evolution, the goal was principally the protection of the Bank of England's gold reserve. When funds flowing into the country were inadequate for that purpose, discount rates were raised to attract funds. To some extent, such a policy did tend toward price stability. Lack of adequate foreign exchange was related to high domestic prices (relative to those in other countries), and the increase in interest rates tended in the direction of discouraging expenditure, which should weaken prices. Full employment was too indirectly related to be fostered effectively. Depressed conditions in foreign countries were readily transmitted, for low exports would be engendered and foreign exchange would be drawn down. The resultant marking-up of interest rates would tend to cut down on domestic activity. The government assumed little or no responsibility for full employment.

Integrated monetary policy in America originated with the Federal Reserve System, which had it roots in lessons drawn from the 1907 recession. It appeared to provide a remedy for currency crises, which at the time represented the prevalent explanation of business cycle recessions, especially of the 1907 recession. Under the National Banking System the money supply had been inflexible because currency expansion depended on the volume of gold and on a fixed and limited volume of specified government obligations (which were available as security for national bank notes); and because deposit expansion depended on the volume of prescribed reserves, causing the banks to become "loaned up" in prosperity. No machinery was available for increasing the deposit volume if an emergency arose; and this was particularly troublesome in view of the fact that "country" banks were expected to keep a part of their reserves in city banks, which used them in profitable loan undertakings in prosperous periods.

Monetary policy, which has come to represent changing cost and supply of credit for the purpose of stabilizing goals, is founded on the machinery made available by the establishment of the Federal Reserve System. The goals, as we see them today, slowly evolved. In the twenties, it seemed that monetary policy had come to provide a basis for maintaining a stable price level. In turn, the stabilization of activity seemed to have been achieved as a bonus value. This was before the advent of employment policy as a national goal; but the outcome of activity stabilization appeared natural, in view of the emphasis which had been placed on eliminating currency crises, and in view of attained recognition that instability represents a variation in total production (see Chapter 7).

THE MAJOR INSTRUMENTALITIES OF MONETARY CONTROL

The instrumentalities of monetary control include (1) changes in the permissive level of credit extension, (2) direct influences on the volume of credit outstanding, (3) changes in the cost of credit, and (4) persuasion or dissuasion, either by token of above instrumentalities or by direct warnings or appeals. These are principally on the level of indirect controls, involving an intentional "shotgun" effect with the purpose of the expansion or contraction of credit generally. Direct controls, involving efforts to influence credit extension in particular uses, are considered in the following section.

We examine indirect control measures employed to counter expansion separately from those employed to counter contraction, for the approaches are not precisely parallel. The permissive level of credit expansion is set by the percentage of reserves required as backing for deposits. The raising of reserve requirements to the legal maximum is looked on as a relatively extreme measure, to be taken only when inflationary conditions appear likely to get out of hand. A more direct influence on the amount of credit outstanding can be achieved by open-market operations (sale of government securities by the Federal Reserve). This is less likely to bring undue hardships in areas where growth may be unusually rapid. Although cash reserves are drawn away from banks by the process of open-market sales of government securities, any individual bank with a relatively large loan portfolio has a better chance of making an orderly adjustment and of avoiding swift curtailment. Aside from needs for seasonal requirements or for refunding operations of the government, however, the process is carried out to reduce credit availability for business in expanding operations.

Advancing the rediscount rate is a complementary measure adding to the cost of borrowing if the measure is taken in advance of rising interest rates in the commercial market, or confirming the rise which has taken place in the commercial market when the measures tightening outstanding credit conditions have already led to rises in commercial interest rates.

Often, all of these measures are applied negatively instead of positively: For instance, the normal seasonal credit requirements are not provided for in the fall when some credit restriction is felt to be necessary. The "moral suasion" involved often is more important than the quantitative measures taken. The fact that the rediscount rate is raised, for instance, provides a public warning that the Federal Reserve feels caution is necessary and that further restrictive action can be anticipated if conditions continue to become increasingly inflationary. Pressure also is brought to bear by official warnings, conferences, and personal contact with key bankers.

Partly because of the moral suasion applied, commercial banks begin to ration credit among applicants. This tends to be done on the basis of personal relationships—largely founded on how well customers are known and liked, and on the past profitability of the lines of credit they provide. Thus, the degree of risk involved and the rate of interest a customer is able to pay may play no greater part in the credit allocation than a qualitative custom factor. New and dynamic needs necessary for appropriate growth of the economy may be cut down, not because of potential risk but because the customers are new and untried; and under these circumstances, the banker finds satisfaction in restricting himself to proved credit lines without encountering any great financial loss. This is the penalty society pays for following a course of limitation. Theoretically, the banker would curb credit extension in riskier ventures and thus improve the average quality in the loan portfolio; but in practice the outcome may not be that simple.

The credit control actions taken by the Federal Reserve, to quote the Federal Reserve Act, are for "accommodating commerce and business." More and more, this means that in an inflationary atmosphere, efforts are made to allay rising prices, but not to the extent that satisfactory employment conditions will be endangered. For another thing, it is clearly recognized that the System does not have complete control over the level of prices, partly because offsetting actions may be taken in other sectors of the economy and partly because price changes often signalize maladjustments after they have occurred so that controls may be too late to influence forces which made prices rise. Furthermore, other considerations of national policy—such, for instance, as the needs of foreign trade— may make it impossible for the Federal Reserve to look too narrowly at domestic price stability and employment requirements. To be sure, all of this is vague, but as Goldenweiser says:

A more precise definition of objectives, even though it were feasible to construct one in understandable terms, would be sure to lack flexibility. Vagueness in the law and precision in responsible thinking are to be preferred to exactitude in the language of the law and indecisiveness in its application. Conditions change in unpredictable ways, and it is as unwise to incorporate current ideas on economic matters into permanent law as it is to build the mistakes of institutional planners into brick and mortar.[1]

In efforts to counter declines, the same methods are employed. The percentage of reserves required may be reduced, government securities may be purchased in the open market by the Federal Reserve, or the rediscount rate may be reduced. Since reserve requirements are changed reluctantly, the percentage requirement is lowered only if it is felt that a general level of credit expansion somewhat higher than current levels will be desirable for some time to come. Open-market purchases of government securities are made to such an extent that commercial banks are encouraged to pursue all loan applications which appear to involve a satisfactory credit rating. A matching reduction occurs in rediscount rates, so that business borrowing is encouraged both by reduced costs and by increased availability of funds.

Just as policy shift in the opposite direction involves a public warning that a tightening of credit is in progress, initiation of a policy of credit ease has significant anticipatory repercussions. However, the intended lesson is less likely to be effective. In prosperity, notice that credit is to be tightened usually leads bankers to get their houses in order because of fear of the effect of further tightening and because of the respect with which they hold the implied advice that inflationary dangers are increasingly imminent. Convic-

---

[1] E. A. Goldenweiser, *American Monetary Policy* (New York: McGraw-Hill Book Co., Inc., 1951), p. 76.

tion that a policy of easing credit is to be followed is less likely to lead to credit expansion. However, in recent recessions, there is little evidence that commercial bankers have become significantly concerned about increasing their liquidity, except, perhaps, in the case of inventory loans when businessmen generally are making strenuous efforts to effect some liquidation. After the recession has spent much of its force, bankers may search for customers and find that reduced interest cost appeals to some borrowers who can visualize favorable markets. In the case of long loans, reduced interest rates have a substantial influence on the total costs of borrowing. Where a steady market appears reasonable, loan agreements may be reached without too much difficulty. Term loans may be increasingly resorted to under these conditions.

The goals of monetary policy, in recession and in early recovery, when the existing level of unemployment is universally accepted to be too high, are principally directed at advance in activity. To an increasing extent, poor performance in terms of total activity in the economy is interpreted as justifying greater and greater credit ease. The money supply is increased, and rediscount rates are cut to very low levels if recession continues. The stable price criterion fades into the background if danger of inflation appears to have receded for the time being. At first, prices are not considered to be a major worry if unemployment remains large. When average prices again rise substantially, less emphasis is placed on employment needs.

QUALITATIVE CREDIT CONTROL

Many persons who believe that credit control is an essential policy in the interests of stabilization nevertheless hold that the effect of the measures discussed above is too indiscriminate to be satisfactory. Credit control may fail to reach areas where it is most needed, and may be damaging or ineffective in areas where control is undesirable. This is because change in the cost of credit may not influence its use in some applications, and because it is felt that credit expansion readily leads to unstable maladjustments in some areas. As an illustration of the first point, the demand for consumer credit appears to be little affected by wide variations in interest rates. As to the second point, since consumer credit tends to recede if disposable income falls, rapid extension in prosperity may be considered unstabilizing; and areas like the stock market, where credit extension is thought to be motivated by speculation, could lead to a large volume of debt which would face liquidation, as in the contraction following 1929.

Because of the debt liquidation which followed from purchase of securities with borrowed funds in 1929, margin requirements, prescribing the proportion of credit which may be extended on the loan value of securities, have become an established practice. These margin requirements are administered by the Federal Reserve, and are increased when dependence of the stock market on credit is thought to point to a disturbing situation. Margin requirements have been raised in each prosperity since the war. They were driven up to 100 per cent in 1946, to 75 per cent during the Korean War, to 70 per cent in 1955, and to 90 per cent late in 1958. So far, this regulation seems to have been effective in keeping stock market credit down to reasonable levels.

Consumer credit regulation (Regulation W) was in effect in the United States from September, 1941, to November, 1947; from September, 1948, to June, 1949; and from September, 1950, to May, 1952. It dealt with minimum down payment and maximum maturity of instalment debt. The first period represented a regulation during the war for the specific purpose of facilitating transfer of productive resources to defense industries, except for continuance for a brief period during reconversion. By December, 1946, regulation was removed on many of the items covered and slightly relaxed on those on which control was continued until November, 1947.

In response to the continued rise in prices after the regulation was removed in 1947, re-enactment as to automobiles, major appliance, furniture, and rugs took effect in September, 1948. Large purchases were made in anticipation of renewed control, and the onset of recession two months after the regulation took effect cast doubt on the effectiveness of any inflationary control achieved. By the spring of 1950 and before the onset of the Korean War, renewed expansion in the demand for consumer durable goods was pressing against the limits of capacity. It was inevitable, therefore, that with the passage of the Defense Production Act, consumer credit control would be re-enacted. It represented a part of the general war control; and in view of the limited influence of the war, it was much less restrictive than the control in effect in World War II. The effect on consumers was also moderated by the very large purchases of consumer durables in the third quarter of 1950 before the control went into operation.

Thus, consumer credit controls have been imposed only during times when the entire economy was being subjected to many direct controls as the outcome of war, except for the brief period of 1948-49. That the 1948 re-enactment was a fiasco as inflationary control does not provide a fair evaluation of the importance of controlling consumer credit in the interest of stabilization. Unquestionably, consumer credit adds to expenditures when disposable income is rising and may become a significant inflationary influence if the purchase of consumer durables rises rapidly when pressure on demand becomes great under highly prosperous conditions. Any measure might, however, do more harm than good if enactment of the regulation is debated when it is most needed, as in 1948. To be effective, stand-by legislation should be available.

Housing credit is a third major type which has been subjected to selective controls. The only important restrictive measures have been enacted during war and are of little help in analyzing controls under peacetime conditions. In the most recent instance, the Federal Reserve Regulation X was operative from October, 1950, to September, 1952. Maximum loan values and maximum maturities permissible for credit provided were set to curb housing activity which might otherwise have drawn away materials and labor needed in the war effort.

Expansionary efforts are almost universal for housing whenever growth in expenditures is accepted as inadequate. A striking illustration is the Federal Housing Administration, which planned in the Great Depression to insure mortgages for lenders and thereby increase their willingness to lend money on housing. Plans were worked out so that any liquidation of FHA-insured mortgages would be orderly rather than demoralized. The plans were further extended after World War II. A special system was set up for mortgages required by veterans of the war. The FHA and VA systems have come to finance approximately 40 per cent of the debt on residential mortgages. The efforts at all times are in the direction of credit ease and can scarcely be said to contribute a great deal to business cycle therapy. A striking illustration of the extremes to which this policy has been carried is illustrated by the fact that, with permissible interest rates under the VA and FHA financing systems falling below market rates in 1956–57, financing through them declined. Thus, housing activity in the 1957–58 recession was down substantially, and significant revival occurred only after the minimum interest rate permissible under these programs was *raised*.

In spite of the fact that, aside from war periods, housing policy measures have almost continuously moved toward credit ease, so far it has been found possible to add substantially to the easement in recessions. In 1949, this appeared unnecessary because housing starts continued to rise in view of continued urgent demand for housing. Early in 1954, interest charges permitted on FHA and VA loans were increased, producing the effect noted at the end of the preceding paragraph. An automatic effect was created by declining commercial interest rates as the recession developed, so that shifts occurred to contracts with more favorable financing terms. As summarized in the *Survey of Current Business* for April, 1954:

One aspect of the improvement in financing may be seen in the rising proportion of Veterans Administration home loans being made with no downpayment and with maturities of 25 years or more. In February over 15 percent of all home loans closed involved no down payment, in contrast to almost 12 percent in the fourth quarter of last year and 9 percent in the third quarter. Similarly, loans with maturities of 25 years or more were 56 percent of the VA total this February as compared with 48 percent in the fourth quarter and 42 percent in the third quarter.

A large number of relaxations were made in the 1957–58 recession in addition to the raising of permissible interest rate charges in the FHA and VA programs, noted above. Minimum down payments were reduced, funds were released for the purchase of mortgages by the Federal National Mortgage Association, rules requiring that closing costs be paid in cash were rescinded, together with other easements in detailed technical requirements.

Reduction in down payment requirements in the spring of 1960 clearly indicated that movements toward credit ease are sensitive to any slight hesitation in advancing expenditures. In other words, the policies taken on housing credit appear to be founded on the same philosophy as the "underwriting of consumer expenditures" summarized in the preceding chapter. Representing an area so much less comprehensive, however, the inflationary potential is far less devastating.

We have but one experience with policy decisions on consumer credit control during recession—in 1949. With the downturn occurring in November, 1948, maximum maturities permissible for instalment credit were first increased early in March and further advanced together with some decreases in down payments late in April. These changes came after the recession was more than a third over. There is no reason to believe that timing could not be at least equally good in future recessions. Actually, most of the desirable influence could be achieved without close timing. Assume that standard terms which are only slightly restrictive were established and subject to change only if the economy is endangered with highly inflationary conditions or if the existence of a recession were obvious to everyone. As the inflationary conditions passed, the control could move back to the standard terms without reliance on a precise forecast of the downturn. After the terms were further relaxed in recession, they could be moved back to the standard terms when it appeared generally obvious that prosperous conditions had returned. In some prosperities, it might be unnecessary to move to terms more restrictive than the standard because the demand pressure on resources might not be excessive. The major excuse for a plan such as outlined here would lie in the fact that indirect monetary control can exert little influence on consumer credit variation because it is insensitive to interest rate changes.

Margin requirements on stock market purchases have been relaxed in each postwar recession. In relation to the first recession, relaxation occurred nearly two years before the downturn—in February, 1947—not because a downturn was anticipated but because stock prices had dropped a fourth from the 1946 peak and speculative dangers had been abated. A further cut was made in response to the recession at the end of March, 1949, some four months after the downturn. The next cut occurred in February, 1953, but not in response to anticipation of the downturn which occurred a half year later. Rather, it was part of a program, with war requirements leveling out, of taking "steps toward freer, more self-reliant markets."[2] Stock market credit was at a low level when the change was made and expanded immediately, but shortly leveled off. As the relaxation was made, stock prices were at their peak and immediately began to *decline* in spite of increased use of credit; and the decline continued for a year, when business upturn was a half year away. No further relaxation was made during the recession.

Margin terms were relaxed in January, 1958, a half year after the downturn in July, 1957. In this case, no ulterior reasons existed before the downturn to warrant relaxation before it occurred, as in the two previous recessions. History reveals that margin requirements were not changed in specific response to business cycle changes, but rather to counter what appeared to be undesirable changes in stock market prices or undesirable use of credit in the stock market. Recognizing our inability to time changes coincidentally with downturns and upturns, the credit and stock market criteria unquestionably appear superior. In fact, one might argue that

---

[2]See Federal Reserve System, *Fortieth Annual Report of the Board of Governors, 1953* (Washington, D.C., 1954), pp. 6–8.

they would be superior even if perfect timing with the business cycle were possible. They are directed at the influences we would wish to avoid, and it is through soundness of stock prices and of the credit supporting them that business fluctuations may be favorably influenced by such control.

CREDIT VARIATION OUT OF FEDERAL RESERVE CONTROL

Control of credit is not neatly centralized in the Federal Reserve. In the first place, many other agencies have specific responsibility for influencing credit in their particular field. Selective control of credit in housing is a good illustration. The Federal Reserve has not had specific responsibility in this field since 1952, as indicated above. In addition to the responsibilities of the Federal Housing Administration and the Federal National Mortgage Association, there are several other agencies under the over-all supervision of the Housing and Home Finance Agency, including the Public Housing Administration and the Home Loan Bank Board. The Veterans Administration has autonomy for control in the VA loan system.

The Veterans Administration also has responsibility for the insurance of farm and business loans to veterans. A labyrinth of control of agricultural credit is also dispersed among many agencies, including the Farm Credit Administration, and involving banks for co-operatives, production credit corporations, intermediate credit banks, and land banks. Also involved are the Rural Electrification Administration, the Commodity Credit Corporation, and Farmers Home Administration.

Additional credit areas are covered by the Export-Import Bank and by the Commodity Credit Corporation in strategic stock-piling arrangements for defense purposes. We shall not recite more agencies which play a part in credit policies; but clearly, there is an undetermined degree of influence out of the control of the Federal Reserve. Generally, the influences relate to provision of credit obtained through the agency of the banking system and to administered interest rates which may be divergent from market conditions, rather than to a money-creating function. Nonetheless, these agencies do exercise an important, although undetermined, influence on credit conditions in the country. Also, the policies pursued usually are not pointed at the stabilization of general business conditions. A truly effective credit policy would have to counter many of the actions taken by these agencies, in addition to countering the movements of general business.

In the second place, control of the cost and amount of credit exerts no necessary influence on the velocity of spending. By faster spending, the same amount of credit will cover more transactions. If the amount of money is greatly increased in pursuance of a policy of credit ease, the velocity may fall enough that transactions are not increased. Another way of saying approximately the same thing is that more or less of the money supply may be held in idle balances.

An important development in recent years involves a mushroom growth of "financial intermediaries" outside of the monetary system of the banks. Good illustrations are credit unions and savings and loan associations, which have increased rapidly in number and in volume of operations. An individual may place idle money which he had been holding for precautionary purposes in such an institution and still retain most or all of the precautionary advantages he had in holding the money idle.

Shares of a savings and loan association are a highly liquid asset involving little or no risk because of insurance features. In New York State, mutual savings banks can pay bills for depositors, making savings deposits a means of payment. The funds obtained by the nonmonetary financial intermediary are loaned in the investment market and pay interest to depositors.

Nonmonetary financial intermediaries may be governmental or private. Among the former may be mentioned federal land banks and government insurance and pension funds. In addition to credit unions and savings and loan associations, life insurance companies and mutual savings banks are important illustrations of private intermediaries. The precise effect of nonmonetary financial intermediaries is still open to question, but they do appear to have provided a secular change in efficiency of the use of money.

Another way by which bank money can be made to go further is represented by a type of "near money" which often substitutes for currency. Tokens, in payment of specific obligations such as for local transportation, are an illustration of a time-honored type, but their use probably has not been increasing. Consumer credit on account is a type which has been increasing. Charge accounts represent another familiar type, but credit cards probably have accounted for a much greater increase in volume in recent years. Credit of this type economizes on money because a pooled precautionary reserve makes possible a smaller aggregate idle balance than if it were held by many individuals.

Although the effects of increasing efficiency in the use of idle balances because of the above influences is unmeasured, we can show that a dollar of final product is paid for with less money, measured by demand deposits plus currency, than in 1955. Money so measured represented over a third of the dollar amount of yearly gross national income in early 1955 and represented less than 30 per cent in 1960. A $500 billion product is now sold with $140 billion in money, while less than $400 billion in product employed $132 billion in money in 1955.

LAGS IN THE APPLICATION OF MONETARY POLICY

If indirect monetary controls are used to counter undesirable changes in prices and in activity, several lags can be recognized in the application and the taking-effect of control:

1. A forecasting lag may occur because forecasts may be unsatisfactory.
2. A brief period may be required to implement the appropriate policy once a forecast is accepted.
3. The availability of credit to the borrower ordinarily will not be effected immediately after the policy action is taken.
4. Some time will elapse after change in availability of credit before it has the desired effect on prices and on gross national product.

1. Clearly, forecasting is necessary in effective application of countering policy. The influence desired relates to future and not to present or past conditions. A forecasting lag in applying controls results partly from the fact that information on current conditions —and, more importantly, on inadequacy of the forecasts made— cannot be made immediately available. The inadequacy of forecasts seems to be overemphasized, however, partly because of the stress placed on inadequacy by Federal Reserve officials. In view of the fact that the Federal Reserve was applying measures to tighten credit after the downturn in July, 1957, it is revealing to find that the tone of discussion in meetings of the Open Market Committee through most of the early part of that year indicated a pessimistic outlook. As summarized by Asher Achinstein:

In the light of the vehemence and the frequency with which Federal Reserve officials publicly stressed during the first 10 months of 1957 the necessity for continuing monetary restraint, it comes as a surprise to read the record of the 1957 meetings of the Open Market Committee. During almost all of the 18 meetings held throughout the year there appeared to be an absence of that confidence in the business outlook and in the continuation of inflationary pressures which was manifested in public statements by top spokesmen for the System.[3]

2. If policy actions exaggerate the extent to which forecasts used by the Open Market Committee are inferior, the second lag—the period required to implement policy—must be assigned increased importance. Perhaps these lags shade into each other—a wavering develops on accepting the predominant forecast. Improvements now being made in forecasting methods can confidently be expected to lead to better forecasting by the Open Market Committee and to reduce the combined length of the first two lags. However, business conditions can never be forecast with certainty, and the Federal Reserve can be expected to hedge its position in order to minimize the danger of being caught in an extreme predicament. An ambivalent position, rather than one in conflict with prevalent optimistic attitudes before a downturn or pessimistic attitudes before an upturn, is to be expected.

If countering actions were taken at those times, they might well be misunderstood. Credit ease produced before the downturn actually occurred would appear to fan the flames of inflation. Policy actions with a deflationary intent before the upturn actually occurs would be condoned by no one.

3. A variety of factors tend to produce some lag in the time it takes to influence borrowers. The lag produced by all such factors is short, perhaps adding to no more than a month, with two possible exceptions. The important lags relate to the slowness with which the policy action is put into effect and the time it may take to transmit the change in credit pressure from the short- to the long-term markets, if only short-term government securities are traded in open-market policy. The Federal Reserve seldom tightens or eases credit suddenly, but generally by small steps spread out over several months. Until the effect has accumulated for some time, the change in the secondary credit market position may be changed so slightly that credit conditions for the private borrower may be little affected. Reading from experience, a great deal of variation exists in the time taken to influence the long-term market if only

---

[3]U.S. Senate, Committee on Banking and Currency, *Federal Reserve Policy and Economic Stability, 1955–57*, Senate Report No. 2500, 85th Cong., 2d sess. (Washington, D.C.: U.S. Government Printing Office, 1958), p. xiii. Shift to a questioning attitude on the current economic situation is evident from the time of the February meeting. The summary Minutes of these meetings are reproduced in Federal Reserve System, *Forty-Fourth Annual Report of the Board of Governors, 1957* (Washington, D.C., 1958), pp. 34–62.

short-term securities are used in policy action; but at times, it seems to have taken several months.[4]

"Bills only,"[5] as the policy of trading only in short-term government securities in open-market operations is called, has been the subject of much controversy. Those opposed to it lay their principal arguments on the time lag required for policy actions to take effect. Those who defend it hold (1) that because of the role of expectations, dealers in government bonds might be encouraged by Federal Reserve action to take market positions which are unsustainable and actually inconsistent with the supply-demand situation and (2) that influences exerted in the long-term market have a greater significance than in the short-term market. With respect to the first point, we may call attention to the 1958 experience, when a thinly margined long position in government bonds was widespread among traders. The open-market policy of the Federal Reserve at the time involved buying government securities to support credit ease. If the purchase of long-term securities had been involved, accusation might have developed that the Federal Reserve was supporting the speculative position of traders in government bonds. Late in 1958 the price of government bonds was falling (with a rise in interest rates) instead of rising, so that many traders suffered severe losses in closing out speculative accounts.

The argument that transactions in the long-term market represent dealings with a heavy hand is founded on the fact that the fluctuation in interest rates on short-term securities is ordinarily associated with a smaller variation in interest rates on longer-term government bonds. If the Federal Reserve dealt in long-term securities, the interest rate variation in government bonds might tend more nearly to approximate that in Treasury bills and certificates, with a devastating influence on the fluctuation in the asset value of government bonds.

A converse argument is that it is the long-term market which needs to be reached, especially in recession. The low level of activity in durable investment is the most crucial, and its financing depends to a substantial degree on the price of long-term bonds.

The "bills only" doctrine is a market factor. We cannot look confidently for any substantial change in lags caused by the time

---

[4]See Alvin H. Hansen, "Monetary Policy," *Review of Economics and Statistics,* May, 1955; and Deane Carson, "Recent Open Market Committee Policy and Techniques," *Quarterly Journal of Economics,* August, 1955.

[5]For a summary defense of the "bills only" doctrine, see "Open-Market Operations in Long-Term Securities," *Federal Reserve Bulletin,* November, 1958.

required for credit pressure to be transmitted from short- to long-term security markets.[6]

4. The time required for policy actions to exert an actual effect on prices and/or output is a most important lag. The time involved arises first of all because the Federal Reserve is trying to counter a part of the private market influences, not to offset them. Thus, one reason why action counters private market influences only to a partial extent is that it is designed that way. If violent and rapid enough action were taken, a complete offset could be produced; but as we have noted above, the Federal Reserve understandably refuses to take so violent a position. It is sometimes said that counter-measures could not be produced in recession because extending credit at such a time is like letting string out on a kite—if the market situation fails to appear promising, private interests will not avail themselves of additional credit in making expenditures. But if all caution were thrown to the winds and the Federal Reserve increased the money supply without limit, sooner or later the fear of inflation would induce major increases in expenditures.

With less consummate measures, a long lag of indeterminate length tends to appear. As for expenditures, the effect is partially or wholly offset by changes in demand. For instance, the investment demand curve shifts. With a rise in demand, this curve moves to the right. Even advanced interest rates thus may be associated with increasing amounts of investment expenditure. Little doubt exists as to the fact that much of the rise in demand is transient. This means that in time the pressure of a rise in interest rates will cut off investment demand, but with a policy of mild pressures the time may differ little from the date at which a downturn would have occurred because of the play of market forces. A major reason for the transient advance in investment demand, as outlined in earlier chapters, is the doubly reinforcing nature of investment expenditures themselves.

The advance in prices may be no more than moderated because of the supplementation of primary money supply with near-money contrivances and active use of many money balances which had been substantially idle. Thus, cutting-off of the supply of bank credit

---

[6]Except for a shift in the Federal Reserve policy. In the fall of 1960, the policy of "bills usually, but not always" was invoked. To evaluate this policy, we must know how often and under what circumstances bills will be preferred. A Federal Reserve announcement on February 20, 1961 was currently interpreted to represent an ending of limitation of open market trading to bills. The extent to which the operations will come to involve longer term securities remains to be determined.

can, for an indefinite time, be largely offset by more efficient monetary use with the aid of nonmonetary institutions. We are not sure of the extent to which these contrivances represent a cyclical stimulation. They may be principally secular developments which nevertheless may adventitiously add to monetary efficiency when the Federal Reserve is trying to cut down on its use. Unfortunately, we know so little about such secular developments that the Federal Reserve is hard put to take them into consideration in making policy decisions.

When supporting action is desirable, about the same kind of a situation develops. The investment demand curve shifts to the left. Even with greatly reduced interest rates, investment projects are substantially curtailed. Increase in the supply of primary money does not change greatly the rate of market expenditure so long as it is not interpreted as a major influence on the prospective price level, and so long as the Federal Reserve is careful to avoid profligate measures.

With improved long-term forecasting the time will surely come when the cyclical shift in the investment demand curve will be reduced. Under these circumstances, the variation in interest rates, where financing is with bonds, should produce a greater effect on the amount of investment expenditure. Even under such conditions, however, it is possible that, in prosperity, stock prices would rise sufficiently that equity financing could offset debt financing and investment expenditures could continue undeterred by tighter monetary policy. (Of course, we could plausibly argue that the long-term planning which is assumed to offset the optimistic forces driving the investment demand curve to the right might also keep down the optimistic sentiment which would account for abnormally high stock prices.)

Furthermore, the time will surely come when we can better anticipate the *secular* changes in efficiency in the use of money originating outside the banking system. Then, in adding to the money supply, the Federal Reserve could better anticipate the need for additional monetary supply to accommodate commerce and business.

Little hope can be held out that the changes anticipated in the two preceding paragraphs will make much difference within the next five to ten years. Under the circumstances, no tight monetary control of average prices or total expenditures appears possible because of extended lags which will arise in the application of monetary policy. The conclusion is not that monetary policy can be of no importance, but that it should be considered a broad modulating force rather than a basis for neat countering of undesirable price and expenditure movements. This point is more fully developed below.

SHOULD WE ADOPT A POLICY OF STEADY GROWTH IN THE MONEY SUPPLY?

In a growing economy a related growth is required in the money supply. If we assume the relation is one-to-one under present conditions, the Federal Reserve might use the major instrumentalities of monetary control to keep as close as possible on the course of the rate of growth of total deflated gross national product. If we assume the basic rate of growth is 4 per cent, the major goal of monetary policy then would be to maintain the growth of money supply at 4 per cent at all times.

Laying aside the question of the exact rate of growth occurring in deflated gross national product and whether a precisely similar growth is required in the money supply, most students feel that the use of a rule requiring a constant growth in the money supply would sacrifice important stabilizing potentialities. Granted the policy has not neatly countered the movement of final expenditures or of average prices, nevertheless it has provided a force which has tended to lighten deflationary forces in recession and which has tended to slow down inflationary movements in prosperity when the economy was threatened with substantial price rises.

Look at the period 1955–57. The monetary supply, represented by demand deposits plus currency,[7] rose 2 per cent instead of the 7 or 8 per cent implied by the above rule. Nevertheless, the Wholesale Price Index rose 6 per cent, and the Consumers Price Index rose nearly as much. It stands to reason that a greater increase in the money supply would have augmented the price increase. The difficulty lies in the increase in the velocity of money (or more rapid use of idle balances) for the reasons explained above.

Or take the nine months of recession from July, 1957, to April, 1958. Unemployment was rising rapidly, and final expenditures were declining. On the other hand, the Wholesale Price Index rose nearly

---

[7]In this sense, demand deposits are adjusted to eliminate interbank and United States government deposits; and currency is adjusted to eliminate holdings of the Treasury, the Federal Reserve banks, and the holdings of vault cash by all banks. The figures employed are seasonally adjusted. For a recent revision of this series, see the *Federal Reserve Bulletin,* October, 1960.

1 per cent and consumer prices about 2 per cent. The money supply was not increased at all. Would conditions have been much improved if the money supply had increased at the rate of secular requirements? Most students would hesitate to give an unequivocal answer. If they gave a "yes" answer, it would be based on the belief that the money supply should be increased because there was a recession, but not necessarily at the secular rate. If they gave a "no" answer, it would be because they felt that the price increase was undesirable and should have been offset. Both of these answers depend on a forecast of current conditions rather than of secular requirements.

Those students who advocate a policy of steady increase in the money supply assign the changing supply of money major causal importance in determining economic change. Rather than answer the questions we have posed in the above paragraph, they would question the probability of achieving as serious a culmination as occurred in 1957 if a sufficient money supply had been made available at all times. The argument is not that no fluctuations would occur in aggregative economic activity, but that culminating forces would be impeded. To take this position, one must be a "quantity theorist" and assign great importance to changes in the quantity of money in the equation of exchange.[8]

RECENT EXPERIENCE WITH GENERAL MONETARY CONTROL

Chart 23-1 contrasts changes in the major applications of indirect monetary control with changes in gross national product (after allowance for growth, since appropriate stabilization policy should point to levels needed with growth rather than just a horizontal level). If we were looking for a prompt countering, monetary stringency should correspond with increases in gross national product and monetary ease with declines in gross national product.

Since purchase of government securities in the open market adds to monetary ease, which is the appropriate policy under depressed conditions, this series is plotted on an inverted scale. It is dangerous to read the relations to open-market operations too precisely because an important part of them is made in response to seasonal needs (especially in the fall) and to maintain an orderly market when the Treasury is engaging in major refinancing opera-

---

[8]See B. W. Sprinkel, "Monetary Growth as a Cyclical Predictor," *Journal of Finance,* September, 1959; and Clark Warburton, "The Misplaced Emphasis in Contemporary Business Fluctuation Theory," *Journal of Business,* October, 1946.

tions. No effective basis is available for adjusting the series for these extraneous factors. The general policy has been to rely on reserve requirements to a decreasing extent, since that policy lends itself less readily to flexible adjustments by the member banks than policies involved in other instrumentalities of control. This largely accounts for the fact that the reserve requirement line declines continuously over the five years plotted on the chart.

CHART 23–1

Monetary Control Factors, 1955–59

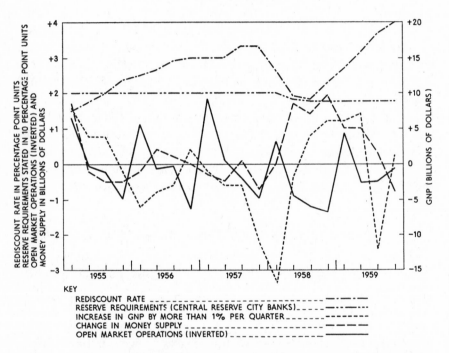

KEY

REDISCOUNT RATE	— ·—·—
RESERVE REQUIREMENTS (CENTRAL RESERVE CITY BANKS)	—··—···
INCREASE IN GNP BY MORE THAN 1% PER QUARTER	————
CHANGE IN MONEY SUPPLY	━━ ━━
OPEN MARKET OPERATIONS (INVERTED)	━━━━

Source: Board of Governors, Federal Reserve System; Office of Business Economics, Department of Commerce.

Note: Changes in money supply are stated in current dollars—the total level at the beginning of 1955 was $131 billion and at the end of 1959, $140 billion. The figures used are demand deposits, seasonally adjusted to exclude interbank, United States government, and cash items reported as in process of collection. The GNP change is stated in constant 1954 dollars, and the change plotted is from 1 per cent above the preceding quarterly figure (to allow for growth).

It should come as no surprise that monetary policy has not countered short-term changes in gross national product. The whole plan of Federal Reserve monetary policy is not patterned to provide quick offsets to changes in activity. Even if it were, the lags described above would balk success.

On a yearly basis, Chart 23–2 shows that Federal Reserve policy

generally represents countering movements in the right direction.
Special conditions existed in the years 1955 and 1959. In 1955 an
unusually rapid increase occurred in consumer durables and in
business investment. Even so, no serious demand pressure was being

CHART 23–2

CHANGE IN MONETARY CONTROL FACTORS, 1955–59°

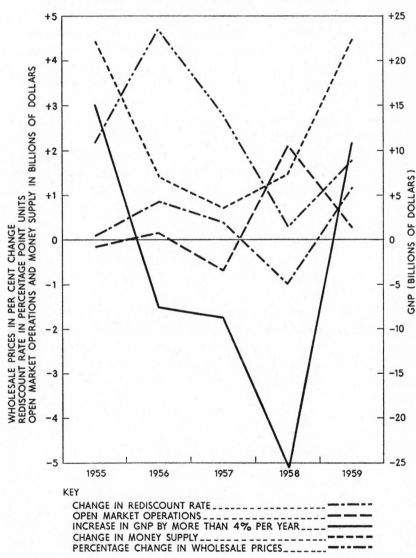

KEY

CHANGE IN REDISCOUNT RATE	—·—·—
OPEN MARKET OPERATIONS	———
INCREASE IN GNP BY MORE THAN 4% PER YEAR	———
CHANGE IN MONEY SUPPLY	▬ ▬ ▬
PERCENTAGE CHANGE IN WHOLESALE PRICES	▬·▬·▬

°For sources and description of series, see footnote to Chart 23–1, except for the percentage
change in wholesale prices. The series used is wholesale prices other than farm products and
foods. The percentage changes refer to percentage changes from one year to another, not to
number of points change in the index.

put on available resources. Unemployment continued to decline slightly in 1956 and early 1957. Under these circumstances, the low rediscount rate and increase in the money supply (shown by a plus position on the chart) can scarcely be severely criticized in spite of the fact that there was a 2 per cent increase in prices in 1955. Unemployment was greater in 1959 than in 1955; but prices increased almost as much in 1959 as in 1955, the advance in gross national product was similar, and the money supply was increased by the same amount. Rediscount rates were increased more, although that was to a considerable extent the result of the movement of the money market in the private economy.

Prices rose nearly 5 per cent in 1956. We might ask if the Federal Reserve should not have engaged in more restrictive policies in that year. The change in gross national product was not as much as our crude 4 per cent growth standard, although it must be admitted that such a criterion is far from precise. Nevertheless, activity did not appear to be excessively high with percentage unemployment greater than in previous postwar prosperity periods. The Federal Reserve had a difficult decision to make; and no doubt, fear of being blamed for a recession, if one should occur, was an influential factor in keeping the restriction relatively mild. In any case the course taken was median between advocacy of more stringent measures to prevent inflation and advocacy of strong measures to minimize unemployment.

We have not reviewed the postwar years before 1955 because they do not provide good lessons on what monetary policy can do under typical peacetime conditions. Until the time of the Korean War the Federal Reserve was involved in supporting the government bond market. An Accord between the Federal Reserve and the Treasury was reached in 1951, and the Korean War created special problems thereafter.

BROAD NEED FOR MONETARY POLICY

The comparison of monetary policy actions with changes in total economic conditions in Charts 23–1 and 23–2 relates only to the extent to which actions were timed correctly, and not to achievement. It is difficult, if not impossible, to isolate the influence monetary policy action had. Partly, this is because of the indeterminate delay before policy actions influence economic conditions. Also, it is because many other factors influence economic conditions, including other types of policy action as well as forces within the private economy. It is much easier to show the apparent influence of fiscal policy actions because these may be reduced to a net expenditure effect.

Although monetary policy is of limited importance as a countering measure, it plays an important role along with other stabilizing measures. All persons, after inspection, will agree that monetary changes do influence changes in aggregate economic conditions, and that this influence is better planned than unplanned. Reflecting on the limited purposes stated in the Federal Reserve Act in 1913, Goldenweiser said:

A sounder and more elastic credit and currency system is not an adequate objective of monetary management in the middle of the twentieth century. What the monetary authorities strive to promote by the means at their disposal is a sounder and more stable economy. These broader objectives may have been foreshadowed by some orators advocating the passage of the Federal Reserve Act, but they were not the cardinal considerations or the moving force for the adoption of the legislation. Money and credit are only a means to an end; they must be made to serve the interests of steadily expanding prosperity and national well-being.[9]

We must not conclude that the kind of policy actions now taken are necessarily inferior to an effort to provide neat countering measures. On the one hand, it is doubtful if such neat measures could be successful, and more disturbance than stabilization might result. On the other hand, what is most needed at the present time is assured financial stability. That, as the major aim of monetary policy as we know it, is at least a plausible reading of the actions now taken. Financial stability would be upset if either serious depression or undue inflation occurred. The method employed to promote financial stability is the application of mild pressures to keep the actions of commercial bankers within limits that are judged to be reasonable for the economy. Bankers are so attuned to this system that "unless the change in requirements comes unexpectedly, banks are likely to be so ready for it when it comes that the actual event will not have much effect on their actions."[10]

Change in requirements is made rapidly when the economy is undergoing movements that carry activity dangerously high or dangerously low, in accordance with the judgment of the monetary authorities. Agreement is universal that the type of judgment in-

---

[9]*Op. cit.,* p. 73.

[10]Paul T. Homan, Albert G. Hart, and Arnold W. Sametz, *The Economic Order* (New York: Harcourt, Brace & Co., Inc., 1958), p. 528.

volved has shifted violently from that held thirty years ago. If descent into a deep depression became obvious, as it was in the early thirties, a rapid shift would be made to credit ease, contrary to the course pursued then. Note the marked difference between this idea of stability and that of immediate countering of current fluctuations in general business conditions.

Nonetheless, the current type of monetary control presents serious problems. We shall call attention to four at this point. In the first place, the timing of Federal Reserve policy at the downturn is particularly unfortunate. A continued tightening of credit conditions after the downturn occurs is scarcely commendable on any score. We may hope, as a minimum, that improved forecasting and/or improved faith in forecasting will bring the Federal Reserve to forswear cautious avoidance of any action when a downturn is imminent. Improvement in forecasting techniques should help in bringing this about.

In the second place, more needs to be done to discourage commerical bankers in shifting credit standards over the business cycle. If standards were tightened in prosperity, something could be said for the shift, but it would appear that increased laxity tends to occur at that time. Progress appears to have been made in this direction, but what is most needed is a better understanding among bankers of the extent of the transientness of demand under the extremes of prosperity and of depression.

In the third place, disturbing questions arise as to the characteristic concentration in the impact of general credit stringency. Certain areas of the economy are particularly affected, not because they are overexpanding unduly or because a dangerous credit unbalance is developing, but simply because they are most sensitive to interest rate changes. This applies notably to housing and to the utility industry. As has often been said, if credit restriction is to have any effect, it will have to pinch somewhere, and those who get pinched will find the experience distasteful. To some persons, however, it is a discovery to find that the pinches are not necessarily related to growing stresses or developing instability. Perhaps a thorough study of the possibilities of co-ordinating general controls with carefully tailored qualitative controls is needed.

In the fourth place, the effectiveness of the Federal Reserve policy surely would be substantially improved if co-ordinated with credit control practices exercised by other agencies. This is another reason for introducing qualitative controls into the general program of monetary policy, for most of the influence exercised by other agencies relates to qualitative control. Granted that the precise effect of any credit measure is not wholly predictable, it still is desirable to narrow the range of variation by bringing all of the controls exercised by government agencies into a co-ordinated policy. To effect such a change would be little short of revolutionary, since other agencies exercising credit influences are governed by very different motivation from the Federal Reserve and face the problems of particular sectors of the economy rather than financial problems which pervade the whole economy. We have no suggestions to make on how the co-ordination may be achieved, but limit our comments to its desirability and perhaps inevitability.

To effect any such co-ordination, the Federal Reserve might find it necessary to operate in a more predictable manner. Part of the technique now employed is the avoidance of explanation of policy actions before they are taken. In order to preserve the character of anonymity, instead of taking positive action to produce credit ease or credit stringency, often contrary action is not taken when other considerations, such as seasonal needs, require it. To co-ordinate with other agencies, the Federal Reserve would have to state policies explicitly and usually in advance.

In the interest of general economic policy a still broader co-ordination is necessary, involving fiscal policy, debt management, and broad planning. Thinking along this line is developed in the following chapter.

FOR REFLECTION AND ANALYSIS

1. High-light the importance of open-market operations.
2. Should the Federal Reserve give us a more precise statement of objectives of monetary policy?
3. How do recession and expansion goals for monetary policy differ?
4. What is the argument for qualitative credit control on consumer credit?
5. Evaluate the experience with consumer credit in 1948–49.
6. Why have FHA loans increased with a rise in permissible interest rates?
7. Is the high level of mortgages on housing as dangerous as in 1929?
8. Should margin-requirement changes on stock market purchases be changed with the business cycle?
9. What do you think of the importance of "near money"?
10. What does the "bills only" doctrine have to do with lags in the application of market policy?
11. How long does it take a change in monetary controls to influence the action of businessmen?

12. What kind of causal influence is implied if one argues that a satisfactory rate of growth in the money supply would insure satisfactory growth in the total economy?
13. Evaluate recent successes in monetary policy.
14. Differentiate between the current monetary policy and that which would exist if a prompt countering action were taken.
15. Outline what you see to be desirable steps toward reform of the policies of monetary control.

Chapter 24

CO-ORDINATION OF EMPLOYMENT AND INFLATION POLICY

We turn in this chapter to co-ordination of policy measures, to their organization and governmental direction, and finally to an evaluation of the prospects that stability in the economy may improve or worsen. This analysis is essential to visualize policy operation in a workable framework. The final evaluation of prospects is necessarily speculative, but should aid the reader in relating policy measures to the inherent instability in the economy.

PUBLIC DEBT MANAGEMENT

Management of the public debt provides a tool complementary to fiscal and monetary policy, and it is therefore given explicit consideration before we take up the co-ordination of policies. By debt management is meant all actions (1) which change the amount of publicly held federal debt and (2) which change the composition of that debt. Change in amount is closely related to fiscal policy, and change in composition is closely related to monetary policy.

As the term is ordinarily used, public holdings include all federal debt except that held in federal government accounts or by the Federal Reserve banks. That amount has kept close to $200 billion since the end of the war. (The amount held in United States government accounts comes to $55 billion, double the figure at the end of the war, and by the Federal Reserve banks to $25 billion, about the same as at the end of the war.) The part of the publicly held debt which is marketable (excluding such securities as savings bonds) is approximately $150 billion and is most significantly concerned in debt management.

Short-term federal debt is a principal liquid or operating reserve asset for banks, other financial institutions, and business corporations. Any change made in it, therefore, has a critical effect on the economy. With the present composition of publicly held, marketable issues of federal debt, about a third is due within one year, and another third matures in between one and five years. With so much in short maturities, management policies are frequently handicapped. In the order of $50 billion has to be refunded nearly every year, and the operation may be upsetting in the capital funds market. An important factor in driving up interest rates in 1959 was the constant maturing of Treasury securities, with the attendant scramble in the open market to recapture the funds. What is needed is a debt distribution with maturities well spaced over a period of years. This would require a substantial shift to securities with intermediate and long-term maturities.

Changing the debt distribution is a tricky and difficult problem. As a matter of economy, the maturity structure would be lengthened in recession when interest rates are relatively low. Unfortunately, however, this is the wrong economic stabilization policy. Reducing the amount of short-term government securities at such a time cuts down on liquid and operating reserve assets just when we would wish to encourage greater activity. Contracyclical policy would be furthered if the shift were made under prosperous conditions; for at that time, cutting down on liquid assets would tend to pinch off further expansion.

As debt management has worked out, the maturity structure has been almost continually shortened rather than lengthened. The length of the federal debt averaged almost six years in 1952 and fell to less than five years by 1959. We might have expected a somewhat better achievement, since the Treasury–Federal Reserve Accord in 1951 laid the foundation for the development of a flexible debt-management policy.[1] Part of the difficulty is that legally established interest rate ceilings on long-term debt shackle the Treasury under prosperous conditions; but during much of the period mentioned, the prevailing interest rates were low enough that the ceiling had little or no effect. More likely, increasing issuance of long-term bonds was resisted in prosperity because of increased cost and public criticism, and resisted in recession because of the harmful influence that would be imposed on economic stabilization. As to public criticism, we may cite the angry public reaction to the announcement of the Treasury in April, 1953, that it would issue $1 billion in thirty-year bonds at 3¼ per cent. Accusations were widespread

---

[1]The pertinent fact at this point is that the Accord freed the Federal Reserve from supporting the government bond market. See pp. 312-13.

that this issue paved the way for a general rise in interest rates and imposed hard money on the economy at the expense of curtailed activity.[2]

Debt maturities better spaced over a period of years would provide the potentiality of influencing liquidity positions in the economy with smaller changes in the interest rate. The liquidity of short-term securities is not much affected by credit and monetary measures. The situation is very different in long-term bonds. When interest rates decline, the market price of bonds rises, improving the liquidity position of the holders. Conversely, when interest rates rise and security prices decline, the long-term bonds will be viewed as less liquid; in many cases, owners will feel "frozen in" and wait for higher prices before liquidating. A little arithmetic will show the substantial changes which occur in bond prices with a point or two change in the interest return on the purchase price. Changes in the liquidity position of federal government bonds could have an important contracyclical effect if long-term government bonds came to represent a larger proportion of private holdings of liquid assets. If the relative holdings of bonds by commercial banks could be increased from the present low levels nearer to that prevailing immediately after the Accord (about 20 per cent of the total United States government securities they then held), changes in their liquidity positions over the cycle would provide greater support for contracyclical policy.

Leverage is increased in the management of fiscal policy if deficits are financed and if surpluses are paid off in the short-term market. This is because of the high liquidity of short-term securities. If short-term securities are increased in recession, more liquid funds are made available than if long-term securities are issued. If short-term securities are withdrawn in prosperity, the liquidity position is pinched more than it would be with reductions in the volume of long-term bonds.

CO-ORDINATION OF POLICY

Theoretically, at least, slight adjustments in the policy "mix" could greatly modify the outturn. For instance, a popular proposal

---

[2]See, for instance, Bertram Gross and Wilfred Lumer, *The Hard Money Crusade* (Washington, D.C.: Public Affairs Institute, 1954). Even Paul Douglas advocates lengthening the debt structure in recession, but for the reason that it is more economical at that time. See Joint Economic Committee, *Employment, Growth, and Price Levels: Minority, Supplemental, and Additional Views* (Washington, D.C.: U.S. Government Printing Office, 1960), pp. 1–61.

at the present time would involve tightening up on fiscal policy and easing up on monetary policy in the interest of fostering more rapid growth.

If personal income taxes were raised, personal consumption expenditures would be reduced. If, at the same time, monetary policy were eased by making credit plentiful and keeping interest rates low, capital expenditures would be fostered. An increase in capital expenditures would tend to increase the advance in productivity. The growth of the economy thus would be fostered; and this is held essential in some circles, so that we may retain a favorable production potential in the face of more rapid growth in Soviet Russia and perhaps also in Communist China.

Simple as this plan is, there are important questions with respect to how effectively it could be put into operation. To the extent that the accelerator describes the motivation for investment, the plan would not work in the straightforward way the model describes. Under the conditions of the accelerator, investments would not be made without rising markets to justify them, no matter how available credit or how low the interest rate.[3] This is another illustration of the problem faced in generalizing on what behavior would be if designed controls were set up in the economy.

Even if investments were made as alleged, the outcome is not entirely clear. In our kind of economy the short resource is labor and not capital. To the extent that capital is already sufficiently available, added capital expenditures might do little more than create difficulties by increasing the capital/output ratio to an unstable level.

To hold that easier credit would provide no stimulation for investment would be too extreme. We know that the accelerator falls far short of a complete explanation of motivating factors which explain investment action. Also, no doubt, some capacity would be added as a result of the easy-credit stimulus, and some of this would add to the effectiveness of production. Nevertheless, the major stimulus for increasing productivity must depend on changing technology, not merely on additional units of capital which may differ little from the average types already in existence.

Perhaps, therefore, research activity will do more toward speed-

---

[3] It is true, of course, that the accelerator is related to the rise in *all* product sales, not just those to consumers. Due to the small proportion investment products represent of total sales, however, it is not very likely that, singly, they would support a large induced investment for long.

ing up growth than easy-credit policy. Certainly, we must depend on research to develop the improved technology which will speed up the rise required in productivity. Any discussion of how this is to be achieved would carry us far afield from our main stream of thought, but we may note that possibly an important research stimulus has been the high rate of corporate income taxes because such outlays are paid with "50-cent dollars" (the income tax would take half of the remainder left for profits if the research expenditures had not been made).

There are many other possibilities for adapting the combination of control instrumentalities to serve particular ends, but none more interesting. In any case, prediction of the changes which would occur in behavior as a result of the modifications resulting from other control measures might, if anything, be more difficult. The above proposal relates to a continuously more stringent fiscal policy and to a continuously easier monetary policy. If a part of the change in policy mix proposed related to neat timing over the business cycle, many difficulties would be encountered, as outlined in the preceding chapters.

The desirable co-ordinated action in either extremely depressed or extremely inflationary conditions is not difficult to prescribe. Essentially, the full force of both monetary and fiscal policy should be applied. Timing and lagged effects are of minor importance, for the intensity of the current problem faced is paramount, and, in contrast, aftereffects fade into unimportance.

Minor fluctuations, such as we have experienced in the postwar, call for a more delicate approach. At the present time, our understanding is too limited for us to expect successful launching of a full-blown scheme of modifying the policy mix. Another line of attack is resolution to eliminate all inconsistencies between monetary and fiscal policy. These arise particularly in connection with debt policy. They may occur, for instance, if the Treasury tries to secure funds at a low interest rate when the Federal Reserve is tightening monetary policy under inflationary conditions.

It is readily seen that the central problem is the pattern needed to guide co-ordination. Cataloguing of various inconsistencies is little more than frustrating unless a principle of evaluation is established. In this connection, a first question relates to how similar the objectives of monetary and fiscal policy should be. Must all other objectives be subordinated to economic stabilization policy? If this is to be the case, the traditional governmental organization can be shown to be largely outdated. An up-dating would be needed such that the responsibility for setting stabilization policy and development of contrivances for doing this would get top billing. Under such circumstances, efforts to refund government securities at low interest rates would be unthinkable if the accepted objective of economic stabilization policy called for anti-inflationary measures.

It is hard to believe that we are ready for so revolutionary a position. It appears, nevertheless, that this is the *direction* in which widely accepted goals point. How soon, if ever, so "advanced" a position will be reached is not a central question at the present time. What is needed now is to see how we can increase the emphasis on economic stabilization measures within the scope of existing governmental organization. Clearly, it would seem essential that the Treasury give full-dress consideration to the actions which should be taken in the interest of economic stabilization. These may then be weighed against other national policy considerations; and, by whatever means available, decisions should be taken to pursue the policy which is deemed to be in the best interests of the country. This proposal merely guarantees that economic stabilization policy will be given equal consideration with other policies deemed to be in the national interest.

A key problem relates to the integration of monetary policy. In spite of the fact that monetary policy is most frequently pointed to as a major deficiency in the co-ordination of stabilization policy, discretionary monetary policy actions have been better timed with the requirements of contracyclical action than fiscal policy. This, of course, is largely because monetary action can be timed more readily than fiscal policy. The better timing of monetary policy does not indicate superiority with respect to the influence of the action or to the extent of the lag before the influence is felt. The influence can be more readily understood in fiscal policy because it can be more or less directly equated into dollar expenditure effect.

The Federal Reserve officials would be the first to admit failures in providing economic stabilization in the administration of monetary policy. They appear, however, to be in a better position to promote financial stability than any other agency, as outlined in Chapter 23.

Monetary measures have been poorly co-ordinated with other policy actions, however. An important reason may be that the Federal Reserve has had longer experience and pursues stabilization policy more directly than other governmental agencies. It would therefore not be irrational to conclude that co-ordination awaits the maturization of stabilization policy in other agencies. There are, nevertheless, two reasons for not accepting this position as representing the whole answer. In the first place, efforts at co-ordination should speed the development of stabilization policy in the other agencies. And in the second place, the difficulties of co-ordination are magnified by the secrecy with which the Federal Reserve conducts its stabilization operations. As stated by M. J. Rossant of *Business Week:*

There's a shroud of secrecy over the Fed's operations. It never reveals the reasons for its operations, lest it tip off the dealers on its intentions. The dealers are free to interpret whether any sale or purchase is defensive or dynamic, but they do so on their own. Like a good poker player, the New York Fed—which dealers call "the big house"—always conceals its hand.[4]

Historically, there are good reasons for the secrecy of Federal Reserve operations. Stabilization operations were experimental, and they were best developed experimentally. For this purpose, all actions were taken tentatively. Under these circumstances, advance announcement of intentions was out of the question. Furthermore, actions taken slowly and experimentally are less likely to create major market disturbances. Finally, forecasts have been viewed with great skepticism, and plans for advance action would have to rest on forecasts.

With the present emphasis on co-ordinated stabilization policy, the Federal Reserve will find it necessary to remove at least part of the shroud of secrecy. The most promising means of moving in that direction is the employment of an explicit co-ordinating body. An informal committee on credit policy, consisting of the President's economic adviser, the Chairman of the Board of Governors of the Federal Reserve System, the Secretary of the Treasury, and the Chairman of the Council of Economic Advisers, has been operating since 1957 and is a step in the right direction. As explained in the second following section (page 536), co-ordinated action at more analytical levels is now required to back up this high-level committee.

Preliminary steps are needed to co-ordinate the monetary policy pursued by agencies other than the Federal Reserve. We may hope

---

[4]Joint Economic Committee, *Employment, Growth, and Price Levels,* Part 6B: *The Government's Management of Its Monetary, Fiscal, and Debt Operations* (Washington, D.C.: U.S. Government Printing Office, 1959), p. 1544. Reprinted from *Business Week,* July 12, 1958.

that the Federal Reserve will assume leadership in such a movement. No doubt, it will require encouragement and prodding by
more general co-ordinating procedures within the executive offices
of the federal government. This is particularly necessary in view
of the failure of other agencies involved in monetary policy[5] to
recognize over-all economic stabilization as an objective which
should be faced in the pursuit of their activities.

The position taken here is that the time has come when co-
ordination of stabilization policies must be more vigorously pursued, but that the movement should be evolutionary. Particularly,
we are not ready to shift the establishment of policy to a co-
ordinating group. The basic development of policies to foster financial stability is best left in the hands of the Federal Reserve, at least
for the time being. Effective development of fiscal policy will be
most promising if left in the hands of the Treasury and the Budget
Bureau.

Policy actions taken in the short term should be integrated in
a longer-term perspective. Founded on growth potential and saving
propensities in the economy, needed policy action may be visualized
to fall into one of three types:

1. Prosperity surpluses should approximately balance depression
   deficits;
2. Prosperity surpluses should be sufficient to permit significant debt
   retirement after allowance is made for depression deficits; or
3. Depression deficits must be expected to come to substantially more
   than prosperity surpluses, so that a secular increase in government
   debt will have to be anticipated.

The first policy type assumes no secular adjustment is required.
Under the conditions assumed, neither inflationary nor deflationary
pressure would be desirable on a secular basis. This is the type of
growth we described as secular in Chapter 6. Some evidence was
there adduced to show that important long-term tendencies tend
to produce this situation.

Possibly, a high secondary growth may tend continuously to
force an inflationary bias. Then, policy actions would need to be
more restrictive to prevent unduly inflationary conditions. If reliance is placed on monetary-fiscal policy, the appropriate prescription is a significant cutting-down on aggregate expenditures during
the most inflationary periods, and minimizing additions to expendi-

---

[5]See pp. 506–9.

tures during recessions. In other words, government surpluses would, on the average, exceed government deficits.

On the other hand, a low secondary growth may almost continuously force a deflationary bias, so that policy actions need to average more inflationary than deflationary. Emphasis would be placed on creating large government deficits in recession and small or no surpluses in the unsatisfactory prosperity which would be expected to develop.

Policy action can be much more effectively evolved if a tentative long-range plan is established. Such a plan will help in deciding on how soon deflationary action should be taken in recovery and how soon inflationary action should be taken in recession. It will also provide a guide as to the extent of the action which should be taken. However, long-term policy guides should not be permitted to make planned action inflexible. If careful analysis indicates the possibility that the long-range plan is at least partially mistaken, adaptive adjustments should be made to face current developments realistically.

REFORMING MARKET STRUCTURES AND OTHER STABILIZATION PROPOSALS

Possibility that reform most needed lies in the market structure weakens the case for fiscal-monetary policy. One line of thinking suggests that monopolistic practices in management of private industry prevent flexible enough adjustment to provide satisfactory activity without undue inflation. Over the short run, there appears to be enough truth to this contention that hopes for preventing all economic fluctuations are not well founded. Over the longer run, such practices seem to have been kept sufficiently in abeyance by antitrust and other action that, on the average, the use of resources is kept at a reasonably satisfactory level.

Recently, a greater worry has developed regarding labor practices. Growing rigidity in employee relationships is often held to represent a major threat to economic stability and growth. One proposal is to force free mobility of labor.[6] Since labor is relatively the scarcest resource in our economy, its complete freedom of movement would go far to produce flexible adjustment. Unfortunately,

---

[6]See particularly A. P. Lerner, *Economics of Employment* (New York: McGraw-Hill Book Co., Inc., 1951), pp. 209 ff.; Sidney Weintraub, *An Approach to the Theory of Income Distribution* (Philadelphia: Chilton Co., 1958), pp. 86 ff.

most persons remain unconvinced of the workability of any proposal which has been made along this line.

Lack of labor mobility has been argued not only to explain intensified inflexibility of adjustments over business fluctuations, but to account for permanently reduced levels of employment. According to Professor John T. Dunlop, when unemployment averages more than 3 per cent over the full business cycle, class rather than mass forces are responsible. He holds that class unemployment will be little influenced by fiscal and monetary policy—in fact, that a

CHART 24-1

NUMBER OF PERSONS UNEMPLOYED FOR A LONG AS FIFTEEN WEEKS
(In Thousands, during Postwar Recessions)

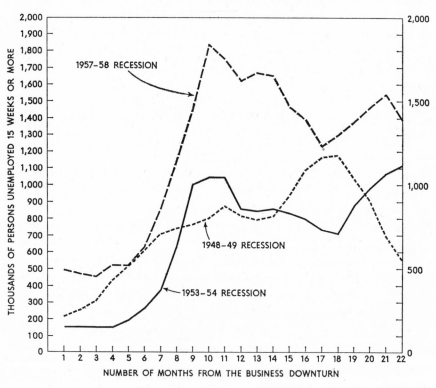

"great deal of mischief has been done in discussions of public policy concerning unemployment by allowing fiscal and monetary policies to preempt and dominate the field."[7] Under class unemployment,

---

[7]"Public Policy and Unemployment," *Studies in Unemployment: Prepared for the Special Committee on Unemployment Problems, United States Senate* (Washington, D.C.: U.S. Government Printing Office, 1960), pp. 1–15.

he lists particularly "unemployment of Detroit, of Negroes, of unskilled workers, or of those over age 50." He contends that "a wide variety of specialized private and public programs rather than any single public program" is required to correct the evil.

CHART 24–2

UNEMPLOYMENT RATE IN POSTWAR RECESSIONS
(Seasonally Adjusted Percentage of the Civilian Labor Force Who are Unemployed)

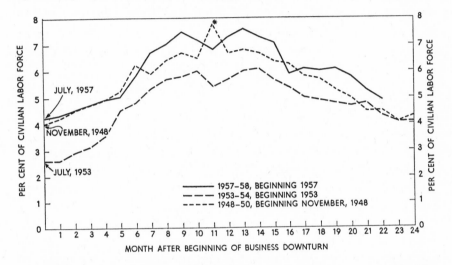

MONTH AFTER BEGINNING OF BUSINESS DOWNTURN

°October, 1949, rate exaggerated by coal miners on strike who reported they were seeking jobs. Source: Bureau of the Census, *Current Population Reports:* Labor Force, Series P–57, No. 203, Washington, D.C., June, 1959. Earlier figures are adjusted for comparability with new definitions adopted in January, 1957.

The fact is that the number of persons unemployed fifteen weeks or more from 1957 to 1959 hung well above the level of the earlier postwar recessions, as shown in Chart 24-1. One factor has been increasing unemployment in heavy industrial plants. Chart 24-2 shows that the total unemployment rate appeared relatively high in the 1957-58 recession. The possibility that some increase may be occurring in the immobility of labor weakens the case for the use of fiscal-monetary policy as a method of perfectly achieving the desired stabilization goals.

Some mention should be made of the use of specific price controls as a stabilization measure in peacetime. A direct approach often is appealing when changes get out of hand. If prices continue to rise in an undesirable fashion, the temptation to dictate price ceilings is great. If ceilings are set, however, to the extent that they work, the flexible adjustments of the market at price levels above the ceiling are forsworn. No possible way could be found to make the market structure more *inadaptable.*

Most students now find the most expeditious definition of inflation the price rise itself. Ordinarily, that definition is workable as long as it is used only in connection with description of change taking place in markets which possess substantial flexibility. When price ceilings are set arbitrarily and no adjustment is made to underlying forces, that definition of inflation is no longer operational. If, for instance, the money supply should rise rapidly and the mood to buy were unabated, little would have been done to the fires of inflation in capitalistic markets by dictating price ceilings. The situation may be very different in war because of other accompanying controls and because of a difference in mood when our very freedom is threatened.

THEORY AND MACHINERY OF ECONOMIC POLICY

In World War II the guaranty of full employment was a popular idea. War prosperity, created by tremendous government expenditures, was set against the background of the Great Depression and its appalling consequences. A British Conservative government took the lead in May, 1944, by issuing a White Paper which stated the unprecedented doctrine that "the Government accept as one of their primary aims and responsibilities the maintenance of a high and stable level of employment after the war." Governments throughout the world were moving in the same direction. In 1945 the Canadian and Australian governments issued rather similar commitments.[8]

Work started on writing a full-employment bill in the United States after President Roosevelt declared in his Message on the State of the Union in January, 1944, that one of the essentials of an Economic Bill of Rights is "the right to a useful and remunerative job." A year later the Murray Full-Employment Bill was introduced. This bill declared it to be the "policy of the United States to assure the existence at all times of sufficient employment opportunities to enable all Americans" to exercise a right to useful employment if they are able to work and are seeking work. The method proposed for achieving this aim was a National Production and Employment Budget, to be transmitted to Congress by the President at the first of each year. This would show the current level of national income, the corresponding level of income required to

---

[8] See United Nations, Department of Economic Affairs, *Maintenance of Full Employment* (Lake Success, July, 1949).

produce full employment, and the levels of these aggregates to be expected in the following year. If a prospective deficiency were indicated, the President would be directed, first, to suggest a program to encourage private expenditure, and, second, if there were a remaining prospective deficiency, to suggest supplementary government expenditures. If the bill had been passed, this would have provided an American declaration comparable to the British White Paper.

Heated arguments on the Murray Full-Employment Bill continued for a year. In February, 1946, a greatly revised measure, the Employment Act of 1946, became law. This act states:

The Congress hereby declares that it is the continuing policy and responsibility of the Federal Government to use all practicable means consistent with its needs and obligations and other essential considerations of national policy, with the assistance and co-operation of industry, agriculture, labor, and State and local governments, to co-ordinate and utilize all its plans, functions, and resources for the purpose of creating and maintaining, in a manner calculated to foster and promote free competitive enterprise and the general welfare, conditions under which there will be afforded useful employment opportunities, including self-employment, for those able, willing, and seeking to work, and to promote maximum employment, production, and purchasing power.

The President shall transmit to the Congress not later than January 20 of each year an economic report setting forth (1) the levels of employment, production, and purchasing power obtaining in the United States and such levels needed to carry out the policy declared [above]; (2) current and foreseeable trends in the levels of employment, production, and purchasing power; (3) a review of the economic program of the Federal Government and a review of economic conditions affecting employment in the United States or any considerable portion thereof during the preceding year and of their effect upon employment, production, and purchasing power; and (4) a program for carrying out the policy declared [above], together with such recommendations for legislation as he may deem necessary or desirable.[9]

This act is the principal foundation in the United States for (1) stabilization policy and (2) machinery for implementation.

1. There is no doubt that the policy enunciated is less forceful than that of many foreign countries. Extended arguments with

---

[9]Public Law 304, chap. 33, 79th Cong., 2d sess. Reproduced in Council of Economic Advisers, *First Annual Report to the President* (Washington, D.C.: U.S. Government Printing Office, December, 1946); also reproduced in *The Economic Reports of the President* (New York: Reynal and Hitchcock, 1948), pp. 167–71; and in U.S. Senate, Committee on Unemployment Problems, *Readings in Unemployment,* 86th Cong., 2d sess. (Washington, D.C.: U.S. Government Printing Office, 1960), pp. 12–15.

regard to the effectiveness of the legislation have arisen from this fact. The qualifications stated in the act, as shown in the part reproduced above, leave the actual course of action largely to the discretion of the President. This is in striking contrast with the Murray Full-Employment Bill, which called for a forecast of deficiency in expenditure expected in the following year and would have required the proposal of suggested lines of action to remedy any indicated deficiency. Actually, the course of action is left quite indefinite. As it stands, policy will be evolved through the process of experience. There has been no disregard for "other essential considerations of national policy." The programs of other countries appear to be somewhat more forthright, although experience has not indicated a great difference in actual operation. In many of the smaller countries, foreign trade is so important an influence on economic fluctuations that the pronouncements on stabilization policy are relatively unimportant in any case.

2. The machinery set up by the act involves a streamlined Council of Economic Advisers in the Executive Department and a Joint Economic Committee in Congress. The Council has pioneered in providing advice on stabilization and in co-ordinating economic analysis for this purpose. A major part of the contribution has been made by work done on the *Economic Report of the President,* which is transmitted to the Congress in January of each year. The influence has spread through the Executive Department and no doubt played a part in the establishment of an economic adviser in the Office of the President.

Originally, the Joint Economic Committee (formerly called the Joint Committee on the Economic Report) was established principally for the purpose of assuring Congressional study of the *Economic Report of the President.* The Committee has advanced far beyond that stage, and has taken on the function of making independent economic studies which far outweigh its yearly consideration of the *Economic Report.* Furthermore, the influence of its studies has spread so that other Congressional committees have taken up the analysis of economic stabilization to an extent that probably would not otherwise have occurred. Notably, a Special Committee on Unemployment Problems was recently set up in the Senate, out of which forthright reports, referred to in footnotes 7 and 9, were made in 1960.

As would be expected, revision of the Employment Act has been a matter of frequent debate. We may refer to the Reuss Bill, introduced in 1958 (H.R. 12785), which was not passed but which created wide discussion.[10] The bill contains two main provisions:

1. The second paragraph of the Employment Act of 1946, quoted on page 537, is revised to note parenthetically that the program for carrying out the prescribed policy should include monetary and credit policies.
2. A subsection is added to assign the Council the duty of collecting information and making studies of such "proposed price and wage increases as may adversely effect maximum employment, production, and purchasing power; and to report to the President instances where the proposed increase is found likely to have such an adverse effect, in order to enable the President to make an appropriate, informed request for voluntary restraint by the parties concerned."

As to the first provision, one group of persons ranged from the feeling that no material change was effected by the bill to the feeling that the change indicated would be mischievous in that the integration of monetary and fiscal policies with other needed measures was not clearly stressed. In the preamble to the bill, it is stated that the amendment is to "provide for the inclusion of recommendations concerning monetary policies in the President's program, and to bring to bear an informed public opinion upon proposed inflationary price increases." Partly because of this statement, some persons were impressed with the anti-inflationary importance of the bill, and others expressed the opinion that badly needed integration of monetary and fiscal policies was implied.

Difference of opinion was even greater on the second provision. At one extreme, A. P. Lerner felt that direct interference in wage and price increases in particular industries was all to the good, but that it did not go far enough.[11] Most economists felt that interference in wage-price relationships in individual industries would be harmful. They indicated that the question at issue is whether or not there is substantial monopoly power, and that, if there is, it should be dealt with directly by antitrust action. Some felt that the nonpolitical character of the Employment Act would be destroyed. A searching question often asked by responding economists was

---

[10]The bill is quoted and a provocative discussion is given in *Amending the Employment Act of 1946 to Include Recommendations on Monetary and Credit Policies and Proposed Price and Wage Increases: Hearings before a Subcommittee of the Committee on Government Operations, House of Representatives* (Washington, D.C.: U.S. Government Printing Office, 1958).

[11]*Op. cit.*, pp. 138–39. See also the reference to Lerner in n. 6.

as to what criteria would be employed to determine whether a proposed price increase would have an adverse effect.

One criticism made was that the language of the act would remain vague. On the other hand, Grover Ensley expressed what many economists appear to believe:

The Employment Act of 1946 is an enabling statute. Its wording, both as to objectives and machinery, leaves considerable discretion to the President and to the Congress. This is as it should be in view of the dynamics of our American economy and the varying economic philosophies and approaches to identifying economic problems, to say nothing of the various approaches to solving them. The lack of specificness in the act, however, has not impeded the formulation or pursuit of public policies to achieve the act's broadly stated objectives. On the contrary, the broadness of language in the act has permitted and encouraged the flexibility and adaptability in public policies which the frequent and rapid changes in the American economy since 1946 have required. If each such change in circumstance and in policy had inspired specific amendment of the act, it might very well have been amended to death.[12]

What, in summary, can be said about the functions of the Joint Economic Committee and of the Council of Economic Advisers? The Joint Economic Committee stimulates discussion in and out of Congress on pertinent economic issues. It also performs yeoman's service in assembling informed opinion across the spectrum of conservatism and liberalism, and makes it readily available in published form.

On the other hand, the Council is responsible for initiating and integrating policy positions. So far, this has been limited to a rathei broad statement in the *Economic Report* of the policies pursued in the preceding year and of a legislative program for the ensuing year. Additionally, the Council has assumed limited leadership throughout the Executive Departments of the federal government on the development of policy questions. Through its Chairman, the Council reports frequently to the President on current economic developments and, as circumstances warrant, submits recommendations for legislative enactments and for administrative actions. It makes analytical reviews of legislative proposals emanating from Congress. It provides leadership on various committees, including the Advisory Board on Economic Growth and Stability, the Cabinet Committee on Price Stability and Economic Growth, and an Informal Committee on Credit Policy. It stimulates some co-ordina-

---

[12]*Amending the Employment Act of 1946 to Include Recommendations on Monetary and Credit Policies and Proposed Price and Wage Increases,* pp. 122–23.

tion of work on problems of stabilization in departments throughout the Executive Department by drawing information from them in the course of finding answers to its own problems.

Important as these activities are, they scarcely measure up to a satisfactory initiation and integration of needed stabilization policy. To face effectively the pertinent questions, five new or expanded approaches appear to be needed.

1. For fiscal-monetary policy to become effective, a pattern of co-ordination must be developed. The responsibility for developing this pattern appears to lie most clearly with the Council.

2. Rather than preparing a statement of needed legislation, the Council could be most effective if an evaluation were made of the type of monetary-fiscal control likely to be needed in the coming year. We do not believe that the most effective process would involve relationships in a precise mechanical model, but rather statements of the general order of policy required (which may have been partially developed earlier in office work by mechanical models). Since the issue has psychological repercussions, tempering of such statements may be desirable until the thinking of decision makers is adjusted to a mature presentation. Misgivings about the willingness of businessmen to face straightforward forecasts frankly are, nevertheless, largely misplaced. The business world now faces forecasting more aggressively than the government. If the Council were to issue a broad policy statement, as suggested, its effectiveness would be increased if the statement were placed in perspective by a tentative judgment on the long-range policy implied by the long-range outlook.

3. Since forecasts play so vital a part in the planning of control, the Council should assume leadership in facing squarely the potentialities of forecasting. Having achieved a mature attitude toward the use of forecasting, the Council would have the responsibility of promoting that position among policy-making agencies. We believe that a primitive prejudice prevails against forecasting. It should not be looked at as an occult or irrational process but should be carefully evaluated and then used to the extent warranted in future planning.

4. Changing market structures need to be carefully evaluated as to their impact on stabilization developments. Although we do not believe that the Council should make recommendations as to reforms of the market structure, we do believe that it should supervise an analysis of their impact on economic stabilization. Otherwise,

the recommendations on monetary-fiscal policy will remain vague in their significance. Neil Jacoby, a one-time member of the Council, stated in 1959: "I would say frankly I was somewhat disappointed in the 'Economic Report of January 1959' in failing to point out the importance of some of these structural rigidities, their relation to the inflation question, and to propose some specific steps for starting to do away with them."[13] Robert Gordon, a famous business cycle analyst, stated about the same time that the "President's Economic Report should be made into a more effective instrument for bringing public pressure to bear on private wage and price decisions."[14]

5. The Council should squarely face all other current influences which are widely considered to have a major impact on the economic outlook. The nature of these influences is certain to vary from time to time. They may be illustrated by the feelings expressed in the late fifties about market structures discussed in point 4, above. At other times, they could be international trade problems, the basis on which our currency rests, or other factors founded on troublesome relationships between institutional foundations and current economic problems. Where there is universal professional agreement, the Council could point clearly to the truth or fallaciousness of prevailing popular opinion. Frequently, perhaps, little more could be accomplished than a clarification of the issues involved. Nevertheless, public confidence of the evaluation called for in point 2 is likely to be seriously impaired if current difficulties appear to be ignored.

IS ACTIVITY BECOMING MORE STABLE?

In December, 1959, in his address as President of the American Economic Association, Arthur F. Burns, who was Chairman of the Council of Economic Advisers from 1953 to 1956, stated: "It is a fact of the highest importance, I think, that although our economy continues to be swayed by the business cycle, its impact on the lives and fortunes of individuals has been substantially reduced in our generation. More than twenty-five years have elapsed since we last had a severe business recession."[15]

Burns goes on to point out that the character, as well as intensity of over-all movement of the business cycle, has changed. For one

---

[13]*Employment, Growth, and Price Levels,* p. 81, Part 1, March, 1959, See n. 4.
[14]*Ibid.,* p. 2961, Part 9A, October, 1959.
[15]"Progress towards Economic Stability," *American Economic Review,* March, 1960, p. 1. The further quotations given below are from succeeding pages of this article.

thing, dividend payments appear to have become more stable. For another, automatic stabilizers, including corporate and graduated personal income taxes as well as Social Security payments, have tended to smooth out disposable income.

Furthermore, the cyclical effect on employment has been moderated by changes in the occupational structure of the labor force, notably by the great relative expansion of "white-collar" workers. Again, consumer spending has declined no more than 1 per cent and risen before production or employment in all of the postwar recessions. Burns concludes that the personal security which derived from living on farms in an earlier age tends to have been restored through new institutions that have developed in both the private and the public branches of our economy.

The institution of financial reforms such as "the insurance of mortgages, the creation of a secondary market for mortgages, the insurance of savings and loan accounts, and—most important of all—the insurance of bank deposits" has served powerfully to limit the propagation of fear. Even more basic is the fact that mass unemployment has come to be regarded as intolerable.

"Long-term interest rates have tended to move down as soon as the cyclical peak in economic activity was reached, in contrast to the long lags that were characteristic of earlier times," which is held to reflect the increased vigor and effectiveness of monetary policies. The phase of inventory disinvestment has tended to cease earlier in recession than formerly, and the inventory problem has been reduced with a secular decline in the inventory/sales ratio. Non-commercial work around the house—such as carpentry, painting, plumbing, and landscaping—has been expanding rapidly in the postwar period, and perhaps has risen most rapidly in recession.

Thus, Burns thinks that "the links that previously tied together the cyclical movements of production, employment, personal income, and consumption have become looser. . . . Yet, it is well to remember that projections of human experience remain descriptions of a limited past no matter how alluringly they are expressed in language of the future." He notes that possibly the rising trend of prices and growing consumer and mortgage debt might serve to complicate future recessions. "The coordination of governmental policies, which may make the difference between success and failure in promoting our national objectives, can be left largely to accidents of personal force and ingenuity or it can be made systematic through an economic policy board under the chairmanship of the President."

In summary, we may point to five different types of influence:

1. Forces increasing instability.
2. Forces reducing instability.
3. Reforms and other countering actions.
4. Forces representing a questionable effect.
5. The influence of a new visualization which is arising as to desirable goals.

1. With the present growth in disposable income, discretionary income is outpacing the advance in essential outlays and in major fixed commitments. A large part of discretionary income goes for durable goods, and the purchase of durable goods can be postponed for a considerable time without fundamentally disturbing prevailing standards of living. Again, the great expansion in consumer and mortgage debt could become unstabilizing. Short- and intermediate-term consumer credit outstanding rose from $7 billion in 1939 to over $50 billion by the end of 1959. If we remember that such debt is invariably paid off to a partial extent in recession, it is not difficult to visualize that further expansions now to be expected may provide a major source for a continuing debt deflation in a future depression. Finally, when we realize the major effect that war has had on economic fluctuations in the past, political instability in the world today throws reasonable doubt on how stable future business fluctuations will be.

2. Pitted against these factors are the points Burns makes about the stability of disposable income and consumer expenditure, growing out of stable dividend payments, the stabilizing effect on disposable income of graduated personal income taxes, the influence of Social Security payments, and the expansion of noncommercial activities in recession. Also, the stabilizing effect of changes occurring in the occupational structure of the labor force is pertinent. Another factor which moderates the danger of an overbuilt situation which we found ourselves facing in the early thirties is the shortened average life of durable capital. This has come about by the rising proportion of equipment, rather than plant expenditures, and the accelerated rate of obsolescence in equipment facilities. With shorter-lived capital, less time will be required to work off an excessive capital stock.

3. The philosophy of fiscal policy has changed; government expenditures will not be cut just because receipts decline. Government receipts will decline in recession because of automatic stabilizers, notably corporate income tax payments. As Burns notes, such

financial reforms as the insurance of bank deposits reduce the danger of propagation of fear. The danger of unstable speculation is lessened—if not eliminated—by close control of margin requirements on trading in securities. The apparent speedier response of long-term interest rates to easier credit conditions in recession is encouraging. Perhaps most important is the acceptance of governmental responsibility for economic stabilization. This is a growing development, and many governmental activities which have been barely touched by its influence will come increasingly under the sway of stabilization goals.

4. We hold that the stabilizing effect of business investment is questionable. There is some promise of taming the wildness of fluctuations in inventory investment. The relative size of the inventory stock has been cut by shop practices, by prompter transportation, and by speedier controls which are available with electronic calculation. Desire to carry inventories for speculative purposes is far less than in the immediate period following World War I. We may hope that manufacturers are coming to see more clearly the reduction needed in inventory variation if ultimate final sales, rather than sales complicated by inventory changes in later stages of distribution, are taken as the standard of inventory requirements (see Chapter 19). If the economy progresses as rapidly as we hope, however, needs for inventories of new types and in shifting channels will be a complicating factor tending to produce unsteadiness of inventory investment.

The danger of overinvestment in durable capital is being reduced as we learn more about the size of existing stocks and the needs for them by long-range planning founded on improved long-range forecasting procedures. Nevertheless, overbuilding is promoted by many factors. Long-range forecasting is far from universally employed; and where it is employed, acceptance is little more than tentative. Major investment stimulus still comes from the level or changes in current market sales plus other transient market factors. Shifting rates of obsolescence, newer technology, and major shifts in demand with higher living standards threaten to increase the difficulty of the effective planning of capital projects. The problem is even further complicated by aggressive attempts of many firms to obtain an increasing share of the market, which has sometimes led to a substantial overinvestment for the industry as a whole.

5. What will shift in goals do to tendency toward improved stabilization? If we become increasingly concerned about inflation,

either the average level of employment will be reduced, or its fluctuation is likely to be increased. Since the failure of prices to fall in recession is an important factor tending to produce "creeping inflation," measures may be taken which will reduce prices at that time, and any such measures are likely to increase recession unemployment. Any reduction in the average level of employment is likely to slow down the rate of growth; and since this is being promoted as an increasingly important goal, that development is likely to be considered unacceptable. The goal of speeding up growth may itself add to instability. One of the important bases of instability in the past has generally been considered to be the rapidity of economic development. Structural adjustments become more difficult. Increasing demands are made on labor mobility. Failures tend to increase in antiquated areas. Strains are intensified as adjustments have to be made to more rapid changes.

FOR REFLECTION AND ANALYSIS

1. What would be the advantage of increasing the proportionate holding of government bonds by commercial banks?
2. What is the relation between monetary policy and changes in composition of the federal debt?
3. Could a continuously easier credit policy with a more stringent fiscal policy increase the rate of growth and keep inflation in check?
4. If monetary policy actions are better timed with respect to contracyclical requirements, how can one hold that the influence on the cyclical movement might be inferior to that of fiscal policy?
5. Should Federal Reserve policy be conducted under a shroud of secrecy?
6. Will good stabilization policy require the paying-off of a substantial part of the federal government debt in near-future years?
7. Does the inflexibility of wages throw a new light on the utility of fiscal and monetary policies?
8. Would specific price controls solve our inflation problems?
9. Should the Employment Act of 1946 be revised to stress anti-inflationary policies?
10. Is it proper that the language of an employment act should be vague?
11. Outline what you think to be the chief weaknesses of the operation of the Council of Economic Advisers.
12. Are the holdings of Arthur Burns on improved stability overoptimistic?
13. Is there some way of striking a golden mean between the arguments that stability is increasing and that the dangers of instability are growing?
14. This is a research question. To answer, it will be necessary to study a number of the issues of the *Economic Report of the President*. In

Part 9A of the Hearings before the Joint Economic Committee of the Congress on *Employment, Growth, and Price Levels,* issued in late October, 1959, Professor Robert A. Gordon, on pages 2961–62, states:

The Economic Report, virtually from the beginning, has tended to run in terms of broad generalities, well meaning exhortations that ask to be ignored, and innocuous platitudes. I have not noticed a great deal of difference between Republican and Democratic administrations in this respect. I should like to see the Economic Report be more explicit about the objectives to be sought during the coming year and the combination of public and private policies needed to attain these objectives. In this connection, the Administration should not be afraid to state frankly what range of wage increases it believes to be compatible with price stability; what needs to be done to accelerate increases in productivity; what policy measures it is prepared to take under various contingencies, and so on.

Comment.

SELECTED READINGS FOR PART FIVE

ACHINSTEIN, ASHER. *Federal Reserve Policy and Economic Stability, 1951–57.* Committee on Banking and Currency, 85th Cong., 2d sess. Washington, D.C.: U.S. Government Printing Office, 1958.

A critical appraisal of monetary policies.

BOULDING, KENNETH E. *Principles of Economic Policy.* Englewood Cliffs, N.J.: Prentice-Hall, Inc., 1958.

Contains a simplified and lucid statement on economic policy by a leading economist.

COMMITTEE FOR ECONOMIC DEVELOPMENT. *Anti-recession Policy for 1958.* Washington, D.C., March, 1958.

May be considered a typical illustration of advice on stabilization policy by enlightened business groups. Note that it was published only one month before the upturn.

DUE, JOHN F. *Government Finance: An Economic Analysis.* Rev. ed. Homewood, Ill.: Richard D. Irwin, Inc., 1959.

Should be helpful in showing what a good undergraduate textbook on public finance covers on fiscal policy.

FEDERAL RESERVE SYSTEM, BOARD OF GOVERNORS. *Consumer Instalment Credit.* 5 vols. Washington, D.C., 1957.

A comprehensive study of the processes and regulation of consumer credit.

————. *Treasury Federal Reserve Study of the Government Securities Market.* 3 vols. Washington, D.C., 1959 and 1960.

A study of the performance of the federal securities market and a survey of opinion about its functioning.

FELLNER, WILLIAM. *Emergence and Content of Modern Economic Analysis.* New York: McGraw-Hill Book Co., Inc., 1960.

Contains interesting observations on compensatory fiscal policy, as well as on dynamic interpretation of Say's Law and on issues of international economic policy.

FIRESTONE, JOHN M. *Federal Receipts and Expenditures during Business Cycles, 1879–1958.* Princeton: Princeton University press, 1960.

Changes in fiscal magnitudes and fiscal policies.

GOLDENWEISER, E. A. *American Monetary Policy.* New York: McGraw-Hill Book Co., Inc., 1951.

Contains uncensored conclusions of an economist who spent his life working on monetary policy.

GURLEY, JOHN G., and SHAW, EDWARD S. *Money in a Theory of Finance.* Washington, D.C.: Brookings Institution, 1960.

A discussion of the needs of monetary policy in light of rapid growth of nonmonetary financial intermediaries.

HALL, CHALLIS A. *Fiscal Policy for Stable Growth: A Study in Dynamic Macroeconomics.* New York: Holt, Rinehart and Winston, 1960.

An application of fiscal policy to the problems of a growing economy, rather than merely to variations.

HANSEN, ALVIN H. *Economic Policy and Full Employment.* New York: McGraw-Hill Book Co., Inc., 1947.

Contains lucid descriptions of postwar plans.

HARRIS, SEYMOUR E. *Economic Planning: The Plans of Fourteen Countries with Analyses of the Plans.* New York: Alfred A. Knopf, Inc., 1949.

Of interest in studying how employment policies were set up after World War II.

JOINT ECONOMIC COMMITTEE. *Employment, Growth, and Price Levels,* Part 7: *The Effects of Monopolistic and Quasi-Monopolistic Practices.* 86th Cong., 1st sess. Washington, D.C.: U.S. Government Printing Office, 1959.

A useful range of opinion on how important monopolistic practices are in stabilization.

————. *Fiscal Policy Implications of the Economic Outlook and Budget Developments.* 2 vols., dated June 3–14, 1957, and April 28–May 1, 1958. 85th Cong. Washington, D.C.: U.S. Government Printing Office, 1957 and 1958.

Gives the opinion of a wide range of analysts on the effectiveness of fiscal policy in the 1957–58 recession.

MUSGRAVE, RICHARD A. *The Theory of Public Finance.* New York: McGraw-Hill Book Co., Inc., 1959.

Contains fundamental statements on fiscal policy.

NATIONAL BUREAU OF ECONOMIC RESEARCH, INC., CONFERENCE OF THE UNIVERSITIES–NATIONAL BUREAU COMMITTEE ON ECONOMIC RESEARCH. *Regularization of Business Investment.* Princeton: Princeton University Press, 1954.

An effort to show what business can do to increase stability.

"REVIEW OF ECONOMICS AND STATISTICS." "Controversial Issues in Recent Monetary Policy: A Symposium," August, 1960, pp. 245–345.

An interesting series of articles on the current problem of monetary policy.

U.S. SENATE, COMMITTEE ON UNEMPLOYMENT PROBLEMS. *Readings in Unemployment.* 86th Cong., 2d sess. Washington, D.C.: U.S. Government Printing Office, 1960.

A good selection of a wide range of articles bearing on employment policy.

PART

SIX

International Repercussions

<table>
<tr><td>

Chapter

25

</td><td>

INTERNATIONAL

SPREADING OF

BUSINESS FLUCTUATIONS

</td></tr>
</table>

Interregional variations in business fluctuations have been overlooked up to this point. Within the country, although the variations are substantial, they are largely explained by the tendency for major industries to concentrate in particular localities. For instance, a recent study indicates that manufacturing employment is most variable in Michigan, and this corresponds with the high concentration of durable manufactures in that state.[1] Because of the predominant importance of industry differentiation in this connection, we have not felt that regional analysis within the country would be very helpful in business cycle analysis.

International repercussions are a different matter. The basic principles are the same, but institutional factors play a more important role in the international case. Differences in variation are not always greater, but they are not so readily explained by differences in industry or by any other single factor. Furthermore, the international repercussions have a graver connotation. They relate to what we do to others or others do to us, which is more significantly out of our control than are interregional reactions within the country. In the international sphere the concern is political or even military as much as economic.

Interregional trade, whether international or within a country, faces certain impediments. These include immobility of resources, concentrated development of know-how, and transportation costs. As to immobility of natural resources, such resources as coal veins or water power are unevenly distributed; and the labor movement fails to keep up with shifts in geographical needs. Concentrated

---

[1]George H. Borts, *Regional Cycles of Manufacturing Employment in the United States, 1914–1953*, Occasional Paper 73 (New York: National Bureau of Economic Research, Inc., 1960).

developments of know-how may be illustrated by the convergence of particular activities, like automobiles in Detroit. Transportation costs hit industries with bulky products especially, and only limited geographical concentration tends to occur in making such products.

These impediments tend to be magnified in the international sphere. Tariffs and other artificial controls limit the freedom with which goods flow across national borders. Fear of confiscation and instability of foreign governments similarly obstruct the flow of capital. Obstacles to trade between states in our country—as, for instance, use taxes on final consumption goods—do occur, but they are unimportant compared to those interfering with international flows.

A more basic and, no doubt, most important reason for differences between foreign and domestic trade is national purpose. This is related to economic development; and we lose perspective if we confuse purpose, as it has developed historically, with action employed to counter business fluctuation. The central issue is economic development of the country; and for fostering that development, measures have frequently been taken to encourage favorable foreign trade balances and the advance of manufacturing at the expense of agriculture. (Many economists would not agree that the measures taken did always foster development.) National purpose has been concerned with the development of new resources and new productive factors. A simple illustration is the development of the British Empire. The specialization which arose made possible an island economy closely geared to world trade—imports of raw materials and exports of finished products. Without national identification, Britain probably could not have achieved so high a specialization as an industrial nation.

The early development of the United States is an illustration of the use of foreign capital to foster rapid growth. Here, too, we have an exemplification of the force of national development. Looking back, it is easy enough to see that the growth potential of America was tremendous, but that was less obvious at the time. The transformation of nations has been at least partly encouraged by national purpose.[2]

Our chief interest in this chapter is how and to what extent

---

[2]For a clear statement of the distinction between external mobility and purposeful control of the international movement of productive factors, see John H. Williams, "The Theory of International Trade Reconsidered," *Readings in the Theory of International Trade* (Philadelphia: Blakiston Co., 1950), pp. 253–71 (reprinted from the *Economic Journal*, June, 1929).

business fluctuations have been transmitted from one country to another. Business annals, as developed by the National Bureau of Economic Research, provide our best evidence on the comparative changes in business conditions in early years. These are pictured in Chart 25-1.

CHART 25-1

Conspectus of Business Cycles in Various Countries, 1890–1925

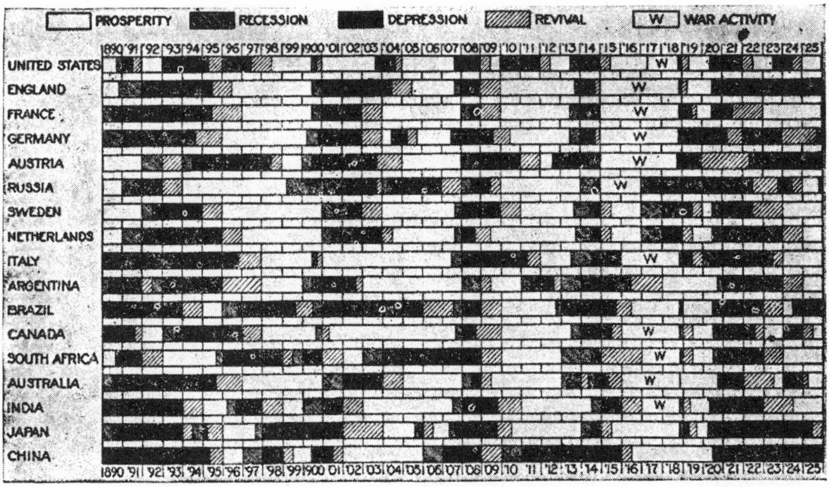

Source: Taken from Willard Thorp and W. C. Mitchell, *Business Annals* (New York: National Bureau of Economic Research, Inc., 1926), pp. 94–95. The reference also shows a similar picture of annals for some countries from 1790 to 1889, including the United States and England beginning with 1790, France beginning with 1806, Germany beginning with 1819, and Austria beginning with 1867. Reproduced with permission.

PROCESSES THROUGH WHICH ACTIVITY IS TRANSMITTED TO FOREIGN COUNTRIES

Economic fluctuation may be carried to foreign countries by six processes:

1. Exports and imports
2. Relative movements of commodity and service prices
3. Flow of investment
4. Relative movements of interest rates
5. Changes in foreign aid
6. Competitive devaluation and other controls

The relation between these processes, as it pertains to changes in economic conditions, is summarized in a later section by appeal to the balance of payments between countries. Clearly, each process will, directly or indirectly, affect that balance. It is not our purpose, however, to set up a rigid model to show the relationships. The spreading of economic change between countries is most effectively explained at the present time by assuming that causal relationships may move in various directions. For instance, repercussions on other countries may be produced by sale or purchase of goods and services (note the American purchase of foreign cars in the late fifties) or by flow of investments.[3] Further illustrations are given below.

1. A rise in exports stimulates domestic activity. It results from increased demand abroad and hence represents the transmission of foreign expansionary conditions to our economy. Imports represent an offset to the stimulation created on our activity by our exports. Import levels depend on the degree of our prosperity. Thirty years ago, half were crude materials, and demand for these rose rapidly with prosperity and advancing industrial production. Now, the proportion of manufactured imports has increased. Manufactured imports are influenced by rising disposable income in prosperity, but it is doubtful that the influence ordinarily will be as great as that experienced by raw materials. Thus, the advancing stimulation produced on foreign countries by rise in our imports in business cycle expansion may have weakened somewhat. The problem comes up for evaluation later in the chapter.

2. If, for any reason, our domestic prices fall, relative to world prices or prices in other countries, our exports will increase, and our imports will decline. Contrary to the contractionary effect of an absolute fall of domestic prices, with the rest of the world disregarded, prices relatively lower than in the rest of the world are expansionary. In the opposite case, the expansionary effect in the domestic economy of rising prices will be partially neutralized if the rise is out of proportion to that occurring in the rest of the world.

3. The flow of investment to foreign countries is expansionary in the countries receiving the investments. A major expansionary factor in prosperous phases of our business cycles in the nineteenth century was the investment funds flowing from abroad, which financed a substantial part of the early railroad development. The effect on any domestic economy of sending investment funds abroad

[3]Many other interrelations can, of course, be noted. For a fuller, but simple explanation, see Delbert A. Snider, *Introduction to International Economics* (Homewood, Ill.: Richard D. Irwin, Inc., 1958), esp. pp. 25–225; and John P. Powelson, *National Income and Flow-of-Funds Analysis* (New York: McGraw-Hill Book Co., Inc., 1960), pp. 461–505.

is partially dependent on the accompanying conditions. If the funds compete severely with domestic investment demand, their export may be disturbing. Actually, domestic investment is more likely to find enough preference that the foreign flow of funds can be said ordinarily to draw from funds not in demand in the domestic economy. For instance, foreign investments of the United States increased most during recessions in the twenties. Furthermore, the sending of funds abroad finances purchases from us and is largely balanced by a similar increase in our exports. The export-import process is described above.

The act of making foreign investments sets up repercussions which tend to work themselves out by increasing foreign trade. Assume country US invests in country C, and call all other countries O. C gains foreign exchange and buys more than it would otherwise in US and in O. The additional purchases made in US leads US to import more goods. In like manner, successive trade accommodations induce further changes in imports and exports. As C imports more goods, it has to pay out funds for them, and the funds US originally sent to C for the purpose of making a foreign investment are at least partially offset. To the extent that they are not, C will have attained a net increase in gold or foreign exchange funds, and the foreign exchange value of its currency will have been driven up. This is most simply explained by the fundamental net foreign investment equation: Disregarding unilateral payments (gifts and aid), exports minus imports equal net foreign investment.

4. A rise in interest rates to a higher level than in foreign countries tends to draw investment funds. Such a rise in interest rates is most likely to occur in a period of prosperity in the domestic economy. In such a period the acquired foreign funds are likely to add to domestic spending, although the result may be an increase in prices rather than in physical activity if full employment has already been achieved. Sooner or later the rise in prices and in interest cost for investment will reduce the attractiveness of domestic investment projects.

If investment funds are placed in the economy only temporarily, to take advantage of high interest rates, they are considered upsetting and are often called "hot money." Turning the above example around, relatively low interest rates in the domestic economy may make domestic investors seek foreign outlets. The interest rate relationship probably accounts to a substantial extent for investment funds flowing to America in the nineteenth century and for the

American placing of investment funds abroad in recessions of the 1920's. Thus, the interest rate relationship is ancillary to the investment flow and influences longer-term investment funds as well as short-term speculative movement of capital.

5. Unilateral payments made available by the government or by individuals of the domestic economy for use in foreign economies are another way influences are transmitted, but change in unilateral payments is not likely to be closely geared to domestic business fluctuations. Rapid changes in these payments, nonetheless, could be very disturbing on foreign economies. Such an induced disturbance on the European economies, especially Britain, was avoided in 1947 when Marshall Plan aid was legislated as funds made available by the earlier "special British loan" were being exhausted. Although we have failed to plan foreign aid on a long-term basis, changes in the aid made available have usually been small enough that only limited disturbances have been superimposed on the economies benefiting from them. With the foreign aid now generally limited to underdeveloped areas, a crutch is being provided with the intention of fostering growth.

6. Finally, note should be made of official acts taken to influence foreign trade. Two possibilities are either to modify the exchange rate or to adopt import restrictions. It is generally agreed that foreign trade is likely to benefit more from exchange policy than from adoption of import restrictions. The devaluation of a country's currency effectively reduces the foreign price of its products and thus increases foreign demand, although the effect is canceled if other countries also devaluate their currencies to protect their foreign trade. We shall not consider these measures further at this point because they reflect efforts to change the results flowing from the first five process types; hence, a consideration of them is more appropriate in the following chapter, where we center our attention on trade policy.

POSTWAR EXPERIENCE

In looking at the processes by which activity is transmitted from one country to another, it is a mistake to limit our attention to short-term fluctuations. Each process can produce a secular influence. Our exports as a share of world exports have recently fluctuated around what looks like a secular level of about 17 per cent, and imports around a secular level of about 14 per cent. These are merely historical figures and do not represent forecasts.

From World War II to the end of the 1950's decade, wholesale prices in the United States rose substantially less than in most other major countries. Switzerland is a notable exception, where prices were very slightly higher at the end of the fifties than at the end of the war. By 1960 the differences were narrowing in many other countries. For instance, from the 1953 recession to 1959, United Kingdom prices increased only slightly more than ours, and Australian prices increased less.

Flow of private investment to foreign countries in the fifties averaged close to $2 billion per year, with two thirds of the total going to Canada and Latin-American Republics. At the end of the decade, as the common market developed in Europe, an increasing proportion of investment was flowing in that direction. Practically all foreign investment was made directly, with American companies maintaining at least a share of control, rather than by outright purchase of portfolio securities.

In many foreign countries—e.g., the United Kingdom—interest rates were higher than in the United States. This was not true of Canada in the early fifties; and yet, Canada was one of the major countries drawing our investments. Since most foreign private investment was direct, the level of interest rates was not particularly at issue. The crucial question related to the profitability of branch plants or of facilities for supplying natural resources (such as iron ore) rather than to interest rates. Thus, the critical advantages were labor supply and markets, or unique availability of raw materials.

Foreign aid held at $4 billion to $5 billion most years in the fifties. Half of this was for military aid, although late in the period a shift was occurring toward increased economic support. Although subject to constant improvisation because the program has not been planned on a long-term basis, aid has become a constant crutch in support of foreign economies. Aid has been shifting from Europe to underdeveloped countries where the need is less temporary. We consider below the questions posed with respect to continuance of aid with the "dollar shortage" disappearing.

Among the major trading countries, surprisingly few changes were made in the exchange rate, and few cases of exchange restrictions occurred in the fifties. In fact, foreign barriers were becoming far less ominous. A notable improvement emanating in Europe was the introduction of free convertibility of foreign currencies. In some countries, such as in South America, however, new measures were constantly required to correct for unfavorable foreign trade developments, largely growing out of desperate inflationary forces.

THE BALANCE OF PAYMENT AS A SUMMARIZATION OF INTERRELATIONSHIP

In an aggregative sense international trade factors must register either in the current or in the prospective balance of payments. This is because the balance of payments pits the flow of receipts against the flow of expenditures made in foreign trade. For activity of a country to be affected, some change must arise in domestic income or expenditures, and foreign influences can do this only by a change in receipts or expenditures. If the balance of payments is zero, in an aggregative sense no influence has been introduced; and if the balance does not change from one time to another, the influence introduced has remained unchanged.

This conclusion overlooks the disturbance which might be produced by a change in structure of either exports or imports. For instance, the great increase in imports of foreign automobiles into the United States in the late fifties would have added a disturbing element in the American economy and a stimulating one in European economies even if the aggregate balance had remained unchanged. While major changes in structure do play an important part in the transmission of business fluctuations throughout the world, they are most frequently caused by short-term variation in the aggregative levels of foreign trade rather than by dynamic changes in growth patterns.

Whenever a recession develops in the United States, our import of raw materials suffers disproportionately because of the exaggerated decline which occurs in our industrial production, since industrial production in the United States is the chief consumer of imported raw materials. The rapid and disturbing decline in our import of British textiles in 1949 was caused by runoff of inventories connected with the recession. Certainly, the most striking pressures put on foreign trade usually grow out of short-term changes in the structure induced by business cycle fluctuations. As business cycle expansion follows recession, the trade types which fell most violently rise with the greatest vigor, and the structural problems are inverted.

We shall examine forces producing changes in the balance of payments in terms of (1) trade flows and (2) financial flows. First, however, we should note that the processes which transmit activity changes between countries, listed in an earlier section, relate also to relative price differences, to relative movements of interest rates, and to devaluation. Each of these influences trade or financial flows. Price changes encourage or discourage trade, relatively high interest rates encourage the flow of investment, and devaluation discourages imports and encourages exports. These other processes are important because they influence trade movements and financial flows. This was indicated by the summary presented earlier in the chapter.

Trade flows influence income in the countries between which the trade occurs. The major types of trade flow involved are:

1. Merchandise trade
2. Service trade and foreign travel
3. Military grants
4. Nonmilitary grants in kind
5. Cash transfer payments by the government
6. Private remittances

Merchandise exports in excess of imports add to our income, and likewise with respect to miscellaneous services we provide abroad. We pay out more in foreign travel than we receive, and that adds to foreign income. Military and nonmilitary grants made by our government to foreign governments represent a kind of transfer payment. Private remittances are a relatively small transfer of income from our citizens to those in foreign countries.

Merchandise trade is by far the largest and most variable income influence. In 1959, merchandise exports came to $16 billion out of a total export of goods and services of $25 billion. Similarly, merchandise imports were $15 billion in a total of $24 billion. Possibly, merchandise exports will tend to be a bit higher and merchandise imports a bit lower in comparison with total foreign trade in future years, but the importance of merchandise trade is illustrated. In the following section, we summarize the factual information on the transmission as reflected by the merchandise trade balance.

The cyclical fluctuations in service transactions cannot be effectively traced because of paucity of data, but it is clear that these transactions vary less than merchandise trade does with business fluctuations. The same can be said of the other four types listed above. The three covering the major types of government grants are subject to erratic influences and may therefore introduce variation in business activity in foreign countries; but the erratic fluctuations would grow out of political—or at least, a type of social —considerations not closely related to business cycle movements. Private remittances to foreigners have not varied with postwar recessions, and the decline shown in them in the Great Depression may be attributed to the depression itself.

Another way of visualizing the balance of payments is by consideration of the financial instrumentalities by which any remaining balance is paid. The payment of balances is not a purely passive factor, however, as investments may be made because of their promise by contrast with payments which are found necessary when exports do not equal imports plus foreign-aid payments. A striking illustration is provided by a large flow of United States investment into Canada in the fifties. The flow of investment funds was so great that merchandise and service trade payments did not move fast enough to balance out the exaggerated flow of American dollars into Canada.

The balance of payments may also be disturbed by the flow of foreign-aid payments. Foreign aid acquits foreigners of the obligation of obtaining sufficient American dollars to pay for at least part of the excess of our exports over our imports. In so far as it is provided in dollars (number 5, above), it reduces the pressure foreign countries may face in paying for the excess of our exports over our imports. In so far as it provides goods freed from commercial payment (numbers 3 and 4, above), a part of the flow of goods and services abroad is removed from commercial transactions. Foreign aid works reasonably well in a "dollar shortage" economy, in the situation where our exports significantly exceed our imports and where we have substantial obligations to assist in advancing foreign standards of living. Such situations largely explain foreign-aid payments in the fifties. The transfers can be made without any embarrassment to the value of the dollar so long as needed dollar payments greatly exceed needed foreign currency payments.

If our exports should fall substantially in relation to our imports, as occurred in much of the depressed period 1957–58, the international exchange value of the dollar would be weakened. Since foreign aid is influenced by commercial considerations only in so far as political factors are guided by market requirements, decisions on foreign aid properly should be made in the light of probable export-import relationships. When foreign investment is made under private auspices rather than through foreign aid, excessive demands for foreign currencies are at least partly deterred by more expensive foreign exchange.

We may put aside the problem of foreign aid and visualize the market factors involved in capital movements in reaching a payments balance. As stated above, to a substantial extent foreign private investments merely raise the whole level of foreign trade because they induce greater exports, which in turn make for higher imports, and thereby raise the demand for imports. If this does not happen, foreign investment raises our claim to foreign assets and produces a positive net foreign investment. The larger our foreign holdings become, the greater will be our flow of earnings, which, to the extent that they are not reinvested in the foreign country, will add to the foreign country's exchange difficulties because they will represent a demand for conversion of the foreign currency into dollars for payment to American citizens.

When exports of goods and services plus return on foreign capital holdings exceed imports, and the excess is not canceled by foreign-aid payments, a transfer of gold ownership or issue of short-term evidences is required. If the short-term capital movement becomes great enough, emergency measures will be required in the interest of the foreign country. A traditional procedure in the world's history involves raising the interest rate in the embarrassed country. This will tend to draw "hot money" to it and thus provide relief in obtaining foreign exchange requirements. It will also be contractionary in the country involved and thus draw down activity, with a consequent reduction of imports, and perhaps a decline in domestic prices which may encourage an increase in exports.

Most persons look unfavorably on the use of procedures for effecting a balance-of-payments adjustment which will tend to reduce the country's activity. As pointed out in the following chapter, a widely accepted opinion now is that monetary policy should be used to promote full employment rather than to protect gold reserves or to protect the foreign exchange rate.

For our present purposes, it is most important to recognize that "the balance of payments tends to affect not only the stock of money, but also the flow of income and hence expenditure."[4] To some extent, adherence to the traditional procedures of balance-of-payments adjustment assumed that conditions could be corrected merely by readjusting the stock of money in the domestic economy. As we have seen, however, changes in the balance of payments will influence exports and imports. Changes in exports and imports will realign the level of activity in the domestic economy. Extent of

---

[4]League of Nations, *International Currency Experience* (Geneva, 1944), p. 100. Reprinted by the United Nations, 1947.

the realignment will depend upon the degree to which the economy depends on foreign trade. In any case, whatever the foreign trade policy adopted, the fact that it will affect employment levels in the domestic economy cannot be ignored.

INTERNATIONAL TRANSMISSION OF FLUCTUATION AT DIFFERENT BUSINESS CYCLE PHASES

Shift in the spread of business cycle influences to other countries can be traced most effectively through changes in merchandise trade balances, because of sensitivity of the merchandise flow to variation in aggregate activity. As we have seen above, most other income-type flows in the foreign trade picture do not vary significantly with the business cycle unless the fluctuation is large, as in the Great Depression. However, Mintz notes that "a brief study of available data on services upholds the decisive role of merchandise trade in determining the movements of the whole balance on current account."[5] Furthermore, the fluctuations in the trade balance have approximately paralleled those in net foreign investment since 1948.

Obviously, the merchandise trade balance, representing the difference between merchandise exports and merchandise imports, is dependent upon the level of these two series. Generally, both merchandise exports and merchandise imports have correlated positively with the business cycle.[6] The rates of movement in these two series, however, have not been the same. In fact, merchandise imports have risen so much faster in expansion and have declined so much faster in recession that the merchandise trade balance generally has moved inversely with the business cycle. This would indicate that foreign trade tends to have a slight stabilizing effect on our business cycle. Imports have risen fast enough in expansion to retard the trade balance and have fallen fast enough in contraction to increase its level.

Although the effect on our business cycle is negative, its relative effect has been small, averaging but a slight fraction of 1 per cent of the total level of gross national product.[7] The mitigating

---

[5]Ilse Mintz, *Trade Balances during Business Cycles: U.S. and Britain since 1880*, Occasional Paper 67 (New York: National Bureau of Economic Research, Inc., 1959), p. 6. Most of the information in this and the following section was developed in that monograph.

[6]See the Mintz chart, *op. cit.*, p. 15. The relation of exports was poor before World War I.

[7]According to the Mintz chart, *op. cit.*, p. 20, the average merchandise trade balance decline in business cycle expansion from 1921 to 1938 was $120 million, while the average GNP level for the period was $84 billion.

effect on our business cycle, looked at reciprocally, means that our business cycle variation has aggravated the movement in foreign countries. The reason is that we have accelerated the rise of activity in foreign countries in business cycle expansion and have induced a slackening effect in recession because of the high elasticity of our demand for imports. Our exports do not react as sensitively to our own business cycle, partly because the business cycle movements in foreign countries, whose demand determines the level of our exports, do not entirely conform with our business cycle movement. The relatively small effect of foreign trade on our business cycle does not necessarily mean that our influence on foreign fluctuations is small. This is because our imports from some countries are relatively large in comparison to the total level of expenditures in those countries. We return to this point later in the chapter.

Late in business cycle contraction the generalization above with regard to movement of the trade balance inverse to our business cycle has not held. This is due more to a shift in the behavior of exports in that cyclical phase than to any change in the characteristic movement of imports. In other words, by late contraction the tendency is such that the induced effect our business cycle creates on the rest of the world ricochets back on the level of our own activity, as evidenced by an acceleration in the slackening of our exports.

The retarding influence of foreign trade on our business cycle in expansion is particularly apparent in the late phases of prosperity. Again, the key is the movement of exports. Higher domestic prices retard foreign purchases when we are experiencing peak prosperity; furthermore, the pressure of domestic demand makes it difficult to find supplies to satisfy foreign demand.

The major influence is so-called "import conformity"—the fact that imports in any country are largely determined by the level of total expenditures in that country. However, import conformity fails to explain the decline in the trade balance late in business cycle contraction or the rapid decline in the trade balance late in business cycle expansion. As noted in the two preceding paragraphs, the explanation in these cases is shift in exports.

The trade balance movement actually is largely concentrated in the neighborhood of the business cycle downturn—late in expansion and early in contraction. At other times, it levels off and produces but a very small effect on changing activity. An important reason for this is declining exports late in expansion and rapid decline in imports as the business cycle downswing gets under way. The rapidity of decline in imports is partly due to inventory runoff. Some import cuts are proportionately more than the decline in final expenditures in this country, with a reduction in inventories accounting for the difference. Later on in the contraction the decline in our exports as the rest of the world reacts to our contraction deadens the expansionary effect in this country. Early in expansion, our demand for imports does not rise rapidly so that, at first, little contractionary force develops.

RELATION OF TRADE BALANCE TO WORLD IMPORTS

Since we think of the trade balance as representative of activity changes carried from country to country, it is natural to seek a simplification in representing activity change of all other countries taken together. This could be achieved by some kind of a representation of the "world business cycle." For that purpose the best measure appears to be the change in world imports aside from those of the country being considered. Mintz finds that such a series conforms closely with changes in manufacturing production representative of the rest of the world.[8]

The American merchandise trade balance conforms to some extent with the movement of world imports in other countries, although the American trade balance shows more cycles. This is partly because of the greater frequency of business cycles in the United States than in other major countries, but it is also due to the fact that cycles in the American merchandise trade balance occur more frequently than American business cycles representing total activity. The inverse movement of the United States trade balance with the American business cycle is principally based on times when our business cycle did not move positively with world imports.[9] The movement of the United States trade balance was irregular when the American business cycle corresponded with movement in world imports. "Thus, if American business cycles had always moved with those abroad, no balance pattern would exist."[10] This means that movements in the American trade balance do not imply contagious spreading of American cyclical influences when American business cycles conform with those in foreign countries.

The degree of independence which the American business cycle can be expected to show in the future is therefore important in-

---

[8]*Op. cit.,* pp. 61–62.
[9]Mintz, *op. cit.,* charts on pp. 11–13.
[10]*Ibid.,* p. 81.

formation. If other countries are experiencing parallel short-term changes, variation in our imports may imply nothing more serious than conformity to business fluctuations which are generally occurring. The statistical evidence on time-series variations here reviewed does not, however, eliminate the possibility that the elasticity of our demand for imports may be great enough to exaggerate the world cyclical movements. As indicated below, there are some reasons for believing that the elasticity may be declining.

INTERDEPENDENCE OF FLUCTUATIONS THROUGHOUT THE WORLD

Business cycles do not wholly conform in various countries. This is not only because of barriers to interregional trade, described early in the chapter, but is due to characteristic differences between countries. These differences may be classified according to (1) the degree of isolation in any country, (2) the differences in phase of industrial development, and (3) various diversities in the structure of trade.

1. The relative isolation of an economy depends partly on its size and its available resources. Large countries with ample resources of most major types, as far as economic considerations are concerned, could maintain substantial barriers to international trade with reasonably impunity. The abandonment of the gold standard in the Great Depression changed the rules so that countries were less bound by trade practices which had tied their own income and employment to the fluctuation occurring in other countries. Increasing recognition of full employment as an objective, to be pursued independently, if necessary, provided a framework for any country to follow if it wished to cut itself adrift from undesirable fluctuations found in the rest of the world. Yet, little of this kind of action has been taken.

2. There is slight reason to believe that business cycle fluctuations will work themselves out in the same way in countries differing greatly in maturity of industrial development. Throughout the world, therefore, differences in timing and amplitude are sure to occur. Entirely aside from world trade which takes place between countries, it is hard to believe that countries in different stages of industrial development would always reach the culminating stages of business cycle expansion and business cycle contraction simultaneously. In fact, the foreign trade influence may provide the causal forces which bring the degree of timing conformance that occurs.

3. Differences in the structure of industry account for dissimilarity of business fluctuations on similar lines of reasoning. To take an extreme illustration, a country largely restricted to the making of short-lived goods would experience a different cyclical movement than one making durable goods. Also, institutional heterogeneity may make for important unlikeness in the cyclical movement. For instance, company practices on inventory control or devices used to foster price and wage flexibility are likely to influence business fluctuation.

These are qualitative forces, and their quantitative relations to the length and amplitude of business cycle phases are unmeasured. Their influences will be important, however, in determining the correspondence of business cycle movements in various countries. We cannot expect trade between nations, however free and unimpeded it may be, to neutralize basic forces which make for fundamental differences in cyclical movements.

Mintz has computed a diffusion index going back to 1880 to show the percentage of countries with a rise in imports in relation to cycles in world (ex United States) imports.[11] The result does not look too different from the comparison we find between diffusion indexes and domestic business cycle movements, except that leads are less prevalent for the diffusion of imports throughout the world. The indication is that cyclical movements in foreign trade have spread any fluctuation which was occurring in the individual countries.

Actual increases or decreases in similarity of movement are difficult to establish with any finality. The National Bureau measures indicate that fluctuations became increasingly alike prior to World War I.[12] Considerable diversity did develop in the thirties despite the universal influence of the Great Depression. Notably, recovery in the United Kingdom far exceeded that in the United States, and expansion in Japan greatly outdistanced that of all other industrial countries. World War II stimulated activity in all countries; and the early postwar period was quite similar in different countries because all nations were faced with urgent demand, and

---

[11]*Op. cit.*, pp. 68–73. Work along these lines is continuing. See National Bureau of Economic Research, Inc., *A Respect for Facts: Fortieth Annual Report* (New York, 1960), pp. 58–59.

[12]See, for instance, summaries in the fourth edition of this book, pp. 265, 277, and 278. By the same methods, Oskar Morgenstern shows that the similarity declined from 1919 to 1938. See *International Financial Transactions and Business Cycles* (Princeton: Princeton University Press, 1959), p. 49.

almost all governments permitted inflationary developments in the face of this situation.

The first substantial postwar recession in the United States, developing in 1948–49, appeared in the United States while the European economies did not show previous signs of faltering. The inventory runoff in the United States, however, "exported" the recession, particularly to Great Britain. British textile stocks in the United States came to be looked on as excessive, and the temporary interruption of our imports induced a slight decline in British activity. Other European economies reflected at least a slackening in the advance of activity. Fundamentally, urgent demand remained so great in the European economies that recession might not have occurred at the time if our imports had not dropped so rapidly.

Although the second recession in the United States was principally related to readjustments following the Korean War, activity either leveled off or declined in most countries in 1953 or in 1954. Our imports declined almost as much as in the previous recession, by 6 to 7 per cent.

In 1957–58, activity leveled off or declined in almost all European countries, although the decline was less than in the United States in all cases, and in some cases less than in the two preceding recessions. The decline in total imports into the United States was very slight, coming to scarcely more than 1 per cent; raw material imports, however, declined as much as in the previous recessions. In several foreign countries the decline continued into 1959; but in those cases, recession did not begin until some time in 1958, as in France, for instance.

The postwar cycles appear to have been nearly world-wide. The United States influence has been greater than in earlier decades when the American cycle was shorter than in most other industrial countries. This conclusion agrees with Mintz in her view that the diffusion index of imports "supports the view that [interdependence of nations] has grown."[13] In spite of the fact that world trade is no longer tied together by the conventional financial relations imposed by the gold standard, the interrelation of activities does not appear to have lessened.

CHANGING INFLUENCE OF THE UNITED STATES

From the Great Depression to the late fifties a "dollar shortage" came to be one of the commonly accepted facts of international

---

[13]*Op. cit.,* p. 73.

relations. Foreign holding of dollars was always in short supply. This was because our exports continuously exceeded our imports, and we were the leading creditor nation.[14] After World War II, much of the discrepancy was redressed by a large flow of foreign aid payments to which we were the major contributor.

Dollar shortages seemed to end abruptly in 1958. The abruptness was partly due to the Suez crisis, with our net exports rising to the abnormally high annual rate of $6 billion in the first quarter of 1957. As that crisis cleared, the 1957–58 recession might have been expected to cut imports enough to provide a large offset to the inevitable decline in exports. But the decline in imports was very slight. This is largely because the structure of our imports had changed, with an increasing shift away from raw materials and toward fabricated products. Our demand for fabricated products holds up better in recession because more of these products go into consumer sales, while materials are mainly for use in manufacturing production which declines disproportionately in depression.

Changes occurring in productivity and advances in production in most other nations were as important an influence on our trade balance as the shift in structure of our imports. (Our relatively efficient branch plants located in foreign countries are an important reason.) Our predominance in supplying desirable goods in world markets was shrinking because of the industrial awakening in other countries. Due to the induced (or multiplier) effect which occurs in foreign trade, the result was more an increase in the total foreign movement of goods than a loss of trade by us. Total world exports doubled in the fifties. Our own exports rose substantially because, as exports of other nations rose rapidly, their induced increase in income added to their own foreign demand. But the rise in our exports was scarcely keeping up with that in the rest of the world.

On the other hand, our import demand was coming to vary less sensitively with changes in our business cycle. This was caused by the changes occurring in the structure of our import demand. Our foreign demand for raw materials was being substituted to an increasing extent by domestic production of synthetic materials, notably in rubber and various new textile products. At the same time, the quality of foreign manufactures had improved, and they were

---

[14]It is not our purpose to attempt an explanation of the long existence of the dollar shortage. Light on the subject will be found in Hal B. Lary and Associates, *The United States in the World Economy* (Washington, D.C.: U.S. Government Printing Office, 1943).

competing more effectively in our markets. The foreign automobile is an excellent illustration because it represents a significant conquest in our markets, and partly because the competition later came to be neutralized by the American "compact" car. Foreign competition has become an increasingly important market factor, but American products are unlikely to fade out of the competition except in cases where advantages relative to other products are outstanding.

This means that the size of our balance of exports over imports has been reduced. At $1 billion, net imports were the largest in peacetime history in 1959. An export balance is to be expected in most future years, but probably less than the $2.5 billion average from 1955 to 1958. We may anticipate that our exports will tend toward less than 17 per cent compared with 18 per cent of world exports in the fifties, and that our imports will average about 14 per cent compared with slightly over 14 per cent of world imports in the fifties. As a consequence, the problems foreign countries have had in financing trade with us may have been largely resolved. Dollar receipts of the rest of the world rose 50 per cent in the fifties. A first reaction of other governments was to bring gold and dollar reserves up to more secure levels.

With our foreign market position on a more competitive basis and with the strengthening of foreign economies, the likelihood of our creating major disturbance in the world by "exporting" our recessions has been reduced. The greater violence of decline in activity, compared with that in the rest of the world, may be expected to continue, but reaction to it may be less sharp with wide prevalence of a more effective buffer of gold and dollar reserves. As Nurkse pointed out, "so long as there are ample liquid reserves to meet the external deficit, there is no reason to worry about it."[15]

If, because of change in structure, our imports have come to vary less sensitively with fluctuations in our total output, we may conclude that instability in the rest of the world is coming to be less dependent on our actions. In business cycle expansion, our total imports may rise less disproportionately, and our increased demand may be moderated and become less inflationary in foreign economies. In recessions, our imports may fall less; hence, we may disturb foreign economies less. Much of the slight stabilizing effect that foreign trade has had on our own domestic economy, as out-

---

[15]Ragnar Nurkse, "Domestic and International Equilibrium," in *The New Economics* (New York: Alfred A. Knopf, Inc., 1947), p. 274.

lined above, may have been eliminated by the same influences. Our export balance may be expected to fall less in expansions and rise less in recessions. This is a small price to pay for the partial exoneration from guilt in creating instability in the world.

But the exoneration is only partial. If our activity continues to be more unstable than in the rest of the world, we shall remain a most likely country to initiate economic disturbance. Furthermore, the improved stability in our total imports is wholly dependent upon a change in the structure of imports. Undeveloped countries, which are critically dependent upon the export of raw materials for use in our production, may be relieved little, if at all. The raw material countries may, of course, find wider markets as a result of the rapid growth in industrial production in the rest of the world, but our influence is likely to remain critical for many years to come.

The stability of the rest of the world thus will not be exempt from what happens in our country. We may be forced to make some adaptation in our foreign-aid payments in view of the narrowing difference between our exports and our imports. Other industrial countries whose trade balances have improved may wish to share more fully the burden of bringing advancement to underdeveloped nations. Another possibility is that, with our increased level of private foreign investment, interest and dividend returns flowing to us may augment foreign exchange funds, as they did for Britain in the nineteenth century. Clearly, important questions on trade policy remain for consideration in the following chapter.

FOR REFLECTION AND ANALYSIS

1. Why is international transmission of business fluctuations emphasized more in this book than interregional fluctuations within the economy?
2. In advocacy of foreign investment, it is sometimes said that "trade follows the dollar." Comment.
3. What dangers are posed by "hot money"?
4. Should underdeveloped countries count on our aid?
5. Does merchandise trade represent the international spreading of business fluctuations?
6. Will foreign investments relieve the scarcity of American dollars in foreign countries?
7. How have the cyclical movements of merchandise exports and merchandise imports differed?
8. Would the world influence of the American business cycle be increased if our cyclical movement came to correspond exactly with those in the rest of the world?
9. Do you agree with the text forecast of the changing influence of the United States in world trade?

Chapter 26

INTERNATIONAL TRADE POLICY

This chapter deals with international trade policy as it relates to our business fluctuation and economic growth. We cover this subject because of its relation to the pursuit of economic goals. Inevitably, controls of one sort or another will be placed on international financial and trade relations. The impact of these controls on economic instability and economic growth warrants attention.

Repercussions would be at a minimum if an economy were completely isolated from the rest of the world, or if fluctuations and growth were precisely similar in all countries. Complete isolation would eliminate all trade and investment flows, and thereby cut off interacting economic forces. For reasons other than economic, this is not a plausible policy in our world; furthermore, we cannot treat lightly the fact that forgoing the advantages of foreign trade would lower living standards. The effect on living standards would be greater in small nations specializing in limited economic activities. Even in the United States, some of our imports might be difficult to develop locally, e.g., coffee or iron ore supplies. A policy of isolationism by us would cripple small nations whose economies have been developed to supply us with raw materials.

By taking thought, we cannot make fluctuations similar throughout the world. Fluctuations differ because of unevenness of economic development and unlikeness in the structure of trade, as explained in the preceding chapter. The chief hope would be to eliminate fluctuation in all countries by continuous maintenance of full employment. If full employment were maintained in each country, it would have to be contrived through domestic policy.

We have found no satisfactory way of achieving continuously full employment in our own economy. There is, however, some basis for hope that our fluctuations have become relatively mild, as noted in Chapter 24. If fluctuations can be kept effectively limited in all countries of the world, the problem is not as neatly solved as it would be with no deviation from full employment anywhere, but policies could be developed which would keep international repercussions at a tolerable level. The chief burden of this chapter is to explain that proposition.

Goals of international trade policy have recently been extended to cover growth as well as fluctuation. We can point with some pride at the rapid advancement in Western Europe during the postwar period because we have played a part in bringing it about. Opportunity for us to contribute further to economic advancement in that part of the world may be more limited. We now face the difficult challenge of speeding advancement in underdeveloped nations. We are committed to the lending of positive support in hastening the development of those nations. That is a vague, but nonetheless critically important, area of foreign policy. Business activity in the underdeveloped nations generates little or no endogenous fluctuating influence, but the business cycle variation of developed countries superimposes fluctuations on them. We shall give heed to the problem of what can be done to short-cut the repercussions of our instability on those nations. Problems of speeding up advancement of underdeveloped nations principally lie outside the province of this book.

MONETARY VERSUS INCOME CRITERIA IN INTERNATIONAL POLICY

An obvious indication of international relations to which every national government must give attention is the level of gold or foreign-money reserves. When these reserves fall below a safe minimum, policy action is called for. One resort is the raising of interest rates. This is achieved by action of the Central Bank. Higher interest rates tend to draw short-term funds from foreign countries, thus easing the demand for them, and to improve the reserve position. The value of the country's foreign exchange rises in terms of foreign moneys. This is important, for presumably that value tends to fall when the country's reserves are approaching inadequacy. The prewar policy was to preserve a stable foreign exchange rate, which is also an accepted gauge of the present Monetary Fund.

In use of income criteria, there is no objection to a change in interest rates if such a change is required for full-employment stability. Difference of opinion turns more on objectives than on the instrumentality. If rising interest rates not only remedy a deteriorating reserve position, but also reduce inflationary pressures without driving activity below the requirements for full employment, those persons favoring income criteria would not object. But that result ordinarily would be hard to achieve. Rising interest rates not only tend to draw in "hot money," which relieves the embarrassment of low monetary reserves, but also are likely to induce effects on activity of the economy. One possibility is that the high interest rates will discourage investment and thus tend to drive down the total level of investment. Under other conditions, investment may be financed predominantly with equity flotations so that high interest rates may not drive income levels down so directly. The high interest rates may be more important in bringing in additional investment funds, which add to inflation for the time being, and rising commodity prices may discourage exports. Whichever line of development occurs, the ultimate end would seem to be a recession. Thus, the raising of interest rates to avoid instability in the international financial field may produce instability in the domestic economy.

Implicitly, we have been assuming that the economy is at full-employment levels when monetary correction is to be made for inadequate gold or foreign-money reserves. But inadequate reserves have arisen at other cyclical phases. One illustration is the United Kingdom with its postwar loss of earning receipts from foreign investments. Another is a situation such that cyclical depression has spread throughout the world when the country whose policy is under consideration has suffered a disproportionate decline in exports so that protection of its foreign-money reserves is called for. Rising interest rates under these circumstances would tend to drive domestic levels of activity to even deeper depression.

Nurkse clearly provided an evaluation based on income criteria:

The behavior of its neighbors need never deflect a country from the pursuit of full employment. The classical free trade doctrine showed that it was both beneficial and practicable for an individual country to abolish its trade barriers even in the face of a protectionist world. In the same way it is always to some extent possible for a single country to pursue a full employment policy unilaterally. The relative importance of foreign markets, the dependence on imported raw materials, and other similar conditions vary, of course, from country to country. Yet, to some extent, it is always possible for a single country to go ahead with a domestic expansion policy even in a world of depression and unemployment. The expansion will inevitably, under these conditions, produce an adverse balance of payments. So long as there are ample liquid reserves to meet the external deficit, there is no reason to worry about it. When liquid reserves have run out or are not available to start with, there is usually some change in the exchange rate that will preserve external equilibrium. Alternatively, there is the possibility of adopting import restrictions, not in order to reduce imports, but just enough to prevent them from increasing. This will prevent the expansion from "spilling over" abroad, but will not actually hurt the outside-world. It is a defensive measure aimed at maintaining the equilibrium of foreign payments, and is to be sharply distinguished from the aggressive and unneighborly policy which operates through a disruption of external equilibrium.

. . . Devaluation or import restrictions may be justifiable, as in the case of a unilaterally expanding country, when they are intended to close a deficit or preserve equilibrium in the balance of payments. They are not justifiable when their purpose is to create a surplus in the balance of payments or to enlarge a surplus already existing.[1]

TREND IN FOREIGN TRADE REGULATION

When contraction in the Great Depression failed to lead to prompt recovery, a rash of "beggar my neighbor" measures spread throughout the world. The Smoot-Hawley Bill, raising American tariffs, was passed in June, 1930. While this did produce a slight expansionary influence domestically, that effect was only temporary. Foreign retaliation followed, and by the summer of 1932 the Ottawa Conference set up preferential tariffs for the British Empire. By the autumn of 1932, President Hoover felt impelled to call attention to the fact that on sixteen broad classes of products, duties were not high enough to protect us from foreign competition. Once "beggar my neighbor" measures are taken in a recession, a chain reaction develops. The measures required become successively more severe as long as business cycle contraction continues. Carried to its limit, a virtual strangulation of foreign trade would be reached.

A reversal of the movement toward restrictive action was started by passage of the Reciprocal Tariff Act in 1934, which authorized the President to raise or lower tariffs by not more than 50 per cent and gave him power to negotiate reciprocal trade agreements. By repassage, with only slight changes in the provisions, this legislation has been kept on the books. The average duty on dutiable imports was already declining, and has since dropped by four fifths, as shown in Table 26-1.

---

[1]Ragnar Nurkse, "Domestic and International Equilibrium," in *The New Economics* (New York: Alfred A. Knopf, Inc., 1947), pp. 273-74.

After World War II the old gold standard was not restored; but on the basis of the Bretton Woods Conference held in New Hampshire in 1944, a system called the International Monetary Fund was established. Resources of the Fund come to some $14 billion of gold and member-country currencies which are made available for stabilizing activities in accordance with the Fund's charter. The Fund is designed to deal with the problems of exchange stability and convertibility. A currency-short nation can meet a temporary shortage by borrowing from the Fund rather than resorting to Central Bank rate increases, exchange readjustment, or trade restrictions when embarrassment does not appear to be lasting.

TABLE 26–1

UNITED STATES IMPORTS AND DUTIES ON IMPORTS

Year	(1) Imports (Billions of Dollars)	(2) Duty-Free Imports (Percentage of Total Imports)	(3) Duties Collected (Percentage of Dutiable Imports)
1931	2.1	66.6	53.2
1932	1.3	66.8	59.1
1933	1.4	63.1	53.6
1934	1.6	60.6	46.7
1935	2.0	59.1	42.9
1936	2.4	57.1	39.3
1937	3.0	58.6	37.8
1938	2.0	60.7	39.3
1946	4.8	60.8	26.4
1947	5.7	61.0	20.1
1948	7.1	58.9	14.3
1949	6.6	58.9	13.8
1950	8.7	54.5	13.3
1951	10.8	55.4	12.5
1952	10.7	58.2	12.8
1953	10.8	54.9	12.3
1954	10.2	55.4	12.2
1955	11.3	53.2	12.6
1956	12.5	49.8	11.7
1957	12.9	46.5	11.0
1958	12.7	41.9	11.3

Source: U.S. Tariff Commission.

If the derangement proves to be more permanent, the Fund has an escape clause which permits any member nation to alter the value of its currency by as much as 10 per cent without formal approval. Further exchange rate changes are supposed to require the sanction of the Fund's board of directors. This procedure is needed to guard against arbitrary and competitive currency devaluations prompted by nations seeking a temporary stimulus to their domestic economies.

Cases have occurred of countries devaluing their currencies without the Fund's approval. These have been related to uncontrolled domestic commodity-price inflation. The Fund has not seen fit to try to control "hot money" movements, even though these have been disturbing. Nevertheless, the Fund has been successful as long as reasonably stable trade conditions were faced. Exchange convertibility has recently become common throughout Europe. Generally, rates of exchange have held at the fixed official levels in recent years. Dealings with the international exchange problems of countries facing substantial commodity-price inflation have been unsatisfactory, and some changes in regulations probably are essential to adapt to those problems.

In 1947, twenty-three nations, including the United States, signed the General Agreement on Tariffs and Trade (GATT). There are now thirty-seven signatory countries. The Agreement has provided a steady pressure in the direction of freer, multilateral trade in contrast with the restrictions and bilateral agreements generated in the Great Depression. It is founded on the principles of equal and nondiscriminatory treatment for all trading nations, reduction of tariffs by negotiations similar to those carried out under the Reciprocal Trade Act, and elimination of import quotas. While some discretion has been essential in invoking these principles, limited progress has clearly been achieved. In a sense, GATT may be characterized as an agreement among many nations which embodies the principles of reciprocal trade policy.

Further advancement through the auspices of GATT appears to be partially blocked by preferential escape clauses of signatory countries. For instance, the United States has insisted on an escape clause which reserves the right to withdraw or modify a concession if, by determination of the Tariff Commission, it would cause serious injury to a domestic industry producing like, or directly competitive, products. Nevertheless, GATT has reduced the likelihood of a return of the vicious "beggar my neighbor" policies which became so strangulating in the Great Depression.

Success of the Common Market in Europe points to the customs union as the most likely direction of further adjustment in international trade regulation. The trade policy of the United States has generally been opposed to preferential arrangements, although we have made them with Cuba and the Philippines as the consequence of a special historical situation. In the case of the customs union the United States has taken the position that resulting discrimination may be justified by the broader interests of the participating countries. The customs union is the only type of trade preference, with the exception of discriminations maintained under postwar transitional arrangements, that GATT sanctions.

The countries of Western Europe were encouraged to grant trade preferences to each other, in which the United States did not share, early in the postwar period under the Organization for European Economic Cooperation (OEEC). The Common Market—a customs union among France, Germany, Italy, the Netherlands, Belgium, and Luxemburg—grew out of the OEEC. It has a great potential, as already indicated by the economic advance which has been achieved by these countries.[2] (See Chart 26–1.)

CHART 26–1

ADVANCE IN DEFLATED GROSS NATIONAL PRODUCT IN THE
COMMON MARKET COUNTRIES

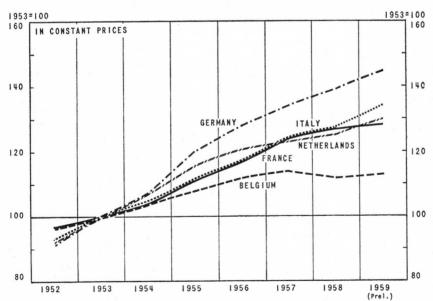

Source: Taken from the June 9, 1960, issue of *Economically Speaking*, issued by Bankers Trust Company of New York, by permission.

---

[2]Transitional problems appear threatening, however. For instance, an early effort in the Common Market to develop a common external tariff in 1960 called for lowering tariffs in high-tariff member countries, but for perceptible raising of tariffs in Germany and the Netherlands, where the resulting increased cost of imported raw materials was being resisted.

Another union, called the Free Trade Association, composed of seven other countries—the United Kingdom, Sweden, Norway, Denmark, Switzerland, Portugal, and Austria—has been formed. This has less promise than the Common Market union, but for various reasons the countries involved have not been able to reach agreements required to enter the Common Market. The salutary influence on world trade of custom union developments in Europe will be greatly reduced if the OEEC countries come to be divided into three groups—the Common Market, the Free Trade Association, and European countries outside of both—which set up stifling multilateral trade arrangements among themselves.

The fact is that the promise of achievement in the Common Market countries is so great that almost everyone has been impressed. The widespread economic prosperity in the Common Market area is remarkable as shown by Chart 26-1 on the advance in deflated gross national product in the Common Market countries. Knowledge of success will go a long way to overcome difficulties. If the outgrowth is freer and more firmly based foreign trade, the upsetting paralysis of the thirties would seem less likely to recur.

FOOD AND RAW MATERIALS PROBLEMS

For convenience, we may divide international raw materials problems into two types, the first relating to nature of the production process in raw materials activity and its impact in developed countries, and the second to the irregularity or inadequacy of the market which may be imposed on underdeveloped countries. As to the first, Bernstein provides an excellent summary:

> The problems concerned with international trade in primary products are extremely complex. They arise from two difficulties. First, the supply of certain primary products, especially agricultural commodities, is relatively insensitive to price for extended periods, so that a persistent tendency for production to increase more rapidly than demand is not easily corrected even by a large fall in prices. Second, the demand for primary products, especially industrial raw materials, varies considerably for cyclical and other reasons, so that the prices of such commodities fluctuate widely over short periods. Most food and raw materials exporting countries, including the United States, are confronted with these problems.
>
> The problems do not all arise from the difficult supply and demand conditions that distinguish primary products. These natural difficulties are accentuated by the fact that international trade in agricultural products is controlled and restricted far more than trade in industrial products.

The great industrial countries of Western Europe, which are net importers of foodstuffs, nevertheless provide a high degree of protection for their domestic production. In practically all of these countries, the price paid to domestic producers of wheat and other foodstuffs is a political rather than an economic price. The United States, too, maintains a very high level of protection for a number of agricultural products.[3]

Because of government surplus crop holdings in the United States, which reached about $10 billion in 1960, half of the American exports of agricultural products are under government programs. These exports are theoretically not of the type which otherwise would enter commercial trade; but in practice, there is no doubt some competition with trade demand. However, donations through private charities, and shipments for famine and emergency relief, generally do not replace private sales.

International trade in agricultural products thus is honeycombed with domestic problems which are almost universal. Actually, we would have much to gain by achievement of better economic balance in the agricultural area, because the spread of technological improvement in American agriculture has brought us some relative cost advantages. The difficulties of putting a satisfactory program on a commercial basis internationally are almost as great as the domestic problems dramatized by the system of price supports. Bernstein states the situation clearly:

> The problem of persistent agricultural surpluses in the United States and other high-income countries and chronic shortages in low-income countries presents a serious dilemma. There is no doubt that world consumption of agricultural products can be increased to a considerable extent by making such goods available at what is equivalent to bargain prices. The net increase in the consumption of agricultural products, however, would be considerably less than the amount made available through aid. The commercial exports of the United States and of other countries are certainly less as a consequence of our surplus disposal program. The adverse effect on some agricultural exporting countries is serious; the effect of terminating the program might be even worse for some of the countries now receiving aid. For there can be little doubt that to many low-income countries aid in the form of agricultural products represents a considerable accretion of resources for development, and these resources might not be available to them except in this form.[4]

---

[3]Edward M. Bernstein, *Study of Employment, Growth, and Price Levels: International Effects of U.S. Economic Policy,* Study Paper No. 16, 86th Cong., 2d sess., January 25, 1960 (Washington, D.C.: U.S. Government Printing Office, 1960), pp. 45–46.

[4]*Op. cit.,* p. 46.

The foundation for the maintenance of sound relationships in foreign trade of agricultural products appears to be no firmer than it was in the Great Depression.

Underdeveloped countries are constantly threatened with the inadequacy or irregularity of our market for their raw materials. In recession, our demand falls off sharply. Crude material imports declined nearly 30 per cent from early in the Korean War to the 1954 recession, and declined 15 per cent in each of the other two postwar recessions. The full brunt is better measured by particular commodities. Crude rubber imports, for instance, dropped two thirds from early in the Korean War to the 1954 recession, and by a third in the 1958 recession. As another illustration, copper imports halved from 1956 to 1958. Underdeveloped economies built around the production of a few crude materials for which we are the principal customer are in recurrent jeopardy of fluctuations in our manufacturing activity. Obviously, little can be done to stabilize such economies in the face of our fluctuating demand.

It is easy enough to say that the solution is for us to maintain a full-employment rate of activity at all times. In the above chapters, we found no competent prescription for that goal, especially in view of the flexible variation which occurs in inventory investment in our economy.

If we cannot stabilize the private demand for raw material purchases in our economy, it is reasonable to suggest that the government should make purchases so timed as to keep total demand stable. Attractive proposals for achieving this involve the acquisition and sale of "buffer" stocks of raw materials. To be practicable for inclusion in a buffer stock composite, the raw material must be storable without too much impairment of economic value, and the cost of storage must lie within reasonable limits. A plan for such raw materials could be economically sound; for when the demand falls off, stocks could be purchased at some reduction in price, although less than represented by the commercial decline which now occurs, and they could be sold at higher prices in periods of active demand.

Carefully described detailed buffer stock proposals are available, but they will not be presented here because they are all impractical at the present time.[5] First, a plan would require international sanc-

---

[5] The most effective evaluation available is that by M. K. Bennett and Associates, *International Commodity Stock-Piling as a Stabilizer* (Stanford, Calif.: Stanford University Press, 1949).

tion, and experience tends to indicate that such sanction is not forthcoming. Second, and perhaps more important, secular decline (relative to total demand) in the use of raw materials makes the establishment of buying and selling prices, to be employed by the government stock-piling agency, highly speculative.

The principal reason for secular decline in the import of natural raw materials is the development of synthetic raw materials which are replacing them to a significant degree. Possibly of some importance also is economy in the use of raw materials in making modern products and some shift in the structure of demand away from products which have been made of natural raw materials.

The raw material problem is not amenable, by itself, to any simple plan for providing adjustment. Of many specific proposals which have been made, none stands out as an effective solution. Nevertheless, we may well quote one of Bernstein's conclusions:

> The best way to deal with the problems created by chronic surplus of primary products is to encourage a lesser dependence among the underdeveloped countries on such output as a field of employment and as a source of export receipts. More and more of their growing labor force must in time be shifted to manufacturing: for their own use, for export to each other, and for export to advanced industrial countries. This does not diminish the importance of having these countries continue to produce and export foods and raw materials, for world demand will grow although not at the same rate as income and industrial production. It is even more important for the underdeveloped countries to improve productive efficiency in agriculture and mining, for higher incomes from the production of primary products is possible only through greater output per worker.[6]

UNITED STATES PRIVATE FOREIGN INVESTMENT

An inspection of the component goods and services imported and component goods and services exported to determine the items which account for major changes which are occurring in the trade balance is helpful in tracking down the forces at work. But part of the initiating forces may lie in investment rather than in imports and exports. The flow of investment to foreign countries generates exports from us, which in turn lead to higher imports to permit the increase in production required to produce the additional goods for export.

American investment in foreign countries has been an important growth factor in their economies. This promises to be as important

---

[6]*Op. cit.*, p. 50.

as British overseas investment in earlier periods. In some cases, as in the Latin American economies, American investment may feed inflation fires, and thus be disturbing. In others, as in the European Common Market, our investments have been a major factor in increasing productivity. We have brought in new technology and new industrial engineering practices which are more effective than the old local plants. Thus, the flow of investment has been important for other reasons than merely the amount of American funds made available.

Aside from Latin America, our private investment in underdeveloped countries does not exceed $200 million a year. This is unfortunate, for those countries now provide the greatest opportunity for us to change productivity by introducing our know-how. But major impediments exist. Weaving new activities into exotic cultures is extremely difficult. The governments usually are unstable, and the chances of expropriation are great. Hence, exploitation of raw materials, where the need in future activity of the company at home can be clearly seen, represents the major outlet for investment in underdeveloped countries. Manufacturing investment has been largely neglected, for the odds against its success are not justified by critical needs expected to develop at home. Fear of expropriation may be allayed to some extent by guaranty by the United States government against loss from political upheaval. Systems are being worked out which promise some success along that line.

In theory, at least, foreign investment should tend to add to the stability of the economies into which it flows rather than be destabilizing. This is because, when investment funds crowd limited markets for financing domestic investment projects, foreign demand should draw the funds, unless business fluctuation in foreign countice, which means that the funds obtained must be spent on Amerinished should help to offset the reduction in imports taken by us in recession. Investment flows appear to have worked that way at least part of the time prior to the collapse of international investment in the Great Depression.

In the postwar period, foreign investment has been principally made directly by companies in locating foreign branch plants or in developing raw material supplies. As in domestic investment the chief motivation has been a rising or a high level of sales in the United States. The cheapness of funds in recession plays a much smaller part in encouraging direct investment. By the late fifties, portfolio foreign investment has again been increasing rapidly, and possibly foreign investment will once more tend to fluctuate inversely with our business cycle. New issues of foreign securities sold in portfolio peaked in both 1954 and 1958.

INTERNATIONAL BANKS

So far, at least, private investment in underdeveloped areas has fallen far short of needs. Three nonprivate institutions are now supplying about $1.5 billion a year for investment in underdeveloped areas. The most important of these is the International Bank for Reconstruction and Development, frequently called the World Bank. This Bank was providing $700 million a year in the late fifties, compared with half as much in the middle of the decade. The capital of the Bank was doubled in 1959, which further increases its potential in placing investments in underdeveloped countries. Technical assistance offered by the World Bank to underdeveloped areas has been an important feature of the Bank's contribution.

The International Finance Corporation was formed in 1956 as an affiliate of the World Bank. Its operations are distinct, however, for the International Finance Corporation deals exclusively with private business, contrasted with large loans made to governments by the World Bank. So far, the loans of the Corporation have been relatively small, coming to $22 million in the year ending in June, 1960, and covering only thirty-three different commitments. The importance is less in the amount of investment funds provided than in the influence the operations may have on private investment: the example given to private investors.

The American Export-Import Bank predates both of these institutions. It was established in 1934 as an agency to help finance American exports to ease unemployment at home. Its character has shifted so that now its principal operations are financing industry in underdeveloped countries. "Tied loans" are a common practice, which means that the funds obtained must be spent on American exports; this no doubt derives from the original legislation, which was for the purpose of increasing United States exports. The Export-Import Bank is now providing investment funds of over $700 million a year.

The World Bank obtains funds for lending by security flotations. Thus, that institution channels some private savings into loans made to underdeveloped nations. There seems to be little promise in the near future of private agencies taking over functions of similar extent in investing in underdeveloped countries, even though satis-factory guaranties against political upheaval may be worked out.

THE FOREIGN-AID PROGRAM

Postwar payments under the foreign-aid program are shown in Table 26–2. The early aid programs, following in the wake of lend-

TABLE 26–2

UNITED STATES GOVERNMENT FOREIGN-AID ASSISTANCE

(In Billions of Dollars)

Year	(1) Total Aid	(2) Military Transfers under Grant	(3) Other Aid
1946......	5.5	0.1	5.4
1947......	5.7	...	5.7
1948......	5.3	0.4	4.9
1949......	5.7	0.2	5.4
1950......	4.2	0.5	3.6
1951......	4.6	1.5	3.2
1952......	5.0	2.7	2.4
1953......	6.4	4.3	2.1
1954......	4.9	3.2	1.7
1955......	4.6	2.4	2.2
1956......	4.9	2.6	2.3
1957......	5.1	2.5	2.6
1958......	4.9	2.4	2.5
1959......	3.9	2.0	1.9

Source: Office of Business Economics, Department of Commerce.

lease payments, were made on the simple principle that the reha-bilitation and reconstruction of the countries whose productive ca-pacity had been destroyed or impaired by the war were indis-pensable to a strong and balanced world economy. In this stage the aid went principally to Europe. When the funds appropriated for the purpose were running out, supplementation was obtained by the Marshall Plan, which provided funds at a declining rate for European reconstruction from 1948 to 1951.

In 1952 and 1953, large increases were made in military grants, as a consequence of the Korean War. As those grants declined in 1954 and 1955, the total aid program was shrinking. Beginning with 1955, however, increasing aid was going to underdeveloped coun-tries, especially in Asia.

It is clear, therefore, that the total aid program has been more stable than its different parts. Continuation of the aid program at present levels turns largely on the questions: (1) Will we continue military aid payments at the current $2 billion per year, and (2) will we continue or extend the aid to underdeveloped countries which is running at nearly as high a level?

Perhaps some indication of what we may find ourselves forced to do on military grants is provided by the change which has been taking place in the additional military expenditures for support of our own establishments that we are making abroad. From $0.5 billion a year in 1946–50, these expenditures have risen steadily to about $4 billion by 1960. (For the purposes of indicating influence on balance of payments, these may be added to the aid program, by which method we reach a total of $8 billion instead of $4 billion.)[7] If we are finding it necessary to increase our own military expenditures abroad, the chances are that military aid will increase rather than decrease.

With world conditions as they are, the argument that reducing aid to underdeveloped countries would be suicidal is difficult to refute. Possibly, appropriations for these purposes might be more vulnerable to Congressional slashing than military appropriations, since their need for defense may be less evident. The extent to which they are tied to surplus disposal programs abroad weakens that argument, however. Also, with a demonstrated need larger than is being met by the present programs, Congress might be expected to try to keep the program at least at present levels.

In spite of the fact that foreign aid has been composed of shifting programs, with the dynamic parts rising rapidly only to ebb away later, it is hard to show that the present program could be shrunk with impunity. In view of the exchange difficulties we now face, this presents a distressing dilemma. For various reasons, mostly noneconomic, we cannot afford to cut our foreign-aid program. However, taken together with military expenditures in foreign countries, required foreign payments are added to, so that avoidance of a negative trade balance is made difficult. In a world without a "dollar shortage," closer approach to a foreign investment balance is highly desirable. One way or another, countries with an improved foreign trade situation must be encouraged to take on a more equitable share of foreign aid and defense.

---

[7] See Bernstein, *op. cit.*, pp. 67–69.

Expenditures for aid and military support do not appear to threaten dangerous spreading of instability to foreign countries. This is because of the apparent necessity of maintaining the present level of expenditures and the unlikelihood that they will be capriciously increased, in view of the balance-of-trade embarrassment in meeting even the present levels. Nevertheless, military expenditure requirements are highly uncertain, and little assurance can be given that they will not vary.

OUTLOOK FOR INTERNATIONAL TRADE POLICY

American trade policy has passed through two stages in the postwar period and is now entering a third:

1. The early postwar years, when business fluctuations in the American economy were looked on as the chief threat to world stability.
2. A period of strengthening in the European economies.
3. End of the dollar shortage, together with recognition of reduced violence in the fluctuations of our imports.

1. The unenviable position of being considered the chief "exporter" of recessions climaxed with the 1949 recession. The European world was greatly disturbed, and the expression was coined that "when the United States sneezes, the rest of the world gets pneumonia." Demand, growing out of shortages created by the war, was still so urgent in Europe that declining demand characteristic of recession was hard to attribute to domestic developments in Europe. Difficulty was experienced, however, in adjusting during the recession to the rapid decline which occurred in our imports of some of their commodities.

2. Even before initiation of payments under the Marshall Plan, much had been accomplished in helping to restore European economies to healthy peacetime conditions with aid contributed by the United Nations Relief and Rehabilitation Administration and by large loans made by us to the United Kingdom, France, and other countries in 1946 and 1947. After the funds obtained were spent, Marshall Plan aid was continued long enough to put the economies back on a reasonable peace time basis. The specter of American instability remained; but the nightmare of an imported recession, when lack of capacity kept the European economies from meeting most urgent domestic demands, had faded.

3. The Treaty of Rome was signed in 1957 by the Common Market countries as a political measure to bolster European defenses. It serves the Common Market as a constitution and code of laws. The startling economic advantages flowing from freer trade

were soon reflected in significant improvement in the rates of growth in Common Market countries. The imagination of American enterprisers was sparked, and private direct American investments in Europe began to increase rapidly by 1959. This in itself was an important factor in increasing productivity, because the industrial engineering practices of American plants were generally more advanced than those of competitive European concerns.

The dollar shortage meant nothing more than that our trade balance was more favorable than the average in the rest of the world. Rapid improvement in foreign countries built a sound foundation for achieving greater exports relative to imports. The stage has now been reached such that our currency in the channels of world trade is no more short than that of many other countries. The reliance of the rest of the world on us has thereby been reduced to more reasonable proportions.

Change in structure of our imports also has reduced the extent to which we are likely to influence foreign domestic economies unfavorably. With a larger proportion of our imports in fabricated products, especially in consumer goods, demand for total imports will fall off less violently in recession. The relative decline in imports of raw materials is due largely to substitution of synthetic materials; but the increase in imports of fabricated products is founded to a substantial extent on industrial advancement in other countries, particularly in Europe and in Japan. A summary on the reaction of our imports as an aggregate does not give adequate consideration to the violence of the influence of our imports on underdeveloped countries producing raw materials principally for us, however. No evidence exists that the variation in our imports of raw materials has lessened.

We are approaching a position such that the accusations that we lie at the center of spreading instability throughout the world sound empty. Our foreign aid offsets to some extent the disturbance our imports of raw materials produce on underdeveloped countries. Change in our import influence on the industrially developed world has canceled much of our uniqueness in introducing disturbance that seemed apparent a decade ago. There is left the possibility that we may have wider business cycle fluctuations than most of the rest of the industrially developed countries, but there is a chance that even this difference may be fading with the developing influences which are tending to improve domestic stability. (See Chapter 24.)

Fundamentally, the objective of all foreign policy is security, not primarily economic considerations as such. To build toward security in our world, it is generally agreed that we cannot afford to reduce foreign aid and assistance programs. They provide us with "St. George's Cavalry"—financial aid in the interest of developing a strong economic position. The total of less than 2 percent of gross national product which we now employ in foreign aid and foreign military support appears very modest in view of the disturbed world in which we live. Our problems in this connection are not in the relative cost of the support we lend foreign economies but in the unbalance of our foreign account. We cannot continue to make net payments abroad in excess of the surplus on private account. We must insist on readjustment in aid burdens or realignment of trade practices so that the international payments of the United States will be restored to balance.

In spite of the problems faced in foreign trade, the current promise appears almost unbounded. The Common Market is providing an object lesson which has no parallel in history, except possibly free trade development within the British Empire in the nineteenth century. The spirit of wider and freer trade surely will spread as peoples note the improvement in well-being that is resulting. The fact is that adapting engineering knowledge in parts of the world where is has been undeveloped and making effective use of differences in relative efficiencies in various types of production in different countries are far less complicated than it has often been made to appear. Although the Common Market grew out of a political compact, its economic implications could be staggering.

The implications relate principally to the long run, rather than to cyclical fluctuations, however. Freer trade can be expected to generate quicker, not slower, transmission of cyclical disturbances. Some gain may have been achieved if delayed foreign trade reactions and the use of "beggar my neighbor" policies have become less ominous. The impressive gain relates to the higher growth potential freer trade makes possible.

FOR REFLECTION AND ANALYSIS

1. What is meant by use of income criteria in formulating international policy?
2. What advantages would accrue to us from putting a larger part of the international movement of agricultural products on a commercial basis?
3. What is the importance of the effect on underdeveloped countries of the variation in our imports of raw materials?

4. Contrast the relative importance of United States foreign investment with the investment activity of the Export-Import Bank.
5. Should we cut off our foreign-aid program?
6. How has foreign trade policy evolved since the war?
7. In mid-1960 a current comment was: "This country is now in some categories a 'have-not' nation, and this situation promises to become more acute with each passing year." Do you agree?

SELECTED READINGS FOR PART SIX

AMERICAN ECONOMIC ASSOCIATION, COMMITTEE OF *Readings in the Theory of International Trade.* Philadelphia: Blakiston Co., 1950 (kept in stock by Richard D. Irwin, Inc., Homewood, Ill.).

Several important papers are reprinted, including Williams on "The Theory of International Trade Reconsidered," and Salant on "Foreign Trade Policy in the Business Cycle."

BENNETT, M. K., and ASSOCIATES. *International Commodity Stock-Piling as a Stabilizer.* Stanford, Calif.: Stanford University Press, 1949.

A research study of the potentialities for setting up an international system of buffer stocks of storable materials.

BERNSTEIN, EDWARD M. *Study of Employment, Growth, and Price Levels: International Effects of U.S. Economic Policy,* Study Paper No. 16, 86th Cong., 2d sess., January 25, 1960. Washington, D.C.: U.S. Government Printing Office, 1960.

A rounded and imaginative study of foreign economic policy.

HARRIS, SEYMOUR E. *The New Economics.* New York: Alfred A. Knopf, Inc., 1947.

Several important papers on international economic relations, including four by Keynes.

JOINT ECONOMIC COMMITTEE. *Employment, Growth, and Price Levels,* Part 5: *International Influences on the American Economy.* 86th Cong., 1st sess., June 29–July 2, 1959. Washington, D.C.: U.S. Government Printing Office, 1959.

A very useful discussion of the effects of the Common Market on our economy.

————. *World Economic Growth and Competition.* 84th Cong., 2d. sess., hearings conducted December 10–13, 1956. Washington, D.C.; U.S. Government Printing Office, 1957.

Reports several opinions on comparable growth of various nations.

LICHTENBERG, ROBERT M. *The Role of Middleman Transactions in World Trade.* Occasional Paper 64. New York: National Bureau of Economic Research, Inc., 1959.

Shows that middleman trade involves not only re-export, but also temporary control without movement of the commodity to the middleman's country of residence.

MINTZ, ILSE. *Trade Balances during Business Cycles: U.S. and Britain since 1880,* Occasional Paper 67. New York: National Bureau of Economic Research, Inc., 1959.

Summarizes the international transmission of business cycle fluctuation.

MORGENSTERN, OSKAR. *International Financial Transactions and Business Cycles.* Princeton: Princeton University Press, 1959.

A study of international money markets, largely in terms of interest and exchange rates, comparing the gold standard conditions before World War I with the different conditions thereafter.

"REVIEW OF ECONOMICS AND STATISTICS," Vol. XL, No. 1, Part 2, Supplement, February, 1958.

Discusses problems in international economics; publication of papers presented at a conference called by the Universities–National Bureau of Economic Research.

Index

INDEX

*This book has been set on the Linotype in 11 point
Caledonia, leaded 2 points, and 10 point Caledonia,
leaded 1 point. Chapter and part numbers and titles
are in 18 point Futura Medium. The size of the type
page is 27 x 47 picas.*